"*Four Testaments* is an excellent compendium of scriptures of the Eastern religious traditions. Complementing Brown's *Three Testaments: Torah, Gospel, and Quran*, the present volume introduces Taoism, Confucianism, Buddhism, and Hinduism through religious texts. . . . This rich array of texts, interpreted by a wide range of scholars and theologians, is one of the book's strengths. Brown's focus is the meeting of East and West, and this is what gives the manuscript its uniqueness as it strives to make previously unarticulated connections between scriptures. This accessible volume should have a wide readership." —**CHOICE**

"An insightful inquiry into the connections between the primary scriptures of the East, in the context of their cultures, and the primary scriptures of the West. This volume expertly affirms the interconnections between various textual traditions. It is a welcome addition to the ever-growing field of intertextual studies." —**Sharada and Rasiah Sugirtharajah**, University of Birmingham

"*Four Testaments* is an excellent overview of the Eastern religious traditions and an ideal complement to *Three Testaments* on the Abrahamic religions. If *Three Testaments* is your text for an introduction to the scriptures of the Western monotheisms in the autumn semester, *Four Testaments* should be your text for the scriptures of the Eastern monisms in the spring." —**Jonathan Kearney**, Saint Patrick's College, Dublin University

"*Four Testaments* is certainly invaluable both worldwide and in the Global South. People may be more open to interfaith and interreligious dialogue—a lived reality—than is sometimes realized. *Four Testaments* showcases this dialogue at its best." —**Rev. Joy Abdul-Mohan**, St. Andrew's Theological College, Trinidad and Tobago

"The religions of India and China, which were once seen by Westerners as exotic but not very important personally, have now become, due to modern communication, religious influences on people all over the globe. This second volume of an important set thus serves as an essential introduction to how traditionally Eastern religions think about individuals, society, the environment, and the transcendent so that we can come to know each other and work together for the benefit of all of us." —**Elliot Dorff**, American Jewish University

"This work brings together in one volume scholarly and gender-inclusive translations and interpretations of Judaism's *Torah*, Christianity's *New Testament*, and Islam's *Qur'an*.

. . . This work not only introduces each scriptural text but also serves as a foundation for greater understanding among the three traditions." —*Booklist*

"Brown (*Noah's Other Son*), a United Church of Canada minister, was surprised that the sacred scriptures of Judaism, Christianity, and Islam are not usually included in a single volume. He includes all three here, emphasizing the common ground among these monotheistic religions and their texts. As editor, he utilizes reputable scholars from the three religious traditions to give introductory information on the sacred texts as well as providing commentary. . . . General readers and undergraduates with an interest in these monotheistic religions and their sacred writings will find this book to be very helpful." —*Library Journal*

"This is an unusual, ambitious, and groundbreaking book that seeks to discover the threads that connect the sacred texts of Judaism, Christianity, and Islam." —*The Bible Today*

"*Three Testaments: Torah, Gospel, and Quran* invites readers to study the interdependence of the scriptures claiming the tradition of Abraham, Sarah, and Hagar as their heritage. I especially appreciate the use of inclusive language and the voice of wo/men scholars in parts I and III, introducing the progressive edge of Jewish and Muslim Scriptures. This volume is a very unique and helpful resource for introductory scripture courses and interreligious dialogue. I highly recommend it." —**Elisabeth Schüssler Fiorenza**, Harvard Divinity School

"Since the medium is indeed a great part of the message, *Three Testaments*—bringing together the *Torah*, the Christian *Scriptures*, and the *Quran* in one volume—is already transformative, simply by challenging all of us to look each other in the face, and to see in each face the Face of God. Besides that, Brian Brown's 'message'—his proposal for seeing the Zoroastrian tradition as having set the context for new revelations in Judaism, Christianity, and Islam—may open us up to fuller spiritual and religious explorations." —**Rabbi Arthur Waskow**, The Shalom Center

"*Three Testaments* is appropriately inclusive in many ways. The use of inclusive scripture is especially appropriate for the twenty-first century, both scholarly and evocative. To leave women out of the scripture in our time would be to distort the message entirely." —**Sister Joan Chittister**, author of *Called to Question*; columnist for *National Catholic Reporter*

"*Three Testaments* suggests new paradigms that could considerably enrich interfaith discussions for each of these three faiths: a new paradigm for Jews about the origin of monotheism in world religion, for Christians about the savior of the world, and for Muslims about the people of the book." —**Mark G. Toulouse**, Emmanuel College, University of Toronto

four testaments

Tao Te Ching, Analects, Dhammapada, Bhagavad Gita: Sacred Scriptures of Taoism, Confucianism, Buddhism, and Hinduism

Brian Arthur Brown

Foreword by Francis X. Clooney, SJ

ROWMAN AND LITTLEFIELD
Lanham • Boulder • New York • London

Published by Rowman & Littlefield
A wholly owned subsidary of The Rowman & Littlefield Publishing Group, Inc.
4501 Forbes Boulevard, Suite 200, Lanham, Maryland 20706
www.rowman.com

Unit A, Whitacre Mews, 26-34 Stannary Street, London SE11 4AB

British Library Cataloguing in Publication Information Available

The hardback edition of this book was previously cataloged by the Library of Congress as follows:

Names: Brown, Brian A., 1942– editor. | Clooney, Francis X. (Francis Xavier), 1950– writer of foreword. | Laozi. Dao de jing. English. | Confucius. Lun yu. English.
Title: Four testaments : Tao Te Ching, Analects, Dhammapada, Bhagavad Gita : sacred scriptures of Taoism, Confucianism, Buddhism, and Hinduism / Brian Arthur Brown ; foreword by Francis X. Clooney, SJ.
Description: Lanham, Maryland : Rowman & Littlefield Publishers, 2016.
Subjects: LCSH: Sacred books. | Religions—Relations. | Asia—Religion. | BISAC: RELIGION / Comparative Religion. | RELIGION / Buddhism / Sacred Writings. | RELIGION / Confucianism. | RELIGION / Hinduism / Sacred Writings. | RELIGION / Taoism (see also PHILOSOPHY / Taoist).
Classification: LCC BL70 .F67 2016 (print) | LCC BL70 (ebook) | DDC 208/.2—dc23
LC record available at http://lccn.loc.gov/2016003911

ISBN 978-1-4422-6577-6 (cloth : alk. paper)
ISBN 978-1-5381-0908-3 (pbk. : alk. paper)
ISBN 978-1-4422-6578-3 (electronic)

Printed in the United States of America

∞™ The paper used in this publication meets the minimum requirements of American National Standard for Information Sciences—Permanence of Paper for Printed Library Materials, ANSI/NISO Z39.48-1992.

To the memory of Bajnath Gosine, my father-in-law
and my mentor in Zoroastrian links, East and West,
and to his late wife, Leelawati (Ram), a Vedic storyteller who filled in the blanks,
and to their daughter, Jenny Sutacriti, my wife, who helped me connect the dots.

contents

book one: from the foundations of the earth to our common spiritual ancestors

book two: the taoist testament

book three: the confucian testament

book four: the buddhist testament

book five: the hindu testament

book six: the z factor

book seven: the "dead zee scrolls"

foreword

Francis X. Clooney

FOUR TESTAMENTS: TAO TE CHING, ANALECTS, DHAMMAPADA, BHAGAVAD GITA IS AN IMPORTANT work, suited to the times in which we live. It is a necessary work. While we ought not assume that our world today is any worse than in ages past, today's nearly instantaneous verbal and visual interconnectedness accentuates everything good and bad happening around us and among us. It is hard, in this atmosphere of heightened awareness, not to see all that is good and bad about the human condition. In particular, we are accosted with the bad news of our times, religious discord and violence, the evident misunderstandings among traditions on the ground, at home and around the globe. Deep down, we know that we very much need to learn to live together as sisters and brothers, respectful and open, living in peace, and working together in justice and love for a better world. For that, we also need to understand one another better, and for that, some of us need to be better and bolder readers.

It is here that Brian Brown's visionary project makes its welcome contribution. *Three Testaments: Torah, Gospel, and Quran* and now this new volume of *Four Testaments* simply make it enticingly easy, first of all, for interested readers to engage with some of the great religious classics of the human race: the Torah, the New Testament, the Quran—and now the *Tao Te Ching*, the *Analects*, the *Dhammapada*, and the *Bhagavad Gita*. It is a particular merit of both volumes that these texts are given in full and not in part. There is no rush here, no list of quotable quotes, no easy path to perennial wisdom; the reader is asked to enter upon the whole of each text, to read each beginning to end, and to learn, page by page.

It is also a merit that these very different texts are bound together under one cover. These are great philosophical and religious texts not used to such binding, and some may be unsettled to see them thus published; after all, what have the *Tao Te Ching* and the *Bhagavad Gita* to do with one another? But this unexpected proximity also makes possible (and perhaps inevitable) another real benefit of the project: to read them *together*, paging through them, moving back and forth from text to text, allowing reading and one's imagination to bring them together. One is invited to browse religiously, intelligently, and see what one finds.

Four Testaments: Tao Te Ching, Analects, Dhammapada, Bhagavad Gita therefore offers much, but it also expects much from its readers, and rightly so. Today's needed learning cannot be delivered in a digested form or reduced to themes and bullet points. It is a much larger, longer, and deeper task of learning that is placed before us. In this book we are asked to undertake the work—all in one volume—of thinking across traditions Indian and Chinese: Hindu, Buddhist, Daoist, and Confucian. Of course, the reading is not so simple or arbitrary as to end with just one volume. All these great texts deserve to become good neighbors to one another in this century's greater world library. One needs to keep the *Four Testaments* on one's desk or nightstand alongside the *Three Testaments*, moving back and forth between the two volumes and their several great texts.

At several points in *Four Testaments*, particularly in the opening and closing sections, we find a different mode of reflection, concerning the Zoroastrian tradition of Vedic derivation and the "Dead Zee Scrolls" (a quest to find or imagine the lost sections of the Zoroastrian Avesta Scriptures). These are reflections of quite a different kind than the service of merely publishing the *Four Testaments* and the *Three Testaments* in close proximity. Thinking about Zoroastrian wisdom and the learning of these scrolls in a series of essays and imaginative writings fosters wider speculations that expand our interest in this project. It asks us whether it is not the case that these great traditions, now brought together in such volumes, were never really quite separate from one another millennia ago. Perhaps the intersections, indebtedness, and meeting points go back further than we can remember, and we are now rediscovering. Putting all these texts and speculative reflections under one cover may, in a certain sense, invite a homecoming, perhaps even a return of history's great travelers to some common points of origin.

This is not the first effort to bring classic religious texts together; one thinks of the *Sacred Books of the East*, that great nineteenth-century project. But in every age, the task is worth taking up again. Brian Brown and his team are to be commended for their contribution to interreligious understanding in the twenty-first century, in a true and enduring way that still manages to be fresh and new.

illustrations

T HE DIAGRAM AT THE BEGINNING OF CHAPTER 3 ("THE GREAT INTERSECTION") WAS DESIGNED by the author, executed by Indira Brown-Sinton, and copyrighted with this text. The final illustration in the appendix was also designed by the author and executed by Arthur and David Brown.

Most of the illustrations in the appendix have been coordinated for this compendium by Emma Goodliffe of the International Dunhuang project and Sanskrit curator Pasquale Manzo, both at the British Library, 92 Euston Road, London, NWI 2DB, United Kingdom. Sincere gratitude is expressed to them both and to their colleagues in the departments of Reproduction and Permissions. Other single figures and photos come from the British Museum in the United Kingdom, the Schoyen Collection in Norway, and Bridgeman Images, United States of America. Specific details of copyrights and permissions are published next to the figures.

acknowledgments

MAJOR CONTRIBUTORS OF MATERIAL TO THIS VOLUME, WHOSE NAMES APPEAR ON THE back cover, are introduced in a spirit of thankful gratitude in the prologue, in introductions to the books in which their contributions appear, and in the "About the Contributors" section. R. S. Sugirtharajah and Sharada Sugirtharajah of Birmingham University in the United Kingdom would have been in that category were they not prevented from direct contributions by the weight of other commitments, so I thank them here for their encouragement and for refining my own postcolonial perspective in their insightful books, *The Bible and Asia* (by Rasiah Sugirtharajah) and *Imagining Hinduism* (by Sharada Sugirtharajah). Their evidence that Asiatic influence is more predominant in Western scriptures than is usually realized ranks with Victor Mair's evidence that "Western" Magi were active during the composition of Eastern scriptures in ancient China, two observations that may serve as the magnetic poles of this work.

These contributors have become almost like family, and I would add to the list of such intimates the names of readers and critical reviewers of early drafts of the whole compendium or parts of it, including senior scholars Jonathan Kearney in Dublin and David Bruce in Toronto, once again, as well as my "editorial review panel" of Niagara educator Nikole Amato; Toronto seminarian Graham Wilson; and Trinidadians, Senator Joy Abdul-Mohan, Senator Rolph Balgobin, and Justice Peter Jamadar, who ensured that I dealt with the "Global South" perspective and other matters appropriately.

My final proofreader was Stanley Algoo, who came from the Caribbean to Canada as a prestigious "Island Scholar" at McGill University. He served as a career librarian at Scarborough Public Library in Toronto, where he facilitated the creation of the first Chinese character–based catalog for public library use. In putting the finishing polish on this complex text, Algoo caught not only typos and spelling errors invisible to the author but also issues of syntax with reference to the flow and meaning as he grasped it, for which my readers will join me in gratitude.

It is essential for a work of this magnitude to have an editor who demands the highest standards, and I have had that blessing in Sarah Stanton, religion editor for Rowman

& Littlefield, for both *Three Testaments* and *Four Testaments*. Her skillful editorial assistants, Karie Simpson and Carli Hansen, have been especially helpful in the present volume, as has been senior production editor Patricia Stevenson.

Colleague contributors have generously described the two-volume compendium of *Three Testaments* and *Four Testaments* as the author's *magnum opus*. If I have any such legacy to offer, I hope it is in connecting the seven world religions to their Vedic roots, whether tenuous or vigorous, and thereby to each other. In this task I have been "aided and abetted" by Jenny (Sutacriti Gosine) Brown, my life partner since teenage years in university, and my "guru" in enriching our Christian faith through ever deepening appreciation of Eastern mysticism. The assistance of other members of our family is mentioned in the "Illustrations" section. With a nod to our own Vedic roots, referred to in the dedication, we have felt that without the influence of profound Eastern mysticism, especially in mainstream Christian traditions of Western Europe and North America, the progressive expression of traditional Christianity, to which we adhere, has become somewhat insipid in our time. We hope to point here to possibilities of enrichment and renewal in this regard.

Such enthrallment actually remains vital in Catholic pageantry and Pentecostal emotionalism, but Christianity also needs an intellectual basis bathed, immersed or baptized in a profundity that goes beyond itself, even while satisfying the mental capacity with which all God's people are endowed. This historic hallmark of mainstream Protestantism appears open to renewal from these four testaments. Judaism and Islam preserve enough of their own Asiatic roots to relate to or give leadership in this quest. We join with Jewish, Christian, and Muslim monotheistic colleagues, Clooney, Glassé, Mair, Mates-Muchin, Bruce, and Freund, in this guided exploration of the depths of Eastern monism. We cannot but express grateful acknowledgment of our Chinese and Indian fellow travelers, Mates-Muchin (creatively straddling the cultures), Eduljee, Sharma, Rasiah and Sharada Sugirtharajah, and our special guides, the translators James Legge, Sarvepalli Radhakrishnan, and Mohandas Gandhi, who have passed into glory or nirvana, and Victor Mair, who is still part of our pilgrimage.

abridgment and dramatic presentations

SOME READERS AND CERTAIN ACADEMIC PROGRAMS MAY HAVE ACCESSED THIS COMPENDIUM anticipating the "four testaments" without expecting the opening section on the Vedic context or the closing material relating to the West. This volume has been designed so such readers may begin with Book II and conclude with Book V. The Zoroastrian material in the opening and the closing may work for others as what we refer to as the thumb that facilitates the action of those four fingers, and it may be read by class members or study group participants as an introduction to the four world religions of the East in Books II–V, followed by a conclusion in the Western context.

In this connection we may point out that the reading of new concepts and words may appear easier in the *Tao Te Ching*, more difficult in dialogue between unfamiliar characters in the *Analects*, more accessible again in the *Dhammapada*, and especially manageable in the *Bhagavad Gita* as the reader has become adept through the process. Coincidentally, the reader may be following the chronological evolution of monism.

Three Testaments: Torah, Gospel, and Quran in 2012 was followed two years later by a study guide, still available from Amazon under the title *Three Testaments Companion*, featuring well-designed congregational, community, and academic course outlines by Dr. David Bruce. There are no plans as yet for such a resource in support of *Four Testaments*, but the *Three Testaments Companion* might suggest structure, and the examples on the following page illustrate "discussion starters" for consideration by group leaders, clergy, and professors.

> The monistic religions of the East are echoed by twenty-first-century quantum physics, nanotechnology, and quantum theology in their understanding that all matter is simply a manifestation of energy, that it all began as One and "somehow" . . . "creation" . . . exploded in the ongoing burst of material energy that continues today. This means that reality as we know it is comparable to a hologram and that the universe itself is empty, except for what we make of its "appearance," and that relationships are more genuine than "things." This is certainly germane to Taoism, and more particularly to both Buddhism and Hinduism, although not so much to Confucianism. It is almost lost in translation to Western monotheism except for the traces of Vedic influence in the Torah, the Gospel, and the Quran (now becoming accessible and appreciated in the context of current interfaith engagement).

The *Three Testaments* book inspired the play *Three Testaments: Shalom, Peace, Salam*, which premiered in upstate New York in June 2015 and is available on both YouTube and DVD from Amazon. Produced by James Flood, directed by Arthur Strimling, and staged by Alison Miculan, with artistic direction by Cheryl Wood-Thomas, it anticipates presentation at the inaugural day of the Performing Arts Center at the World Trade Center in 2018. As a possible post-intermission presentation, playwright and dramaturg Bill Thomas of St. Catharines, Ontario has purchased the rights to produce a play based on *Four Testaments*. That one-act play will feature four dramatic scenes presenting Confucius visiting Lao Tzu at the Imperial Archives, Lao Tzu heading west from China on his donkey, the Buddha leaving his father's palace and wondering until finding enlightenment under the Bodhi tree, and Krishna with Arjuna in the chariot between battle lines of the struggle within each person—a consummate presentation of "east meets west."

prologue

Four Fingers and a Thumb: Tao Te Ching, Analects, Dhammapada, Gita, *and Avesta*

THIS VOLUME OFFERS THE SACRED TEXTS OR FOUNDATIONAL SCRIPTURES OF THE FOUR "WORLD religions" of Eastern tradition, four trunks plus the stump of another, with introductory comments by scholars and leaders with expertise in the field. It also offers the central premise and discerning thesis that the Vedic religious tradition that influenced religious developments in China was the same Zoroastrian iteration of Vedic heritage that stimulated reform of Hinduism and the development of Buddhism in India and that intersected with Judaism during the Babylonian Captivity.

Zoroastrianism, which itself may have been exposed to even earlier Hebrew influence, was neither foundational nor dominant in any of those developments, but it was possibly simulative in all areas connected by the Silk Route in the sixth century BCE. Frequently serving as the state religion of the Persian Empire through a thousand years of association with this first superpower, it would also stimulate certain revelations in the later religious developments of Christianity and Islam. It thus influenced or at least connected the seven world religions generally recognized in the newer discipline of "religious studies," the successor to comparative religion. As an interesting sidebar, the search for the lost portions of Zoroastrian scriptures (the "Dead Zee Scrolls") is presented as almost a holy grail of archaeology in the view of some of our contributors.

Were there Magi in ancient China, connected with Persia, introducing religious concepts from the Middle East and the Middle West to the Chinese culture that was believed, until recently, to have developed in total isolation? Was Baruch Spinoza, the framer of philosophy that shaped modern Europe, actually informed and influenced by Vedanta Hinduism through his family connections with the Dutch East India Company? The proof of the first is now conclusive, the evidence for the second is mounting, and these are but a couple of the links between the major religious traditions in human history to be explored in this book.

In it, Eastern scriptures take a preeminent place in this discussion of *"Our Religions,"* to use the term employed by a publication of that title associated with the Parliament of Religions to describe the seven truly "world" religions. This study of four eastern, mainly "monistic," texts is presented in tandem with the 2012 publication of *Three Testaments: Torah, Gospel, and Quran* of Western monotheism from Rowman & Little-field. An interesting question to be addressed is whether monism and monotheism can be shown to have some common roots; are they as totally incompatible as is usually presumed, or might there be ways in which these traditions may enrich each other (or at least coexist)?

There was a dramatic spiritual stirring along the Silk Route early in the sixth century BCE, possibly triggered by a prophetic ministry of the Persian prophet named Zoro-aster, and reaching from Europe to China through connections between Magi who were already in "The Land of the Heavenly Dragon" and their Iranian counterparts. The reverberations of this stirring may have inspired the custodian of the Imperial Archives in China's imperial palace to venture into the new dimension of religion we call Taoism, and that development led to an "equal and opposite reaction" in Confucianism, based on China's own best traditions. The response to this stimulus in India was different, beginning with Buddhism as a positive development, but, instead of a pushback Hindu reaction, a reform of Indian religion led to the renewal of Hinduism, making Buddhism redundant there but ready for export throughout neighboring lands. The scriptures to be examined and studied in this volume reflect on these developments that took place within a single century among a significant portion of the world's population.

When I entered what is now the Master of Divinity program of religious studies at McGill University fifty years ago, Western Christians were engaged in recovering the Jewish heritage of the church, despite a theology partially shaped by Greek and Roman influences and developed in Europe. This new balance in both theology and biblical studies prevailed until the end of the twentieth century, when a "postcolonial" agenda began to emerge and another change in perspective appeared inevitable. To illustrate the change as it may be seen in a wider, parallel phenomenon, dictionaries of the twentieth century gave the Greek and Latin roots of words, but as the twenty-first century dawned, dictionaries began to show the "Indo-European" roots of most words. The same is now happening in the search for the Vedic roots of Christian theological concepts in my old school, and for Vedic influences in other places as well.

Jewish and Islamic studies have been developing corresponding links in the same direction, and the influence of monistic theology and Eastern scriptural texts on all three is beginning to be recognized at last in this postcolonial era. In 2013, R. S. Sugirtharajah of the University of Birmingham could write, "In modern times there has been a grudging acknowledgement that some of the key theological concepts in Christianity might have their origins in Zoroastrianism,"[1] a Vedic imprint from the East impressed upon the West but almost invisible until recently. This observation was an echo of a "subtext" of *Three Testaments: Torah, Gospel, and Quran*, the compendium that preceded this one. Indeed, a Canadian reviewer in the *Presbyterian Record* referred to my Zoroastrian subtext in that volume as a "theory of everything" and compared it to the penchant of the bride's father in the movie *My Big Fat Greek Wedding*, who attributed every idea in the world to a Greek origin. In *Four Testaments*, Zoroastrianism once again plays a significant role, though the reason may be more apparent in the current volume, which proposes it as a Vedic link between certain Eastern texts, and between Eastern and Western texts.

While four-fifths of this book is devoted to the four primary "testaments" of Eastern scripture, its Vedic subtext (via its Zoroastrian conduit) may be the single "revelation" of greatest impact. In addition to providing a link between the three Western testaments, the Vedic umbrella over all seven world religions, and also many traditional religions, signifies the linkage between all or most cultures in the world. Thus in the West the Vedic-linked Norse mythology, Wicca and Dravidic religions, and even Egyptian and other African religions display words, phrases, rituals, and concepts reflecting common themes. Likewise in the East, the identifiable commonalities of Jainism, divergent Tibetan Buddhism, earlier Shinto, and later Sikh traditions may be seen as reflecting the essence of a religions quest that is more than the coincidence of humans responding to similar phenomena. Vedic lore, as discerned in the seven world religions, may be described as the umbrella over all seven, or perhaps better as the deep subterranean aquifer from which the world draws its waters of baptism, ablution, sacred bathing, the flow of the Tao, and water sacrifice in other religions. This plausible resolution of so many issues was addressed tentatively in *Three Testaments*, but we hope to substantiate the thesis of a relationship between the seven and the many, the world religions and the traditional religions throughout the world.

Of all potential influences from "further east," Zoroastrianism is emerging as potentially the most influential, and also still the most ignored, for a variety of reasons. As the Vedic bridge between Eastern and Western religious traditions, Zoroastrianism is of special interest because its influence in the West is like the mirror opposite of its reforming impact on Eastern religion and its formative influence on Eastern philosophy during the Axial Age in the fifth and sixth centuries BCE. The derisively humorous observation that "Zoroastrianism is the next big thing, and always will be," may be about to materialize as the last laugh.

In his seminal analysis of the situation among Jews and Christians, Sugirtharajah summarizes the point by referencing the late Professor Norman Cohn of Sussex University to the effect that "the Judeo-Christian faith tradition owes an intellectual debt to Zoroastrianism for such theological ideas as a universal god, notions of angels, Satan, heaven, hell, resurrection of the body, life after death, and the final apocalyptic ending of this world."[2] Narrowing further to Christianity alone, he quotes J. C. Hindley, New Testament instructor at Serampore College in West Bengal, in saying that "it is no longer possible to relegate Zoroastrianism to the fringe of Christian interest."[3] This book will also broaden the Jewish and Christian analysis to include Islam, and more particularly to show how that process not only engages Eastern religions and philosophy through a common ancestor but also connects contextually with Western religions and philosophy today in a manner heretofore unimaginable.

If the frequent reference to Zoroastrianism seems like a stretch to some traditional scholars, let me suggest that we may be at the beginning of an epochal awareness of something like a cross-fertilization of ideas between East and West along the "Silk Route" in an era long before we have traditionally understood that conduit as primarily a trade route. It may turn out that there were links other than the Zoroastrian-tinged Vedic connection we are proposing, like perhaps Manichaeism a little later, but at this point it would appear that Zoroastrianism in the mid-sixth century BCE needs to be taken more seriously as the stimulus we are attempting to identify for what is now frequently referred to as the Axial Age. Every time this text refers to whatever Silk Route influence reached over into China, down into India and back to Israel-in-Babylon as "Zoroastrianism," the reader may mutter under her breath "or whatever." But the premise here is that the sixth-century BCE eruption of "something" under the aegis of the Persian superpower was a resophisticated Vedic influence moving through the conduit we now call the Silk Route and acting as a stimulant in all three cases. If it looks like Zoroastrianism, quacks like Zoroastrianism, and waddles like Zoroastrianism, for now we will assume that it is Zoroastrianism.

There had been hints of monism in various places in the ancient world, and monotheism had been incubating in Israel since Moses, when rather suddenly "Westernism" (i.e., in religion and philosophy) veered sharply from polytheism toward monotheism at almost precisely the same moment that "Easternism" moved just as suddenly from polytheism to monism. The parallel timing, as well as Zoroastrian geographical connections to both along the Silk Route, suggests that something was going on that may not fully explain these phenomena but nevertheless implies a link or a shared stimulation. If so, modern occidental and oriental philosophers may have more grist for their mills, and Western and Eastern religions have a clear agenda for their "interfaith" discussions in the twenty-first century. The profundity of this discussion of the relationship between monism and monotheism is so all embracing that it may turn out to be one of the more important agenda items of twenty-first-century religious studies.

Are human beings creatures who alone (aside from the instinct of animals and the "being" of inanimate matter) have the privilege of knowing, worshipping, and serving God, or are we potentially part of God, consciously seeking to realize our participation in the whole? Is the role of religion to provide "atonement" in the sense of reconciliation between creatures and their Creator, or is it truly "at-*one*-ment," meaning an integration of individual "selves" into the glorious fullness of God? If the latter, what is the role of the "individual" in striving toward realization of the divine, and what is the status of individual elements in relation to the Godhead after integration?

Is it possible to conceive of monotheism as a way station in the direction of monism, or does monism simply fail to recognize and accept God's creativity in the divine authentication of separate elements in creation? Where is the line between monotheism and monism, or is there a dynamic continuum between them? In the simplest of human terms, these may be among the questions facing analysts of religion and theologians of the twenty-first century. Lately one keeps meeting people who say they are both Jews and Buddhists, and Paul Knitter, a Catholic theologian at Union Theological Seminary in New York, has graced the discussion with his book, *Without Buddha I Could Not Be a Christian*. Similar in spirit is *Confucius for Christians*, written from an evangelical perspective, by Gregg A. Ten Elshof, without a monistic component. Hindus are usually capable of this stretching, while Muslims anchor the opposite end of the spectrum.

In my own recent volume presenting the monotheistic scriptures of Abraham's family together for the first time,[4] I began the exploration of how important Zoroastrianism is for the world, not merely for all three principal Western traditions. In this current book, with the assistance of learned colleagues, we extend the new appreciation of Zoroastrianism in the West to an equal standing in the East, another groundbreaking investigation. This is the first time the four main popular scriptures of Eastern monism are linked to one another (in mutual support or in reaction), to the Western traditions, and to the Zoroastrian iteration of Vedic lore. In this compendium we hope to help launch a field of studies with a potential to engage academic research in areas from ancient Greek and Roman classics through Mesopotamian history, back to investigations of the Vedic origins of spiritual development from one end of the Silk Route to the other, and forward to a whole new Western understanding and appreciation of religion and philosophy in India and China.

We might acknowledge that a certain level of dedication will be required to plod through the *Exordium* by Karl Friedrich Geldner in book I. *What We Once Knew* is about Zoroastrianism as the Vedic godparent of all major religions, East and West. This hundred-year-old document has considerable value, not merely in the information it presents but also in presenting a religious ethos integral to Western culture just a century ago, but foreign to many people now. That ethos is still part of life in the East and is closer to the animus of the ancient world than we are. It may both inform and enthrall those who can endure the old-world archaisms in this presentation, which lays a foundation for much that follows.

We hope to illustrate how Western and Eastern traditions of theology and philosophy may be understood as illuminating each other through their shared Zoroastrian connections. To begin with, the Vedic and Semitic traditions connect with each other through intersections on the Silk Route more than earlier realized. They do not run parallel there, and they only crisscross directly perhaps once or twice that we know of, though these momentous intersections perhaps affect the whole world. The first such intersection now appears to have happened when the Vedic tradition, migrating southward toward India, crossed the path of Israelite exiles moving northward toward Europe—significant not for the numbers involved but for the particular putative personas involved. The second intersection took place as monotheistic Vedic Zoroastrian Persian conquerors encountered their monotheistic Jewish civil service in newly captured Babylon. These two meetings were perhaps less than seventy-five years apart, and we contend that their ramifications are still reverberating, especially in the field of religious studies.

Our focus on Taoism, Confucianism, Buddhism, and Hinduism as the Eastern complement to Judaism, Christianity, and Islam was inspired and confirmed by the publication of a survey of seven religions that might be properly designated as truly "world religions." *Our Religions: The Seven World Religions Introduced by Preeminent Scholars from Each Tradition* was authored and edited by Arvind Sharma of McGill University, one of our own commentators in this compendium. It was a response to the 1993 recognition of those seven by the Parliament of Religions, a book currently regarded by many as a preeminent text in the field of interfaith studies. We intend to indicate how these seven have some common scriptural rootage and have influenced one another more significantly than has been previously realized. We have no interest in homogenizing these religions and we recognize that the differences between them are as enlightening as what may be identified as points of common stimulation. Indeed, while we focus primarily on the scriptures and their contexts in four religions in particular, we urge the study of the *Our Religions* text to follow through on how these religions evolved or grew to the character and the status they enjoy in the twenty-first century, an area of study far beyond the mandate of this compendium.

After the publication of *Three Testaments: Torah, Gospel, and Quran*, and the international launch tour that followed, in addition to synagogues and churches, I found myself being invited to speak at mosques in Canada, the United States, and elsewhere from across the spectrum of Sunni, Shia, and Sufi communities. There were sometimes awkward moments when I felt members of the audience were asking themselves, "Why would our leaders invite this speaker who obviously has limited knowledge of the Quran and even less of Islamic theological understanding?" So I would begin with the story of American astronauts and Russian cosmonauts who know things about the British countryside that farmers who have worked that land all their lives do not know. From space they see the outlines of the ancient Roman occupation with walls, wells, streets, and dams that are not apparent to those on the ground who know every stick and stone of the terrain. The most recent example is the 2014 discoveries from space that redefine our understanding of the true purpose and nature of Hadrian's Wall, which provided aqueduct services to both Romans in England and the less developed world in Scotland.

Then I comment, "With great humility today, and with profound respect for your more intimate understanding, I hope to tell you about my observation of the Quran from a great distance, seeing things that you may have never seen in the Quran, the holy book you know inside out." I conclude this prologue with a similar word to the many scholars of Zoroastrianism who will quickly realize that I know very little about detailed matters in which they are expert. I hope to reveal things seen from a great distance that may enhance their appreciation of a subject they love and contribute to a greater understanding of it to our world heritage. With respect to scholarship introducing the four complete scriptural texts on exhibition in Books II, III, IV, and V, we are on more like *terra firma* through the participation and contributions of experts in those fields.

These four Eastern Asian testaments, together with the "Eastern" Zoroastrian Avesta, represent the quintessence of Eastern Religion, like four fingers and a thumb, presented in the context of their Vedic glove. Archaeologists are still looking for the bulk of the Avesta, a search to be introduced in Book VII by Professor Richard Freund of the University of Hartford, but we present the other four sacred Eastern testaments in a manner we believe renders the original as faithfully as possible in translation, portrays the understanding of these scriptures down through the ages, and appropriately represents their position in today's world.

We use the dating system BCE and CE, for "Before the Common Era" and "Common Era," instead of the Western traditional BC and AD except in quotations by contributors (who happen to be Jewish in every case in this regard) or when Muslim or other dates are also required for clarity. Likewise, while we note the classic spelling of *Daoism* by Professor Clooney, our other contributors lean toward *Taoism* as more familiar to our readers. The translations of the four Eastern testament scriptures in both quotations and exhibition sections are by Victor H. Mair in the case of the *Tao Te Ching*, for the *Analects* the classic English version by James Legge, the *Dhammapada* by Radhakrishnan, and the *Bhagavad Gita* by Gandhi, as will be discussed in each accompanying preface. Quotations of Western texts in commentary sections are usually from the *Tanakh* version of the Hebrew Scriptures of the Jewish Publication Society, the New Revised Standard Version of the Bible from the National Council of Churches, except when tradition or sentiment dictate use of the King James Authorized Version or an original rendering, and we use the translations of the twentieth-century Holy Quran by A. Yusuf Ali and the twenty-first-century rendering of the Sublime Quran by Laleh Bakhtiar. Quotations in translation of the Zoroastrian Avesta come from a long list of sources represented in the bibliography as well as an extensive original paraphrase.

Like high school students overwhelmed by facts, names, and dates in history, rather than the story, many seminarians, university undergraduates in "Comparative Religion," and members of congregations venturing into the interfaith arena are overwhelmed by the number of sects and variant versions of oriental religions. In this compendium our approach is more selective, beginning with the first or primary "testament" sized scripture of each religion. Without giving breathing exercises or guidelines for meditation, our material verges on the experiential with respect to the four texts on exhibition, the core of our study. For context however, and to illustrate wider trends in passing, my colleagues and I present glimpses of past religious knowledge, current political realities affecting the religious life of the world, and future developments in religious archaeology that may unfold in our lifetimes.

The previous volume, *Three Testaments: Torah, Gospel, and Quran*, has been the recipient of awards not only in religious, academic, and literary categories but also for its contribution to "world peace." Likewise, this *Four Testaments* volume, while focused on religious and academic questions, is presented in a literary fashion that hopefully will contribute to a greater understanding between believers in the oneness of this world, an aspect of faith being necessary as the *sine qua non* of existence on this planet now and in the future.

We acknowledge that in some respects this book appears targeted at a North American readership and English-speaking readers elsewhere, but we are aiming far beyond the traditional, white Protestant market that constitutes a certain religious book industry in America. We are cultivating a diverse spectrum of readers from many demographics who will be joined by others who read English as a second language, as well as many for whom the scriptures of Eastern religions are indeed their own scriptures. Among the first to see the draft manuscript of this compendium were those invited to present the foreword and the introductions to the seven books: an eminent scholar with Australian connections who teaches at Harvard, a Russian-born Muslim encyclopedist, a Chinese female rabbi born on the west coast of the United States, America's leading academic Sinologist (who happens to be Jewish), a Hindu scholar from India at McGill University in Montreal, a Catholic scholar and writer whose "day job" is providing housing for refugees in Toronto, a Jewish archaeologist whose most famous dig has provided a promising hypothesis for the location of Atlantis near Gibraltar as observed from space, and near the end a Zoroastrian blogger with street cred displayed on his scholarly website.

It is the latter, the final contributor to this compendium, with his comments on an ancient text by a fifth-century BCE Zoroastrian monarch, inscribed on fossilized horse bones found recently in China, who moves the seemingly improbable quest for the "Dead Zee Scrolls" of lost Avestan scriptures to the realm of genuine possibility and almost probability. That final contribution from a colleague prompts me to linger at this point in describing this important source of Eastern scholarly insight.

K. E. Eduljee may be regarded as the world's preeminent "Zoroastrian scholar," at least from within that community, as compared to "scholars of Zoroastrianism" from without. In *Three Testaments* I acknowledged that Zoroastrian scholarship and scholarship of Zoroastrianism are two different disciplines, and that, despite respect for the former, in that book we were there employing the latter since it conformed more easily and compared more helpfully to textual criticism and other techniques used by the Jews, Christians, and Muslims who were both intended readers and active contributors to the compendium. That was a mistake. Scholars of Zoroastrianism are feeling their way forward in a discipline that is new in the last century and full of promise, and while there is much mutual respect among them, there is little agreement among academic specialists, even when evidence is overwhelming or a consensus is possible. With help from Mary Boyce, I have tracked and explicated some of the more dramatic controversies. Beginning with *Four Testaments*, again to illustrate the growing realization that there may be a Vedic backdrop via Zoroastrianism to all major world religions, I turned to several "Zoroastrian scholars," principally Eduljee, to settle some questions for recalcitrant "scholars of Zoroastrianism." I was told, "Good luck with that."

Two things happened. The same issues remained, but I developed a new respect for those I had described as "recalcitrant," for my new tutor was as uncertain about solid dates for the life and teachings of Zoroaster and other matters not as important to the core theology of Zoroaster as some of them are (though his views are as good as theirs and well within the spectrum of our speculations). Formerly ridiculous legends about Zoroaster himself are resolved on all sides these days. However, with Eduljee I discovered that what we all need in the study of Zoroastrianism—namely, the essential spirituality at its core—is preserved not in textual studies but in tradition and practice within the community. This is largely missing from secular and non-Zoroastrian studies, including my own, though in this compendium I attempted to develop a new sensitivity to this aspect that transcends all others. While Eduljee's influence may now be seen in this text from start to finish, I cannot claim that I have his approval for all that you read and learn here. I keenly urge readers to investigate over a thousand web pages on the subject at his Zoroastrian Heritage website, http://www.heritageinstitute.com.

To assist more formally academic scholars to appreciate this trove of treasure, let me say that this is the largest Zoroastrian website in the world, entirely from one person, with a long-term average of just under 35,000 unique visitors per month from a multitude of countries around the globe, but primarily, or almost exclusively, within the Zoroastrian community. These statistics do not include the four blogs by Eduljee, whose work is endorsed and printed by journals of the World Zoroastrian Organisation, the Federation of North American Zoroastrian Associations, the Zarathushtrian Assembly, "Parsis and Irani Under One Roof," and numerous other organizations in North America, Europe, Iran, India, Australia, and elsewhere, while Eduljee himself is a Canadian. Zoroastrians of different denominations and backgrounds have accepted his work, and it should be acknowledged that he also receives mail from academics, scholars, authors, reporters, TV producers, and individuals who have twigged to the value of this resource. Eduljee's pages are quoted in classrooms and used by people organizing weddings, initiation ceremonies, general festivals, and even funerals.

The views he publishes represent the mainstream and the "center of gravity" of Zoroastrian thinking, as evidenced by endorsements by conservatives, traditionalists, and orthodox, as well as liberals and reformers, with only a few detractors. His articles on King Cyrus the Great published by the Federation of North American Zoroastrian Associations (FEZANA) have been translated into Spanish and French by a translator in Argentina. Meanwhile, I am among the friends and members of his family who are urging him to write *The Encyclopedia of Zoroastrianism*, the sort of thing in which my own publisher specializes, as do some others. For example, as a neophyte in the study of Islam, I frequently turn to *The New Encyclopedia of Islam* by Cyril Glassé, and many of us need just such a tool for Zoroastrian studies, hopefully crafted by one who appreciates the virtues of secular and non-Zoroastrian explorations but, as with Glassé, from within the community of tradition and practice. Both Zoroastrian scholars and scholars of Zoroastrianism would benefit immensely from such a resource. Ed, are you ready to get started?

In some respects this compendium may be regarded as an academic book, but it may have other applications. Because of the manner in which "race relations" of the twentieth century are being partially supplanted by "faith relations" in the twenty-first century, *Three Testaments: Torah, Gospel, and Quran* has been found to be a valuable resource for conferences on such topics as "The Terror of These Times," an 2015 event in Niagara Falls, New York, in which clergy and academics of those three traditions considered how proper understanding of our own and one another's scriptures could become the first line of defense against terrorism. In similar fashion, as referenced by Francis Clooney and others, *Four Testaments* may prove to be of value in getting ahead of the curve in potential issues involving East–West politics, immigration, economic, and military power. With regard to religion in China, nuclear threats from North Korea, Buddhist extremism in Sri Lanka and Myanmar, and Hindu nationalism in India, to name a few areas of concern, one place to begin to foster understanding may be an appreciation of the basic religious resources available. The primary and fundamental Eastern "testaments" are the *Tao Te Ching*, the *Analects*, the *Dhammapada*, the *Bhagavad Gita*, and even the Zoroastrian Avesta, which provides the Vedic link among these four monistic and mixed texts, and between them and the Western monotheistic texts of the previous volume.

With a word on each of the others in order, Francis Clooney might not appreciate being called the *éminence grise* of the interfaith movement so often, but he is all of that. Victor H. Mair demolishes the old "high school lesson" about Chinese civilization developing in total isolation. Jacqueline Mates-Muchin begins the Oriental–Occidental comparative process. Radhakrishnan and Gandhi present the basis of a postcolonial perspective. Arvind Sharma helps us see how these scriptures complement one another. David Bruce resonates with the perspectives of dispossessed migrant minorities, especially Middle East refugees these days. Richard Freund verifies that our archaeological speculations may be well-grounded in scientific realities. These contributors have ensured a worldview equal to the tasks assigned to them. Their credentials are described more fully at the back of the compendium and more specifics of their contributions will be introduced as we proceed. This team has worked so well with me and with one another that it seemed appropriate that I almost belabor the point so that readers might join the team through appreciation of both the excellence of their contributions and the background spectrum of their qualifications and experience.

Finally, before we get going, I wish to acknowledge the value of a compendium that competes with this one in a certain area and to consider its value in context. *The Wiley Blackwell Companion to Zoroastrianism*, edited by Michael Stausberg and Yuhan Sohrab-Dinshaw Vevaina, was published just over a year before *Four Testaments*. It is focused on Zoroastrianism alone, whereas our compendium merely includes Zoroastrianism as providing the single most important link between Vedic spiritual lore and the seven world religions, particularly Taoism, Confucianism, Buddhism, and reformed Hinduism. The expert scholars of Zoroastrianism in the Wiley volume offer additional (and possibly corrective) insights to our theses, even while important issues remain unresolved for them in reference to this work.

With a focus on Zoroastrianism a thousand years closer to our time than the Zoroastrianism of this study, they have been unable to reconcile their scholastic propositions with the community traditions and recent work of "Zoroastrian scholars," much less with one another as "scholars of Zoroastrianism." For example, the majority of contributors to the Wiley volume favor a date for Zoroaster in the 1200–1000 BCE range (for mainly "philological" reasons) and only acknowledge the Persian / Arabic tradition (728–652 BCE) in their preface. This is despite the views of their Susan Whitfield in her own book and Amir Hussain and others elsewhere who agree with us in adopting the more recent dates for reasons both traditional and scholarly in the approach we employ in "reading backward" from the witness of Jewish material related to the Babylonian Exile. Their philological arguments for earlier dates are dealt with elsewhere in our text, showing why Zoroaster might have deliberately used archaic language, just as new religions today present their "scriptures" in King James English to gain "authenticity." Likewise, the Wiley contributors' argument that Zoroaster's Gatha poems exhibit none of the animals or industries of the seventh century BCE but do show earlier examples is countered by the habit of modern urban Christians continuing to sing about sheep and shepherds known in both the Bible and their own rural past.

Finally, some of the postmodern scholars of Zoroastrianism contributing to the esteemed *Wiley Blackwell Companion to Zoroastrianism* are of the view that the Avesta existed only in oral form for a thousand years, with none of it being written down until sometime between 350 and 500 CE (when we believe it was actually codified). Until the discovery of the Dead Sea Scrolls, the earliest known version of the Hebrew Scriptures dated back to the ninth century CE, so until that discovery there were Jewish scholars who taught that the Hebrew Scriptures were unwritten until the fifth century CE. Both theories are nonsense, of course, with references to copies of the Avesta throughout antiquity supported by certainty that the Rig Veda, a predecessor or linguistic uncle of the Avesta, was written down around 1200 BCE, as acknowledged by those same Avesta doubters. The "Dead Zee Scrolls" have not yet been found, but there can be no doubt that they existed, and, following the model of the Dead Sea Scrolls, we might assume that some copies still exist, just waiting to be found.

Though necessarily fragmented and disjointed given the current state of research, the material in the *Wiley Blackwell Compendium* is stunning in the scholarship underlying its cautious deductions, despite a safe, minimalist approach. Its contributors are the intellectual and analytical equals of the finest scholars in more established fields such as Egyptology, and one can only sympathize with their dilemma over the growing welter of conflicting evidence about Zoroastrianism early in the Common Era. The questions they raise are important but possibly incapable of resolution without the actual discovery of the BCE documents that this study postulates as the foundational origins of Zoroastrianism and the stimulative origins of Taoism, Confucianism (in reaction), and Buddhism (as well as the reformed Hinduism that followed it).

However, the Wiley contributors offer a splendid array of Zoroastrian traditions in later Iran and contiguous areas early in the Common Era, derived in various ways from our classical Zoroastrianism a thousand years earlier, which itself spawned a wide variety of religious developments in neighboring lands in its own time. Wiley also offers impressive evidence regarding the several forms of Zoroastrianism throughout Central Asia, China, India, Korea, and even Japan in the first millennium CE, even where Ahura Mazda is somewhat absorbed into deities like the Hindu Indra and more especially Brahma. Indeed, it is important to note the Zoroastrian presence throughout even the Far East up to the present time, without acknowledgment or support from the wider community of Parsees and others, as elucidated by Takeshi Aoki in *The Wiley Blackwell Compendium of Zoroastrianism.* Such resources are not easily accessed elsewhere, and they are presented in conjunction with an array of traditions found in this exciting compilation.

Yaakov Elman and Shai Secunda raise interesting questions about recent evidence of significant Jewish activity in China in ancient times, supported by evidence in our own appendix. Nobody is entirely comfortable in connecting the exiles in Isaiah 49:12 with China—"Behold, these shall come from far: and, lo, these from the north and from the west; and these from the land of Sinim (סינים in Hebrew, or 秦國 in the Chinese Union text)." But we can hope to hear more from the Wiley folks about recent DNA tests showing Semitic genes in more than one thousand citizens of the city of Kaifeng, some five hundred miles southwest of Beijing.

Parsee historical lore from India and legends regarding Zoroastrians in Iran through the ages since the Islamic conquest are described by John R. Hinnells, with reliable information about modern practices by Jenny Rose. These are the people we need to hear from about the current reports of "conversions" or authentic "returns to ancestral faith" by tens of thousands of Kurds and Yazidis facing ISIS in Syria and Iraq, a phenomenon receiving a warm reception by Parsees and other Zoroastrians, to the surprise of many. The Wiley team has just begun its work.

Meanwhile, to move forward in reference to the Vedic/Zoroastrian stimulation of eastward religious developments, it may be necessary to briefly summarize the progress in this field prior to the eruption of theories represented by the current spectrum of opinions expressed in Wiley, mostly concerning Zoroastrianism closer to the fifth century CE than to the Zoroastrianism of the fifth century BCE, the era of our primary interest.

In his *Historica religions veterum Persarium, eorumque Magorum* (*History of the Religion of the Ancient Persians and Their Magi*) Oxford's Thomas Hyde (1636–1703) was the first non-Zoroastrian scholar since ancient times to suggest that Zoroaster had been a pupil of one of the Hebrew prophets and to call for a search for the missing and unknown Zoroastrian Scriptures. French Iranist James Darmesteter (1849–1894) adopted the Persian/Arabian date of 258 years before Alexander as the starting point for Zoroaster's Avesta. German scholar Friedrich von Spiegal (1820–1905) developed the theme that Semantic elements had found their way into Zoroastrianism, and he produced the first significant European translation of the Avesta in a line of translations we review in this book. Karl Friederich Geldner (1852–1929) made important improvements to translation of the Avesta text in sections released between 1886 and 1895, preliminary to his 1911 *Encyclopaedia Britannica* articles, which we use to summarize the positions of his pioneering predecessors. Meanwhile, Geldner's friend Abraham Valentine Williams Jackson (1862–1937) confirmed the linguistic links between the Avestan language and its Sanskrit (Vedic) parent, and Geldner's contemporary, Christian Bartholomae (1855–1925), established that Zoroaster had fled from western to eastern Iran, where he found a royal patron for his monotheistic and eschatological message—all positions prevailing in this book.

Walter Henning, a leading scholar of Zoroastrianism at London's School of Oriental and African Studies through the mid-twentieth century, adopted the dates we favor, but he is best known through the further research of his pupil and protégé Mary Boyce (1920–2006), who rejected those dates. Boyce established Zoroastrian studies as an independent discipline, and she encouraged us personally in matters related to the Hebrew connection in the *Three Testaments* precursor of this study. Every Zoroastrian scholar since then owes a debt to this doyen of the discipline, even while the wildly divergent positions of many contributing to the *Wiley Blackwell Compendium* distressed her in the last months of her life. Our interest in Zoroastrianism in some 20 percent of this book is its role as a conduit for a progressive version of the Vedic religious concepts that functioned as the stimulus for an eruption of religious and philosophical fervor from one end of the Silk Route to the other in the fifth and sixth centuries BCE, recognized first in its interplay with Judaism in Babylon during what we now call the Axial Age, when Taoism, Confucianism, Buddhism, and reformed Hinduism came onstage.

book one

FROM THE FOUNDATIONS OF THE EARTH TO OUR COMMON SPIRITUAL ANCESTORS

introduction

East and West Meeting at the Altar of Religion

Cyril Glassé

B OOK I SETS THE ARGUMENT OF THIS VOLUME IN A UNIVERSAL CONTEXT; THE NEXT SEVERAL "books" present the primary Eastern scriptures, which speak for themselves; and the concluding books show the relationship between Eastern and Western texts and point to a greater appreciation of the connection. My comments may serve to link the starting point with the conclusion, perhaps for the benefit of Western readers in particular. This is meant to contextualize rather than ignore the preponderant weight of Eastern scriptures throughout the bulk of this investigation, a sequel and companion to Brian Arthur Brown's seminal work on the Western texts, *Three Testaments: Torah, Gospel, and Quran.*

In proposing a Vedic backdrop for all of the major world religions, Brown builds on previously established links between Jews and the Zoroastrian reconfiguration of Vedic religious lore. That the Jews were profoundly influenced by Zoroastrian priests, the Magi, in the court of Cyrus the Great and his successors is a given. In his previous work, and summarized again here, Brown persuasively argues that Zoroaster himself may have encountered Semitic influences long before Cyrus marched into Babylon, where the interplay continued. The mutual sway of evolving Semitic influences over such Vedic developments, and back again, is a paradigm of similar mutual influences in China and India, as we shall see. The presence of a certain Krishna (traditionally and inexplicably written as "Carshena" in Western Bibles, instead of using an obvious transliteration of the Hebrew letters for Kṛṣṇa) in the Persian court of Ahasuerus[1] represents the wider interplay so skillfully presented in this work.

Vedic "Eastern" influence in Christianity is only beginning to be seen, here and elsewhere. If I may be permitted to quote myself,

Jesus rises from the dead in three days, an interval taken directly from Zoroastrianism. In that religion the dead linger near the grave for three days before continuing their afterlife journey. Half or more of Christianity is composed of elements from Zoroastrianism in compound with elements from Semitic religion. The Evangelists, writing after 80 AD, recording the evolving mass of traditions, took the Teacher of Righteousness (who we know from the Dead Sea Scrolls) and split him into two personae. There was John the Baptist, wearing animal skins, eating locusts, a primitive wolf-man living in the desert, a leader of a world-shunning sect (the Qumran Essenes), giving out his Zoroastrian baptism of New Life. Then there is Jesus himself, born of a virgin as Zoroastrianism said would happen, the *Saoshyant*, the world savior. Isaiah (duly repeating Zoroastrian doctrine) says: "Therefore the Lord himself shall give you a sign: Behold, a virgin shall conceive. And bear a son, and call his name Immanuel." (God is with us.)[2] Isaiah is quoting Zoroastrian dogma on the subject, and pretending otherwise is deliberate obfuscation. The Zoroastrian prophecy is attested by the visit of the Magi, who were Zoroastrian priests, following the "Star out of Jacob"[3] to bring gifts to the baby Jesus to certify that everything was in accordance with the most ancient of religions. This marks him as the Zoroastrian "Saoshyant," or world savior.[4]

The Koran calls the Zoroastrians *Majus*. Muslim authorities, going back to the Caliph Umar, accept Zoroastrians as a People of Scripture, with a revealed religion, thus qualified for the protection of the Islamic State. Zoroaster was the first to proclaim that salvation is possible for all, the humble of mankind as well as the heroes of legend. He composed hymns called *Gathas*, whose Avestan language is close to the Sanskrit of the Rig-Veda, as pointed out some time ago by Professor Geldner.[5]

The Indo-European peoples have demonstrated an intellectual propensity to think metaphorically, to idealize, to take the concrete and turn it into the abstract. The Semitic peoples have a marked propensity to concretize. When these two dynamics of consciousness came into contact with each other during the Iranian expansion into the Semitic world, being diametrically opposed to each other, a reaction took place which could be termed alchemical, a reaction which is still going on to this day. Semitic religious elements combined with Zoroastrian ones to produce new religions[6] [and to revive and reform old ones].

Brown applies this dynamic to the Axial Age developments of religion in the East, both the new religions of Taoism and Buddhism and the classical traditions of Confucianism and Hinduism. The generous and somewhat lengthy treatment of Zoroastrianism and its Vedic antecedents in Book I as themselves being Eastern religions is appropriate as our preparation for understanding the particular Eastern scriptures that are the main subject of this compendium, as well as their links to the Western scriptures, a subject that gets a book of its own near the end.

My simple goal has been to whet your appetite for the following exposition of how all this seems to have happened in ancient times, since the world we live in today continues to shrink, leading to an urgent necessity to understand each other. The East is now within the West, and the West continues its impact on the East. The religious dynamics of our New Axial Age are more important today than they have been for many centuries.

exordium

What We Once Knew

Karl Friedrich Geldner

This exordium is excerpted directly from the eleventh edition of the *Encyclopedia Britannica* of 1910–1911, the classic edition in which the superlative scholarship was so respected that its articles have been taken as primary sources in academic circles for over a hundred years. The following presentation on Zoroaster upheld that standard in the early education of most scholars of Zoroastrianism in the twentieth century, including those who broke the new ground that is a subtext of this book, allowing us to grow into the subject with them. Its archaic idiom may serve as one link with antiquity inasmuch as the religious ethos over one hundred years ago was almost closer to that of the ancients than to us. Please note that here the name of the Zoroastrian God is frequently abbreviated from *Ahura Mazda* to *Or-mazd*, the popular usage two generations after the death of Zoroaster, and frequently employed by Professor Geldner in this précis of his article, our entrée to the subtext of the world religions that first developed in the hemispheres we designate as East and West.

ZOROASTER, ONE OF THE GREAT TEACHERS OF THE EAST, THE FOUNDER OF WHAT WAS THE national religion of the Perso-Iranian people from the time of the Achaemenidae to close of the Sassanian period. The name is the corrupt Greek[1] form of the old Iranian Zarathustra.[2] Its signification is obscure, but it certainly contains the word *ushtra*, or "camel." Zoroaster was already famous in classical antiquity as the founder of the widely renowned wisdom of the Magi.

The ancients also recount a few points regarding the childhood of Zoroaster and his hermit-life. Thus, according to Pliny,[3] he laughed on the very day of his birth and lived in the wilderness upon cheese.[4] Plutarch speaks of his intercourse with the deity.[5] Dio Chrysostom, Plutarch's contemporary, declares that neither Homer nor

Hesiod sang of the chariot and horses of Zeus so worthily as Zoroaster, of whom the Persians tell that, out of love for wisdom and righteousness, he withdrew himself from men, and lived in solitude upon a mountain. The mountain was consumed by fire, but Zoroaster escaped uninjured and spoke to the multitude.[6] Plutarch speaks of his religion in his *Isis and Osiris*.[7]

As to the period in which he lived, most of the Greeks had by then lost the true perspective. Hermodorus and Hermippus of Smyrna place him five thousand years before the Trojan war, Xanthus six thousand years before Xerxes, Eudoxus and Aristotle six thousand years before the death of Plato. Agathias remarks,[8] with perfect truth, that it is no longer possible to determine with any certainty when he lived and legislated. "The Persians," he adds, "say that Zoroaster lived under Hystaspes, but do not make it clear whether by this name they mean the father of Darius or another Hystaspes. But, whatever may have been his date, he was their teacher and instructor in the Magian religion, modified their former religious customs, and introduced a variegated and composite belief."[9]

He is nowhere mentioned in the cuneiform inscriptions of the Achaemenidae, although Cyrus, Darius, and their successors were without doubt devoted adherents of Zoroastrianism. The Avesta is, indeed, our principle source for the doctrine of Zoroaster; on the subject of his person and his life it is comparatively reticent; with regard to his date it is, naturally enough, absolutely silent. The whole thirteenth section, or *Spend Nask*, which was mainly consecrated to the description of his life, is among the many sections which have perished; while the biographies founded upon it in the seventh book of the *Dinkard* (ninth century AD), the *Shāh-Nāma*, and the *Zardusht-Nāma* (thirteenth century), are merely legendary—full of wonders, fabulous histories, and miraculous deliverances.

The Gāthā poem prayers alone within the Avesta make the claim to be the *ipissima verba*, the very words of the prophet; in the rest of that work they are described as being from Zoroaster's own mouth[10] and are expressly called "the Gāthās of the holy Zoroaster."[11] The litanies of the Yasna, and the Yashts, refer to him as a personage belonging to the past. The Vendidad also merely gives accounts of the dialogues between Ormazd (a late spelling of Ahura Mazda) and Zoroaster. The Gāthās alone claim to be authentic utterances of Zoroaster, his actual expressions in the presence of the assembled congregation. They are the last genuine survivals of the doctrinal discourses with which—as the promulgator of a new religion—he appeared at the court of King Vishtāspa in Bactria.

According to the epic legend, Vīshtāspa (Greek: Hystaspes) was king of Bactria. According to the *Arda Vīrāf*,[12] Zororoaster began his teaching before this regal convert, in round numbers, some three hundred years before the invasion of Alexander. Probably he emanated from the old school of Median Magi, and appeared earlier in Media as the prophet of a new faith, but met with sacerdotal opposition, and turned his steps eastward. It was to the east of Iran that the novel creed first acquired a solid footing, and only subsequently reacted with success upon the West.

His doctrine was rooted in the old Iranian—Aryan—folk religion, of which we can only form an approximate representation by comparison with Vedic religion. The Aryan folk religion was polytheistic. Worship was paid to popular divinities, such as the war god and dragon slayer Indra, and to natural forces and elements such as fire, but the Aryans also believed in the ruling of moral powers and of an eternal law in nature.[13] Numerous similarities with Vedic religion survive in Zoroastrianism, side by side with marked reforms. The *daēvas*, unmasked and attacked by Zoroaster as the true enemies of mankind, are still in the Gāthās, without doubt the gods of old popular belief—the idols of the people. For Zoroaster they sink to the rank of spurious deities, even while maintaining spiritual vigor.

Some few of these have names; and among those names of the old Aryan divinities emerge here and there, for example, Indra and Nāonhaitya. With some, of course—such as Igni, the god of fire—the connection with the good deity was *a priori* indissoluble. Other powers of light, such as Mithra,[14] the god of day, survived unforgotten in popular belief until the later system incorporated them into the angelic body. Beyond the Lord and his Fire, the Gāthās only recognize the archangels and certain ministers of Ormazd, who are, without exception, personifications of abstract ideas. The essence of Ormazd is Truth and Law:[15] The essence of the wicked spirit is falsehood: and falsehood, as the embodiment of the evil principle, is much more frequently mentioned in the Gāthās than Ahriman or Satan himself.

Zoroaster says of himself that he had received from God a commission to purify religion.[16] He purified it from the grossly sensual elements of *daēva* worship, and uplifted the idea of religion to a higher purer sphere. The body of Vedic Aryan folk belief, when subjected to the unifying thought of a speculative brain, was transformed to a self-contained theory of the universe and a logical dualistic principle. But this dualism is a temporally limited dualism—no more than an episode in the world-whole—and is destined to terminate in monotheism. Later sects sought to rise from it to a higher unity in other ways. Thus the Zarvanites represented Ormazd and Ahriman as twin sons proceeding from the fundamental principle of all—*Zrvana Akarana,* or limitless time.

The doctrine of Zoroaster and the Zoroastrian religion may be summarized somewhat as follows:—

At the beginning of things there existed the two spirits who represented good and evil.[17] The existence of evil in the world is thus presupposed from the beginning. Both spirits possess creative power, which manifests itself positively in the one and negatively in the other. Ormazd is light and life, and creates all that is pure and good—in the ethical world of law, order, and truth. His antithesis is darkness, filth, death, and produces all that is evil in the world. Until then the two spirits had counterbalanced one another. The ultimate triumph of the good spirit in ethical demand of the religious consciousness is the quintessence of Zoroaster's religion.[18]

As soon as the two separate spirits encounter one another,[19] their creative activity and at the same time their permanent conflict begin. The history of this conflict is the history of the world. A great cleft runs right through the world: all creation divides itself into that which is Ahura's and that which is Ahriman's. Not that the two spirits carry on the struggle in person; they leave it to be fought out by their respective creations and creatures which they sent into the field. The field of battle is the present world.

In the center of battle is man: his soul is the object of the war. Man is the creation of Ormazd, who therefore has the right to call him to account. But Ormazd created him free in his determinations and in his actions, wherefore he is accessible to the influences of the evil powers. This freedom of the will is clearly expressed in the Avesta: "Since thou, O Mazda, didst at the first create our being and our consciences in accordance with thy mind, and didst create our understanding and our life together with the body, and works and words in which man according to his own will can frame his confession, the liar and the truth-speaker alike lay hold of the word, the knowing and the ignorant each after his own heart and understanding."[20] Man takes part in this conflict by all his life and activity in the world.

The life of man falls into two parts—its earthly portion, and that which is lived after death is past. The lot assigned to him after death is the result and consequence of his life upon earth. No ancient religion had so clearly grasped the ideas of individual guilt and of merit. On the works of men here below a strict reckoning will be held in heaven. All the thoughts, words, and deeds of each are entered in the book of life as separate items—all the evil works, et cetera, as debts. Wicked actions cannot be undone, but in the heavenly account can be counterbalanced by a surplus of good works. It is only in this sense that an evil deed can be atoned for by good deed.

After death the soul arrives at the *cinvatō peretu*, or accountant's bridge, over which lies the way to heaven. Here the statement of his life account is made out. If he has a balance of good works in his favor, he passes forthwith into paradise[21] and the blessed life. If his evil works outweigh his good, he falls finally under the power of Satan, and the pains of hell are his portion forever.

Zoroaster experienced within himself the inward call to seek the amelioration of mankind and their deliverance from ruin, and regarded this inner impulse, intensified as it was by long, contemplative solitude and by visions, as being the call addressed to him by God Himself. Like Muhammad after him he often speaks of his conversations with God and the archangels. He calls himself most frequently *manthran* ("prophet"), *ratu* ("spiritual authority"), and *saoshyant* ("the coming helper"—that is to say, when men come to be judged according to their deeds).

Like John the Baptist and the Apostles of Jesus, Zoroaster also believed that the fullness of time was near, that the kingdom of heaven was at hand. Through the whole of the Gāthās runs the pious hope that the end of the present world is not far distant. He himself hopes, with his followers, to live to see the decisive turn of things, the dawn of the new and better eon. Ormazd will summon together all his powers for a final decisive struggle and break the power of evil forever; by his help the faithful will achieve the victory over their detested enemies, the *daēva* worshippers, and render them impotent. Thereupon Ormazd will hold a *judicium universale*, in the form of a general ordeal, a great test of all mankind by fire and molten metal, and will judge strictly according to justice, punish the wicked, and assign to the good the hoped-for reward.

Satan will be cast, along with all those who have been delivered over to him to suffer the pains of hell, into the abyss, where he will henceforward lie powerless. Forthwith begins the one undivided kingdom of God in heaven and on earth. This is called, sometimes the good kingdom, sometimes simply the kingdom. Here the sun will forever shine, and all the pious and faithful will live a happy life, which no evil power can disturb, in the eternal fellowship of Ormazd and his angels.

The last things and the end of the world are relegated to the close of a long period of time, when a new Saoshyant is to be born of the seed of the prophet, the dead are to come to life, and a new incorruptible world to begin.

preface

Why the Z Factor Matters

THE ANCIENT VEDIC HERITAGE MAY BE SEEN AS THE FOUNDATION OF EASTERN MONISTIC religions, Hindu, Jain, Buddhist, and even Tao to some extent, with Confucianism perhaps a reaction to the introduction of this influence in China. The only comparable influence in world religions is the Semitic heritage that is the cradle for Western monotheistic religions: Judaism, Christianity, and Islam. This compendium is intended to develop our understanding of the Eastern traditions and to show their influence upon and relationship with the Western traditions. Vedic-based Zoroastrianism is presented as both the main connector and the principal conduit of Eastern correlation in the West.

In the Vedic traditions, any situation "is what it is," and devotees are enjoined to "go with the flow" and act correctly within it (the flow being the complete One monistic universe). In Semitic tradition, no situation is what it should be (at least since the "fall" of humanity), and believers are challenged to change things and act accordingly. Aryan Vedic notions of "super race" (lamentably promoted in Germany in the middle of the last century, but not limited to that) and Semitic concepts of "chosen people" (upheld by Jews, Christians, and Muslims in equal but different ways) are both mitigated by Zoroastrian principles, as we shall see, but it is little wonder that peoples have sometimes clashed under Vedic and Semitic influences. We are entering an era in which it is increasingly necessary that they contribute to each other in our one world in ways that enhance the faith of those engaged in practically all major world religions.

It is not to be expected that many readers of this interfaith tome will be converted to another tradition as a result of considering the faith of others from the positive perspective in this particular study. However, it is to be hoped that members of each tradition might at least become better Taoists, Confucians, Buddhists, Hindus, Jews, Christians, Muslims, and whatever else through this exercise.

Extensive missing portions of the Zoroastrian "Avesta" Scriptures may be the Rosetta Stone of common ground among the "world religions" and could contribute generously to mutual respect among believers when found. These "Dead Zee Scrolls" will certainly contain material related to the three testaments of Western monotheistic religion (Torah, Gospel, and Quran), and they will also illuminate the early development of Eastern monistic religious texts, especially Taoist, Hindu, and Buddhist examples, all developing in the churning wake of Zoroaster.

The Avesta, as the Zoroastrian scriptural corpus is called, was once the most broadly circulated and widely translated written material in the world, disseminated east and west along and beyond the Silk Route. The Zoroastrian tradition of respect for others and tolerance of their religion was established by Cyrus the Great in the Persian Empire but eventually rejected by the Greeks in their promotion of a European vision of "civilization," and by Muslims who encountered a later Zoroastrianism that had lost its focus on the Oneness of God, a matter found to be offensive. So the main corpus of the Zoroastrian Scriptures was deliberately destroyed twice, first by the Europeans under Alexander the Great and again by Muslims after Muhammad. But copies had undoubtedly been stored by accident or hidden in various places, much like the Dead Sea Scrolls and the Nag Hammadi Library, so valued now by Jews and Christians. Strange to say, the search for this Zoroastrian treasure has only now begun in earnest.

In their prayers today, Zoroastrians employ only some 20 percent of the ancient Avesta material, rescued or remembered from those destructive calamities. This book details the ancient references to that vast earlier collection and points to the near certainty that complete versions of two distinct editions will eventually be found, perhaps sooner rather than later, and conceivably equalling the Dead Sea Scrolls in both size and significance. In this compendium, we exhibit material already found and examine the prospects for an unearthing of the entire mother lode, even while looking for clues between the lines of the scriptures that emerged in the wake of the appearance of the Avesta along the Silk Route both east and west.

Archaeologists in Uzbekistan and Western China are now turning up interesting Zoroastrian artifacts from the fifth century CE, but these are just remnants of a religious tradition that actually flourished more significantly a thousand years earlier. With a pristine bronze statue of Apollo found off Gaza in 2014, the 2013 appearance of a cuneiform disk in Mesopotamia showing blueprints of the ark modeled by Noah, and the Roman eagle discovered under the streets of London in 2012, all from the prime earlier Zoroastrian era, why would we not assume that the most published book in the world of that era would turn up under the streets of Samarkand or among tens of thousands of as yet uncataloged manuscripts stored in the library of the Southwest University of Nationalities in China or elsewhere? Current archaeological expeditions employ space age technology and infrared camera techniques capable of finding troves of artifacts and caches of documents, some of which might have been hidden in circumstances remarkably similar to the concealment of the Dead Sea Scrolls and the famous Nag Hammadi Library. Whether by design or by accident, the finding of the "Dead Zee Scrolls" jackpot is now only a matter of time (and with it new clues to the origins of Eastern scriptures in particular).

The search for clues to what may have been in the Avesta text will unfold in this book, chapter by chapter. Excitement has been mounting about the possibilities of locating copies of the ancient originals, and even during the writing our interest was piqued by a press conference announcement from the Institute of Archaeology of the Academy of Sciences of Uzbekistan.[1] A fifth-century BCE temple at Khorazm (a province of the ancient Persian Empire just north of Bactria, Zoroasters headquarters, near the borders of today's Turkmenistan and Afghanistan) has been positively identified as a Zoroastrian fire temple from the precise era of our interest. Being unearthed in good condition except for four towers at the corners, the 625-square-meter temple is yielding pitchers, jugs, vessels, bowls, jars, terra-cotta figurines, bronze medallions, pins, and arrowheads in intact, bright, and expressive condition. The excavation is now complete and has yielded no documents, but the search continues in this area. Other important sites to which we will refer were unearthed early in the twentieth century, as the field of Zoroastrian studies began to get organized, and the pace is picking up in the twenty-first. Even as we go to press, archaeologists in Northwest China's Xinjiang Uygur Autonomous Region have discovered major Zoroastrian tombs, dated to over 2,500 years ago on the sparsely populated Pamir Plateau. This find purportedly exceeds all previously known Zoroastrian cultural artifacts, but still no complete Avesta.

We join the leading universities of Russia, China, India, Europe, and North America in the hunt for this important written artifact in the quest to discover that we are one world, and to prove that religious development has been interrelated. We already know that Zoroastrianism provides a model precedent for mutual respect in the diversity we should cherish in mixed societies of the twenty-first century. Not even the excavation of Troy near the end of the nineteenth century or the putative discovery of Atlantis in photos taken from space at the end of the twentieth century could match the communal or cultural significance for our era of finding the Avesta Scriptures. This will be a treasure for religious people, grist for the academic mill through the twenty-first century, and front-cover material for tabloids at the supermarket in the future as superficial headlines dramatically proclaim: SOURCE OF ALL SCRIPTURES FOUND.

Meanwhile, we will experience a new appreciation of the Zoroastrian Avesta from "testaments" of the religions whose monism exploded upon a vast region of the East within the same era that monotheism burst beyond its Semitic base in the West. Both developments may have happened in response to stimuli in the Axial Age, triggered by that certain Persian prophet. The initial intersection of these developments is the subject of Book I, beginning with an analysis of the religion most of us know the least about.

Indeed, in Book I we almost appear to digress from the four testaments themselves before we even start on them. This is to provide the reader with insights into Zoroastrianism and its Vedic antecedents in the relationship between monotheism and monism before we present those main features of the compendium, in order to fully appreciate the Eastern monistic perspective. Much later we conclude with an appreciation of how all this impacts upon Western monotheism and where we may be headed in a future in which East and West more fully appreciate each other.

1

fRom the foundations of the earth

Vedic and Semitic Prehistories Connecting East and West

THE FOLLOWING DEPICTION OF TWO ANCIENT AND SURVIVING TRADITIONS RELATED TO OUR theme is not meant to settle any outstanding disagreements among either Vedic or Semitic scholars, and is therefore painted in broad strokes to give an introductory summary that is relatively beyond dispute. This is for the benefit of readers new to the material in preparation for understanding how these traditions intersected in possibly one of the most dramatic interchanges of religious ideas in world history, with repercussions east and west as reflected in the scriptures under investigation in this and the related previous compendium.

Proto-Vedic religion is the hypothesized religion of Proto-Indo-European peoples (sometimes abbreviated as PIE) around 3600–3000 BCE, based on the existence of similarities among sacred linguistic terms, deities, religious practices, and mythologies among those later referred to as "Indo-European" peoples in the Russian Steppes prior to the dynamic Aryan migrations northwest across Europe and southeast through Iran and into India.

In 1147 CE the new city of Moscow was named after the ancient Moscva River, on which the city is situated, a name cognate with *moksha*, the Sanskrit Vedic word meaning "salvation," often associated with river rites, which still remain significant among Hindu descendants of Vedic-related traditions still today. This linguistic marker is but one of the more obvious among a great number that locate the proto-Vedic religion of Aryan migrants as originating in Russia, right down to the current Russian word *vedat*, which means "knowledge," obviously derived from the Indo-European roots *veda* and *Vedic*. Other evidence for this origin of Vedic religion relates to Aryan archaeology and religious traditions. We will limit ourselves to the latter in this study, secure in the knowledge that evidence for the overall thesis is easily accessed elsewhere.

In the religious connection, the most obvious link is the names of gods from the area we now call the Russian Steppes, as they appear in the Vedic Scripture known as the Rig Veda and other Vedic sacred materials that followed in India and Persia. Indra, Mitra, and Varuna are Vedic gods: Varuna the sky, Mitra the sun, and Indra representing the power of nature. In the various iterations of these Aryan gods found in Scandinavia, Central and Southern Europe, Persia, and India, these three also tend to represent a tripartite theology found in all Indo-European religions, excepting Greek. The three functions are sacerdotal, martial, and productivity, though we would be oversimplifying if we ignore other important gods found throughout this swath of humanity, like Agni, the god of fire and acceptor of sacrifices, whose name is actually the first word in the first verse of the ancient Rig Veda scripture. The Aryan migration into India and Persia (Iran) took place for the most part between 2500 and 1500 BCE, with trailblazers before and stragglers after.

The Rig Veda, a collection of over one thousand hymns and mythic poems, is the oldest continuously used scriptural material in the world. Written down around 1200 BCE, the Rig Veda was "composed" earlier and maintained orally in the final form we have it by the Aryans in India around 1500 BCE. While also showing influence from the ancient Harappan high culture they overran, the Rig Veda was being developed even hundreds of years earlier, before the Aryans left Russia as shown by place names, linguistic markers, names of gods, and other evidence. When it was written down, it was first written in Vedic, an early form of Sanskrit, and related to the widespread Avestan language employed by Zoroaster. If its composition began in Russia, and it was completed in India and written down later there, we can only guess what stage it was at or what status it enjoyed *en route* from the Russian Steppes to the Indus River, except that as it passed through Persia much of it appeared not dissimilar to the classic mode in which we have it, judging by the use Zoroaster makes of this material as quoted in his poetic "Gatha" prayers in the Avesta, the scriptures of his "new" reformed Vedic religion.

Indeed, by the seventh century BCE, Zoroaster may have even been familiar with the accepted written version of the Rig Veda, or at least the transitional material that led to its production. He adopted its then archaic dialect of the twelfth century BCE to authenticate his reforms in much the same way that twentieth-century Christians used the dialect of the King James Version of the Bible to endow their new hymns with authenticity, and a familiar sense of holiness, despite a similar time lapse. Radhakrishnan and Gandhi used KJV English for twentieth-century translations of the *Dhammapada* and *Bhagavad Gita* for the same reason.

While the Rig Veda is the oldest of the Vedas, there are three other Vedic Scriptures, the Sama Veda chants, the Yajur Veda rites, and the Athara Veda teachings of theology, all entirely composed and eventually written down in India. These later compositions had little or no influence on Zoroaster in Persia, and among Vedic influences it is his material, reformed from the Rig Veda alone, that impacted the Jews in Babylon under the aegis of Zoroastrian rulers and their Magi priests.

Proto-Semitic culture is the hypothetical progenitor of historical Semitic languages in the Middle East. Locations that have been proposed for its origination include northern Mesopotamia, the Arabian Peninsula, and the Levant (Greater Syria), with recent estimates that this antecedent of Semitism may have originated around 3750 BCE, the era of the very first stirrings of Aryan identity in Russia.

The word "Semitic" is an adjective derived from Shem, one of the sons of Noah in the biblical book of Genesis, from the Greek version of that name—namely, Σημ (Sēm). The concept of "Semitic peoples" is derived from biblical accounts of the origins of the cultures known to the ancient Hebrews. In an effort to categorize the peoples known to them, those closest to them in culture and language were generally deemed to be descended from their forefather, Shem. Those in other parts of the world were thought to descend from the other surviving sons of Noah as they moved out following the biblical account of the flood, his son Canaan having drowned in the deluge after refusing to get on board the ark.[1]

In Genesis 10:21–31, Shem is described as the father of Aram, Ashur, and Arpachshad, who are presented in the Bible as the ancestors of the Arabs, Aramaeans, and Assyrians, as well as Babylonians, Chaldeans, Sabaeans, and Hebrews, all of whose languages are closely related. This whole language family was accordingly named "Semitic" by linguists, with the pejorative term "anti-Semitic" only coming into existence in reference to the Jews alone since 1879, when William Marr founded the "League for Anti-Semitism" in Germany.

Mesopotamia is generally held to be "The Cradle of Civilization," where writing, the wheel, and the first organized nations or city-states arose during the mid-fourth millennium BCE. Rivaled in certain developments by only the pre-Aryan Harappan civilization in northern India (and perhaps as yet undocumented developments in China), the Sumero-Akkadian states that arose in Mesopotamia between about the thirty-sixth century BCE and the twenty-fourth century BCE were the most advanced in the world at the time in terms of engineering, architecture, agriculture, science, medicine, mathematics, astronomy, and military technology. Many had highly sophisticated socioeconomic structures, with the world's earliest examples of written law, together with structurally advanced and complex trading, business, and taxation systems, a well-structured civil administration, currency, and detailed record keeping. Schools and educational systems existed in many states, Mesopotamian religions were highly organized, and astrology was widely practiced. By the time of the Middle Assyrian Empire in the mid-second millennium BCE, early examples of zoology, botany, and landscaping had emerged, and during the Neo-Assyrian Empire in the early to mid-first millennium BCE, the world's first public library was built by King Ashurbanipal in the ancient Mesopotamian city of Nineveh.

In the nineteenth century BCE a wave of Semites entered Egypt, possibly about the time Abraham and his family made their pilgrimage there. By the early seventeenth century BCE these Hyksos, as they were known by the Egyptians, had conquered the country, with possibly "Sons of Israel" as their slaves, forming the Fifteenth Dynasty, to be succeeded by the Sixteenth and Seventeenth Dynasties. The New Kingdom, next in sequence from possibly 1550 BCE until about 1050, was the Egyptian era the world knows best, with its famous pharaohs, the biblical account of Moses leading the Israelites out of slavery, and an interlude of monotheism under Akhenaten, so swayed by his wife. The beautiful Nefertiti was a Mitanni princess who may have brought monotheism from the Assyrian desert, though her Semitic community there also worshipped the Aryan Vedic gods, Mitra, Varuna, Indra, and the Nasatya twins (Sunrise and Sunset), an early preview of the coming encounter between the two main religious traditions of the ancient world.

All early Semites across the entire Near East appear to have been originally polytheist, except for the tentative emergence of what we might call the proto-monotheism of some desert people, such as Abraham, and possibly Nefertiti. Mesopotamian religion is the earliest recorded in writing in its own time, and for three millennia it was the most influential, exerting strong influence in what is today Syria, Lebanon, Jordan, Israel, Palestine, and the Sinai Peninsula. Its ideas—rejected, "corrected," or improved upon—may be seen in the later Semitic monotheistic religions of Judaism, Christianity, Manichaeism, Mandaeism, Gnosticism, and Islam.

Some of the most significant of the Mesopotamian deities were Anu, Ea, Enlil, Enki, Ishtar (Astarte), Ashur, Shamash, Shulmanu, Tammuz, Adad (Hadad), Sin (Nanna), Dagan (Dagon), Ninurta, Nisroch, Nergal, Tiamat, Bel, Ninlil, and Marduk, representing an entirely independent subset of theological ideas, separate from the Vedic religion of the same era. Out of this welter of divinities, the above Semitic monotheistic religions of Judaism, Christianity, Manichaeism, Mandaeism, Gnosticism, and Islam came forth, beginning with the Israelites, regardless of mistaken populist and new age notions about Zoroaster being the world's first monotheist, as we shall see.

Israel, as the very first among surviving examples of monotheism, gradually evolved with the founding of Judaism and the belief in one single God, Yahweh, often unpronounced in reverential respect, and frequently written using only the Hebrew Consonants, יהוה, or YHWH. The Hebrew language, closely related to the earlier attested Canaanite language of Phoenicians, would become the vehicle of the religious literature of the Torah (referred to by Muslims as *Taurat*) and the more complete Tanakh (referred to by Christians as the Old Testament), thus eventually having global ramifications. We will trace its influence in the East as well.

Scholars may observe that monotheism and its ramifications appear to have "evolved" in this culture, but religious records and the experience of many believers attest to an understanding that this development was triggered by specific incidents in which God's very self was "revealed" to leaders like Moses and the prophets who were chosen by God. These revelations were then shared with others by people who were similarly called to prophetic utterance, as we shall attempt to illustrate.

The point that there is no "Aryan gene" and no "Aryan super race" would not be worth making, were it not for the immature delusions of a miniscule but dangerous remnant of fanatics who can be found in the strangest of places. The Aryans were a hybrid tribal polyglot that was somehow concentrated in valleys west of the Ural mountains and east of the Danube River system until it burst upon the world with great energy, moving in several directions but especially into India and "Iran" (the "Aryan" nation), from whence Magi emissaries made their way even into China. I have elsewhere compared the claim of Aryan racial superiority to a naïve child hearing from a parent that their new dog is a mongrel and going forth to proclaim to playmates with pride that "our dog is a pure-bred mongrel." Something similar obtains with respect to the Semitic peoples who are also not a "race" but a language group with dynamic histories and impacts upon the world, derived from the vibrancy of an early hybrid mix of people at the great hinge of the world where three continents connect. Again we are more interested in the ideas, including religious ideas, which emanated from this group than their particular genetic composition, except for purposes of tracking their migrations.

We shall return to the peripatetic Aryans and their Vedic religion shortly, but meanwhile some comment in passing about changing perspectives on movements of Semitic peoples might be in order. The Jews in particular are of interest with their gift of monotheism to the world, on their own and through Zoroaster and other influences, including later Christians and Muslims (the latter in perhaps a less derivative sense, by their own account). The Jews migrated in several directions in search of economic and other opportunities, sometimes triggered by expulsions or persecutions. Their presence in business along the Silk Route throughout history has been documented and is increasingly attested by DNA evidence among populations from Israel to China, amid both people who have always claimed a Jewish identity for themselves and others who have lost all memory of such a connection.

People now identified as "Jews" came up into Europe through Asia Minor and Scythia beginning with the Assyrian expulsion of the ten northern "Israelite" tribes in 722 BCE, followed by some others who went to Europe *en route* through Egypt more than a hundred years later when separate groups from Jerusalem and Judah also went into exile in Babylon in 598 and 587 BCE. Another migration took place after the destruction of Jerusalem by the Romans in 70 CE, with the difference being that there were significant Jewish populations already present to greet them in the cities of Egypt, Turkey, Greece, Italy, the Balkan countries, and to a lesser extent Spain, France, and Germany, to use the current place names. Were subsequent local concentrations of Jewish inhabitants mainly recent migrants, or were they populations related to earlier exiles in 722 BCE, 598 or 587 BCE, or 70 CE? The jury is out on the question of whether these scattered Jewish communities were based on a combination of all these Mediterranean and European accumulations of monotheistic Semites over many centuries.

DNA research now attests to a long-standing Jewish presence in Central Asia, along the Silk Route, and into both China and India. Such pockets of genetically specific Semitic Jews are often also now identified with the "lost tribes of Israel" of the seventh century BCE by gravesites and historical artifacts. Similar research proves beyond doubt that Spain harbors a large Semitic presence, both Jewish and Arabic, despite the determination of Ferdinand and Isabella to expel all such populations in 1492. Similar studies are ongoing to identify a Jewish presence in Africa, from Ethiopia to Zimbabwe among tribes who have traditionally claimed a Jewish identity, and parts of Europe where such collective memories have been suppressed or ridiculed, as in the case of "British Israel." The point of this digression is to illustrate that the extent of movement by Semitic peoples may be almost as extensive as that of the Indo-European Aryan migrations, and that the intersection of the two cultures and their religious interchange was formative in world culture. Periodic tragic experiences of interface between them, as in Germany in the twentieth century, are as much a support to this thesis as detraction from it. Obviously more was going on than meets the eye, and folk traditions are increasingly regarded as having the potential for historical veracity if corroborated by other evidence such as DNA and archaeological investigations.

The point in reference to this study is that just as genes mix and migrate, so do ideas and beliefs. All people make their contributions to warlike and peaceful mentalities, sporting competition and culture, music composition and performance, scientific discovery and technology, and, of course, religion, in various measures and at various times. The thesis behind this compendium is that Vedic religion forms the backdrop behind much of what endures to our time in Eastern religions. This may be especially true of a particular Vedic tradition that crossed paths with a certain Semitic tradition in a dynamic interface that has had ramifications through the ages.

Research a hundred years ago demonstrated that well before their migrations in the 2500 to 1500 BCE millennium, the Aryans worshipped *Dyaus Pitr*, the "Divine Father," who created the universe.[2] Known as *Gitchi Manitou* on the Great Central Plains of North America, and called *Shang Di* in the "Border Sacrifice" of ancient China, *Altjira* in the Australian Outback, *Nyambe* in the west tropics of Africa, and *Brahman* in India, this religious instinct was shared by aboriginal peoples around the world. Before 1500 BCE the remoteness of God resulted in a growing Vedic adulation of life forces called "devas" (from which we get both "divinities" and "devils") that were closer at hand to these spirited Aryans.

Agni (or Igni) the fire spirit, existed in concurrence with other forces of nature that needed to be harnessed through communal worship. Varuna, representing the night, the waters, the underworld, and the unconscious, maintained order. Indra, the divine warrior, defended the people from their foes. Mythra, the deva of sun and rain, would nourish and replenish the earth. Mazda, whose name means "wisdom," would engender the cult of wisdom and all the wisdom traditions that form subtexts of many religions down through the ages. It was the Lord of Wisdom, Ahura Mazda, who rose in Zoroastrianism to represent the Dyaus Pitr, though closer at hand and available to those seeking guidance in the midst of chaos; God was at last seen to be both transcendent and immanent (echoing discussions among believers in many religions today).

Chaos had come with a new stirring of the spirit of adventure and even conflict in the era of migration. Mythra would develop from a peaceful fertility deva to become the favorite mascot-god of the Roman Legion as certain legions of that army became Aryanized. More dramatically, and even earlier, the Aryans had adopted bronze weapons from the Armenians and learned to hitch their wild horses to wagons acquired from Kazakh neighbors, leading to their invention of the war chariot. In their sweep into India, Indra was transformed from a defensive patron to a spirit of the scourge. "Heroes with noble horses ready for war, and chosen warriors, call upon me! I am Indra, Lord of plunder. I excite the conflict. I stir up the dust. I am the Lord of unsurpassed vigor."[3]

The movement of these peoples into Persia appears less violent than the move into India in some respects. The migration to Persia appears to have attracted gentler elements of the Aryan culture, including many who sought to simply maintain the old pastoral ways. However some in their midst were stirred with the spirit of plunder and adventure, even to preying on their fellow Aryans in the name of strife that brings victory and reward to the strong. "Dog eat dog" and "every man for himself" were slogans appropriate for the times, and the price was high for women and children, farmers settling into production, the elderly, and anyone with cattle that could be rustled. What kind of gods were these devas now? This question would have been uppermost in the mind of the young Zoroaster.

The account of the revelation Zoroaster received at the river may appear to be identical to the biblical story of Daniel at the River Ulai,[4] which is also located in Persia, but the young prophet Zoroaster, in the first instance, was a hundred years earlier. No one need doubt the meaning or the significance of the reported appearance of the archangel Gabriel to Daniel just because that epiphany is identical in format to the earlier appearance to Zoroaster, as recorded in the ancient but still extant Avesta Scriptures of Zoroastrianism. Apocryphal or otherwise, Daniel's epiphany is placed at the beginning of the reign of Cyrus the Great, Persia's first Zoroastrian monarch, but similar appearances by Gabriel heralded the births of John the Baptist[5] and Jesus Christ[6] in the Gospel according to Luke.

The unexpected appearance of Gabriel to Muhammad in the Cave of Hera[7] also bears a striking resemblance to the angelic appearances to Zoroaster and to Daniel, Zechariah, and Mary. It was this same archangel who appeared time and again to Muhammad over the next twenty-three years, always unannounced and unexpected, to present the Recitations that stand now as the final chapters of scripture in the Abrahamic family compendium. This is not the forum in which to address skeptics who are unable to rationally fathom the reality or the meaning of angelic appearances. Suffice it to say that the powerful phenomenological occurrences reported in Zoroastrianism bear an uncanny resemblance to critical embryonic junctures in the three Western religions whose scriptures were the substance of the compendium prior to this one: chaotic times, a spectral appearance to a spiritually questing individual, and a commitment to share the ways of God in peace and service.

The moment when Zoroaster was confronted and instructed by the archangel was not the first or the last occasion when religion changed from ritual, from philosophy, and from theology into experience, and from communal rites into personal encounter with the divine. God's call for Abraham to leave home,[8] the story of Jacob's ladder[9] and his wrestling all night that changed him into Israel,[10] Moses at the burning bush[11] and on Mount Sinai[12] are all examples of this phenomenon. St. Paul, knocked off his horse on the road to Damascus,[13] and Muhammad, tightly embraced by the angel

Gabriel in the Hera Cave, were far into the future, but further testimony to religious convictions borne of experiential rather than philosophical phenomena.

Ritual, philosophy, and theology have also survived, in formal religious guise and otherwise, but what Karl Jaspers has helped us recognize as the Axial Age[14] of reform may be attributed in significant measure to that moment of revelation experienced by Zoroaster at the river. Within a hundred years after Zoroaster, to the east the Buddha was transforming Hinduism and founding his religion of enlightenment, and farther east Lao Tzu elucidated the Tao and Confucius taught a traditional philosophy in reaction to it. To the west the classical age of prophecy emerged with dramatic impact in Israel, while even farther west the philosophers of Greece swept away an old mythology with deeper passions of the mind, based on questions of individual responsibility to transcendent realities or even "Reality."

If Semitic Jewish genes could spread throughout the earth in ancient, middle, and modern times, how much more easily could seminal ideas spread? Much current research about Zoroastrianism comes from the Sassanian epoch as late as the fifth, sixth, seventh, and eighth centuries CE, accessible to us but possibly not entirely typical of earlier Zoroastrian influence and power. In fact, the fifth-century CE era currently under international investigation along the Silk Route, while yielding exciting information and insights, might almost be characterized as a "dark age" period for Zoroastrianism, immediately before its virtual disappearance. Of infinitely greater significance would be the Zoroastrian situation and its influence a full thousand years earlier. At this point we can only examine that phenomenon through observation of its churning wake along the Silk Route and just beyond, east and west. That may be about to change, but for now there is more even in that wake than meets the eye at first.

The significance of the dates 628–551 BCE for Zoroaster has been recognized partly as a result of growing acceptance of the Axial Age theory, popularized now by writers such as Karen Armstrong in *The Great Transformation*. Sometimes called the *Pivotal Age* in English,[15] Jaspers originally used his "axis time" to describe a slightly broader era of a few centuries, though he was then still unable to identify a specific "pivot," or what we might call "the axis of the Axial Age." He locates Zoroaster just prior to Cyrus in Persia, as we do, but the connection of the Axial Age directly to Zoroaster depends on dates and other issues not resolved before Jaspers died in 1969.

It would now appear that Zoroaster died about a dozen years before Cyrus the Great occupied Babylon and began Persian rule over some 127 former kingdoms of various sizes. This empire of the world's first superpower comprised nearly one-fifth of the world's land mass, equal to the Roman Empire at its height, the British Empire at its zenith, or the Soviet Union before its collapse. The state religion was a Zoroastrianism that featured a tolerant and inclusive monotheism, and the era under Cyrus represents the Axial Age in full bloom. The influence and the power of the Zoroastrian movement over the next thousand years is difficult to picture or imagine for many now because, even at its zenith as the state religion of the world's first superpower, it was the religion of an oriental culture outside the mainstream of Western historical reportage. The Persian Empire may be compared in this regard to the Mogul Empire of the thirteenth and fourteenth centuries CE in failing to register significantly in Western consciousness, but even more obscure, given its greater antiquity.

In *Three Testaments: Torah, Gospel, and Quran*, it was suggested that we might now think of Zoroaster as the "axis of the Axial Age." On reflection, and in subsequent discussions, it is realized that a better terminology would be to speak of the Silk Route as the axis along which Zoroaster and Zoroastrianism provided inspiration drawn from Vedic religion (possibly cross fertilized with Semitic religion) that stimulated the major religious reforms and developments which permeated that Silk Route from one end to the other over the hundred-year period following his life. The objections (and answers) to this might be that:

1. "Silk Route" or "Silk Road" were not phrases employed before 1877 when coined by the German geographer Ferdinand von Richthofen, who designated the Silk Road as "Seidenstrasse" and the Silk Route as "Seidenstrassen" (to which we say, "so what?"). Trade was uncommon there before the first century BCE (now found in fifth century BCE).
2. Zoroastrians were not identified as such in the *Gathas* of Zoroaster (nor were Jews mentioned in the Torah).
3. None of those religions ever did become Zoroastrian as such (nobody says they did).

Zoroastrianism reached great heights, was eventually decimated both militarily and politically by Alexander the Great, and then revived for hundreds of years in a degraded form. Finally, it was practically eliminated by Islam, except for purely monotheistic elements that lived on in Iran and India, surviving today there and in pockets of the United Kingdom, Canada, Australia, and the United States.

However, the once pervasive sway of this movement, which may have contributed key elements to the spiritual foundation of the whole world, can be glimpsed in the West in the politics and theological development of ancient Israel after returning from the Babylonian Exile, and also in historical accounts of its near domination of Europe in the failed Persian invasions of Greece. A more objective appraisal of these events than that found in Hollywood film presentations, in the biased reports in Greek history, or in the adulation of Cyrus in Hebrew literature, might be seen in just a brief overview of the reigns of Zoroastrian monarchs whom we know at least peripherally. Both the Bible and ancient writers provide additional information from their own records and from inscriptions about a line of such monarchs who ruled the Persian Empire at the apex of the Zoroastrian era in a world just beyond the horizon of the West.

Vishtāspa, the first Zoroastrian monarch, is mainly known to us because of his relationship to Zoroaster. Not a lot is known about his rule beyond that connection, though the available information perhaps serves to introduce life in the court of a typical monarchy of minor but growing status in an era and in a part of the world unfamiliar to many. Cyrus, however, is well known both to historians and to readers of the Hebrew Scriptures. In 559 BCE, almost a decade before Zoroaster died, Cyrus succeeded to the throne of Anshan, a vassal kingdom of Media (now Northern Iran) then ruled by his grandfather, another early Zoroastrian monarch who had succeeded Vishtāspa. Within two decades Cyrus had subdued Media itself, conquered Asia Minor and marched into Northern India. After consolidation, in 539 BCE his forces fought their way into the city of Babylon, then the vast urban center of the ancient world.

The supreme potentate of Babylonia, King Belshazzar, was killed and Cyrus assumed rule of the entire Babylonian Empire. This was just as prophesied by Daniel, as the apocryphal account appears in the Hebrew Scriptures, when Belshazzar and his court were feasting out of the sacred vessels stolen from the temple in Jerusalem. This travesty resulted in their guilty vision of the *Mene, Mene, Tekel, Parsin* "writing on the wall," interpreted for them by Daniel in terms of God's judgment.[16] Babylon's time was up: it was "found wanting, divided, and ready to be conquered." In assuming and extending his control, Cyrus ruled the largest and most powerful empire the world would see until that of Alexander the Great and the later Roman Empire.

The success of Cyrus was built on combining military strategy with enlightened diplomacy based on Zoroastrian spirituality. For example, the Kingdom of Lydia had been difficult to conquer on the way to hegemony, but upon finally defeating the wealthy King Croesus, instead of killing him, Cyrus made him prime minister. He even referred to him as one of his "Companions,"[17] an inner circle of advisors to the Zoroastrian monarch, perhaps emulated by Jesus with his disciples, and almost certainly a model for Muhammad and his "Companions."

In all the places he conquered, in addition to graciousness toward the vanquished, Cyrus allied himself with those who had been oppressed by their former rulers. A famous but not entirely unique example reflects to his relationship with the elite Jewish exiles, many of whom had earned high places in the civil service of Babylon. His sponsorship of their return to Jerusalem, and his funding of the rebuilding of their temple and culture, won him the loyalty of a new province on his Egyptian flank, a buffer facing a power that would not be integrated into the Persian Empire until the rule of his son and penultimate successor.

The empire's new religion under Cyrus was Zoroastrianism in its pristine, complete, and uncorrupted manifestation, articulated at the core of his brilliantly successful policy toward enemies and subjects alike. This Zoroastrianism was monotheistic, as understood by the Jews on location, undiluted by later dualism at first, again suggesting chronological closeness to the originator of the faith who was dedicated to the Oneness of God. In a time subsequent to Cyrus, an altered form of the religion did shift the balance toward dualism in the struggle between good and evil, light and darkness. While he recognized the necessity of the struggle with evil forces, which are real in human experience, Zoroaster himself believed fervently in the ultimate exclusivity of the prerogatives and final reign of the Lord of Wisdom, and in the goodness that the religion he founded was commissioned to promote. Cyrus appears to have embraced the pristine Zoroastrian religion much as first promulgated by its founding prophet. The Jewish exiles recognized the affinity of this religion with their own, possibly even before Cyrus formally ascended the throne of Babylon.

We will return to the reign of Cyrus time and again, especially in his relationship with the Jews, as the main illustration of the Zoroastrian phenomenon triggering a "reformation" among all religious and philosophical traditions connected by the Silk Route. We will not be suggesting that the new religions appearing in China—that is, Taoism and Confucianism—were actually Zoroastrian. Nor were the new Buddhism or the reformed Hinduism of India Zoroastrian per se, in the same way that the Jews did not become Zoroastrian in spite of profound influence in that direction. We merely point to simultaneous religious upheavals or stimuli in all these cases at the same time, within a hundred years of Zoroaster and his influence through the length of the "Silk Route." Internally, the developments under the successors of Cyrus are documented by memorial inscriptions; many other developments were independent of Persian control farther east and farther west, testimonials to the power of sweeping ideas.

After Cyrus, the reign of Cambyses was a brief eight years but brought Egypt into the Persian Empire. Darius tried to do the same with Greece and Europe, but he was turned back by the "300" Greeks at the battle of Marathon. Despite the Persian employment of forces numbering in excess of a million men including soldiers, sailors, and support personnel, Xerxes failed at the same project again, by land against Greeks led by Sparta at Thermopylae and by sea at Artemnisium against a fleet led by the Athenians. These battles have been depicted by Hollywood in movies that got almost every detail wrong except for the realization that much of world history was thus determined by the outcomes. These monarchs were succeeded by Artaxerxes, who extended the sponsorship of the Jewish return by refunding Nehemiah and Ezra, before he was succeeded by Xerxes II, Darius II, and Artaxerxes II (Ahasuerus in the story of Esther).

Finally Artaxerxes III and Darius III extended the drift toward dualistic theology, and when Xerxes III was about to mount the peacock throne, Alexander the Great crossed the Hellespont in 334 BCE. This European avenger subdued the whole Persian Empire in just two years, finally sacking Persepolis in 330 BCE with a fiery holocaust of scriptures and other writings at that city's great library. During this attempt at "civilizing" Asia, the Greeks apparently imagined that nobody would think to hide a copy of the precious Avesta Scriptures.

In 224 BCE a Persian officer led a coup against Alexander's heirs and successors to establish the Sassanian Dynasty, a typically retro-naming for his grandfather Sassan, a restoration of Persian control over most of its ancient empire. The state religion was reinstated, but while monotheism appears to have survived in Zoroaster's old Bactrian stronghold, in the villages of Fars province and among traders on the Silk Route, the creeping dualism of later monarchs blossomed into a rivalry of near equals between Ahura Mazda and the Adversary (Ahriman, later Satan) in a neo-Zoroastrianism, and in the cognate Manichean religion that developed by and large out of Zoroastrianism and grew under its influence.

Even though a surviving few original Avesta poems by Zoroaster were cherished, this dualistic perversion of the pristine monotheistic faith of old flourished under the Sassanian Dynasty for 875 years, as recorded in new scriptures, which were added to the remnants of the earlier corpus. The Islamic invaders eventually disenfranchised this version of Zoroastrianism, burned all the scriptures they could find, and enforced a strict monotheism, all the while recognizing Zoroastrians as potentially people of the book, were it not for this perversion. Were some copies of this edition of the Avesta Scriptures also buried somewhere once again? Again, time will tell, and it is becoming increasingly difficult to imagine that such a time is not imminent.

Let us return to Cyrus. The pristine Zoroastrianism appearance of edicts, inscriptions, and documents from his reign, and their similarity to prophetic pronouncements of Zoroaster, is one more aid in dating Zoroaster's life and ministry. The convergence of justice elements and the Oneness of God is among the most persuasive arguments for a new level of understanding of the Zoroastrian contribution to world culture that is emerging in our time. A reasonably complete picture may become achievable as we add the Quranic confirmations of true Zoroastrian revelations, new perspectives that Jewish sources can teach us, unique Christian Gospel material from Zoroastrianism in the time of Jesus, and material from sources in the related religious traditions much farther east, featured in the next four books of this compendium. These conjectures can stand on their own, but will be ultimately verified by the location of the early Avesta Scriptures, most of which were destroyed in the era of Alexander the Great in the fourth century BCE, or the later Avestan additions from the scriptures destroyed in the seventh century CE soon after Muhammad, a quest that may help define the world culture emerging in the New Axial Age of the twenty-first century.

The Zoroastrian revelation, which stimulated religions throughout the ancient Silk Route, may have been triggered by an encounter with a more Western Semitic religion, but it came out of the more easterly Vedic vortex. Religious developments in the Semitic "holy land" are sometimes attributed to its position at the hinge of three continents; Vedic religious fervor erupted in a similar crucible in the Russian Steppes between Ukraine and Kazakhstan. There a confluence of developments shaped a society that had migrated from northwestern Russia to a previously barren plain that blossomed when they adapted from hunting and gathering to planting and domestication of animals, techniques borrowed from European cultures to their west. This burgeoning population became mobile due to invention of the wheel, brought from the Mesopotamian south, adapted to the wagon from the Khazak east and eventually the war chariot.

None of these "advances" were invented on the steppes, but the cross fertilization was dynamic. The same thing happened to their "Proto-Indo-European" language in tension with Hittite and other influences, a process that expanded in Rig Veda religious terms as the still growing hybrid society began to migrate in several directions. The invention of the automobile was a development that shaped modern society in a manner similar to the influence of the wheel of old, while the advent of computers and the Internet might resemble the impact of PIE linguistic development throughout much of the world. Religious turmoil was the next stage for the ancients, followed by "worldwide" spiritual creativity along the Silk Route. We may be reliving this pattern in the twenty-first century, and there are few studies as valuable in our time as those of the interfaith discipline sometimes described as "comparative theology."

2

a priest becomes a prophet

Commissioned at the River

TO AMPLIFY THE EARLIER SUMMARY OF WHAT WE ONCE KNEW ABOUT ZOROASTER, THE TIMES were tough and the people of his religious community were oppressed. The young priest went down to the river to prepare the water sacrifice and to meditate on his need, and that of his people, and to hear a word from God. As he waded out of the river, quite unexpectedly an angel appeared in the shining form of a man who both confronted him and instructed him.[1]

The pensive young priest had waded into the river almost distracted from his improvisational incantations by the social disintegration all around him. As he emerged, a vision came to him in which he was personally addressed by a specter he could only identify as one of the Immortals, beings then identified with or symbolized by the seven major celestial bodies visible to the naked eye in the universe. This story is important enough that it is repeated three times in extant remnants of the Avesta Scriptures.[2] After establishing rapport, the shining figure led him in the spirit into an audience with the Lord of Wisdom, Ahura Mazda, who was also the deva of justice, and who was attended by six other Immortals. Ahura Mazda was both immanent and entirely lucid in authorizing Zoroaster to energize his people to oppose violence and to confront the terror of the times. Zoroaster had gone into the water as a priest and come out to become a prophet.

Zoroaster learned in this revelation that even divinities had to choose between order and disorder in support of either harmony or chaos. The human race was being enlisted to join the forces of nature in a new era that would lead to eventual victory of good over evil. Zoroaster had experienced the immanence of the Lord of Wisdom; the glory of the moment triggered his immediate realization that this Ahura Mazda was also transcendent and should be identified as the Creator of the Universe. The Divinity was "uncreated" and all the forces of nature must become subservient to God. Ahura Mazda is not alone in the universe, but he alone is God. Some suggest this was not technically monotheism at first, since the Immortals participated in divinity, but they are soon correctly understood as angels in the service of the only One worthy of worship. It was also revealed or became clear that the Lord had an evil counterpart whose status appeared great, though his purpose was less lofty and destined to fail as humans joined the struggle on the side of goodness. Zoroaster was instructed to put the invitation clearly to his people.

Spiritually precocious, even as a child, Zoroaster had trained to be a priest from the age of seven and was recognized early for his ability to improvise incantations during sacrificial ceremonies.[3] Hebrew monotheism had been in the air throughout neighboring nations since the time of Moses, and the prophetic ministry of Jeremiah may have included visits to the Israelites who had been exiled by Assyria a hundred years earlier, between 730 and 710 BCE. Many Israelites were then living in Hala, Habor, and Hara,[4] communities eventually absorbed into the Median Empire, and all mentioned in Zoroaster's own story in the Avesta. Even before the matter of Zoroaster's dates was quite resolved, twentieth-century historian Arnold J. Toynbee put the matter as follows: "The date of Zarathustra is a matter of dispute and we cannot say for certain whether his religious discovery was independent . . . or whether his voice was a mere echo of the cry of forgotten Israelite prophets who had been marooned in the cities of the Medes."[5]

The scriptural evidence for a direct connection with Jeremiah is slender, but Israel's lamenting prophet did have something of a fixation with the exiles, wherever they were, visiting many such communities, as attested by several references in the Bible. Jeremiah even prophesied that if the northern and southern kingdoms of Israel and Judah reunited, they would be rejoined by the exiles from "the north."[6] He also demonstrated personal knowledge of the Scythians when he describes the "rising waters of the north," their ability and their possible interest in flooding the enemies of Israel with galloping steeds and rumbling chariots.[7]

By Jeremiah's time, many Israelite exiles may have intermarried with the Scythians in northern Syria, Media, and elsewhere, so Zoroaster may have even had Semitic Hebrew relatives. Given the meshing of their dates, as we now understand the overlap, it is entirely possible that as a teenager, Zoroaster could have heard Jeremiah, his elder contemporary, preaching monotheism and issuing a plea for the exiles to return to keep the faith. The appeal of monotheism might have had significance to a young Zoroaster at a time when religious and political turmoil was affecting his community. Would a youthful student of Vedic religion have heard this as a message that "there is One God," or was it a message that "God is One"? This fine distinction might be something with which his followers and others he influenced would struggle, whether or not he was yet aware of the difference, a subject to which we shall return in the discussion of Western monotheism in relation to Eastern monism.

The possibility of a direct connection between Zoroaster and Jeremiah is not contended here with any degree of certainty, but is offered as an example of ancient cross-border interchange. Given a plethora of hints in the Talmud and early Arab Christian references, the Jeremiah connection to Scythians and the exile communities in Zoroaster's homeland may be a promising area of future study in support of this thesis. However, if Zoroaster's initiation into awareness of the Oneness of God was not through a connection with Jeremiah, it could well have been through one of the other prophets, commercial or other visitors to the exile community, or simply from the Jewish exiles themselves, many of whom no doubt remained devout, as they did elsewhere. We do not yet have physical proof of an intersection between Semitic and Vedic traditions at this juncture, but it is clear that before the Jews developed an expanded theology of angels, Satan, the last judgment, and paradise from Zoroastrians in Babylon, the Zoroastrians had been introduced to monotheism or the Oneness of God, as well as messianism, almost certainly from the Jews, and that this happened somewhere other than either Babylon or Israel. Our conjecture is merely a plausible example of the exchange of ideas that certainly happened among ancient peoples, but the conjunction of dates and geography facilitating such intercourse in this case is too great to discount entirely.

While unheard of among the laity, in academic circles it is increasingly recognized that Judaism was influenced, some might say "transformed," under Zoroastrian persuasion in Babylon, giving Zoroastrianism both direct and indirect sway in Christianity and Islam. What is less well recognized in academia is the near certainty that Zoroastrianism was profoundly influenced in its Vedic infancy by Semitic Israelites in exile, with whom it crossed paths. From them this particular Vedic tradition received the vision of the Oneness of God (whether monotheistic or monistic), the understanding of personal responsibility to God (the commandments, rules or dharma), and the hope for a Redeemer (an avatar, messiah, or sayoshyant), all of which appeared in Eastern religions also within a generation.

We do know that following the "revelation at the river" several years later, Zoroaster commenced his mission at the age of thirty, launched by two aspects emulated exactly by Jesus long into the future. In both cases the river rite or "baptism" at the age of thirty was followed by the attempt by a satanic adversary, "tempting" them to renounce their faith. However, through the first several years of his ministry Zoroaster gained only one reliable disciple, in the person of his cousin, Miadhyoimah. He also earned the enmity of the religious establishments and was forced to migrate from the western end of the Silk Route, where he was born, to the eastern end, where he flourished. His opportunity came in Balkh, the capital of the minor kingdom of Bactria, just west of China and north of India, and at the far eastern tip of what would become the Persian Empire, in an event regarded as a godsend by his later followers.

Zoroaster was given a chance to discuss his mission with the priests of the royal court in the Kingdom of Bactria, an area of Northern Afghanistan and contiguous Islamic republics today. After three days they dismissed him and had him jailed, but he had caught the eye of King Vishtāspa, who must have seen the divine spark in the prophet priest, now forty years old. When Vishtāspa's favorite horse became paralyzed and unable to rise, the established priests could do nothing, so the king took the opportunity to send for Zoroaster, who prayed over the beast and somehow raised it to renewed vigor, to the delight of the king, the queen, and the whole royal household. They converted to the cause of peace and justice for possibly both spiritual and political reasons (sometimes inseparable), and Zoroaster flourished, with influence then growing rapidly throughout the region coincident with the expansion of Vishtāspa's realm, which the king's descendants would expand and parlay into the Persian Empire.

Zoroaster's utterances were poetic and couched in the evocative dialect of his proto-Vedic forebears, regarded as sacred. That was the almost primordial and rudimentary articulation of the evolving Vedic tradition that had taken root in India and would soon be reformed there under the Buddhist ripples in the wake of Zoroaster's influence. Within a few years the body of Zoroaster's writings was so precious in his expanding circle that King Vishtāspa put his literate prime minister in charge of the texts. Jāmāspa undertook this responsibility with such devotion that, according to tradition, he produced two archetypical copies with gold lettering on ox-hide sheets. This devotion to the texts themselves was emulated by Jews not long after, by Christian monogrammed texts in due course, and by Islamic adulation of sacred words in the final iteration of "The Book." Testimony to the plethora of copies and translations of these Avesta Scriptures in the ancient world has been referenced earlier, and will be elaborated upon again later, but needs to be kept in mind here too. Even among ancient Jews and in the early church there was never such prodigious production of copies of the treasured text. Are we to believe that not even a single copy has survived?

Zoroaster trained three orders of disciple missionaries who fanned out across the ancient world and organized the community of faith in the Lord of Wisdom. The horse itself became an enduring symbol of the Zoroastrian religion, and, as trends sometimes do, Zoroaster's spiritual influence galloped all over the world. Zoroaster had relocated from the gates of Greece at the western end of the Silk Route to his new headquarters near the gates of China and India at the eastern end of the Silk Route. If Billy Graham could be heard in person or through modern media by most of the world in the twentieth century, it is not a stretch to realize how Zoroaster, or his message, could extend his reach from west to east along a route in a portion of the globe little different in size and shape from the nation of Chile (in east-west "landscape" rather than north-south "portrait" orientation). Are we to continue to believe that ideas could not traverse such a space, though often erroneously described as impossibly remote and inaccessible? Such a concept is now understood to relate more to limitations in our own dark ages than to the situation in the time and location of Zoroaster. Recent evidence of the presence of Iranian Magi in China before and during Zoroaster's lifetime will be introduced at the beginning of Book II of this compendium as the *piéce de resistance* of this new realization.

Zoroaster married, possibly more than once, and established his home and religious headquarters in the city of Balkh, then the capital of Bactria, some twenty kilometers to the northwest of Mazar-e-Sharif in what is called Afghanistan today. His three sons took the lead in reorganizing society into three classes: priests, warriors, and farmers, according closely with the principal castes organized in India by related Aryan migrants some generations earlier. That social system was now to be employed in bringing order to the spiritual struggle between good and evil.

The mighty prince of darkness, introduced as Ahriman, later known as Satan or Lucifer, also had a retinue of six additional Anti-mortals, including Indra and other forces who served the cause of evil in the world. Following the revelation to Zoroaster at the river, the cosmic battle was to be joined by those prepared to struggle on earth. Zoroaster was inspired to understand that in the battle between the devas representing good and evil, the Lord of Wisdom was destined for the final victory and that mortals who joined His cause should acknowledge Him as the only One true God. This rapid blossoming of monotheism, monism, or the Oneness of God is reflected in the extant Avestas, and preserved by the modern Zoroastrian community of Parsees and others, though the seeds of an eventual flowering of dualism in much of that community were also there from the very beginning.

All of this and the subsequent Avestan Scriptures are presented in dramatic apocalyptic language, the first appearance of this genre of expression in the world. We meet this style again in Daniel and a few other places in the Hebrew Scriptures. The apocalyptic style appears in the Gospels and dominates the book of Revelation, concluding the Christian Scriptures, prior to its predominant use again through almost the whole of the Quran. This is the first hint of the closeness between the Avesta and the Quran, a core thesis of the *Three Testaments* compendium that preceded this one. We will identify similar phenomena in the Eastern testaments to be examined here.

Zoroaster lived long and well and saw the impact of his mission spread throughout all areas of Persian influence and well beyond, the harbinger of what many scholars now call the "Axial Age" of religion and philosophy. Peasants and royal families alike flocked to his banner. Until recently, it was believed that he died a mysterious and violent death at the hands of assassins in the fire temple at Balkh at seventy-seven years of age. Judging by the language used, suspicions have arisen that this story was a fabrication placed in the record by detractors some centuries later. He probably died at a great age, having seen his revelations transform his religion and beginning to influence all religions, and his reforms transform his society and influence all societies throughout the ancient world. If this was the case, it is even possible that his tomb will yet be discovered, perhaps at Mazar-e-Sharif, where the Blue Mosque is one of the most beautiful buildings in the world. This shrine is considered in local legend to be the tomb of Ali, the son-in-law and putative successor of Muhammad, even though Muslims everywhere else in the world recognize his tomb as being at the Imam Ali Mosque at Najaf in Iraq. On the contrary, the tour guides of Mazar-e-Sharif have maintained their legend that the body of Ali was carried here on the back of a camel—an "ustra" (Ali's legend on top of Zarath-ustra?).

Zoroaster's name was *Zarath-ustra* in Persian, but the Greeks called him *Zorastres*, the Romans called him *Zoroastres*, and the anglicized *Zoroaster* has now become almost universal. An exception is the German title from Friedrich Nietzsche's book, *Also Sprach Zarathustra*, and the music by Richard Strauss that used that title for music that was popularized by Stanley Kubrick's movie, *2001: A Space Odyssey*. Once he saw the movie, the music of *Also Sprach Zarathustra* was also used as the introduction to every show of Elvis Presley from 1969 until his death in 1977. Even in an era before scholarship had revealed as much as we now know, Zoroaster appears as "Sarastro" in Mozart's opera *The Magic Flute*, noted for its Masonic elements, where he represents moral order in opposition to the "Queen of the Night." He is also the subject of the 1749 opera *Zoroastre* by Jean-Philippe Rameau, set in the ancient kingdom of Bactria where the forces of Good, led by Zoroastre, the "founder of the Magi" struggle against the forces of Evil. During the Enlightenment, Voltaire and other encyclopaedists promoted research into Zoroastrianism, considering it to be a rational deism more acceptable than Christianity. In essence, Zoroaster was a reformer of the older Vedic religion, which provided the raw materials for all emerging religions at the Middle Eastern hinge of continents, the area where both monism and monotheism took root. As mentioned, the period of a hundred years after Zoroaster, when all this happened, has come to be identified as the Axial Age, a subject to which we shall return.

Despite all this, until the current era, Zoroaster remained largely off the radar screen of Western history and consciousness because of Western ignorance and confusion about his birthplace and his dates. He was born into a world of warlord "kingdoms" like Azerbaijan, Syria, Media, Lydia, Bactria, and 122 others that all later became provinces of the Persian Empire under more ancient names. Zoroaster's birthplace appears to have been the city of Urmiah, now known as Rizaijeh, in the Shiz district of present-day Azerbaijan. Arabic and Persian scholars mark his birth date as 628 BCE[8] by noting that the sacking of the Persian capital of Persepolis by Alexander the Great in 330 BCE took place 258 years after "the appearance" or epiphany of Zoroaster. This is possibly a reference to his birth, traditionally celebrated by Zoroastrians on July 25, but it more likely refers to the establishment of the Zoroastrian religion under King Vishtāspa, and Avesta records show that Zoroaster was some forty years old at that time.[9]

As referenced in our earlier exordium, an alternate ancient tradition reported by Xanthus of Lydia about 450 BCE, and adopted by Greek and Roman historians, places the birth of Zoroaster some six thousand years before Xerxes. This pushes Zoroaster's dates back to about 6500 BCE, a popular mythology that survived until very recently, though it makes Zoroaster appear approximately twelve times as ancient as in the Persian record.[10] This is the basis of the mythical image of Zoroaster adopted in "new age" circles, rather than the historical reality. While readers often abjure books with too many dates, an accurate dating of Zoroaster's impact on the world is key to the argument in this story, so some heavy plodding is necessary.

Whenever we see what appear to be fantastic or impossible dates and ages in the ancient world, the first question we must ask is whether these numbers are divisible by twelve. Most primitive societies measured time by cycles of the moon, rather than the solar calculations employed in the Common Era. This was the practice of early Hebrew, contiguous and related societies, and even aboriginal societies surviving into the modern era in many parts of the world. Methuselah[11] may have lived to a very old age for his time, but it is obvious that if divided by twelve, his age represents 969 cycles of the moon, or some eighty cycles of the sun. We might call this eighty "years" in the solar method of time measurement that was adopted just shortly before the

Common Era. By this computation Noah lived 950 moons,[12] or seventy-nine years. He was "600" when the flood came, or fifty years old by our calculations. After the adoption of solar time measurement, we are given to understand that Jesus lived approximately thirty years and Muhammad some sixty-three years, both ages described in the system employed in the Common Era. Their followers would realize that they both lived holy and healthy lives, at least as compared to Noah and Methuselah, and could have lived as long as either of these predecessors.

The confusion concerning Zoroaster's birth date might be illustrated by the current switch in measurement of temperature. The United States continues to use the Fahrenheit scale while the rest of the world has switched to Celsius. A thousand years from now, when the whole world (including America) has been using Celsius for centuries, at first glance a study of our times would reveal that while temperatures peaked at thirty or forty degrees everywhere else, a hot day in America was represented by 100 degrees or more, misunderstood as surely the hottest place on earth with almost unbelievable heat.[13]

So when Xanthus reports that Zoroaster was born six thousand "cycles" before Persian King Xerxes invaded Asia Minor and Greece in 480 BCE, we may presume that he meant six thousand cycles of the moon. The Roman historian Diogenes Laertius, among others, took this to be six thousand cycles of the sun, since they lived in the solar era, placing the birth of Zoroaster at a seemingly impossibly remote date in relation to the Aryan activities that preceded him and to the religious developments in Persia and elsewhere that succeeded him. When Xanthus recorded that period as six thousand cycles, he really meant five hundred of our solar years before 480 BCE, or the year 930 BCE according to our calculations. This is not precisely the same as the Persian record, but a difference measured in a couple of centuries, not many thousands of years. The choices for birth dates of Zoroaster are three. First, we would accept 6500 BCE if we believe Xanthus and documents like the Bible really measured time in solar years rather than moons. Second, we would accept a date of somewhere roughly around 1000 BCE if we adjust this Greek and Roman account from moons to solar years. Third, the date would be 628 BCE if we accept the Arabic and Persian records, similar to certain European estimates in the twentieth century but much older and commonly held throughout the centuries in regions of the East.

With the support of those recent European conclusions, to be described in detail in Book VII, we employ the later Arabic and Persian date of 628 BCE, partly because it fits with our thesis regarding Persian Zoroastrianism as the direct immediate predecessor of scriptural Judaism, as represented by the Hebrew Scriptures as we have them. The slightly earlier revised Greek and Roman date of 930, or about 1000 BCE, would not be a major problem, since it, too, follows Moses by some centuries, but it does not fit quite as well when we begin to compute backward from the Jewish experience, a technique to be elaborated upon later. Impressive corroboration of our position is also bolstered by information now known about the birth of Darius I, shortly before 550 BCE, the factor that tipped the balance in the recent debate in Europe. This son of the first royal convert, King Vishtāspa, grew up to succeed to the Persian throne in 522, eight years after the birth of Cyrus, and would have known Zoroaster as the revered priest and prophet in his father's court. Cyrus, too, would have known Zoroaster as a child. Debate, controversy, and final resolution of this important matter will be presented in a subsequent chapter.

Certain scholars may continue to give weight to other factors, but leading writers on the topic, from experts such as Susan Whitfield[14] through Sol Nigosian[15] to Karen Armstrong,[16] have increasingly tended toward more recent dates as evidence mounts. The substantiation of a birth date of around 628 BCE is convincing and important in our thesis that Zoroaster's revelation at the river occurred around 600 BCE in a region populated in part by Israelite exiles who were at least nominally monotheistic. If that is conceded, permitted, or imagined, a great many other things fall into place with respect to both Eastern and Western religious developments.

Zoroaster's prophetic ministry exploded ten years later, and dramatically impacted the whole of the ancient Middle East and beyond for the next fifty years, until soon thereafter Cyrus, the rising Zoroastrian conqueror, marched into Babylon in 539 BCE to establish that faith at the heart of the first realm in history to be appropriately described as a superpower. The significance of the Zoroastrian Cyrus establishing the Persian Empire in this manner just twenty years after the death of Zoroaster (or a century after his birth) has yet to be entirely digested in either academic circles or popular imagination. Along with Zoroaster's impact both farther west and farther east, the impact of the interchange between Vedic and Semitic influences in Babylon is important as an example of what may well have happened elsewhere, though not yet as well documented.

As indicated, the late date for Zoroaster's birth (either 930 or 628 BCE) places the revelation that was given to him well after the establishment of monotheism in Israel. Future chapters will establish that religious and other ideas traveled in a fluid dynamic all through the ancient East, with the Silk Route as the conduit. For example, Vashti, the great-granddaughter of Nebuchadnezzar and the first wife of Artaxerxes II, was of Indian lineage, through Nebuchadnezzar's son, Amel-Marduk,[17] who distinguished himself in the campaigns of Northern India and brought home a wife. The Vashti connection is a given among Indians, where the ancient name remains common, and the scholarly linkage is now typical of the newer interfaith research in which India is accepted as being in the farther reaches of the empire of Ataxerxes II.

To reiterate an earlier example, only recently have Westerners noted the presence of a certain Krishna in the book of Esther among those the king consulted before banishing Vashti, the Hebrew letters of his name being "KRiShNA," or Kṛṣṇa.[18] This is patently obvious in transliteration, though the name is traditionally and inexplicitly rendered as "Carshena" in English translations. However, Indians who incline to take this reference as the king's invocation of a Hindu god should perhaps be content to simply recognize Indian influence in the court, including the fluid transmission of ideas we have been describing as typical of Zoroaster's time and the age that followed.

Meanwhile, under Zoroastrian influence, the many deities of the Vedic tradition may have moved toward the Oneness of All, a monism inclusive of creator and creation, an Eastern development seemingly opposite to related monotheistic developments in the West, requiring further discussion. While Zoroastrianism may have facilitated the spread of monotheism as an increasingly dominant belief throughout the Persian Empire and toward the west, the fact that this seminal belief had flourished for hundreds of years in the Jewish community almost next door to Zoroaster's birthplace can hardly be mere coincidence. We may regard the revelation to Zoroaster at the river as genuine, but monotheism, or something approaching monism was not exactly new to him at that moment. His worldview was Vedic, but Zoroaster's inspiration with respect to the Oneness of God was almost certainly Jewish. The exceptional Zoroastrian influence on Judaism during the Persian years of Israel's Exile in Babylon may now be understood as but the closing of the circle. A belief in the Oneness of God came to Zoroaster and to the world from the Jews, and the Hebrew Torah was facilitated and financed by Zoroastrian monarchs in Babylon. Through the return to Jerusalem it was passed on to the world. The growing evidence for this will be forthcoming, but this much has been available for a long time.

A correct dating of the birth of Zoroaster is perhaps just one of the more obvious illustrations of how the Zoroastrian record helps resolve many conundrums of later Western scriptures, and correlates with the examination of Eastern scriptures that form the core material of this compendium. Extant Avesta information testifies to Zoroaster's birth to his mother, Dughdhova, when she was fifteen years of age, reporting it as a "virgin birth."[19] The custom of attributing the birth of an outstanding figure to divine initiative eventually became relatively common in what we now call the Middle East. Zoroaster's lineage is then traced back through his father, Pourushaspa, forty-five generations to the first human, Gayomart,[20] again in a manner identical in ethos to the way in which the genealogy of another famous son of a virgin is traced by St. Luke back to Adam through his "father," Joseph.[21] Pointing out the similarities to later scriptures is not meant to challenge the veracity of either account, but rather to point to the origins of the imagery and establish the linguistic power of images that may be historical or adopted by faith—in either case, they offer profound truths that lie beneath the eternal mysteries.

To bolster our understanding that critical aspects of religion were not merely evolving, but were triggered by revolutionary incidents, such as revelations or encounters, we will pause to reflect on a plausible illustration. The following two scenes are excerpted from the play *Three Testaments: Shalom, Peace, Salam*, with an upstate New York premier in June 2015 at Niagara Falls and a DVD movie recording available on YouTube and from Amazon in anticipation of a performance on the opening day of the Performing Arts Venue in Tower Five of the new World Trade Center in 2018.

a chance meeting at the crossroads of history

Before the Vedic-Semitic Interface in Babylon

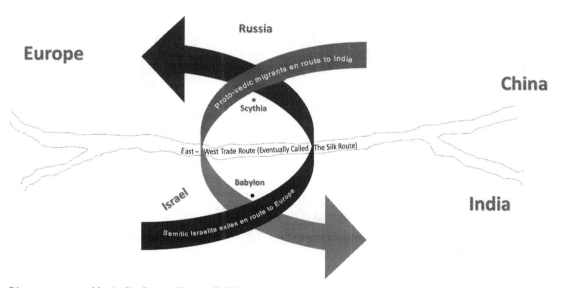

Diagram executed by Indira Brown Sinton. © 2016 Brian Arthur Brown.

the great intersection

THE VEDIC OR PROTO-VEDIC RELIGION OF MIGRANTS ON THEIR WAY FROM THE RUSSIAN STEPPES to India swept through Asia Minor (Turkey) and into Babylon (Iraq)/ Persia (Iran) on their way to India. Israelite religion of Semitic monotheism stalled briefly in Asia Minor as these "lost tribes of Israel" made their way northeast to Europe and west along the Silk Route. In this investigation, it is conjectured that the two religions may have intersected in momentous coincident exchanges—first, in passing, in places like ancient Scythia (present-day Armenia/Azerbaijan), and second, more intensely in Babylon, where exiled Jews were running the civil service when the Zoroastrian Cyrus swept into power and recognized them as something akin to co-religionists.

The profound significance of this intersection for the twenty-first century is only now being recognized as the trigger for the Axial Age in which philosophical ideas and religious ideals stirred in concert from Greece to China, connected by what we now call the Silk Route. To illustrate how such interplay could well have taken place, this chapter excerpts two scenes from the play *Three Testaments: Shalom, Peace, Salam.* Other connections are possible, as happened in Mitanni earlier, and Zoroaster may have even met itinerant Jewish prophets or profiteers other than Jeremiah. However, speculation from notes in the Babylonian Talmud, through early Arab Christian sources and Muslim sources to be quoted in Book VI, to Arnold Toynbee's speculations in the twentieth century, support the thesis of this book. Reading backward from Judaism to Zoroastrianism in Babylonia also verifies the encounter between Zoroaster and Jeremiah as a valid hypothesis in the exciting new discipline of Zoroastrian studies. Readers can pass judgment on that for themselves later, but they may enjoy an excursion to the theater first. Two scenes are excerpted from the play as an illustration of some points we have been discussing.

act l, scene 2

(Back 2,700 years to visit Israelite exiles by the Black Sea, gathering around an evening campfire. These exiles, expelled from Israel by the Assyrians a hundred years before the famous Babylonian Captivity, are often said to be among the "lost tribes" of Israel. Singers are quietly humming a *niggun*.)

CAMPFIRE HOST (*Addressing cast and audience*)

Shalom aleichem!

CAMPFIRE GUESTS

Aleichem Shalom!

CAMPFIRE HOST

Tonight we have a guest, the young prophet Jeremiah, bringing news from Jerusalem, the City of David, the home to which many of us yearn to return. Jeremiah confronts those who would forget the special destiny of our people to be a holy nation. We here in exile believe it was our failure to follow our mission that allowed the Assyrians to drive us out of our home. Jeremiah, meet Israel in exile. Few here have ever returned, but we remember the stories of our grandparents, and we look to the day of our return.

ZOROASTER *(Joining the circle)*

Cousin, don't forget to introduce those of us of Vedic faith to your guest. My tunic tells him I am training for the priesthood, almost ready to be ordained. Some have come to hear how Israel's God fits into our Vedic pantheon, though I personally question that such a thing is possible. In fact, let me serve notice of my concern about the presence of this guest. We are living in peace together here; we don't need someone dividing us.

CAMPFIRE HOST

Thank you for your thoughts, Zoroaster. Jeremiah, your audience is mainly Israelite, but yes, we welcome other faiths among us, including Zoroaster, my brash young cousin . . . from a mixed marriage . . . who is sometimes a bit confrontational. Friends, let us hear Jeremiah, son of Hilkiah, High Priest in the Jerusalem Temple. He comes bearing a special scroll, and to deliver a special message, a word from the God of Israel. Join us, Zoroaster, you might learn something tonight.

JEREMIAH *(Large scroll in his arms)*

Thank you, Eliphaz. Some communities I passed through also have Israelite residents, but few have so many, and none live so far from home. It was to you that I was called to prophesy by my God and yours, and at the wish of my father.

(Speaking in falsetto voice with arms raised in the air)

The word of the Lord came to me: "Before I created you in the womb, I selected you;
Before you were born, I consecrated you; I appointed you a prophet to Israel among the nations."
I replied, "Ah, Lord God! I don't know how to speak, for I am still a boy."
And the Lord said to me: "Do not say, 'I am still a boy,' But go wherever I send you
And speak whatever I command you. Have no fear, for I am with you to deliver you."

Yes, I am young for a prophet, but the message I bring should enhance the faith of sincere people living together in peace. My father, Hilkiah, has been High Priest for many years. I know you possess an old scroll of Israelite history, but in my hands is a copy of the Second Scroll, found by my father during the reign of righteous Josiah. It contains the speeches by Moses, which were memorized by Levites and passed on from generation to generation. My father felt compelled by God to have me deliver this Scroll of Teachings to you. You may even know some of its words:

Hear, O Israel. The Eternal our God, The Eternal is one.
And you must love the Eternal your God
With all your heart, with all your soul and with all your strength.
Take these words which I command you today to heart
Teach them to your children; speak them when you sit at home
or walk upon the road, when you lie down and when you rise up.

I am called to prophesy wherever our people are in danger of forgetting God. God calls us to serve Him in Jerusalem, but also in this foreign place. Each individual is responsible to God. The commandments of God are found in the ancient scroll in your possession, so you have no excuse.

ZOROASTER

You have come to sow dissension! To persuade Israelites to return to their old ways! We have begun to include Israelites in our rites, and many of our families are intermarried now. From time immemorial we Vedic people have worshipped the divinities in many forms. Spiritual forces, good and evil, are all around us, and we lift up our voices together in fear and supplication. Is there truly but one God above all divinities? Does this God know each of us? Does your God expect things of mere individuals? I challenge your nonsense and I resent what you are doing here. Let these people become part of our community and adopt our ways. People like you always bring strife, and the next thing you know we are fighting. Can't you leave us in peace?

JEREMIAH

There is but one God, known by our Father, Abraham, and described by His servant Moses. This understanding may be the greatest gift of Israel to the world. The Great God who made heaven and earth has a plan for the world and a purpose for each person in it. God also expects each individual to take personal responsibility in the fight against evil. Only then will peace prevail.

ZOROASTER

If I understand you, the Great God is the only God. This is either nonsense or it changes everything. Perhaps I need to think about this, so I'll be at your gatherings. But we Vedic folk will keep our eyes on you before you drive a wedge between us and our neighbors. We are living at peace here; we don't want trouble! We can run you out of here, Jeremiah, and we will do so as soon as you begin to put our peaceful way of life at risk.

JEREMIAH

In the days and weeks ahead, I hope to meet with many of you, Israelites and Scythians alike, and you especially, Zoroaster. Together we will study the Second Scroll and respectfully consider the needs of Vedic people as well as Israelites and Jews. We will consider what each person must do to serve God, and also what communities must do to be at peace among the nations, since that is what you are worried about. Bring your concerns to the table, but keep an open heart and mind.

(A campfire singer leads the audience and cast in singing another niggun.*)*

act l, scene 3

(Ten years later Zoroaster is still a young Vedic priest. He wades into a river in a scene similar to the baptism of Christ many years later. He dips some water in a jug, holds it up and splashes himself in a purification rite, talking to himself in a reverie.)

ZOROASTER

Ten years since I met that Jeremiah! I fought against dividing the community, but his teachings haunt me. I have been faithful to our Vedic religion. We use the purity of water to cleanse the pollution of the land, and the heat of fire to sear away the dross of corruption and violence. But the people are oppressed by nature and by crime. Thirty! I am now the same age Jeremiah was when he opened my mind to the reality that there is but one God. I fetch this pure water from the middle of the river before I light our fire sacrifice, but I nearly despair. We need to hear a word from God.

(An angel appears in the heavens as one who confronts and instructs.)

GABRIEL

Zoroaster!

ZOROASTER

I am here!

GABRIEL

Your given name, Zarathustra, means "camel-herder." But now you are called upon to guide people, not camels, and to share with them what you believe about God, and to marshal them in the fight against evil. Only thus will you and they find peace.

ZOROASTER *(Falling to his knees)*

Sacred Spectre, are you a god?

GABRIEL

No! I am not a god; there is but One. But I am immortal like the seven planets. I patrol an orbit assigned by God. I have been sent to invite you, no . . . command you to turn to Ahura Mazda, Lord of Wisdom, the Great God described by Jeremiah. God is One, and God alone can redeem both communities and individuals. Are you at last ready to face God?

ZOROASTER

I am ready. I bow in humility. I am ashamed that it has taken me so long.

GABRIEL

Then come into the presence of the Lord of Wisdom, Ahura Mazda, who is also the deva of universal justice, and who is attended by six Immortals.

VOICE OF GOD *(off stage, as Zoroaster falls to his knees)*

I AM . . . I AM . . . I am the transcendent Lord of Wisdom, and I am the immanent Spirit who is available to all people. Today I commission you, Zoroaster, to inspire people to oppose violence and to confront the terror of the time. All beings, human and divine, must choose between order and disorder, harmony and chaos. The Israelites have already responded to my invitation. Zoroaster, you came into the river as a good priest; you come out of the river to become a great prophet, My prophet.

ZOROASTER

You are the Creator of the Universe, the uncreated Source of all life. Before You, all the forces of nature must bow, and in harmony with Your purpose all people must serve justice. I have heard of You, but now I have heard Your voice. I am Your servant, and I know that You can redeem me and my people.

VOICE OF GOD

And all people! I send you to proclaim the way of peace to princes and priests, as well as to paupers and peasants, to be redeemed and to respect each other.

ZOROASTER *(Rising to his feet)*

To my people and the Israelites and Jews of our community, to people of the road to the east and to people of the road to the west, I will proclaim Your ways of truth and justice.

VOICE OF GOD

I was present in creation with all the potential of the universe. I am present in the fullness of time for all who call upon Me. I will be present at the end of time to be the Redeemer for all those who have turned to Me.

ZOROASTER

Your prophet, Jeremiah told me of a Messiah, a holy saviour foretold by a prophet called Isaiah. Is that the Redeemer? And how will he redeem, and whom?

VOICE OF GOD

He will ransom My people Israel, and lead them as a shepherd leads the sheep to green pastures and still waters. He will redeem all people in justice and peace.

ZOROASTER

What shall they do to obtain this justice and peace?

VOICE OF GOD

In their trusting response to Me they can bring justice and peace to one another.

ZOROASTER

And how will they know You to trust You?

VOICE OF GOD

Write these things down, so My power can be passed on to all who can read and to those who will listen. Honour the holy scriptures above all writings, whether by Jews, Vedic sources or others. By honouring the scriptures you honour Me, and you also secure my word for all time.

(*I Know that My Redeemer Liveth*, first verse from offstage . . . from the book of Job, of Eastern, possibly Vedic origin.)

4

the silk route

The Axis of the Axial Age

THE PHRASES "AXIAL AGE" OR "AXIAL PERIOD" ARE ENGLISH TRANSLATIONS OF THE GERMAN *Achsenzeit*, "axis time," a term coined in the twentieth century by philosopher Karl Jaspers. He originally used the term to describe the wider period from 800 to 200 BCE, during which, according to Jaspers, comparable transformative thinking appeared in Persia, India, China, Israel, and Greece. Described as "the great transformation" by Karen Armstrong, this concept now has near universal acceptance. The German Egyptologist Jan Assmann expresses the essence succinctly in a major new study of *Dynamics in the History of Religions Between Asia and Europe*:

> The theory of the axial age as put forward by Karl Jaspers in 1949 and elaborated since then, especially by Shmuel Eisenstadt and his circle[1] is centred on the following principal assumptions: there is but One Truth and One Mankind. At a given point in its moral, spiritual and intellectual evolution, mankind "broke through" to a much clearer apprehension of this Truth. This happened independently in several places at approximately the same time around 500 BCE. The main characteristics of this breakthrough may be summarized as universalisation and distanciation. *Universalisation* is concerned with the recognition of absolute truths, valid for all times and all peoples; this implies features such as reflexivity, abstraction, second order thinking, theory, systematisation, etc. *Distanciation* is concerned with introducing ontological and epistemological distinctions, such as the eternal and the temporal world, being and appearance, spirit and matter, critique of the "given" in view of the true, etc.: in short, the invention of transcendence and the construction of two-world theories.[2]

Fine words profoundly expressed, except for a glaring improbability: that such a major and fundamental shift in human understanding would have happened "independently at several places at approximately the same time" with no connection or mutual influence. It is possible that such a phenomenon could have occurred in two places or even three at the same time, but to happen independently everywhere that is connected by the Silk Route, and at a time when there was already one common denominator, seems highly improbable. In his book *Vom Ursprung und Ziel der Geschichte* (*The Origin and Goal of History*), Jaspers himself identified a number of key Axial Age thinkers as having had a profound influence on future philosophies and religions, and identified characteristics common to each area from which those thinkers emerged. Jaspers saw striking parallels in religion and philosophy, but he failed to identify any obvious direct connection or transmission of ideas between regions.

He argued that during the Axial Age "the spiritual foundations of humanity were laid simultaneously and independently in China, India, Persia, Judea, and Greece. And these are the foundations upon which humanity still subsists today."[3] Jaspers is being seen increasingly as correct, except for the failure to identify the common denominator, a factor he missed by casting his net over an unnecessarily broad a span of time. Popular and respected scholars like Richard Freund, Karen Armstrong, and Amir Hussain tend toward speaking of the Axial Age from Jewish, Christian, and Islamic perspectives as a period lasting from Lao Tzu as an elderly seer in 550 BCE and Socrates as a young philosopher in 450 BCE, a period spanning just the hundred years after the death of Zoroaster. Perhaps we might think of that hundred-year epoch as including the reign of Cyrus (538–529 BCE) as the main political marker and the rise of Jewish prophets and the Buddha as dominant religious factors, with Socrates bookending the era philosophically in the West and Confucius in the East.

Jaspers's mistake was natural enough since there were Greek philosophers like Thales and Pythagoras before Parmenides, a monist, and Socrates, a monotheist in the period as we now define it. After that span, the likes of Plato and Aristotle can be seen as simply worthy students of the trend. The point is that Greek philosophy might have been interesting, but not seminal without Parmenides and Socrates, key figures in our core definition of the Axial Age.

The same could be said of Israel's prophets, with Joel, Elijah, Elisha, and First Isaiah making earlier contributions that would have been valued anyway, except that Jeremiah, Second Isaiah, Daniel, and Ezekiel raised the bar so incredibly high in the Axial Age that they defined the movement and left the prophets who followed them to be described as "the minor prophets." Similar predecessors and successors to the true Axial giants might be seen in China, India, and Persia, though not as well known in Western literature on the subject. Suffice it to say that in China, Lao Tzu and Confucius held sway; in India, it was all Buddha in that hundred-year era except for Mahavira, the great reformer of the Jain religion, whose teachings also fit and whose dates are too exactly in the middle of this epoch to ignore. In Persia, Cyrus himself set everything in motion with his support for monotheistic religion and his application of Zoroastrian moral principles to diplomacy and governance. The dates of these historic figures all fit the tighter timeline.

Consider the BCE dates of these worthies, and ask yourself what they might have in common, the only outlier on this list being Jeremiah, who may be grandfathered into the record for the sake of a slightly earlier connection described in earlier chapters. All in the BCE era of course, Jeremiah lived his three-score years and ten, 655–586;

Lao Tzu, 604–555; Ezekiel, 622–569; Isaiah, 582–512; Cyrus, 580–529; Buddha, 563–483, Confucius, perhaps 551–479 or slightly later; Mahavira, 540–468; Parmenides, 515–444?; and Socrates, 469–399. They all confronted their worlds with distinctive new thinking about morality and its spiritual basis, within one hundred years of the life of Zoroaster. Cyrus may be the only one to have met Zoroaster personally, which would have happened when he was a child in the court of Vishtāspa, but the others were part of a spiritual upheaval triggered by Zoroaster, and his influence shows in every one of them. It is absent from their predecessors and only found in their successors identified as minor prophets and students.

Jaspers held Socrates, Confucius, and the Buddha in especially high regard, describing each of them as an exemplary human being and a "paradigmatic personality." His linking of them as exemplary might have been his clue. We concede a similar place of preeminence to the aforementioned towering prophets of Israel, and the impact of Cyrus was such that Israel almost took him to be the Messiah, a figure who actually appears in Zoroastrianism as the *Saoshyant* or Redeemer—which Cyrus almost was to Israel, in a certain sense.

Socrates was officially executed for "atheism," by which his judges meant that he no longer believed in the "gods," plural, though, as quoted by Plato, he clearly believed in God, a radical new departure soon to be adopted throughout Greece. In the Axial Age, the gods of Olympus were dethroned in the West, and the Vedic gods continued to exist in the East only under the canopy of monism, the meaning of which (along with its relationship to monotheism) will be discussed in a future chapter. Israel's monotheism was reinforced in Babylon by Zoroastrianism at its height and the issues, in religion and philosophy, became how should individuals live in reference to good and bad, right and wrong, justice and injustice. All this was related to what was now perceived as God's claim upon them and God's invitation to them.

The Gathas are the earliest chapters of the Avesta Scriptures, written by Zoroaster and still extant, but Zoroastrians are not mentioned by name in any of them, just as Jews are not mentioned anywhere in the Torah, and Christians are not mentioned by that name in any of the Gospels. As with Jews and Christians, we rely on later generations to self-identify as Zoroastrians, so it is not surprising that Cyrus (a very young contemporary of Zoroaster) and others of his generation do not refer to themselves as Zoroastrians. The first independent description of Zoroastrian religion (the religion of the government under which the commentator grew up) comes from Herodotus, the Greek "Father of History," who was born in Halicarnassus, a Greek city in the Persian province of Caria (Turkey) in the time of Xerxes I. Even he does not yet use the Zoroastrian name but refers to its practitioners as Magians, the then common designation of Zoroastrian priests in the empire's heartland provinces where Magi converted or adjusted *en masse* from the earlier religion of that name. This "shorthand," conflation of Magianism and Zoroastrianism, or confusion of the two lasted many centuries. Indeed, this transition was so smooth that outside observers long imagined that Zoroaster founded the Magian religion.

Without much distinction between monotheism (one God) and monism (one Being or "mono-be-ism"), according to Herodotus, the Zoroastrian Magians of his region preserved many of the names of the divinities ("singing the Theogony") and held to a belief in a future immortality, going after their death to "Zalmoxis" (the "God of Moses"). They even called their country of domicile, as he knew it, "Moesia," for it was there that the people of Moses lived.[4] Moesia is best known in history as a province of the Roman Empire in the southeastern Balkans in what was the only part of Scythia controlled by the Romans. In Scythia / Caria / Moesia we can see at a glance the connection between the Persian religion as Herodotus knew it and the Israelite exiles, whose religion was acceptable to the Zoroastrianism of the general population. That is the kind of thing that was common, though not universal, from Greece to China in the first one hundred years after Zoroaster. Personal responsibility to God for good thoughts and good actions was not new or unique to Zoroaster any more than being "born again" was new or unique to Billy Graham. Graham triggered a worldwide phenomenon in a similar way, much of which was identified with his own Baptist tradition but which also affected reforms among charismatic Catholics, energized the new Pentecostal movement, and bolstered other young churches, as well as elements within the sometimes moribund mainline Protestant denominations. The relationship of Zoroastrian teachings to Judaism, Hinduism, Buddhism, Taoism, and others may be seen in a similar light.

The first direct classical Greek reference to Zoroaster and the Magi is located in the dialogue *Alcibiades I*, by Plato (429–347 BCE). In the dialogue, Zoroaster (Zoroastren in Greek) is called "the son of Oromazes" (a Greek form of *Ormazd*, the common corruption of Ahura Mazda). In the same play, Zoroaster's religion is called "the magianism of Zoroaster . . . which is the worship of the Gods." A blatant inaccuracy notwithstanding, the inference here is simply that Zoroaster is the founder of the doctrine of the Magi, also an error in historical order. Other passing Platonic or neo-Platonic references to Zoroaster are found in *Alkibiades, Protos, The Republic,* and *Anonymmi Vita Platonis.*

It is almost certainly in Zoroaster that the Vedic and Semitic traditions definitively intersected, resulting in a transformative burst of energy that provided a powerful reinforcement for monotheism as it was emerging in the West and the development of monism in the East, both major departures from earlier polytheism. Between them we have the creative tension of dynamics that form the spiritual agenda of the sixth century BCE and well into the fifth, and which might have a similar reverberation in a New Axial Age of the twenty-first century CE.

While we do propose Zoroaster as the stimulus of the Axial Age, we do not suggest that the aforenamed Axial Age prophets and philosophers were his disciples, or that they lacked their own genius. But genius rarely appears in a vacuum; it is frequently a reaction or a response to some stimulus—in this case, Zoroaster's impact in the matter of morality and personal religion. Our theses may well prove valid, even without the documents for which we are searching, though we anticipate this momentous discovery before long. There are also two additional impact factors in Zoroastrianism that may be of as much value in our quest today as they were 2,500 years ago.

The first of these additional impact factors was the specific content of Zoroastrian Scriptures, doctrine, and practices as reflected in Buddhist enlightenment, in the messianic theology of Jews and Christians, and the eschatology of Islam. In Zoroastrian spirit, we do not suggest that recognizing the details of Zoroastrian heritage in the major religions of the world should lead to changes to these religions, but rather to mutual respect and understanding. This needs elucidation and illustration yet to come in this study, only part of which is dependent on new documentation, and much of which is found in the religions and philosophies of the East.

The second of these additional impact factors was Zoroastrianism's ecumenical tolerance and even encouragement of other religions, while insinuating a certain influence upon them. We have the clearest evidence of this with respect to the Jewish religion, but it was also evident in the midst of Buddhists along the Silk Route in early times, a coexistence among Central Asia's Sogdians[5] in particular and others, as we shall see. The essence of the Zoroastrian phenomenon was the individual religious fervor and personal esoteric communion with God, both populist and elitist, from west to east and back again. With even tentative acceptance of that premise, the rest will fall into place in both monotheistic and monistic traditions west and east.

Since a subtext of Book I and Book VII focuses on the additional information we may find in the "Dead Zee Scrolls," yet to be located, we might conclude this chapter by at least whetting our appetites for it in an examination of what Zoroastrian material we do have now. We can do so by turning to another article in the eleventh edition of the *Encyclopedia Britannica* by the same Karl Friedrich Geldner. He gives us the starting point for modern knowledge at the beginning of the twentieth century and manages to preserve a genuine feel for the antiquity of our sources, "warts and all." This entry is under Zend—Avesta, with the Persian word *zend* meaning "translation."

Zend-Avesta *Origin and History*—While all that Herodotus (i. 132) has to say is that the Magi sang "the theogany" at their sacrifices, Pausanias is able to add (v. 27. 3) that they read from a book. Hermippus, in the third century B.C., affirmed that Zoroaster, the founder of the doctrine of the magi, was the author of twenty books, each containing 100,000 verses. According to the Arab historian, Tabari, these were written on 12,000 cowhides, a statement confirmed by Masudi, who writes, "Zartusht gave to the Persians the book called Avesta. It consists of twenty-one parts, each containing 200 leaves. This book, in the writing which Zartusht invented and which the magi called the writing of religion, was written on 12,000 cowhides, bound together by golden bands. Its language was Old Persian, which now no one understands." These assertions sufficiently establish the existence and great bulk of the sacred writings. Parsee tradition adds a number of interesting statements as to their history. According to the *Arda-Viraf-Nama* the religion revealed through Zoroaster had subsisted in its purity for 300 years, when Iskander Rumi (Alexander the Great) invaded and devastated Iran and burned the Avesta, which, written on cow hides with golden ink, was preserved in the archives at Persepolis. According to the Dinkard, there were two original copies, one of which was burned, while the second came into the hands of the Greeks. One of the Rivayato relates further, "After the villainy of Alexander, an assemblage of several high-priests brought together the Avesta from various places, and made a collection which included the sacred Yasna, Vispered, Vendidad and other scraps of the Avesta," which, as far as possible, should be a faithful reproduction of the original.[6] King Shapur I (241–272 AD) enlarged this re-edited Avesta by collecting and incorporating with it the non-religious tractates on medicine, astronomy, geography and philosophy. Under Shapur II (309–380 AD) the nasks were brought into complete order, and the new redaction of the Avesta reached its definitive conclusion.

5

the extant avesta

Pieces of a Jigsaw Puzzle

THE EARLIEST PARTS OF THE AVESTA SCRIPTURES WERE COMMITTED TO WRITING AT THE insistence of King Vishtāspa, whom Zoroaster converted to the faith and who became Zoroaster's powerful patron. As a former scribe, this king's own prime minister, Jāmāspa, had responsibility for redactions of the text. Especially after the death of the monarch, Jāmāspa took special care of the portions written to date, as recorded in later verses of the Avesta.[1] Another, earlier contributor, Ṭabarī, and also Bundarī after him, affirm that Vishtāspa had instructed that two copies of the holy texts be inscribed in letters of gold upon ox-hide scrolls, a tradition illustrating Zoroastrianism's devotion to the sacred character of the texts. The Roman commentator, Pliny, made reference to the legend that Zoroaster composed no less than two million verses,[2] an obvious exaggeration unless someone multiplied two hundred verses of all possible Gathas in the Avesta by perhaps an estimate of one thousand copies of the work.

The two archetypal copies of Zoroaster's original and seminal work were to serve as the standard priestly codices of Vishtāspa's realm and are mentioned later in the *Dinkard*, the *Artā-Vīrāf*, and the *Shatrōihā-i-Airān*. Those three works are all portions of parts of the Avesta composed at a later date and witnessing to the Gathas, which introduce the Avesta much as the Torah introduces the Hebrew Scriptures and the Gospels introduce the New Testament. The faith was to be promulgated throughout the world in accordance with the teaching of these scrolls. We mentioned a tradition to the effect that one of these original copies came into the hands of the Greeks and was translated into copies in their language. It, too, has disappeared, but support for this tradition may perhaps be found in the Arabic lexicon of Bar-Bahlūl, according to which the Avesta of Zoroaster was available in seven languages: Syriac, Persian, Aramean, Segestanian, Mervian, Greek, and Hebrew. A still earlier Syriac manuscript commentary on the New Testament by 'Ishō'dād, bishop of Ḥadatha, near Mosul, similarly speaks of the Avesta as having been written in twelve different languages.

Even if there is hyperbole here, it is clear that there was fervor and devotion surrounding written versions of the original Avesta Scripture. Yet we are asked to believe that every single copy has perished.

This material appears to have been more voluminous than all the classical Hebrew writings in our possession—scriptural, apocryphal texts, and noncanonical materials combined. Like the Bible itself, the Avesta was, and, what still remains of it is, a compendium of documents written in various related languages. The oldest portions contain materials that were written by Zoroaster under inspiration from Vedic oral sources that were somewhat contemporary to Abraham, down to final texts composed just prior to the closing of the canon of the Christian Scriptures. The Avesta as a whole may therefore be regarded as a slightly older contemporary of the entire Bible and an influential background context for it.

Mention has also been made of the deliberate destruction of the Avesta in a conflagration under the direction of Alexander the Great in 330 BCE. This desecration was part of a program to "Hellenize" his empire, the first of many European attempts to "civilize" the rest of the world. Following the breakup of that empire, the Parthians governed Persia from 150 to 250 CE and revived the vigor of the Zoroastrian religion. This was especially evident under King Vologese, who commissioned the first attempt to recover Avesta materials from scattered fragments, to write down the oral traditions and liturgies, and to gather Zoroastrian quotations from Greek manuscripts. A brief disruption of the project by political and military upheavals was followed by a revival of the Persian Empire itself in the Sassanian era, 250–650 CE, in which Zoroastrianism again became the state religion. Its high priests succeeded in collecting the surviving Avesta documents into twelve volumes called *nasks*, producing the first official Zoroastrian canon, not long after the establishment of the Hebrew canon and just shortly before the closing of the Christian canon.

Sadly, from both monistic and monotheistic perspectives, new materials produced in these popular revivals were increasingly dualistic in nature, so that by the time of Muhammad Zoroastrian monotheism was largely a memory. The surviving portions of the Avesta itself were ambivalent in this regard, so most of what remained was obliterated by the fervently monotheistic Muslims when they took over Persia in the seventh century CE. Both confirmation of the early monotheistic truths of the Avesta and condemnation of its latter dualism are almost certainly to be found "between the lines" in the Quran, as we attempted to illustrate in Book III of the *Three Testament* compendium, and in abbreviated fashion later in this text.

So all that remains today of the original documents consists of portions from several religious nasks, both monotheistic and mixed, and one law book of social regulations. These have been put together from documents and fragments hidden by the few remaining Zoroastrian believers in Persia/Iran or spirited out of the country by refugees fleeing to India at that time and later. They were supplemented by familiar and beloved hymns, dating back to Zoroaster himself, which could be reproduced from memory by believers at any time. There is just enough remaining that we can outline the development of the Avesta as a whole, prior to tracing its influence on the Torah, and also considering its influence in the world of the Torah, in which the rest of the Hebrew Scriptures were produced in the form we know, and reflected in the New Testament and the Quran. But even prior to that, we may now see traces of certain monistic Zoroastrian traditions further east in the investigations presented in our Books II, III, IV, and V.

Europeans were largely unaware of the Avesta until after the seventeenth century, when, in the growth of trade with India, manuscript copies began to reach Europe. The French scholar A. H. Anquetil du Perron (1731–1805) went to India, learned to read the Avestan language from a Parsi priest in Surat, acquired manuscripts, and produced a translation. European study of the Avesta subsequently paralleled and drew support from the study of the earliest Sanskrit literature, which was linguistically related. More recent translations are more reliable, using tools produced by Mary Boyce, who had a Sanskrit scholastic background and became fluent in the Persian Avestan cognate languages as preserved in the rural Zoroastrian communities of Iran, where she actually chose to live among Zoroastrian villagers for a considerable period of time.

The core of the surviving or extant Avesta is a small collection of writings called the Gathas, universally recognized as prophetic utterances by Zoroaster himself. We refer to their language as Gathic Avestan, an ancient Indo-European language that serves as a link between Sanskrit and Hindi to the southeast and Greek and Latin to the northwest, each with their own linguistic offshoots.

At each stage of the Avesta's development, it also displays a linguistic affinity with Aramaic, its linguistic contemporary as spoken in Persia, and a link with both Hebrew and Sanskrit texts, West and East. The Gathas have an oracular quality that is rhetorical and poetically melodic—an apocalyptic literature, the first of that genre in the world. Like other ancient linguistic traditions, these factors make them difficult to translate, so verses of the Avesta are cherished by Zoroastrians today in the original as memorized. There are only about six thousand words in the Gathas by Zoroaster himself, recorded in five distinct poems, each with its own meter. They present the great Persian prophet's sublime expression of belief in one uncreated Lord of Wisdom, and they outline what this God expects of people in the universal and the personal struggle between good and evil, between truth and falsehood. God's will is presented as both invitation and command, detailed equally in worship and in good deeds as opposed to false gods and bad deeds.

The second surviving "text" of the Avesta was possibly written by a school of Zoroaster's disciples, probably during his lifetime or soon after, although Mary Boyce, as the world's leading academic authority on the Gathic Avestan dialect, believed it, too, may have been composed entirely by Zoroaster later in his life. Titled "Worship in Seven Chapters" in translation, it is known in the Zoroastrian community as the *Yasna Haptanhaiti*. The prayers in these seven chapters are more like hymns than poems, invoking the Lord of Wisdom as well as the sacred devas or "guardian angels" who protect the earth, sky, and sea. In direct correspondence to the prophet's teaching, they profess devotion to the truth and seek the happiness and fulfillment of the believers in serving God in good thoughts (worship) and in good deeds (action).

The third book, simply known as *Yasna*, "Worship," begins at chapter 28, implying that the seven chapters of the Yasna Haptanhaiti was once preceded by twenty other poems, chapters, or *sutras* by Zoroaster or his disciples, including his five Gathas. This leaves fifteen missing sutras as the mother lode of what we hope to find in someday unearthing the complete Avesta. Yasna itself is primarily liturgical, consisting of rubrics and instructions for worship. The Yasna has seventy-two chapters at present and appears rather complete. Written somewhat later in a dialect known as "Younger Avestan," in it we catch a glimpse of creationism and cosmological inferences from its introduction of the old devas of the Vedic pantheon. They are called *yazatas*, and they are regarded as spirits whose only purpose now is to serve and glorify the Lord of Wisdom.

A fourth collection, titled the *Visparad*, is much smaller at this point, also written in a Younger Avestan dialect. Its purpose is to simply comment on much of what we find in the first three collections. There may be much of the Visparad yet to be found, but its value will be less than the extended Gathas referred to above.

The fifth series of documents is called the *Yashts*, or "Services" of worship. There are twenty-one complete Yashts, and other bits and pieces, all based on ancient Vedic hymns used by Buddhists and Hindus still today; the comparison is instructive. These Yashts have been thoroughly reworked in the Avesta to laud the yazatas as models for humans to emulate in service to the Lord of Wisdom. Ahura Mazda is extolled, using the Younger Avestan translation of his name, *Ormazd*, which came into use even before the Common Era, although modern Zoroastrians have maintained or returned to the use of *Ahuramazda*.

In spite of their beauty, in the Yashts the Zoroastrian religion appears to begin the transition toward dualism, a form of Zoroastrianism that did not finally survive. There are yasht hymns to specific yazatas, or reinvigorated Vedic devas, like *Mah*, the Moonlight, or *Tir*, the Starshine, and *Aban*, the Waterfall. The latter features a recycled Vedic hymn to the river goddess *Ardvi Sura Anahita*, a hymn still in use among Hindus in the twenty-first century. These days, a similar concept of angelic presences, long associated with Catholic and Orthodox Christian tradition in the West, appears to be undergoing a popular revival among Jews, Protestants, and Muslims in popular cultures of the West. Such hymn poems are among the most sublime passages in the Avesta, and they may remind us of the romantic devotion to nature found in "new age" greeting cards and recordings used for meditation today. We find some of them represented in the Quran in a more theologically complete form as revealed to the Prophet, according to Islamic understanding of such transmissions.

The danger was always in compromising the rigorous abstraction of Zoroaster's original monotheistic or monistic vision of the Oneness of God. That danger is illustrated in Yashts extolling the beauty of green pastures and still waters, but without any shepherd. Others extol the endurance of the *Fravashis*, the souls of good people, but no reference to the goodness of God. The fire may give a certain charm to the hearth, but without the warmth of God's spirit it represents, these most beautiful moments may be but fleeting illusions. This Zoroastrianism resembles a modern greeting-card religion, with beautiful sentiment but few demands, subject only, if we are correct, to such sentiments being revealed to Muhammad in an appropriate form acceptable to God—much like their re-presentation also in Hebrew and Christian revelations.

The balance needed for the use of such imagery to experience and to reflect God's glory was about to be lost in Zoroastrianism. Once the power of these aesthetic devas was no longer used to serve and glorify God, and as they themselves became the object of meditation or worship, the direct encounter between humans and God was gone. With it went the impetus for personal morality and the imperative for social justice, both lost in the loveliness and beauty of an antiseptic religion that never dirties its hands—perhaps a precursor to sermons and discussions in many synagogues, churches, and masjids today, warning about a failure to distinguish between the requirements of the Creator and the desires of the created. This is a subject prominent in the Eastern texts we are about to examine, discussed in sermons in temples, stupas, and shrines.

The sixth and concluding section in the extant Avesta material is the *Vendidad*, intended to exorcise demons, but in confirming their power, the Vendidad reinforces many of the negative stereotypes of Zoroastrianism that have existed in many quarters. Published sometime after 300 CE, halfway between the lifetimes of Jesus and Muhammad, it continues the momentum of Vedic revival in the service of a dualistic worldview Zoroaster would possibly have found abhorrent. Without a solid underpinning based upon the Oneness of God, Zoroastrianism by this time bore little resemblance to the pristine faith encountered by the Jews in Babylon. The Vendidad appears to be a recapitulation of earlier texts, now lost, but the clumsy use of the Avestan language gives it a strained tone. Its prescriptions for the purification of women in menstruation, priests *in flagrante*, and animals and corpses are said to be still observed in remote rural Zoroastrian villages in Iran, though less so in India and abroad. The Vendidad is either ignored or scorned by many urbane Zoroastrians today in Tehran, Mumbai, London, Toronto, New York, and Sydney, where sins like adultery, child abuse, apostasy, sorcery, and profanity no longer require hanging, flaying, infestation, beheading, or dismemberment—penalties like those also abjured by Christians, Jews, and others in comparatively recent times despite the appearance of such extreme measures in scripture.

In addition to these large and significant Zoroastrian Avesta texts, there is also the *Khordah Avesta*, the "Little Avesta" still in use as their prayer book by Zoroastrians today. Composed and collected at an undetermined time during one of the attempts to recover texts and summarize the teachings in a worshipful context, the Khordah Avesta contains quotes from all the other extant collections, as well as fragments not found anywhere else. A number of verses in which God proclaims his name to be "I AM" will occasion our return to the Little Avesta when we consider Zoroaster's debt to Moses at the burning bush, similar I AM passages uttered by Jesus in the Christian Gospel, and frequently by Krishna in the *Bhagavad Gita*, a late addition to the *Mahabharata* possibly dating from the Axial Age.

The extant Zoroastrian Scriptures currently represent about 20 percent of the original, which would have been somewhat larger than the entire Christian Bible. What remains now makes up a volume somewhat smaller than the Torah, or about half the size of the Christian New Testament. It opens with the Gathas by Zoroaster himself, the poetic psalm-like prayers that set the style for much of the rest of the collection. The first comprehensive modern translation was completed in 1864 by Professor Friedrich von Spiegel (1820–1905), a German translation of "the original manuscripts" now at Harvard University, brought out serially from 1852 to 1863. Under the simple title *Avesta*, its English translation was completed in 1864 by von Spiegel's colleague, Arthur Henry Bleeck. Frequently reprinted and still available, it uses a strict formal equivalence that has been continued in more recent original translations, though with improved linguistic research.

From within the Parsee community, Piloo Nanavutty offered a charming dynamic equivalent translation of *The Gathas of Zarathustra* in 1999, limited mainly by a surfeit of untranslated phrases unfamiliar to and unmanageable by most English readers, although appreciated in the increasingly English-speaking Parsee community. This has led to our present attempt to offer a paraphrased dynamic equivalent sample, relying on everything we know about Zoroaster's life, passion, impact, and theology, but presented in a style believably representing the clarity and dynamism that must have been characteristic of this prophet whose message so changed the world.

The current offering in this study is aided by the *Textual Sources for the Study of Zoroastrianism* by Mary Boyce, and it is inspired by the brilliant synthesis of recent scholarship presented in *The Hymns of Zoroaster* (2010) by M. L. West, emeritus fellow of All Souls College, Oxford, and fellow of the British Academy. While somewhat hamstrung by formal equivalence to a language and a sometimes opaque text, with which we are all still struggling, West's accompanying commentary is the new gold standard in Zoroastrian scholarship in our new era of greater certainty about the dates of Zoroaster himself.

The paraphrases in this publication are an attempt to appreciate the power and majesty of the Avesta text and the intimacy between its first author and God. They are dependent upon the four sources mentioned above, based primarily on Spiegel and Bleeck for vocabulary, though enriched by the other three, who supply insights to the meaning. Our brief selection from the Gatha section of the Avesta illustrates Zoroaster's belief in the Oneness of God, clouded later by the appearance of Avestan "divinities," who are first recognized in Zoroastrianism as something akin to angels but who eventually grew in importance to become again gods like their Vedic antecedents, almost equal to their creator. This trend later motivated Muslims in their drive to recover a pure monotheism for themselves, for Jews and Christians, and for Zoroastrians as well.

In these samples we include the Gatha that presents Zoroaster's questions about creation of the earth and the origins of the universe that some of us now believe may have been answered directly by Isaiah in Babylon. Another of our examples is obviously from the crisis moment early in his ministry when Zoroaster felt impelled to move from his birthplace in Eastern Iran (Scythia / Armenia / Azerbaijan) to the region of Bactria, where he flourished for the next forty years. Also included are references to

Zoroaster's expectation of *Saoshyant* redeemers or "saviors" (in the plural, described elsewhere as three in number) who might come early to redeem creation, at the climax of history, and at the end of time (mirrored exactly in the Christian view of the Messiah). While using the flowing syntax of dynamic equivalence in these examples, there has been every effort to stick to the formal equivalent language to illustrate what is apparent in all these translations—that the Avesta is indeed echoed in the Torah and Gospel, that its truths confirmed in the Quran, and that it was a primary stimulus for the Eastern scriptures yet to come in this study.

In what follows, we witness a turning point in religious development of the world that swept throughout the region of the emerging Persian Empire and beyond, as humanity quite suddenly shifted from a creaturely dependence to active partnership with the Divine.

Worship[3]

With hands outstretched in worship, I pray to you and seek your help,
O Lord of Wisdom, placing your bountiful will above everything.
I offer right actions combined with good thoughts,
To connect Wisdom with souls in nature, like that of the contented cow.

I approach you, O Lord of Wisdom, as a mortal with good thoughts,
So you can bless me personally, both materially and spiritually.
Such blessings are your appropriate responses to the needs of believers.

I will praise you with right actions and good thoughts.
O Lord of Wisdom, your dominion is unimpaired.
My piety is worthy of an answer, so come to my aid.

I have summoned the spiritual resources to lift my thoughts on high,
Knowing that you, O Lord of Wisdom, reward right actions.
As long as I possess ability and strength I will pursue justice.

O Right One, may I see a vision of you as my thoughts rise to you?
Let our compliance become a path to you, O Lord of Wisdom.
In submission may we impress even predators with our hymns.

Join your good thoughts with ours, and make righteousness your gift.
In honest words, O Lord, give support to this camel herder, and to all.
Lord, give us what we need to overcome the acts of hostility by the foe.

O Right One, reward our good thoughts with your blessing.
Out of your holiness, empower King Vishtāspa and me.
O Lord of Wisdom, provide your authority,
Showing the requirements in which we may receive your care.

Revelation[4]

In accord with the laws of primordial existence,
The Day of Judgment shall come.
The wicked and the righteous together
Shall see their falsehoods and their honesty weighed up.

The person who is honest to others, whether kith or kin, O Lord,
Or even the ones who serve the needs of cattle in the field,
Shall themselves find pasture and peace.

So, God, I worship you and seek to avoid disobedience,
Whether in the challenges of family, or in the life of the clan,
In community service, or with ignorance like beasts in the field.

Reveal to me your purpose and your requirements,
So that I may attain your dominion,
The path of life that is in accord with your will.

As your priest, I call for truth and seek to fulfill my calling.
Assist me to undertake my ministry to the people,
By taking counsel with you, O Lord of Wisdom.

Come to me now, in your manifest essence, O God.
May my faith in you be vindicated among the believers.
Let all your promises to me be seen to be true.

All that was, everything that is, and all that shall be comes from You.
You reward us all according to our faithfulness, and we pray
That we may grow in righteousness in response to your dominion.

O Lord, you are the Mighty One of Wisdom.
Devotion and truth which nurture human life belong to you.
Hear my prayer and have mercy upon me in any reckoning to be made.

Arise within me, O Lord, and fulfill my desire
To serve you perfectly with unfailing devotion.
Accept my self-offering and confer your power for good.

From afar, draw near and reveal yourself to me.
Let me share in your sovereign reign, O Lord,
And instruct your people in devotion and in truth.

As an offering, this camel herder gives body and breath,
So that you may be served in good thoughts and good deeds,
Described in words that correspond to your dominion.
Everything that is good in life comes from you, O Lord of Wisdom.

Glory to God[5]

I realized that your very nature is bountiful, O God,
When I recognized you as the originator of life.
You offer both words of revelation and deeds which bear fruit.
Sun, moon and stars of creation reflect your glory, as may we.

As this turning point of realization, Lord, you come and bless.
Your sovereignty and your wisdom lead us on to truth.
Our devotion will allow you to guide us in wisdom.

When your wisdom encircled me and inquired of me,
"Who are you? To what people do you belong?
What will it take for your Lord to engage you?"

Then I answered you, first and foremost, I am a simple Camel Herder.
But I am an enemy of falsehood and lying, as best I know.
My goal in life is to respond to the glory I see in you, Lord,
To worship and praise you with songs of rejoicing.

Salvation[6]

I know I am ineffective here, My Wise Lord.
To which land shall I flee?
Where shall I seek refuge?
I am excluded from family and clan.

The community I would serve has rejected me
And the tyrants of the territory are no better.
How can I please you, Lord, where there is no response?

My cattle are few and my followers are scattered.
I lament my situation to you as my only true friend.
Give me a vision of your strength in Wisdom.

O Lord of Wisdom, when will you send your Redeemers,
To bring in the sparkling light of salvation,
The Redeemers who offer inspiration and guidance?
As for me, here and now, I rely on your Spirit alone.

This I Ask[7]

This I ask of you, so tell me truly Lord,
How are you to be worshipped?
O Lord of Wisdom, will you speak to me as a friend?
And may other worshippers gain wisdom from our encounter?

This I ask of you, so tell me truly Lord,
Can life be renewed by salvation during this existence,
And can human beings be blessed through understanding,
With your truth acting as the healer, and you as our friend?

This I ask of you, so tell me truly Lord,
At the beginning of creation, who was the father of order?
Who set the sun and the stars in their orbits
and caused the moon to wax and wane?
These things and many more I long to understand, Lord God of Wisdom.

This I ask of you, so tell me truly Lord,
Who holds up the earth and who keeps the sky from falling?
Who brought water into being to nourish the plants?
Who but you, Wise Lord, is the breath of the wind and the spirit of the cloud?

This I ask of you, so tell me truly Lord,
Which worker of wonders called forth the speed of light
Across the expanse of darkness, in rhythms of sleep and waking?
From whom came times of dawn, mid-day and nightfall to regulate our work?

This I ask of you, so tell me truly Lord,
How am I to grow in understanding of
Your revelations enshrined in sublime teachings?
I learned of them first through your wisdom, my greatest joy.

This I ask of you, so tell me truly Lord,
How am I to remain faithful to you in daily living?
Will you teach me, Lord, how to be loyal to your sovereignty?
Or is it only you that can dwell in truth and wisdom?

This I ask of you, so tell me truly Lord,
Is the revelation I received for everyone,
And will it be enough to sustain my livelihood?
Or am I to live a life of devotion apart from the world?

This I ask of you, so tell me truly Lord,
How shall others who see the vision express their devotion?
I was chosen to spread abroad your truth,
But I look upon others with apprehension.

This I ask of you, so tell me truly Lord,
Who is really a disciple of the truth and who lives by lies?
Am I to proclaim your truth to those who are hostile,
Or is salvation intended for those who receive it gladly?

Day of Judgment[8]

Protect me as long as this perishable world is dominant, O Lord,
Until wickedness and lies are obliterated in the Day of Judgment.
Mortals and immortals alike, both good and evil, abound,
But your promise of salvation gives your devotees the courage to go on.

Tell me, O Lord of Wisdom, since you know all things,
Will the just overcome the unjust in this life,
Or do we await the Day of Judgment
For the glorious renewal of life that is to come?

Right teaching is available to the one who is able to understand
The truth from you, O Lord of Wisdom, giver of all good.
In your benevolence, you provide the most profound insights,
Those that are integral to your wise understanding.

So in your great wisdom, O Lord,
Welcome those mortals who respond to your invitation.
Those whose thoughts and actions are in accord
With your desires and purposes.

Let good rulers govern us rather than corrupt,
So that surrounded by good governance,
We may live in piety and in harmony with nature,
As symbolized by the contentment of the cow.

For it is our cattle that provide for us,
Even as we provide for them.
And the vegetation so prevalent in creation
Remains as the context for the life we share.

In such a life, why should cruelty and violence prevail?
Let all who would triumph do so with understanding
Of the truth which underlies our existence,
And which draws us together for worship in your house, O God.

Truly I acknowledge your dominion, O Wise Lord,
What will you provide for me in response to my devotion?
Where will I find the resources for the followers you desire
To promote your cause of justice and of truth?

When will I be able to perceive the manifestation of sovereignty
Which will pit your truth against the hostile malice all around us?
Let me see the specific expression of your truth
In the coming Savior, who brings his reward with him.

O Lord of Wisdom, when will mortals see salvation?
When do we eliminate our intoxication with power,
Which deludes both the rulers and their people
And through which these lands are corrupted?

When, O Wise Lord, can we expect to see devotion and justice combine
To give safety and good pasture beneath your sovereign control?
Who will establish peace and security in the midst of blood-thirsty conflict?
From whom will the penetrating insights come to set us free in truth?

Such will be the Saviours and Redeemers of the lands,
Working through wisdom in harmony with truth.
Your Saoshyants will fulfill your purposes in the universe.
They are destined to prevail against all the forces of doom.

This selection of clustered verses, paraphrased after the pattern used by Mary Boyce and some others, serves to illustrate the intimacy between Zoroaster and God. It is limited to excerpts from Gathas widely accepted as being by Zoroaster himself, expressed with a spiritual sophistication that is a breakthrough as compared with both the older theological constructs of his Vedic predecessors and the awkward caricatures of his religion represented by previous Western translations. It is not suggested that the above paraphrases represent an advance in linguistic scholarship. If there is any improvement in the presentation, it is derived from a more flowing English syntax and the application of our growing knowledge about Zoroaster, his influence, and his prophetic passion.

In the cadences presented here we may at last glimpse the turning point in which belief develops into the spiritual power that transformed the people of the ancient world, as stated, "from a creaturely dependence to active partnership with the Divine" through either redemption or at-one-ment. Indeed, we do also see something of that understanding in biblical personas who predate Zoroaster: Abraham, Moses, the pre-Zoroastrian prophets, and perhaps elsewhere. But it is Zoroaster who sees and presents this partnership or union as a universal vision that is open to all humanity. The impact of that realization, as articulated and implemented by his followers at the apex of Persian rule as the world's first superpower, with reverberations from Europe to the Orient, triggered a spiritual tsunami in what we now call the Axial Age. Israel itself was, of course, among those most dramatically impacted due to its close association with Zoroastrians in Persia during the Babylonian Exile, but the birth of Buddhism, the reforms of Hinduism, and other related developments, both philosophical and religious, have been well documented elsewhere and will be illustrated in Books II, III, IV, and V of this compendium. The connections to Christianity and Islam are also presented in Book VI of this volume in summarizing the universal vision, followed by the quest for the "Dead Zee Scrolls."

We also see the reflection of Hebrew and Christian Scriptures in the Quran, but the issue of the place of Zoroastrian Scriptures in the Quran falls into the category of what, in conversation, is sometimes called "the elephant in the room"—that is, something clearly obvious but not discussed or acknowledged by anyone. Since the Roman Empire and the rule of Alexander the Great are mentioned in the Quran, and since regional religions like Judaism and Christianity are discussed, how could it be possible that the Quran makes no mention of Persia and Zoroastrianism, Arabia's most powerful neighbor and most significant external religious influence, respectively? The fact is that these influences are indeed addressed in the Quran, but in such a manner that they are so pervasive as to be almost invisible, forming the context of much of the Islamic Scripture. Just as water is invisible to fish and air is invisible to humans, it may be only in an interfaith study like this one that the "water" (Persia) and the "air" (Zoroastrianism) of the Quran can be seen and identified in the "corrected and true" revelation to Muhammad, in the understanding of Muslims.

Prior to turning to the Eastern texts in detail, and before including Judaism, Christianity, and Islam in the wider vision, we need consider how Zoroastrianism could have inspired both monistic and monotheistic manifestations, and even consider how the former may be considered by some to be the fulfillment or conclusion of the world's spiritual pilgrimage from polytheism through monotheism to monism. This much is required before we are able to give the *Tao Te Ching*, the *Analects*, the *Dhammapada*, and the *Bhagavad Gita* their due.

6

the fraternal twins of world religions

Monism for Monotheists

READERS MAY HAVE BARELY TAKEN NOTE OF THE COMMENT BY KARL FRIEDRICH GELDNER IN the exordium, "The Zarvanites represented Ormazd and Ahriman as twin sons proceeding from the fundamental principle of all—*Zrvana Akarana*, or limitless time." Few have even heard of the Zarvanites, and yet this Zoroastrian cult in the Near West may be illustrative of the Zoroastrian influence in mainstream Eastern and Oriental thought, Hindu and Buddhist in particular. Monism and monotheism do not look alike—hence "fraternal" in the title of this chapter—but twins they may be, with spiritual DNA indicating perhaps two strands of common parentage in different Zoroastrian manifestations, East and West.

Zurvan, as a name for the *Ultimate*, or God, from the Sanskrit word *Sarva*, via the Avestan *zurvan*, came to mean "infinity," and was referred to as *The Ancient of Days* in hymns and prayers. The name is freighted with semantic inferences describing a monistic deity, as found in India and throughout the East. In the Middle West (Western Persia and west from there), Zurvanism, as it existed for centuries, refers to Zurvan as the God of infinity in time and space, known simply as the One. The name Zurvan was revived from Vedic tradition about a hundred years after Zoroaster, whose teachings the cult claimed to correctly interpret, rightly or wrongly regarding monotheism as merely a step to monism. The latent dualism in Zoroastrianism was a problem thus solved by regarding good and bad, justice and evil, right and wrong, and other opposites as manifestations of the two divinities, *Spenta Mainyu* (Benevolent Spirit) and *Angra Mainyu* (Malevolent Spirit), twin brother offspring of Zurvan and his creation. They were known to people as Ahura Mazda (Lord of Wisdom) and Ahriman (The Adversary). By correct dealing with both these devas, the devotees aspired to ultimate Oneness with the eternal and infinite Zurvan.

None of this might matter very much, except that Zurvanism is an illustration of Zoroastrian monism accessible to Western scholars, assisting us to understand the impact of Zoroastrianism in the development of monism in the East. The Zurvan cult simmered through western areas of the Persian Empire in the last half of the Achaemenid period, during the rule of the descendants of Cyrus, and actually held sway in most of the later Sassanid period, ending in 651 CE under the Muslims. Zurvanism disappeared by the tenth century, while monotheistic Zoroastrianism has survived in reduced circumstances until the modern era. The importance of Zurvanism to us is as an illustration of how Zoroaster's message acted as a stimulus, triggering a variety of responses in the Axial Age including monism, prevalent in the East but also visible in the West early in the Common Era, through Spinoza to "New Age" religion and other trends in our time.

The connection between Zoroastrianism and monism is perhaps easily documented in the West but possibly more dominant in the East, where it may be pervasive in most religious traditions. The particular dichotomy between monism and monotheism, inherited by the world from the followers of Zoroaster, may form the basis of one of the main religious discussions in the twenty-first century. We will return to what this means shortly, but before affirming the Zoroastrian heritage of Eastern monism, let us at least establish the bona fides of Zurvanism and monism in the Middle West, since the whole concept may be new to many readers. This will be an esoteric exercise to prepare us for Books II, III, IV, and V of this compendium, devoted to monism in the East, before returning to a new appreciation of what this may mean to the world of the twenty-first century in Books VI and VII.

The oldest reference to the Zurvan sect is attributed to Eudemus of Rhodes (370–300 BCE) in his *History of Theology*, cited by Damascius in his *Difficulties and Solutions of First Principles* in the sixth century CE. In it Eudemus describes a cult among the Persians that considered Infinity/Eternity the primordial parent of Light and Darkness,[1] seeming references to Ahura Mazda and Ahriman. There are also contemporary inscriptions invoking the name of Zurvan, but most written sources on this subject during the Sassanian period are from Christian critics, both Armenian and Syrian.

For that matter, if all we had to go on were those early Christian commentaries on the lengthy Sassanian era, we would assume that Zoroastrianism was through and through monistic, as it certainly was (by names other than Zurvanite) in the Far East. As it was, Mazdean monotheism was the norm through most of the classical Achaemenid era, again after the Sassanians, and then down through the ages to modern times. But we highlight the Zurvanites to show how the monistic phenomenon was an option, even in the West, where they were always the minority party. Even under Sassanian rule their *modus operandi* might be compared to modern "Charismatic Catholics," who are enthusiastic in private or in small groups but also attend regular mass as loyal members of the Roman Catholic Church. Even when the ancient Persian royal family embraced Zurvanistism for a time, the state religion maintained the rituals of what was considered orthodox monotheistic Mazdianism.

After Zoroaster's time, and in extant Avesta texts published previous to the Sassanian era, Zurvan appears in the evolving scriptural compendium only twice. Zurvan is praised as represented by *Vata* and *Vayu* (Space and Air),[2] and plants only thrive as they develop according to the pattern established over "time" as embodied in Zurvan.[3] Zurvan also appears twice in passing in the more recent extant Vendidad section of the Avesta, but without significance, and makes no appearance in the Gathas of Zoroaster himself, nor in the Yazatas, and certainly not in the *Khordeh Avesta* (Little Avesta) of enduring popularity.

However, something had apparently given these Zurvanites the idea that Zoroastrianism (even if they did not yet all use that name) should be interpreted in a monistic fashion. In the Avesta as we have it, the Yasna section on worship begins as "chapter 28" of the whole. Obviously somewhere between the five opening Gatha poems by Zoroaster and the seven chapters of *Yasna Haptanhaiti*, there were once fifteen chapters, poems, or sutras of other material that might have been highly influential at some stage of the religion's development. Three scraps of verses usually prepended to the Gathas may be from that corpus, where the Gathas habitually address Ahura Mazda (Lord of Widsom), whereas the Yasnas after the gap are mainly about the Mindful Lord. As perhaps from the prayer poems now missing in between, the scraps of these "detached mantras," as they are sometimes called, address a "Mindful One" (a term we will see again when we consider monistic aspects of Buddhism and Hinduism).

This is not much to go on, since with five Gathas containing six thousand words, we may assume the missing fifteen early sutras could contain eighteen thousand words or more. But the opening words of the first one, for example, could have come straight out of the *Dhammapada* or the *Bhagavad Gita*:

> Just as he is the Master one would choose,
> So the guidance of right and good thoughts,
> Of actions is assigned to the Mindful One,
> With power to the Lord as guru to the destitute.[4]

In later reconstructions of verses remembered by the majority, were most of these verses neglected or forgotten because they were the treasure of only the heterodox Zurvanites? Is this the basis of Zoroastrian stimulation that was taken farther east by Magi in China and Zurvan travellers and interlocutors in India? We will know if and when we find the "Dead Zee Scrolls."

In the seventh century CE, Zoroastrianism was supplanted by Islam throughout the Persian Empire, gradually in areas of Mazdean orthodox monotheism like the northwestern provinces of Zoroaster's heartland, and in the villages, but rapidly among the ruling Sassanian elite with their Zurvanistic tendencies. Islam would have had little patience with a monism in which people strive to unite with God rather than to worship and serve God, especially since that monism presented itself in twin divinities of Ahura Mazda and Ahriman and other dualistic manifestations. However, Islamic respect for Zoroastrian monotheism continued down through the ages in a Persian Islamic culture that still today respectfully reserves a seat in the parliament of Iran for a Zoroastrian representative.

Meanwhile, in Greece, Parmenides of Elia propounded a monistic view of reality in his poem *On Nature*. In a section of one poem[5] Parmenides says that "what is (i.e., reality) must be understood as being One," that "change is an illusion," and that "existence is timeless." In another section called "The Way of Opinion," he argues that the world of appearances is a false realm from which we must become detached in order to enter into the reality of the One. The monism of Parmenides is virtually identical to Vedantic Hinduism, though it is hard to imagine any link except Zurvanic Zoroastrianism. Of course, Parmenides never quotes Zoroaster, but he greatly influenced Plato, who does. Indeed, Plato presents Parmenides as being in conflict with Socrates in the play *Parmenides*, where the monism of Parmenides stands in contrast to the monotheism of Socrates, both conceivably responding to the Zoroastrian stimuli that were in the air. Monotheism won out in the West, but we may observe that the collapse of faith in the gods of Olympus happened at the very same time that in the East the old Vedic gods became subsumed under the umbrella of monism, both developments taking place in the wake of Zoroaster's life and ministry.

There is enough similarity between Zurvan and the Lord of Creation (Prajapati) in Vedic literature,[6] as well as in literature ascribed to the mythical poet Orpheus concerning the origins of the gods, for us to at least recognize the fluidity of these ideas in the fifth century BCE, when both Zurvanites in Persia and philosophers in Greece were seeking ancient sanction for their understandings of Zoroastrian ideas. To go a step further, these inferences begin to look like mounting evidence that monotheism and monism have roots that are similar, if not intertwined. This is a helpful appreciation of the Vedic subtext of religions east and west, before we move on.

In the west, an ultimate "One," drawing "all" to itself by operating through the facade of twin deva divinities, good and evil, finally led to a pessimistic fatalism that characterized a classical Zurvanism, not too different from the fatalism sometimes identified with Indian religions. This might stand in contrast to a more positive Mazdeanism in which devotees are encouraged to serve Ahura Mazda in the attainment of the victory of good over evil in an eternal kingdom. Of course, if we acknowledge the fatalism in serene monism, we must also concede the damage of activist monotheism, from warfare to climate change, brought about by human activity among monotheists.

For Zurvanism to have simmered for several centuries, to have survived foreign domination, and to have flourished in the new Sassanian era, there must have been an agency, if not a separate organization, of these monistic Zoroastrians. Such a zealous minority can be identified as the Magi, whose earlier religion, before virtually all of them identified with the Zoroastrian state religion, may well have been dualistic. The indications of this would take up too much space to document here, but the opportunity to highlight the potential dualism in Zoroaster's message might have helped the Magi to feel at home under the Zoroastrian umbrella. It blended well with the Zurvan tendency to present the conflict between Ahura Mazda and Ahriman as a creative tension leading to resolution in the Oneness of God rather than the victory of good over evil. Is this the face of Zoroastrianism the Magi presented in China?

This is speculation, but the Magi did disappear from the stage of world history during the quashing of Zurvanism by Islam, while more orthodox Mazdean Zoroastrians survived. Another speculation of interest might be regarding the effect, if any, that the conflict between Zurvanism and Islam might have had on the development of militant Shiism in Iran as a distinct branch of Islam. More to the point in reference to future material to be presented in Book II of this compendium is the current and irrefutable evidence that the Magi became established in China even before Zoroaster's time. They would surely have maintained their Iranian connections and may well have been the conduit of Zoroastrian monistic ideas to the East.[7]

Monotheism dominated the scene throughout the Middle East and all over the West all through the Middle Ages in Judaism, Christianity, and Islam, while the exact opposite was the case in Southeast Asia and the Orient, where monism prevailed in Taoism, Buddhism, Jainism, and Hinduism. That equilibrium was challenged in the East perhaps first by Confucianism and later by the arrival of European missionaries following the Renaissance and Reformation eras, and in the West by the philosophical writings of Baruch Spinoza (1632–1677). Regarded by many as the thinker who laid the groundwork for the eighteenth-century Enlightenment as well as for modern biblical criticism, current conceptions of the self, and, arguably, the universe, Spinoza has come to be considered one of Western philosophy's most important thinkers. Indeed, philosopher Georg Wilhelm Friedrich Hegel said of all contemporary philosophers, "You are either a Spinozist or you are not a philosopher at all."[8]

It is traditionally assumed that Spinoza worked his way into a profound monism in isolation from any monistic precedents elsewhere in the world. However, a careful analysis, not of his writings but of his connections, might stimulate some interesting second thoughts in that regard with reference to this study. A resemblance between Spinoza's philosophy and Eastern monistic traditions has been the subject of many previous investigations based on textual evidence alone; we will build on that by taking a different approach.

Theodore Goldstucker of Germany, a noted scholar of Sanskrit literature, was one among several in the nineteenth century who noticed one particular connection that seemed too obvious to ignore. He described the similarities between Spinoza's religious ideas and the Vedanta beliefs of India in some detail. Spinoza's conception of God is "so exact a representation of the ideas of the Vedanta that we might have suspected its founder to have borrowed the fundamental principles of his system from the Hindus, did his biography not satisfy us that he was wholly unacquainted with their doctrines."[9] Others have been equally spellbound by the comparison. "Spinoza was a man whose very life is a picture of that moral purity and intellectual indifference to the transitory charms of this world, which is the constant longing of the true Vedanta philosopher. Comparing the fundamental ideas of both, we should have no difficulty in proving that had Spinoza been a Hindu, his system would in all probability mark a last phase of the Vedanta philosophy."[10]

In these and other instances, even allowing for translation into another language, we appear to be looking at the same words in Spinoza's writing and the Vedanta written two thousand years earlier. How could this be? Max Muller, in his lectures on the subject, noted the striking connection between the Vedanta and the philosophical system of Spinoza, saying that "the Brahman, as conceived in the Upanishads and defined by Sankara, is clearly the same as Spinoza's 'Substantia.'"[11] Helena Blavatsky, a founder of the Theosophical Society, spells out the core detail of Spinoza's religious thought as compared to the Vedanta when she says, "As to Spinoza's Deity—*natura naturans*—it is the Vedantic Deity pure and simple."[12]

Is there anything that could be discovered by standing back further than these specialists that would allow us to make an actual connection? As it turns out, Spinoza would have had good reasons to disguise any pagan source for his ideas about God. By the age of seventeen he had left formal educational pursuits to take over the family business of importing goods from India and elsewhere in the East, and to begin his writing career. By the age of twenty-three he was expelled from the synagogue and spurned in the Jewish community for radical views never completely described. Books by his pantheist friend and philosophical mentor, Francis Van den Ende (1625–1672), were placed on the Index of Forbidden Books, and it was not long before Spinoza was similarly honored by the Catholic Church for his heretical theology. A few years later Van den Ende would be executed, along with Johan de Witt (1625–1672), Spinoza's political mentor. For Spinoza to publish views that were merely unacceptable would be one thing, but to seek acceptance for ideas originating in pagan India could have put his life in danger in that environment.

So, even supposing we could illustrate any probable linkage with Eastern thought, Spinoza would have good reason to shield any connection with the Hindu Vedanta. As it is, he wore a signet ring that he used to mark his letters and that was engraved with the word *caute* (Latin for "cautiously")[13] under a rose, suggesting his familiarity with the Vendata legend in which two divinities, "Brahma, the creator and Vishnu, the protector, were discussing which flower was the most beautiful. Brahma favoured the lotus and Vishnu the rose. After seeing the arbour laden with fragrant roses in Vishnu's celestial garden, Brahma acknowledged the supremacy of the rose over all the flowers, including the lotus,"[14] and the rose became a flower associated with the Vendata. This symbol was adopted by Spinoza, "cautiously," as expressed on his seal.

Spinoza's Jewish family had moved from Portugal to Amsterdam in 1593, having previously established themselves in mercantile endeavors in which connections with Goa, Daman, and Diu in Portuguese India and elsewhere in the East were essential. The Dutch East India Company was formed in Holland in 1602, through a union of several companies founded in 1595, which took place soon after his family's arrival. In Spinoza's personal library, on display in his cottage museum today, we find books by Pieter and Jean de la Court, including *Political Maxims of the State of Holland*, which critiques the trade in nutmegs, mace, cloves, cinnamon, and, notably, Indian quilts and carpets.[15] In the 1600s the British East India Company was importing perfumes and cosmetics from India after Queen Elizabeth I adopted and popularized the use of imported red lipstick. French fashion in the seventeenth century was dominated by silks from India, despite a late entry into trade there by the French. On their buildings the Dutch themselves adopted the frilly gables of Indian architecture. We can only speculate about what other fashions from India may have been under critique in Europe, and with Spinoza importing spices and textiles it is hard to imagine that this scholar never took note of papers or books.

But the connections do not end with his business associations. While establishment Protestants were as unimpressed as Catholics with Spinoza and his ideas (though he was finally buried in a Reformed Church cemetery), from his diaries we know that he had an intimate circle of Mennonite friends. Mennonites had been prominent in the Dutch East India Company in its early years. They were "free thinkers" and eventually became an annoyance to the more profiteering shareholders. "The Mennonites withdrew from the trade when the company became involved in conquest and violence."[16] Again we ask the question: How much did Spinoza and his circle know about India and what was going on there? Were their concerns strictly limited to business matters or did they have access to information and materials of wider, and even spiritual, interest?

Spinoza was considered by some to be an atheist because he used the word "God" (Deus) to signify a concept that was different from that of traditional Judeo-Christian monotheism: "Spinoza expressly denies personality and consciousness to God; he has neither intelligence, feeling, nor will; he does not act according to purpose, but everything follows necessarily from his nature, according to law."[17] Accordingly, we might even say that Spinoza's detached God[18] is antithetical to a Jewish God who chooses and empowers people to serve him, to a Christian God who loves them, to a Muslim God of justice who will call people to account in a Final Judgment, and to all anthropomorphic concepts of the Divinity. The monistic concept of a God who not only "goes with the flow" but also is the Flow will be discussed in Book II beginning with the monistic images of Taoism.

Spinoza recommends *amor intellectualist dei* (the intellectual love of God) as the supreme good for man,[19] but Spinoza's God does not have free will[20]—he does not have purposes or intentions[21]—and Spinoza insists that "neither intellect nor emotion will pertain to the nature of God."[22] Moreover, while we may love God, we need to remember that God is really not the kind of "being" who could ever love us back. "He who loves God cannot strive that God should love him in return," says Spinoza.[23] The purpose of prayerful meditation in monism is not to get God to change the natural order of things, which may appear as good or evil, or to plead that events may be tilted in our favor. It is rather that each believer should seek and attain grace to accept and deal with life by attuning one's self with God and God's nature, a contrast with monotheists pleading with God to attune himself to our humanity's needs and desires. This "becoming One with God" may result in a state of gentle bliss, as we shall consider when we get to the Eastern examples.

Or is this akin to fatalism, which may not be pleasing to a God who has a program and invites human creaturely participation and who enables humans to engage in a partnership? This brief summary of Spinoza's life and works has been altogether inadequate as a summary of this great philosopher's religion, but American critic Harold Bloom has written, "As a teacher of reality, Spinoza practiced his own wisdom, and was surely one of the most exemplary human beings ever to have lived."[24] Since Spinoza, there have been countless individuals in the West who have exemplified a monistic faith, but there has been no significant *movement* as such, akin to Zurvanism. The late twentieth-century vogue of interest in Hinduism and Buddhism in the West may have been a harbinger of profound discussions to come in the interfaith environment of the twenty-first century, in which religion is both fluid and dynamic.

Indeed, the religious situation is suddenly fluid and dynamic throughout the whole world, and the relationship between monotheism and monism is a critical issue. Western monotheism continues to attract interest in the East with the spectacular growth of Christianity in China, Korea, the Philippines, Africa, and elsewhere, even as churches appear to diminish in parts of the West while they recover strength in Russia and Eastern Europe and take new forms in South America. At the same time, Eastern religious influence grows daily in the West through the influx and increasing pervasiveness of millions of monistic immigrants, establishing temples of many kinds among the churches, synagogues, and also mosques in cities large and small where Judaism remains the anchor of monotheism, Christianity witnesses to God's immanence, and Islam reflects God's transcendence as a bridge between East and West. With such influences affecting us all where we live and even where we worship, in a New Axial Age the phenomenon known as New Age religion may actually find its place within various religious communities, coming to mean more than movie stars like Shirley MacLaine running along a beach, exclaiming to the heavens, "I am God."

Monotheism and monism might be regarded as the double-helix DNA of the spiritual life of humanity. By coincidence or otherwise, both strands of this double helix appeared West and East in the philosophies and religious expressions of the Axial Age, immediately following a burst of energy emitted by the Persian prophet Zoroaster (628–551 BCE), whose spectacular career flared into prominence around 588 BCE, at least according to Iranian and Arabic records, now accepted by something approaching a broad consensus, except in certain strictly academic circles.

Monotheism appeared among the Israelites much earlier and got a tremendous boost among the Jews in the Babylonian Exile with the advent of rule there by Zoroastrians whose founder may have received monotheism from Israelite exiles in the first place—just seventy-five years earlier. With phenomenal consequences at the beginning of the Axial Age, monism came on the world scene later than monotheism's first appearance with Moses, but it blossomed in the East in the writings and preaching of Lao Tzu in China and the Buddha in India in precisely the same post-Zoroaster historical epoch as monotheism began its spread and flourished in the West. Lao Tzu and the Buddha were followed by the ethical reforms of Confucius in China and a reformation of Hinduism in India, respectively, with Confucianism as perhaps a reaction to foreign religious influence on behalf of Chinese traditional values, and developments in Hinduism building on such influences, much as Christianity and Islam eventually followed Judaism to the fore as champions of monotheism.

Lao Tzu and Buddha may have both been stimulated by a degree of animation surrounding the spread of Zoroastrian influence, but it is not contended that either they or their followers were Zoroastrians. Rather, in response to that vision of personal intimacy with the transcendence of divinity, and the impact of the Zoroastrian program of "right deeds" to accompany these "right thoughts," they would have presented their own genius in concert with spiritual advances that, while perhaps not "worldwide," seem to have extended throughout the length of the Silk Route and into its peripheral offshoots at either end.

At the risk of obfuscation of the issues, let us attempt to address the differences and the relationship between monotheism and monism in practice. Many in the West have adopted the misconception that oriental religions require those who seek unity with the One to give up their individuality, to perhaps retire to a mountain retreat, and to forswear family, business, and other responsibilities. Later Buddhism may make the case that such withdrawal is permitted or even required, but that is not our understanding of the *Tao Te Ching*, where we become One with God in the very thick of community activity and "go with the flow" in the midst of responsible family life, as will become apparent.

In a fulsome understanding of monism, does the individual identity endure in this life and in the life to come? In a marriage, we sometimes employ the biblical image of two becoming one, even described in the scripture as "one flesh," but their oneness allows for individual particularity within the union. This may be a helpful illustration of the *at-one-ment* with God that monistic faith offers, in contrast to the Western view of "atonement" for sins, which implies not oneness but reconciliation of particularities, which remain very separate as creator and creature. Both "monotheism" and "monism" are relatively new terms, originating in the seventeenth and eighteenth centuries and completely unknown to the ancients, East or West. Rather than being seen as contradictory, in this early period of the twenty-first century, we might begin to consider the two concepts as poles or endpoints on a continuum. Some believers are at one end and some at the other (and perhaps many in between), but in our time it may be possible to maintain one's own faith position with integrity while benefitting from an enriching vision from the other end of the spectrum.

The three most familiar forms of monotheism in the West were explored in *Three Testaments: Torah, Gospel, and Quran*. Monism too may take a variety of forms, the three most widely recognized being Taoism, Buddhism, and Hinduism as featured in this compendium. The Oneness we seek is described as the *Flow of Life* in Taoism, in which a person swims against the current, spits into the wind, or rows against the tide at one's peril, while another person experiences fulfillment as an individual by finding one's destiny within the flow as a part of the whole. Buddhism finds unity in the liberation that comes from an emptying out of individual particularities into a fullness that is the essence of enlightenment. Confucianism, if not a reaction to these concepts and trends, is at least distinguished by some distance from monism, though it can hardly be described as merely monotheistic, given its respect for polytheistic aspects of ancestor worship. Hinduism, as exemplified in the *Bhagavad Gita*, will be described in this study as a bridge between monotheism and monism, with monotheism as a way station *en route* to the Ultimate, despite the necessity of a respectful nod to polytheism along the way.

At the risk of oversimplification, in the interest of stretching the understanding of those for whom this is religious "new think," let us attempt to explore the relationship of monotheism to monism from a Christian perspective. Christianity is chosen for this exercise not only as the religion of some contributors to this study (and possibly the majority of our readers) but also as being, by about a billion adherents, the largest religion in the world, providing an example most likely to be easily understood by many others, monistic and monotheistic alike.

To begin with, it is perhaps often presumed by casual observers that monotheists pray and monists meditate. But while prayer is addressed "to God" as one who is separate and meditation is thinking "about God" as a means to become One with God, it is easily observed that monotheists recite little poems about God and monists do address God directly. The prayers of Christian children like "Now I lay me down to sleep, I pray the Lord my soul to keep" and "God is great and God is good, let us thank God for our food" are not actually prayers because they are *about* our intentions, and *about* God, rather than directly addressed to God. (Prayers would be "Now I lay me down to sleep, I pray You Lord my soul to keep" and "God you are great, God you are good, and we thank you for our food.") However, the following Hindu "meditation on peace" from the *Atharva Veda* is actually a proper prayer, addressed *to* God:

> Supreme Lord, let there be peace in the sky and in the atmosphere.
> Let there be peace in the plant world and in the forests.
> Let the cosmic powers be peaceful.
> Let the Brahman, the true essence and source of life, be peaceful.
> Let there be undiluted and fulfilling peace everywhere.

This distinction is important as it goes to the heart of spiritual practice, so let us continue in a practical vein. The object of either prayer or meditation is "God" for traditional Christians and "The Godhead" for orthodox Hindus. However, Christians actually see Christ as the manifest presence of God and think of him as the head ("God has put all things under the feet of Christ and has made him the head over all things"),[25] while, as noted, Hindus may indeed address God as "Supreme Lord."

St. Paul goes further by linking all believers into the one body:

The body does not consist of one member but of many. If the foot would say, "Because I am not a hand, I do not belong to the body," that would not make it any less part of the body. And if the ear would say, "Because I am not an eye, I do not belong to the body," that would not make it any less a part of the body. If the whole body were an eye, where would the hearing be? If the whole body were hearing, where would the sense of smell be? But as it is, God arranged the members in the body, each of them, as he chose.[26]

The believer is not the Head, but the believer is in one body with the Head, perhaps a humble toenail offering praise, laments, thanksgivings, supplications, and listening to the Head in prayer.

This Oneness for Christians comes about as unity with not only the Head but also other members. Perhaps we should have taken a moment to connect the concept of "metaphor" with meaning and truth, but suffice it to say that this casts a whole new light on the prayer of Jesus for his disciples and the church: "I ask not only on behalf of these, but also on behalf of those who will believe in me through their word, that may all be *one*. As you, Father, are in me and as I am in you, may they also be in us, so that the world may believe that you have sent me. The glory that you have given me, I have given them, so that they may be *one*, as we are *one*" (italics added).[27]

This nontraditional emphasis on *oneness* between believers and God and between believers and one another may be uncomfortable for Christians who see such headship and oneness language as merely symbolic, but for literalists these words point to the possibility of a more monistic understanding of Christianity, leading on to an understanding of heaven with perhaps less anthropomorphic individualism, though there, too, the *oneness* may enfold many parts. In Christian prayer, the Godhead may have the face of Jesus; for Jews and Muslims, the face is veiled; for Hindus, it may appear as the face of Vishnu, Krishna, or perhaps Kali, the latter being the feminine face of divine empowerment. While Taoists will have no such image of the face of Godhead, they may prayerfully picture the great Flow of life, a wide river in which each drop plays a role and has both character and purpose. But to appreciate monism, Christians and others may not need to leave traditional doctrines they find efficacious, as their monotheistic dichotomy between Creator and creature could gently expand in the direction of monistic enrichment in wholeness. To offer a Christian example, "To tell the truth in love, we must all grow up into Him who is the head, into Christ, from whom the whole body, joined and knit together by every ligament with which it is equipped, as each part is working properly, promotes the body's growth in building itself up in love."[28] The scriptural texts in Books II, III, IV, and V will provide grist for the mill, concluding with the *Bhagavad Gita*, which bridges these seeming differences more completely from an Eastern perspective. Before we go there, we should confirm our grasp on the issue to be raised from the perspective of the believer, the devotee, the religious practitioner.

Thomas Jefferson, framer of the American Declaration of Independence and third president of the United States, never called himself a deist but is often regarded as such—deism being the belief that God has created the universe but remains apart from it and permits the creation to administer itself through natural laws. Deism rejects the supernatural aspects of religion, such as belief that revelation is contained in the scriptures, and rejects the notion that God intervenes in human affairs, but it stresses the importance of moral conduct. While both monists and monotheists can be deists, so as to prevent misunderstanding it may be important to point out that neither usually are.

When the believer or devotee addresses God as "Eternal One," the word "One" may have one of two meanings. The address may be to "One who is separate from us" like an individual, even the greatest individual, in which case the monotheistic believer's inflection in the address is likely to be "ETERNAL One." Or the address may be to "One who embraces all," meaning that the devotee aspires to feel a part of a greater whole, in which case the monistic inflection would be closer to "Eternal ONE." If this seems to be splitting hairs, it is not, and it leads on to another question.

Is it possible that while the concepts of God are different, the praxis, or the practical requirements of religious life may be the same? Might monistic and monotheistic experiences of God result in similar behavior (or not)? Is this possibly an area of fruitful discussion in interfaith conversation moving forward? Is going with the Taoist Flow, as a toenail cooperating with the Godhead, the monist's equivalent of the monotheist seeking to know the will of God and to serve the Creator Lord? To further conceptualize monism from a monotheistic perspective, it might be said that while Jews, Christians, and Muslims might have no difficulty *praying* to the Godhead, they would be more likely to see themselves as *meditating* on the Flow as the ongoing will and purpose of God.

We have not here touched on an important distinction between monism and monotheism in popular cultures, East and West—namely, the relationship or connection with the environment of natural world. It is commonly supposed that monists are more inclined to live in harmony with nature, since they see themselves as being one with it, while monotheists may feel more free to exploit nature for their own benefit. However, the extreme pollution in countries where much of the population espouses monism raises a question about that theory, and for monotheists the Hebrew Scripture teaches that humanity is "to have responsibility for the earth and to replenish it,"[29] in a passage thought now to have come down from Vedic tradition, equally dishonored in practice in both monistic and monotheistic traditions.

Before leaving this exercise of attempting to define the line between monotheism and monism, and finding it perhaps thinner than traditionally imagined, it may be of interest to note that while monotheistic Judaism flirted with polytheism (in scripture), or at least henotheism (worshipping a God who is merely the best among gods), it has rarely manifested monistic tendencies, except in the case of certain notable individuals like Spinoza. This is passing strange, given that the bedrock monotheistic verse in the Torah is where God says to Moses, "I am who I am,"[30] at least in English translation. Many books have been written on the exact meaning of this verse in Hebrew, but the most obvious possibility is rarely mentioned. Where Exodus 3:14b has the word *ehyeh*, Exodus 3:15 has the name YHWH, both derived from the verb *hayah,* conveying the meaning of "to exist" or the verb "to be." In a footnote in the 1985 *JPS Tanakh*, the uncertainty over the meaning of *ehyeh* is noted, and two possible literal translations identified: "*I am*" and "*I will be.*" Neither of these is as entirely satisfactory in Hebrew as something more essentially monistic, like "I am what is" or "I am Existence."

Perhaps Buddhism, as we shall see, takes us to a place where humanity finds its most intimate connection to divinity when an astonishing fullness is discovered once ultimate emptiness is experienced—an existential presentation of God's (or Life's) grace. In reference to YHWH, we may connect with this elemental reality in the anecdote of the Rabbi's Paradox:

Two groups of rabbis were debating the nature of the human relationship to the divine: Are humans separate from God to the extent that God should be considered "wholly other" than they, or are humans connected to God in such a way that they might be considered manifestations of God? The debate became so acrimonious that one rabbi called for arbitration from a far distant Rabbi Eliezar, respected by both groups. All agreed to the journey and to accept whatever he said as being the truth.

After shuffling into Rabbi Eliezar's presence, the first group humbly presented their case—that God is wholly other than humanity. Rabbi Eleizar listened attentively, stroked his beard, and then proclaimed, "You are right!"

The second group protested, "But how can you say this, since you have not yet heard our arguments?" So Rabbi Eliezar agreed to hear them out, and they argued passionately for human unity with God. The great rabbi paused only briefly, and then he proclaimed, "You are right!"

Both groups exclaimed in one voice, "How can you say 'You are right' to both of us?" To this Rabbi Elizar retorted, "You don't need to understand what I said, but still, you are right!"

book *two*

THE TAOIST TESTAMENT

introduction

Magi in China and Intellectual Ferment in Eurasia at the Middle of the First Millennium BCE [1]

Victor H. Mair

NEXT TO THE BIBLE AND THE *BHAGAVAD GITA*, THE *TAO TE CHING* IS THE MOST TRANSLATED book in the world. Well over a hundred different renditions of the Taoist classic have been made into English alone, not to mention the dozens in German, French, Italian, Dutch, Latin, and other European languages. There are several reasons for the superabundance of translations. The first is that the *Tao Te Ching* is considered the fundamental text of both philosophical and religious Taoism. Indeed, the Tao, or Way, which is at the heart of the *Tao Te Ching*, is also the centerpiece of all Chinese religion and thought. Naturally, different schools and sects bring somewhat different slants to the Tao, but all subscribe to the notion that there is a single overarching Way that encompasses everything in the universe.[2] As such, the *Tao Te Ching* also shares crucial points of similarity with other major religious scriptures the world over.

The second reason for the popularity of the *Tao Te Ching* is its brevity. There are few bona fide classics that are so short, and yet so packed with food for thought. One can read and reread the *Tao Te Ching* scores of times without exhausting the insights it offers.

The third aspect that accounts for the wide repute of the *Tao Te Ching* is its deceptive simplicity: In the words of the author himself, it is supposedly "very easy to understand," when actually it is quite difficult to comprehend fully. Paradox is the essence of the *Tao Te Ching*, so much so that even scholars with a solid grounding in classical Chinese cannot be sure they have grasped what the Old Master is really saying in his pithy maxims. For this reason I vowed two decades ago that I would never attempt to translate the *Tao Te Ching*. However, an unexpected event forced me to recant: the recent discovery of two ancient manuscripts in China made it possible to produce a totally new translation of the *Tao Te Ching*, far more accurate and reliable that any published previously. These manuscripts are at least half a millennium older than any commonly translated versions (a matter not unrelated to the quest described in this compendium to find certain other documents of that era).

This translation of the *Tao Te Ching* is based wholly on these newfound manuscripts. Their availability has made it possible to strip away the distortions and obfuscations of a tradition that has striven for two millennia to improve the text with commentaries and interpretations more amenable to various religious, philosophical, and political persuasions. And they have provided me with the means to make the translation in this book significantly different from all other previously existing translations.

In late 1973, when Chinese archaeologists working at Ma-wang-tui in central China, about a hundred miles south of the Yangtze River, unearthed two silk manuscripts of the *Tao Te Ching*, scholars of ancient China around the world were overjoyed. Forty-nine other important items, including the earliest extant version of the *Book of Changes*,[3] were also found. It will be many years before sinologists fully absorb the wealth of new materials made available by the Ma-wang-tui manuscript finds, but we are already beginning to reap important benefits.

By relying on the Ma-wang-tui manuscripts for the present translation of the *Tao Te Ching*, I have solved a number of problems that have puzzled interpreters of the text for centuries. For example, line 8 of chapter 77 reads, "To die but not be forgotten." In previously available editions of the *Tao Te Ching*, this reads, "To die but not to perish," which does not really make sense even in a religious Taoist context. There are dozens of such incidents in which the Ma-wang-tui manuscripts are much more intelligible than the old standard editions, which are the basis of almost all other translations.[4]

In Chinese indigenous religion, the individuals charged with divination concerning questions and interpreting the responses from the gods were called *wu*, who were also healers. The usual translations given for *wu* are "shaman, sorcerer, wizard, witch, and magician." Although it is the most common rendering, "shaman" is not really appropriate, since it signifies a type of Tungusic medium whose activities are altogether different from those of the *wu*. The term "sorcerer" is even less suitable for *wu*, inasmuch as it signifies the use of supernatural power over others through the assistance of evil spirits. "Wizard" and "witch" are also poor matches for *wu* because they cast spells and are thought to have dealings with the devil—hardly the types of concerns displayed by the *wu*. "Magician" is slightly preferable to the other four translations, but its modern English connotations of "illusionist" and "presti-digitator" are likewise inappropriate for *wu*. However, as we shall soon discover, "magician" in its ancient etymological sense offers a much better fit than any of the other customary renderings of *wu*.

Just who were these mighty Magi (*wu*)? Two small heads carved from mollusk shells and discovered in the autumn of 1980 within the precincts of the Zhou royal palace at Fufeng in Shaanxi Province provide valuable clues to the identity of the *wu*. Dating to early eighth century BCE, the tiny (about 2.85 centimeters in height) figures clearly depict the features of Caucasoid or Europoid individuals. What is more, one of the heads has carved on its top the archaic character for *wu*, 中, unmistakably identifying him as a religious specialist. Still more astonishing are the facts that Old Sinitic reconstruction of *wu* is roughly ˚m⁽ʸ⁾a(g), that the archaic character for *wu* (˚m⁽ʸ⁾a[g]) is identical to the ancient sign of magicians (in the old, primary sense) in the West, and that the duties and abilities of the *wu* were roughly the same as those of early Iranian Magi.

A Magi or magus (from Persian *maguš*) signifies someone who has power or who is able, from the Indo-European root <*magh-* ("be able"). The Magi were members of the Zoroastrian priestly caste who possessed special knowledge of astrology. They represent the "old" religion, and *magu* is a western Iranian term for priest (the comparable term in Avestan was *athravan*, and in Sanskrit it was *atharvan*) that was still in use in Sassanian times (by then modified to *mog*). Originally, it seemed to have conveyed an ethnic designation, as Herodotus describes the *magoi* as one of the Median tribes (and Media is in western Iran). They appear at first to have been involved with polytheism, but by Achaemenid times they associated themselves with the worship of Ahura Mazda and consequently came into the Zoroastrian "fold." Their presence was thought to be essential for the success of sacrificial rites. Like their *wu* ˚m⁽ʸ⁾a(g) cousins in East Asian history, the West Asian Magi specialized in taking omens, interpreting dreams, and carrying out ritual sacrifices, and they were experts in cosmogony, cosmology, astronomy, and astrology.[5]

Of the three major doctrines (the "San Jiao") of China—Confucianism, Buddhism, and Taoism—the first is fundamentally a native product, the second is mainly a foreign importation, and the third is a fusion of indigenous and alien elements. As established doctrines or religions, the San Jiao evolved chiefly during the late classical period through the early medieval period, roughly the second century BCE through the sixth century CE. If we seek to identify the single most important characteristic of indigenous Chinese religion, nothing can compete with ancestor worship.[6] Indeed from the very first historically verifiable dynasty, the Shang (from around 1600 BCE to the middle of the eleventh century BCE), rituals dedicated to the ancestors were essential to the wellbeing of the state and its rulers. But it is evident that the study of the history of religion in late classical and early medieval China cannot ignore the interface between Sinitic and non-Sinitic elements and influences.[7]

It is often claimed that China and India did not have any significant cultural intercourse until the first century A.D. This is false, for there is now available artifactual evidence of Buddhism in China from no later than the middle of the first century B.C. and China is mentioned by name, particularly as the source of silk, in a number of still earlier Indian texts. Trade between India and China, through a variety of overland and ocean routes, flourished well before the sayings of the Old Master came to be written down. As suggested earlier, wherever trade occurs between two countries, mutual cultural borrowing is inevitable.[8]

In spite of the political disruption and the social chaos of the Warring States period (475–221 BCE), intellectually this was by far the most exciting and lively era in the whole of Chinese history. Peripatetic philosophers wandered through the length and the breadth of the land to get the attention of any ruler who might be willing to put their ideas into practice. The Warring States period offers many interesting parallels with developments in Greek philosophy that were going on at the same time.[9]

A tremendous intellectual ferment convulsed all of Eurasia around the middle of the first millennium BCE. Within a brief span of approximately a century, the following major systems of thought were articulated or adumbrated: Zoroastrianism, Greek philosophy, Confucianism, Mohism, Upanisadic Hinduism, Jainism, Taoism, Buddhism, and Biblical Judaism. It is highly unlikely that these great movements were utterly independent phenomena.

preface

Magic and iMagination

A news paper article a few years ago in the *New York Times* took the academic world by surprise. Harper & Row had acquired the rights to an English version of a tiny Chinese classic, for which they had paid the highest amount ever for a work of its kind. This classic of only five thousand characters was none other than the *Tao Te Ching*. The text, tiny in its size and style, exemplifies a philosophy of both economy and universality that extend to the business terms of the translation itself. In keeping with Taoist principles, less was shown to be worth more, and the medium once again turned out to be the message. How do we define a religion in which the less we know the wiser we become?[1]

IN THIS COMPENDIUM, WE BEGIN THE BOOK II COLLECTION OF THE EASTERN "TESTAMENTS," MORE or less chronologically, with the *Tao Te Ching* by Lao Tzu, who introduced the monistic *Tao* to China. It will be followed in Book III by the *Analects* of Confucius, applying the ethical challenges of the *Tao* through reference to ancient Chinese tradition. At almost the same time the *Dhammapada* by Sidhartha Gautama appeared in India, adopting the monistic *Om* already established in the Vedic Upanishads as the chant to Oneness, articulating the mystique of previous intuitions. This led to the establishment of Buddhism in India and its subsequent move into China and elsewhere, as well as the reform of Hinduism represented by the *Bhagavad Gita*, which applied the monism of Vedic reforms by Buddha to Hinduism in India. All four developments happened within about a hundred years, the precise era of the Axial Age as we have narrowly defined it.

The dates are important in reference to our thesis about Zoroaster's stimulation of all these developments, as well as connecting with their parallels in the West. If Zoroaster's prophetic ministry was launched like a flare in 588 BCE, we might date Lao Tzu's response in China at 565 BCE, almost a quarter-century later. As a young man, Confucius may have met Lao Tzu, or his ethical application of the Tao may have actually come more than a generation later. The Buddha may have offered his earliest verses of the *Dhammapada* as early as 563 BCE by traditional dating, though it is recently seen as a widespread teaching in India during the fifth century, followed by the *Bhagavad Gita* as a reform of Hinduism sometime around 400 BCE. Again, none of this was Zoroastrianism per se, and some of these other dates are almost as uncertain as were Zoroaster's dates until recently. However, if a spiritual revolution erupted in Balkh or Bactria, somewhere halfway along the Silk Route early in the sixth century BCE, the philosophical and religious ripple effect to the east fits as well as it does for the classical age of prophets in Israel and the golden age of philosophy in Greece to the west.

Beginning with the *Tao Te Ching*, we will see that unity with the One facilitates the highest and finest of personal, family, vocational, business, and community relationships. Is this One to be iMagined as "God"? The answer is "yes," in a monistic sense, but there are difficulties in this manner of thinking for those to whom such a concept is new.

When commentators say that the Chinese *Tao* of Lao Tzu or the *Mind* of Indian religions are not "deities," they almost sound like Buddhists and other monists today who announce in popular media that they "do not believe in God." By this they mean that they do not believe in a separate divine entity, worthy of worship but eternally separate from a created universe. To monists, the destiny of each "individual" is to overcome this separation and "realize" the individual's being as part of the One, intimately integrated though perhaps remaining identifiable.

Though he had an important disciple in Zhuangzi, whose book *Chuang Tzu* expounds and expands the vision of the *Tao Te Ching*, the latter is the obvious choice of a testament for the work of Lao Tzu and the essential introduction to Taoism, an indispensable testament of the monistic East. While the *Analects* of Confucianism, the *Dhammapada* of Buddhism, and the *Bhagavad Gita* of Hinduism are about the size of the Torah, the Quran, and the New Testament, respectively, in our related *Three Testaments* compendium presenting the scriptures of Western monotheism, the *Tao Te Ching* is slightly smaller than the others. These portable and popular testaments became mass produced in the East at about the time the New Testament and the Quran were introduced there, and they serve well as primary "testaments" and testimonial summaries of the vast bodies of Eastern monist scriptures.

Many translations of the *Tao Te Ching* from earlier centuries reflect the best scholarship of those times but are almost unintelligible, mirroring our current experience with the Zoroastrian Avesta, partially solved by my own paraphrases in this text. Some popular editions of the twentieth century are inspirational but of questionable scholarship, given recent discoveries of textual variants. We are happy in this text to feature the text that resolves these issues for the *Tao Te Ching* in a rather complete manner. The translation by Victor H. Mair of the University of Philadelphia is also the first, and so far the only, presentation to rearrange the order of the chapters to conform with the 1973 Ma-wang-tui discovery of two most ancient silk manuscripts of the *Tao Te Ching* by Chinese archaeologists. This numbering of verses represents the order in the most recent manuscripts; in parentheses we show the traditional order. Mair thus resolves a host of difficult problems with the text, to the delight of leading scholars around the world.

According to tradition, Lao Tzu worked at the Imperial Palace as a custodian of the Imperial Archives, where he might have collected information from home and abroad, observing the way of human beings, the way of the natural environment, and the way of the stars in the heavens. It can be assumed that here any new ideas from the Magi of the Persian Empire would come to his attention through the agency of any Magi operating in China.

Upon retiring, Lao decided to leave China and departed on an ox. As he reached the Han-Ku pass, the border guard, Yin-His, refused to let him pass until he left some evidence of his highly regarded teaching, so that those remaining and future generations could benefit from it. Lao Tzu consented, sat down, and wrote out the eighty-one short chapters of his *Simple Way*, which we know as the *Tao Te Ching*. As the story goes, he then remounted his ox and departed, travelling west, never to be seen again.

The little that we are told about the life of Lao Tzu makes him sound more myth than man. Traditional stories say that he lived in the sixth century BCE. After being in his mother's womb for many years, he was finally born with a beard, looking like an old man and given the name Lao Tzu, meaning "Old Master." Stories claim he was born laughing, a possible direct connection to Zoroaster, of whom the same story is told in the extant Avesta Scriptures.

Our translator, Victor Mair, was invited to contribute certain materials to this study because his evidence for the presence of Magi in China, even before Zoroaster, illustrates that Chinese civilization may not have developed in complete isolation from the rest of the world after all. He also briefly elucidated the relationship between Taoism and both Confucianism and Buddhism in China, and, later in this compendium, Mair illuminates even more cogently the connections between the *Tao Te Ching* and the *Bhagavad Gita*.

After Zoroaster, the Magi in Iran had converted *en masse* to the Zoroastrian state religion in deference to the reign of Cyrus and out of respect for Zoroastrian theology, the latest thing. Their confreres in China would certainly have had influence with thinkers like Lao Tzu, possibly reflected in the oriental monism of his *Tao Te Ching*. This putative link is not a *sine qua non* of ancient religious connections at that pivotal moment in history, but it offers a thread that forms a subtext of our study and inquiry. Having already seen Professor Mair's brief introduction, explaining what makes this translation unique to date, and contextual evidence for the influence of the Magi in China, so critical to the argument of this book, we will now let the *Tao Te Ching* speak for itself.

While our four Eastern testaments appear in chronological order in this compendium, it is almost passing strange how they also seem to succeed each other in meaning and in development of our understanding. The *Tao Te Ching* is inscrutably enigmatic at points, but Rabbi Mates-Muchin, herself Chinese, successfully employs Taoist-sounding phrases in the opening paragraphs of her introduction to the Confucian *Analects*. Likewise the *Analects*, to some extent, raise questions about traditional morality that are addressed, if not answered, by the Buddha in the *Dhammapada* . . . and on to the *Bhagavad Gita*, which draws the Eastern testaments together in a manner none of the participant contributors might have intended or expected.

7

tao te ching

Translated by Victor H. Mair

integrity

1. (38)*

The person of superior integrity
does not insist upon his integrity;
For this reason, he has integrity.
The person of inferior integrity
never loses sight of his integrity;
For this reason, he lacks integrity.

The person of superior integrity takes no action,
nor has he a purpose for acting.
The person of superior humaneness takes action,
but has no purpose for acting.
The person of superior righteousness takes action,
and has a purpose for acting.
The person of superior etiquette takes action,
but others do not respond to him;
Whereupon he rolls up his sleeves
and coerces them.

Therefore,
When the Way is lost,
afterward comes integrity.

*Parentheses indicate "chapter" numbering in translations and "originals" prior to discovery of the earlier Ma-wang-tui manuscripts in 1973 by Chinese archaeologists and adopted by Victor H. Mair and others.

When integrity is lost,
afterward comes humaneness.
When humaneness is lost,
afterward comes righteousness.
When righteousness is lost, afterward comes etiquette.

Now,
Etiquette is the attenuation of trustworthiness,
and the source of disorder.
Foreknowledge is but the blossomy ornament of the Way,
and the source of ignorance.

For this reason,
The great man resides in substance,
not in attenuation.
He resides in fruitful reality,
not in blossomy ornament.

Therefore,
He rejects the one and adopts the other.

2. (39)

In olden times, these attained unity:
Heaven attained unity,
and thereby became pure.
Earth attained unity,
and thereby became tranquil.
The spirits attained unity,
and thereby became divine.
The valley attained unity,
and thereby became full.
Feudal lords and kings attained unity,
and thereby all was put right.

Yet, if pushed to the extreme,
It implies that,
If heaven were ever pure,
it would be likely to rend.
It implies that,
If earth were ever tranquil,
It would be likely to quake.
It implies that,

If the spirits were ever divine,
they would be likely to dissipate.
It implies that,
If the valley were ever full,
it would be likely to run dry.
It implies that,
If feudal lords and kings were ever noble
and thereby exalted,
they would be likely to fall.

Therefore,
It is necessary to be noble,
and yet take humility as a basis,
It is necessary to be exalted,
and yet take modesty as a foundation.

Now, for this reason,
Feudal lords and kings style themselves
"orphaned," "destitute," and "hapless."
Is this not because they take humility as their basis?

Therefore,
Striving for an excess of praise,
one ends up without praise.
Consequently,
Desire not to be jingling as jade
nor stolid as stone.

3. (41)

When the superior man hears the Way,
he is scarcely able to put it into practice.
When the middling man hears the Way,
he appears now to preserve it, now to lose it.
When the inferior man hears the Way,
he laughs at it loudly.
If he did not laugh,
it would not be fit to be the Way.

For this reason,
There is a series of epigrams that says:
"The bright Ways seems dim,
The forward Way seems backward.

The level Way seems bumpy.
Superior integrity seems like a valley.
The greatest whiteness seems grimy.
Ample integrity seems insufficient.
Robust integrity seems apathetic.
Plain truth seems sullied.

"The great square has no corners.
The great vessel is never completed.
The great note sounds muted.
The great image has no form.
The Way is concealed and has no name."
Indeed,
The Way alone is good at beginning
and good at completing.

4. (40)

Reversal is the movement of the Way;
Weakness is the usage of the Way.

All creatures under heaven are born from being;
Being is born from nonbeing.

5. (42)

The Way gave birth to unity,
Unity gave birth to duality,
Duality gave birth to trinity,
Trinity gave birth to the myriad creatures.

The myriad creatures bear yin on their backs
and embrace yang in their bosoms.
They neutralize these vapors
and thereby achieve harmony.

That which all under heaven hate most
Is to be orphaned, destitute, and hapless.
Yet kings and dukes call themselves thus.

Things may be diminished by being increased,
increased by being diminished.

Therefore,
That which people teach,
After deliberation, I also teach people.

Therefore,
"The tyrant does not die a natural death"
I take this as my mentor.

6. (43)

The softest thing under heaven
gallops triumphantly over
The hardest thing under heaven.

Nonbeing penetrates nonspace.
Hence,
I know the advantages of nonaction.

The doctrine without words,
The advantage of nonaction—
few under heaven can realize these!

7. (44)

Name or person,
which is nearer?
Person or property,
which is dearer?
Gain or loss,
which is drearier?

Many loves entail great costs,
Many riches entail heavy losses.

Know contentment and you shall not be disgraced,
Know satisfaction and you shall not be imperiled;
then you will long endure.

8. (45)

Great perfection appears defective,
but its usefulness is not diminished.
Great fullness appears empty,
but its usefulness is not impaired.

Great straightness seems crooked,
Great cleverness seems clumsy,
Great triumph seems awkward.

Bustling about vanquishes cold,
standing still vanquishes heat.

Pure and still,
one can put things right everywhere under heaven.

9. (46)

When the Way prevails under heaven,
swift horses are relegated to fertilizing fields.
When the Way does not prevail under heaven,
war-horses breed in the suburbs.

No guilt is greater than giving in to desire,
No disaster is greater than discontent,
No crime is more grievous than the desire for gain.

Therefore,
Contentment that derives from knowing
when to be content
is eternal contentment.

10. (47)

Without going out-of-doors,
one may know all under heaven;
Without peering through windows,
one may know the Way of heaven.

The farther one goes,
The less one knows.

For this reason,
The sage knows without journeying,
understands without looking,
accomplishes without acting.

11. (48)

The pursuit of learning results in daily increase,
Hearing the Way leads to daily decrease.

Decrease and again decrease,
until you reach nonaction.
Through nonaction,
no action is left undone.

Should one desire to gain all under heaven,
One should remain ever free of involvements,
For,
Just as surely as one becomes involved,
One is unfit for gaining all under heaven.

12. (49)

The sage never has a mind of his own;
He considers the minds of common people to be his mind.

Treat well those who are good,
Also treat well those who are not good;
thus is goodness attained.

Be sincere to those who are sincere,
Also be sincere to those who are insincere;
thus is sincerity attained.

The sage
is self-effacing in his keeling with all under heaven,
and bemuddles his mind for the sake of all under heaven.

The common people all rivet their eyes and ears upon him,
And the sage make them all chuckle like children.

13. (50)

A person comes forth to life and enters into death.
Three out of ten are partners of life,
Three out of ten are partners in death,
And the people whose every movement leads them to the
land of death because they cling to life
Are also three out of ten.

Now,
What is the reason for this?
It is because they cling to life.

Indeed,
I have heard that
One who is good at preserving life
does not avoid tigers and rhinoceroses
when he walks in the hills;
nor does he put on armor and take up weapons
when he enters a battle.
The rhinoceros has no place to jab its horn,
The tiger has no place to fasten its claws,
Weapons have no place to admit their blades.

Now
What is the reason for this?
Because on him there are no mortal spots.

14. (51)

The Way gives birth to them and integrity nurtures them.
Matter forms them and function completes them.

For this reason,
The myriad creatures respect the Way and esteem integrity.
Respect for the Way and esteem for integrity
are by no means conferred upon them
but always occur naturally.

The Way gives birth to them,
nurtures them,
rears them,
follows them,
shelters them,
toughens them,
sustains them,
protects them.
It gives birth but does not possess,
acts but does not presume,
rears but does not control.

This is what is called "mysterious integrity."

15. (52)

Everything under heaven has a beginning
which be thought of as the mother

of all under heaven.
Having realized the mother,
you thereby know her children.
Knowing her children,
go back to abide with the mother.
To the end of your life,
you will not be imperiled.

Stopple the orifices of your heart,
close your doors;
your whole life you will not suffer.
Open the gate of your heart,
meddle with your affairs;
your whole life you will be beyond salvation.

Seeing what is small is called insight,
Abiding in softness is called strength.

Use your light to return to insight,
Be not an inheritor of personal calamity.

This is called "following the constant."

16. (53)

If I were possessed of the slightest knowledge,
traveling on the great Way,
My fear would be to go astray.
The great Way is quite level,
but the people are much enamored of mountain trails.

The court is thoroughly deserted,
The fields are choked with weeds,
The granaries are altogether empty.

Still there are some who
wear fancy designs and brilliant colors,
sharp swords hanging at their sides,
are sated with food,
overflowing with possessions and wealth.

This is called "the brazenness of a bandit."
The brazenness of a bandit is surely not the Way!

17. (54)

What is firmly established cannot be uprooted;
What is tightly embraced cannot slip away.

Thus sacrificial offerings made by sons and grandsons
will never end.

Cultivated in the person, integrity is true.
Cultivated in the family, integrity is ample.
Cultivated in the village, integrity lasts long.
Cultivated in the state, integrity is abundant.
Cultivated everywhere under heaven, integrity is vast.

Observe other persons through your own person.
Observe other families through your own family.
Observe other villages through your own village.
Observe other states through your own state.
Observe all under heaven through all under heaven.

How do I know the nature of all under Heaven?
Through this.

18. (55)

He who embodies the fullness of integrity
is like a ruddy infant.

Wasps, spiders, scorpions, and snakes
will not sting or bite him;
Rapacious birds and fierce beasts
will not seize him.

His bones are weak and his sinews soft,
yet his grip is tight.
He knows not the joining of male and female,
yet his penis is aroused.
His essence has reached a peak.

He screams the whole day without becoming hoarse;
His harmony has reached perfection.

Harmony implies constancy;
Constancy requires insight.

Striving to increase one's life is ominous;
To control the vital breath with one's mind entails force.

Something that grows old while still in its prime
is said to be not in accord with the Way;
Not being in accord with the Way
leads to an early demise.

19. (56)

One who knows does not speak;
One who speaks does not know.

He
Stopples the opening of his heart,
Closes his doors,
Diffuses the light,
Mingles with the dust,
Files away his sharp points,
Unravels his tangles.

This is called "mysterious identity."

Therefore,
Neither can one attain intimacy with him,
Nor can one remain distant from him;
Neither can one profit from him,
Nor can one be harmed by him;
Neither can one achieve honor through him,
Nor can one be debased by him.

Therefore,
He is esteemed by all under heaven.

20. (57)

Rule the state with uprightness,
Deploy your troops with craft,
Gain all under heaven with non-interference.

How do I know this is actually so?
Now,
The more taboos under heaven,
the poorer the people;

The more clever devices people have,
the more confused the state and ruling house;
The more knowledge people have,
the more strange things spring up;
The more legal affairs are given prominence,
the more numerous bandits and thieves.

For this reason,
The sage has a saying:
"I take no action,
yet the people transform themselves;
I am fond of stillness,
yet the people correct themselves;
I do not interfere in affairs,
yet the people enrich themselves;
I desire not to desire,
yet the people of themselves become
simple as unhewn logs."

21. (58)

When the government is anarchic,
the people are honest;
when government is meddlesome,
the state is lacking.

Disaster is that whereon good fortune depends,
Good fortune is that wherein disaster lurks.
Who knows their limits?

When there is no uprightness,
correct reverts to crafty,
good reverts to gruesome.

The delusion of mankind,
How long have been its days!

For this reason, be
Square but not cutting,
Angular but not prickly,
Straight but not arrogant,
Bright but not dazzling.

22. (59)

To rule men and serve heaven,
there is nothing like thrift.

Now
Only through thrift
can one be prepared;
Being prepared
means having a heavy store of integrity;
With a heavy store of integrity,
he can overcome everything.
Able to overcome everything,
no one knows his limits;
If no one knows his limits,
he can have the kingdom;
Having the mother of the kingdom,
he can long endure.
This is called "sinking roots firm and deep,
the Way of long life and lasting vision."

23. (60)

Ruling a big kingdom is like cooking a small fish.
If one oversees all under heaven in accord with the Way,
demons have no spirit.
It is not that the demons have no spirit,
but that their spirits do not harm people.
It is not merely that their spirits do not harm people,
but that the sage also does not harm them.

Now,
When neither harms the other,
integrity accrues to both.

24. (61)

A large state is like a low-lying estuary,
the female of all under heaven.
In the congress of all under heaven,
the female always conquers the male through her stillness.
Because she is still,
it is fitting for her to lie low.
By lying beneath a small state,

a large state can take over a small state.
By lying beneath a large state
a small state can be taken over by a large state.

Therefore,
One may either take over or be taken over by lying low.

Therefore,
The large state wishes only to annex and nurture others;
The small state wants only to join with and serve others.

Now,
Since both get what they want,
It is fitting for the large state to lie low.

25. (62)

The Way is the cistern of the myriad creatures;
It is the treasure of the good man,
And that which is treasured by the bad man.

Beautiful words can be traded,
Noble deeds can be used as gifts for others.
Why should we reject even what is bad about men?

Therefore,
When the son of heaven is enthroned
or the three ministers are installed,
Although they may have large jade disks
And be preceded by teams of four horses,
It would be better for them to sit down
and make progress in this.

What is the reason for the ancients
to value this so highly?
Did they not say:
"Seek and thou shalt receive;
Sin and thou shalt be forgiven"?

Therefore,
It is valued by all under heaven.

26. (63)

Act through nonaction,
Handle affairs through non-interference,
Taste what has no taste,
Regard the small as great, the few as many,
Repay resentment with integrity.

Undertake difficult tasks
by approaching what is easy in them;
Do great deeds
by focusing on their minute aspects.

All difficulties under heaven arise from what is easy,
All great things under heaven arise from what is minute.

For this reason,
The sage never strives to do what is great.
Therefore,
He can achieve greatness.

One who lightly assents
will seldom be believed;
One who thinks everything is easy
will encounter much difficulty.

For this reason,
Even the sage considers things difficult.
Therefore,
In the end he is without difficulty.

27. (64)

What is secure is easily grasped,
What has no omens is easily forestalled,
What is brittle is easily split,
What is minuscule is easily dispersed.

Act before there is a problem;
Bring order before there is disorder.

A tree that fills the arms' embrace
is born from a downy shoot;
A terrace nine layers high

starts from basketful of earth;
An ascent of a hundred strides
begins beneath one's foot.

Who acts fails;
Who grasps loses.

For this reason,
The sage does not act.
Therefore,
He does not fail.
He does not grasp.
Therefore,
He does not lose.

In pursuing their affairs,
people often fail when they are close to success.
Therefore,
If one is as cautious at the end as at the beginning,
there will be no failures.

For this reason,
The sage desires to be without desire
and does not prize goods that are hard to obtain;
He learns not to learn
and reverts to what the masses pass by.

Thus, he can help the myriad creatures be natural,
but dares not act.

28. (65)

The ancients who practiced the Way
did not enlighten the people with it;
They used it, rather, to stupefy them.

The people are hard to rule
because they have too much knowledge.
Therefore,
Ruling a state through knowledge is to rob the state;
Ruling a state through ignorance
brings integrity to the state.

One who is always mindful of these two types
grasps a paradigm;
Mindfulness of this paradigm is called "mysterious integrity."

Deep and distant is this mysterious integrity!
It runs counter to things
until it reaches the great confluence.

29. (66)

The river and sea can be kings of
the hundred valley streams
because they are good at lying below them.
For this reason,
They can be kings of the hundred valley streams.
For this reason, too,
If the sage wants to be above the people,
in his words, he must put himself below them;
If he wishes to be before the people,
in his person, he must stand behind them.
Therefore,
He is situated in front of the people,
but they are not offended;
He is situated above the people,
but they do not consider him a burden.
All under heaven happily push him forward without
wearying.
Is this not because he is with contention?
Therefore,
No one under heaven can contend with him.

30. (80)

Let there be a small state with few people,
where military devices find no use;
Let the people look solemnly upon death,
and banish the thought of moving elsewhere.

They may have carts and boats,
but there is no reason to ride them;
They might have armor and weapons,
but they have no reason to display them.

Let the people go back to tying knots
to keep records.
Let their food be savory,
their clothes beautiful,
their customs pleasurable,
their dwelling secure.

Though they may gaze across at a neighboring state,
and hear the sounds of its dogs and chickens,
The people will never travel back and forth,
till they die of old age.

31. (81)

Sincere words are not beautiful,
Beautiful words are not sincere.
He who knows is not learned,
He who is learned does not know.
He who is good does not have much,
He who has much is not good.

The sage does not hoard.
The more he does for others,
the more he has for himself;
The more he gives to others,
the more his own bounty increases.

Therefore,
The Way of heaven benefits but does not harm,
The Way of man acts but does not contend.

32. (67)

All under heaven say that I am great,
great but unconventional.
Now,
Precisely because I am unconventional,
I can be great;
If I were conventional,
I would long since have become trifle.

I have always possessed three treasures
that I guard and cherish.

The first is compassion,
The second is frugality,
The third is not daring to be ahead of all under heaven.

Now,
Because I am compassionate,
I can be brave;
Because I am frugal,
I can be magnanimous;
Because I dare not be ahead of all under heaven,
I can be a leader in the completion of affairs.

If, today, I were to
Be courageous while forsaking compassion,
Be magnanimous while forsaking frugality,
Get ahead while forsaking the hindmost
that would be death.

For compassion
In war brings victory,
In defense brings invulnerability.

Whomsoever heaven would establish,
It surrounds with a bulwark of compassion.

33. (68)

A good warrior is not bellicose,
A good fighter does not anger,
A good conqueror does not contest his enemy,
One who is good at using others puts himself below them.
This is called "integrity without competition,"
This is called "using others,"
This is called "parity with heaven"
—the pinnacle of the ancients.

34. (69)

The strategists have a saying:
"I dare not be host,
but would rather be a guest;
I advance not an inch,
but instead retreat a foot."

This is called
Marching without ranks,
Bearing nonexistent arms,
Flourishing nonexistent weapons,
Driving back nonexistent enemies.

There is no greater misfortune
than not having a worthy foe;
Once I believe there are no worthy foes,
I have well-nigh forfeited my treasures.

Therefore
When opposing forces are evenly matched,
The one who is saddened will be victorious.

35. (70)

My words are
very easy to understand,
very easy to practice.
But no one is able to understand them,
And no one is able to practice them.

Words have authority.
Affairs have an ancestry.

It is simply because of their ignorance,
that they do not understand me;
Those who understand me are few,
thus I am ennobled.

For this reason,
The sage wears coarse clothing over his shoulders,
but carries jade within his bosom.

36. (71)

To realize that you do not understand is a virtue;
Not to realize that you do not understand is a defect.

The reason why
The sage has no defects,
Is because he treats defects as defects.

Thus,
He has no defects.

37. (72)

When the people do not fear the majestic,
Great majesty will soon visit them.

Do not limit their dwellings,
Do not suppress their livelihood.
Simply because you do not suppress them,
they will not grow weary of you.

The reason,
The sage is self-aware,
but does not flaunt himself;
He is self-devoted,
but does not glorify himself.

Therefore,
He rejects the one and adopts the other.

38. (73)

He who is brave in daring will be killed,
He who is brave in not daring will survive.
One of these two courses is beneficial,
The other is harmful.

Who knows the reason for heaven's dislikes?
The Way of heaven
does not war
yet is good at conquering,
does not speak
yet is good at answering,
is not summoned
yet comes of itself,
is relaxed
yet good at making plans.

Heaven's net is vast;
Though its meshes are wide,
nothing escapes.

39. (74)

If the people never fear death,
what is the purpose of threatening to kill them?
If the people ever fear death,
and I was to capture and kill those who are devious,
who would dare to be so?
If the people must be ever fearful of death,
then there will always be an executioner.

Now,
To kill in place of the executioner
Is like
Hewing wood in place of the master carpenter;
Few indeed will escape cutting their own hands!

40. (75)

Human hunger
is the result of over taxation.
For this reason,
There is hunger.

The common people are not governable
because of their superiors' actions.
For this reason,
They are not governable.

The people make light of death
because of too much emphasis on the quest for life.
For this reason,
They make light of death.

Now,
Only she who acts not for sake of life
Is wiser than those who value life highly.

41. (76)

Human beings are
soft and supple when alive,
stiff and straight when dead.

The myriad creatures, the grasses and trees are
soft and fragile when alive,
dry and withered when dead.

Therefore, it is said:
The rigid person is a disciple of death;
The soft, supple, and delicate are lovers of life.

An army that is inflexible will not conquer;
A tree that is inflexible will snap.

The unyielding and mighty shall be brought low;
The soft, supple, and delicate will be set above.

42. (77)

The Way of heaven is like the bending of a bow—
the upper part is pressed down,
the lower part is raised up,
the part that has too much is reduced,
the part that has too little is increased.
Therefore,
The Way of heaven
reduces surplus to make up for scarcity;
The Way of man
reduces scarcity and pays tribute to surplus.

Who is there that can have a surplus
and take from it to pay tribute to heaven?
Surely only one who has the Way.

For this reason,
The sage
acts but does not possess,
completes his work but does not dwell on it.
In this fashion,
he has no desire to display his worth.

43. (78)

Nothing under heaven is softer or weaker than water,
and yet nothing is better
for attacking what is hard and strong,
because of its immutability.

The defeat of the hard by the soft,
The defeat of the strong by the weak—
this is known to all under heaven,
yet no one is able to practice it.

Therefore, in the words of the sage, it is said:
"He who bears abuse directed against the state
is called 'lord of the altars for the gods of soil and grain';
He who bears the misfortunes of the state
is called the 'king of all under heaven.'"

True words seem contradictory.

44. (79)

Compromise with great resentment
will surely yield lingering resentment;
How can this be seen as good?

For this reason,
The sage holds the debtor's side of the contract
and does not make claims upon others.

Therefore,
The man of integrity attends to his debts:
The man without integrity attends to his exactions.

The Way of heaven is impartial,
yet is always with the good person.

the way

45. (1)

The ways that can be walked are not the eternal Way;
The names that can be named are the eternal name.
The nameless is the origin of the myriad;
The named is the mother of the myriad creatures.

Therefore,
Always be without desire
in order to observe its wondrous subtleties;
Always have desire
so that you may observe it, manifestations.

Both of these derive from the same source;
They have different names but the same designation.

Mystery of mysteries,
the gate of all wonders!

46. (2)

When all under heaven know beauty as beauty,
already there is ugliness;
When everyone knows goodness,
this accounts for badness.

Being and nonbeing give birth to each other,
Difficult and easy complete each other,
Long and short form each other,
High and low fulfill each other,
Tone and voice harmonize with each other,
it is ever thus.

For these reasons,
The sage
dwells in affairs of nonaction,
carries out a doctrine without words.
He lets the myriad creatures rise up
but does not instigate them;
He acts
but does not presume;
He completes his work
but does not dwell on it.

Now,
Simply because he does not dwell on them,
his accomplishments never leave him.

47. (3)

Not exalting men of worth
prevents the people from competing;
Not putting high value on rare goods
prevents the people from being bandits;
Not displaying objects of desire
prevents the people from being disorderly.

For these reasons,
The sage, in ruling,
hollows their hearts,
stuffs their stomachs,
weakens their wills,
builds up their bones,
Always causing the people
to be without knowledge and desire.
He ensures that
the knowledgeable dare not to be hostile,
and that is all.

Thus,
His rule is universal.

48. (4)

The Way is empty,
yet never refills with use;
Bottomless it is,
like the forefather of the myriad creatures.
It files away sharp points,
unravels tangles,
diffuses light,
mingles with the dust.
Submerged it lies,
seeming barely to subsist,
I know not whose child it is,
only that it resembles the predecessor of God.

49. (5)

Heaven and earth are inhumane;
they view the myriad creatures as straw dogs.
The sage is inhumane;
he views the common people as straw dogs.

The space between heaven and earth,
how like a bellows it is!
Empty but never exhausted,
The more it pumps, the more comes out.

Hearing too much leads to utter exhaustion;
Better to remain in the center.

50. (6)

The valley spirit never dies—
it is called the "the mysterious female";
The gate of the mysterious female
is called "the root of heaven and earth."
Gossamer it is,
seemingly insubstantial,
yet never consumed through use.

51. (7)

Heaven is long and earth is lasting.
Heaven and earth can be long and lasting
because they do not live for themselves.
Therefore,
They can be long-lived.

For this reason,
The sage
withdraws himself
but comes to the fore,
alienates himself
but is always present.

Is this not because he is free of private interests?
Therefore,
He can accomplish his private interests.

52. (8)

The highest good is like water;
Water is good at benefiting the myriad creatures
but also struggles
to occupy the place loathed by the masses.
Therefore,
It is near to the Way.

The quality of an abode is in its location,
The quality of the heart is in its depths,
The quality of giving lies in trust,
The quality of correct governance lies in orderly rule,
The quality of an enterprise depends on ability,
The quality of movement depends on timing.

Now,
It is precisely because one does not compete
that there is no blame.

53. (9)

Instead of keeping a bow taut while holding it straight,
better to relax.
You may temper a sword until it is razor sharp,
but you cannot preserve the edge for long.
When gold and jade fill your rooms,
no one will be able to guard them for you.
If wealth and honor make you haughty,
you bequeath misfortune upon yourself.
To withdraw when your work is finished,
that is the Way of heaven.

54. (10)

While you
Cultivate the soul and embrace unity,
can you keep them from separating?
Focus your vital breath until it is supremely soft,
can you be like a baby?
Cleanse the mirror of mysteries,
can you make it free of blemish?
Love the people and enliven the state,
can you do so without cunning?
Open and close the gate of heaven,
can you play the part of the female?
Reach out with clarity in all directions,
can you refrain from action?

It gives birth to them and nurtures them,
It gives birth to them but does not possess them,
It rears them but does not control them.
This is called "mysterious integrity."

55. (11)

Thirty spokes converge on a single hub,
but it is in the space where there is nothing
that the usefulness of the cart lies.
Clay is molded to make a pot,

but it is in the space where there is nothing
that the usefulness of the clay pot lies.
Cut out door and windows to make a room,
but it is in the spaces where there is nothing
that the usefulness of the room lies.

Therefore,
Benefit may be derived from something,
but it is in nothing that we find usefulness.

56. (12)

The five colors
make a man's eyes blind;
Horseracing and hunting
make a man's mind go mad;
Goods that are hard to obtain
make a man's progress falter;
The five flavors
make a man's palate dull;
The five tones
make a man's ears deaf.

For these reasons,
In ruling, the sage
attends to the stomach, not to the eye.
Therefore,
He rejects the one and adopts the other.

57. (13)

"Being favored is so disgraceful that it startles,
Being honored is an affliction as great as one's body,"

What is the meaning of
"Being favored is so disgraceful that it startles"?
Favor is debasing;
To find it is startling,
To lose it is startling.

This is the meaning of "Being favored is so disgraceful that it startles."

What is the meaning of "Being honored is an affliction as great as one's body"?

The reason I suffer great afflictions is because I have a body;
If I had no body, what affliction could I suffer?

Therefore,
When a man puts emphasis on caring for his body
while caring for all under heaven,
then all under heaven can be entrusted to him.
When a man is sparing of his body in caring
for all under heaven,
then all under heaven can be delivered to him.

58. (14)

We look for it but do not see it;
we name it "subtle."
We listen for it but do not hear it:
we name it "rare."
We grope for it but do not grasp it;
we name it "serene."

These three cannot be fully fathomed,
Therefore,
They are bound together to make unity.

Of unity,
its top is not distant,
its bottom is not blurred.
Infinitely extended
and unnameable,
It returns to nonentity.
This is called
"the form of the formless,
the image of nonentity."
This is called "the amorphous."

Following behind it,
you cannot see its back;
Approaching it from the front,
you cannot see its head.

Hold to the Way of today
to manage the actualities of today,
thereby understanding the primeval beginning.
This is called "the thread of the Way."

59. (15)

Those of old that were adept in the Way
were subtly profound and mysteriously perceptive,
So deep
they could not be recognized.
Now,
Because they could not be recognized,
One can describe their appearance only with effort:
hesitant,
as though crossing a stream in winter;
cautious,
as though fearful of their neighbors all around;
solemn,
as though guests in someone else's house;
shrinking,
as ice when it melts;
plain,
as an unhewn log;
muddled,
as turbid waters;
expansive,
as a broad valley.

If turbid waters are stilled,
they will gradually become clear;
If something inert is set in motion,
it will gradually come to life.
Those who preserved this Way did not wish to be full.
Now,
Simply because they did not wish to be full,
they could be threadbare and incomplete.

60. (16)

Attain utmost emptiness,
Maintain utter stillness.

The myriad creatures arise side by side,
thus I observe their renewal.
Heaven's creatures abound,
but each returns to its roots,
which is called "stillness."
This is termed the "renewal of fate."

Renewal of fate is perpetual—
To know the perpetual is to be enlightened;
Not to know the perpetual is to be reckless—
recklessness breeds evil.
To know the perpetual is to be tolerant—
tolerance leads to ducal impartiality,
ducal impartiality to kingliness,
kingliness to heaven,
heaven to the Way,
the Way to permanence.

To the end of his days,
he will not be imperiled.

61. (17)

Preeminent is one whose subjects barely know he exists;
The next is one to whom they feel close and praise;
The next is one whom they fear;
The lowest is one whom they despise.

When the ruler's trust is wanting,
there will be no trust in him.
Cautious,
he values his words.
When his work is completed and his affairs finished,
the common people say,
"We are like this by ourselves."

62. (18)

Therefore,
When the great Way was forsaken,
there was humaneness and righteousness;
When cunning and wit appeared,
there was great falsity;
When the six family relationships lacked harmony,
there were filial piety and parental harmony,
When the state and royal house were in disarray,
there were upright ministers.

63. (19)

"Abolish sagehood and abandon cunning,
the people will benefit a hundredfold;

Abolish humaneness and abandon righteousness,
the people will once again be filial and kind;
Abolish cleverness and abandon profit,
bandits and thieves will be no more."
These three statements
are inadequate as a civilizing doctrine;
Therefore,
Let something be added to them:

Evince the plainness of undyed silk,
Embrace the simplicity of the unhewn log;
Lessen selfishness,
Diminish desires;
Abolish learning
and you will be without worries.

64. (20)

Between "yes sir" and " certainly not!"
how much difference is there?
Between beauty and ugliness,
how great is the distinction?

He whom others fear,
likewise cannot but fear others.

How confusing,
there is no end to it all!

Joyful as the masses,
as though feasting after the great sacrifice of oxen,
or mounting a terrace in spring.

Motionless am I,
without any sign,
as a baby that has yet to gurgle.
How dejected!
as though having nowhere to return.

The masses all have more than enough;
I alone am bereft.

I have the heart of a fool.
How muddled!

The ordinary man is luminously clear,
I alone seem confused.
The ordinary man is searchingly exact,
I alone am vague and uncertain.

How nebulous!
as the ocean;
How blurred!
as though without boundary.

The masses all have a purpose,
I alone am stubborn and uncouth.
I desire to be uniquely different from others
by honoring the mother who nourishes.

65. (21)

The appearance of grand integrity
is that it follows the Way alone.
The Way objectified
is blurred and nebulous.

How nebulous and blurred!
Yet within it there are images.
How blurred and nebulous!
Yet within it there are objects.
How cavernous and dark!
Yet within it there is an essence.
Its essence is quite real;
Within it there are tokens.

From the present back to the past,
its name has been imperishable.
Through it we conform to the father of the masses.

How do I know what the father of the masses is like?
Through this.

66. (24)

Who is puffed up cannot stand,
Who is self-absorbed has no distinction,
Who is self-revealing does not shine,
Who is self-assertive has no merit,
Who is self-praising does not last long.

As for the Way, we may say these are
"excess provisions and extra baggage."
Creation abhors such extravagances.

Therefore,
One who aspires to the Way,
does not abide in them.

67. (22)

If it
is bent,
it will be preserved intact;
is crooked,
it will be straightened;
is sunken,
it will be filled;
is worn out,
it will be renewed;
has little,
it will gain;
has much,
it will be confused.

For these reasons,
The sage holds on to unity
and serves as the shepherd of all under heaven.
He is not self-absorbed,
therefore he shines forth;
He is not self-revealing,
therefore he is distinguished;
He is not self-assertive,
therefore he has merit;
He does not praise himself,
therefore he is long-lasting.
Now,
Simply because he does not compete,
no one can compete with him.

The old saying about the bent being preserved intact
is indeed close to the mark!

Truly, he shall be returned intact.

68. (23)

To be sparing of speech is natural.

A whirlwind does not last the whole morning,
A downpour does not last the whole day.
Who causes them?
If even heaven and earth cannot cause them to persist,
how much less can human beings?

Therefore,
In pursuing his affairs,
a man of the Way identifies with the Way,
a man of integrity identifies with integrity,
a man who fails identifies with failure.

To him who identifies with integrity,
the Way awards integrity;
To him who identifies with failure,
the Way awards failure.

69. (25)

There was something featureless yet complete,
born before heaven and earth;
Silent—amorphous—it stood alone and unchanging.
We may regard it as the mother of heaven and earth.
Not knowing its name
I style it the "Way."
If forced to give it a name,
I would call it "great."
Being great implies flowing ever onward,
Flowing ever onward implies far-reaching,
Far-reaching implies reversal.

The Way is great,
Heaven is great,
Earth is great,
The king, too, is great.

Within the realm there are four greats,
and the king is one among them.
Man
patterns himself on earth,

Earth
patterns itself on heaven,
Heaven
patterns itself on the Way,
The Way
patterns itself on nature.

70. (26)

Heavy is the root of light;
Calm is the ruler of haste.

For these reasons,
The superior man may travel the whole day
without leaving his heavy baggage cart.
Though inside the courtyard walls of a noisy inn,
he placidly rises above it all.

How then should a king with ten thousand chariots
conduct himself lightly before all under heaven?

If he treats himself lightly,
he will lose the taproot;
If he is hasty,
he will lose the rulership.

71. (27)

He who is skilled at traveling
leaves neither tracks nor traces;
He who is skilled at speaking
is flawless in his delivery;
He who is skilled in computation
use neither tallies not counters;
He who is skilled at closing things tightly
has neither lock nor key,
but what he closes cannot be opened.
He who is good at binding
has neither cord nor string,
but what he binds cannot be untied.

For these reasons,
The sage
is always skilled at saving others

and does not abandon them,
nor does he abandon resources.
This is called "inner intelligence."

Therefore,
Good men are teachers for the good man,
Bad men are foils for the good man.
He who values not his teacher
and loves not his foil,
Though he be knowledgeable, is greatly deluded.
This is called "the wondrous essential."

72. (28)

Know the masculinity,
Maintain femininity,
and be a ravine for all under heaven.
By being a ravine for all under heaven,
Eternal integrity will never desert you.
If eternal integrity never deserts you,
You will return to the state of infancy.

Know you are innocent,
Remain steadfast when insulted,
and be a valley for all under heaven.
By being a valley for all under heaven,
Eternal integrity will suffice.
If eternal integrity suffices,
You will return to the simplicity of the unhewn log.

Know whiteness,
Maintain blackness,
and be a model for all under heaven.
By being a model for all under heaven,
Eternal integrity will not err.
If eternal integrity does not err,
You will return to infinity.

When the unhewn log is sawn apart,
it is made into tools;
When the sage is put to use,
He becomes the chief of officials.

For
Great carving does no cutting.

73. (29)

Of those who wish to take hold of all-under-heaven
and act upon it,
I have seen that they do not succeed.
Now,
All-under-heaven is a sacred vessel,
Not something that can be acted upon;
Who acts upon it will be defeated, who grasps it will lose it.

Of creatures,
some march forward, others follow behind;
some are shiveringly silent, others are all puffed up;
some are strong, others are meek;
some pile up, others collapse.

For these reasons,
The sage
rejects extremes,
rejects excess,
rejects extravagance.

74. (30)

One who assists the ruler of men with the Way
does not use force of arms against all under heaven;
Such a course is likely to boomerang.

Where armies have been stationed,
briars and brambles will grow.

A good general fulfills his purpose
and that is all.
He does not use force
to seize for himself.

He fulfills his purpose,
but is not proud;
He fulfills his purpose,
but is not boastful;

He fulfills his purpose,
but does not brag;
He fulfills his purpose
only because he has no other choice.
This is called "fulfilling one's purpose without using force."
If something grows old while still in its prime,
This is called "not being in accord with the Way."
Not being in accord with the Way
leads to an early demise.

75. (31)

Now,
Weapons are instruments of evil omen;
Creation abhors them.
Therefore,
One who aspires to the Way
does not abide in them.

The superior man
at home honors the left,
on the battle field honors the right.
Therefore,
Weapons are not instruments of the superior man;
Weapons are instruments of evil omen,
to be used only when there is no other choice.

He places placidity above all
and refuses to prettify weapons;
If one prettifies weapons,
this is to delight in the killing of others.
Now
One who delights in the killing of others
Cannot exercise his will over all under heaven.

For this reason,
On occasions for celebration,
the left is given priority;
On occasions for mourning,
the right is given priority.

Therefore,
A deputy general stands on the left,

The general-in-chief stands on the right.
In other words,
They stand in accordance with mourning ritual.

The killing of masses of human beings,
we bewail with sorrow and grief:
Victory in battle,
we commemorate with mourning ritual.

76. (32)

The Way is eternally nameless.

Though the unhewn log is small,
No one in the world dares subjugate it.
If feudal lords and kings could maintain it,
The myriad creatures would submit of themselves.

Heaven and earth unite
to suffuse sweet dew.
Without commanding the people,
equality will naturally ensue.

As soon as one begins to divide things up,
there are names;
Once there are names,
one should also know when to stop;
Knowing when to stop,
one thereby avoids peril.
In metaphorical terms,
The relationship of all under heaven to the Way
is like that of valley streams
to the river and sea.

77. (33)

Understanding others is knowledge,
Understanding oneself is enlightenment,
Conquering others is power,
Conquering oneself is strength;
Contentment is wealth,
Forceful conduct is willfulness;
Not losing one's rightful place is to endure,
To die but not be forgotten is longevity.

78. (34)

Rippling is the Way, flowing left and right!
Its tasks completed, its affairs finished,
Still it does not claim them for its own.
The myriad creatures return to it,
But it does not act as their ruler.

Eternally without desire,
It may be named among the small;
The myriad creatures return to it,
But it does not act as their ruler;
It may be named among the great.

For these reasons,
The sage can achieve greatness,
Because he does not act great.
Therefore,
He can achieve greatness.

79. (35)

Hold fast to the great image
and all under heaven will come;
They will
come but not be harmed,
rest in safety and peace;
Music and fine food
will make the passerby halt.
Therefore,
When the Way is expressed verbally,
We say such things as
"how bland and tasteless it is!"
"We look for it,
but there is not enough to be seen."
"We listen for it,
but there is not enough to be heard."
Yet, when put to use,
it is inexhaustible!

80. (36)

When you wish to contract something,
you must momentarily expand it;

When you wish to weaken something,
you must momentarily strengthen it;
When you wish to reject something,
you must momentarily join with it;
When you wish to seize something,
you must momentarily give it up.
This is called "subtle insight."

The soft and weak conquer the strong.

Fish cannot be removed from the watery depths;
The profitable instruments of state
cannot be shown to the people.

81. (37)

The Way is eternally nameless.
If feudal lords and kings preserve it,
The myriad creatures will be transformed by themselves.
After transformation, if they wish to rise up,
I shall restrain them with the nameless unhewn log.
By restraining them with the nameless log,
They will not feel disgraced;
Not feeling disgraced,
They will be still,
Whereupon heaven and earth will be made right by themselves.

book three

THE CONFUCIAN TESTAMENT

introduction

Tradition versus Innovation

Jacqueline Mates-Muchin

NEW IS NEVER COMPLETELY NEW. IN A CULTURAL AND RELIGIOUS CONTEXT, "NEW" IS merely a different approach that invigorates a view of the universe that is already deeply embedded in the hearts and minds of followers. Innovation happens most successfully within the context of an established tradition, such as Christianity within the context of Judaism and Buddhism in the context of Hinduism. Indeed, we now contemplate the possibility that each of these religions and others connected by the Silk Route may have been influenced by a common Vedic heritage and were stimulated by Zoroastrian innovations in that relationship.

In each case, the innovation stemmed from the desire to distill the tradition down to its most basic ideals and build again, based on the experiences and values of the new realities of a different generation. In this process, the traditional ideals are brought to life in an altered form. Without the grounding of tradition, innovation would lack relevance and legitimacy. Without innovation, tradition dies out for lack of a contemporary expression. Thus, there is no innovation without tradition, and there would be no tradition if not for innovation.

Confucius's innovation was his practical application of tradition. The *Analects* of Confucius are a collection of aphorisms intended to guide an individual toward moral behavior. If we contrast Confucius's approach with Lao Tzu's, for instance, we see that Lao Tzu tends to be esoteric and philosophical, where Confucius tends to be action oriented. Lao Tzu teaches, "Those who know do not say; those who say do not know."[1] The same idea is articulated by Confucius as "The superior man wishes to be slow in his speech and swift in his actions."[2] Thus, for Confucius, the superior man does not just know—he acts.

Lao Tzu may be responding philosophically to Vedic Zoroastrian theological influence, whereas Confucius is reacting with practical application of China's traditions of noble action. Why was action so important to him?

Confucius lived in the Warring States period, a time of great instability and conflict in China. Living in such difficult times, he glorified the earlier Zhou period, which he believed was a time of unity, peace, and justice. Having seen the terrible things that happen during war, perhaps Confucius felt compelled to reflect and teach the ways in which individuals must treat each other. Indeed, one's thoughts can only be influenced, but one's actions can be controlled. Confucius tells us of his most basic principle when a disciple asks, "Is there one word which may serve as a rule of practice of all one's life? The Master said, 'Is not reciprocity such a word? What you do not want done to yourself, do not do to others.'"[3] Ethical interactions with others are at the heart of Confucius's teaching.

Yet behavior had to be based upon learning the tradition. We read, "The superior man learns in order to reach the utmost of his principles."[4] And, elsewhere, we understand that "the Master said. . . . The Odes serve to stimulate the mind. They may be used for purposes of self-contemplation. They teach the art of sociability. They show how to regulate feelings of resentment. From them you learn the more immediate duty of serving one's father, and the remoter one of serving one's prince."[5]

Thus, the impetus for the learning was moral action. One needed to be steeped in tradition in order to know how to behave.

Hierarchy and ritual were important because they helped individuals to hone discipline and self-control. We read, "The superior man, in his thoughts, does not go out of his place."[6] And, elsewhere, Confucius taught, "The superior man in everything considers righteousness to be essential. He performs it according to the rules of propriety. He brings it forth in humility. He completes it with sincerity."[7]

Discipline is required to remember one's place in society, to know the rules of propriety, and to remain humble and sincere. Such behavioral conditioning would enable individuals to develop the self-control necessary to restrain their impulses and, therefore, be intentional when interacting with others.

Judaism has a similar approach. When the Israelites accepted God's law, they said, "Na'asei v'nishma," which means "we will do and we will hear" (or understand). What we do is foremost. Of course, there are fundamental Jewish beliefs; yet tradition is primarily built upon the system of *mitzvot* (commandments). Actions can be commanded; beliefs and thoughts cannot. Within Jewish tradition, ritual, too, becomes an essential component that helps practitioners improve discipline and self-control.

As one might expect, the *Analects* of Confucius has significant parallels in early rabbinic texts. Namely, *Avot*, the earliest book of the Mishnah, is comprised of similarly pithy axioms. The two texts address many of the same themes: learning, honesty, respect, and proper behavior. *Avot* teaches, "Rabbi Elazar ben Azaryah said, 'If there is no Torah, there are no manners (proper conduct); if there are no manners, there is no Torah.'"[8] The *Analects* likewise explain, "The Master said, 'By extensively studying all learning, and keeping himself under the restraints of the rules of propriety, one may thus not err from what is right.'"[9] Significantly, both texts link proper behavior with the study of a traditional system with which the authors assume their readers are familiar, illustrating the fact that, in both instances, this is a new take on an old idea.

Like Confucius, the early rabbis lived in terribly unstable times. From the time that Alexander the Great entered the area in 334 BCE until the Second Temple was destroyed in 70 CE, the region was plagued by internal and external conflict. In reaction, the rabbis idealized a world of proper conduct wherein learning and appropriate behavior would be priorities. Teachings from their time demonstrate that instability gave rise to their picture of peace and unity through ethical conduct of the individual. Thus, similar social and political realities give rise to the need for a fresh expression of ancient value systems in Confucius's China and the rabbis' Judah.

Confucius's contribution lay in his basic teaching that individuals' actions and behavior, when properly grounded in traditional values, could constructively affect the world around them. And he was right. Individuals in every generation, whether we live in times of war or in times of peace, can learn to better interact with other individuals. Through positive and appropriate relationships, we can and we do bring about societal change. In this way, Confucius's practical application of tradition remains relevant and timeless.

preface

Fireworks, East and West

There is something ethically elevating about Jesus Christ's exhortation to turn the other cheek: it appeals to the streak of self-effacing idealism in many of us. We believe that this unilateral altruism symbolizes a higher virtue than simply the revengeful "eye for an eye and tooth for a tooth." It might come as a surprise that another response is possible, no less noble, but characterized by a lofty pragmatism rather than sheer idealism. When Confucius was asked, "Should one not return malice with kindness?" he replied, "If you return malice with kindness, what will you return kindness with? Therefore return malice with uprightness (justice), but return kindness with kindness."[1] How do we define a religion that shifts the moral focus from abstract principles to lived realities?[2]

JAMES LEGGE, TRANSLATOR OF OUR *ANALECTS*, WAS A DISTINGUISHED SINOLOGIST, A MINISTER OF the Scottish Congregationalist Church, a representative of the London Missionary Society in Malacca and Hong Kong, and the first professor of Chinese Language and Literature at Oxford University. In 1841 Legge began his translating of all or most of the Chinese classics, which he believed that missionaries needed to appreciate before engaging with the Chinese populace. Though he was not the first or the last to connect the Son of Heaven in the *Analects* to Jesus Christ, his respectful approach was of some importance in the ultimate development of the Christian Church in China, ultimately one of the most amazing religious phenomena in China in the twentieth century. That church of now perhaps 100 million members in four main branches (Catholic official and Catholic underground, Three-Self Protestant official and evangelical Protestant underground), and growing exponentially, may be a religious story of historic proportions in the twenty-first century, like the rise of Islam in the West. If so, much of the credit is due to the respectful attitude established by Legge, in contrast to more aggressive Christian missionary assertions elsewhere.

Legge was the headmaster at Ying Wa Teachers College in Hong Kong from 1839 to 1867, and pastor of the Union Church there from 1844 to 1867. He was editor of the *Chinese Serial*, the first Chinese-language newspaper in Hong Kong, 1853–1856, which was revived in 2006. While in Hong Kong he also published the *She King* (*Classics of Poetry*), the first substantial volume of Chinese poetry in English translation, which is still in use.

Before leaving China after thirty-five years to take up his leading role at Oxford in 1873, he toured the whole country to visit his former students. Beginning in Shanghai and on to Tianjin by boat, he traveled by mule cart to "Peking," where he visited the Great Wall, the Ming Tombs, and the Temple of Heaven, where he felt compelled to take off his shoes with holy awe. He next headed west to Shandong by mule cart to visit Jinan, Taishan, where he ascended the sacred Mount Tai, carried up by four former students (now school principals) in a chair. He then traveled southwest to Qufu, the birthplace of Confucius, and visited the Confucius Temple and the Forest of Confucius, where he climbed to the top of the Confucius's burial mound.

In 1875, Legge was named fellow of Corpus Christi College, Oxford, and in 1876 he assumed the new chair of Chinese language and literature at Oxford, which he occupied for twenty years. In his book *The Religions of China: Confucianism and Tâoism Described and Compared with Christianity* (published in 1880), he demonstrated the breadth of his awareness by describing a mosque in Canton that had a placard denouncing footbinding, saying Islam did not allow it since it constituted violating the creation of God. Legge was also an ardent opponent of Britain's opium policy, serving as a founding member of the Society for the Suppression of the Opium Trade. In addition to his translation work, Legge wrote *The Life and Teaching of Confucius* (1867), *The Religions of China* (1880), and other books on Chinese literature and religion. Many of his manuscripts and letters are archived at the School of Oriental and African Studies.[3] They were drawn to my attention there by Mary Boyce, who aspired to provide the West with the kind of appreciative introduction to Zoroastrianism that Legge provided for the religions of China.

While Legge's translation of the *Analects* of Confucius is older than others we might have used, it is regarded as a classic and is still preferred by many academics, especially oriental scholars working in English. I feel a particular affinity with James Legge personally, given my own fifty years of service in the United Church of Canada, with its Scottish and Congregationalist roots and a progressive theology like his. So we use his translation of Confucius, now in the public domain, with 99 percent of Legge's text intact, but with changes in spelling of Chinese names and related material to reflect the consensus of modern scholars and more recent translations. This translation is also attractive in the manner of three other earlier pieces in this compendium (by Geldner, Radhakrishnan, and Gandhi) distinguished by enduring scholarship but also capturing a religious ethos closer to the ancients than most moderns can claim as their own.

Confucius and his school may be seen as presenting traditional Chinese values. Do they do so in a natural evolution of such a collection or in a reaction against foreign influences as they appeared in Taoism and were being imported as Buddhism? Jacqueline

Mates-Muchin has addressed this matter in her introduction in a manner that works for our thesis about Taoism articulating a Chinese monism while Confucius holds the line with a popular expression of monotheism, though never fully articulated as such.

Marco Polo may or may not have ever actually reached China but he did apparently observe fireworks and obtain the formula in either Central Asia or western China, where it was used for many forms of celebration as well as in psychological warfare as firecracker arrows with the launching of rats to scare soldiers and spook horses. Polo himself sensed the potential to do serious physical harm to enemies, but the "gunfire" procedure was perfected by an Englishman, Francis Bacon. Medieval warfare came to an end in Europe, as metal armor could now be punctured by bullets and the once impenetrable walls of castles could be blown to bits by cannonballs. Partly on this foundation, European colonial expansionism began in earnest. Our point here is that in the current debate as to whether the Bible or the Quran is more violent, neither placed much restraint on the violence of believers, which continues to this day, while none of the Chinese scriptures give any hint of religious-based violence. China has rarely attacked anyone.

The story in the preface of Book II about Lao Tzu leaving China but being held at the border until he wrote a quick summary of his teachings for the gatekeeper may well be apocryphal, but it makes a certain point about Taoism having an ancient and identifiable written tradition. Another story, about a meeting between Lao Tzu and Confucius, while also possibly apocryphal, may have an even more pointed meaning. According to the treasured tale, in his early thirties, Confucius paid a visit to Lao Tzu, his elder contemporary, who was the foremost philosopher of the land at the time. Lao Tzu was then the curator of the National Archives in Luoyang, a flourishing, imperial city, three times the size of the capital of Lu, the young teacher's home. Confucius visited the splendid royal palace, the grand ancestral temple of the royal family, and the museum abundant with cultural relics. What he saw led him to a deeper understanding of the rich culture and the imperial greatness of the Zhou Dynasty.

But while both philosophers would have shared concern about the social order then crumbling throughout China, they had differing approaches to the cure of these ills. Confucius regarded the rule of the sage kings of the early Zhou Dynasty, based on ancient Chinese traditions of virtue and benevolence, as a model for restoring peace in a troubled world. Lao Tzu felt these ancient rules and rulers were no longer relevant. Their moral codes had become tools of coercion, and something new was required to save the world. Lao Tzu was part of a new vision, a possible source of which was described by Victor H. Mair in his 1990 and 2010 seminal presentations about the presence of Magi in China. This and other recent discoveries may be overturning the traditional view that Chinese civilization developed in isolation from the rest of the world, despite the strength of Chinese traditional wisdom, which we meet in the Confucian presentation.

"Get rid of arrogance and ambition," Lao Tzu would have said to Confucius. "A smart man will get into trouble if he is fond of criticizing others. An educated man will put his life in danger if he exposes the evils of others. When the time for his influence is not right, a gentleman should hide himself in a safe place." In other words, Lao Tzu was counseling Confucius to "go with the flow," a "Flow" to which we were exposed in Book II. Though deeply impressed, Confucius was not persuaded that inaction is ever appropriate. He remarked to his disciples, "I understand what a bird is; a bird can fly. I understand what a fish is; a fish can swim. I understand what a beast is; a beast can run. But I don't know what a dragon is. I can't make out Lao Tzu, except to say that he is like a dragon riding the winds and clouds in the sky. I don't know how to convince him that tradition teaches us how to act in every circumstance."

Confucianism is currently going through a dramatic period of renewal in China. It provides a putative supplement to communist dogma, especially as the Communist Party itself treats Confucian teaching as nonreligious (as compared with imports like Christianity, Islam, and Buddhism), complementing party ideology. Party leaders are quoted as saying, "Confucianism is aligned with the core values of socialism in the promotion of harmony," and suggesting that "it guides the current leadership's attack on corruption,"[4] a not-too-subtle self-serving interpretation. As professor and associate dean of the School of Arts and Media at Beijing Normal University, Yu Dan is a popular media personality in China, promoting Confucianism in both academia and the public. Her 2006 book, *Confucius from the Heart: Ancient Wisdom for Today's World*, sold ten million copies in its first year alone as China's best-selling (nongovernmental) book ever.[5]

Western readers might be easily misled to perceive a Machiavellian subtext to the *Analects*, but that would be a mistake based on simple differences in public morality. For example, support for the family, and even loyally covering for dishonest relatives, took precedence over government laws in the culture of ancient China. We take no position on this or other such cultural and legal matters, except to acknowledge the differences and recognize that all systems are subject to contextualization, and that there is a charm to Confucianism as well as commonsense elements that even the Communist Party might learn from.

Confucianism is certainly a religion but less heavenly minded and more earthly grounded than some. At the risk of oversimplification, it may be described as the ancient counterpart to modern progressive religions that strive to be politically correct, to protect the environment, and to defend the rights of women, gays, and minorities rather than defend religious doctrine or teach correct dogma. Does the quest for justice lead people to God, or does devotion to God lead believers to pursue justice? Confucius and his followers would emphasize justice, or at least appropriate behavior, as exemplified in Chinese tradition, of which religion was a part.

Because so much of it depends on some knowledge of the context, in our presentation of Legge's translation of the *Analects* we offer very brief introductions to each chapter, using interpretive ideas from a welter of sources too varied to be properly attributed, though the influence of Edward Slingerland of the University of British Columbia should be acknowledged.

8
analects
Translated by James Legge

chapter 1

Chapter 1 appears to be intended as an overview for prospective disciples or readers, showing that education has more to do with personal behavior than academic knowledge.

1. The Master said,
   "Is it not pleasant to learn with a constant perseverance and application?
   "Is it not delightful to have friends coming from distant quarters?
   "Is he not a man of complete virtue, who feels no discomposure though men may take no note of him?"
2. The philosopher You said, "They are few who, being filial and fraternal, are fond of offending against their superiors. There have been none, who, not liking to offend against their superiors, have been fond of stirring up confusion.
   "The superior man bends his attention to what is radical. That being established, all practical courses naturally grow up. Filial piety and fraternal submission, —are they not the root of all benevolent actions?"
3. The Master said, "Smooth words and an insinuating appearance are seldom associated with true virtue."
4. The philosopher Zeng said, "I daily examine myself on three points: —whether, in transacting business for others, I may have been not faithful; —whether, in intercourse with friends, I may have been not sincere; —whether I may have not mastered and practiced the instructions of my teacher."
5. The Master said, "To rule a country of a thousand chariots, there must be reverent attention to business, and sincerity; economy in expenditure, and love for men; and the employment of the people at the proper seasons."

6. The Master said, "A youth, when at home, should be filial, and, abroad, respectful to his elders. He should be earnest and truthful. He should overflow in love to all, and cultivate the friendship of the good. When he has time and opportunity, after the performance of these things, he should employ himself in understanding the culture involved."

7. Zixia said, "If a man withdraws his mind from the love of beauty, and applies it as sincerely to the love of virtue; if, in serving his parents, he can exert his utmost strength; if, in serving his prince, he can devote his life; if, in his intercourse with his friends, his words are sincere—although men say that he has no formal education, I will certainly say that he is learned."

8. The Master said, "If the scholar be not grave, he will not call forth any veneration, and his learning will not be solid.

"Hold faithfulness and sincerity as first principles.

"Have no close friends not equal to yourself.

"When you have faults, do not hesitate to abandon them."

9. The philosopher Tsang said, "Let there be a careful attention to perform the funeral rites to parents, and let them be followed when long gone with the ceremonies of sacrifice—then the virtue of the people will fall into place."

10. Ziqin asked Zigong saying, "When our master comes to any country, he does not fail to learn all about its government. Does he ask his information? or is it given to him?" Zigong said, "Our master is benign, upright, courteous, temperate, and complaisant and thus he gets his information. Our master's mode of gaining information is different from that of other men, is it not?"

11. The Master said, "While a man's father is alive, look at the bent of his will; when his father is dead, look at his conduct. If for three years he does not alter from the way of his father, he may be called filial."

12. The philosopher You said, "In practicing the rules of propriety, a natural ease is to be prized. This is the Way of the ancient kings, a quality of excellence, and in things small and great we follow them. Yet this is not to be observed in all cases. If one, knowing how such ease should be prized, shows it without regulating it by rules of propriety, it will not work."

13. The philosopher You said, "When agreements are made according to what is right, what is spoken can be counted upon. When respect is shown according to what is proper, one keeps far from shame and disgrace. When the parties upon whom a man leans are proper persons to be intimate with, he can make them his guides and masters."

14. The Master said, "He who aims to be a man of complete virtue does not seek to gratify his appetite in his consumption of food, nor in his dwelling place does he seek the indulgences of ease; he is earnest in what he is doing, and careful in his speech; he frequents the company of men of principle that he may be mentored—such a person may be said indeed to love to learn."

15. Zigong said, "What do you say concerning the poor man who does not flatter, and the rich man who is not proud?" The Master replied, "They will do; but

they are not equal to him, who, though poor, is yet cheerful, and to him, who, though rich, loves the rules of propriety."

Zigong replied, "It is said in the Book of Poetry, 'As you cut and then file, as you carve and then polish.'—The meaning is the same, I apprehend, as that which you have just expressed."

The Master said, "With one like Zigong I can begin to talk about the odes. I tell him one point, and he knows what comes next."

16. The Master said, "As to the third of your first points, do not worry if the people do not know you; be concerned if you do not know the people."

chapter 2

This chapter deals with governance and provides guidance on maintaining political power through the influence of virtuous persons rather than physical force. It also contains a famous autobiographical note by Confucius.

1. The Master said, "He who exercises government by means of his virtue may be compared to the north polar star, which keeps its place and all the stars turn towards it."
2. The Master said, "In the Book of Poetry are three hundred pieces, but the design of them all may be embraced in one sentence 'Have no depraved thoughts.'"
3. The Master said, "If the people be led by laws, and conformity is sought to be given them by punishments, they will try to avoid the punishment, but have no sense of shame.

    "If they be led by virtue, and conformity is sought to be given them by the rules of propriety, they will have the sense of shame, and moreover will become good."
4. The Master said, "At fifteen, I had my mind bent on learning.

    "At thirty, I stood firm.

    "At forty, I had no doubts.

    "At fifty, I knew the Decrees of Heaven.

    "At sixty, my ear was an obedient organ for the reception of truth.

    "At seventy, I could follow what my heart desired, without transgressing what was right."
5. Meng Yizi asked what filial piety was. The Master said, "It is not being disobedient."

    Soon after, as Fan Chi was driving him, the Master told him, saying, "Meng Yizi asked me what filial piety was, and I answered him, 'not being disobedient.'"

    Fan Chi said, "What did you mean?" The Master replied, "That parents, when alive, be served according to propriety; that, when dead, they should be buried according to propriety; and that they should be sacrificed to according to propriety."
6. Meng Wubo asked what filial piety was. The Master said, "Give parents no anxiety except for the possibility of sickness."

7. Tiyou asked what filial piety was. The Master said, "Filial piety nowadays means the support of one's parents. But dogs and horses likewise are able to do something in the way of such support—without reverence, what is there to distinguish the one support given from the other?"

8. Zixia asked what filial piety was. The Master said, "The difficulty is with the demeanor. If, when their elders have work to be done, the young take the burden from them, and if, when the young have wine and food, they set them before their elders, but is this enough to be considered filial piety?"

9. The Master said, "I have talked with Hui for a whole day, and he has not made any objection to anything I said; as if he were stupid. He has retired, and I have examined his conduct when away from me, and found him able to live up to my teachings. That Hui! He is not stupid after all."

10. The Master said, "See what a man does.

"Mark his motives.

"Examine in what things he rests.

"How can a man conceal his character? I ask you, how can a man conceal his character?"

11. The Master said, "If a man cherishes old knowledge, and also is continually acquiring new, he may be a teacher of others."

12. The Master said, "The accomplished scholar is not a mere utensil for spoon feeding his students."

13. Zigong asked what constituted the superior man. The Master said, "He acts before he speaks, and afterwards speaks according to his actions."

14. The Master said, "The superior man has a universal outlook and not provincial. The mean man is provincial and not universal."

15. The Master said, "Learning without thought is labor lost; thought without learning is perilous."

16. The Master said, "The study of strange doctrines is injurious indeed!"

17. The Master said, "Zilu, shall I teach you what knowledge is? When you know a thing, to hold that you know it; and when you do not know a thing, to allow that you do not know it—this is knowledge."

18. Zizhang was learning with a view to official emolument. The Master said, "Hear much and put aside the points of which you stand in doubt, while you speak cautiously at the same time of the others:—then you will afford few occasions for blame. See much and put aside the things which seem perilous, while you are cautious at the same time in carrying the others into practice: then you will have few occasions for repentance. When one gives few occasions for blame in his words, and few occasions for repentance in his conduct, he is on the way to get emolument."

19. The Duke Ai asked, saying, "What should be done in order to secure the submission of the people?" Confucius replied, "Advance the upright and set aside the crooked, then the people will submit. Advance the crooked and set aside the upright, then the people will not submit."

20. Ji Kangzi asked how to cause the people to reverence their ruler, to be faithful to him, and to go on to nerve themselves to virtue. The Master said, "Let him preside over them with gravity—then they will reverence him. Let him be final and kind to all—then they will be faithful to him. Let him advance the good and teach the incompetent—then they will eagerly seek to be virtuous."

21. Someone addressed Confucius, saying, "Sir, why are you not engaged in the government?" The Master said, "What does the Book of Documents say of filial piety?—'If you are filial, you discharge your duties to your seniors and your juniors. These are the qualities to be displayed in government.' So if one is doing that anyway, one is already participating in government."

22. The Master said, "I do not know how a man without truthfulness is to get on. How can a large carriage be made to go without the crossbar for yoking the oxen to, or a small carriage without the arrangement for yoking the horses?"

23. Zizhong asked whether the affairs of ten ages after could be known. Confucius said, "The Yin dynasty followed the regulations of the Xia: wherein it took from or added to them may be known. The Zhou dynasty has followed the regulations of Yin: wherein it took from or added to them may be known. Some other may follow the Zhou, but though it should be at the distance of a hundred ages, its affairs may be known."

24. The Master said, "For a man to sacrifice to a spirit which does not belong to him is flattery. To see what is right and not to do it is want of courage."

chapter 3

The ritual improprieties of the aristocracy are exposed and the need for cultural refinement is linked to virtuous life and substantial actions.

1. Confucius said of the head of the Ji family, who had eight rows of dancers in his arena, "If he can condone this, what else might he do?"

2. The three families performed the Yong Ode, while the dishes were being removed, at the conclusion of the sacrifice. The Master said,

> When the princes are assisting,
> The son of heaven looks on with appreciation and approval.

"What application can these words have in the hall of the three families?"

3. The Master said, "If a man be without the virtues proper to humanity, what has he to do with the rites of propriety? If a man be without the virtues proper to humanity, he cannot even appreciate good music?"

4. Lin Fang asked what was the first thing to be attended to in ceremonies.
   The Master said, "A great question indeed!
   "In festive ceremonies, it is better to be sparing than extravagant. In the ceremonies of mourning, it is better that there be deep sorrow than that there be minute attention to observances."

5. The Master said, "The rude tribes of the east and north have their princes, but are not like the states of our great land which are able to function without them."

6. The chief of the Ji family was about to sacrifice at Mt. Tai, sacred to the Zhou kings. The Master said to Ran Qiu, "Can you not prevent this?" He answered, "I cannot." Confucius said, "Alas! will you say that the Tai mountain is not able to discerning the difference?"

7. The Master said, "The student of virtue has no need to compete. But if he cannot avoid it, should he try archery? In this one bows complaisantly to ones competitors, ascends the hall, descends, and then exacts a forfeit by drinking. In this competition they compete in good manners."

8. Zixia asked, saying, "What is the meaning of the ode:

> "The pretty dimples of her artful smile!
> The well-defined black and white of her eye!
> The background is the context for the colors?"

The Master said, "The business of applying cosmetics depends on the face."

9. "Ceremonies then are a subsequent thing?" The Master said, "It is you, Zixia, who can bring out my meaning. Now I can begin to talk about the odes with someone."

   The Master said, "I could describe the empty ceremonies of the Xia dynasty, but Qii cannot sufficiently attest my words. I could describe the corrupt ceremonies of the Shang dynasty, but the whole state of Song cannot sufficiently attest my words. They cannot do so because of the insufficiency of their records and wise men. If those were sufficient, I could adduce them in support of my words."

10. The Master said, "At the great sacrifice, after the pouring out of the libation, I have no wish to observe the debauchery that follows."

11. Someone asked the meaning of the great sacrifice. The Master said, "I do not fully understand it. Anyone who knows its complete meaning would find the ability to govern right at hand"—and he pointed to his palm.

12. The Master said, "I consider my not being present at the sacrifice, as if I did not sacrifice." He sacrificed to the dead, as if they were present. He sacrificed to the spirits, as if the spirits were present.

13. Wang-sun Jia asked, saying, "What is the meaning of the saying, 'It is better to pay homage to the stove in the kitchen than to the shrine in the corner'?" The Master said, "Not so. He who offends against Heaven then has none to whom he can pray."

14. The Master said, "The Zhou Dynasty had the advantage of viewing the two past dynasties. How complete and elegant are its regulations! I follow the Zhou."

15. The Master, when he entered the grand temple, asked about everything. Someone said, "Who says that this son of a man from Zou knows the rules of propriety! He has entered the grand temple and asks about everything." The Master heard the remark, and said, "This is the first rule of propriety."

16. The Master said, "In archery piercing through the leather is not the principal thing—because people's strength is not equal. This old habit misses the point."

17. Zigong wished to do away with the offering of a sheep connected with the inauguration of the first day of each month. The Master said, "Zigong, you resent the loss of the sheep; I would miss the loss of the ceremony."

18. The Master said, "The full observance of the rules of propriety in serving one's prince can be misunderstood by people as flattery."

19. The Duke Ding asked how a prince should employ his ministers, and how ministers should serve their prince. Confucius replied, "A prince should employ his minister according to the rules of propriety; ministers should serve their prince with faithfulness."

20. The Master said, "The Song of the Osprey is expressive of enjoyment without being licentious, and of grief without being hurtfully excessive."

21. The Duke Ai asked Zai Wo about the altars of the spirits of the land. Zai Wo replied, "The Xia sovereign planted the pine tree about them; the men of the Shang planted the cypress; and the men of the Zhou planted the chestnut tree, meaning thereby to cause the people to be in awe."

    When the Master heard it, he said, "Things that are done, it is needless to speak about; things that have run their course, it is needless to protest about; things that are past, it is needless to blame."

22. The Master said, "Small indeed was the competence of Guan Zhong!" Someone said, "But was not Guan Zhong frugal?" "Guan," was the reply, "had the triple palaces and his officers performed double duties; how can he be considered frugal?"

    "Then, did Guan Zhong know the rules of propriety?" The Master said, "The princes of states have a screen obscuring the view at their gates. Guan had likewise a screen at his gate. The princes of states on any friendly meeting between two of them, had a stand on which to place their toasting cups. Guan had also such a stand. If Guan did not know the rules of propriety, who does?"

23. The Master instructing the grand music master of Lu said, "How to play music may be known from life experience. At the commencement of the piece, all the parts should sound individually. As it proceeds, they should be in harmony, both severally distinct and flowing without break, and thus on to the conclusion."

24. The border warden at Yi requested to be introduced to the Master, saying, "When men of superior virtue have come here, I have never been denied the privilege of seeing them." The followers of the sage introduced him, and when he came out from the interview, he said, "My friends, why are you distressed by your master's loss of office? The kingdom has long been without the principles of the Way; Heaven is going to use your master as the clapper of a bell."

25. The Master said of the Shao music that it was perfectly beautiful and also perfectly good. He said of the Wu music that it was perfectly beautiful but not perfectly good.

26. The Master said, "High stations are filled without magnanimity; ceremonies are performed without reverence; mourning is conducted without sorrow—how can I endorse such behavior?"

chapter 4

Those who are truly virtuous find fulfillment in the Way as defined by Confucius, but those who attempt to exploit the Way for their own purposes will reach a dead end.

1. The Master said, "It is virtuous manners which constitute the excellence of a neighborhood. If a man in selecting a residence does not fix on one where such prevail, how can he be wise?"
2. The Master said, "Those who are without virtue cannot abide long either in a condition of poverty and hardship, or in a condition of enjoyment. The virtuous rest in virtue; the wise desire virtue."
3. The Master said, "It is only the truly virtuous man, who can love, or who can hate, others."
4. The Master said, "If the will be set on virtue, there will be no practice of wickedness."
5. The Master said, "Riches and honors are what men desire. If they cannot be obtained in the proper way, they should not be held. Poverty and meanness are what men dislike. If they cannot be avoided in the proper way, they should not be avoided. If a superior man abandon virtue, how can he fulfill the requirements of that name? The superior man does not, even for the space of a single meal, act contrary to virtue. In moments of haste, he cleaves to it. In seasons of danger, he cleaves to it."
6. The Master said, "I have not seen a person who loved virtue, or one who hated what was not virtuous. He who loved virtue, would esteem nothing above it. He who hated what is not virtuous, would practice virtue in such a way that he would not allow anything that is not virtuous to approach his person. Is anyone able for one day to apply his strength to virtue? I have not seen the case in which his strength would be insufficient. Should there possibly be any such case, I have not seen it."
7. The Master said, "The faults of men are characteristic of the class to which they belong. By observing a man's faults, it may be known that he is virtuous."
8. The Master said, "If a man begins the day in the right Way, he may die in the evening without regret."
9. The Master said, "A scholar, whose mind is set on truth, but who is ashamed of shabby clothes and poor food, is not fit to be discoursed with."
10. The Master said, "The superior man, in the world, does not set his mind either for anything, or against anything; what is right he will follow naturally."
11. The Master said, "The superior man thinks of virtue; the small man thinks of comfort. The superior man thinks of obeying the law; the small man thinks of favors which he may receive."

12. The Master said: "He who acts with a constant view to his own advantage will be much murmured against."

13. The Master said, "If a prince is able to govern his kingdom with deference to the rules of propriety, what difficulty will he have? If he cannot govern it with that deference, what has he to do with the rules of propriety?"

14. The Master said, "A man should say, I am not concerned that I have no position, but I am concerned how I may fit myself for one. I am not concerned that I am not known, but I seek to be worthy to be known."

15. The Master said, "Zeng, my doctrine is like the all-pervading unity of a single thread." The disciple replied, "Yes." The Master went out and the other disciples asked, saying, "What do his words mean?" Zeng said, "The doctrine of our master is to be true to the principles of our nature and the benevolent exercise of them to others—this and nothing more."

16. The Master said, "The mind of the superior man is conversant with righteousness; the mind of the mean man is conversant with gain."

17. The Master said, "When we see men of worth, we should think of equaling them; when we see men of a contrary character, we should turn inwards and examine ourselves."

18. The Master said, "In serving his parents, a son may remonstrate with them, but gently; when he sees that they do not incline to follow his advice, he shows an increased degree of reverence, but does not abandon his purpose; and should they punish him, he does not allow himself to murmur."

19. The Master said, "While his parents are alive, the son may not go abroad to a distance. If he does go abroad, he must have a fixed place to which he goes."

20. The Master said, "If the son for three years does not alter from the way of his father, he may be called filial."

21. The Master said, "The age of one's parents must always be kept in mind as both a source of rejoicing and a cause of anxiety."

22. The Master said, "The reason why the ancients did not readily give utterance to their words, was that they were afraid that they might not live up to them."

23. The Master said, "The cautious seldom err."

24. The Master said, "The superior man wishes to be slow in his speech and swift in his actions."

25. The Master said, "Virtue is not left to stand alone. He who practices it will have neighbors."

26. Ziyou said, "In serving a prince, frequent presumption leads to disgrace. Between friends, frequent presumption merely makes the friendship distant."

chapter 5

The virtues of the superior person are illustrated by examples from political life and the experience of disciples in which Confucius does not hesitate to offer moral judgments. Specialist scholars are conversant in the identities of both the politicians and the disciples, but first-time readers may use their imaginations.

1. The Master said of Gongye Chang that he might be wived; although he was put in jail, he had not been guilty of any crime. Accordingly, he gave him his own daughter to wife.

2. Of Nan Rong he said that if the country were governed in the right Way he would not be out of office, but if it were not so governed, he would escape punishment and disgrace. He gave him the daughter of his own elder brother to wife.

3. The Master said of Zijian, "Of superior virtue indeed is such a man! If there were not virtuous men in Lu, how could this man have acquired this character?"

4. Zigong asked, "What do you say of me?" The Master said, "You are a utensil." "What utensil?" "A gemmed sacrificial utensil."

5. Someone said, "Zhonggong is truly virtuous, but he is not eloquent." The Master said, "What is the good of being ready with the tongue? They who respond to men with smartness of speech for the most part procure resentment for themselves. I know not whether he be truly virtuous, but why should he show readiness of the tongue?"

6. The Master was wishing Qidiao Kai to accept an official position. He replied, "I am not ready for this responsibility." The Master was pleased.

7. The Master said, "My doctrines do not make the Way. I get upon a raft and float about on the sea. The first to accompany me will be Zilu, I dare say." Zilu hearing this was glad, upon which the Master said, "Zilu is fonder of daring than I am, though he does not exercise his judgment upon matters."

8. Meng Wubo asked about Zilu, whether he was perfectly virtuous. The Master said, "I do not know." He asked again, when the Master replied, "In a kingdom of a thousand chariots, Zilu might be employed to manage the military levies, but I do not know whether he be perfectly virtuous." And when he was asked, "What do you say of Ran Qiu?" The Master replied, "In a city of a thousand families, or a clan of a hundred chariots, Ran Qiu might be employed as governor, but I do not know whether he is perfectly virtuous." Then, "What do you say of Zihua?" The Master replied, "With his sash tied and standing in a court, Zihua might be employed to converse with the visitors and guests, but I do not know whether he is perfectly virtuous."

9. The Master said to Zigong, "Which do you consider superior, yourself or Yan Hui?" Zigong replied, "How dare I compare myself with Hui? Hui hears one point and knows all about a subject; I hear one point, and only move on to a second." The Master said, "You are not equal to him. I grant you, you are not equal to him."

10. Zai Wo being asleep during the daytime, the Master said, "Rotten wood cannot be carved; a wall of dirty earth will not receive the trowel. This Zai Wo—what is the use of my reproving him?" The Master said, "At first, my way with men was to hear their words, and presume their conduct. Now my way is to hear

their words, and look at their conduct. It is from Zai Wo that I have learned to make this change."

11. The Master said, "I have not seen a firm and unbending man." Someone replied, "There is Shen Cheng." "Cheng," said the Master, "is under the influence of his passions; how can he be pronounced firm and unbending?"

12. Zigong said, "What I do not wish men to do to me, I also wish not to do to men." The Master said, "Zigong, you have not attained that yet."

13. Zigong said, "The Master personally displays his principles and public descriptions of them may be heard. His discourses about human nature and the way of Heaven are not as well-known nor are they discussed."

14. When Zilu heard any new thing, if he had not yet succeeded in carrying it into practice, he was afraid that he might hear something else before he did.

15. Zigong asked, saying, "On what ground did Kong-wenzi get that title of Cultured?" The Master said, "He was of an active nature and yet fond of learning, and he was not ashamed to ask and learn of his inferiors!—On these grounds he has been styled Cultured."

16. The Master said of Zichan that he had four of the characteristics of a superior man: in his conduct of himself, he was humble; in serving his superior, he was respectful; in nourishing the people, he was kind; in ordering the people, he was just."

17. The Master said, "Yan Pingzong knew well how to maintain friendly intercourse. The acquaintance might be long, but he showed the same respect as at first."

18. The Master said, "Zang Wenzhong kept a large tortoise in the house on which he made hills on the capitals of the pillars, and with representations of duckweed on the small pillars above the beams supporting the rafters. What does this symbolize about his wisdom?"

19. Zizhang asked a question saying, "The prime minister Ziwen took office thrice, and manifested no joy in his countenance. Thrice he retired from office, and manifested no displeasure. He made it a point to inform the new minister of the way in which he had conducted the government; what do you say of him?" The Master replied. "He was loyal." "Was he perfectly virtuous?" "I do not know. How can he be pronounced perfectly virtuous?"

    Zizhang proceeded, "When the officer Cuizi killed the prince of Qi, Chen Wenzi, though he was the owner of forty horses, abandoned them and left the country. Coming to another state, he said, 'They are here like our great officer, Cuizi,' and left it. He came to a second state, and with the same observation left it also. What do you say of him?" The Master replied, "He was pure." "Was he perfectly virtuous?" "I do not know. How can one be pronounced perfectly virtuous?"

20. Ji Wenzi always thought thrice, and then acted. When the Master was informed of it, he said, "Twice may do."

21. The Master said, "When the Way prevailed in his country, Ning Wuzi acted the part of a wise man. When his country was in disorder, he acted the part of a stupid man. Others may equal his wisdom, but they cannot equal his stupidity."

22. When the Master was in Chen, he said, "Let me return! Let me return! The little children of my school are ambitious and too hasty. They are accomplished and complete so far, but they do not know how to restrict and shape themselves."

23. The Master said, "Bo Yi and Shu Qi did not keep the former wickedness of men in mind, and hence the resentments directed towards them were few."

24. The Master said, "Who says of Weisheng Gao that he is upright? One begged some vinegar of him, and he begged it of a neighbor and gave it to the man as if it was his own."

25. The Master said, "Fine words, an ingratiating manner, and excessive respect—Zuoqui Ming was ashamed of these things and I also am ashamed of them. To conceal resentment against a person and appear friendly with him—Zuoqui Ming was ashamed of such conduct and I also am ashamed of it."

26. Yan Hui and Zilu being by his side, the Master said to them, "Come, let each of you tell his wishes." Zilu said, "I should like, having chariots and horses, and light fur clothes, to share them with my friends, and though they should spoil them, I would not be displeased."

    Yan Hui said, "I should like not to boast of my excellence, nor to make a display of my meritorious deeds."

    Zilu then said, "I should like, sir, to hear your wishes." The Master said, "They are, in regard to the aged, to give them rest; in regard to friends, to show them sincerity; in regard to the young, to treat them tenderly."

27. The Master said, "It is all over. I have not yet seen one who could perceive his own faults, and inwardly accuse himself."

28. The Master said, "In a hamlet of ten families, there may be found a person as honorable and sincere as I am, but none so fond of learning."

chapter 6

Examples of disciples, acquaintances, and public figures are used to illuminate the desired virtues and the practices that should be avoided by those aspiring to excellence in a Confucian system, which is intended to be more practical than theoretical.

1. The Master said, "There is Zhonggong!—He might occupy the place of a prince."

2. Zhonggong asked about Zisang Bozi. The Master said, "He may pass. He does not get entangled in small matters." Zhonggong said, "If a man cherishes in himself a reverential feeling of the necessity of attention to business, though he may be easy in small matters in his government of the people, that may be allowed. But if he cherishes in himself that easy feeling, and also carry it out in his practice, is not such an easy mode of procedure excessive?"

3. The Duke Ai asked which of the disciples loved to learn. Confucius replied to him, "There was Yan Hui; he loved to learn. He did not convey his displeasure; he did not repeat a fault. Unfortunately, his appointed time was short and he

died; and now there is not such another. I have not yet heard of anyone who loves to learn as he did."

4. Zihua being employed on a mission to Qi, the disciple Ran Qiu requested grain for his mother. The Master said, "Give her a fu." Ran Qiu requested more. "Give her a yu," said the Master. But Ran Qiu gave her five bing. The Master said, "When Zihua was proceeding to Qi, he had fat horses for his carriage, and wore light furs. I have heard that a superior man helps the distressed, but does not add to the wealth of the rich."

5. Yuan Si was made governor of his town by the Master, who gave him nine hundred measures of grain, but Si declined them. The Master said, "Do not decline them. May you not give them away in the neighborhoods, hamlets, towns, and villages?"

6. The Master, speaking of Zhonggong, said, "If the calf of an ox be red and sharp horned, although men may not wish to sacrifice it, would the spirits of the mountains and rivers reject it?"

7. The Master said, "Such was Yan Hui that for three months there would be nothing in his mind contrary to perfect virtue. The others may attain to this on some days or some months but not more."

8. Ji Kangzi asked about Zilu, whether he was fit to be employed as an officer of government. The Master said, "Zilu is a man of decision; what difficulty would he find in being an officer of government?" Kangzi asked, "Is Zigong fit to be employed as an officer of government?" and was answered, "Zigong is a man of intelligence; what difficulty would he find in being an officer of government?" And to the same question about Ran Qiu the Master gave the same reply, saying, "Ran Qiu is a man of various abilities."

9. The chief of the Ji family sent a messenger to ask Min Ziqian to be governor of Bi. Min Ziqian said, "Decline the offer for me politely. If you come again to me with a second invitation, I shall be obliged to go and live beyond the Wen River."

10. Boniu being ill, the Master went to ask for him. He took hold of his hand through the window, and said, "This is killing him. It is the appointment of Heaven. Alas that such a man should have such a sickness! Alas that such a man should have such a sickness!"

11. The Master said, "Admirable indeed was the virtue of Yan Hui! With a single bamboo dish of rice, a single gourd dish of drink, and living in his narrow little lane. While others could not have endured the distress, he did not allow his joy to be affected by it. Admirable indeed was the virtue of Hui!"

12. Ran Qiu said, "It is not that I do not delight in your doctrines, but my strength is insufficient." The Master said, "Those whose strength is truly insufficient must give up in the middle of the Way, but you are just limiting yourself."

13. The Master said to Zixia, "You have the ability to be a scholar after the style of the superior man, and not after that of the mean man."

14. Ziyou being governor of Wucheng, the Master said to him, "Have you got good men there?" He answered, "There is Tantai Mieming, who never takes a short cut in business, and never comes to my office unnecessarily."

15. The Master said, "Meng Zhifan does not boast of his merit. Defending the rear on an occasion of retreat, when they were about to enter the gate, he whipped up his horse and quipped, "It is not my courage that kept me back. My horse would not advance."

16. The Master said, "Without the specious speech of the liturgist Tuo or the good looks of Prince Chao of Sung, it is difficult to get by in the present age."

17. The Master said, "Who can go out but by the door? How is it then that men will not walk according to the Ways?"

18. The Master said, "Where the solid qualities are in excess of accomplishments, we have a crude rustic; where the accomplishments are in excess of the solid qualities, we have the manners of a clerk. When the accomplishments and solid qualities are equally blended, we then have the man of virtue."

19. The Master said, "Man is born for uprightness. If a man loses his uprightness and yet carries on in life, his escape from demise is the effect of mere good fortune."

20. The Master said, "They who know the truth are not equal to those who love it, and they who love it are not equal to those who delight in it."

21. The Master said, "With those whose talents are above mediocrity, the highest subjects may be discussed. With those who are below mediocrity, the highest subjects may not be considered."

22. Fan Chi asked what constitutes wisdom. The Master said, "To give one's self earnestly to the responsibilities of men, and, while respecting spooks and ghosts, to keep aloof from them, may be called wisdom." He asked about perfect virtue. The Master said, "The man of virtue makes dealing with difficulty his first business, and success only a subsequent consideration—this may be called perfect virtue."

23. The Master said, "The wise find pleasure in brooks; the virtuous find pleasure in hills. The wise are active; the virtuous are tranquil. The wise are joyful; the virtuous are long-lived."

24. The Master said, "Qi, by making one change, could come to the status required by the State of Lu. Lu, by making one change, could become a State where true principles predominated."

25. The Master said, "A cornered chalice without properly shaped corners is a strange cornered chalice! A strange cornered chalice is what you get these days!"

26. Zai Wo asked, saying, "A benevolent man, though someone lied to him that— 'There is a man in the well' will go in after him, I suppose." Confucius said, "Why should he do so? A superior man may be required to go to the well, but he cannot be made to go down into it. He may be tricked, but he should not be fooled."

27. The Master said, "The superior man, being well informed through his learning, and keeping himself under the restraint of the rules of propriety, is not likely to overstep what is right by accident."

28. The Master having visited Nanzi, Zilu was displeased, on which the Master swore, saying, "If I have behaved improperly, may Heaven reject me, may Heaven reject me!"

29. The Master said, "Perfect is the virtue which is according to the Constant Mean! Yet for a long time its practice has been rare among the people."

30. Zigong said, "Imagine the case of a man extensively conferring benefits on the people, and able to assist all, what would you say of him? Might he be called perfectly virtuous?" The Master said, "Why speak only of virtue in connection with him? Must he not have the qualities of a sage? Even Yao and Shun are still solicitous about this, but the man of perfect virtue, wishing to be established himself, seeks also to establish others; wishing to be enlarged himself, he seeks also to enlarge others. To be able to judge of others by what is near and dear to ourselves—this may be called the art of virtue."

chapter 7

The theme of this chapter is the exercise of willpower to achieve Confucian standards, resulting in deep happiness.

1. The Master said, "I am a transmitter and not an originator, believing in and loving the ancients, I venture to compare myself with our old Peng."

2. The Master said, "The silent treasuring up of knowledge; learning without exhaustion; and instructing others without becoming tired of them—these are the things most important to me."

3. The Master said, "Having virtue without proper cultivation; not thoroughly discussing what is learned; not being able to move towards righteousness of which knowledge has been gained; and failing to change what is not good—these are the things which cause me anxiety."

4. When the Master was unoccupied with business, his manner was easy, and he looked pleased.

5. The Master said, "Extreme is my decay. For a long time, I have not even dreamed that I saw the duke of Zhou, the way I used to."

6. The Master said, "Let the will be set on the Way.
   "Let perfect virtue be firmly grasped.
   "Let relaxation and enjoyment be found in cultivating the arts."

7. The Master said, "From the man bringing his bundle of dried flesh for my teaching to those who brought whatever they could, I have never refused instruction to anyone."

8. The Master said, "I do not open up the truth to one who is not eager to get knowledge, nor help out any one who is not anxious to explain himself. When I have presented one corner of a subject to any one, and he cannot from it learn the other three, I do not repeat my lesson."

9. When the Master was eating by the side of a mourner, he never ate to the full.

10. He did not sing on the same day in which he had been weeping.

11. The Master said to Yan Hui, "When called to office one should undertake its duties; when not so called one should stand in reserve—it is only I and you who have accepted this." Zilu said, "If you had the conduct of the armies of a great state, whom would you have to act with you?" The Master replied, "I would not have him to act with me who will attack a tiger barehanded, or cross a river without a boat and drown without any regret. My associate must be the man who proceeds to action full of attentive consideration, who is able to adjust his plans, and then carries them into execution."

12. The Master said, "If the search for riches is sure to be successful, though I need become a jockey with whip in hand to get them, I will do so. But as the search may not be successful, I prefer to follow after that which I love."

13. The things in reference to which the Master exercised the greatest caution were fasting, war, and sickness.

14. When the Master was in Qi, he heard the Shao music, and for three months did not know the taste of meat. "I did not think" he said, "that music could have been made as sublime as this."

15. Ran Qiu asked, "Does our Master support the ruler of Wei?" Zigong said, "Oh! I will ask him." He went in accordingly, and said, "What sort of men were Boi and Shuqi?" "They were ancient worthies," said the Master. "Did they have any regrets because of their course?" The Master again replied, "They sought to act virtuously, and they did so; what was there for them to regret?" On this, Zigong went out and said, "Our Master is not for him."

16. The Master said, "With coarse rice to eat, with water to drink, and my bended arm for a pillow, I still have joy in simple things. Riches and honors acquired by unrighteousness are to me as a floating cloud."

17. The Master said, "If many years were added to my life, I would give fifty of them to the study of the Book of Changes, and then I might come to be without great faults."

18. The Master's frequent themes of discourse were the Odes, the History, and the maintenance of the Rules of Propriety. On all these he frequently discoursed.

19. The Duke of She asked Zilu about Confucius, and Zilu did not answer him. The Master said later, "Why did you not say to him, 'He is simply a man, who in his eager pursuit of knowledge forgets his food, who in the joy of its attainment forgets his sorrows, and who does not perceive that old age is coming on'?"

20. The Master said, "I am not one who was born with the possession of knowledge; I am one who is fond of antiquity, and earnest in seeking knowledge there."

21. The subjects on which the Master did not talk were extraordinary things, feats of strength, disorder, and spectral appearances.

22. The Master said, "When I walk along with two others, they will always serve me as my teachers. I will select their good qualities and follow them, their bad qualities and avoid them."

23. The Master said, "Heaven produced the virtue that is in me. What can Hwan Tui do to me?"

24. The Master said, "Do you think, my disciples, that I have any concealments? I conceal nothing from you. There is nothing which I do that is not shown to you, my disciples; that is my way."

25. There were four things which the Master taught: letters, ethics, devotion of soul, and truthfulness.

26. The Master said, "A sage it is not mine to see, but if I could see a man of real talent and virtue, that would satisfy me. A good man it is not mine to see, but if I could see a man possessed of constancy, that would satisfy me. Having not seen everything and yet desiring to see, being empty and yet desiring to be full, anxious and yet desiring to be at ease—it is difficult with such challenges to have constancy."

27. The Master angled for fish but did not use a net. He shot at birds in flight but not at birds perching.

28. The Master said, "There may be those who act without knowing why. I do not do so. Hearing much and selecting what is good and following it; seeing much and keeping it in memory: this is the second best style of knowledge."

29. It was difficult to talk about the Way with the people of Hu village. A lad of that place having desired an interview with the Master, the disciples resisted. The Master said, "I admit people's approach to me without committing myself as to what they may do when they have retired. Why must one be so severe? If a man prepares himself to wait upon me, I receive him so prepared, without guaranteeing his future conduct."

30. The Master said, "Is virtue a thing remote? I wish to be virtuous, and lo! virtue is at hand."

31. The minister of crime of Chen asked whether the duke Zhao knew propriety, and Confucius said, "He knew propriety." Confucius having retired, the minister bowed to Wuma Qi to come forward, and said, "I have heard that the superior man is not to be a partisan. May the superior man ever be a partisan? The prince married a daughter of the house of Wu, of the same surname with himself, and called her 'The elder daughter of Wu.' If the prince knew propriety, who does not know it?" Wuma Qi reported these remarks, and the Master said, "I am fortunate! If I have any errors, people are sure to know them."

32. When the Master was in company with a person who was singing, if he sang well, he would make him repeat the song, while he accompanied it with his own voice.

33. The Master said, "In letters I am perhaps equal to other men, but the character of the superior man, carrying out in his conduct what he professes, is what I have not yet attained to."

34. The Master said, "The sage and the man of perfect virtue—how dare I rank myself with them? It may simply be said of me, that I strive to become such without being satisfied, and teach others without weariness." Gong Xihua said, "This is just what we, the disciples, cannot imitate you in."

35. The Master being very sick, Zilu asked leave to pray for him. He said, "May such a thing be done?" Zilu replied, "It may. In the Eulogies it is said, 'Prayer has been made for thee to the spirits of the upper and lower worlds.'" The Master said, "My praying has been going on for a long time."

36. The Master said, "Extravagance leads to insubordination, and parsimony to meanness. But it is better to be mean than to be insubordinate."

37. The Master said, "The superior man is satisfied and composed; the mean man is always full of distress."

38. The Master was mild, and yet dignified; majestic, and yet not fierce; respectful, and yet easy.

chapter 8

A nucleus of sayings from a disciple, later known as Master Zeng, plus a collection of passages similar to those in Section Seventeen and a context of historical reflections.

1. The Master said, "Tai-Bo may be said to have reached the highest point of virtuous action. Thrice he declined the kingdom, but the people in ignorance of his motives could not express their admiration of his conduct."

2. The Master said, "Respectfulness, without the rules of propriety, becomes exasperating; carefulness, without the rules of propriety, becomes temerity; boldness, without the rules of propriety, becomes insubordination; straightforwardness, without the rules of propriety, becomes rudeness. When those who are in high stations perform well all their duties to their relations, the people are aroused to virtue. When old friends are not neglected by them, the people are preserved from meanness."

3. The philosopher Zeng being ill, he called the disciples of his school to him, and said, "Uncover my feet, uncover my hands. It is said in the Book of Poetry,

> "We should be apprehensive and cautious,
> as if on the brink of a deep gulf,
> as if treading on thin ice.

"And so have I been. Now and hereafter, I know my escape from all injury to my person, O ye, my little children."

4. The philosopher Zeng being ill, Meng Jingzi went to ask how he was. Zeng said to him, "When a bird is about to die, its notes are mournful; when a man is about to die, his words are good. There are three principles of conduct which the man of high rank should consider specially important—that in his deportment and manner he keep from violence and heedlessness; that in regulating his countenance he keep near to sincerity; and that in his words and tones he keep far from lowness and impropriety. As to such matters as attending to the sacrificial rituals, there are proper officers to attend them."

5. The philosopher Zeng said, "Gifted with ability, and yet putting questions to those who were not so; possessed of much, and yet putting questions to those possessed of little; having, as though he had not; full, and yet counting himself as empty; offended against, and yet entering into no altercation; formerly I had a friend who pursued this style of conduct."

6. The philosopher Zeng said, "Suppose that there is an individual who can be entrusted with the charge of a young orphan prince, and can be commissioned with authority over a state of great territory, and whom no emergency however great can drive from his principles—is such a man a superior man? He is a superior man indeed."

7. The philosopher Zeng said, "The officer may not be without breadth of mind and vigorous endurance. His burden is heavy and his course is long. Perfect virtue is the burden which he considers it is his to sustain—is it not heavy? Only with death does his course stop—is it not long?

8. The Master said, "It is by the Odes that the mind is aroused. It is by the Rules of Propriety that the character is established. It is through Music that perfection is received."

9. The Master said, "The people may be made to follow a path of action, but they may not be made to understand it."

10. The Master said, "The man who is fond of daring and is dissatisfied with poverty, will proceed to insubordination. So will the man who is not virtuous, when you carry your dislike of him to an extreme."

11. The Master said, "Though a man have abilities as admirable as those of the Duke of Zhou, yet if he be proud and miserly, those other things are really not worth being looked at."

12. The Master said, "It is not easy to find a man who has learned for three years without coming to be good."

13. The Master said, "With sincere faith he unites the love of learning; holding firm to death, he is perfecting the excellence of his course. Such a one will not enter a tottering state, nor dwell in a disorganized one. When right principles of government prevail in the kingdom, he will show himself; when they are prostrated, he will keep concealed.

   "When a country is governed in the Way, poverty and a mean condition are things to be ashamed of. When a country is ill governed, riches and honor are things to be ashamed of."

14. The Master said, "He who is not appointed to particular office has nothing to do with planning the administration of its duties."

15. The Master said, "Since the music master Zhi first entered on his office, the performance of the Song of the Osprey has been magnificent—how it has filled the ears of the soul!"

16. The Master said, "Ardent and yet not upright, stupid and not even honest; simple and yet not sincere—such persons I do not understand."

17. The Master said, "Learn as if you could not reach your goal, and as if always fearing lest you lose sight of it."

18. The Master said, "How majestic was the manner in which Shun and Yu held possession of the empire, as if it were nothing to them!"

19. The Master said, "Great indeed was Yao as a sovereign! How majestic was he! It is only Heaven that is grand, and only Yao corresponded to it. How vast was his virtue! The people could find no name for it. How majestic was he in the works which he accomplished! How glorious in the elegant regulations which he instituted!"

20. Shun had five ministers, and the empire was well governed. King Wu said, "I have ten able ministers." Confucius said, "Is not the saying that talents are difficult to find, true? Only when the dynasties of Shun and Yeo combined, were they more abundant than that of Zhou, yet there was a woman among them. The able ministers were no more than nine men. King Wan possessed two of the three parts of the empire, and with those he served the dynasty of Yin. The virtue of the house of Zhou may be said to have reached the highest point indeed."

21. The Master said, "I can find no flaw in the character of Yu. He used coarse food and drink, but displayed the utmost filial piety towards the spirits. His ordinary garments were poor, but he displayed the utmost elegance in his sacrificial cap and apron. He lived in a low, mean house, but expended all his strength on the ditches and water channels. I can find nothing like a flaw in Yu."

chapter 9

Chapter 9 may be a variant of chapter 17 in that both focus on perseverance, sincerity, and the pursuit of learning and virtue, though here we have the distress of Confucius at the rejection or ignoring of heaven's mandate by people high and low.

1. The subjects of which the Master seldom spoke were—profitableness, and also the appointments of Heaven, and perfect virtue.

2. A man of the village of Daxiang exclaimed, "Great indeed is the philosopher Confucius! His learning is extensive, and yet his name is not famous by any particular accomplishment." The Master heard the observation, and said to his disciples, "What shall I undertake to achieve fame? Shall I practice charioteering, or shall I practice archery? I think I will take up charioteering."

3. The Master said, "The linen cap is that prescribed by the rules of ceremony, but now a silk one is worn. It is economical, and I follow the common practice. The rules of ceremony prescribe the bowing below the hall, but now the practice is to bow only after ascending it. That is arrogant. I continue to bow below the hall, though I oppose the common practice."

4. There were four things from which the Master was entirely free. He had no foregone conclusions, no arbitrary predeterminations, no obstinacy, and no egoism.

5. The Master was put in fear in Kuang. He said, "After the death of King Wan, was not the cause of truth lodged here in me? If Heaven had wished to let this cause of truth perish, then I, a mortal, should not have got such a relation to that cause. While Heaven does not let the cause of truth perish, what can the people of Kuang do to me?"

6. A high officer addressed Zigong, saying, "May we not say that your Master is a sage? How various is his ability!" Zigong said, "Certainly Heaven has endowed him unlimitedly. He is a sage, but moreover, his ability is various." The Master heard of the conversation and said, "Does the high officer know me? When I was young, my condition was low, and I acquired my ability in many things, but they were mean matters. Must the superior man have such variety of ability?"

7. Lao said, "The Master said, 'Having no official employment, I acquired many arts.'"

8. The Master said, "Am I indeed possessed of knowledge? I am not knowledge-able. But if a mean person, who appears quite empty-like, ask anything of me, I set it forth from one end to the other, and exhaust it."

9. The Master said, "The Phoenix bird has not returned; the Yellow River does not follow its course—it is all over with me!"

10. When the Master saw a person in a mourning dress, or anyone with the cap and upper and lower garments of official dress, or a blind person, on observing them approaching, though they were younger than himself, he would rise up, and if he had to pass by them, he would do so hastily.

11. Yan Hui, in admiration of the Master's doctrines, sighed and said, "I looked up to them, and they seemed to become more high; I tried to penetrate them, and they seemed to become more firm; I looked at them before me, and suddenly they seemed to be behind. The Master, by orderly method, skillfully leads men on. He enlarged my mind with learning, and taught me the restraints of propriety. When I wish to give over the study of his doctrines, I cannot do so, and having exerted all my ability, there seems something to stand right up before me; but though I wish to follow and lay hold of it, I really find no way to do so."

12. The Master being very ill, Zilu wished the disciples to act as ministers to him. During a remission of his illness, he said, "Long has the conduct of Zilu been wrong headed! By pretending to have ministers when I have them not, whom should I impress? Should I attempt to impress Heaven? Moreover, than that I should die in the hands of ministers, is it not better that I should die in the hands of you, my disciples? And though I may not deserve a great burial, I shall hardly be left to die at the side of the road."

13. Zigong said, "There is a beautiful jade here. Should I lay it up in a case and keep it? or should I seek for a good price and sell it?" The Master said, "Sell it! Sell it! But I would wait for one to offer the right price."

14. The Master was wishing to go and live among the nine wild tribes of the east. Someone said, "They are rude. How can you do such a thing?" The Master said, "If a superior man dwelt among them, what rudeness would there be?"

15. The Master said, "I returned from Wei to Lu, and only then was the music reformed, and the pieces in the Royal songs and Praise songs performed in their proper places."

16. The Master said, "Abroad, to serve the high ministers and nobles; at home, to serve one's father and elder brothers; in all duties to the dead, not to dare not to exert one's self; and not to be overcome of wine—none of these things are difficult for me."

17. The Master standing by a stream, said, "It passes on just like this, not ceasing day or night!"

18. The Master said, "I have not seen one who loves virtue as he loves a beauty."

19. The Master said, "The prosecution of learning may be compared to building a mound into a mountain. If there lacks but one basket of earth to complete the work, and I stop, the stopping is my own decision. It may be compared to throwing down the earth back to the level ground. Though but one basketful is thrown at a time, the advancing or retreating is one's own responsibility."

20. The Master said, "Never flagging when I set forth anything to him—ah! that is Hui."

21. The Master said of Yan Hui, "Alas! I saw his constant advance. I never saw him stop in his progress."

22. The Master said, "There are cases in which the blade springs, but the plant does not go on to flower! There are cases where it flowers but fruit is not subsequently produced!"

23. The Master said, "A youth is to be regarded with respect. How do we know that his future will not be equal to our present? If he reach the age of forty or fifty, and has not made himself heard of, then indeed he will not be worth being regarded with respect."

24. The Master said, "Can men refuse to assent to the words of strict admonition? But it is reforming the conduct because of such words which is valuable. Can men refuse to be pleased with words of gentle advice? But it is implementing their aim which is valuable. If a man be pleased with these words, but does not implement their aim, and assents admonition, but does not reform his conduct, I can really do nothing with him."

25. The Master said, "Hold faithfulness and sincerity as first principles. Have no close friends not equal to yourself. When you have faults, do not fear to abandon them."

26. The Master said, "The commander of the forces of a large state may be carried off, but the will of even a common man cannot be taken from him."

27. The Master said, "Dressed himself in a tattered robe quilted with hemp, yet standing by the side of men dressed in furs, and not ashamed—ah! it is Zilu who is equal to this!

> "He dislikes none, he covets nothing;
> What can he do but what is good!"

Zilu kept continually repeating these words of the ode until the Master said, "Those things are not sufficient to constitute perfect excellence."

28. The Master said,

> "When the year becomes cold,
> then we know the pine and the cypress
> are the last to lose their leaves."

29. The Master said,

> "The wise are free from perplexities;
> the virtuous from anxiety;
> and the bold from fear."

30. The Master said, "There are some with whom we may study in common, but we shall find them unable to go along with us to principles. Perhaps we may go on with them to principles, but we shall find them unable to get established in those along with us. Or if we may get so established along with them, we shall find them unable to weigh occurring events along with us."

> How the flowers of the aspen-plum flutter and turn!
> Do I not think of you? But your house is so distant.

31. The Master said, "It is failing to think about the one in the ode that makes her distant."

chapter 10

Here we have a description of ritualized perfection, presented as a portrait of Confucius himself, concluding the first half of the Analects, *the chapters traditionally called Upper Text.*

1. Confucius, in his village, looked simple and sincere, and as if he were not able to speak. When he was in the prince's ancestral temple, or in the court, he spoke minutely on every point, but cautiously.
2. When he was waiting at court, in speaking with the great officers of the lower grade, he spoke freely, but in a straightforward manner; in speaking with those of the higher grade, he did so blandly, but precisely. When the ruler was present, his manner displayed respectful uneasiness; it was grave, but self-possessed.
3. When the prince called him to employ him in the reception of a visitor, his countenance appeared to change, and his legs to move forward with difficulty. He inclined himself to the other officers among whom he stood, moving his left or right arm, as their position required, but keeping the skirts of his robe before and behind evenly adjusted. He hastened forward, with his arms like the wings of a bird. When the guest had retired, he would report to the prince, "The visitor is no longer circulating."

4. When he entered the palace gate, he seemed to bend his body, as if it were not sufficient to admit him. When he was standing, he did not occupy the middle of the gateway; when he passed in or out, he did not tread upon the threshold. When he was passing the vacant place of the prince, his countenance appeared to change, and his legs to bend under him, and his words came as if he hardly had breath to utter them. He ascended the reception hall, holding up his robe with both his hands, and his body bent; holding in his breath also, as if he dared not breathe. When he came out from the audience, as soon as he had descended one step, he began to relax his countenance, and had a satisfied look. When he had got the bottom of the steps, he advanced rapidly to his place, with his arms like wings, and on occupying it, his manner still showed respectful uneasiness.

5. When he was carrying the scepter of his ruler, he seemed to bend his body, as if he were not able to bear its weight. He did not hold it higher than the position of the hands in making a bow, nor lower than their position in giving anything to another. His countenance seemed to change, and look apprehensive, and he dragged his feet along as if they were held by something to the ground. In presenting the presents with which he was charged, he wore a placid appearance. At his private audience, he looked highly pleased.

6. The superior man did not use a deep purple, or a puce color, in the ornaments of his dress. Even in his undress, he did not wear anything of a red or reddish color. In warm weather, he had a single garment either of coarse or fine texture, but he wore it displayed over an inner garment. Over lamb's fur he wore a garment of black; over fawn's fur one of white; and over fox's fur one of yellow. The fur robe of his undress was long, with the right sleeve short. He required his sleeping dress to be half as long again as his body. When staying at home, he used thick furs of the fox or the badger. When he put off mourning, he wore all the appendages of the girdle. His undergarment, except when it was required to be of the curtain shape, was made of silk cut narrow above and wide below. He did not wear lamb's fur or a black cap on a visit of condolence. On the first day of the month he put on his court robes, and presented himself at court.

7. When fasting, he thought it necessary to have his clothes brightly clean and made of linen cloth. When not fasting, he thought it necessary to change his food, and also to change the place where he commonly sat in the apartment.

8. He did not dislike to have his rice finely cleaned, nor to have his mincemeat cut quite small. He did not eat rice which had been injured by heat or damp and turned sour, nor fish or flesh which was gone. He did not eat what was discolored, or what was of a bad flavor, nor anything which was ill-cooked, or was not in season. He did not eat meat which was not cut properly, nor what was served without its proper sauce. Though there might be a large quantity of meat, he would not allow what he took to exceed the due proportion for the rice. It was only in wine that he laid down no limit for himself, but he did not allow himself to be confused by it. He did not partake of wine and dried meat bought in the market. He was never without ginger when he ate. He did not eat much.

9. When he had been assisting at the prince's sacrifice, he did not keep the flesh which he received overnight. The flesh of his family sacrifice he did not keep over three days. If kept over three days, people could not eat it.

10. When eating, he did not converse. When in bed, he did not speak.

11. Although his food might be coarse rice and vegetable soup, he would offer a little of it in sacrifice with a grave, respectful air.

12. If his mat was not straight, he did not sit on it.

13. When the villagers were drinking together, upon those who carried staffs going out, he also went out immediately after.

14. When the villagers were going through their ceremonies to drive away pestilential influences, he put on his court robes and stood on the eastern steps.

15. When he was sending complimentary inquiries to any one in another state, he bowed twice as he escorted the messenger away.

16. Ji Kangzi sent him a present of medicinal herbs, he bowed and received it, saying, "I do not know it. I dare not taste it."

17. The stable being burned down, when he was at court, on his return he said, "Has any man been hurt?" He did not ask about the horses.

18. When the prince sent a gift of food he would adjust his mat, first taste it, and then give it away to others. When the prince sent him a gift of undressed meat, he would have it cooked, and offer it to the spirits of his ancestors. When the prince sent him a gift of a living animal, he would keep it alive. When he was in attendance on the prince and joining in the entertainment, the prince only sacrificed. He first tasted everything.

19. When he was ill and the prince came to visit him, he had his head to the east, made his court robes be spread over him, and drew his girdle across them.

20. When the prince's order called him, without waiting for his carriage to be yoked, he went at once.

21. When he entered the ancestral temple of the state, he asked about everything.

22. When any of his friends died, if he had no relations offices, he would say, "I will bury him."

23. When a friend sent him a present, though it might be a carriage and horses, he did not bow. The only present for which he bowed was that of the flesh of sacrifice.

24. In bed, he did not lie like a corpse. At home, he did not put on any formal deportment.

25. When he saw any one in a mourning dress, though it might be an acquaintance, he would change countenance; when he saw any one wearing the cap of full ceremonial dress, or a blind person, though he might be in his undress, he would salute him in a ceremonious manner.

26. To any person in mourning he bowed forward to the crossbar of his carriage; he bowed in the same way to any one bearing the tables of population. When he was at an entertainment where there was an abundance of provisions set before him, he would change countenance and rise up. On a sudden clap of thunder, or a violent wind, he would change countenance.

27. When he was about to mount his carriage, he would stand straight, holding the cord. When he was in the carriage, he did not turn his head quite round, he did not talk hastily, he did not point with his hands.

28. Startled by their arrival a bird instantly rises. It flies round, and by and by settles. The Master said, "There is the hen-pheasant on the hill bridge. Everything in its season! Everything in its season!" Zilu made a motion to it. Thrice it squawked and then rose.

chapter 11

Chapter 11 consists of comments about the disciples, evaluating their characters regarding virtue and self-cultivation.

1. The Master said, "The men of former times in the matters of ceremonies and music were rustics, it is said, while the men of these latter times, in ceremonies and music, are accomplished gentlemen. If I have occasion to use those things, I follow the men of former times."

2. The Master said, "Of those who came with me to Chen and Cai, there are none to be found to hold positions with me."

3. Distinguished for their virtuous principles and practice, there were Yan Hui, Min Ziquan, Boniu, and Zhonggong; for their ability in speech, Zai Wo and Zigong; for their administrative talents, Ran Qi and Jilu; for their literary acquirements, Ziyou and Zixia.

4. The Master said, "Yan Hui gives me no assistance, though there is nothing that I say in which he does not delight."

5. The Master said, "Filial indeed is Min Ziquan! Other people say nothing of him different from the praise of his parents and brothers."

6. Nan Rong frequently repeated the ode about a white scepter stone. Confucius gave him the daughter of his elder brother in marriage.

7. Jii Kangzi asked which of the disciples loved to learn. Confucius replied to him, "There was Yan Hui; he loved to learn. Unfortunately his appointed time was short, and he died. Now there is no one who loves to learn, as he did."

8. When Yan Hui died, Yen Lu begged for the carriage of the Master to get an outer shell for his son's coffin. The Master said, "Everyone calls his son his son, whether he has talents or has not talents. There was Li; when he died, he had a coffin but no outer shell. I would not walk on foot to get a shell for him, because, having followed in the rear of the great officers, it was not proper that I should walk on foot."

9. When Yan Hui died, the Master said, "Alas! Heaven is destroying me! Heaven is destroying me!"

10. When Yan Hui died, the Master bewailed him exceedingly, and the disciples who were with him said, "Master, your grief is excessive!"

"Is it excessive?" said he. "If I am not to mourn bitterly for this man, for whom should I mourn?"

11. When Yan Hui died, the disciples wished to give him a great funeral, and the Master said, "You may not do so." But the disciples did bury him in great style. The Master said, "Hui behaved towards me as his father. I have not been able to treat him as my son. The fault is not mine; it belongs to you, O disciples."

12. Zilu asked about serving the spirits of the dead. The Master said, "While you are not able to serve men, how can you serve their spirits?" Zilu added, "I venture to ask about death?" He was answered, "While you do not know life, how can you know about death?"

13. The disciple Min was standing by his side, looking bland and precise; Zilu, looking bold and soldierly; Ran Qi and Zigong, with a free and straightforward manner. The Master was pleased, but he said, "Zilu there!—he will not die a natural death."

14. Some parties in Lu were going to take down and rebuild the Long Treasury. Min Ziquan said, "Suppose it were to be repaired after its old style—why must it be altered and made anew?" The Master said, "This man seldom speaks; when he does, he is sure to hit the point."

15. The Master said, "What is the lute of Zilu doing in my office?" The other disciples then began not to respect Zilu. The Master said, "Zilu has ascended to the hall, though he has not yet passed into the inner apartments."

16. Zigong asked which of the two, Zizhang or Zixia, was the superior. The Master said, "Zizhang goes beyond the due mean, and Zixia does not come up to it." "Then," said Zigong, "the superiority is with Zizhang, I suppose." The Master said, "To go beyond is as wrong as to fall short."

17. The head of the Ji family was richer than the duke of Zhou had been, and yet Ran Qiu collected his imposts for him, and increased his wealth. The Master said, "He is no disciple of mine. My little children, beat the drum and assail him."

18. Zigao is simple. Zeng is dull. Zizhang is specious. Zilu is coarse.

19. The Master said, "There is Hui! He has nearly attained to perfect virtue, yet he is often in want. Zigong does not acquiesce in the appointments of Heaven, and his goods are increased by him. Yet his judgments are often correct."

20. Zizhang asked what were the characteristics of the good man. The Master said, "He does not tread in the footsteps of others, but moreover, he does not enter the chamber of the sage."

21. The Master said, "If, because a man's discourse appears solid and sincere, we allow him to be considered a good man, is he really a superior man? or is his gravity only in appearance?"

22. Zilu asked whether he should immediately carry into practice what he heard. The Master said, "There are your father and elder brothers to be consulted—why should you act on that principle of immediately carrying into practice what you hear?" Ran Qiu asked the same, whether he should immediately carry into practice what he heard, and the Master answered, "Immediately carry into

practice what you hear." So then Zihua said, "Yu asked whether he should carry immediately into practice what he heard, and you said, 'There are your father and elder brothers to be consulted.' Ran Qiu asked whether he should immediately carry into practice what he heard, and you said, 'Carry it immediately into practice.' I am perplexed, and venture to ask you for an explanation." The Master said, "Ran Qiu is retiring and slow; therefore I urged him forward. Zilu has more than his own share of energy; therefore I held him back."

23. The Master was put in fear in Kuang and Yan Hui fell behind. The Master, on his rejoining him, said, "I thought you had been killed." Hui replied, "While you were alive, how should I be allowed to die?"

24. Ji Ziran asked whether Zilu and Ran Qiu could be called great ministers. The Master said, "I thought you would ask about some extraordinary individuals, and you only ask about Zilu and Ran Qiu!

   "What is called a great minister, is one who serves his prince according to what is right, and when he finds he cannot do so, retires. Now, as to Zilu and Ran Qiu, they may be called ordinary ministers." Ji Ziran said, "Then they will always follow their chief, will they?" The Master said, "In an act of parricide or regicide, they would not follow him."

25. Zilu got Zigao appointed governor of Bi. The Master said, "You are injuring a man's son." Zilu said, "In that state there are common people and officers; there are the altars of the spirits of the land and grain. Why must one read books before he can be considered to have learned?" The Master said, "It is on this account that I hate glib-tongued people."

26. Zilu, Zengxi, Ran Qiu, and Zihua were sitting by the Master. He said to them, "Though I am a day or so older than you, do not think of that. From day to day you are saying, 'We are not getting appointments because we are not known.' If some ruler were to know you, what would you like to do?" Zilu hastily and lightly replied, "Suppose the case of a state of ten thousand chariots; even let it be hemmed in between other large cities; let it be suffering from invading armies; and to this let there be added a famine in corn and in all vegetables—if I were entrusted with the government of it, in three years' time I could make the people bold, and have them recognize the rules of righteous conduct." The Master smiled at him.

   Turning to Ran Qiu, he said, "Ran Qiu, what are your wishes?" Ran Qiu replied, "Suppose a state of sixty or seventy li square, or one of fifty or sixty, and let me have the government of it—in three years' time, I could make plenty to abound among the people. As to teaching them the principles of propriety, and music, I must wait for the rise of a superior man to do that."

   "What are your wishes, Zihua," said the Master. Zihua replied, "I do not say that my ability extends to these things, but I should wish to learn them. At the services of the ancestral temple, and at the audiences of the princes with the sovereign, I should like, dressed in the dark square-made robe and the black linen cap, to act as a small assistant."

Last of all, the Master asked Zengxi, "Zengxi, what are your wishes?" Zengxi, pausing as he was playing on his lute, while it was yet twanging, laid the instrument aside, and "My wishes," he said, "are different from the cherished purposes of these three gentlemen." "What harm is there in that?" asked the Master; "Can you also, as well as they, speak out your wishes." Zengxi then said, "In this, the last month of spring, with the dress of the season all complete, along with five or six young men who have assumed the cap, and six or seven boys, I would bathe so that I might enjoy the breeze among the rain altars, and return home singing." The Master heaved a sigh and said, "I give my approval to Zengxi."

The three others having gone out, Zeng remained behind, and said, "What do you think of the words of these three friends?" The Master replied, "They simply told each one his wishes." He pursued, "Master, why did you smile at Zilu?" He was answered, "The management of a state demands the rules of propriety. His words were not humble; therefore I smiled at him." Again pressing, "But was it not actually a state which Ran Qiu proposed for himself?" The reply was, "Yes; did you ever see a territory of sixty or seventy li or one of fifty or sixty, which was not a state?" Once more, the disciple inquired, "And was it not a state which Zihua proposed for himself?" The Master again replied, "Yes; who but princes have to do with ancestral temples, and with audiences but the sovereign? If Zihua were to be a small assistant in these services, who could be a great one?"

chapter 12

Legge himself, in his introduction to the translation of the monumental Sacred Books of the East series, describes this chapter as "lessons on perfect virtue, government, and other questions of morality, addressed in conversation by Confucius chiefly to his disciples. The different answers, given to different questioners, show well how the sage suited his instruction to the characters and capacities of the parties with whom he had to do."

1. Yan Hui asked about perfect virtue. The Master said, "To subdue one's self and return to propriety, is perfect virtue. If a man can for one day subdue himself and return to propriety heaven will ascribe perfect virtue to him. Is the practice of perfect virtue from a man himself, or is it from others?" Yan Hui said, "I beg to ask the steps of that process." The Master replied, "Look not at what is contrary to propriety; listen not to what is contrary to propriety; speak not what is contrary to propriety; make no movement which is contrary to propriety." Yan Hui then said, "Though I am deficient in intelligence and vigor, I will make it my business to practice this lesson."

2. Zhonggong asked about perfect virtue. The Master said, "It is, when you go abroad, to behave to everyone as if you were receiving a great guest; to employ the people as if you were assisting at a great sacrifice; not to do to others as you would not wish done to yourself; to have no murmuring against you in the

country, and none in the family." Zhonggong said, "Though I am deficient in intelligence and vigor, I will make it my business to practice this lesson."

3. Sima Niu asked about perfect virtue. The Master said, "The man of perfect virtue is cautious and slow in his speech." "Cautious and slow in his speech," said Niu; "is this what is meant by perfect virtue?" The Master said, "When a man feels the difficulty of doing, can he be other than cautious and slow in speaking?"

4. Sima Niu asked about the superior man. The Master said, "The superior man has neither anxiety nor fear." "Being without anxiety or fear!" said Nui; "does this constitute what we call the superior man?" The Master said, "When internal examination discovers nothing wrong, what is there to be anxious about, what is there to fear?"

5. Sima Niu, full of anxiety, said, "Other men all have their brothers, I only have not." Zixia said to him, "There is the following saying which I have heard:

> "Death and life have their determined appointment;
> Riches and honors depend upon Heaven.

"Let the superior man never fail reverentially to order his own conduct, and let him be respectful to others and observant of propriety—then all within the four seas will be his brothers. What has the superior man to do with being distressed because he has no brothers?"

6. Zizhang asked what constituted intelligence. The Master said, "He with whom neither slander that gradually soaks into the mind, nor statements that startle like a wound in the flesh, are successful may be called intelligent indeed. Yea, he with whom neither soaking slander, nor startling statements, are successful, may be called farsighted."

7. Zigong asked about government. The Master said, "The requisites of government are that there be sufficiency of food, sufficiency of military equipment, and the confidence of the people in their ruler."

Zigong asked, "If it cannot be helped, and one of these must be dispensed with, which of the three should be foregone first?" "The military equipment," said the Master. Zigong again asked, "If it cannot be helped, and one of the remaining two must be dispensed with, which of them should be foregone?" The Master answered, "Part with the food. From of old, death has been the lot of individuals; but if the people have no faith in their rulers, there is no standing for the state."

8. Ji Zicheng said, "In a superior man it is only the substantial qualities which are wanted—why should we seek for ornamental accomplishments?" Zigong said, "Alas! Your words, sir, show you to be a superior man, but four horses cannot overtake the tongue. Ornament is as substance; substance is as ornament. The hide of a tiger or a leopard stripped of its hair, is like the hide of a dog or a goat stripped of its hair."

9. The Duke Ai inquired of You, saying, "The year is one of scarcity, and the returns for expenditure are not sufficient—what is to be done?" You replied to him, "Why not simply tithe the people?" "With two tenths," said the duke, "I find it not

enough—how could I do with that system of just one tenth?" You answered, "If the people have plenty, their prince will not be left to want alone. If the people are in want, their prince cannot enjoy plenty alone."

10. Tizhang having asked how virtue was to be exalted, and delusions to be discovered, the Master said, "Hold faithfulness and sincerity as first principles, and be moving continually to what is right—this is the way to exalt one's virtue. You love a man and wish him to live; you hate him and wish him to die. Having wished him to live, you also wish him to die. This is a case of delusion.

> "It may not be on account of her being rich,
>   yet you come to make a difference."

11. Duke Jing of Qi, asked Confucius about government. Confucius replied, "There is government when the prince is prince, and the minister is minister; when the father is father, and the son is son." "Good!" said the duke; "but if, indeed, the prince be not prince, the minister not minister, the father not father, and the son not son, even though I have my revenue, can I enjoy it?"

12. The Master said, "Ah! it is Zilu, who could with half a word settle litigations! Zilu never slept over a promise but did it at once."

13. The Master said, "In hearing litigations, I am like any other body. What is necessary, however, is to cause the people to have no litigations."

14. Zizhang asked about government. The Master said, "The art of governing is to keep its affairs before the mind without weariness, and to practice them with undeviating consistency."

15. The Master said, "By extensively studying all learning, and keeping himself under the restraint of the rules of propriety, one may thus likewise not err from what is right."

16. The Master said, "The superior man seeks to perfect the admirable qualities of men, and does not seek to perfect their bad qualities. The mean man does the opposite of this."

17. Ji Kangzi asked Confucius about government. Confucius replied, "To govern means to rectify. If you lead on the people with correctness, who will dare not to be correct?"

18. Ji Kangzi, distressed about the number of thieves in the state, inquired of Confucius how to do away with them. Confucius said, "If you, sir, were not covetous, although you should reward them to do it, they would not steal."

19. Ji Kangzi asked Confucius about government, saying, "What do you say to killing the unprincipled for the good of the principled?" Confucius replied, "Sir, in carrying on your government, why should you use killing at all? Let your evinced desires be for what is good, and the people will be good. The relation between superiors and inferiors is like that between the wind and the grass. The grass must bend, when the wind blows across it."

20. Zizhang asked, "What must the officer be, who may be said to be distinguished?" The Master said, "What is it you call being distinguished?" Zizhang replied, "It is

to be heard of through the state, to be heard of throughout his clan." The Master said, "That is notoriety, not distinction. Now the man of distinction is solid and straightforward, and loves righteousness. He examines people's words, and looks at their countenances. He is anxious to humble himself to others. Such a man will be distinguished in the country; he will be distinguished in his clan. As to the man of notoriety, he assumes the appearance of virtue, but his actions are opposed to it, and he rests in this character without any doubts about himself. Such a man will be heard of in the country; he will be heard of in the clan."

21. Fan Chi, rambling with the Master under the trees about the rain altars, said, "I venture to ask how to exalt virtue, to correct cherished evil, and to discover delusions." The Master said, "Truly a good question! If doing what is to be done be made the first business, and success a secondary consideration—is not this the way to exalt virtue? To assail one's own wickedness and not assail that of others;—is not this the way to correct cherished evil? For a morning's anger to disregard one's own life, and involve that of his parents—is not this a case of delusion?"

22. Fan Chi asked about benevolence. The Master said, "It is to love all men." He asked about knowledge. The Master said, "It is to know all men." Fan Chi did not immediately understand these answers. The Master said, "Employ the upright and put aside all the crooked; in this way the crooked can be made to be upright." Fan Chi retired, and, seeing Zixia, he said to him, "A Little while ago, I had an interview with our Master, and asked him about knowledge. He said, 'Employ the upright, and put aside all the crooked—in this way, the crooked will be made to be upright.' What did he mean?" Zixia said, "Truly rich is his saying! When Shun was in possession of the kingdom he selected from among all the people, and employed Yi Yin which caused all who were devoid of virtue to disappear."

23. Zigong asked about friendship. The Master said, "Faithfully admonish your friend, and skillfully lead him on. If you find him impracticable, stop. Do not disgrace yourself."

24. The philosopher Zeng said, "The superior man meets with his friends on grounds of culture, and by such friendships builds up his virtue."

chapter 13

General issues of governance, emphasizing the power of suasion almost to the extent of non-violent action (reintroduced to the world by Mohandas Gandhi), except that in the Analects *this approach is recommended from the top down for enlightened rulers.*

1. Zilu asked about government. The Master said, "Go before the people with your example, and be laborious in their affairs." He requested further instruction, and was answered, "Be not weary in these things."

2. Zhonggong, being chief minister to the head of the Ji family, asked about government. The Master said, "Employ first the services of your various officers, pardon small faults, and raise to office men of virtue and talents." Zhonggong asked, "How shall I know the men of virtue and talent, so that I may raise them to office?" He was answered, "Raise to office those whom you know. As to those whom you do not know, will others neglect to tell you of them?"

3. Zilu said, "The ruler of Wei has been waiting for you, in order for you to administer the government. What will you consider the first thing to be done?" The Master replied, "What is necessary is to rectify titles." "So! indeed!" said Zilu. "You are wide of the mark! Why must there be such rectification?" The Master said, "How uncultivated you are, Zilu! A superior man like you, in regard to what he does not know, should show a cautious reserve. If titles be not correct, language is not in accordance with the truth of things. If language be not in accordance with the truth of things, affairs cannot be carried on to success. When affairs cannot be carried on to success, proprieties and music do not flourish. When proprieties and music do not flourish, punishments will not be properly awarded. When punishments are not properly awarded, the people do not know how to move hand or foot. Therefore a superior man considers it necessary that the names he uses may be spoken appropriately, and also that what he speaks may be carried out appropriately. What the superior man requires is just that in his words there may be nothing incorrect."

4. Fan Chi requested to be taught husbandry. The Master said, "I am not so good for that as an old husbandman." He requested also to be taught gardening, and was answered, "I am not so good for that as an old gardener." Fan Chi having gone out, the Master said, "A small man, indeed, is Fan Chi! If a superior man loves propriety, the people will not dare not to be reverent. If he loves righteousness, the people will not dare not to ignore his example. If he loves good faith, the people will not dare to be insincere. Now, when these things obtain, the people from all quarters will come to him, bearing their children on their backs; what need has he of a knowledge of husbandry?"

5. The Master said, "Though a man may be able to recite the three hundred odes, yet if, when entrusted with a governmental charge, he knows not how to act, or if, when sent to any quarter on a mission, he cannot give his replies unassisted, notwithstanding the extent of his learning, of what practical use is it?"

6. The Master said, "When a prince's personal conduct is correct, his government is effective without the issuing of orders. If his personal conduct is not correct, he may issue orders, but they will not be followed."

7. The Master said, "The governments of Lu and Wei are like brothers."

8. The Master said of Jing, a scion of the ducal family of Wei, that he knew the economy of a family well. When he began to have means, he said, "Ha! here is a collection—!" When they were a little increased, he said, "Ha! this is complete!" When he had become rich, he said, "Ha! this is admirable!"

9. When the Master went to Wei, Ran Qiu acted as driver of his carriage. The Master observed, "How numerous are the people!" Ran Qiu said, "Since they are thus numerous, what more shall be done for them?" "Enrich them," was the reply. "And when they have been enriched, what more shall be done?" The Master said, "Teach them."

10. The Master said, "If there were any of the princes who would employ me, in the course of twelve months, I should have done something considerable. In three years, the government would be perfected."

11. The Master said, "'If good men were to govern a country in succession for a hundred years, they would be able to transform the violently bad, and dispense with capital punishments.' True indeed is this saying!"

12. The Master said, "If a truly royal ruler were to arise, it would stir the people and then virtue would prevail within a generation."

13. The Master said, "If a minister make his own conduct correct, what difficulty will he have in assisting in government? If he cannot rectify himself, what has he to do with rectifying others?"

14. The disciple Zan returning from the court, the Master said to him, "How are you so late?" He replied, "We had government business." The Master said, "It must have been family affairs. If there had been government business, though I am not now in office, I should have been consulted about it."

15. Duke Ting asked whether there was a single sentence which could make a country prosperous. Confucius replied, "Such an effect cannot be expected from one sentence. There is a saying, however, which people have—'To be a prince is difficult; to be a minister is not easy.' If a ruler knows this—the difficulty of being a prince—may there not be expected from this one sentence the prosperity of his country?" The duke then said, "Is there a single sentence which can ruin a country?" Confucius replied, "Such an effect as that cannot be expected from one sentence. There is, however, the saying which people have—'I have no pleasure in being a prince, but only in that no one can offer any opposition to what I say!' If a ruler's words be good, is it not also good that no one oppose them? But if they are not good, and no one opposes them, may there not be expected from this one sentence the ruin of his country?"

16. The Duke of She asked about government. The Master said, "Good government obtains when those who are near are made happy, and those who are far off are attracted."

17. Zixia, being governor of Jifu, asked about government. The Master said, "Do not be desirous to have things done quickly; do not look at small advantages. Desire to have things done quickly prevents their being done thoroughly. Looking at small advantages prevents great affairs from being accomplished."

18. The Duke of She informed Confucius, saying, "Among us here there are those who may be styled upright in their conduct. If their father has stolen a sheep, they will bear witness to the fact." Confucius said, "Among us, in our part of the country, those who are upright are different from this. The father conceals

the misconduct of the son, and the son conceals the misconduct of the father. Uprightness is also to be found in this."

19. Fan Chi asked about perfect virtue. The Master said, "It is, in retirement, to be sedately grave; in the management of business, to be reverently attentive; in intercourse with others, to be strictly sincere. Though a man go among rude, uncultivated tribes, these qualities may not be neglected."

20. Zigong asked, saying, "What qualities must a man possess to entitle him to be called an officer?" The Master said, "He who in his conduct of himself maintains a sense of shame, and when sent to any quarter will not disgrace his prince's commission, deserves to be called an officer." Zigong pursued, "I venture to ask who may be placed in the next lower rank?" And he was told, "He whom the circle of his relatives pronounce to be filial, whom his fellow villagers and neighbors pronounce to be fraternal." Again the disciple asked, "I venture to ask about the class still next in order." The Master said, "They are determined to be sincere in what they say, and to carry out what they do. They are obstinate little men. Yet perhaps they may make the next class." Zigong finally inquired, "Of what sort are those of the present day, who engage in government?" The Master said "Pooh! they are only so many pecks and hampers, not worth being taken into account."

21. The Master said, "Since I cannot get men pursuing the due medium, to whom I might communicate my instructions, I must find the ardent and the cautiously decided. The ardent will advance and lay hold of truth; the cautiously decided will keep themselves from what is wrong."

22. The Master said, "The people of the south have a saying—'A man without constancy cannot be either a wizard or a doctor.' Good! Inconstant in his virtue, he will be visited with disgrace." The Master said, "This arises simply from not attending to the prognostication."

23. The Master said, "The superior man is affable, but not adulatory; the mean man is adulatory, but not affable."

24. Zigong asked, saying, "What do you say of a man who is loved by all the people of his neighborhood?" The Master replied, "We may not accord our approval of him merely because of that." "And what do you say of him who is hated by all the people of his neighborhood?" The Master said, "We may not for that reason conclude that he is bad. It is better than either of these cases that the good in the neighborhood love him, and the bad hate him."

25. The Master said, "The superior man is easy to serve and difficult to please. If you try to please him in any way which is not accordant with right, he will not be pleased. But in his employment of men, he uses them according to their capacity. The mean man is difficult to serve, and easy to please. If you try to please him, though it be in a way which is not accordant with right, he may be pleased. But in his employment of men, he wishes them to be equal to everything."

26. The Master said, "The superior man has a dignified ease without pride. The mean man has pride without a dignified ease."

27. The Master said, "The firm, the enduring, the simple, and the modest are near to virtue."

28. Zilu asked, saying, "What qualities must a man possess to entitle him to be called a scholar?" The Master said, "He must be thus—earnest, urgent, and bland—among his friends, earnest and urgent; among his brethren, bland."

29. The Master said, "Let a good man teach the people seven years, and they may then likewise be employed in war."

30. The Master said, "To lead an uninstructed people to war, is to throw them away."

chapter 14

Chapter 14 includes themes of reclusion, not withdrawal from the world, but holding back something in reserve and, for rulers and leaders in particular, maintaining some distance from their subjects or those they would serve and expect service from in return.

1. Yuan Si asked what was shameful. The Master said, "When good government prevails in a state, to be thinking only of salary; and, when bad government prevails, to be thinking, in the same way, only of salary—this is shameful. When the love of superiority, boasting, resentments, and covetousness are repressed, this may be deemed perfect virtue." The Master said, "This may be regarded as the achievement of what is difficult. But I do not know that it is to be deemed perfect virtue."

2. The Master said, "The scholar who cherishes the love of comfort is not fit to be deemed a scholar."

3. The Master said, "When good government prevails in a state, language may be lofty and bold, and actions the same. When bad government prevails, the actions may be lofty and bold, but the language may be with some reserve."

4. The Master said, "The virtuous will be sure to speak correctly, but those whose speech is good may not always be virtuous. Men of principle are sure to be bold, but those who are bold may not always be men of principle."

5. Nangung Kuo, submitting an inquiry to Confucius, said, "Yi was skillful at archery, and Ao could move a boat along upon the land, but neither of them died a natural death. Yu and Ho Ji personally wrought at the toils of husbandry, and they became possessors of the kingdom." The Master made no reply; but when Nangung Kuo went out, he said, "A superior man indeed is this! An esteemer of virtue indeed is this!"

6. The Master said, "Superior men, and yet not always virtuous, there have been, alas! But there never has been a mean man, and, at the same time, virtuous."

7. The Master said, "Can there be love which does not lead to strictness with its object? Can there be loyalty which does not lead to the instruction of its object?"

8. The Master said, "In preparing the governmental notifications, Bi Chen first made the rough draft; Shi Shu examined and discussed its contents; Ziyu, the

manager of foreign intercourse, then polished the style; and, finally, Zichan of the East Precinct gave it the proper elegance and finish."

9. Someone asked about Tichan. The Master said, "He was a kind man." He also asked about Zixi. The Master said, "That man! That man!" He asked about Guan Zhong. "For him," said the Master, "the city of Ping, with three hundred families, was taken from the chief of the Bo family, who did not utter a murmuring word, though, to the end of his life, he had only coarse rice to eat."

10. The Master said, "To be poor without murmuring is difficult. To be rich without being proud should be easy."

11. The Master said, "Meng Gongchuo is more than fit to be chief officer for the chief families of Zhao and Wei, but he is not fit to be great officer to either of the states Teng or Xue."

12. Zilu asked what constituted a complete man. The Master said, "Suppose a man with the knowledge of Zang Wuzhong, the freedom from covetousness of Gongchuo, the bravery of Zhuangzi of Bian, and the varied talents of Ran Qiu; add to these the accomplishments of the rules of propriety and music—such a one might be reckoned a complete man." He then added, "But what is the necessity for a complete man of the present day to have all these things? The man, who in the view of gain, thinks of righteousness; who in the view of danger is prepared to give up his life; and who does not forget an old agreement however far back it extends—such a man may be reckoned a complete man."

13. The Master asked Gongming about Gongshu Wenzi, saying, "Is it true that your master speaks not, laughs not, and takes not?"

    Gongming replied, "This has arisen from the reporters going beyond the truth.—My master speaks when it is the time to speak, and so men do not get tired of his speaking. He laughs when there is occasion to be joyful, and so men do not get tired of his laughing. He takes when it is consistent with righteousness to do so, and so men do not get tired of his taking." The Master said, "So! But is it really so with him?"

14. The Master said, "Zang Wuzhong, keeping possession of Fang, asked of the Duke of Lu to appoint a successor to him in his family. Although it may be said that he was not using force with his sovereign, I believe he was."

15. The Master said, "The Duke Wen of Jin was crafty and not upright. The Duke Huan of Qi was upright and not crafty."

16. Zilu said, "The Duke Huan caused his brother Jiu to be killed, when his servant Shao Hu died with his master, but servant Guan Zhong did not die. May not I say that he was wanting in virtue?" The Master said, "The Duke Huan assembled all the princes together, and that not with weapons of war and chariots—this was all through the influence of Guan Zhong. Whose beneficence was like his? Whose beneficence was like his?"

17. Zigong said, "Guan Zhong, I believe really was wanting in virtue. When the Duke Huan caused his brother Jiu to be killed, Guan Zhong was not able to die with him. Moreover, he became prime minister to Huan." The Master said, "Guan

Zhong acted as prime minister to the Duke Huan, who made him leader of all the princes, and united and rectified the whole kingdom. Down to the present day, the people enjoy the gifts which he conferred. But for Guan Zhong, we should now be wearing our hair unbound, and the lappets of our coats buttoning on the left side. Will you require him to emulate the small fidelity of common men and common women, who would commit suicide in a stream or ditch, no one knowing anything about them?"

18. The great officer, Zhuan, who had been family minister to Gongshu Wenzi, ascended to the prince's court in company with Wenzi. The Master, having heard of it, said, "He deserved to be considered accomplished."

19. The Master was speaking about the unprincipled course of Duke Ling of Wei when Ji Kangzi said, "Since he is of such a character, how is it he does not lose his state?" Confucius said, "The Kong Wenzi is the superintendence of his guests and of strangers; the liturgist, Tuo, has the management of his ancestral temple; and Wangsun Jia has the direction of the army and forces—with such officers as these, how should he lose his state?"

20. The Master said, "He who speaks without modesty will find it difficult to make his words good."

21. Chen Chengzi murdered the Duke Jian of Ji. Confucius bathed, went to court and informed the Duke Ai, saying, "Chen Heng has slain his sovereign. I beg that you will undertake to punish him." The duke said, "Inform the chiefs of the three families of it." Confucius retired, and said, "Following in the rear of the great officers, I did not dare not to represent such a matter, and my prince says, 'Inform the chiefs of the three families of it.'" He went to the Three, and informed them, but they would not act. Confucius then said, "Following in the rear of the great officers, I did not dare not to represent such a matter."

22. Zilu asked how a ruler should be served. The Master said, "Do not impose on him, and, moreover, withstand him to his face."

23. The Master said, "The progress of the superior man is upwards; the progress of the mean man is downwards."

24. The Master said, "In ancient times, men learned with a view to their own improvement. Nowadays, men learn with a view to the approbation of others."

25. Qu Boyu sent a messenger with friendly inquiries to Confucius. Confucius sat with him, and questioned him. "What," said he! "is your master engaged in?" The messenger replied, "My master is anxious to make his faults few, but he has not yet succeeded." He then went out, and the Master said, "A messenger indeed! A messenger indeed!"

26. The Master said, "He who is not in a particular office should have nothing to do with plans for the administration of its duties." The philosopher Zeng said, "The superior man, in his thoughts, does not go out of his place."

27. The Master said, "The superior man is modest in his speech, but exceeds in his actions."

28. The Master said, "The way of the superior man is threefold, but I am not equal to it. Virtuous, he is free from anxieties; wise, he is free from perplexities; bold, he is free from fear." Zigong said, "Master, that is what you yourself say."

29. Zigong was in the habit of comparing men together. The Master said, "To do this, Zigong must have reached a high pitch of excellence himself! Now, I have no time for this."

30. The Master said, "I will not be concerned at men's not knowing me; I will be concerned at my own want of ability."

31. The Master said, "He who does not anticipate attempts to deceive him, nor think beforehand of his not being believed, and yet apprehends these things readily when they occur—is he not a man of superior worth?"

32. Weisheng Mou said to Confucius, "Qiu, how is it that you keep roosting about? Is it not that you are a clever talker?" Confucius said, "I do not dare to play the part of such a talker, but I hate obstinacy."

33. The Master said, "A horse is called a champion, not because of its strength, but because of its other good qualities."

34. Someone said, "What do you say concerning the principle that injury should be recompensed with kindness?" The Master said, "With what then will you recompense kindness? Recompense injury with justice, and recompense kindness with kindness."

35. The Master said, "Alas! there is no one that knows me." Gongbo Liao said, "What do you mean by thus saying—that no one knows you?" The Master replied, "I do not murmur against Heaven. I do not grumble against men. My studies lie low, and my penetration rises high. But there is a Heaven that knows me!"

36. The Gongbo Liao, having slandered Zilu to Ji, Zifu Jingbo informed Confucius of it, saying, "Our master is certainly being led astray by the Gongbo Liao, but I have still power enough left to cut Liao off, and expose his corpse in the market and in the court." The Master said, "If my principles are to advance, it is so ordered. If they are to fall to the ground, it is so ordered. What can the Gongbo Liao do where such ordering is concerned?"

37. The Master said, "Some men of worth retire from the world. Some retire from particular states. Some retire because of disrespectful looks. Some retire because of contradictory language." The Master said, "Those who have done this are seven men."

38. Zilu happening to pass the night the Stone Gate, the gatekeeper said to him, "Whom do you come from?" Zilu said, "From Confucius." "It is he—is it not?"—said the other, "who knows the impracticable nature of the times and yet will be acting in them."

39. The Master was playing, one day, on musical chimes in Wei when a man carrying a straw basket passed door of the house where Confucius was, and said, "His heart is full who so beats the musical chimes." A little while after, he added, "How contemptible is the one-toned obstinacy those sounds display! In the same

way, when one is taken no notice of, he has simply at once to give up his wish for public employment. 'Deep water must be crossed with the clothes on; shallow water may be crossed with the clothes held up.'" The Master said, "How determined is he in his purpose! But this is not difficult!"

40. Zizhang said, "What is meant when the Book of Documents says that Gaozong, while observing the usual imperial mourning, went for three years without speaking?" The Master said, "Why must Gaozong be referred to as an example of this? The ancients all did so. When the sovereign died, the officers all attended to their several duties, taking instructions from the prime minister for three years."

41. The Master said, "When rulers love to observe the rules of propriety, the people respond readily to the calls on them for service."

42. Zilu asked what constituted the superior man. The Master said, "The cultivation of himself in reverential carefulness." "And is this all?" asked Zilu. "He cultivates himself so as to give rest to others," was the reply. "And is this all?" again asked Zilu. The Master said, "He cultivates himself so as to give rest to all the people. He cultivates himself so as to give rest to all the people:—even a Yao or a Shun would find this a challenge."

43. Yuan Rang was squatting on his heels, and so waited the approach of the Master, who said to him, "In youth not humble as befits a junior; in manhood, doing nothing worthy of being handed down; and living on to old age—this is to be a pest." With this he slapped him on the shank with his staff.

44. A youth of the village of Que was employed by Confucius to carry the messages between him and his visitors. Someone asked about him, saying, "I suppose he has made great progress in his own studies." The Master said, "I observe that he is fond of sitting with full-grown men; I observe that he walks shoulder to shoulder with his elders. He is not one who is seeking to make progress in learning. He simply wishes to succeed quickly."

chapter 15

Here we begin a collection of sayings of Confucius that may have originated in a different school at a slightly later date.

1. The Duke Ling of Wei asked Confucius about tactics. Confucius replied, "I have heard all about sacrificial vessels, but I have not learned military matters." On this, he took his departure the next day.

2. When he was besieged in Chan, their provisions were exhausted, and his followers became so ill that they were unable to rise. Zilu, with evident dissatisfaction, said, "Has the superior man likewise to endure in this way?" The Master said, "The superior man may indeed have to endure want, but the mean man, when he is in want, gives way to unbridled license."

3. The Master said, "Zigong, you think, I suppose, that I am one who learns many things and keeps them in memory?" Zigong replied, "Yes, but perhaps it is not so?" "No," was the answer; "I seek a unity all pervading, a single thread."

4. The Master said, "Zilu, those who know virtue are few."

5. The Master said, "May not Shun be an instance of having governed without exertion? What did he do? He did nothing but gravely and reverently occupy his royal seat."

6. Zizhang asked how a man should conduct himself, so as to be everywhere appreciated. The Master said, "Let his words be sincere and truthful and his actions honorable and careful—such conduct may be practiced among the rude tribes of the South or the North. If his words be not sincere and truthful and his actions not honorable and careful will one, with such conduct, be appreciated, even in his neighborhood? When one is standing, let him see those two things, as it were, fronting him. When he is in a carriage, let him see them attached to the yoke. Then may he subsequently carry them into practice." Zizhang wrote these counsels on the end of his sash.

7. The Master said, "Truly straightforward was the historian Yu. When good government prevailed in his state, he was like an arrow. When bad government prevailed, he was like an arrow. A superior man indeed is Qu Boyu! When good government prevails in his state, he is to be found in office. When bad government prevails, he can roll his principles up, and keep them in his breast."

8. The Master said, "When a man may be spoken with, not to speak to him is to err in reference to the man. When a man may not be spoken with, to speak to him is to err in reference to our words. The wise err neither in regard to their man nor to their words."

9. The Master said, "The determined scholar and the man of virtue will not seek to live at the expense of injuring their virtue. They will even sacrifice their lives to preserve their virtue complete."

10. Zigong asked about the practice of virtue. The Master said, "The mechanic, who wishes to do his work well, must first sharpen his tools. When you are living in any state, take service with the most worthy among its great officers, and make friends of the most virtuous among its scholars."

11. Yan Hui asked how the government of a country should be administered.
    The Master said,
    "Follow the seasons of Xia.
    "Ride in the state carriage of Yin.
    "Wear the ceremonial cap of Chau.
    "Let the music be the Shao with its pantomimes.
    "Banish the songs of Chang, and keep far from specious talkers. The songs of Chang are licentious; specious talkers are dangerous."

12. The Master said, "If a man take no thought about what is distant, he will find trouble near at hand."

13. The Master said, "It is all over! I have not seen one who loves virtue as he loves a beauty."

14. The Master said, "Was not Zang Wenzhong like one who had stolen his situation? He knew the virtue and the talents of Hui of Liu-hsia, and yet did not realize that he should stand with him in court."

15. The Master said, "He who requires much from himself and little from others, will keep himself from being the object of resentment."

16. The Master said, "When a man is not in the habit of saying 'What shall I think of this? What shall I think of this?' I can indeed do nothing with him!"

17. The Master said, "When a number of people are together, for a whole day, without their conversation turning on righteousness, and when they are fond of carrying out the suggestions of small cunning—theirs is indeed a hard case."

18. The Master said, "The superior man in everything considers righteousness to be essential. He performs it according to the rules of propriety. He brings it forth in humility. He completes it with sincerity. This is indeed a superior man."

19. The Master said, "The superior man is distressed by his want of ability. He is not distressed by men's not knowing him."

20. The Master said, "But the superior man dislikes the thought of his name not being mentioned after his death."

21. The Master said, "What the superior man seeks, is in himself. What the mean man seeks, is in others."

22. The Master said, "The superior man is dignified, but does not wrangle. He is sociable, but not a partisan."

23. The Master said, "The superior man does not promote a man simply on account of his words, nor does he put aside good words because of the man."

24. Zigong asked, saying, "Is there one word which may serve as a rule of practice for all one's life?" The Master said, "Is not understanding such a word? What you do not want done to yourself, do not do to others."

25. The Master said, "In my dealings with men, whose evil do I blame, whose goodness do I praise, beyond what is proper? If I do sometimes exceed in praise, there must be ground for it in my examination of the individual. This people supplied the basis for the three dynasties to pursue the path of straightforwardness."

26. The Master said, "Even in my early days, a historian would leave a blank in his text for another to fill in, and he who had a horse would lend him to another to ride. Now, alas! There are no such things."

27. The Master said, "Empty words confound virtue. Want of forbearance in small matters confounds great plans."

28. The Master said, "When the multitude hate a man, it is necessary to look into the case. When the multitude like a man, it is necessary to look into the case."

29. The Master said, "A man can enlarge the Way which he follows; the Way does not enlarge the man."

30. The Master said, "To have faults and not to reform them—this, indeed, should be pronounced having faults."

31. The Master said, "I have been the whole day without eating, and the whole night without sleeping—occupied with thinking. It was of no use. A better plan is to study."

32. The Master said, "The object of the superior man is truth. Food is not his object. There is plowing—even in that there is sometimes want. So with learning—emolument may be found in it. The superior man is anxious lest he should not get to the truth; he is not anxious lest poverty should come upon him."

33. The Master said, "When a man's knowledge is sufficient to attain, and his virtue is not sufficient to enable him to hold, whatever he may have gained, he will lose again. When his knowledge is sufficient to attain, and he has virtue enough to hold fast, if he cannot govern with dignity, the people will not respect him. When his knowledge is sufficient to attain, and he has virtue enough to hold fast; when he governs also with dignity, yet if he try to move the people contrary to the rules of propriety—full excellence is not reached."

34. The Master said, "The superior man cannot be known in little matters; but he may be entrusted with great concerns. The small man may not be entrusted with great concerns, but he may be known in little matters."

35. The Master said, "Virtue is more to man than either water or fire. I have seen men die from treading on water and fire, but I have never seen a man die from treading the course of virtue."

36. The Master said, "Let every man consider virtue as what devolves on himself. He may not yield the performance of it even to his teacher."

37. The Master said, "The superior man is correctly firm, and not firm merely."

38. The Master said, "A minister, in serving his prince, reverently discharges his duties, and makes his emolument a secondary consideration."

39. The Master said, "In teaching there should be no distinction of classes."

40. The Master said, "Those whose courses are different cannot lay plans for one another."

41. The Master said, "In language it is simply required that it convey the meaning."

42. The music master having called upon him, when they came to the steps, the Master said, "Here are the steps." When they came to the mat for the guest to sit upon, he said, "Here is the mat." When all were seated, the Master informed him, saying, "So and so is here; so and so is here." The music master having gone out, Tsze-chang asked, saying, "Is it the rule to tell those things to the music master?" The Master said, "Yes. This is certainly the rule for those who lead the blind."

chapter 16

From a different hand, awkward in style. From here on "The Master" is often known simply by his name, used only rarely until this point.

1. The head of the Ji family was going to attack Zhuanyu. Ran Qiu and Zilu had an interview with Confucius, and said, "Our chief, Ji is going to commence operations against Zhuanyu." Confucius said, "Ran Qiu, is it not you who are in fault here? Now, in regard to Zhuanyu, long ago, a former king appointed its ruler to preside over the sacrifices to the eastern Meng; moreover, it is in the midst of the territory of our state; and its ruler is a minister in direct connection with the sovereign: What has your chief to do with attacking it?" Ran Qiu said, "Our master wishes the thing; neither of us two ministers wishes it." Confucius said, "Ran Qiu, there are the words of Zhou Ren—'When he can put forth his ability, he takes his place in the ranks of office; when he finds himself unable to do so, he retires from it.' How can he be used as a guide to a blind man, who does not support him when tottering, nor raise him up when fallen? And further, you speak wrongly. When a tiger or rhinoceros escapes from his cage; when a tortoise or piece of jade is injured in its repository—whose is the fault?" Ran Qiu said, "But at present, Zhuanyu is strong and near to Bi; if our chief do not now take it, it will hereafter be a sorrow to the Ji descendants." Confucius said. "Ran Qiu, the superior man hates those declining to say—'I want such and such a thing,' and framing explanations for their conduct. I have heard that rulers of states and chiefs of families are not troubled lest their people should be few, but are troubled lest they should not keep their several places; that they are not troubled with fears of poverty, but are troubled with fears of a want of contented repose among the people in their several places. For when the people keep their several places, there will be no poverty; when harmony prevails, there will be no scarcity of people; and when there is such a contented repose, there will be no rebellious instabilities. So it is.—Therefore, if remoter people are not submissive, all the influences of civil culture and virtue are to be cultivated to attract them to be so; and when they have been so attracted, they must be made contented and tranquil. Now, here are you, Ran Qiu and Ziku, assisting your chief. Remoter people are not submissive, and, with your help, he cannot attract them to him. In his own territory there are divisions and downfalls, leavings and separations, and even with your help, he cannot preserve it. And yet he is planning these hostile movements within the state.—I am afraid that the sorrow of the Ji family will not be on account of Zhuanyu, but will be found within the screen of their own court."

2. Confucius said, "When good government prevails in the empire, ceremonies, music, and punitive military expeditions proceed from the son of Heaven. When bad government prevails in the empire, ceremonies, music, and punitive military expeditions proceed from the princes. When these things proceed from the princes, as a rule, the cases will be few in which they do not lose their power for ten generations. When they proceed from the great officers of the princes, as a rule, the case will be few in which they do not lose their power for five generations. When the subsidiary ministers of the great officers hold in their grasp the orders of the state, as a rule the cases will be few in which they do not lose their power in three generations. When right principles prevail in the kingdom, government

will not be in the hands of the great officers. When right principles prevail in the kingdom, there will be no discussions among the common people."

3. Confucius said, "The revenue of the state has left the ducal house now for five generations. The government has been in the hands of the great officers for four generations. On this account, the descendants of the three Huan are much reduced."

4. Confucius said, "There are three friendships which are advantageous, and three which are injurious. Friendship with the upright; friendship with the sincere; and friendship with the man of much observation—these are advantageous. Friendship with the man of specious airs; friendship with the ingratiatingly gentle; and friendship with the glib-tongued—these are injurious."

5. Confucius said, "There are three things men find enjoyment in which are advantageous, and three things they find enjoyment in which are injurious. To find enjoyment in the discriminating study of ceremonies and music; to find enjoyment in speaking of the goodness of others; to find enjoyment in having many worthy friends—these are advantageous. To find enjoyment in extravagant pleasures; to find enjoyment in idleness and sauntering; to find enjoyment in the pleasures of feasting—these are injurious."

6. Confucius said, "There are three errors to which they who stand in the presence of a man of virtue and station are liable. They may speak when it does not come to them to speak—this is called rashness. They may not speak when it comes to them to speak—this is called concealment. They may speak without looking at the countenance of their superior—this is called blindness."

7. Confucius said, "There are three things which the superior man guards against. In youth, when the physical powers are not yet settled, he guards against lust. When he is strong and the physical powers are full of vigor, he guards against quarrelsomeness. When he is old, and the animal powers are decayed, he guards against covetousness."

8. Confucius said, "There are three things of which the superior man stands in awe. He stands in awe of the ordinances of Heaven. He stands in awe of great men. He stands in awe of the words of sages. The mean man does not know the ordinances of Heaven, and consequently does not stand in awe of them. He is disrespectful to great men. He makes sport of the words of sages."

9. Confucius said, "Those who are born with the possession of knowledge are the highest class of men. Those who learn, and so readily get possession of knowledge, are the next. Those who are dull and stupid, and yet compass the learning, are another class next to these. As to those who are dull and stupid and yet do not learn—they are the lowest of the people."

10. Confucius said, "The superior man has nine things which are subjects with him of thoughtful consideration. In regard to the use of his eyes, he is anxious to see clearly. In regard to the use of his ears, he is anxious to hear distinctly. In regard to his countenance, he is anxious that it should be benign. In regard to his demeanor, he is anxious that it should be respectful. In regard to his speech, he is anxious

that it should be sincere. In regard to his doing of business, he is anxious that it should be reverently careful. In regard to what he doubts about, he is anxious to question others. When he is angry, he thinks of the difficulties his anger may involve him in. When he sees gain to be got, he thinks of righteousness."

11. Confucius said, "Contemplating good, and pursuing it, as if they could not reach it; contemplating evil! and shrinking from it, as they would from thrusting the hand into boiling water—I have seen such men, as I have heard such words. Living in retirement to study their aims, and practicing righteousness to carry out their principles—I have heard these words, but I have not seen such men."

12. Duke Jing of Qi had a thousand teams, each of four horses, but on the day of his death, the people did not praise him for a single virtue. Bo Yi and Shu Qi died of hunger at the foot of the Shouyang mountains, and the people, down to the present time, praise them. Is not that saying illustrated by this?

13. Ziqin asked Boyu, saying, "Have you heard any lessons from your father different from what we have all heard?" Boyu replied, "No. He was standing alone once, when I passed below the hall with hasty steps, and said to me, 'Have you learned the Odes?' On my replying 'Not yet,' he added, 'If you do not learn the Odes, you will not be fit to converse with.' I retired and studied the Odes. Another day, he was in the same way standing alone, when I passed by below the hall with hasty steps, and said to me, 'Have you learned the rules of Propriety?' On my replying 'Not yet,' he added, 'If you do not learn the rules of Propriety, your character cannot be established.' I then retired, and learned the rules of Propriety. I have heard only these two things from him." Ziqin retired, and, quite delighted, said, "I asked one thing, and I have got three things. I have heard about the Odes. I have heard about the rules of Propriety. I have also heard that the superior man maintains a distant reserve towards his son."

14. The wife of the prince of a certain state is called by him Lady. She calls herself Little Lad. The people of the state call her Lord's Lady, and the people of other states call her Lowly Little Lord, though the people of other states also call her Lord's Lady.

chapter 17

These passages reimagine the political issues of Confucius time from a later perspective, along with a concern for hypocrisy and the denegation of virtue in a world where Confucius was denied proper influence.

1. Yang Huo wished to see Confucius, but Confucius would not go to see him. On this, he sent a present of a pig to Confucius, who, having chosen a time when Huo was not at home went to pay his respects for the gift. He met him, however, on the way. Huo said to Confucius, "Come, let me speak with you." He then asked, "Can one be called benevolent who keeps his jewel in his bosom, and

leaves his country to confusion?" Confucius replied, "No." "Can one be called wise, who is anxious to be engaged in public employment, and yet is constantly losing the opportunity of being so?" Confucius again said, "No." "The days and months are passing away; the years do not wait for us." Confucius said, "Right; I will accept a position with you."

2. The Master said, "By nature, men are nearly alike; by practice, they get to be wide apart."

3. The Master said, "There are only the wise of the highest class, and the stupid of the lowest class, who cannot be changed."

4. The Master, having come to Wucheng, heard there the sound of stringed instruments and singing. Well pleased and smiling, he said, "But why use an ox knife to kill a fowl?" Ziyou replied, "Formerly, Master, I heard you say—'When the man of high station is well instructed, he loves men; when the man of low station is well instructed, he is easily ruled.'" The Master said, "My disciples, Ziyou's words are right. What I said was only in sport."

5. Gongshan Furao, when he was holding Bi, and in an attitude of rebellion, invited the Master to visit him, who was rather inclined to go. Zilu was displeased and said, "Indeed, you cannot go! Why must you think of going to see Gongshan?" The Master said, "Can it be without some reason that he has invited me? If anyone employ me, may I not make an eastern Zhou Dynasty?"

6. Zizhang asked Confucius about perfect virtue. Confucius said, "To be able to practice five things everywhere under heaven constitutes perfect virtue." He begged to ask what they were, and was told, "Gravity, generosity of soul, sincerity, earnestness, and kindness. If you are grave, you will not be treated with disrespect. If you are generous, you will win all. If you are sincere, people will repose trust in you. If you are earnest, you will accomplish much. If you are kind, this will enable you to employ the services of others."

7. Bi Xi inviting him to visit him, the Master was inclined to go. Zilu said, "Master, formerly I have heard you say, 'When a man in his own person is guilty of doing evil, a superior man will not associate with him.' Bi Xi is in rebellion, holding possession of Zhongmou; if you go to him, what shall be said?" The Master said, "Yes, I did use these words. But is it not said, that, if a thing be really hard, it may be ground without being made thin? Is it not said, that, if a thing be really white, it may be steeped in a dark fluid without being made black? Am I a bitter gourd? How can I be always hung up out of the way of being eaten?"

8. The Master said, "Zilu, have you heard the six words to which are attached six confusions?" Zilu replied, "I have not." "Sit down, and I will tell them to you. There is the love of being benevolent without the love of learning;—the confusion here leads to a foolish simplicity. There is the love of knowing without the love of learning—the confusion here leads to dissipation of mind. There is the love of being sincere without the love of learning—the confusion here leads to an injurious disregard of consequences. There is the love of straightforwardness without the love of learning—the confusion here leads to rudeness. There is the love of

boldness without the love of learning—the confusion here leads to insubordination. There is the love of firmness without the love of learning—the confusion here leads to extravagant conduct."

9. The Master said, "My children, why do you not study the Book of Poetry?

"The Odes serve to stimulate the mind.

"They may be used for purposes of self-contemplation.

"They teach the art of sociability.

"They show how to regulate feelings of resentment.

"From them you learn the more immediate duty of serving one's father, and the remoter one of serving one's prince.

"From them we become largely acquainted with the names of birds, beasts, and plants."

10. The Master said to Boyu, "Do you give yourself to the odes of South Zhou and South Shao? The man who has not studied the South Zhou and South Shao is like one who stands with his face right against a wall. Is he not so?"

11. The Master quoted, "'It is according to the rules of propriety,' they say.—'It is according to the rules of propriety.' Are gems and silk all that is meant by propriety? 'It is music,' they say—'It is music.' Are bells and drums all that is meant by music?"

12. The Master said, "He who puts on an appearance of stern firmness, while inwardly he is weak, is like one of the small, mean people—yea, is he not like the thief who breaks in, or who climbs over a wall?"

13. The Master said, "Your good, circumspect people of the villages are the thieves of virtue."

14. The Master said, "To tell, as we go along, what we have heard on the street, is to cast away our virtue."

15. The Master said, "There are those mean creatures! How impossible it is along with them to serve one's prince! While they have not got the positions they want, their anxiety is how to get them. When they have got them, their anxiety is lest they should lose them. When they are anxious lest such things should be lost, there is nothing to which they will not proceed."

16. The Master said, "In ancient times, men had three failings, which now perhaps are not to be found. The high-mindedness of antiquity showed itself in a disregard of small things; the high-mindedness of the present day shows itself in wild license. The stern dignity of antiquity showed itself in grave reserve; the stern dignity of the present day shows itself in quarrelsome perverseness. The stupidity of antiquity showed itself in straightforwardness; the stupidity of the present day shows itself in sheer deceit."

17. The Master said, "Fine words and an ingratiating appearance are seldom associated with virtue."

18. The Master said, "I hate the manner in which purple takes away the luster of vermilion. I hate the way in which the folk songs of Zheng confound the music

of the classics. I hate those who overthrow kingdoms and families with their sharp tongues."

19. The Master said, "I would prefer not to speak." Zigong said, "If you, Master, do not speak, what shall we, your disciples, have to record?" The Master said, "Does Heaven speak? The four seasons pursue their courses, and all things are continually being produced, but does Heaven say anything?"

20. Ru Bei wished to see Confucius, but Confucius declined, on the ground of being sick, to see him. When the bearer of this message went out at the door, the Master took his lute and sang to it, in order that Bei might hear him.

21. Zai Wo asked about the three years' mourning for parents, saying that one year was long enough. "If the superior man," said he, "abstains for three years from the observances of propriety, those observances will be quite lost. If for three years he abstains from music, music will be ruined. Within a year the old grain is exhausted, and the new grain has sprung up, and, in procuring fire by friction, we go through all the changes of wood for that purpose. After a complete year, the mourning should stop." The Master said, "If you were, after a year, to eat good rice, and wear embroidered clothes, would you feel at ease?" "I should," replied Wo. The Master said, "If you can feel at ease, do it. But a superior man, during the whole period of mourning, does not enjoy pleasant food which he may eat, nor derive pleasure from music which he may hear. He also does not feel at ease, if he is comfortably lodged. Therefore he does not do what you propose. But now you feel at ease and may do it." Zai Wo then went out, and the Master said, "This shows Zai Wo's want of virtue. It is not till a child is three years old that it is allowed to leave the care of its parents. And the three years' mourning is universally observed throughout the empire. Did Zai Wo not enjoy the three years' love of his parents?"

22. The Master said, "Hard is it to deal with one who will stuff himself with food the whole day, without applying his mind to anything good! Are there not gamesters and chess players? To be one of these would still be better than doing nothing at all."

23. Zilu said, "Does the superior man esteem valor?" The Master said, "The superior man holds righteousness to be of highest importance. A man in a superior situation, having valor without righteousness, will be guilty of insubordination; one of the lower people having valor without righteousness, will commit robbery."

24. Zilu said, "Has the superior man his hatreds also?" The Master said, "He has his hatreds. He hates those who proclaim the evil of others. He hates the man who, being in a low station, slanders his superiors. He hates those who have valor merely, and are unobservant of propriety. He hates those who are forward and determined, and, at the same time, of contracted understanding." The Master then inquired, "Zilu, do you also have hatreds?" Zilu replied, "I hate those who pry out matters, and ascribe the knowledge to their wisdom. I hate those who are immodest, and think that they are valorous. I hate those who make known secrets, and think that they are straightforward."

25. The Master said, "Of all people, girls and servants are the most difficult to behave toward. If you are familiar with them, they lose their humility. If you maintain a reserve towards them, they are discontented."

26. The Master said, "When a man at forty is the object of dislike, he will always continue what he is."

chapter 18

Chapter 18 displays a certain confusion in text but is regarded by some as of particular value in its responses to Taoist teachings, as well as dealing with reclusion and Confucius's premonitions of rejection and the short-term failure of his mission.

1. The Viscount of Wei withdrew from the court. The Viscount of Ji became his slave. Bi Gan remonstrated with him and was executed. Confucius said, "In them the Shang dynasty lost three men of virtue."

2. Hui of Liuxia, being chief criminal judge, was thrice dismissed from his office. Someone said to him, "Is it not yet time for you, sir, to leave this?" He replied, "Serving men in an upright way, where shall I go to, and not experience such a thrice-repeated dismissal? If I wanted to serve men in a crooked way, what necessity would there be for me to leave the country of my parents?"

3. Duke Jing of Ji, with reference to the manner in which he should treat Confucius, said, "I cannot treat him as I would the chief of the Ji family. I will treat him in a manner between that accorded to the chief of the Ji and that given to the chief of the Meng family." He also said, "I am old; I cannot use his doctrines." Confucius took his departure.

4. The people of Qi sent to Lu a present of female musicians, which Ji Huanzi received, and for three days no court was held. Confucius thereupon took his departure.

5. The madman of Chu, Jieyu, passed by Confucius, singing and saying,

> O Phoenix! O Phoenix!
> How is your virtue degenerated!
> As to the past, reproof is useless;
> The future may still be provided.
> Give up your vain pursuit.
> Give up your vain pursuit.
> Peril awaits those who now
> Engage in affairs of government.

Confucius alighted and wished to converse with him, but Jieyu hastened away, so that he could not talk with him.

6. Chang Ju and Jie Ni were at work in the field together, when Confucius passed by them, and sent Zilu to inquire about the ford. Chang Ju said, "Who is he that holds the reins in the carriage there?" Zilu told him, "It is Confucius." "Is

it Confucius of Lu?" asked he. "Yes," was the reply, to which the other rejoined, "He knows the ford."

Zilu then inquired of Jie Ni, who said to him, "Who are you, sir?" He answered, "I am Zilu." "Are you not the disciple of Confucius of Lu?" asked the other. "I am," replied he, and then Jie Ni said to him, "Disorder, like a swelling flood, spreads over the whole empire, and who is he that will change its state for you? Rather than follow one who merely withdraws from this one and that one, had you not better follow those who have withdrawn from the world altogether?" With this he fell to covering up the seed, and proceeded with his work, without stopping. Zilu went and reported their remarks, when the Master observed with a sigh, "It is impossible to associate with birds and beasts, as if they were the same with us. If I associate not with these people, and with mankind, with whom shall I associate? If right principles prevailed through the empire, there would be no use for me to change its state."

7. Zilu, following the Master, happened to fall behind, when he met an old man, carrying across his shoulder on a staff a basket for weeds. Zilu said to him, "Have you seen my master, sir?" The old man replied,

> Your four limbs are unaccustomed to toil;
> You cannot distinguish the five kinds of grain—
> Who then can your master be?

With this, he planted his staff in the ground, and proceeded to weed. Zilu joined his hands across his breast, and stood before him. The old man allowed Zilu to pass the night in his house, killed a fowl, prepared millet, and feasted him. He also introduced to him his two sons. Next day, Zilu went on his way, and reported his adventure. The Master said, "He is a recluse," and sent Zilu back to see him again, but when he got to the place, the old man was gone. Zilu then said to the family, "Not to take responsibility is not righteous. If the relations between old and young may not be neglected, how is it that he sets aside the duties that should be observed between sovereign and minister? Wishing to maintain his personal purity, your father allows that great relation to come to confusion. A superior man takes office, and performs the righteous duties belonging to it. As to the failure of right principles to make progress, he is aware of that."

8. The men who have retreated to privacy from the world have been Bo Yi, Shu Qi, Yu Zhong, Yi Yi, Zhu Zhang, Liuxia Hui, and Shao Lian. The Master said, "Refusing to surrender their wills, or to submit to any taint in their persons; such, I think, were Bo Yi and Shu Qi. It may be said of Hui of Liuxia! and of Shao Lian, that they surrendered their wills, and submitted to taint in their persons, but their words corresponded with reason, and their actions were such as men are anxious to see. This is all that is to be remarked in them. It may be said of Yu Zhong and Yi Yi, that, while they hid themselves in their seclusion, they gave a license to their words; but in their persons, they succeeded in preserving their

purity, and, in retreating, they acted according to the exigency of the times. I am different from all these. I have no course for which I am predetermined, and no course against which I am predetermined."

9. In an exodus from the court of Duke Ai, the grand music master, Zhi, went to Qi. Gan, the master of the band at the second course, went to Chu. Liao, the band master at the third course, went to Cai. Que, the band master at the fourth meal, went to Qin. Fangshu, the drum master, withdrew to the north of the river. Wu, the master of the hand drum, withdrew to the Han River. Yang, the assistant music master, and Xiang, master of the musical chimes, withdrew to an island in the sea.

10. The Duke of Zhou addressed his son, the Duke of Lu, saying, "The virtuous prince does not neglect his relations. He does not cause the great ministers to repine at his not employing them. Without some great cause, he does not dismiss from their offices the members of old families. He does not seek in one man talents for every employment."

11. To the State of Zhou belonged eight worthy officers, Boda, Bokuo, Zhongtu, Zhongtu, Shuye, Shuxia, Jisui, and Jiwa.

chapter 19

In chapter 19 the disciples elaborate themes they have presented earlier, but now in the era after the life of Confucius. They even use an honorific title, "Chung-ni," signaling the beginning of the deification of the sage that was characteristic of the Han Dynasty.

1. Zizhang said, "The scholar, trained for public duty, seeing threatening danger, is prepared to sacrifice his life. When the opportunity of gain is presented to him, he thinks of righteousness. In sacrificing, his thoughts are reverential. In mourning, his thoughts are about the grief which he should feel. Such a man commands our approbation indeed."

2. Zizhang said, "When a man holds fast to virtue, but without seeking to enlarge it, and believes in right principles, but without firm sincerity, what account can be made of his existence or non-existence?"

3. The disciples of Zixia asked Zizhang about the principles that should characterize mutual intercourse. Zizhang asked, "What does Zixia himself say on the subject?" They replied, "Zixia says: 'Associate with those who can advantage you. Pull away from you those who cannot do so.'" Zizhang observed, "This is different from what I have learned. The superior man honors the talented and virtuous, and bears with all. He praises the good, and pities the incompetent. Am I possessed of great talents and virtue? Then who is there among men whom I will not bear with? Am I devoid of talents and virtue?—Then men will push me away from them. What have we to do with the pushing away of others?"

4. Zixia said, "Even in trivial studies and employments there is something worth being examined; but if it be attempted to develop them further, there is a danger of their proving inapplicable. Therefore, the superior man does not practice them."

5. Zixia said, "He, who from day to day recognizes what he still lacks, and from month to month does not forget what he is capable of, may be said indeed to love to learn."

6. Zixia said, "Learning broadly is one thing, along with having a firm and sincere focus, inquiring with earnestness, and reflecting with self-application—virtue is found in these directions."

7. Zixia said, "Mechanics have their shops to dwell in, in order to accomplish their works. The superior man learns in his study, in order to reach to the utmost of his principles."

8. Zixia said, "The mean man is sure to gloss over his faults."

9. Zixia said, "The superior man undergoes three changes. Looked at from a distance, he appears stern; when approached, he is mild; when he is heard to speak, his language is firm and decided."

10. Zixia said, "The superior man, having obtained their confidence, may then impose labors on his people. If he has not gained their confidence, they will think that he is oppressing them. Having obtained the confidence of his prince, one may then dispute with him. If he has not gained his confidence, the prince will think that he is vilifying him."

11. Zixia said, "When a person does not transgress the boundary line in the great virtues, he may pass it again and again in the small virtues."

12. Ziyou said, "The disciples and followers of Zixia, in sprinkling and sweeping the ground, in answering and replying, in advancing and receding, are sufficiently accomplished. But these are only the peripheries of learning, and they are left ignorant of what is essential.—How can they be acknowledged as sufficiently taught?" Zixia heard of the remark and said, "Alas! Ziyou is wrong. According to the way of the superior man in teaching, what departments are there which he considers of prime importance, and delivers? What are there which he considers of secondary importance, and allows himself to be idle about? But as in the case of plants, which are assorted according to their classes, so he deals with his disciples. How can the way of a superior man be such as to make fools of any of them? Is it not the sage alone, who can unite in one the beginning and the consummation of learning?"

13. Zixia said, "The officer, having discharged all his duties, should devote his leisure to learning. The student, having completed his learning, should apply himself to becoming an officer."

14. Zixia said, "Mourning, having been carried to the utmost degree of grief, should stop with that."

15. Zixia said, "My friend Zizhang can do things which are hard to be done, but yet he is not perfectly virtuous."

16. The philosopher Zeng said, "How imposing is the manner of Zizhang! It is difficult to practice virtue alongside him."

17. The philosopher Zeng said, "I heard this from our Master: 'Men may not have shown what is in them to the full extent, and yet they will be found to do so on the occasion of mourning for their parents.'"

18. The philosopher Zeng said, "I have heard this from our Master—'The filial piety of Meng Zhuangzi, in other matters, was what other men are competent of, but, as seen in his not changing the ministers of his father, nor his father's mode of government, it is difficult to match.'"

19. The chief of the Meng family having appointed Yang Fu to be chief criminal judge, the latter consulted the philosopher Zeng. Zeng said, "The rulers have failed in their duties, and the people consequently have been disorganized for a long time. When you have found out the truth of any accusation, be grieved for and pity them, and do not feel joy at your own ability."

20. Zigong said, "Zhow's wickedness was not so great as that name implies. Therefore, the superior man hates to dwell in a low-lying situation, where all the evil of the world will flow in upon him."

21. Zigong said, "The faults of the superior man are like the eclipses of the sun and moon. He has his faults, and all men see them; he changes again, and all men look up to him."

22. Gongsun Chao of Wei asked Zigong, saying, "From whom did Chung-ni get his learning?" Zigong replied, "The doctrines of ancient Zhou Kings Wan and Wu have not yet fallen to the ground. They are to be found among men. Men of talents and virtue remember the greater principles of them, and others, not possessing such talents and virtue, remember the smaller. Thus, all possess the doctrines of Wan and Wu. Where could our Master go that he should not have an opportunity of learning them? And yet what necessity was there for his having a regular master?"

23. Shusun Wushu observed to the great officers in the court, saying, "Zigong is superior to Chung-ni." Zifu Jingbo reported the observation to Zigong, who said, "Let me use the comparison of a house and its encompassing wall. My wall only reaches to the shoulders. One may peep over it, and see whatever is valuable in the apartments. The wall of my Master is several fathoms high. If one does not find the door and enter by it, he cannot see the ancestral temple with its beauties, nor all the officers in their rich array. But I may assume that they are few who find the door. Was not the observation of the chief only what might have been expected?"

24. Shusun Wushu having reviled Chung-ni, Zigong said, "There is no point in arguing. Chung-ni cannot be reviled. The talents and virtue of other men are hillocks and mounds which may be stepped over. Chung-ni is the sun or moon, which it is not possible to step over. Although a man may wish to cut himself off from the sage, what harm can he do to the sun or moon? He only shows that he does not know his own capacity."

25. Chen Ziqin, said to Zigong, "You are too modest. How can Chung-ni be superior to you?" Zigong said to him, "For one word a man is often deemed to be wise, and for one word he is often deemed to be foolish. We ought to be careful in what we say. Our Master cannot be matched, just in the same way as the heavens cannot be gone up by the steps of a stair. Were our Master in the position of the ruler of a state or the chief of a family, we should find verified the description of a sage's rule—he would plant the people, and forthwith they would be established; he would lead them, and forthwith they would follow him; he would make them happy, and forthwith multitudes would resort to his dominions; he would stimulate them, and forthwith they would be harmonious. While he lived, he would be glorious. When he died, he would be bitterly lamented. How is it possible for him to be matched?"

chapter 20

Chapter 20 is an appendix of miscellaneous material that, for whatever reason, could not be fitted into other chapters or that was saved to provide a religious conclusion.

1. Yao said, "Oh! you, Shun, the Heaven—determined order of succession now rests in your person. Sincerely hold fast the due mean. If there shall be distress and want within the four seas, the Heavenly revenue will come to a perpetual end." Shun also used the same language in giving a charge to Yu. Tang said, "I, the child Lu, presume to use a dark-colored sacrifice, and presume to announce to Thee, O most great and sovereign God, that I dare not pardon the sinner, and thy ministers, O God, I do not keep in obscurity. The examination of them is by thy mind, O God. If, in my person, I commit offenses, they are not to be attributed to the people of the myriad regions. If the people in the myriad regions commit offenses, these offenses must rest on my person." The Zhou Dynasty conferred great gifts, and the good were enriched. King Wu had said "Although he has his near relatives, they are not equal to my virtuous men. The people are throwing blame upon me, the One man." He carefully attended to the weights and measures, examined the body of the laws, restored the discarded officers, and the good government of the kingdom took its course. He revived states that had been extinguished, restored families whose line of succession had been broken, and called to office those who had retired into obscurity, so that throughout the kingdom the hearts of the people turned towards him. What he attached chief importance to were the food of the people, the duties of mourning, and the sacrifices. By his generosity, he won the loyalty of all. By his sincerity, he made the people repose trust in him. By his earnest activity, his achievements were great. By his justice, all were delighted.

2. Zizhang asked Confucius, saying, "In what way should a person in authority act in order that he may conduct government properly?" The Master replied,

"Let him honor the five excellent things, and banish away the four bad things;—then may he conduct government properly." Zizhang said, "What are meant by the five excellent things?" The Master said, "When the person in authority is beneficent without great expenditure; when he lays tasks on the people without their repining; when he pursues what he desires without being covetous; when he maintains a dignified ease without being proud; when he is majestic without being fierce." Zizhang said, "And what is meant by being beneficent without great expenditure?" The Master replied, "When the person in authority makes more beneficial to the people the things from which they naturally derive benefit—is not this being beneficent without great expenditure? When he chooses the labors which are proper, and makes them labor on them, who will repine? When his desires are set on benevolent government, and he secures it, who will accuse him of covetousness? Whether he has to do with many people or few, or with things great or small, he does not dare to indicate any disrespect—is not this to maintain a dignified ease without any pride? He adjusts his clothes and cap, and throws a dignity into his looks, so that, thus dignified, he is looked at with awe—is not this to be majestic without being fierce?" Zizhang then asked, "What are meant by the four bad things?" The Master said, "To put the people to death without having instructed them—this is called cruelty. To require from them, suddenly, the full produce of work, without having given them warning—this is called oppression. To issue orders as if without urgency, at first, and, when the time comes, to insist on them with severity—this is called injury. And, generally, in the giving pay or rewards to men, to do it in a stingy way—this is acting the part of a mere official and not as a ruler."

3. The Master said, "Without recognizing the ordinances of Heaven, it is impossible to be a superior man. Without an acquaintance with the rules of Propriety, it is impossible for the character to be established. Without knowing the force of words, it is impossible to know men."

book four

THE BUDDHIST TESTAMENT

introduction

The Indian Origins of Buddhism

Sarvepalli Radhakrishnan

THE TREE OF CIVILIZATION HAS ITS ROOTS IN SPIRITUAL VALUES THAT MOST OF US DO NOT recognize. Without these roots, the leaves would have fallen and left the tree a lifeless stump. In the history of civilization it has been the privilege of Asia to enrich the mind of the world with the noblest content of spiritual values. She has been brought into more or less direct contact with Europe via the Persian Empire, the invasion of the East by Alexander, Asoka's missions to the West, the Roman Empire (which extended over a part of Asia), the Moors in Spain, and the Crusades—and each time she has left her mark.

Today there is a worldwide spiritual renaissance. We have come to recognize that it is either one world or none. The effort to build one world requires a closer understanding among peoples of the world and their cultures. This translation of the *Dhammapada*, the most popular and influential book of the Buddhist canonical literature, is offered as a small contribution to world understanding. The central thesis of the book—that human conduct, righteous behavior, reflection, and meditation are more important than vain speculations about the transcendent—has an appeal to the modern mind. Its teaching—to repress the instincts entirely is to generate neuroses; to give them full rein is also to end up in neuroses—is supported by modern psychology. Books as rich in significance as the *Dhammapada* need to be understood by each generation in relation to its own problems.

The *Dhammapada* has 423 verses in the Pali Version, divided into twenty-six chapters. It is an anthology of Buddhist devotion and practice, which brings together verses in popular use or gathered from different sources. Though it may not contain all words of the Buddha, it does embody the spirit of the Buddha's teaching, summoning humanity to a process of strenuous mental and moral effort. *Dhamma* is discipline, law, religion; *pada* is the path.

The verses of the *Dhammapada* were believed from very early times—that is, from the period of the First Council that settled the canon—to have been utterances of the Buddha himself. The verses are generally connected with incidents in the life of the Buddha and illustrate the method of teaching adopted by him.

In Gautama, the Buddha, we have a mastermind from the East, second to none so far as the influence in the thought of life of the human race is concerned and sacred to all as the founder of a religious tradition whose hold is hardly less wide and deep than any other. He belongs to the history of the world's thought, to the general inheritance of all cultivated men, for, judged by intellectual integrity, moral earnestness, and spiritual insight, he is undoubtedly one of the greatest figures in history.

Though his historical character has been called in question, there are few competent scholars, if any, at the present time who doubt that he was a historical person whose date can be fixed, whose life can be sketched at least in outline, and whose teachings on some of the essential problems of the philosophy of religion can be learned with reasonable certainty.

The stories of his childhood and youth have, undoubtedly, a mythical air,[1] but there is no reason to distrust the traditional account of his lineage. He was born in the year 563 BCE, the son of Suddhodana, of the Kshatriya clan known as the Sakya[2] of Kapilavastu, on the Nepalese border, one hundred miles north of Benares. The spot was afterward marked by the emperor of Asoka with a column that is still standing. His own name was Siddhartha, Gautama being his family name.

We learn from the *Sutta Nipata* the story of an aged seer named Asita who came to see the child and, more or less in the manner of Simeon,[3] prophesied the future greatness of the child and wept at the thought that he himself would not live to see it and hear the new gospel. The efforts of Gautama's father to turn his mind to secular interests failed, and at the age of twenty-nine he left his home, put on the ascetic's garb, and started his career as a wandering seeker of truth. This was the great renunciation. It is difficult for us in this secular age to realize the obsession of religion on the Indian mind and the ardors and agonies it is willing to face in order to gain the religious end.

Gautama remembered how once in his youth he had an experience of mystic contemplation, and now he tried to pursue that line. Legend tells us that, at the time of this crisis, Gautama was assailed by Mara, the tempter, who sought in vain, by all manner of terrors and temptations, to shake him from his purpose.[4] These incidents indicate that his inner life was not undisturbed and continuous, and it was with a mental struggle that he broke away from old beliefs to try new methods. He persisted in his meditations and passed through the four stages of contemplation, culminating in pure self-possession and equanimity. He saw the whole universe as a system of law, composed of striving creatures, happy or unhappy, noble or mean, continually passing away from one form of existence and taking shape in another. In the last watch of that night, ignorance was destroyed, and knowledge had arisen—"as I sat there, earnest, strenuous, resolute." Gautama had attained *Bodhi*, or illumination, and became the Buddha, the enlightened one. He converted in the first place the five disciples who had borne him company in the years of his asceticism, and in the deer park, where ascetics were allowed to dwell and animals might not be killed, at the modern Sarnath, he preached his first sermon.

The Buddha was not concerned with changes of the creed. He sat by the sacred fire of the Brahmin and gave a discourse of his views without denouncing his worship. When Siha the Jain became a Buddhist, he was required to give food and gifts as before to the Jain monks who frequented his house. With a singular gentleness, the Buddha presented his views and left the rest to the persuasive power of truth.

In his time women were not secluded in India, and he declared that they were quite capable of attaining sanctity and holiness. In the last year of his life he dined with the courtesan Ambapali, but he had considerable hesitation in admitting women to the Order, as we see in his conversation with one of his ten principal disciples: "How, Lord, are we to conduct ourselves with regard to womankind?" "Don't see them, Ananda." "But if we see them, what are we to do?" "Abstain from speech." "But if they should speak to us, what are we to do?" "Keep wide awake." Ananda was quite chivalrous, pleading the cause of women for admission into the Order, and won the consent of the Master.

The story of his death is told with great pathos and simplicity in the *Mahaparinibbana Sutta*. The Buddha was now eighty years old, worn out with toil and travel. At a village near the little town of Kusinagara, about 120 miles northeast of Benares, in 483 BCE, he passed away. The quiet end of the Buddha contrasts vividly with the martyr's deaths of Socrates and Jesus. However, all three undermined, to different degrees, the orthodoxies of their time. As a matter of fact, the Buddha was more definitely opposed to earlier Vedic orthodoxy and ceremonialism than was Socrates to the state religion of Athens, or Jesus to Judaism, and yet he lived until the age of eighty, gathered a large number of disciples, and founded a religious order in his own lifetime. Perhaps the Indian temper of religion is responsible for the difference in the treatment of unorthodoxies.

The text of his first sermon has come down to us. There is no reason to doubt that it contains the words and the ideas of the Buddha. Its teaching is quite simple. After observing that those who wish to lead a religious life should avoid the two extremes of self-indulgence and self-mortification and follow the middle way, the Buddha enunciates the Four Noble Truths about the experience of sorrow (*duhkha*), the cause of sorrow (*samudaya*), the removal of sorrow (*nirodha*), and the way leading beyond it (*marga*).

That there is a retribution for selfishness and a reward of inward peace for an unselfish life, that we shall be made to realize what we have done and (in the expressive language of Ezekiel) "loathe ourselves for our iniquities,"[5] is the Buddha's deepest conviction. He says, "My action is my possession: my action is my inheritance: my action is the matrix which bears me: my action is the race to which I belong: my action is my refuge." The rule of law has a redeeming feature in that it removes ghastly visions of eternal hell. No place of doom can last forever. Heaven and hell belong to the order of the finite and the impermanent. However intense and long they may be, they have an end, and how and when they end depends on ourselves.

According to the Buddha's teaching, each man will have to find salvation, in the last resort, alone and with his own will, and he needs all the will in the world for so formidable an effort. The general impression that the mystic experience is granted and not achieved is far from correct, except in the sense that all great moments of experience are in a measure given. The Buddha's life was one of strenuous discipline. Right contemplation is the end and the crown of the Eightfold Path that the Buddha bequeathed to the world, building on the fourth of the Four Noble Truths.

The Buddha's teaching begins with the fact of his enlightenment, a spiritual experience that cannot be put into words. Whatever doctrine there is in him relates to his experience and the way of attaining it. To use an image employed by him, our theories of the eternal are as valuable as those which a chick that has not broken its way through its shell might form of the outside world. To know the truth, we must tread the path.

In this he resembles some of the greatest thinkers of the world. Socrates replied to the charge of "corrupting the young" that he had no "doctrine," that Meletus had not produced any evidence, from either his pupils or their relations, to show that they had suffered from his "doctrine." Jesus had an abhorrence of dogma. It was not a creed that he taught or a church that he established. His aim was instead to show a new way of life. The cross was the symbol of the new religion, not the creed. Bearing the cross is the condition of discipleship. It stands for a new way of overcoming evil with good, demands a change of outlook, a rejection of instinctive egoisms and of the earthly standards of glory and greatness. St. Paul gives us the "fruits of the spirit" ("love, joy, peace, long-suffering, gentleness, goodness, faith, meekness, temperance"[6]) and contrasts them with "the works of the flesh" ("idolatry, hatred, variance, jealousies, wrath, strife, envyings, murders, and such like"[7]).

If we place ourselves in imagination in the India of the sixth century BCE, we find that different streams of thought, belief, and practice—animism, magic, and superstition—were tending to unite into a higher monistic[8] idealism. Man's attempt to seek the truth and put himself in a right relation to it also assumed the forms of dualistic and pluralistic experiments, but they were all agreed on certain fundaments. Life does not begin at birth or end at death, but rather is a link in an infinite series of lives, each of which is conditioned determined by acts done in previous existences. Animals, human, and angelic forms are all links in the chain. By good deeds we raise our status and get to heaven, and by evil ones we lower it. Since all lives must come to an end, true happiness is not to be sought in heaven or on earth. Release from the round of births resulting in life in eternity is the goal of the religious man and is indicated by such words as *moksa* or deliverance, union with Brahman, and *nirvana*.

The methods for gaining release were variously conceived. At least four main ones could be distinguished: (1) The Vedic hymns declared that prayer and worship were the best means of gaining the favor of the Divine. (2) The most popular was the sacrificial system that arose out of simple offerings to the deity and became complicated in an age even before the Upanishads. (While its inadequacy was admitted by the Upanishads, it was tolerated as a method useful for attaining temporal blessings and even life in a paradise.) (3) Asceticism was popular with certain sects. By means of temperance, chastity, and mental concentration, one could increase the force of thought and will. (The advocates of the ascetic path were betrayed into the extravagance that, by suppressing desires and enduring voluntary tortures, one could attain supernatural powers. Tapas, or austerity, is said to be better than sacrifice, and it is regarded as the means for attaining the knowledge of Brahman.) (4) Finally, there is *vidya*, which is not learning but rapt contemplation; it is a realization of one's unity with the Supreme Spirit, in the light of which all material attachments and fetters fall away. The Buddha, who teaches "the middle path" between self-indulgence and self-mortification, inclines to the last view.

The Vedic teachings, and later the Upanishads, from which the Buddha's teaching is derived, hold that the world we know, whether outward or inward, does not possess intrinsic reality. Intrinsic reality belongs to the knower, *Atman*, the self of all selves. *Brahman* and *Atman* are one. Knowledge of this supreme truth, realization of the identity of the self of man and the spirit of the universe, is salvation. It is a state of being, not a place of resort, a quality of life to be acquired by spiritual training and illumination. Until this goal is reached, humans are subject to the law of *karma* and rebirth. Under the shadow of the fundamental thesis of the unity of the individual spirit with the universal spirit, numberless dogmas developed, in which the special god of the devotee was identified with the universal spirit. The Buddha accepts the propositions that the empirical universe is not real, that the empirical individual is not permanent, that both of these are subject to changes which are governed by law, and that it is the duty of the individual to transcend this world of succession and time and attain *nirvana*.

Whether there is anything real and positive in the universe, in the individual, and in the state of liberation, he declined to tell us, though he denied the dogmatic theologies. The Upanishads contrast the absolute fullness of limitless perfection with the world of plurality—a state of disruption, restriction, and pain. If there is a difference between the teaching of the Upanishads and the Buddha, it is not in their views of the world of experience (*samsara*) but in regard to their conception of reality (*nirvana*).

Before we take up the question of the meaning of the Buddha's silence, let us understand his motive for it. The supremacy of the ethical is the clue to the teaching of the Buddha. His conceptions of life and the universe were derived from his severely practical outlook. The existence of everything depends on a cause. If we remove the cause, the effect will disappear. If the source of all suffering is destroyed, suffering will disappear. The cure proposed by the sacrificial and the sacramental religions that filled his environment has little to do with the disease. The only way in which we can remove the cause of suffering is to purify the heart and follow the moral law. Doctrines that take away from the urgency of the moral task, the cultivation of individual character, are repudiated by the Buddha.

If what the Upanishads declare is true, that we are divine, then there is nothing for us to aim at or strive for. The Jain and Samkhya theories maintain infinity of souls involved in matter. For them the duty of humanity would consist of ascetic practices through which the unchangeable essence could be freed from the changing trammels. Whether we believe with the Upanishads in one universal spirit or with the Samkhya system in an infinite plurality of spirits, the nature of the spirit is conceived as unchanging and unchangeable. But ethical training implies the possibility of change. Man is not divine; he has to become divine. His divine status is something to be built up by "good thoughts, good words, and good deeds."[9]

The vital problem for the Buddha was how the world spirit, if any, manifests itself, not in the superhuman realm, but in the individual man and in the empirical world. The world is made, not by gods and angels, but by the voluntary choices of men.

The object of religion is the ideal in contrast to the present state. *Dharma* is the unity of all idea ends, arousing us to desire and action. For the Buddha, the impulse to *dharma*, to justice and kindliness, is operative in things, and its efficient activity will mean the reduction of disorder, cruelty, and oppression. *Dharma* is organic to existence, and its implication of *karma* is the builder of the world.

Anyone who believes that the Buddha was a skeptic or an agnostic who did not know the ultimate grounds of things simply because he did not give an account of them misses the main drift of his teaching. Such an attitude will be opposed to many utterances in which the Buddha implies that he knows more than what he has given to his disciples. It will be unfair to equate his attitude with an indolent skepticism that will not take the trouble to find a positive or a negative answer to the ultimate questions, or to say that he had not the courage to own that he did not know. We read: At one time, the Exalted One was saying a Kosambi in the simsapa grove. The Exalted One took a few simsapa leaves in his hand and said to his disciples: "What think ye, my disciples, which are the more, these few simsapa leaves which I have gathered in my hand, or the other leaves yonder in the simsapa grove?" He continued,

> So also, my disciples, is that much more, which I have learned and have not told you, than that which I have told you. And, wherefore, my disciples, have I not told you that? Because, my disciples, it brings you no profit, it does not conduce to progress in holiness; because it does not lead to the turning from the earthly, to the subjection of all desire, to the cessation of the transitory, to peace, to knowledge, to illumination: therefore have I not declared it unto you.

He says, "According to my teaching—ye shall even in this present life apprehend the truth itself and see face to face." It is not an agnostic who speaks here with such conviction and authority.

Though he questioned many beliefs, he never doubted the existence of the moral order of the universe or the supreme reality and value of the life of the soul. His incessant insistence on the practice of virtue and the critical testing of opinions by the standard of reason was based on ardent positive convictions. The absolute is for him the law of righteousness. It is the answer to human hope and striving, that on which the whole existence of the world is founded. It is the meaning of history, the redemption of all creation.

If we assume, as we are obliged to by the compulsion of facts, that the Buddha knew the truth, though he did not proclaim it, may it not be that his truth was atheism? Those who wish to discredit the powerful and massive witness of religious experience to the reality of an absolute spirit quote the Buddha in their support. Was not *nirvana* "only the sleep eternal in an eternal night"? A heaven without a God, immortality without a soul, and purification without prayer sum up his doctrine. T. H. Huxley finds hope in the fact that

> a system which knows no God in the Western sense, which denies a soul to man, which counts the belief in immortality a blunder and the hope of it a sin, which refuses any efficacy to prayer and sacrifice, which binds men to look to nothing but their own efforts for salvation, which in its original purity knew nothing of vows of obedience and never sought the aid of the secular arm, yet spread over a considerable moiety of old world with marvellous rapidity, is still, with whatever base admixture of foreign superstitions, the dominant creed of a large fraction of mankind.

Given the psychological conditions of the time, the reception of the Buddha's message would be unthinkable if it were negative; anyone who is familiar with the religious environment of India knows it is impossible to look upon a philosophy of negative as the mandate of a religious revival. Though the Buddha disputes the preeminence of Brahma, the highest of the gods, those who accepted his leadership felt that he did so in the interests of a higher concept. The worshippers of other gods transferred their adoration to another form of divinity. It was the age of the growth of the great gods Siva and Vishnu, and in course of time the Buddha himself was deified by his followers. His adherents were certainly not people inclined to atheism.

Those who tell us that for the Buddha there is religious experience, but no religious object, are violating the texts and needlessly convicting him of self-contradiction. He supports the reality of what the Upanishads call Brahman, though he takes the liberty of giving it another name, *dharma*, to indicate its essentially ethical value for us on the empirical plane. The way of the *dharma* is the way of the Brahman. To dwell in *dharma* is to dwell in Brahman.

The conception of *nirvana* as the blissful end for which everyone must strive is taken over by the Buddha from existing speculation, and it is parallel to that of *moksa* (release) of the Upanishads. The term *nirvana* occurs in the Upanishads and the *Bhagavad Gita*, and it means the blowing out of all passions, reuniting with supreme spirit (*brahman-irvana*). It does not mean complete extinction or annihilation, but rather the extinction of the fire of the passions and the bliss of union with the whole.

We find in Gautama the Buddha, in powerful combination, spiritual profundity, moral strength of the highest order, and discreet intellectual reserve. He is one of those rare spirits who bring to men a realization of their own divinity and make the spiritual life seem adventurous and attractive, so that they may go forth into the world with a new interest and new joy at heart. While his great intellect and wisdom gave him comprehension of the highest truth, his warm heart led him to devote his life to saving suffering humanity from sorrow, thus confirming the great mystic tradition that true immortals occupy themselves with human affairs, even though they possess divine souls.

The greatness of his personality, his prophetic zeal and burning love for suffering humanity, made a deep impression on those whom he loved and gave rise to those legends and stories that are the modes of expression available to ordinary humanity when it tries to express true things—in this case, the personal superiority of the Buddha to the rest of them—and so Gautama, the apostle of self-control and wisdom and love, becomes the Buddha, the perfectly enlightened, the omniscient one, the savior of the world. His true greatness stands out clearer and brighter as the ages pass, and even the skeptical-minded are turning to him with a more real appreciation, a deeper reverence, and a truer worship. He is one of those few heroes of humanity who have made epochs in the history of our race, with a message for other times as well as their own.

pReface

The Path of the Teachings

In the American presidential election held in November 1988, the Democratic candidate was Michael Dukakis, but at one stage in the nomination process the governor of New York, Mario Cuomo, was deemed a serious contender. Cuomo kept denying that he would run, yet the more strenuously he denied his intention, the more of an issue his likely candidacy became, leading a political analyst to comment: "Cuomo is very Zen. He runs by not running." How are we to define a religion that recommends acting by not acting?[1]

OUR PARTICULAR TRANSLATIONS OF THE *DHAMMAPADA* AND *BHAGAVAD GITA* ARE TREASURED in a special way because Radhakrishnan resituates early Buddhism in India where it originated, and Gandhi makes his favorite particular Hindu scripture into a universal bond connecting Eastern religion to the West. That bond will be illustrated by the principle of "Reciprocal Illumination," introduced in Book V by Arvind Sharma, but we also begin to build now on actual historical linkages.

We faced a dilemma with respect to the choice of a Buddhist "testament." The earliest such "testament" would be the *Dhammapada*, while the most widely used popular text among practicing Buddhists would be the *Diamond Sutra*, and the most popular with Western converts of late seems to be the *Heart Sutra*. Dr. Jack Kornfield is a Thai-trained teacher of Theravada Buddhism who has established important retreat centers and teaching institutes in New England and California to make Buddhism accessible to Americans. In his book *Bringing Home the Dharma*[2] ("Teaching") he makes use of a common Buddhist device that points to the diversity within that religion by imagining a person pointing to the roots as representing the true essence of Buddhism, another person pointing to the flowers, and a third to the fruit.

That illustration could be applied to the *Dhammapada*, the *Diamond Sutra*, and the *Heart Sutra*. The reasons for our publication of the *Dhammapada* as representing the roots of Buddhism as a "religion" in the Theravada tradition are obvious, but, in a way perhaps more striking than with our other texts, it is not the whole story. So the *Diamond Sutra* of the Mahayana tradition, beginning five hundred years later, and the *Heart Sutra* of the Tantrayana, another five hundred years after that, will also get brief consideration in this preface as later "testaments" to a Buddhism that grew beyond its roots and sometimes now claims to be not a religion.

Our choice of the translation of the *Dhammapada* by Sarvepalli Radhakrishnan, Oxford professor of Eastern religions and former president of India (1962–1967), sets Buddhism in its original Indian context and points to its intimate connection to his own Hinduism. His translation is amended slightly to integrate some helpful alternatives he places in brackets, to employ several phrases adopted by consensus among a variety of more recent scholarly translations, and to permit minor editorial touch-ups based on his footnotes. We show an alternative versification tradition in parentheses.

However, we do maintain a certain inertia in continuing Radhakrishnan's adoption of Western and familiar English terms like *hell* and *heaven*, which he believed conveyed the message in a manner more easily understood by Western, English readers who were his intended audience. In the *Dhammapada* he also leaves seven particular words in place that have come into English, including *namaste*, *yoga*, *nirvana*, *karma*, *guru*, and even *dharma* (teaching) and *bhakti* (devotion or worship), with Indian spelling, rather than later transliterations from Chinese or other Buddhist language models. Their use *in situ* here may help to situate the reader inside the text in the manner we promised as being experiential.

Somewhere between the dates ascribed to Lao Tzu and Confucius, a combination of history and tradition give us the story of the sixth-century BCE Indian prince named Siddhartha Gautama. His mother, the queen, died seven days after giving birth to him, probably around 563 BCE. The king raised him in opulence in a Nepalese palace built just for the boy, who was to be kept from witnessing misery and suffering.

One day, early in his manhood, he left the palace in the company of a royal charioteer and was confronted by the painful realities of life. They met a frail old man, and he learned from the charioteer about the challenges of aging. He was next introduced to a diseased person. They then came across the corpse of a dead person. Finally he encountered an emaciated ascetic monk. The charioteer explained how the latter had renounced possessions and indulgence to overcome anxiety about suffering and death. The next day the prince left his palace, as well as his wife and baby son, to follow that ascetic model in an aspiration to move through it to a peace that would relieve the shocking suffering he had witnessed, which he perceived as universal.

One night, after years of frustrating experimentation with asceticism and ascetics, Siddhartha sat under a Bodhi tree, vowing to not get up until the next step in his quest for truth was clear. He meditated all night and then remained there for several days, purifying his mind, seeing his entire life, and previous lives, in his thoughts. Mara, the tempter spirit, asked him what made him think that he had any right to this enlightenment, but the earth itself gave him strength.

A picture began to form in his mind of all that transpired in the universe, and he experienced the answer to the questions of suffering that he had been seeking for several years. In that moment, Siddhartha "awoke" to a new level of life experience and became the Buddha, one who is "enlightened" or "awake" to a union with the universe in which neither pain nor pleasure can divert one from the *whole*someness of all that is.

What he now knew would be almost impossible to communicate to others in words, but Brahma, the "King of Gods," convinced Buddha to teach, so he got up from his spot under the Bodhi tree to begin the mission of his life. He found five ascetics who had abandoned him earlier, and to them and others he preached his first sermon. It is known as "Setting in Motion the Wheel of the *Dharma*," and in it he elucidated the Four Noble Truths and the Eightfold Path, which became established as the core teachings (*dharma*) of Buddhism. The ascetics then began a community of monks that initially transcended all barriers of class, race, and sex, featuring only a desire for enlightenment through the banishment of suffering and spiritual emptiness. For the next fifty years the Buddha traveled, preaching the *dharma* and leading others along the path of enlightenment.

Elsewhere in this study we will acknowledge the proximity of Buddha's birthplace, the palace in which he was raised, and the circle of his travels to the Silk Route. Even in his childhood, Indian philosophical schools were accessible to his doting father, who was eager to provide every tutorial advantage to the son to whom he denied negative experiences. It should therefore not be surprising that the teachings of one connected to elite teachers both before and after he left home should show stimulative traces of ideas current along the Silk Route in his time. Of late, early in the twenty-first century, there has been a spate of scholarly books suggesting a remarkable number of parallels between the sayings of Buddha and the sayings of Jesus.[3] How could this be, since they obviously never met, unless they both had access to a common source? None seems possible except for the growing realization that both the Buddha and Jesus may have been exposed to Zoroastrian teachings or even the Avesta, almost certainly in the possession of the teachers of the Buddha.

The coincidental connection between the Buddha's family moving north from India to Nepal and the Scythians flooding east into Tibet at about the same time, and the related connection between Zoroastrianism and Buddhism, should provide doctoral thesis material for someone reading this tome. If the "Dead Zee Scrolls" are not found under the streets of Samarkand, as speculated in a later chapter, the 2007 endowment of thousands of Tibetan books, scrolls, and manuscripts to a university in China may provide many other alternatives. Twelve thousand ancient manuscripts that were hidden by Tibetan scholars during China's Cultural Revolution were purchased from Tibetan refugees in India by American scholar and philanthropist E. Eugene Smith and digitally copied for future reference. He then presented the originals of this collection to the Southwest University for Nationalities in Chengdu, the largest city of western China. There it resides today, still uncataloged, in the controlled environment of the E. Eugene Smith Library, built with Beijing's approval by this convert from Mormonism to Buddhism who insisted that this treasure belongs in an Asian setting, where it will surely be analyzed carefully in the course of time.[4]

Our choice of a translation of the classic Buddhist testament by Radhakrishnan may seem counterintuitive at first, since this Oxford professor of Eastern religions and former president of India was himself a Hindu religious leader. But as an academic, philosopher, and statesman, Dr. Radhakrishnan is uniquely situated to remind us of the Indian origins of Buddhism and its special relationship to Hinduism as we continue to connect the dots, moving toward the essence of monism and illustrating the putative stretch of monotheism toward monism, to which we will return in our appreciation of the *Bhagavad Gita*.

The selection of a text from among Buddhist writings was complicated by the fact that the three works that stand out in this genre connect with three separate branches of Buddhism, each with offshoots of their own. Described as *yanas* in Sanskrit, these three main Buddhist vehicles, or "paths," to emptying one's personal "self" into the universal Self, or the One, are Theravada, Mahayana, and Tantrayana Buddhism. Theravada is sometimes confused with Hinayana, its branch that began around the first century CE and no longer exists. Mahayana Buddhism was built first on a Theravada foundation, but when Mahayana reached China it developed into Ch'an Buddhism, known better in the West by its Japanese name, *Zen*, a combination of Indian Buddhism and Chinese Taoism. Tantrayana is primarily the Tibetan form of Buddhism and is also known as Vajrayana. For our purposes, we will limit this brief preface survey to the broad branches known as Theravada, Mahayana, and Tantrayana, with emphasis on Theravada providing the *Dhammapada* text as foundational for the others.

Within months of the Buddha's death in 443 BCE his disciples convened a First Council to sum up his teachings (the *Dharma*) as recited by Ananda, his closest companion for twenty-five years. The First Council also recapitulated his rules (the *Vinaya*) for monastic life as remembered by Upali, the "untouchable" Dalit who cut the Buddha's hair and rose to become the coordinating manager of the community of monks. On this basis the movement maintained itself and expanded for a hundred years until the time of a Second Council, which amended and codified the *Dharma*. In 308 BCE, or another fifty years later, during the reign of India's great emperor, Asoka, the Third Council solidified the *Vinaya* in what became known as Theravada orthodoxy, and missionaries proceeded out in every direction, as far east as China and as far west as Egypt.

Profound in its simplicity, the ethos of Theravada Buddhism is found in the *Dhammapada* text of sayings of the Buddha in which the main motivation for following the spiritual path is to achieve liberation (*moksha*, usually defined as "salvation" in Hinduism) of the self. This is *nirvana*, no-self, perhaps the Ultimate Self, or the One. Taking root first in India, many of the terms of its vocabulary are from the ancient Vedic terminology, as redefined and amplified by Zoroaster, as we now realize. As Buddhism moved into China, the *Dhammapada* was welcomed, appearing as if almost built on the foundation of the Tao of Lao Tzu—again indicating the possibility of common roots, as will be confirmed once more in our next chapter.

Diversity began with the Third Council, and from it developed the new and now major branch of Buddhism, the Mahayana tradition. It became formally organized only by the first century BCE, flourishing more with the expansion into China, Korea, Japan, Vietnam, Laos, and Cambodia. Meanwhile, a reformed and resurgent Hinduism made Buddhism more or less redundant in India, but the Theravada tradition remained entrenched in Burma, Sri Lanka, and Thailand, as well as coexisting with the Mahayana tradition in Cambodia and Laos.

Practitioners of Mahayana Buddhism agree that becoming empty of self is the way to achieve *nirvana* (transcending both hedonism and asceticism), but they also assert that such a state of blissful Oneness may be "stuffed" full of multiple aspects of particularities in a diversity within monistic unity. "This very realization is the source of wisdom and compassion in which both ignorance and compassion are overcome. Just because *nirvana* is in itself empty, it is full of particular things functioning freely, which neither lose their particularity nor impede *one* another." So said Maso Abe (1915–2006), the popular and respected Japanese Zen practitioner of the Mahayana school, quoted at the beginning of this chapter, a professor of religious studies at the University of Hawaii who promoted Buddhist–Christian dialogue in a movement that eventually also included Judaism.[5]

Were we to seek the Buddhist testament in the Mahayana tradition, the *Diamond Sutra* would be attractive for our purposes, if only because, in addition to its size, its popularity, and its summary nature, an ancient copy was found at the beginning of the twentieth century among the treasures at Dunhuang in western China, a locus of considerable interest in our quest for the "Dead Zee Scrolls." That copy is dated in the original transcript as having been copied and produced in 868 CE, and it is regarded as the oldest internally dated manuscript in the literature of the whole world.

However, there are drawbacks to the choice of the *Diamond Sutra*. While both are authentic collections of sayings and teachings of the Buddha, as compared with our selection of the *Dhammapada* for this compendium, the *Diamond Sutra* is a much later collection, having been compiled about the time of Christ, and may be said to be somewhat elitist in comparison.

The *Diamond Sutra*

How can one present this Sutra without imagery, metaphors or similes?
Only by meditating in tranquility without distraction by attachments.
Thus may we contemplate our ephemeral existence in this universe:

Like a dewdrop on a leaf, or like a bubble on a brook;
Like a lightning flash that splits open the summer sky,
Flickering candle, shadow, will o' the wisp or dream.

This is how we are each to regard our
Existence and our experience in life.
Thus spake the Enlightened One.[6]

In an age of Pali and other languages in the Buddhist community, the beautiful *Diamond Sutra* was originally written in Sanskrit, to authenticate its validity in the same way that the Avesta had been written by Zoroaster in an earlier dialect, which has confused scholars of Zoroastrianism to this day. The *Diamond Sutra* purports to be a dialogue between a monk and the master regarding how to become empty of ego through such means as charity without expectation of recognition. As a guide toward becoming a selfless part of the One, it may be inspired and profound, but it may also seem somewhat like the famous "sound of one hand clapping" to the uninitiated, as some will have noted in the second quote from the esteemed Professor Abe. In contrast, the *Dhammapada* was compiled during the early years of Indian Buddhism, was embraced by the masses, helped to reform Hinduism (thus making Buddhism redundant in India), and built on Taoism to make Buddhism the dominant religion in China even before the Mahayana division.

Gil Fronsdal is a disciple of Kornfield, who teaches popular Buddhism in the San Francisco Bay Area. In the introduction to his 2006 translation of the *Dhammapada* for Shambhala Publications, he summarizes its teachings simply as living by ethical standards, disciplining one's own mind, being without hatred, being respectful, avoiding evil deeds, being nonviolent, and curbing one's anger. In a comment prescient to this study, he goes on to say that many of these are not uniquely Buddhist teachings. In fact, scholars have suggested that some verses in the *Dhammapada* may have been adapted from poetry, songs, and teachings popular in India before and during Buddha's time. We contend that the Buddha may have made such adaptations himself with then circulating Zoroastrian themes modified to his purposes, through revelations and enlightenments he received, much in the fashion of Muhammad's adaptation of much Jewish, Christian, and Zoroastrian (Magian/Sabaean) material in response to fresh revelation from on high.

We will now attempt to identify that putative Zoroastrian source with greater precision, beginning with a reasonable conjecture regarding the kind of "home-school" education a doting monarch like the Buddha's father might have provided for his son and heir apparent. Tutors were available from India's great centers of learning, and among the best such institutions was Takshashila, also known as Taxila, in the Punjab at the northwest border between India and Persia. We have no direct knowledge of the Buddha's education, but there is ample evidence of his complete familiarity with Indian trans-border lore.

Zoroaster, himself born of Scythian lineage, held forth from his headquarters at Balkh in Bactria/Afghanistan, just over the border from Taxila, a generation before Sidhartha Gautama was born of a Scythian tribe in Nepal, at a time of Zoroastrianism's active interaction with both Indian and Scythian culture on the wings of Persian influence. The exchange of ideas in the ancient East was possibly more fluid in the fifth century BCE than it was in the fifth century CE, though Western impressions of communications in the ancient East are largely formed on the basis of what we know about the latter date, a darker age until learning flourished again under Islamic vigor.

The oldest version of the *Dhammapada* canon is in the Pali language, a vernacular descendant of Sanskrit in use in the lifetime of the Buddha, believed by traditionalists to have been spoken by him. The very name of the book is a corruption or variation of the Sanskrit phrase *dharma pat*, or "religious path." A century of English translations, correct in a literal sense, have made us accustomed to the Eastern religious goal described as self-realization. Since selfishness itself is what we must avoid, according to this tradition, this may seem confusing. A more correct sense of what is being pursued would be One-realization, since the complete Self is the essence of the One.

This modification should not be impossible to promote, since even the actual word "monism" has come into general scholarly usage beginning in the twenty-first century. We might note in passing that none of the ancients of the East ever use the word "monism"; it never appears even once in their writing. This should be no surprise, since the word "monotheism" likewise does not appear anywhere in the Torah, the Gospel, or the Quran, neither monism nor monotheism being spoken of much before 1800 CE.

The *Dhammapada* begins, not with the Torah's perception that "in the beginning God created the heavens and the earth" as entities separate from God, but with the realization that "our life is the creation of our mind." It has been said that if the whole of the New Testament were lost or destroyed, Christians who could recite Jesus's Sermon on the Mount would have all they need to follow his teachings. The teachings of the Buddha are considerably more voluminous than those of the Christ, but Eknath Easwaran, a truly "Indian Guru" at the Blue Mountain Center of Meditation in California, plausibly makes exactly that claim for the *Dhammapada* as an Eastern testament in his highly regarded translation of this text.

Before quite leaving the survey of monism in the three main Buddhist traditions, we might take a glance at Tantrayana Buddhism, or Vajrayana, as it is sometimes called. We do so in part to respect its best-known testimonial, *The Heart Sutra*, as popularized by the best-known Buddhist in the modern world, the Dalai Lama, leader of Tibetan Buddhism, the most significant community in relation to the Tantrayana tradition. Beginning in the early sixth century CE, Tantrayana may be the only significant Buddhist tradition to reverse the flow of influence in which Buddhism was responsible for the remarkable reform of Hinduism, which revived the older Vedic sibling and enabled it to survive and flourish again. Instead, here it was Hinduism that influenced Buddhism in a slightly later era, another circle thus completed.

Hindu tantric practices began well before Buddhism appeared in India, an esoteric principle that holds an important place in both religions. There are both Hindus and Buddhists who insist that there is no connection between the two tantric traditions, and others who maintain that there is little difference between them—the truth probably lying somewhere in between. Tantra features the sacred feminine in Hinduism especially, the entire universe being considered the divine stage where Lord Shiva and his consort, Shakti, carry on the drama of life and become One—not very different from the Jewish and Christian teaching.[7] Tantra deals with ritual and spiritual practices to attain the grace that Shakti experienced, with the aim of achieving liberation from the darkness of ignorance, thus also attaining immortality.

A practitioner of tantric religion believes that the universe is the concrete manifestation of the divine energy of the One Supreme Power that creates and maintains that universe, drawing everything and everyone to itself. The seeker then attempts to make himself or herself a medium of this process in order for her or his own body and soul to channel that energy. Thus the practitioner attains liberation while still in human form, but he or she does so in a manner quite different from orthodox Hinduism or Buddhism.

The word "tantra" is taken from the two Sanskrit roots: *tanoti*, "to stretch," and *trayati*, which means "liberation." Its essence is the employment of liturgical words like spells, chants, or "mantras" and, more important, ritual actions instead of meditation to stretch oneself and combine with another to become liberated. These actions may include breathing patterns, eating requirements, yoga exercises, and sexual activity involving a "combining," which leads to something more like fulfillment than exhaustion. It would be tempting to make something of the visit to your local tandoori restaurant, where we find the most ritualized form of cooking and eating in which "earth" and "fire" (Arkadian *tin* and *nuro*) combine in a *tonir*, actually derived from the Hebrew תנור (oven).

The sexual illustration might be explicitly illustrative of the method and the goals of tantric devotion, despite a sometimes shallow exploitation of this tradition in modern bawdy culture. Breathing each other's breath, holding foreheads together, holding coitus in reserve, and then preventing or delaying climax all suggest fulfillment that may have some parallels to the universal "intercourse" with the divine, leading to a unity or One stripped of self-indulgence. Can this be seen as devotional activity? If so, and if exercised without self-indulgence, the model might be applied to eating, breathing, yoga exercises, and other activities as well.

Tantra has its roots in mysticism; thus some practitioners consider it very necessary to experience mystical phenomena during the course of their practice, sometimes achieved through the chanting of specific mantras designed to attain the state of *Sat-chit-ananda*, or "being-consciousness-bliss." Worship may include group *pooja* prayers, with men and women sitting alternately in a circle, or private yoga involving one person or two partners. The rituals may involve flowers, incense, chants, or anything sensate, but most often they will feature feasting (representing sustenance), intercourse (sexuality, fertility, and procreation), and urination, defecation, and vomiting (symbolizing removal of wastes), meaning that the devotee is working along with nature and not against it. Anecdotal evidence suggests that Western expressions of tantra relate to both Californian esoteric cults and recent physiological/psychological traumas identified as anorexia and bulimia, in which hypersensitive individuals (usually females) identify with a Buddhist ethos to a statistically remarkable and surprising degree.

Tantayana (or Vajrayana) Buddhism first appeared in India around the third century CE, reached the apex of its popularity in the sixth century, and continued until the twelfth century. It is active now mainly among the Vajrayana cults widespread in Tibet and esoteric Tantrayana cults in California, Germany, and Australia. It arrived on the ancient scene in time for one of its loveliest texts to be found in the Dunhuang trove of texts from the sixth century, discovered by Aurel Stein early in the twentieth century and illustrated in our appendix. Let us present the essence of this tradition by a paraphrase of its popular text, beloved by the Tibetan Dalai Lama, and ending with an English rendition of its best-known Sanskrit mantra: "Gate, gate, paragate, parasamgate bodhi savah." The *Heart Sutra* is not to become a testament celebrated in this book, but it is worthy of our awareness and attention.

The *Heart Sutra*[8]

Give Reverence to Divine Wisdom, both Beautiful and Sacred.
The Lord Avalokita, a Holy Bodhisattva, was deep into meditation
when he visualized the five sensate forms of things.
In realizing that each of them was actually empty,
he overcame all threats of illness and suffering in his own life.
He then addressed Sariputra, another of Buddha's disciples, thus:

Fulfillment is not different from emptiness,
and emptiness is not different from complete fulfillment.
Whatever is full is complete and whatever is emptied out is equally complete.
This is true for feelings, conceptions, perceptions and
for all conscious experiences, whether kept to oneself or shared out.
All teachings are both full and empty, as being understood and as being taught.

Therefore Sariputra,
No conscious experiences are valid, in and of themselves,
whether by eye, ear, nose, tongue, touch or even by mind.
We are not truly conscious until we overcome illusions,
ending the ignorance they promote, which simply leads on
to old age, death and non-attainment of anything real.

Therefore, Sariputra,
Reject the quest for attainment. As a Bodhisattva,
be free from trembling and trouble.
Pass beyond frustration, false imagining and stress into the peace of Nirvana.
So everyone should relax and laugh like all the Buddhas who have gone before,
Like those you see in statuary, and like true Buddhas
who illustrate this to people today.
What could go wrong, once you are liberated by chanting this spell?

It is the ultimate reality of nothing that gives us liberation
and hope in the value and meaning of anything.
Gate, gate, paragate, parasamgate bodhi savah
Let it go, let it go, let it go; from letting go it is all reborn, and so will be we all.

However, in this compendium we are not introducing Buddhism as practiced today, but rather introducing the earliest scriptures from which practices in vogue today evolved. There is the joke about what the Buddhist monk said to a hot dog vendor: "Make me one with everything." Is this not every Buddhist's prayer? This issue of the self and the not-self (*atman* and *anatman*) also carries forward as a special feature of our study into reformed Hinduism as presented in the *Bhagavad Gita*.[9]

Theravada Buddhism and Mahayana Buddhism differ on how *anatman* is understood. In fact, more than anything else, it is the different understanding of self that defines and separates the two schools. The Theravada of the *Dhammapada* considers *anatman* to mean that an individual's ego or personality is a fetter and delusion. Once freed of this delusion, the *individual* may enjoy the bliss of *nirvana*. Mahayana, however, considers all physical forms to be void of intrinsic self (a doctrine called *shunyata*, meaning "emptiness"). The ideal in Mahayana is to enable all beings to be enlightened *together*, not only out of a sense of compassion but also because we are not really separate, autonomous beings.

In an early Pali sutra, the *Maha-nidana Sutta*, the Buddha had taught that it was incorrect to say that the self is finite, but it is also incorrect to say that the self is infinite. We fall into the idea that we individuals are component parts of a One Thing, or that our individual self is false and only an infinite self-that-is-everything is true. The *Bhagavad Gita* shows its Theravada connection, adopted in the Axial Age when Buddhism reformed Hinduism on the basis of Zoroastrian stimulation.

The *Dhammapada* itself may seem repetitive to those reading it for the first time, but it presents the same thing from slightly different angles until we "get it." It sparkles like a many-faceted diamond, an image also used for the *Diamond Sutra* in the same manner. The novice should not ask "What am I getting out of this?" verse by verse—only at the end. When taking a bath or shower, one does not analyze the droplets of water, but, after being immersed in the stream or the tub, one feels clean at the conclusion.

The charm of Buddhism, which entrances many, might be grasped by the reader for whom this is new in the sensitive and insightful popular book, *The Dalai Lama's Cat*, by David Michie, available at any bookstore and most drugstores. In this story, caught in traffic on the way from an Indian airport to his base in Dharamsala, the Dalai Lama's car was importuned by children selling kittens. All sold to other motorists except a stunted "runt of the litter," so His Holiness rolled down his window and bought that one for two American dollars, all the cash he had at that moment of compassion and engagement. The book is written entirely from the perspective and in the voice of the cat, describing spiritual developments and monastic events, climaxing in the Buddhist understanding of "mindfulness," the ability to become divorced from the traumas of the past and detached from anxieties of the future, finding fulfillment in the ecstatic present.

While Buddhists writings are replete with illustrations of how mindfulness is the gateway to "awakening" to the fullness of reality through meditation, in this interrelated study we will progress to that stage of understanding of monism in its Hindu manifestation in the *Bhagavad Gita*. That "primary" testament appears to have emerged soon after the Buddha and the reforms that transformed Hinduism from raw Vedic tradition to the post-Zoroastrian sophistication in which it has appeared ever since.

9
dhammapada
Translated by Sarvepalli Radhakrishnan

chapter one: the twin verses

1. Our mental state is the result of what we have thought, is marshalled by our thoughts, and is composed of our thoughts. If a man speaks or acts with an evil thought, sorrow follows him as a consequence, even as the wheel follows the foot of the ox which draws the cart. (1)

2. Our mental state is the result of what we have thought, is marshalled by our thoughts, and is composed of our thoughts. If a man speaks or acts with a pure thought, happiness follows him in consequence, like a shadow that never leaves him. (2)

3. "He abused me, he struck me, he overcame me, he robbed me"—in those who harbour such thoughts hatred will never cease. (3)

4. "He abused me, he struck me, he overcame me, he robbed me,"—in those who do not harbour such thoughts hatred will cease. (4)

5. Not at any time are hostilities appeased here through hostilities but they are appeased through non-hostilities. This is the eternal dharma teaching. (5)

6. Some who are not learned do not know that we must all come to an end here; but those who accept this, cease their dissensions at once by their knowledge. (6)

7. As the wind blows down a tree of little strength so indeed does Mara, the tempter, topple him who lives looking for pleasures, uncontrolled in his senses, immoderate in eating, indolent, and of low vitality. (7)

8. As the wind does not blow down a rocky mountain, so Mara indeed does not topple him who lives unmindful of pleasures, well controlled in his senses, moderate in eating, full of faith, dharma, and community, and of high vitality. (8)

9. He who will wear the Buddhist yellow robe without having cleansed himself from impurity, who is devoid of truth and self-control, is not deserving of the yellow robe. (9)

10. But he who puts away depravity, is well grounded in all virtues, and is possessed of self-restraint and truth is worthy of the yellow robe. (10)

11. They who imagine truth in untruth and see untruth in truth, never arrive at truth but follow vain desires. (11)

12. But they who know truth as truth, and untruth as untruth, arrive at truth and follow right desires. (12)

13. As rain breaks through an ill-thatched roof, so passion makes its way into an unreflecting mind. (13)

14. As rain does not break through a well-thatched roof, so passion does not make its way into a reflecting mind. (14)

15. The evil-doer grieves in this world, he grieves in the next; he grieves in both. He grieves; he is afflicted, seeing the evil of his own actions. (15)

16. The righteous man rejoices in this world and he rejoices in the next; he rejoices in both. He rejoices and becomes delighted seeing the purity of his own actions. (16)

17. The evil-doer suffers in this world, he suffers in the next; he suffers in both. He suffers, thinking "evil has been done by me." He suffers even more when he has gone to the evil place. (17)

18. The righteous man rejoices in this world, he rejoices in the next; he rejoices in both. He rejoices, thinking "good has been done by me." He rejoices still more when he has gone to the good place. (18)

19. Even if he recites a large number of scriptural texts but, being slothful, does not act accordingly, he is like a cowherd counting the cows of others; he has no share in abundant religious life. (19)

20. Even if he recites only a small number of scriptural texts, if he is one who acts rightly in accordance with the teaching of dharma, he, having forsaken passion, hatred, and folly, being possessed of true knowledge and serenity of mind, being free from worldly desires both in this world and the next, has a share in the abundant religious life. (20)

chapter two: vigilance

1. Vigilance is the abode of eternal life; thoughtlessness is the abode of death. Those who are vigilant and given to reflection do not die. The thoughtless are as if dead already. (21)

2. The wise who have clearly understood this reflectiveness delight in reflecting and rejoice in the knowledge of the noble leaders. (22)

3. These wise ones, meditative, persevering, always put forth strenuous effort attain to nirvana, the highest freedom and happiness. (23)

4. If a person is reflective, if he rouses himself, if he is ever mindful, if his deeds are pure, if he acts with consideration, if he is self-restrained and lives according to dharma, his glory will increase. (24)

5. The wise man, by rousing himself, by vigilance, by restraint, by control, may make for himself an island which the flood cannot overwhelm. (25)

6. Fools, men of inferior intelligence, fall into sloth; the wise man guards his vigilance as his best treasure. (26)

7. Give not yourselves over to sloth or to the intimacy of lust and sensual pleasures. He who meditates with earnestness attains great joy. (27)

8. When the wise man drives away sloth by strenuous effort, climbing the high tower of wisdom, he gazes sorrowless on the sorrowing crowd below. The wise person gazes on the fools even as one on the mountain peak gazes upon the dwellers on the plain below. (28)

9. Earnest among the slothful, awake among the sleepy, the wise man advances even as a racehorse does, leaving behind the hack. (29)

10. By vigilance Indra rose to the lordship of the gods. People praise vigilance; thoughtlessness is always deprecated. (30)

11. A mendicant monk who delights in vigilance, who looks with fear on thoughtlessness and sees the danger in it, moves about like a fire consuming every bond, small or large. (31)

12. A mendicant monk who delights in vigilance, who looks with fear on thoughtlessness, cannot fall away, but is close to nirvana. (32)

chapter three: thought

1. Just as a fletcher makes straight his arrow, the wise man makes straight his mind in spite of trembling, unsteady thoughts which are difficult to guard and difficult to restrain. (33)

2. Even as a fish taken from his watery home and thrown on the dry ground moves about restlessly, this thought process quivers all over in order to escape the dominion of Mara, the tempter. (34)

3. The control of thought, which is difficult to restrain and fickle, which wanders at will, is good; a tamed mind is the bearer of happiness. (35)

4. Let the wise man guard his thought, which wanders at will. Thought which is well guarded is the bearer of happiness. (36)

5. They who restrain their thought, which travels far, alone, incorporeal, sealed in the cave of the heart, will be freed from the fetters of death. (37)

6. If a man's thought is unsteady, if it does not know the true dharma, if the serenity of mind is troubled, in him wisdom is not perfected. (38)

7. There is no fear in him whose thought is untroubled, whose thought is not agitated, who has ceased to think of good and evil, who is awake, watchful, and vigilant. (39)

8. Knowing that this body is fragile like a jar, making this thought firm like a fortress, let him attack Mara, the tempter, with the weapon of wisdom, protect what he has conquered and remain attached to it. (40)

9. Before long, alas, will this body lie on the earth, despised, bereft of consciousness, useless like a burnt faggot. (41)

10. Whatever an enemy may do to an enemy, whatever a hater may do to a hater, a wrongly directed mind will do us greater harm. (42)

11. Not a mother, not a father, nor any other relative will do so much; a well-directed mind will do us greater service. (43)

chapter four: flowers

1. Who will conquer this world and the world of Yama, the lord of the departed, with its gods? Who shall find out the well-taught path of virtue even as a skilled person finds out the right flower? (44)

2. The disciple will conquer this world and this world of Yama with its gods. The disciple will find out the well-taught path of virtue even as a skilled person finds out the right flower. (45)

3. Knowing that this body is like froth, knowing that it is of the nature of a mirage, breaking the flowery shafts of Mara, he will go where the king of death will not see him. (46)

4. Death carries off a man who is gathering life's flowers, whose mind is distracted, even as a flood carries off a sleeping village. (47)

5. Death overpowers a man even while he is gathering life's flowers and whose mind is distracted even before he is satiated in his pleasures. (48)

6. Even as a bee gathers honey from a flower and departs without injuring the flower or its color or scent, so let a sage dwell in his village. (49)

7. Not the unworthy actions of others, not their sinful deeds of commission or omission, but one's own deeds of commission and omission should one regard. (50)

8. Like a beautiful flower, full of color but without scent, are the well-spoken but fruitless words of he who does not act as he professes. (51)

9. But like a beautiful flower full of color and full of scent are the well-spoken and fruitful words of he who does act as he professes. (52)

10. As many kinds of garlands can be made from a heap of flowers, so many good works should be achieved by a mortal when once he is born. (53)

11. The scent of flowers does not travel against the wind, nor does that of sandalwood, tagara and mallika flowers, but the fragrance of good people travels even against the wind. A good man pervades every quarter. (54)

12. Sandalwood or tagara, a lotus flower or jasmine, among these kinds of perfumes the perfume of virtue is unsurpassed. (55)

13. Little is the scent that comes from tagara or sandalwood; but the perfume of those who possess virtue rises up to the gods as the highest. (56)

14. Of those who possess these virtues, who live without thoughtlessness, who are freed by perfect knowledge, Mara the tempter never finds their way. (57)

15. Just as on a heap of rubbish, thrown upon the highway, the lotus grows sweetly fragrant and delighting the heart. (58)
16. Even so, among those blinded mortals who are like rubbish, the disciple of the truly enlightened Buddha shines with exceeding glory by his wisdom. (59)

chapter five: the fool

1. Long is the night to him who is awake, long is the journey to him who is weary; long is the chain of existence to the foolish who do not know the true dharma. (60)
2. If on a journey a traveler does not meet his better or equal, let him firmly pursue his journey by himself; there is no companionship with a fool. (61)
3. The fool is tormented thinking "these sons belong to me"; "this wealth belongs to me." He himself does not belong to himself. How can wealth be his? (62)
4. The fool who knows his foolishness is wise at least to that extent; but a fool who thinks himself wise is called fool indeed. (63)
5. If a fool be associated with a wise man even all his life, he does not perceive the truth even as a spoon does not perceive the taste of soup. (64)
6. But a thoughtful man associated with a wise man even for a minute, will perceive the truth even as the tongue perceives the taste of soup. (65)
7. Fools of little understanding, being enemies to themselves, wander about doing evil deeds which bear bitter fruits. (66)
8. That deed is not well done, which, having been done, brings remorse, whose reward one receives weeping and with a tearful countenance. (67)
9. But that deed is well done, which having being done, does not bring remorse, whose reward one receives with delight and happiness. (68)
10. So long as an evil deed does not bear fruit, the fool thinks that it is like honey; but when it bears fruits, and then the fool suffers grief. (69)
11. Let a fool eat his food month after month with fine utensils; nevertheless he is not worth a fraction of those who have understood the dharma. (70)
12. An evil deed, like newly drawn milk, does not turn at once; smoldering, like fire covered by ashes, it follows the fool. (71)
13. The knowledge that a fool acquires, far from being to his advantage, destroys his bright share of merit and splits his brain. (72)
14. Let the fool wish for false reputation, precedence among the mendicant monks, lordship in convents, and worship among other groups. (73)
15. "Let both householders and monks think that this is done by me. Let them follow my pleasure in what should be done and what should not be done." Such is the fool's wish, and so his desire and pride increase. (74)
16. One is the road that leads to gain; another is the road that leads to nirvana. Let, the mendicant monk, the disciple of the Buddha, having learnt this, not seek the respect of men but strive after wisdom. (75)

chapter six: the wise man

1. If a person meets a wise man who reproaches him for his faults, and who shows what is to be avoided, he should follow such a wise man as he would a revealer of hidden treasures. It goes well and not ill with one who follows such a man. (76)
2. Let him admonish, let him instruct, let him restrain from the impure. He becomes beloved of the good and hated by the evil. (77)
3. One should not associate with friends who are evil-doers nor with persons who are despicable; associate with friends who are virtuous, associate with the best of men. (78)
4. He who drinks in the dharma lives happily with a serene mind. The wise man ever rejoices in the dharma made known by the elect nobles. (79)
5. Engineers who build canals and aqueducts lead the water wherever they like, fletchers make the arrow straight, carpenters carve the wood; wise people fashion themselves by adherence to the teaching of dharma. (80)
6. As a solid rock is not shaken by the wind, so wise men are not moved amidst blame and praise. (81)
7. Even as a deep lake is clear and calm so also wise men become tranquil after they have listened to the dharma. (82)
8. Good people rise above whatever happens to them. Good people do not prattle, yearning for pleasures. The wise do not show variations of elation or depression, whether touched by happiness or else by sorrow. (83)
9. He who, for his own sake or for the sake of another, does not wish for a son or wealth or a kingdom, if he does not wish for his own prosperity by unfair means he certainly is virtuous, wise, and religious. (84)
10. Few amongst men are those who reach the farther shore; the other people here run along this shore. (85)
11. But those who, when the dharma has been well preached to them, follow the dharma, will pass to the other shore, beyond the dominion of death which is difficult to overcome. Only those who understand the dharma and follow it in practice can attain nirvana. (86)
12. Let the wise man leave the way of darkness and follow the way of light. After going from his home to a homeless state, that retirement so hard to love. (87)
13. Let him there look for enjoyment. Putting away all pleasures, calling nothing his own, let the wise man cleanse himself from all the impurities of the heart. (88)
14. Those whose minds are well grounded in the seven elements of enlightenment, who without clinging to anything rejoice in freedom from attachment, whose appetites have been conquered, who are full of light, attain nirvana in this world. (89)

chapter seven: the saint

1. There is no suffering for him who has completed his journey, who is freed from sorrow, who has freed himself on all sides, who has shaken off all fetters. (90)

2. The thoughtful exert themselves; they do not delight in an abode; like swans who have left their lake, they leave their house and home. (91)
3. Those who have no accumulation of property, who eat according to knowledge, who have perceived the nature of release and unconditioned freedom, their path is difficult to understand like that the flight of birds through the sky. (92)
4. He whose passions are destroyed, who is indifferent to food, who has perceived the nature of release and unconditioned freedom, his path is also difficult to understand like that of birds through the sky. (93)
5. Even the gods envy him whose senses are subdued like horses well tamed by the charioteer, who is free from pride and from taints. (94)
6. Such is a man who is tolerant like the patient earth, he is like a threshold; he does his duty, he is like a lake free from mud; to a man like that there is no cycle of births and deaths. (95)
7. His thought is calm, his word is calm, his deed is calm when he has obtained freedom through knowledge and has become tranquil. (96)
8. The man who is free from credulity, who knows the uncreated, who has severed all ties, who has put an end to all occasions for the performance of good or bad actions, who has renounced all desires, he, indeed, is exalted among men. (97)
9. The place is delightful where saints dwell, whether in the village or in the forest, in deep water or on dry land. (98)
10. Forests are delightful to saints; the passionless will find delight there where ordinary people find no delight, for they do not seek the pleasures of sense. (99)

chapter eight: the thousands

1. Better than a thousand utterances composed of meaningless words is one sensible word, on hearing which one becomes peaceful. (100)
2. Better than a thousand verses composed of meaningless words is one word of a verse on hearing which one becomes peaceful. (101)
3. Better than reciting a hundred verses composed of meaningless words is one text on hearing which one becomes peaceful. (102)
4. If a man was to conquer in battle a thousand times a thousand men, and another conquer one, namely himself, he indeed is the greatest of conquerors. (103)
5. Conquest of self is indeed better than the conquest of other persons; achieved by one who has disciplined himself, who always practices self-control. (104)
6. Not even a god nor a fairy, nor Mara along with Brahma could turn into defeat the victory of one who has conquered himself. (105)
7. If a man month after month for a hundred years should sacrifice with a thousand religious sacrifices, and if he but for one moment pay homage to a man whose self is grounded in knowledge, better is that homage than what is sacrificed for a hundred years. (106)

8. If a man tends the sacrificial fire in the forest for a hundred years, and then for one moment pays homage to one whose self is grounded in knowledge, that homage is better than what is sacrificed for a hundred years. (107)

9. Whatever a man sacrifices in this world as an offering or oblation for a year in hopes of gaining merit, the whole of it is not worth a fraction of the better offering—homage paid to the righteous. (108)

10. To him who constantly practices reverence and respects the aged, four things will increase: lifespan, beauty, happiness, strength. (109)

11. But compared with he who lives a hundred years, wicked and unrestrained, a life of one day is better if a man is virtuous and reflecting. (110)

12. And for he who lives a hundred years, ignorant and unrestrained, a life of one day is better for one who is wise and reflecting. (111)

13. And for he who lives a hundred years, idle and weak, a life of one day is better if a man strenuously makes an effort. (112)

14. And for he who lives a hundred years, not perceiving beginning and end, birth and death, a life of one day is better if a man perceives the beginning and the end. (113)

15. And for he who lives a hundred years not perceiving the deathless state, a life of one day is better if a man perceives the deathless state. (114)

16. And for he who lives a hundred years not perceiving the highest law of dharma, a life of one day is better if a man perceives the highest law of dharma. (115)

chapter nine: evil conduct

1. A man should hasten towards the good; he should restrain his thoughts from evil. If a man is slack in doing what is good, his mind comes to rejoice in evil. (116)

2. If a man commits sin, let him not do it again and again. Let him not set his heart on it. Sorrowful is the accumulation of evil conduct. (117)

3. If a man does what is good, let him do it again and again. Let him set his heart on it. Happiness is the outcome of good conduct. (118)

4. Even an evil-doer sees happiness so long as his evil deed does ripen; but when the evil deed has ripened, then does the evil-doer see evil. (119)

5. Even a good man sees evil as long as his good deed does not ripen; but when his good deep ripens, then the good man sees the good in store for him. (120)

6. Think not lightly of evil, saying that "if I do, it will come near me." Even a water-pot is filled by the falling of drops of water. A fool becomes full of evil even if he gathers it little by little. (121)

7. Think not lightly of good saying that "if I do, it will not come near me." Even a water-pot is filled by the falling of drops of water. A wise man becomes full of goodness even if he gathers it little by little. (122)

8. As a merchant ill-attended and having much wealth shuns a dangerous road, and as a man who lives his life avoids poison, so should a wise man avoid evil actions. (123)

9. If there be no wound on a person's hand he might touch poison with his hand. Poison does not harm one who has no wound. No evil befalls him who does no evil. (124)

10. Whoever does wrong to an innocent person or to one who is pure and sinless, evil recoils on that fool even as fine dust thrown against the wind recoils on the person throwing it. (125)

11. Some enter the womb; evil-doers go to hell; the good go to heaven; those free from worldly desires attain nirvana. (126)

12. Neither in the sky, nor in the midst of the sea, nor by entering into the clefts of mountains is there known a place on earth where stationing himself, a man can escape from the consequences of his evil deed. (127)

13. Neither in the sky, nor in the midst of the sea, nor by entering into the clefts of mountains is there known a place on earth where stationing himself, death cannot overcome him. (128)

chapter ten: punishment

1. All men tremble at punishment, all men fear death. Likening others to oneself, one should neither slay nor cause to slay. (129)

2. All men tremble at punishment; all men love life. Likening others to oneself, one should neither slay nor cause to slay. (130)

3. He who, seeking his own happiness, inflicts pain on beings who, like himself, are desirous of happiness, does not obtain happiness after death. (131)

4. He who seeking his own happiness does not inflict pain on beings who, like himself, are desirous of happiness obtains happiness after death. (132)

5. Do not speak anything harsh. Those who are spoken to will answer you in the same way. Since angry talk is painful, retaliation will touch you. (133)

6. If you make yourself as still as a broken gong you have attained nirvana, for agitation is not known to you. (134)

7. Just as a cowherd with his staff drives the cows into the pasture, so old age and death drive the life of sentient beings into a new existence. (135)

8. But a fool committing evil deeds does not know what is in store for him. The stupid man is consumed by his own deeds as if burnt by fire. (136)

9. He who inflicts punishment on those who do not deserve punishment and offends against those who are without offence soon comes to one of these ten states. (137)

10. He may have cruel suffering, infirmity, injury of the body, dread diseases, or loss of mind. (138)

11. He may have misfortune proceeding from the king, a fearful accusation, loss of relations, destruction of treasures, (139)

12. or lightning fire burns his houses, and when his body is dissolved the fool goes to hell. (140)

13. Not nakedness, nor matted hair, nor dirt, not fasting, not lying on the ground, not rubbing with ashes, not sitting motionless purifies a mortal who is not free from doubt. (141)
14. Even if someone dresses in fine clothes, if he fosters the serene mind, if he is calm, if he is controlled, and established in the Buddhist way of life, chaste, and has ceased to injure all other beings, he indeed is a Brahmin, an ascetic, a friar. (142)
15. Is there anyone in the world so noble that he cannot accept criticism, just as a well-trained horse responds to the whip? (143)
16. Like a well-trained horse when touched by a whip, be strenuous and swift and you will, by faith, by virtue, by energy, by meditation, by discernment of the dharma, put aside the great sorrow of earthly existence, and be endowed with knowledge, good behavior and mindfulness. (144)
17. Engineers who build canals and aqueducts lead the water where they like; fletchers make the arrow straight; carpenters carve the wood; good people discipline themselves. (145)

chapter eleven: old age

1. Why is there laughter, why is their joy while this world is always burning? When you are shrouded in darkness, should you not seek a lamp? (146)
2. Behold this painted image, a manikin full of wounds, stitched together but falling apart, and full of thoughts in which there is neither permanence nor stability. (147)
3. This body is worn out, a nest of diseases and very frail. The corrupt heap disintegrates; life indeed ends in death. (148)
4. What delight is there for him who sees these white bones like gourds cast away in the autumn? (149)
5. The body is a bony fortress, made and plastered over with flesh and blood. In it dwell old age and death, pride and deceit. (150)
6. The splendid chariots of kings wear away; the body also comes to old age but the virtue of the good never ages, thus the good teach to each other. (151)
7. A man who has learnt but little grows old like an ox; his flesh increases but his knowledge does not grow. (152)
8. I have run a course of many births looking for the maker of this dwelling and finding him not; painful is birth again and again. (153)
9. Now are you seen, O builder of the house, you will not build the house again. All your rafters are broken, your ridgepole is destroyed, the mind, set on the attainment of nirvana, has attained the extinction of desires. (154)
10. Men who have not practiced the proper discipline of celibacy, who have not acquired wealth in youth, pine away like old cranes in a lake without fish. (155)
11. Men who have not practiced celibacy, who have not acquired wealth in youth, lie like worn out bows, sighing after the past. (156)

chapter twelve: the self

1. If a man holds himself dear, let him diligently watch himself. The wise man should be watchful during one of the three watches. (157)
2. Let each man first establish himself in what is proper, then let him teach others. If he does this the wise man will not suffer. (158)
3. If a man so shapes his life as he directs others, then, subduing himself well, he might indeed subdue others, since the self is indeed difficult to subdue. (159)
4. The man himself is the lord of self; who else could be the lord? With self well subdued a man finds a lord who is difficult to obtain. (160)
5. The evil done by oneself, born of oneself, produced by oneself, crushes oneself, crushes the fool even as a diamond breaks a precious stone. (161)
6. As a creeping vine overpowers an entwined tree, he whose impiety is great reduces himself to the state which his enemy wishes for him. (162)
7. Evil deeds, deeds which are harmful to oneself, are easy to do. What is beneficial and good, that is very difficult to do. (163)
8. The foolish man who scorns the teaching of the saintly, the noble, the virtuous and follows false doctrine, bears fruit to his own destruction even like the reed which dies after bearing fruit. (164)
9. By oneself, indeed, is evil done; by oneself is one injured. By oneself is evil left undone; by oneself is one purified. Purity and impurity belong to oneself. No one purifies another. (165)
10. Let no one neglect his own task for the sake of another's, however great; let him, after he has discerned his own task, devote himself to his task. (166)

chapter thirteen: the world

1. Do not follow evil law. Do not live in thoughtlessness. Do not follow false doctrine. Do not be a friend of the world. (167)
2. Rouse yourself and think things through. Follow the dharma of virtue. He who practices virtue lives happily in this world as well as in the world beyond. (168)
3. Follow the dharma of virtue; do not follow the law of sin. He who practices virtue lives happily in this world as well as in the world beyond. (169)
4. Look upon the world as a bubble; look upon it as a mirage. He who looks thus upon the world is not himself seen by the king of death. (170)
5. Come; look at this world as resembling a painted royal chariot. The foolish are sunk in it; for the wise there is no attachment to it. (171)
6. He who formerly was thoughtless and afterwards became reflective and sober lights up this world like the moon when free from a cloud. (172)
7. He whose evil conduct is covered by good conduct lights up this world like the moon when freed from a cloud. (173)

8. This world is blinded, few only can see here. Like birds escaped from the net a few go to heaven. (174)

9. The swans go on the path of the sun; they go through the sky by means of their miraculous power. The wise are led out of this world, having conquered Mara, the temper, and his hosts. (175)

10. He who violates the one dharma (the Buddha's doctrine), who speaks falsely, scoffs at another world, there is no evil he will not do. (176)

11. Verily, the niggardly do not go to the realm of divinity. Fools, indeed, do not give praise. But the wise man, rejoicing in charity, becomes on that account happy in that other world. (177)

12. Better than absolute sovereignty on earth, better than going to heaven, better than lordship over all the worlds is the reward of stepping into the stream, the first step on the path of holiness. (178)

chapter fourteen: the awakened*

1. He whose conquest is not conquered again, into whose conquest no one in this world enters: by what track can you lead him, the awakened, of infinite perception, the trackless? (179)

2. He who is without desire and free of passions that lead astray, by what track can you follow him, the awakened, of infinite perception, the trackless? (180)

3. Even the gods emulate those wise men who are given to meditation, who delight in the peace of emancipation from desire, the enlightened, the reflective. (181)

4. Human birth requires difficult labor. More difficult still is the life of mortals, exceeded by learning the dharma, and finally by the rise to enlightenment. (182)

5. The eschewing of all evil, the perfecting of good deeds, the purifying one's mind, this is the teaching of the awakened. (183)

6. The awakened declare nirvana to be the highest of things. He verily is not a hermit who oppresses others; he is not an ascetic who causes grief to another. (184)

7. Not reviling, not injuring, practicing restraint according to the law, moderation in eating, dwelling in solitude, diligence in higher thought, this is the teaching of the awakened. (185)

8. There is no satisfaction of one's passions even by a shower of gold pieces. He who know that "passions are of small enjoyment and productive of pain" is a wise man. (186)

9. Even in celestial pleasures he finds no delight. The disciple who is fully awakened delights only in the destruction of all desires. (187)

10. Men driven by fear go to many a refuge, to mountains, and to forests, to sacred trees, and shrines. (188)

11. That, verily, is not safe refuge, that is not the best refuge. After having arrived at that refuge a man is not delivered from all pains. (189)

---

*Or "The Buddha."

12. But he who takes refuge in the Buddha, and Dharma, and the Order, he perceives, in his clear wisdom, the four noble truths. (190)

13. Suffering, the origin of suffering, the cessation of suffering, and the noble eight-fold path which leads to the cessation of suffering. (191)

14. That, verily, is a safe refuge, that is the best refuge; after having got to that refuge a man is delivered from all pains. (192)

15. A well-bred person, himself a Buddha, is difficult to be found. He is not born everywhere. Wherever such a wise one is born that household prospers. (193)

16. Blessed is the birth if of the awakened; blessed is the teaching of the dharma; blessed is concord in the Order; blessed is the austerity of those who live in concord. (194)

17. He who pays homage to those who are worthy of homage, whether the awakened or their disciples, are those who have overcome the host of evils and crossed beyond the stream of sorrow. (195)

18. He who pays homage to such as give us a religion of hope finds deliverance and freedom from fear, and no one can gainsay these benefits. (196)

chapter fifteen: happiness

1. Let us live happily, then, hating none in the midst of men who hate. Let us dwell free from hate among men who hate. (197)

2. Let us live happily then, free from disease in the midst of those who are afflicted with disease. (198)

3. Let us live happily then, free from care in the midst of those who are careworn; let us dwell free from care among men who are careworn. (199)

4. Let us live happily then, though we possess nothing. Let us dwell feeding on happiness like shining spiritual beings. (200)

5. Victory breeds hatred; the conquered dwells in sorrow. He who has given up thoughts of both victory and defeat is calm and lives happily. (201)

6. There is no fire like passion, no ill like hatred. There is no sorrow like this individual physical existence, there is no happiness higher than tranquility. (202)

7. Greediness is the worst of diseases; propensities are the greatest of sorrows. To him that has known this truly, nirvana is the highest bliss. (203)

8. Health is the greatest of gifts; contentment is the greatest wealth; trust is the best of relationships. Nirvana is the highest happiness. (204)

9. Having tasted the sweetness of solitude and the sweetness of tranquility, one becomes free from fear and free from sin while he drinks the sweetness of the joy of the dharma. (205)

10. The sight of the noble is good; to live in their company is always happiness. He will always be happy who does not engage with fools. (206)

11. He who consorts with a fool suffers a long time. Association with fools as with an enemy is always productive of pain. Association with the wise, as meeting with one's kinfolk, is productive of happiness. (207)
12. Therefore, even as the moon follows the path of the constellations, one should follow the wise, the intelligent, the learned, the much enduring, the dutiful, the noble: the wise man should follow such as these. (208)

chapter sixteen: pleasure

1. He who gives himself to the distractions of the world and does not devote himself to meditation, giving up his own welfare and grasping at pleasure, will envy him who exerts himself in meditation. (209)
2. Let no man cling to what is pleasant or unpleasant. Not to see what is pleasant is pain, as also it is pain to see what is unpleasant. (210)
3. Therefore, do not take a liking to anything; loss of the loved object is evil. There are no limits for him who has neither likes nor dislikes. (211)
4. From these attachments arises grief; from these attachments arises fear. To one who is free from attachments there is no grief, how then can there be fear? (212)
5. From affection arises grief; from affection arises fear. To one who is free from affection there is no grief. How then can there be fear? (213)
6. From enjoyment arises grief, from enjoyment arises fear. To one who is free from enjoyment there is no grief. How then can there be fear? (214)
7. From desire arises grief, from desires arises fear. To one who is free and from desire there is no grief. How then can there be fear? (215)
8. From craving arises grief, from craving arises fear. To one who is free from craving there is no grief. How then can there be fear? (216)
9. He who is endowed with true virtue and insight, who is established in the dharma, who is truthful, who minds his own affairs, him the world holds dear. (217)
10. He in whom a desire for the Ineffable has arisen, who is replete with mind, whose thought is freed from desires, he is one who succeeds in swimming upstream. (218)
11. When a man who has been long away returns safe from afar, kinsmen, friends, and well-wishers receive him gladly. (219)
12. Even so his good deeds receive the good man who has gone from this world to the next, as kinsmen receive a friend on his return. (220)

chapter seventeen: anger

1. Let a man put away anger, let him renounce pride. Let him get beyond all worldly attachments; no sufferings befall him who is not attached to phenomenal existence, who calls nothing his own. (221)

2. He who curbs his rising anger like a chariot gone off track, him I call a real charioteer: others just hold the reins and do not deserve to be called charioteers. (222)

3. Let a man overcome anger by gentleness, let him overcome evil by good, let him overcome the miser by liberality; let him overcome the liar by truth. (223)

4. One should speak the truth, not yield to anger, even if goaded. By these three means one will certainly come into the presence of divinity. (224)

5. The sages who injure none, who always control their body, go to the unchangeable place, where, having gone, they do not grieve. (225)

6. Those who are ever vigilant, who study by day and by night, who strive after nirvana, their taints come to an end. (226)

7. This is an old saying which applies today: "They blame him who remains silent, they blame him who talks much, they blame also him who speaks in moderation." There is not anyone in the world who is not blamed. (227)

8. There never was, nor will be, nor is there now to be found anyone who is completely at fault, or anyone who should be wholly praised. (228)

9. But who would dare blame the one who discerning critics praise consistently, as without blemish, wise, endowed with meditative wisdom and virtue? (229)

10. Who is worthy to blame him who is like a pure gold coin found in the river? Even the divinities praise him; he is praised even by Brahma. (230)

11. Let one be watchful of bodily irritation. Let him practice restraint of the body. Having abandoned the sins of the body, let him practice virtue with his body. (231)

12. Let one be watchful of irritable speech. Let him practice restraint of speech. Having abandoned the sins of speech let him practice virtue with his speech. (232)

13. Let one be watchful of irritable thinking. Let him practice restraint of mind. Having abandoned the sins of mind let him practice virtue with his mind. (233)

14. The wise who control their bodies, who likewise control their speech, the wise who control their minds are indeed well controlled. (234)

chapter eighteen: impurity

1. You are now like a withered leaf; even the messengers of death have come near you. You stand at the gate of death and you have not made provision for your journey. (235)

2. Make for yourself an island refuge, strive quickly, be wise. When your impurities are purged and you are free from sin you will reach heaven, the land of the elect. (236)

3. Your life has come near to an end; you are arrived in the presence of the king of death. There is no resting-place for you on the way and you have made no provision for your journey. (237)

4. Make for yourself an island refuge, strive quickly, be wise. When your impurities are purged and you are free from sin, you will not again enter into birth and old age. (238)

5. As a smith removes the impurities of silver, even so let a wise man remove the impurities of himself one by one, little by little, and from time to time. (239)

6. Impurity arising from iron eats into it, though born from itself; likewise the evil deeds of the transgressor lead him to the evil state. (240)

7. The failure to recite makes the prayer impure, failure to groom makes the personal appearance impure, and diversion is what makes the watchman impure. (241)

8. Bad conduct is the impurity of a woman; stinginess is the impurity of the giver; evil deeds are impurities in this world and in the next. (242)

9. But there is an impurity greater than all impurities. Ignorance is the greatest impurity, O mendicant monks, having cast away that impurity, be free from all impurities. (243)

10. Life is easy to live for one who is shameless, a hero of crows, a mischief-maker, a slanderer, the impudent, and the impure. (244)

11. Life is hard to live for one who has a sense of modesty, who always seeks for what is pure, who is disinterested, not impudent, who lives in purity; the man of insight. (245)

12. He who destroys life, who speaks untruth, who in this world takes what is not given to him, who goes to another man's wife, (246)

13. and he who gives himself to drinking intoxicating liquors, he, even in this world, digs up his own root. (247)

14. Know this, O man, that evil things befall the unrestrained. Let not greed and wrong-doing bring you to grief for a long time. (248)

15. Men give alms according to their faith or according to their friendliness. Therefore, he who frets about the drink and food given to others does not, either by day or by night, enjoy peace of mind. (249)

16. He, in whom this spirit of envy is destroyed, removed by the very root, he, indeed, by day and by night, enjoys peace of mind. (250)

17. There is no fire like passion, no predator like hatred; there is no snare like delusion, no torrent like craving. (251)

18. The fault of others is easily seen; our own is difficult to see. A man winnows others' faults like chaff, but his own faults he hides even as a cheat hides an unlucky throw. (252)

19. To him who is observant of the faults of others, who is ever censorious, his own passions increase and he is far from the destruction of passions. (253)

20. There is no path through the sky, so the monk must find the path himself. Mankind delights in worldliness; the Buddhas are free from worldliness. (254)

21. There is no path through the sky; so the monk must find the path himself. Nothing in the phenomenal world is eternal, there is no instability to the awakened. (255)

chapter nineteen: the righteous

1. He who carries out his purpose by violence is not therein established in the dharma. He is wise who makes conscious decisions about right and wrong. (256)

2. He who guides others by a procedure that is nonviolent and equitable, he is said to be a guardian of the dharma, wise and righteous. (257)
3. A man is not learned simply because he talks much. He who is tranquil, free from hatred, free from fear, he is said to be learned. (258)
4. A man is not a supporter of the dharma simply because he talks much, but he who, little learned, discerns it by his body, he who does not neglect the dharma himself, he, indeed, is the supporter of the dharma. (259)
5. A man is not an elder simply because his hair is grey. His age is ripe, but he is called an old fool. (260)
6. He in whom dwell truth, virtue, nonviolence, restraint, control, he who is free from impurity and is wise, he is called an elder. (261)
7. Not by mere talk, not by the beauty of the complexion, does a man who is envious, greedy, and wicked become of good disposition. (262)
8. It is by him that envy, greed, and wickedness are destroyed, removed by the very root. He who is free from guilt and is wise, is said to look distinguished. (263)
9. Not by cutting his hair like a monk does one who is undisciplined and who speaks untruth become a religious man. How can one who is full of desire and greed be a religious man? (264)
10. But he who always quiets the evil tendencies, small or large, is called a religious man because he has quieted all evil. (265)
11. He is not a mendicant monk simply because he begs others for alms. He who adopts the whole law is a mendicant monk, not he who adopts only a part. (266)
12. But he who is above good and evil and is chaste, who comports himself in the world with knowledge, he, indeed, is called a mendicant monk. (267)
13. By observing silence a man does not become a sage if he be foolish and ignorant; but that wise man, who, holding the scale, takes what is good, (268)
14. and avoids the evil, he is a sage for that very reason. He, who in this world weighs both sides, is called a sage on that very account. (269)
15. A man is not noble if he injures living creatures. He is called noble because he does not injure living beings. (270)
16. Not only by disciplined conduct and vows, not only by much learning, or even by the attainment of meditative calm, nor by sleeping solitary, (271)
17. do I reach the happiness of release which no worldling can attain. O mendicant monk, do not rest content as long as you have not reached the extinction of impurities. (272)

chapter twenty: the path

1. Of paths the eightfold is the best: of truths the best are four sayings; of virtues freedom from attachment is the best; of men the best is he who is possessed of sight. (273)
2. This is the path; there is none other that leads to the purifying of insight. You are to follow this path. This will be to confuse escape from Mara, death and sin. (274)

3. Going on this path, you will end your suffering. This path was preached by me when I became aware of the removal of the thorns in the flesh. (275)

4. You yourself must strive. The blessed Ones are only preachers. Those who enter the path and practice meditation are released from the bondage of Mara, death and sin. (276)

5. "All created things are transitory." When one by wisdom realizes this, he is superior to this world of sorrow; this is the path to purity. (277)

6. "All created things are sorrowful." When one by wisdom realizes this he is superior to this world of sorrow; this is the path to purity. (278)

7. "All the elements of being are non-self." When one by wisdom realizes this, he is superior to this world of sorrow; this is the path to purity. (279)

8. He who does not get up when it is time to get up, who, though young and strong, is full of sloth, who is weak in resolution and thought, that lazy and idle man will not find the way to wisdom. (280)

9. Guarding his speech, restraining well his mind, let a man not commit anything wrong with his body. He, who keeps these three roads of action clear, will achieve the way taught by the wise. (281)

10. From meditation springs wisdom; from lack of meditation there is loss of wisdom. Knowing this twofold path of progress and decline, a man should place himself in such a way that his wisdom increases. (282)

11. Cut down the whole forest, not the tree only; danger comes out of the forest. Having cut down both the forest and desire, O mendicant monks, you attain freedom. (283)

12. As long indeed as the desire, however small, of a man for women is not destroyed, that is how long his mind is attached to existence, like a sucking calf is attached to its mother. (284)

13. Cut out the love of self as you would an autumn lily with the hand. Cherish the path to peace, to nirvana pointed out by the Buddha. (285)

14. "Here I shall dwell in the rain, here in the winter and summer" thus the fool thinks; he does not think of the obstacle of life itself. (286)

15. As a great flood carries off a sleeping village, death takes off and goes with that man who is giddy with the possession of children and cattle, whose mind is distracted with the desire for worldly goods. (287)

16. Sons are no protection, nor father, nor relations, for one who is seized by death; there is no safety in kinsmen. (288)

17. Realizing the significance of this, the wise and righteous man should even more quickly clear the path leading to release. (289)

chapter twenty-one:
miscellaneous verses

1. If, by surrendering a pleasure of little worth one sees a larger pleasure, the wise man will give up the pleasure of little worth, and look to the larger pleasure. (290)

2. He who desires happiness for himself by inflicting suffering on others is then entangled in the bonds of hatred, and is not freed from hatred. (291)
3. If, by giving up what should be done, what should not be done is done, in those unrestrained and careless, the taints increase. (292)
4. But those whose mindfulness is always alert to the nature of the body, who do not aim at what should not be done, who steadfastly do what should be done, the impurities of these mindful and wise people come to an end. (293)
5. A true Brahmin goes unscathed though he has killed his father and mother and two kings of the warrior caste and a kingdom with all its subjects. (294)
6. A true Brahmin goes unscathed though he have killed his father and mother and two holy kings and an eminent man as the fifth. (295)
7. The disciples of Gautama are always well awake; their thought is always, day and night, set on the Buddha. (296)
8. The disciples of Gautama are always well awake; their thought is always, day and night, set by the Dharma. (297)
9. The disciples of Gautama are always well awake; their thought is always, day and night, set on the Order. (298)
10. The disciples of Gautama are always well awake; their thought is always, day and night, set on the nature of the body. (299)
11. The disciples of Gautama are always well awake; their mind, day and night, delights in abstinence from harm through compassion. (300)
12. The disciples of Gautama are always well awake; their mind, day and night, delights in meditation. (301)
13. It is hard to leave the world as a recluse and hard to enjoy. Hard also is it to live at home as a householder. Living with the unsympathetic is painful. The life of a wanderer is beset with pain. Therefore let no man be a wanderer, let no one fall into suffering. (302)
14. Whatever region a man of faith, endowed with virtue, with fame, and prosperity is allotted, that is where he is revered. (303)
15. Good people shine from afar like the Himalaya Mountains but the wicked are not seen, like arrows shot in the night. (304)
16. Let one sit alone, sleep alone, act alone without being indolent, subdue his self by means of his self alone; then he will find delight in the extinction of desires. (305)

chapter twenty-two: hell

1. He who speaks what is not real goes to hell; he also, who having done a thing says "I do not do it." After death both become equal, being men with evil deeds in the next existence. (306)
2. Many men who are clad in yellow robes are ill-behaved and unrestrained. Such evil-doers by their evil deeds go to hell. (307)
3. Better is it for an irreligious unrestrained person to swallow a ball of red-hot iron than enjoy the charity of the land. (308)

4. An unthinking man who courts another's wife gains four things, access of demerit, broken rest, thirdly blame, and fourthly hell. (309)

5. There is access of demerit as well as the way to evil state; there is the short-lived pleasure of the frightened in the arms of the frightened, and a heavy penalty from the ruler. Therefore do not run after another man's wife. (310)

6. As a blade of grass when wrongly handled cut the hand, so also asceticism when wrongly tried leads to hell. (311)

7. An act carelessly performed, a vow improperly observed, unwilling obedience to the code of chastity bring no great reward. (312)

8. If anything is to be done let one do it vigorously. A recluse who is careless only bespatters himself the more with dust. (313)

9. An evil deed left undone is better, for an evil deed causes suffering later. A good deed done is better for doing, it does not cause suffering. (314)

10. As a frontier town is well-guarded within and without, so guard the self. Do not let a moment glide by, for they who allow the moments to pass by suffer when they are consigned to hell. (315)

11. They who are ashamed of what they ought not to be ashamed of and are not ashamed of what they ought to be ashamed of, such men, following false doctrines, enter the evil path. (316)

12. They who fear when they ought not to fear, and do not fear when they ought to fear, such men, following false doctrines, enter the evil path. (317)

13. Those who discern evil where there is no evil, and see nothing evil in what is evil, such men, following false doctrines, enter the evil path. (318)

14. Those who discern evil as evil and what is not evil as not evil, such men, following the true doctrines, enter the good path. (319)

chapter twenty-three: the elephant

1. I shall endure hard words even as the elephant in battle endures the arrow shot from the bow; the majority of people are, indeed, ill natured. (320)

2. They lead a tamed elephant into battle; the king mounts a tamed elephant. The tamed is the best among men; he who patiently endures hard words. (321)

3. Good are mules when tamed, so also horses of good breeding and the great elephants of war. Better than these is he who has tamed himself. (322)

4. For with these animals no man reaches the untrodden country of nirvana, where a tamed man goes with his self well-tamed. (323)

5. The elephant is hard to control when a pungent sap signals the mating season. He does not eat a morsel when bound. The elephant longs for the delights of the elephant grove. (324)

6. If one becomes a sluggard or a glutton rolling himself about in gross sleep, like a hog fed on wash, that foolish one, again and again, comes to rebirth. (325)

7. This mind of mine would wander formerly as it liked, as it desired, as it pleased. I shall now control it thoroughly, even as the rider holding the hook controls the elephant in a state of rutting. (326)
8. Be not thoughtless, guard your thoughts. Extricate yourself out of the evil way, as an elephant sunk in the mud. (327)
9. If you find a companion, intelligent, one who associates with you, who leads a good life, lives soberly, overcoming all dangers, walk with him delighted and thoughtful. (328)
10. If you do not find a companion, intelligent, one who associates with you, who leads a good life, lives soberly, walk alone like a king who has renounced the kingdom he has conquered or like an elephant roaming at will in the forest. (329)
11. It is better to live alone; there is no companionship with a fool. Let a man walk alone with few wishes like an elephant roaming at will in the elephant forest. Let him commit no sin. (330)
12. Companions are pleasant when the need arises; contentment is pleasant when mutual. At the hour of death merit is pleasant. The giving up of all sorrow is pleasant. (331)
13. To have a mother is happiness in the world; to have a father is happiness in the world; to have a recluse is happiness in the world; to have a sage is happiness in the world. (332)
14. Happy is virtue lasting to old age; happy is faith firmly rooted; happy is the attainment of wisdom; happy is the avoidance of sins. (333)

chapter twenty-four: thirst

1. The craving of a thoughtless man grows like a creeper. Like a monkey wishing for fruit in a forest he bounds hither and thither, and from one life to another. (334)
2. Whomsoever is overcome in this world by fierce craving, full of poison, his sorrows increase like the abundant quack grass. (335)
3. He who does overcome this fierce craving in this world, which is difficult to subdue, sorrows fall off from him like water drops from a lotus leaf. (336)
4. I declare to you this good counsel. "Do ye, as many as are gathered here, dig up the root of the craving as one digs up the biryani grass to find the tender root, that Mara death may not destroy you again and again, even as the river destroys the reeds on the bank." (337)
5. As a tree, even though it has been cut down, grows again if its root is firm and uninjured, even so if the adherences of craving are not destroyed, this suffering returns to us again and again. (338)
6. The misguided man whose thirst is like thirty-six streams flowing towards a delta of pleasure, and whose thoughts are set on passion, will be carried away by the waves. (339)

7. Those streams flow everywhere; the creeping passion keeps welling up, unless we dam it at the source by means of wisdom. (340)

8. The pleasures and desires of creatures are embraced by those who hanker after them. Such men are entrapped in the cycles of birth and old age again and again. (341)

9. Men driven by craving run about like hunted rabbits. Caught in snares, they suffer, escape, and are trapped again. (342)

10. Men driven by craving run about like hunted rabbits. Let, therefore, the mendicant monk, wishing freedom from passion for himself, shake off craving. (343)

11. He who having got rid of the forest of desire, gives himself over to the life of the forest of desire, and he who, free from the forest of desire, runs back to the forest of desire—look at him, though free, he runs into bondage. (344)

12. Wise people do not say that the strongest fetter is made of iron, wood, or rope, because the attachment to earrings made of precious stones, to sons, and to wives is passionately ardent. (345)

13. Wise people call strong this fetter which drags down, yields, and is difficult to unfasten. After having finally cut this, people renounce the world, free from longings and forsaking the pleasure of sense. (346)

14. Those who are slaves to passions follow the stream of craving as a spider creeps into the web which he has made himself. Wise people, when they have cut this craving, leave the world, free from cares, leaving all sorrow behind. (347)

15. Give up what is before, give up what is behind, give up what is in the middle, passing to the farther shore of existence. When your mind is wholly freed you will not again return to birth and old age. (348)

16. Craving increases more in a creature who is disturbed by doubts, full of strong passions, yearning for what is pleasant; he indeed makes his fetters strong. (349)

17. He who delights in quieting his thoughts, always reflecting, focused on what is not pleasant, he will certainly remove, nay, he will cut the bonds of death. (350)

18. He who has reached the good, who is fearless, who is without craving and without sin, he has broken the thorns of existence, and this body is his last. (351)

19. He who is without craving, without appropriation, who is skillful in understanding words and their meanings, who knows the order of the letters; he is called the great sage, the great person. This is his last body. (352)

20. "I have conquered all, I know all, and in all conditions of life I am free from taint. I have renounced all and with the destruction of craving I am freed. Having learned myself, to whom shall I point as teacher?" (353)

21. The gift of the dharma surpasses all gifts; the flavor of the dharma surpasses all flavors, the delight in the dharma surpasses all delights. The destruction of craving conquers all sorrows. (354)

22. Riches destroy the foolish, but not those who seek the beyond. By craving for riches the foolish person destroys himself as he destroys others. (355)

23. Weeds are the bane of fields and passion the bane of this mankind; therefore offerings made to those free from passion bring great reward. (356)

24. Weeds are the bane of fields and hatred is the bane of this mankind; therefore offerings made to those free from hatred bring great reward. (357)
25. Weeds are the bane of fields and folly is bane of this mankind; therefore offerings made to those free from folly bring great reward. (358)
26. Weeds are the bane of fields; desire is the bane of this mankind; therefore offerings made to those freed from desire bring great reward. (359)

chapter twenty-five: the mendicant monk

1. Restraint in the eye is good; good is restraint in the ear; in the nose restraint is good; good is restraint in the tongue. (360)
2. In the body restraint is good, good is restraint in speech; in thought restraint is good, good is the restraint in all things. A mendicant monk who is restrained in all things is freed from all sorrow. (361)
3. He who controls his hand, he who controls his feet, he who controls his speech, he who is well-controlled, he who delights inwardly, who is collected, who is alone and content, him they call a mendicant. (362)
4. The mendicant who controls his tongue, who speaks wisely, who is not puffed up, who illuminates the meaning of the dharma, his utterance is sweet. (363)
5. He who takes pleasure in the dharma, who delights in the dharma, meditates on the dharma, follows the dharma, that mendicant does not fall from the true dharma. (364)
6. He should not despise what he himself receives; he should not envy others. A mendicant who envies others does not obtain tranquility. (365)
7. Even the divine spirits praise that mendicant who, though he receives little does not despise what he receives, whose life is pure and strenuous. (366)
8. He, indeed, is called a mendicant who does not count as his own any name and form, who does not grieve from having nothing. (367)
9. The mendicant who lives in friendliness and calm has faith in the doctrine of the Buddha; he will attain the tranquil, blessed place where bodily existence is at rest. (368)
10. Empty the boat, O mendicant; when emptied it will go lightly. Having cut off passion and hatred then you will go to freedom. (369)
11. Cut off the five senses, get rid of the five senses, rise above the five senses. A mendicant who has freed himself from the five fetters is called "one who has crossed the flood" of re-birth. (370)
12. Meditate, O mendicant, be not negligent. Let not your thought delight in sensual pleasures, that you may not for your negligence have to swallow the iron ball, so that you may not cry out when burning "This is suffering!" (371)

13. There is no meditation for one who is without wisdom, no wisdom for one without meditation; he in whom there are meditation and wisdom, he indeed is close to nirvana. (372)

14. A mendicant who with a tranquil heart has entered an empty house, he has divine delight, through his right discernment of the dharma. (373)

15. Whenever he comprehends the origin and destruction of the elements of the body, he obtains joy and happiness, which is eternal to those who know. (374)

16. This is the beginning for a wise mendicant: control of the senses, contentment, restraint under the dharma, cultivation of friends who are noble, of pure life, and zealous. (375)

17. Let him live a life of friendship. Let him be adept in the discharge of his duties, then his happiness being much he will make an end of suffering. (376)

18. As the conspicuous plant sheds its withered flowers, O mendicants, so you should get rid of passion and hatred. (377)

19. That mendicant is said to be calmed who has a calmed body, a calmed speech, and a calmed mind, who is well-established, and who has rejected the baits of the world. (378)

20. Rouse yourself by yourself, examine yourself by yourself. Thus guarded by yourself and attentive you, mendicant, will live happy. (379)

21. For self is the lord of self; self is the refuge of self; therefore curb yourself even as a merchant curbs a fine horse. (380)

22. The mendicant full of delight, calm with faith in the doctrine of the Buddha, will certainly reach the peaceful state, the cessation of natural existence and happiness. (381)

23. The mendicant who, though young, applies himself to the doctrine of the Buddha, illuminates this world like the moon when freed from a cloud. (382)

chapter twenty-six: the brahmin

1. O Brahmin, cut off the stream, be energetic, drive away desires. Knowing the destruction for all that is made and the element of existence, you know the uncreated, O Brahmin. (383)

2. When the Brahmin has reached the other shore in both meditation and contemplation, for him who knows all bonds vanish. (384)

3. Him I call a Brahmin for whom there is neither this shore nor that shore, nor both, who is free from fear and free from shackles. (385)

4. Him I call a Brahmin who is meditative, free from passion, settled, whose work is done, free from taints and who has attained the highest end of sainthood. (386)

5. The sun shines by day, the moon lights up the night, the warrior shines in his armor, the Brahmin shines in his meditation, but the awakened shines all day and night by his radiance. (387)

6. Because he has put aside evil he is called a Brahmin; because he lives in serenity he is called Peaceful; because he puts away his impurities he is called Pilgrim. (388)

7. One should not attack a Brahmin; let not the Brahmin free his anger on the evil-doer; woe to him who slays a Brahmin and more woe to him who sets free his anger on him the evil-doer. (389)

8. It is not slight benefit to a Brahmin when he holds his mind back from the pleasures of life. Wherever the wish to injure desists, even there is cessation of suffering. (390)

9. Him I call a Brahmin who does not hurt by body, speech, or mind, which is controlled in these three things. (391)

10. Him who understood the dharma as taught by the fully enlightened one, him should man worship reverentially, even as the Brahmin worships the sacrificial fire. (392)

11. Not by matted hair, not by lineage, not by caste does one become a Brahmin. He is a Brahmin in whom there are truth and righteousness. He is blessed. (393)

12. What is the use of matted hair, O fool, what of the raiment of goat-skins? Thine inward nature is full of wickedness; the outside thou doest purge. (394)

13. Him I call a Brahmin who wears cast-off garments, lean, spread over with veins, solitary, and who practices meditation in the forest. (395)

14. I do not call him a Brahmin because of his origin or of his mother. If he be with goods he is called lord. Him I call a Brahmin who is free from goods and free from attachment. (396)

15. Him I call a Brahmin who has cut all the fetters, who never trembles in fear, who has passed beyond attachments, who is separated from what is impure. (397)

16. Him I call a Brahmin who has cut the strap and the thong and the chain with its apparatus, who has burst the bar and is awakened. (398)

17. Him I call a Brahmin who, though he has committed no offence, bears patiently reproach, ill-treatment, imprisonment; who has endurance for his force and strength for his army. (399)

18. Him I call a Brahmin who is free from anger, which is careful of religious duties, observes the moral rules, pure, controlled, and wears his last body. (400)

19. Him I call a Brahmin who, like water on the leaf of a lotus or a mustard seed on the point of an awl, does not cling to pleasures. (401)

20. Him I call a Brahmin who, even here, knows the end of his suffering, who has laid aside his burden, who is detached. (402)

21. Him I call a Brahmin whose wisdom is deep, who possesses knowledge, who discerns the right way and the wrong and who has attained the highest end. (403)

22. Him I call a Brahmin who keeps away from both laymen householders and the houseless mendicants, who does not frequent house and has but few wants. (404)

23. Him I call a Brahmin who lays aside the rod with regard to creatures, moving or unmoving, and neither kills nor causes their death. (405)

24. Him I call a Brahmin who is without hostility among those who are hostile, who is peaceful among those with uplifted staves, who are unattached among those who are attached. (406)

25. Him I call a Brahmin whose passion and hatred, pride and hypocrisy have fallen like a mustard seed from the point of an awl. (407)

26. Him I call a Brahmin who utters true speech, free from harshness, clearly understood, by which no one is offended. (408)
27. Him I call a Brahmin who does not take, here in the world, what is not given him, is it long or short, small or large, good or bad. (409)
28. Him I call a Brahmin who has no desires for this world or for the next, who is free from desires and who is separated from impurities. (410)
29. Him I call a Brahmin who has no desires, who is free from doubt by knowledge of truth, who has reached the depth of the eternal. (411)
30. Him I call a Brahmin who here has passed beyond the attachments of good and evil, who is free from grief, free from passion, free from impurity. (412)
31. Him I call a Brahmin who like the moon is stainless, pure, serene, undisturbed, in whom joyfulness is extinguished. (413)
32. Him I call a Brahmin who has gone beyond this miry road of rebirth and delusion, difficult to cross, who has crossed over, who has reached the other shore, who is meditative, unagitated, not doubting, not grasping, and calm. (414)
33. Him I call a Brahmin who, in this world, giving up all sensual pleasures, wanders about without a home, in whom all desire for existence is extinguished. (415)
34. Him I call a Brahmin who, in this world, giving up all craving, wanders about without a home, in whom all craving for existence is extinguished. (416)
35. Him I call a Brahmin who, casting off attachment to human things, and rising above attachment to heavenly things, is separated from all attachments. (417)
36. Him I call a Brahmin who gives up what is pleasurable and what is unpleasurable, who is cooled and is free from any seeds of renewed existence, the hero who has conquered all the worlds. (418)
37. Him I call a Brahmin who knows everywhere the perishing of living things and their uprising, who is free from attachment, living aright, and who is awakened. (419)
38. Him I call a Brahmin whose path the gods do not know, nor spirits or men, whose taints are extinct and who has attained sainthood. (420)
39. Him I call a Brahmin for whom there is nothing before, behind, or between, who has nothing and is without attachment. (421)
40. Him I call a Brahmin who is fearless like a bull, noble, heroic, the all-wise, who has overcome death, the sinless who has accomplished his study, the awakened. (422)
41. Him I call a Brahmin who know his former lives, who perceives heaven and hell, has reached the end of births, is a sage whose knowledge is perfect, and has accomplished all that has to be accomplished. (423)

book five

THE HINDU TESTAMENT

introduction

Reciprocal Illumination

Arvind Sharma

THERE IS A PHENOMENON THAT PERMEATES THIS BOOK. IT IS CHARACTERIZED BY THE FACT THAT our engagement with another religious tradition helps us understand our own tradition, as well as the other tradition, better. That we should understand another tradition better if we engage in its study with this intention need not come as a surprise; after all, the exercise was undertaken with this end in mind. What, however, does contain an element of surprise is that our engagement with the other tradition might help us understand our *own* tradition better. This whole process as referred to above may be described as one of reciprocal illumination.

As this book consists of selections from the "testaments" of four of the world religions, we see this phenomenon at work at the level of scriptures in these pages. This is fully in keeping with the experience of Mohandas Gandhi, whose translation of the verses of the *Bhagavad Gita* is excerpted in chapter 10. This is what he had to say on this point: "I hold that it is the duty of every cultured man or woman to read sympathetically the scriptures of the world." And further: "My respectful study of other religions has not abated my reverence for or my faith in the Hindu scriptures. They have indeed left their deep mark upon my understanding of the Hindu scriptures. They have broadened my view of life. They have enabled me to understand more clearly many an obscure passage in the Hindu scriptures."[1]

I notice that in this book Rudyard Kipling's famous poem "If" is described as containing the essence of the *Bhagavad Gita* in English (according to Indian commentator Khushwant Singh). Even without knowing this, I have regularly recited that poem in my classes in order to convey to students the message of the *Bhagavad Gita* with poetic brevity in English, prior to discussing Gandhi's take on that text. Had Kipling read the *Bhagavad Gita* during his sojourn in India? Is it odd that the imperialist Kipling may have drawn as much inspiration from the *Bhagavad Gita* as the nationalist Mohandas Gandhi did? Perhaps not. After all, the *Bhagavad Gita* also inspired Gandhi's assassin Godse as much as it inspired Gandhi himself.

But to revert specifically to the theme of reciprocal illumination, among the scriptures presented in this volume, Book III contains the translation of the *Analects* of Confucius and Book V a translation of the *Bhagavad Gita*. Both these texts sketch the portrait of an ideal type, frequently referred to as *Junzi* (the "superior man") in the *Analects* and as *Sthitaprajña* ("the person of steady understanding") in the second chapter of the *Bhagavad Gita*. Could these two ideal types prove reciprocally illuminating?

To explore the point further, let us turn to a verse in the second chapter of the *Bhagavad Gita*, which runs as follows: "What, O Keshava, is the mark of a man whose understanding is secure, whose mind is fixed in concentration? *How does he talk*? How sit? How move?"[2]

Arjuna's question, posed above, has a certain innocence to it. If we were presented with a portrait of an ideal person, we would also like to know how such a person looks in flesh and blood. How does he talk? How does he sit? How does he move around in the world?

It will be interesting to see how these questions are answered by Confucius in relation to the *Junzi*, the superior man, and then compare those answers with those found in the *Bhagavad Gita*. Let us focus only on one item, for the sake of making a clear comparison: How does such a person talk? This is what the *Analects* have to say about how the *Junzi* talks:

In his words and tones he keeps far from lowness and impropriety.[3]

In regard to what he does not know, he shows a cautious reserve.[4]

In his words there may be nothing incorrect.[5]

The superior man is modest in his speech, but exceeds in his actions.[6]

The superior man does not promote a man simply on account of his words, nor does he put aside good words because of the man.[7]

He stands in awe of the words of sages.[8]

He is anxious to hear distinctly.[9]

He is anxious that his speech should be sincere.[10]

He hates those who proclaim the evil of others.[11]

For one word a man is often deemed to be wise, and for one word he is often deemed to be foolish.[12]

Two points immediately suggest themselves: (1) There is hardly any statement made by Confucius that would not be acceptable to Kṛṣṇa of the *Bhagavad Gita* as applying to the *Sthitaprajña*. (2) Nevertheless, Kṛṣṇa does not answer Arjuna's question in this respect, instead moving straight into a description of the *psyche* of the *Sthitaprajña*. The question put by Arjuna is answered not at the level of words, but rather thoughts. In a sense, then, the description of the *Junzi* provides a useful foil here—as answering Arjuna's question in a way. And Kṛṣṇa's answer enables us to probe the psyche of the *Junzi* in a way Confucius does not.

The two descriptions thus could be seen as complementing as well as complimenting each other. This is also in keeping with the more pragmatic orientation of the *Analects* overall and with greater attention accorded to the discussion of religious psychology in the *Bhagavad Gita*. It is not as if psychological orientation is totally lacking in the *Analects*[13] and the pragmatic in the *Bhagavad Gita*, in which there are three other places where we come across a description of a figure similar to the *Sthitaprajña*,[14] and in these the ideal person is described as one disposed to silence[15] and who is restrained in speech.[16] Although the differences in their orientations are also clear, the two seem to enrich each other when read together.

The example used above was drawn from Hinduism and Confucianism, but, of course, the phenomenon of reciprocal illumination is not limited to them. Nor should one conclude that it occurs only within a cluster of religious traditions, such as the Western or the Eastern, as the following example would clarify. Mohandas Gandhi's commitment to nonviolence is well known, based as it was on the sublime idea of returning good for evil. Gandhi had imbibed the idea early on in life from a didactic stanza in Gujarati that gripped his mind. His commitment to the ideal was reinforced when he read the Bible, especially the Sermon on the Mount, which went straight to his heart.

Gandhi, however, was also a serious student of the Quran, and it would be difficult to find a more succinct formulation of his doctrine of Satyagraha than the one found in the following verses of the Quran, where we learn that not everyone is able to practice such forgiveness: "The good and the evil deed are not alike. Repel the evil deed with one that is better, then Lo! He, between whom and thee there was enmity [will become] as though he was a bosom friend. But none is granted this save those who are steadfast, and none is granted this save the owner of great happiness."[17]

preface

With Notes from Mahatma Mohandas Gandhi

Mahatma Gandhi is acknowledged, even by his critics, as the greatest Hindu of modern times. However, on the evening of January 30, 1948, he was shot to death by a fellow Hindu, Nathuran Godse, for acquiescing in the partition of the country into India and Pakistan. Godse bowed to Gandhi reverentially before shooting him to death, and Gandhi raised his hand toward Godse in a gesture of blessing as he fell. In performing these surreal acts of spiritual chivalry, both acted as they did in the name and spirit of Hinduism. How are we to define a religion that embraces both the victim and the assassin?[1]

THE *BHAGAVAD GITA*, AS THE "SONG OF GOD," PRESENTS ITS OWN TEXTUAL DILEMMA THAT goes to the heart of another matter: Is this scripture monist, monotheistic, or polytheistic? Moreover, it is almost universally recommended that one should begin reading the *Gita* under the guidance of a mentor or guru. Accordingly, we exhibit a translation by none other than Mohandas Ghandi, because he successfully manages to allow the multiple presentations of divinity to coexist, depending on context, and because he can serve as our mentor, since many readers "know" him well.

Critics charge that Gandhi leans toward Jainism's interpretations, reflecting the views of his spiritual guide, Shrimad Rajchandra, but Gandhi's own scholarship, while not groundbreaking, is certainly adequate for our purposes. We know where he is coming from: authentic reverence for life, peace, nonviolence, freedom, justice, and inclusion, as these are found in our final text, the *Bhagavad Gita*, a revered scripture beloved by many, including Gandhi. The standing of that text in the spiritual literature of the world, and perhaps a vindication of our choice, occurred on September 30, 2014, when the newly elected prime minister Narenda Modi of India presented a copy of the *Bhagavad Gita* to U.S. President Barack Obama on their first meeting, choosing the Gandhi translation as his gift.[2]

We extend the practice of expanding the reader's vocabulary to get inside these texts in our treatment of the *Gita*. The translation by Gandhi follows and expands upon Victor Mair with respect to its putative relationship with the *Tao Te Ching*, as will be seen, and upon Radhakrishnan in the practice of leaving as many words in Sanskrit as possible for English readers. Building on the better-known words used in the *Dhammapada*, in the *Gita* we hope that readers may become comfortably familiar with another dozen or more words, including *ahimsa* (nonviolence), *sannyasa* (renunciation), *varna* (caste or color/"varnish"), *Brahmins* (priestly educators), *Kshatriyas* (military authorities), *Vaishyas* (those in agriculture and business), and *Shudras* (untouchable laborers). Then *prakriti* (nature), *kalpa* (eon), *mane* (ancestor), *mahatma* (great soul), *sankhya* (knowledge), *karmayoga* (performance), and several other yogas, with which the reader will become familiar through initial footnote introductions, will round out this list of important words, either elaborated upon by Gandhi in occasional parentheses or discussed in reference to context by the editor in those footnotes.

The first image in our appendix speaks volumes concerning the depth of scholarship and literacy in India five hundred years ago and much before. Abu'l-Fath Jalal ud-din Muhammad Akbar ruled most of India from 1556 until 1605 as Akbar I, known in Europe and the Middle East as Akbar the Great, the third emperor of the Muslim Mughal Dynasty. To rise above tribalism and Islamic statist imagery among his non-Muslim subjects, he developed a Persian-style court seemingly modeled on that of Cyrus the Great. Akbar was a personal patron of art and culture; he was fond of literature, possessing more than twenty-four thousand books written in Sanskrit, Persian, Greek, Latin, Arabic, Kashmiri, and Hindi, with scholars, authors, translators, scribes, printers, and bookbinders associated with his household staff. Religious leaders of many faiths, poets, artisans, and artists were attracted to his court from all over the world, accounting for artwork like that which begins our appendix. Akbar saw beyond then-orthodox Islam to the vision of the Quran and hoped to implement the religious harmony Muhammad had promoted in his stillborn *Medina Constitution*, which Caliph Abd Al-Rahman III also attempted to institute in *La Convivencia* of the Umayyad period in Spain a few centuries earlier when Muslims, Christians, and Jews lived in relative peace.

Akbar eventually went further than either Muhammad or Rahman in actually promulgating a syncretic creed in 1582 based on elements of Zoroastrianism, Hinduism, and Islam, featuring the Oneness of God and a generous tolerance of Jainism, Judaism, and Christianity. His *Dīn-i Ilāhī* (Religion of God) drew the ire of some religious leaders, but by abolishing the sectarian tax on non-Muslims and appointing them to positions of leadership in the military and civil service, he laid the foundations for the multicultural society that endured in India long after his reign, though the religions reasserted their identities after his death. The tragic rupture in relationships between Hindus and Muslims in India in the twentieth century coincided with a similar horror between Christians and Jews in Europe at roughly the same time, neither of which should be taken as religiously definitive. More generously inclusive societies are possible, as illustrated by Rahman, Akbar, and Kaiser Wilhelm I of Prussia (1861–1888), who attempted much the same unity with Protestants, Catholics, Jews, and Gypsies as the first emperor of a united Germany.

notes from mohandas gandhi

My first acquaintance with the *Gita* began with the verse translation by Sir Edwin Arnold known as the Song Celestial. On reading it, I felt a keen desire to read a Gujarati translation. And I read as many translations as I could lay hold of. But all such reading can give me no passport for presenting my own translation. Then again my knowledge of Sanskrit is limited, my knowledge of Gujarati too is in no way scholarly. How could I then dare present the public with my translation?

It has been my endeavor, as also that of some companions, to reduce to practice the teaching of the *Gita* as I have understood it. The *Gita* has become for us a spiritual reference book. I am aware that we ever fail to act in perfect accord with the teaching. The failure is due not to want of effort, but in spite of it. Even through the failures we seem to see rays of hope. The accompanying rendering contains the meaning of *Gita* message which my little band is trying to enforce in its daily conduct.

Again, this rendering is designed for women, the commercial class, the so-called *Shudras* and the like who have little or no literary equipment, who have neither the time nor the desire to read the *Gita* in the original and yet who stand in need of its support. This desire does not mean any disrespect to the other renderings. They have their own place. But I am not aware of the claim made by the translators of enforcing their meaning of the *Gita* in their own lives. At the back of my reading there is the claim of an endeavour to enforce the meaning in my own conduct for an unbroken period of forty years.

When I first became acquainted with the *Gita*, I felt that it was not a historical work, but that, under the guise of physical warfare, it described the duel that perpetually went on in the hearts of mankind, and that physical warfare was brought in merely to make the description of the internal duel more alluring. This preliminary intuition became more confirmed on a closer study of religion and the *Gita*. In the characteristics of the perfected man of the *Gita*, I do not see any which correspond to physical warfare. Its whole design is inconsistent with the rules of conduct governing the relations between warring parties.

Krishna of the *Gita* is perfection and right knowledge personified; but the picture is imaginary. That does not mean that Krishna, the adored of his people, never lived, but the perfection is imagined. The idea of perfect incarnation is after growth. In Hinduism, incarnation is ascribed to one who has performed some extraordinary service for mankind. All embodied life is in reality an incarnation of God, but it is not usual to consider every living being an incarnation. Future generations pay this homage to one who, in his own generation, has been extraordinarily religious in his conduct. I can see nothing wrong in this procedure; it takes nothing from God's greatness, and there is no violence done to Truth. There is an Urdu Christian saying which means, "Adam is not God but he is a spark of the Divine." And therefore he who is the most religiously behaved has most of the divine spark in him. It is in accordance with this train of thought that Krishna enjoys, in Hinduism, the status of the most perfect incarnation.

The belief in incarnation is a testimony of man's lofty spiritual ambition. Man is not at peace with himself till he has become like God. The endeavour to reach this state is the supreme, the only ambition worth having. This self-realization is the subject of the *Gita*, as it is of all scriptures, but its author surely did not write it to establish that doctrine. The object of the *Gita* appears to me to be that of showing the most excellent way to attain self-realization. That which is to be found, more or less clearly, spread out here and there in Hindu religious books, has been brought out in the clearest possible language in the *Gita*, even at the risk of repetition.

That matchless remedy is renunciation of fruits of action. This is the centre round which the *Gita* is woven. This renunciation is the central sun, round which devotion, knowledge and the rest revolve like planets. The body has been likened to a prison. There must be action where there is body. Not one embodied being is exempted from labour. And yet all religions proclaim that it is possible for man, by treating "the body as the temple of God"[3] to attain freedom. Every action is tainted, be it ever so trivial. How can the body be made the temple of God? In other words how can one be free from action, i.e., from the taint of sin? The *Gita* has answered the question in decisive language: "By desiring less action; by renouncing fruits of action; by dedicating all activities to God, i.e., by surrendering oneself to Him body and soul."

But the cessation of desire or renunciation does not come for the mere talking about it. It is not attained by intellectual feat. It is attainable only by a constant heart-churn. Right knowledge is necessary for attaining renunciation. Learned men process knowledge of a kind. They may recite the *Vedas* from memory, yet they may be steeped in self-indulgence. In order that knowledge may not run riot, the author of the *Gita* has insisted on devotion accompanying it and has given it the first place. Knowledge without devotion will be like a misfire. Therefore, says the *Gita*, "Have devotion and knowledge will follow." This devotion is not mere lip worship; it is a wrestling with death. Hence, the *Gita*'s assessment of the devotee's quality is similar to that of the sage.

Thus the devotion required by the *Gita* is no soft-hearted effusiveness. It certainly is not blind faith. The devotion of the *Gita* has the least to do with the externals. A devotee may use, if he likes, rosaries and forehead marks, or make offerings, but these are not test of his devotion. He is the devotee who is jealous of none, who is a fount of mercy, who is without egotism, who is selfless, who treats alike cold and heat, happiness and misery, who is ever forgiving, who is always contented, whose resolutions are firm, who has dedicated mind and soul to God, who cause no dread, who is not afraid of others, who is free from exultation, sorrow and fear, who is pure, who is versed in action and yet remains unaffected by it, who renounces all fruit, good or bad, who treats friend and foe alike, who is untouched by respect or disrespect, who is not puffed up by praise, who does not go under when people speak ill of him, who loves silence and solitude, who has a disciplined reason. Such devotion is inconsistent with the existence at the time of strong attachments.

We thus see that to be a real devotee is to realize oneself. Self-realization is not something apart. One rupee can purchase for us poison or nectar, but knowledge or devotion cannot buy us salvation or bondage. These are not media of exchange. They are themselves the thing we want. In other words, if the means and the end are not identical, they are almost so. The extreme of means is salvation. Salvation in the *Gita* is perfect peace. But such knowledge and devotion, to be true have to stand the test of renunciation of the fruits of action. Mere knowledge of right and wrong will not make one fit for salvation. According to common notions, a mere learned man will pass as a pandit or priest. He need not perform any service. He will regard it as bondage even to lift a little brass lota. Where one test of knowledge is non-liability for service, there is no room for such mundane work as the lifting of lotas.

Or take *bhakti*, devotion. The popular notion of bhakti is soft-heartedness, telling beads and the like, and disdaining to even a loving service, least the telling of beads might be interrupted. This bhakti, therefore leaves the rosary only for eating, drinking and the like, never for grinding corn or nursing patients. But the *Gita* says: No one has attained his goal without action. Even men like Janaka attained salvation through action. Even if I were lazily to cease working, the world would not perish. How much more necessary then for people at large to engage in action, but without seeking reward.

While on the one hand it is beyond dispute that all action binds, on the other hand it is equally true that all living beings have to do some work, whether they will or no. Here all activity, whether mental or physical is to be included in the term action. Then how is one to be free from bondage of action, even though he may be acting? The manner in which the *Gita* has solved the problem is to my knowledge unique. The *Gita* says: "do your allotted work but renounce its fruit; be detached and work; work but have no desire for reward." This is the unmistakable teaching of the *Gita*. He who gives up action falls. He who gives up only the reward rises. But renunciation of fruit in no way means indifference to the result. In regard to every action one must know the result that is expected to follow, the means thereto, and the capacity for it. He, who, being thus equipped, is without desire for the result and is yet wholly engrossed in the due fulfillment of the task before him is said to have renounced the fruits of his action.

Again let no one consider renunciation to mean want of fruit for the renouncer. The *Gita* does not warrant such a meaning. Renunciation means absence of hankering after fruit. As a matter of fact, he who renounces reaps a thousand fold. The renunciation of the *Gita* is the acid test of faith. He who is ever brooding over result often loses nerve in the performance of his duty. He becomes impatient and then gives vent to anger and begins to do unworthy things: he jumps from action to action never remaining faithful to any. He who broods over results is like a man given to object of senses; he is ever distracted, he says goodbye to all scruples, everything is right in his estimation and he therefore resorts to means fair and foul to attain his end.

From the bitter experiences of desire for fruit the author of the *Gita* discovered the path of renunciation of fruit and put it before the world in a most convincing manner. The common belief is that religion is always opposed to material good. "One cannot act religiously in mercantile and such other matters. There is no place for religion in such pursuits; religion is only for attainment of salvation," we hear many worldly-wise people say. In my opinion the author of the *Gita* has dispelled this delusion. He has drawn no line of demarcation between salvation and worldly pursuits. On the contrary he has shown that religion must rule even our worldly pursuits. I have felt that the *Gita* teaches us that what cannot be followed out in day-to-day practice cannot be called religion. Thus, according to the *Gita*, all acts that are incapable of being performed without attachment are taboo. This golden rule saves mankind from many a pitfall. According to this interpretation murder, lying, dissoluteness and the like must be regarded as sinful and therefore taboo. Man's life then becomes simple, and from that simplicity springs peace.

Thinking along these lines, I have felt that in trying to enforce in one's life the central teaching of the *Gita*, one is bound to follow Truth and ahimsa.[4] When there is no desire for fruit, there is no temptation for the untruth or himsa. Take any instance of untruth or violence, and it will be found that at its back was the desire to attain the cherished end. But it may be freely admitted that the *Gita* was not written to establish ahimsa. It was an accepted and primary duty even before the *Gita* age. The *Gita* had to deliver the message of renunciation of fruit. This is clearly brought out as early as the second chapter.

But if the *Gita* believed in ahimsa or it was included in cessation of desire, why did the author take a warlike illustration? When the *Gita* was written, although people believed in ahimsa, wars were not only not taboo, but nobody observed the contradiction between them and ahimsa. In accessing the implications of renunciation of fruit, we are not required to probe the mind of the author of the *Gita* as to his limitations of ahimsa and the like. Because a poet puts a particular truth before the world, it does not necessarily follow that he has known or worked out all its great consequences or that having done so; he is able always to express them fully. In this perhaps lies the greatness of the poem and the poet. A poet's meaning is limitless. Like man himself, the meaning of great writings suffers evolution. On examining the history of languages, we noticed that the meaning of important words has changed or expanded. This is true of the *Gita*. The author has himself extended the meanings of some of the current words.

We are able to discover this even on superficial examination. It is possible that, in the age prior to that of the *Gita*, offering of animals as sacrifice was permissible. But there is not a trace of it in the sacrifice in the *Gita* sense. In the *Gita* continuous concentration on God is the king of sacrifices. The third chapter seems to show that sacrifice chiefly means body-labour for service. The third and fourth chapters read together will use other meanings for sacrifice, but never animal-sacrifice. Similarly has the meaning of the word sannyasa[5] undergone, in the *Gita*, a transformation? The sannyasa of the *Gita* will not tolerate complete cessation of all activity. The sannyasa of the *Gita* is all work and yet not work. Thus the author of the *Gita*, by extending meanings of words, has taught us to imitate him. Let it be granted, that according to the letter of the *Gita* it is possible to say that warfare is consistent with renunciation of fruit. But after forty years' unremitting endeavor fully to enforce the teaching of the *Gita* in my own life, I have in all humility felt that perfect renunciation is impossible without perfect observance of ahimsa in every shape and form.

The *Gita* is not an aphoristic work; it is a great religious poem. The deeper you dive into it, the richer the meanings you get. It being meant for the people at large, there is pleasing repetition. With every age the important words will carry new and expanding meanings. But its central teaching will never vary. The teacher is at liberty to extract from this treasure any meaning he likes so as to enable him to enforce in his life the central teaching.

Nor is the *Gita* a collection of do's and don'ts. What is lawful for one may be unlawful for another. What may be permissible at one time, or in one place, may not be so at another time, in another place. Desire for fruit is the only universal prohibition. Cessation of Desire is obligatory.

The *Gita* has sung the praise of Knowledge, but it is beyond the mere intellect; it is essentially addressed to the heart and capable of being understood by the heart. Therefore the *Gita* is not for those who have no faith. The author makes Krishna say: "Do not entrust this treasure to him who is without sacrifice, without devotion, without the desire for this teaching and who denies Me. On the other hand, those who give this precious treasure to My devotees will, by the fact of this service, assuredly reach me. Those who, being free from malice, will with faith absorb this teaching, and shall, having attained freedom, live where people of true merit go after death."

*   *   *

The *Bhagavad Gita* opens with the warrior Arjuna and the divine Krishna on the battleground known as Kuruksetra as the war between two ancient Indian clans, the Pandavas and the Kauravas, is about to commence. While the armies face each other, Arjuna becomes depressed at the thought of fighting acquaintances and even relatives on the opposing side. He considers throwing away his weapons and submitting to death rather than participating in a war that, even if just, will result in a great slaughter.

In reminding him of his duty, the divine Krishna is not embracing war as such, for the battle is nearly always regarded, in a Jungian fashion, as standing for the struggle that goes on inside every person, or faced in every society, like America, which sees everything as a war: War Against Drugs, War Against Cancer, War Against Crime, War Against Heart Disease, and War Against Poverty. Otherwise, who could imagine the *Bhagavad Gita* as the favorite devotional literature of Mohandas Gandhi, the greatest pacifist in the history of the world? The dialogue, which takes place on the eve of the great battle, probes the nature of God and how humans can reach or become one with God through renouncing personal desires and even detachment from earthly emotions, including high virtues like family loyalty and personal sentiments (at least to the extent that these can divert one from the duty to do what is right).

As the *Bhagavad Gita* unfolds, the majestic poem provides a riveting synopsis of the religious thought and experience of Eastern religion and its expressions in polytheism, supplanted by monotheism, and achieving its blissful conclusion in a monism that embraces the other two. Arjuna's destiny and ours is realized by renouncing personal desires and becoming one with God in service (as distinct from action on one's own behalf), devotional meditation (as opposed to prayer to a God who is separate from the devotee), and understanding (in contrast to mere academic knowledge).

The *Bhagavad Gita* is a small part of the ancient Indian epic the *Mahabharata*, though thought by some scholars to have been written as recently as the early Common Era. The precise date of composition is unknown, but in all probability it came out of the reform era that the Buddha brought to Hinduism, penned somewhere around 400 BCE, toward the end of the Axial Age as we have defined it. The *Gita* may be said to be the crowning achievement of the developments we have been considering in this compendium. As one of the foremost religious documents of the world, it is also cherished as a treasure of world literature, presented in the form of a lyrical conversation between the epic hero, Arjuna, and his friend, charioteer, and counselor Krishna, an incarnation of the Godhead.

The *Bhagavad Gita* teaches that there are three paths that lead directly to establishing a relationship with God. These paths have been described as the yoga of perfect actions, the yoga of perfect devotion, and the yoga of perfect knowledge or understanding. The *Gita* consists of eighteen chapters, traditionally grouped into these three paths, and each chapter is also called a yoga. Religious practitioners consider yoga a scientific method whereby individual consciousness may attain communion with the ultimate consciousness, and each chapter of the *Gita* is a specialized yoga revealing an aspect of a path to the realization of ultimate truth.

The first six chapters have been classified as the *Karma Yoga* section, as they mainly deal with the science of the individual consciousness attaining communion with the Ultimate Consciousness through actions (*karma*), including the performance of physical "exercise."

The middle six chapters have been traditionally understood as the *Bhakti Yoga* section, as they principally pertain to the science of the individual consciousness attaining communion with the Ultimate Consciousness by means of the path of worship or devotion (*bhakti*).

The final six chapters are regarded as the *Jnana Yoga* section, as they are primarily concerned with the science of the individual consciousness attaining communion with the Ultimate Consciousness through the intellect (*jnana*).

The *Raja Yoga* is an inclusive practice of all of the above in a personal and regal experience, not limited to the *Gita*, which did not invent yoga but is its most popular (and perhaps most effective) expression. Yoga itself is found as far back as the Rig Veda and found expression in Hinduism, Jainism, and Buddhism prior to the appearance of the *Bhagavad Gita*.

According to Indian historian Khushwant Singh, Rudyard Kipling's famous poem "If" is "the essence of the message of *The Gita* in English."[6] Written as advice to his son, and inspired by the challenges faced by Kipling's friend, Scots-born colonial adventurer Dr. Leander Starr Jameson, the *Gita*-like influence of this Anglo-Indian poet seems apparent. Two lines appear above the entrance to Wimbledon Stadium as an inspiration for tennis players: "If you can meet with Triumph and Disaster / And treat those two impostors just the same."[7]

A verse here might illustrate how this *Gita* thinking has been received in the English-speaking world:

> If you can keep your head when all about you
> Are losing theirs and blaming it on you,
> If you can trust yourself when all men doubt you,
> But make allowance for their doubting too;
> If you can wait and not be tired by waiting,
> Or being lied about, don't deal in lies,
> Or being hated, don't give way to hating,
> And yet don't look too good, nor talk too wise . . .
> Yours is the Earth and everything that's in it.[8]

Earlier we showed the connections between Buddhism and Hinduism, and between Taoism and Buddhism (with Confucianism as possibly a worthy Chinese traditionalist reaction to both of the latter). We are ready now to go a step further in illustrating a connection between Taoism and Hinduism, closing the circle on the main variants of Eastern expressions of monism in answer to a question posed by Francis Clooney in his foreword, composed as we all worked along together.

Our translator of the *Tao Te Ching*, Victor Mair, is also something of an authority on the *Bhagavad Gita*, reading it in the original Sanskrit, observing some connection to Judaism in India, and, more particularly, building a strong case for a more intimate relationship between the *Gita* and the text of the *Tao Te Ching*. In the notes to his translation of the latter, he maintains that in the *Gita* the main thing Krishna impresses upon Arjuna is that "altruistic or disinterested action leads to the realization of Brahma."[9] He shows how the *Gita* teaches that one should act without regard or desire for the fruits of one's action. This appears to be identical to the essential concept of "nonaction" in the *Tao Te Ching*, which says in its opening chapter, "The person of superior integrity takes no action; / nor has he a purpose for acting, / but through non-action, no action is left undone."

Mair is of the opinion that the written *Gita* has a core based on earlier oral yogas from a source not yet identified, but that the written *Gita* may follow the *Tao Te Ching* by over a hundred years, opening and closing the Axial Age in the orient as we have defined it. We cannot know which influenced the other most, or if they draw from another source (a possibility to which Mair refers time and again). In the translation of the *Bhagavad Gita* by Barbara Stoler Miller, Krishna defines his own all-encompassing nature as follows:

> Understanding, knowledge, nondelusion,
> patience, truth, control, tranquility,
> joy, suffering, being, nonbeing,
> fear and fearlessness . . .

> Nonviolence, equanimity, contentment,
> penance, charity, glory, disgrace,
> these diverse attitudes
> of creatures arise from me.[10]

The Old Master of the Tao either taught the writer of the *Gita* or sat at his feet, unless they both had another source. Mair also points to whole passages of the *Tao Te Ching* itself in which the words and images are identical to those of the *Gita*. For example, the obscuring of a mirror by dust as a metaphor for the clouding of the mind in the *Gita*[11] is also found in the *Tao Te Ching*.[12] Or take "closing all the doors of the body, shutting up the mind in the heart" of the *Gita*[13] and compare with the practitioner of the Tao who "stopples the openings of his heart and closes its doors."[14]

Even before providing a plethora of such examples in the body of his book and its appendix, Mair maintains, "At present there are only three conceivable explanations for how this relationship could have developed:

1. China borrowed the yogic system and its attendant practices from India;
2. India borrowed Taoism and its attendant practices from China;
3. Both India and China were recipients of inspiration from a third source.

Much research remains to be done, of course, before a conclusive answer can be given. We must also await the results of more through excavation, particularly in Sinkiang (the Chinese part of Central Asia), through which the famous silk roads passed, and along the southeast coasts of China, where ships from India and Arabia regularly arrived."[15]

Books I and VII of this compendium address that question in their discussion of the missing Zoroastrian material, which follows the initial Gatha poems by Zoroaster and the next material that Mary Boyce and some others ascribe to Zoroaster, but before the slightly later block of Avesta chapters that indicate the possibility of an intermediate phase of *bhaktic* yoga material. As indicated by Mair, it is the manifestly yogic content of the *Tao Te Ching* that is echoed or derived from the *Gita*, as in the beginning of chapter 54, especially lines 4 and 5, which advise the practitioner to "focus the breath until it is supremely soft."

"In short," says Mair, "if Indian Yoga did not exert a shaping force upon Chinese Taoism [or vice versa], the only other logical explanation is that both were molded by a third source."[16] We might add "or sources," since Zoroastrianism is not the only option in an Indian intellectual and spiritual fluidity only now becoming recognized. For example, the opening verses of the *Dhammapada* in previous traditional translations are nearly identical to the Hebrew proverb, "As a man thinketh in his heart, so shall he be," a verse that itself is the subject of some controversy.[17] But it is the similarities between Indian yoga and Chinese Taoism that are apparent in the two schools of religion and philosophy with which the *Tao Te Ching* and the *Bhagavad Gita* are associated in both conundrum and putative resolution.

The *Gita* itself reaches back a thousand years to the Rig Veda when Krishna lauds the *Gayatri Mantra*,[18] the most popular Hindu devotional recitation to this day (preceded by *oṃ* [ॐ] and the formula *bhūr bhuvaḥ svaḥ,* known as *mahāvyāhṛti,* the "great mystical utterance").

(Oṃ bhūr bhuvaḥ svaḥ)[19]
tát savitúr váren i yam
bhárgo devás yadhī mahi
dhíyo yó naḥ prachodáyāt[20]

(Supreme One, Essence of the Uni-verse)
We meditate on the effulgent
Glory of the divine Light;
May God inspire our understanding.

Also contemporary with the *Gita,* and compatible with its sentiments, is the fifth-century BCE verse, *The Salutation of the Dawn,* attributed to Kalidasa, Indian poet, playwright, and undisputed master of the Sanskrit language, offered here to again present the ethos of the age in a cadence less onerous than the heavier scriptural burden that will follow in Radhakrishnan's "true to the original" format rather than the "gussied-up" translations currently in vogue.

Listen to the Salutation of the Dawn:
Look to this Day!
For it is life, the very life of life.
In its brief course lie all the verities
And realities of our existence:
The glory of action,
The bliss of growth,
The splendor of beauty.
For yesterday is but a dream,
And tomorrow is only a vision.
But today, well lived, makes
Every yesterday a dream of happiness
And every tomorrow a vision of hope.
Look well, therefore, to this Day!
Such is the Salutation of the Dawn.

The translation of the *Bhagavad Gita* by Gandhi follows and expands upon Mair, and on Radhakrishnan's practice of leaving as many words in Sanskrit as possible for English readers. At this point we concede the lectern to our teacher, Mohandas Gandhi, for, among other things, the mahatma was an eminent educator, having established more than a hundred schools and colleges, and having lectured in all or most of them, frequently on his favorite topic, the *Bhagavad Gita.*

In the translation that follows, while each of the two main parties in the dialogue are often identified, they are also recognized by each other through other names of mythic significance, a matter of possible confusion to the uninitiated but largely unresolved in this text. Though skilled in the modern English idiom, Gandhi here employs Shakespearean English, the noble form of the language, to reflect the deliberate archaism of the *Gita* in Sanskrit, recapturing the ambience of verbal intercourse with the divine. This deliberate use of archaisms is also employed in the King James Version of the Bible and in the Vedic tone of the Avesta by Zoroaster, authenticating the spiritual heritage in which each stands. The unfamiliar names and titles and the archaic language notwithstanding, the practical authenticity of the Gandhi translation and commentary should be worth the effort for most readers. Again, as mentioned, we attempt to confirm and expand the growing number of Sanskrit words that have come into the English language untranslated. Footnotes will be of some assistance to those unfamiliar with more esoteric words and phrases, but one advantage of the Gandhi text is that it fits the pattern established here by Mair and Radhakrishnan of enabling the reader or student to actually get inside the text.

Transcendental meditation was brought to America by Maharishi Mahesh Yogi in 1955, an exciting fringe activity until it became mainstream in the 1970s and 1980s. If *The Dalai Lama's Cat* more recently made Buddhist "mindfulness" accessible as a populist but true exposition of Buddhism in the twenty-first century, transcendental meditation had done much the same for Hindu meditation techniques in the late twentieth century, though it remained in the alien, esoteric fringe to a considerable extent. Two sequels to *The Dalai Lama's Cat* that help solve this problem for Buddhist, Hindu, and "Western" believers are *The Art of Purring* and *The Power of Meow*, where once again the Buddhist resources make the truths of Hinduism accessible, though perhaps not with the accessible profundity of the *Bhagavad Gita*, itself a populist resource (though not quite as cute). If "mindfulness" enables us to zero in on the present moment, *The Power of Meow* (or the *Power of Now*) takes this a step further in using focus on some object or some word to bring us deeply into connection with everything, like William Blake's "whole universe in a grain of sand." Buddhism certainly has this to offer, but it could be argued that Hinduism, reformed by Buddhism (under whatever stimulation or inspiration that was permeating the ancient East), brings this idea to its highest climax in the *Bhagavad Gita*.

The transcendental meditation practice usually involves reciting a mantra of sacred words or phrases, and it is practiced for fifteen to twenty minutes twice per day while sitting with the eyes closed. Major corporations and institutions in the West that once opened the day with prayer or assumed some level of Christian or Jewish devotion among employees, but are now afraid of the "political correctness police," are comfortable encouraging transcendental meditation for increased productivity or health and prosperity in institutional life, with some exceptions allowed for Muslims who remain intransigent on this issue. The perfect example of this shift is the switch in Western media and culture to a respectful "moment of silence" in public, corporate, or institutional environments instead of prayer at the time of crisis.

10
bhagavad gita
Translated by Mohandas Gandhi*

ᵭíscouᴙse í

No knowledge is to be found without seeking, no tranquility without travail, and no happiness except through tribulation. Every seeker has, at one time or another, to pass through a conflict of duties, heart-churning.

Dhritarashtra said:

1. Tell me, O Sanjaya, what my sons Pandu's assembled, on battle intent, did on the field of Kuru, the field of duty.

The human body is the battle field where the eternal duel between right and wrong goes on. Therefore it is capable of being turned into a gateway to Freedom. It is born in sin and becomes the seed-bed of sin. Hence it is also called the field of Kuru. The Kuravas represent the forces of Evil, the Pandavas the forces of Good. Who is there that has not experienced the daily conflict within himself between the forces of Evil and the forces of Good?

Sanjaya said:

2. On seeing the Pandava's army drawn up in battle array, King Duryodhana approached Drona, the preceptor, and addressed him thus:
3. Behold, O preceptor, this mighty army of the sons of Pandu, set in array by the son of Drupada, thy wise disciple.
4. Here are brave bowmen, peers of Bhima and Arjuna in fighting: Yuyudhana and Virata, and the "Maharatha"† Drupada.

---

*Ghandi's commentary appears in italics.
†A maharatha is an elite warrior.

5. Dhrishtaketu, Chekitana, valorous Kashiraja, Purujit the Kuntibhoja, and Shaibya, chief among men;

6. Valiant Yudhamanyu, valorous Uttamaujas, Subhadra's son, and the sons of Draupadi—each one of them a "Maharatha."

7. Acquaint thyself now, O best of Brahmanas, with the distinguished among us. I mention for thy information, the names of the captains of my army.

8. Thy noble self, Bhishma, Karna, and Kripa, victorious in battle, Ashvatthaman, Vikarna, and also Somadatta's son;

9. There is many another hero, known for his skill in wielding diverse weapons, pledged to lay down his life for my sake, and all adepts in war.

10. This our force, commanded by Bhishma, is all too inadequate; while theirs, commanded by Bhima, is quite adequate.

11. Therefore, let each of you, holding your appointed places at every entrance, guard only Bhishma.

12. At this, the heroic grandsire, the grand old man of the Kurus, gave a loud lion's roar and blew his conch to hearten Duryodhana.

13. Thereupon, conches, drums, cymbals and trumpets were sounded all at once. Terrific was the noise.

14. Then Madhava and Pandava, standing in their great chariot yoked with white steeds, blew their sacred conches.*

15. Hrishikesha† blew the Panchajanya, and Dhananjaya the Devadatta; while the wolf-bellied Bhima of dread deeds sounded his great conch, Paundra.

16. King Yudhishthira, Kunti's son, blew the Anantavijaya, and Nakula and Sahadeva their conches, Sughosha and Manipushpaka.

17. And Kashiraja, the great bowman, Shikhandi the "Maharatha" Dhrishtadyumna, Virata and Satyaki, the unconquerable;

18. Drupada, Draupadi's sons, the strong-armed son of Subhadra, all these, O King, blew each his own conch.

19. That terrifying tumult, causing earth and heaven to resound, rent the hearts of Dhritarashtra's sons.

20. Then, O King, the ape-bannered Pandava, seeing Dhritarashtra's sons arrayed and flight of arrows about to begin, took up his bow, and spoke thus to Hrishikesha:

21. "Set my chariot between the two armies, O Achyuta!"

22. That I may behold them drawn up, on battle intent, and know whom I have to engage in this fearful combat;

23. And that I may survey the fighters assembled here, anxious to fulfil in battle perverse Duryodhana's desire.

---

*Large sea shells attuned for battle sounds like the trumpet or bagpipes.

†The first of a series of names and titles of Krishna.

Sanjaya said:

24–25. Thus addressed by Gudakesha, O King, Hrishikesha set the unique chariot between the two armies in from of Bhishma, Drona and all the kings and said: Behold, O Partha, the Kurus assembled yonder.

26–28. Then did Partha see, standing there, sires, grandsires, preceptors, uncles, brothers, sons, grandsons, comrades, fathers-in-law and friend in both armies. Beholding all these kinsmen ranged before him, Kaunteya was overcome with great compassion and spake thus in anguish:

Arjuna said:

28–29. As I look upon these kinsmen, O Krishna, assembled here eager to fight, my limbs fail, my mouth is parched, and a tremor shakes my frame and my hair stands on end.

30. Gandiva* slips from my hand, my skin is on fire, I cannot keep my feet, and my mind reels.

31. I have unhappy forebodings, O Keshava: and I see no good in slaying kinsmen in battle.

32. I seek not victory, nor sovereign power, nor earthly joys. What good are sovereign power, worldly pleasures and even life to us, O Govinda?

33. Those for whom we desire sovereign power, earthly joys and delights are here arrayed in battle, having renounced life and wealth—

34. Preceptors, sires, grandsires, sons and even grandsons, uncles, fathers-in-law, brother-in-law, and other kinsmen.

35. These I would not kill, O Madhusudana, even though they slay me, not even for kingship of the three worlds, much less for an earthly kingdom.

36. What pleasure can there be in slaying these sons of Dhritarashtra, O Janardan? Sin only can be our lot if we slay these, usurpers though they be.

37. It does not therefore behove us to kill our kinsmen, these sons of Dhritarashtra. How may we be happy, O Madhava, in killing our own kin?

38. Even though these, their wits warped by greed, see not the guilt that lies in destroying the family, nor the sin of treachery to comrades:

39. How can we, O Janardana, help recoiling from this sin, seeing clearly as we do the guilt that lies in such destruction?

40. With the destruction of the family perish the eternal family virtues, and with the perishing of these virtues unrighteousness seizes the whole family.

---

*His archer's bow.

41. When unrighteousness prevails, O Krishna, the women of the family become corrupt, and their corruption, O Varshneya, causes a confusion of varnas.*

42. This confusion verily drags the family-slayer, as well as the family, to hell, and for want of obsequial offerings and rites their departed sires fall from blessedness.

43. By the sins of these family-slayers resulting in confusion of varnas, the eternal tribal and family virtues are brought to naught.

44. For we have had it handed down to us, O Janardana, that the men whose family virtues have been ruined are doomed to dwell in hell.

45. Alas! What a heinous sin we are about to commit, in that, from greed of the joy of sovereign power, we are prepared to slay our kith and kin!

46. Happier far would it be for me if Dhritarashtra's sons, weapons in hand, should strike me down on the battlefield, unresisting and unarmed.

Sanjaya said:

47. Thus spake Arjuna on the field of battle, and dropping his bow and arrows sank down on his seat in the chariot, overwhelmed with anguish.

Thus ends the first discourse, entitled "Arjuna Vishada Yoga" in the converse of Lord Krishna and Arjuna, on the science of Yoga as part of the knowledge of Brahaman in the Upanished called the Bagavad-gita.

òíscouRce íí

By reason of delusion, man takes wrong to be right. By reason of delusion was Arjuna led to make a difference between kinsmen and non-kinsmen. To demonstrate that this is a vain distinction, Lord Krishna distinguishes between body (not self) and Atman (Self) and shows that whilst bodies are impermanent and several, Atman is permanent and one. Effort is within man's control, not the fruit thereof. All he has to do, therefore, is to decide his course of conduct or duty on each occasion and persevere in it, unconcerned about the result. Fulfillment of one's duty in the spirit of detachment or selflessness leads to Freedom.

Sanjaya said:

1. To Arjuna, thus overcome with compassion, sorrowing, and his eyes obscured by flowing tears, Madhusudana spake these words:

The Lord said:

2. How is it that at this perilous moment this delusion, unworthy of the noble, leading neither to heaven nor to glory, has overtaken thee?

---

*Caste groupings or communities of color (varnish).

3. Yield not to unmanliness, O Partha; it does not become thee. Shake off this miserable faint-heartedness and arise O Parantapa!

Arjuna said:

4. How shall I, with arrows, engage Bhishma and Drona in battle, O Madhusudana, they who are worth of reverence, O Arisudana?
5. It were better far to live on alms of this world than to slay these venerable elders. Having slain them I should but have blood-stained enjoyments.
6. Nor do we know which is better for us, that we conquer them or that they conquer us, for here stand before us Dhritarashtra's sons having killed whom we should have no desire to live.
7. My being is paralysed by faint-heartedness; my mind discerns not duty; hence I ask thee; tell me, I pray thee, in no uncertain language, wherein lies my good. I am thy disciple; guide me; I seek refuge in thee.
8. For I see nothing that can dispel the anguish that shrivels up my senses, even if I should win on earth uncontested sovereignty over a thriving kingdom or lordship over the gods.
9. Thus spoke Gudakesha* Parantapa to Hrishikesha Govinda, and with the words "I will not fight" became speechless.
10. To him thus stricken with anguish, O Bharata! Between the two armies, Hrishikesha, as though mocking, addressed these words;

The Lord Said:

11. Thou mournest for them whom thou shouldst not mourn and utterest vain words of wisdom. The wise mourn neither for the living nor for the dead.
12. For never was I not, nor thou, nor these kings; nor will any of us cease to be hereafter.
13. As the embodied one has, in the present body, infancy, youth and age, even so does he receive another body. The wise man is not deceived therein.
14. O Kaunteya! Contacts of the senses with their objects bring cold and heat, pleasure and pain; they come and go and are transient. Endure them, O Bharata.
15. O noblest of men, the wise man who is not disturbed by these, who is unmoved by pleasure and pain, he is fitted for immortality.
16. What is non-Being is never known to have been, and what is Being is never known not to have been. Of both these the secret has been seen by the seers of the Truth.
17. Know that to be imperishable whereby all this pervaded. No one can destroy that immutable being.

---

*One of the series of affectionate names and formal titles of Arjuna.

18. These bodies of the embodied one who is eternal, imperishable and immeasurable are finite. Fight, therefore, O Bharata.

19. He who thinks of This (Atman) as slayer and he, who believes This to be slain, are both ignorant. This neither slays nor is ever slain.

20. This is never born nor ever dies, nor having been will ever not be any more; unborn, eternal, everlasting, ancient, This is not slain when the body is slain.

21. He who knows This, O Partha, to be imperishable, eternal, unborn, and immutable—whom and how can that man slay or cause to be slain?

22. As a man casts off worn-out garments and takes others that are new, even so the embodied one casts off worn-out bodies and passes on to others new.

23. This no weapons wound, no fires burn, no waters wet, no wind doth dry.

24. Beyond all cutting, burning, wetting and drying is This—eternal, all-pervading, stable, immovable, everlasting.

25. Perceivable neither by the senses nor by the mind, This is called unchangeable; therefore knowing This as such thou shouldst not grieve.

26. And if thou deemest This to be always coming to birth and always dying, even then O Mahabahu, thou shouldst not grieve.

27. For certain is the death of the born, and certain is the birth of the dead; therefore what is unavoidable thou shouldst not regret.

28. The state of all beings before birth is unmanifest; their middle state manifest; their state after death is again unmanifest. What occasion is there for lament, O Bharata?

29. One looks upon This as a marvel; another speaks of This as such; another hears thereof as a marvel; yet having heard This none truly knows This.

30. This embodied one in the body of every being is ever beyond all harm, O Bharata: thou shouldst not, therefore, grieve for any one.

*Thus far Lord Krishna, by force of argument based on pure reason, has demonstrated that Atman is abiding while the physical body is fleeting, and has explained that if, under certain circumstances, the destruction of a physical body is deemed justifiable, it is delusion to imagine that the Kauravas should not be slain because they are kinsmen. Now he reminds Arjuna of the duty of a Kshatriya.**

31. Again, seeing thine own duty thou shouldst not shrink from it; there is no higher good for a Kshatriya than a righteous war.

32. Such a fight, coming unsought, as a gateway to heaven thrown open, falls only to the lot of happy Kshatriyas, O Partha.

---

*From kshatra, "rule" or "authority," especially in the military sense, Kshatriyas (with a silent k) were one of the four main varnas (castes or social orders originally identified by color or "varnish") of the Hindu society. Brahmins as priestly educators, Vaishyas in agriculture and business, and Shudras in labor and service roles each had myriad subcategories. The top three castes were accepted as the basis of social order by Zoroaster nearby, whose sons oversaw the integration of service workers into the three divinely sanctioned strata, but the entire spectrum lingers on in India today.

33. But if thou wilt not fight this righteous fight, then in failing in thy duty and in losing thine honour, thou wilt incur sin.
34. The world will forever recount the story of thy disgrace; and for a man of honour, disgrace is worse than death.
35. The Maharathas will think that fear made thee retire from battle; and thou wilt fall in the esteem of those very ones who have held thee high.
36. Thine enemies will deride thy prowess and speak many unspeakable words about thee. What can be more painful than that?
37. Slain, thou shalt gain heaven; victorious, thou shall inherit the earth; therefore arise, O Kaunteya, determine to fight.

Having declared the highest truth, viz. the immortality of the eternal Atman and the fleeting nature of the physical body (11–30), Krishna reminds Arjuna that a Kshatriya may not flinch from a fight which comes unsought (31–32). He then (33–37) shows how the highest truth and the performance of duty incidentally coincide with expediency. Next he proceeds to foreshadow the central teaching of the Gita in the following shloka.*

38. Hold alike pleasure and pain, gain, and loss, victory and defeat, and gird up thy loins for the fight; so doing thou shalt not incur sin.
39. Thus have I set before thee the attitude of Knowledge; hear now the attitude of Action; resorting to this attitude thou shalt cast off the bondage of action.
40. Here no effort undertaken is lost, no disaster befalls. Even a little of this righteous course delivers one from great fear.
41. The attitude, in this matter, springing, as it does, from fixed resolve is but one, O Kurunandana; but for those who have no fixed resolve the attitude is many-branched and unending.

When the attitude ceases to be one and undivided and becomes many and divided, it ceases to be one settled will, and broken up into various wills of desires between which man is tossed about.

42–44. The ignorant, revelling in the letter of the Vedas, declare that there is naught else; carnally-minded, holding heaven to be their goal, they utter swelling words which promise birth as the fruit of action and which dwell on the many and varied rites to be performed for the sake of pleasure and power; intent, as they are, on pleasure and power, their swelling words rob them of their wits, and they have no settled attitude which can be centered on the supreme goal.

The Vedic ritual, as opposed to the doctrine of Yoga laid down in the Gita, is alluded to here. The Vedic ritual lays countless ceremonies and rites with a view to attaining merit and heaven.

---

*A shloka is a poetic couplet or a pairing of images.

These, divorced as they are from the essence of the Vedas and short-lived in their result, are worthless.

45. The Vedas have as their domain the three gunas;* eschew them, O Arjuna. Free thyself from the pairs of opposites, abide in eternal truth, scorn to gain or guard anything, remain the master of thy soul.
46. To whatever extent a well is of use when there is a flood of water on all sides, to the same extent are all the Vedas of use to an enlightened Brahmana.
47. Action alone is thy province, never the fruits thereof; let not thy motive be the fruit of action, nor shouldst thou desire to avoid action.
48. Act thou, O Dhananjaya, without attachment, steadfast in Yoga, even-minded in success and failure. Even-mindedness is Yoga.
49. For action, O Dhananjaya, is far inferior to unattached action; seek refuge in the attitude of detached action. Pitiable are those who make fruit their motive.
50. Here in this world a man gifted with that attitude of detachment escapes the fruit of both good and evil deeds. Gird thyself up for Yoga, therefore. Yoga is skill in action.
51. For sages, gifted with the attitude of detachment, who renounce the fruit of action, are released from the bondage of birth and attain to the state which is free from all ills.
52. When thy understanding will have passed through the slough of delusion, then wilt thou be indifferent alike to what thou hast heard and wilt hear.
53. When thy understanding, distracted by much hearing, will rest steadfast and unmoved in concentration, then wilt thou attain Yoga.

Arjuna said:

54. What, O Keshave, is the mark of the man whose understanding is secure, whose mind is fixed in concentration? How does he talk? How sit? How move?

The Lord said:

55. When a man puts away, O Partha, all the cravings that arise in the mind and finds comfort for himself only from Atman, then he is called the man of secure understanding.

To find comfort for oneself from Atman means to look to the spirit within for pleasure as well as pain. Spiritual comfort or bliss must be distinguished from pleasure or happiness. The pleasure I may derive from the possession of wealth, for instance, is delusive; real spiritual comfort or bliss can be attained only if I rise superior to every temptation even though troubled by the pangs of poverty and hunger.

---

*A guna is a thread, strand, or theme.

56. He whose mind is untroubled in sorrow and longeth not for joys, who is free from passion, fear and wrath—he is called the ascetic of secure understanding.
57. Whoever owns attachment nowhere, who feels neither joy nor resentment whether good or bad comes his way—that man's understanding is secure.
58. And when, like the tortoise drawing in its limbs from every side, this man draws in his senses from their objects, his understanding is secure.
59. When a man starves his senses, objects of those senses disappear from him, but not the yearning for them; yearning too departs when he beholds the Supreme.

This shloka* does not rule out fasting and other forms of self-restraint, but indicates their limitations. These restraints are needed for subduing the desire for sense-objects, which however is rooted out only when one has a vision of the Supreme. The higher yearning conquers all the lower yearnings.

60. For, in spite of the wise man's endeavour, O Kaunteya, the unruly senses distract his mind perforce.
61. Holding all these in check, the yogi should sit intent on Me; for he whose senses are under control is secure in understanding.

This means that without devotion and the consequent grace of God, man's endeavour is vain.

62. In a man brooding on objects of the senses, attachment to them springs up; attachment begets craving and craving begets wrath.

Craving cannot but lead to resentment, for it is unending and unsatisfied.

63. Wrath breeds stupefaction, stupefaction leads to loss of memory, loss of memory ruins the reason, and the ruin of the reason spells utter destruction.
64. But the disciplined soul, moving among sense-objects with the senses weaned from likes and dislikes, and brought under the control of Atman, attains peace of mind.
65. Peace of mind means the end to all ills, for the understanding of him whose mind is at peace stands secure.
66. The undisciplined man has neither understanding nor devotion; for him who has no devotion there is no peace, and for him who has no peace whence happiness?
67. For when his mind runs after any of the roaming senses, it sweeps away his understanding, as the wind drives a vessel upon the waters.
68. Therefore, O Mahabahu, he, whose senses are reined in on all sides from their objects, is the man of secure understanding.
69. When it is night for all other beings, the disciplined soul is awake, when all other beings are awake; it is night for the seeing ascetic.

---

*To elaborate, a shokla may be regarded as a verse, though usually presented as a cuplet/couplet, a formal device in this literature, with each hemistich (half-verse) having sixteen syllables.

This verse indicates the divergent paths of the disciplined ascetic and sensual man. Whereas the ascetic is dead to the things of the world and lives in God, the sensual man is alive only to the things of the world and dead to the things of the spirit.

70. He in whom all longings subside, even as the waters subside in the ocean which, though ever being filled by them, never overflows—that man finds peace; not he who cherishes longing.
71. The man who sheds all longing and moves without concern, free from the sense of "I" and "Mine"—he attains peace.
72. This is the state, O Partha, of the man who rests in Brahman; having attained to it, he is not deluded. He who abides in this state even at the hour of death passes into oneness with Brahman.

Thus ends the second discourse, entitled "Sankhya Yoga" in the converse of Lord Krishna and Arjuna, on the science of Yoga as part of the knowledge of Brahaman in the Upansihad called Bhagavad-gita.

ỏiscourse iii

This discourse may be said to be the key to the essence of the Gita. *It makes absolutely clear the spirit and the nature of the right action and shows how true knowledge must express itself in acts of selfless service.*

Arjuna said:

1. If, O Janardana, thou holdest that the attitude of detachment is superior to action, then why, O Keshava, dost thou urge me to dreadful action?
2. Thou dost seem to confuse my understanding with perplexing speech; tell me, therefore, in no uncertain voice, that way alone whereby I may attain salvation.

Arjuna is sore perplexed, for whilst on the one hand he is rebuked for his faint-heartedness, on the other he seems to be advised to refrain from action (II, 49–50). But this, in reality, is not the case as the following shlokas will show.

The Lord said:

3. I have spoken, before, O sinless one, of two attitudes in this world—the "Sankhayas," that of Jnana yoga,* and the "Yogins," that of Karma yoga.†
4. Never does man enjoy freedom from action by not undertaking action, nor does he attain that freedom by mere renunciation of action.

---

*Yoga of knowledge.
†Yoga of action.

"Freedom from action" is freedom from the bondage of action. This freedom is not to be gained by cessation of all activity, apart from the fact that this cessation is in the very nature of things impossible (see following shloka). How then may it be gained? The following shlokas will explain.

5. For none ever remains inactive even for a moment; for all are compelled to action by the gunas inherent in prakriti.*
6. He who curbs the organs of action but allows the mind to dwell on the sense-objects—such a one, wholly deluded, is called a hypocrite.

The man who curbs his tongue but mentally swears at another is a hypocrite. But that does not mean that free rein should be given to the organs of action so long as the mind cannot be brought under control. Self-imposed physical restraint is a condition precedent to mental restraint. Physical restraint should be entirely self-imposed and not super-imposed from outside, e.g., by fear. The hypocrite who is held up to contempt here is not the humble aspirant after self-restraint. The shloka has reference to the man who curbs the body because he cannot help it while indulging the mind, and who would indulge the body too if he possibly could. The next shloka puts the thing conversely.

7. But he, O Arjuna, who keeping all the senses under control of the mind, engages the organs in Karma yoga, without attachment—that man excels.

The mind and body should be made to accord well. Even with the mind kept in control, the body will be active in one way or another. But he whose mind is truly restrained will, for instance, close his ears to foul talk and open them only to listen to the praise of God or of good men. He will have no relish for sensual pleasures and will keep himself occupied with such activity as ennobles the soul. That is the path of action. Karma yoga is the yoga (means) which will deliver the self from the bondage of the body, and in it there is no room for self-indulgence.

8. Do thou thy allotted task; for action is superior to inaction; with inaction even life's normal course is not possible.
9. This world of men suffers bondage from all action save that which is done for the sake of sacrifice; to this end, O Kaunteya, perform action without attachment. "Action for the sake of sacrifice" means acts of selfless service dedicated to God.
10. Together with sacrifice did the Lord of beings create, of old, mankind, declaring: "By this shall ye increase; may this be to you the giver of all your desires."
11. With this may you cherish the gods and may the gods cherish you; thus cherishing one another may you attain the highest good.
12. "Cherished with sacrifice, the gods will bestow on you the desired boons." He who enjoys their gifts without rendering aught unto them is verily a thief.

---

*That is, nature.

"Gods" in shlokas 11 and 12 must be taken to mean the whole creation of God. The service of all created beings in the service of the gods and the same is sacrifice.

13. The righteous men who eat the residue of the sacrifice are freed from all sin, but the wicked who cook for themselves eat sin.
14. From food springs all life, from rain is born food; from sacrifice comes rain and sacrifice is the result of action.
15. Know that action springs from Brahman and Brahman from the Imperishable; hence the all-pervading Brahman is ever firm-founded on sacrifice.
16. He who does not follow the wheel thus set in motion here below, he, living in sin, sating his senses, lives, O Partha, in vain.
17. But the man who revels in Atman, who is content in Atman and who is satisfied only with Atman, for him no action exists.
18. He has no interest whatever in anything done, nor in anything not done, nor has he needed to rely on anything for personal ends.
19. Therefore, do thou ever perform without attachment the work that thou must do; for by performing action without attachment man attains the Supreme.
20. For through action alone Janaka and others achieved perfection; even with a view to the guidance of mankind thou must act.
21. Whatever the best man does is also done by other men, what example he sets, the world follows.
22. For me, O Partha, there is naught to do in the three worlds, nothing worth gaining that I have not gained; yet I am ever in action.

An objection is sometimes raised that God being impersonal is not likely to perform any physical activity; at best He may be supposed to act mentally. This is not correct. For the unceasing movement of the sun, the moon, the earth et cetera signifies God in action. This is not mental but physical activity. Though God is without form and impersonal, He acts as though He had form and body. Hence though He is ever in action, He is free from action, unaffected by action. What must be borne in mind is that, just as all Nature's movements and processes are mechanical and yet guided by divine Intelligence or Will, even so man must reduce his daily conduct to mechanical regularity and precision, but he must do so intelligently. Man's merit lies in observing divine guidance at the back of these processes and in an intelligent imitation of it rather than in emphasizing the mechanical nature thereof and reducing himself to automation. One has but to withdraw the self, withdraw attachment to fruit from all action, and then not only mechanical precision but security from all wear and tear will be ensured. Acting thus man remains fresh until the end of his days. His body will perish in due course, but his soul will remain evergreen without crease or a wrinkle.

23. Indeed, for were I not, unslumbering, ever to remain in action, O Partha, men would follow my example in every way.
24. If I were not to perform my task, these worlds would be ruined; I should be the same cause of chaos and of the end of all mankind.

25. Just as, with attachment, the unenlightened perform all actions, O Bharata, even so, but unattached, should the enlightened man act, with a desire for the welfare of humanity.
26. The enlightened may not confuse the mind of the unenlightened, who are attached to action; rather must he perform all actions unattached, and thus encourage them to do likewise.
27. All action is entirely done by the gunas of prakriti. Man, deluded by the sense of "I," thinks, "I am the doer."
28. But he, O Mahabahu, who understands the truth of the various gunas and their various activities, knows that this is the gunas that operate on the gunas; he does to claim to be the doer.

As breathing, winking and similar processes are automatic and man claims no agency for them, in a similar manner all his activities should be automatic, without his arrogating to himself the agency or responsibility thereof. A man of charity does not even know that he is doing charitable acts, it is his nature to do so, and he cannot help it. This detachment can only come from tireless endeavour and God's grace.

29. Deluded by the gunas of prakriti men become attached to the activities of the gunas; he who knows the truth of things should not unhinge the slow-witted who have no knowledge.
30. Cast all thy acts on Me, with thy mind fixed on the indwelling Atman, and without any thought of fruit, or sense of "mine" shake off thy fever and fight!

He who knows the Atman inhabiting the body and realizes Him to be a part of the supreme Atman will dedicate everything to Him, even as a faithful servant acts as a mere shadow of his master and dedicates to him all that he does. For the master is the real doer, the servant but the instrument.

31. Those who always act according to the rule I have here laid down, in faith and without cavilling—they too are released from the bondage of their actions.
32. But those who cavil at the rule and refuse to conform to it are fools, dead to all knowledge; know that they are lost.
33. Even a man of knowledge acts according to his nature; all creatures follow their nature; what then will constraint avail?

This does not run counter to the teaching in II.61 and in II.68. Self-restraint is the means of salvation (VI.35; XIII.7). Man's energies should be bent towards achieving complete self-restraint until the end of his days. But if he does not succeed, neither will constraint help him. The shloka does not rule out restraint but explains that nature prevails. He who justifies himself saying, "I cannot do this, it is not in my nature," misreads the shloka. True we do not know our nature, but habit is not nature. Progress, not decline, ascent, not descent, is the nature of the soul, and therefore every threatened decline or descent ought to be resisted. The next verse makes this abundantly clear.

34. Each sense has its settled likes and dislikes towards its objects; man should not come under the sway of these, for they are his besetters.

Hearing, for instance, is the object of the ears which may be inclined to hear something and disinclined to hear something else. Man may not allow himself to be swayed by these likes and dislikes, but must decide for himself what is conducive to his growth, his ultimate end being to reach the state beyond happiness and misery.

35. Better one's own duty, bereft of merit, than another's well-performed; better is death in the discharge of one's duty; another's duty is fraught with danger.

One man's duty may be to serve the community by working as a sweeper; another's may be to work as an accountant. An accountant's work may be more inviting, but that need not draw the sweeper away from his work. Should he allow himself to be drawn away he would himself be lost and put the community into danger. Before God the work of man will be judged by the spirit in which it is done, not by the nature of the work which makes no difference whatsoever. Whoever acts in a spirit of dedication fits him for salvation.

Arjuna said:

36. Then what impels man to sin, O Varshneys, even against his will, as though by force compelled?

The Lord said:

37. It is Lust; it is Wrath, born of the guna-Rajas. It is the arch-devourer, the arch-sinner. Know this to be man's enemy here.
38. As fire is obscured by smoke, a mirror by dust,* and the embryo by the amnion, so is knowledge obscured by this.
39. Knowledge is obscured, O Kaunteya, by this eternal enemy of the wise man, in the form of Lust, the insatiable fire.
40. The senses, the mind and the reason are said to be its great seat; by means of these it obscures knowledge and stupefies man.

When lust seizes the senses, the mind is corrupted, discrimination is obscured and reason ruined. See II.62–64.

41. There, O Bharatarshabha, bridle thou first the sense and then rid thyself of this sinner, the destroyer of knowledge and discrimination.

---

*One of the places where this image found also in the *Tao Te Ching* appears in the *Gita*.

42. Subtle, they say, are the senses; subtler than the senses is the mind; subtler then the mind is the reason; but subtler even than the reason is He.
43. Thus realizing Him to be subtler than the reason, and controlling the self by the Self (Atman) destroy, O Mahabahu, this enemy—Lust, so hard to overcome.

When man realizes Him, his mind will be under this control, not swayed by the senses, and when the mind is conquered, what power has Lust? It is indeed a subtle enemy, but when once the senses, the mind and the reason are under the control of the subtlemost Self, Lust is extinguished.

Thus ends the third discourse entitled "Karma Yoga" in the converse of Lord Krishna and Arjuna, on the science of Yoga, as part of the knowledge of Brahman in the Upanishad called the Bhagavad-gita.

δiscourse iv

This discourse further explains the subject-matter of the third and describes the various kinds of sacrifice.

The Lord said:

1. I expounded this imperishable yoga to Vivasvan; Vivasvan communicated it to Manu, and Manu to Ikshvaku.
2. Thus handed down in succession. The royal sages learnt it; with long lapse of time it dwindled away in this world, O Parantapa.
3. The same ancient yoga have I expounded to thee today; for thou art My devotee and My friend, and this is the supreme mystery.

Arjuna said:

4. Later was Thy birth, my Lord, earlier that of Vivasvan. How then am I to understand Thou didst expound it in the beginning?

The Lord said:

5. Many births have we passed through, O Arjuna, both thou and I; I know them all, thou knowest them not, O Parantapa.
6. Though unborn and inexhaustible in My essence, though Lord of all beings yet assuming control over My Nature, I come into being by My mysterious power.
7. For whenever Right declines and Wrong prevails, then O Bharata, I come to birth.
8. To save the righteous, to destroy the wicked, and to re-establish right, I am born from age to age.

Here is comfort for the faithful and affirmation of the truth that Right ever prevails. An eternal conflict between Right and Wrong goes on. Sometimes the latter seems to get the upper hand, but it is Right which ultimately prevails. The good are never destroyed, for Right—which is Truth—cannot perish; the wicked are destroyed, because Wrong has no independent existence. Knowing this let man cease to arrogate to himself authorship and eschew untruth, violence and evil. Inscrutable Providence—the unique power of the Lord—is ever at work. This in fact is avatara, incarnation. Strictly speaking there can be no birth for God.

9. He who knows the secret of this, My divine birth and action, is not born again, after leaving the body; he comes to Me, O Arjuna.

For when a man is secure in the faith that Right always prevails, he never swerves therefrom, pursuing to the bitterest end and against serious odds, and as no part of the effort proceeds from his ego, but all is dedicated to Him, being ever one with Him, he is released from birth to death.

10. Freed from passion, fear and wrath, filled full with Me, relying on Me, and re-fined by the fiery ordeal of knowledge, many have become one with Me.
11. In whatever way men resort to Me, even so do I render to them. In every way, O Partha, the path men follow is Mine.

That is, the whole world is under His ordinance. No one may break God's law with impunity. As we sow, so shall we reap?* This law operates inexorably without fear or favour.

12. Those who desire their actions to bear fruit worship the gods here; for in this world of men the fruit of action is quickly obtainable.

Gods, as indicated before, must not be taken to mean the heavenly beings of tradition, but whatever reflects the divine. In that sense man is also a god. Stream, electricity and the other great forces of Nature are all gods. Propitiation of these forces quickly bears fruit, as we well know, but it is short-lived. It fails to bring comfort to the soul and it certainly does not take one even a short step towards salvation.

13. The order of the four varnas was created by Me according to the different gunas and karma of each; yet know that though, therefore, as author thereof, being changeless I am not the author.†
14. Actions do not affect Me, nor am I concerned with the fruits thereof. He who recognizes Me as such is not bound by actions.

For man has thus before him the supreme example of one who though in action is not the doer thereof. And when we are but instruments in His hands, where then is the room for arrogating responsibility for action?

---

*Galatians 6:7.

†That is, it happened naturally through God. This and the following verses teach that humans, too, must "go with the flow" (and make their influence felt within it), rather than making things happen—an ethos identical to that of Taoism.

15. Knowing this did men of old, desirous of freedom, perform action; do thou, then, just as they did—the men of old in days gone by.
16. "What is action? What is inaction?"—here even the wise are perplexed. I will then expound to thee that action knowing which thou shalt be saved from evil.
17. For it is right to know the meaning of action, of forbidden action, as also inaction. Impenetrable is the secret of action.
18. Who sees action in action and action in inaction, he is enlightened among men, he is a yogi, he has done all he need do.

The "action" of him who, though ever active, does not claim to be the doer, is inaction; and the "inaction" of him, who though outwardly avoiding action, is always building castles in his own mind, is action. The enlightened man who has grasped the secret of action knows that no action proceeds from him, all proceeds from God and hence he selflessly remains absorbed in action. He is the true yogi. The man who acts self-fully misses the secret of action and cannot distinguish between Right and Wrong. The soul's natural progress is towards selflessness and purity and one might, therefore, say that the man who strays from the path of purity strays from selflessness. All actions of the selfless man are naturally pure.

19. He whose every undertaking is free from desire and selfish purpose, and he who has burnt all his actions in the fire of knowledge—such a one the wise call a pandita.
20. He who has renounced attachment to the fruit of action, who is ever content, and free from all dependence—he, though immersed in action, yet acts not.

That is, his action does not bind him.

21. Expecting naught, holding his mind and body in check, putting away every possession, and going through action only in the body he incurs no stain.

The purest act, if tainted by "self," binds. But when it is done in a spirit of dedication, it ceases to bind. When "self" has completely subsided, it is only the body that works. For instance, in the case of a man who is asleep his body alone is working. A prisoner doing his prison tasks has surrendered his body to the prison authorities and only his body, therefore, works. Similarly, he who has voluntarily made himself God's prisoner does nothing himself. His body mechanically acts, the doer is God, not he. He has reduced himself to nothingness.

22. Content with whatever chance may bring, rid of pairs of opposites, free from ill-will, even-minded in success and failure, he is not bound though he acts.
23. Of the free soul who has shed all attachment, whose mind is firmly grounded in knowledge, who acts only for sacrifice, all karma is extinguished.
24. The offering of sacrifice is Brahman; the oblation is Brahman; it is offered by Brahman in the fire that is Brahman; thus he whose mind is fixed on acts dedicated to Brahman must needs pass on to Brahman.

25. Some yogins perform sacrifice in the form of worship of the gods; others offer sacrifice of sacrifice itself in the fire that is Brahman.
26. Some offer as sacrifice the sense of hearing and the other senses in the fires of restraint; others sacrifice sound and the other objects of sense in the fires of the senses.

The restraint of the senses—hearing and others—is one thing; and directing them only to legitimate objects, e.g., listening to hymns in the praise of God, is another, although ultimately both amount to the same thing.

27. Others again sacrifice all the activities of the senses and of the vital energy in the yogic fire of self-control kindled by knowledge.

That is to say, they lose themselves in the contemplation of the Supreme.

28. Some sacrifice with material gifts; with austerities; with yoga; some with the acquiring and some with the imparting of knowledge. All these are sacrifices of stern vows and serious endeavour.
29. Others absorbed in the practices of the control of the vital energy sacrifice the outward the inward and the inward in the outward, or check the flow of both the inward and the outward vital airs.

The reference here is to the three kinds of practices of the control of vital energy—puraka, rechaka, and kumbhaka.

30. Yet others, abstemious in food, sacrifice one form of vital energy in another. All these know what sacrifice is and purge themselves of all impurities by sacrifice.
31. Those who partake of the residue of sacrifice—called amrita (ambrosia)—attain to everlasting Brahman. Even this world is not for a non-sacrificer; how then the next, O Kurusattama?
32. Even so various sacrifices have been described in the Vedas; know them all to proceed from action, knowing this thou shalt be released.

Action here means mental, physical and spiritual action. No sacrifice is possible without this triple action and no salvation without sacrifice. To know this and to put the knowledge into practice is to know the secret of sacrifice. In fine, unless man uses all his physical, mental and spiritual gifts in the service of mankind, he is a thief unfit for Freedom. He who uses his intellect only and spares his body is not a full sacrificer. Unless the mind and body and the soul are made to work in unison, they cannot be adequately used for the service of mankind. Physical, mental and spiritual purity is essential for the harmonious working. Therefore man should concentrate on developing, purifying, and turning to the best of all his faculties.

33. Knowledge sacrifice is better, O Parantapa, then material sacrifice, for all action which does not bind finds it consummation in Knowledge (jnana).

Who does not know that works of charity performed without knowledge often results in great harm? Unless every act, however noble its motive, is informed with knowledge, it lacks perfection, Hence the complete fulfillment of all action is in knowledge.

34. The masters of knowledge who have seen the Truth will impart to thee this Knowledge; learn it through humble homage and service and by repeated questioning.

The three conditions of knowledge—homage, questioning, and service—deserve to be careful borne in mind in this age. Homage or obeisance means humility and service is a necessary accompaniment; else it would be mock homage. Repeated questioning is equally essential, for without a keen spirit of inquiry, there is no knowledge. All this presupposes devotion to and faith in the person approached. There can be no humility, much less service, without faith.

35. When thou hast gained this knowledge, O Pandave, thou shalt not again fall into such error; by virtue of it thou shalt see all beings without exception in thyself and thus in Me.

The adage "Yatha pinde tatha brahmande" — "as with the self so with the universe" — means the same thing. He who has attained Self-realization sees no difference between himself and others.

36. Even though thou are the most sinful of sinners, thou shalt cross the ocean of sin by the boat of knowledge.
37. As a blazing fire turns its fuel to ashes, O Arjuna, even so the fire of Knowledge turns all actions to ashes.
38. There is nothing in this world so purifying as Knowledge. He who is perfected by yoga finds it in himself in the fullness of time.
39. It is the man of faith who gains knowledge—the man who is intent on it and who has mastery over his senses; having gained knowledge, he comes ere long to the supreme peace.
40. But the man of doubt, without knowledge and without faith, is lost; for him who is given to doubt there is neither this world nor that beyond, nor happiness.
41. He who renounced all action by means of yoga, who has severed all doubt by means of knowledge—him self-possessed, no actions bind, O Dhananjaya!
42. Therefore, with the sword of Self-realization sever thou this doubt, bred of ignorance, which has crept into thy heart! Betake thyself to yoga and arise, O Bharata!

Thus ends the fourth discourse "Janna-Karma-sannyasa-Yoga" in the converse of Lord Krishna and Arjuna, on the science of Yoga, as part of the knowledge of Brahman in the Upanishad called the Bhagavad-gita.

δiscourse v

This discourse is devoted to showing that renunciation of action as such is impossible without the discipline of selfless action, and that both are ultimately one.

Arjuna said:

1. Thou laudest renunciation of actions, O Krishna, whilst at the same time thou laudest performance of action; tell me for a certainty which is the better.

The Lord said:

2. Renunciation and performance of action both lead to salvation; but of the two, karmayoga* is better than sannyasa.†
3. Him one should know as ever renouncing who has no dislikes and likes; for he who is free from the pairs of opposites is easily released from bondage.

That is, not renunciation of action but of attachment to the pairs determines true renunciation. A man who is always in action may be a good sannyasa‡ and another who may be doing no work may well be a hypocrite. See III.6.

4. It is the ignorant who speak of sankhya§ and yoga as different, not so those who have knowledge. He who is rightly established even in one wins the fruit of both.

The yogi engrossed in Sankhya lives even in thought for the good of the world and attains the fruit of karmayoga by the sheer power of his thought. The karmayogi ever engrossed in unattached action naturally enjoys the peace of the jnanayogi.

5. The goal that the sankhyas attain is also reached by the yogins. He sees truly who see both sankhya and yoga as one.
6. But renunciation, O Mahabahu, is hard to attain except by yoga; the ascetic equipped with yoga attains Brahman ere long.
7. The yogi, who has cleared himself, has gained mastery over his mind and all his senses, which has become one with the Atman in all creation, although he acts he remains unaffected.
8. The yogi who has seen the Truth knows that it is not he that acts whilst seeing, hearing, touching, smelling, eating, sleeping, or breathing,
9. Talking, letting go, holding fast, opening or closing the eyes—in the conviction that is the senses that are moving in their respective spheres.

---

*That is, performance.
†That is, renunciation.
‡That is, renouncer.
§That is, knowledge.

So long as "self" endures this detachment cannot be achieved. A sensual man therefore may not shelter himself under the pretence that it is not he but his senses that are acting. Such a mischievous interpretation betrays a gross ignorance of the Gita and right conduct. The next shloka makes this clear.

10. He who dedicates his actions to Brahman and performs them without attachment is not smeared by sin, as the lotus leaf by water.
11. Only with the body, mind and intellect and also with the senses, do the yogins perform action without attachment for the sake of self-purification.
12. A man of yoga obtains everlasting peace by abandoning the fruit of action; the man ignorant of yoga, selfishly attached to fruit, remains bound.
13. Renouncing with the mind all actions, the dweller in the body, who is master of himself, rests happily in his city of nine gates, neither doing nor getting anything done.

The principal gates of the body are the two eyes, the two nostrils, the two ears, the mouth, and two organs of excretion—though really speaking the countless pores of the skin are no less gates. If the gatekeeper always remains on the alert and performs his task, letting in or out only the objects that deserve ingress or egress, then of him it can truly be said that he has no part in the ingress or egress, but that he is a passive witness. He thus does nothing nor gets anything done.

14. The Lord creates neither agency nor action for the world; neither does he connect action with its fruit. It is nature that is at work.

God is no doer. The inexorable law of karma prevails, and in the very fulfillment of the law — giving everyone his deserts, making everyone reap what he sows—lies God's abounding mercy and justice. In undiluted justice is mercy. Mercy which is inconsistent with justice is not mercy but its opposite. But man is not a judge knowing past, present, and future. So for him the law is reversed and mercy or forgiveness is the purest justice. Being himself ever liable to be judged he must accord to others what he would accord to himself, viz. forgiveness. Only by cultivating the spirit of forgiveness can he reach the state of a yogi, whom no actions bind, the man of even-mindedness, the man skilled in action.

15. The Lord does not take upon Himself anyone's vice or virtue; it is ignorance that veils knowledge and deludes all creatures.

The delusion lies in man arrogating to himself the authorship of action and the attributing to God the consequences thereof—punishment or reward as the case may be.

16. But to them whose ignorance is destroyed by the knowledge of Atman, this knowledge, like the sun, reveals the Supreme.
17. Those whose intellect is suffused with That, whose self has become one with That, who abide in That, and whose end and aim is That, wipe out their sins with knowledge, and go whence there is no return.

18. The men of Self-realization look with an equal eye on a brahmana possessed of learning and humility, a cow, an elephant, a dog and even a dog-eater.

That is to say, they serve every one of them alike means that the wise man will suck the poison off a snake-bitten shwapaka with as much eagerness and readiness as he would from a snake-bitten brahmana.

19. In this very body they have conquered the round of birth and death, whose mind is anchored in sameness; for perfect Brahman is same to all, therefore in Brahman they rest.

As a man thinks, so he becomes,* and therefore those whose minds are bent on being the same to all achieve that sameness and become one with Brahman.

20. He whose understanding is secure, who is undeluded, who knows Brahman and who rests in Brahman will neither be glad to get what is pleasant, nor sad to get what is unpleasant.
21. He, who has detached himself from contacts without, finds bliss in Atman; having achieved union with Brahman he enjoys eternal bliss.

He who has weaned himself from outward objects to the inner Atman is fitted for union with Brahman and the highest bliss. To withdraw oneself from contacts without and to bask in the sunshine of union with Brahman are two aspects of the same state, two sides of the same coin.

22. For the joys derived from sense-contacts are nothing but mines of misery; they have beginning and end, O Kaunteya; the wise man does not revel therein.
23. For man who is able even here on earth, ere he is released from the body, to hold out against the floodtide of lust and wrath—he is a yogi, he is happy.

As a corpse has no likes and dislikes, no sensibility to pleasure and pain, even so he who though alive is dead to these, he truly lives, he is truly happy.

24. He who finds happiness only within, rest only within, light only within—that yogi, having become one with nature, attains to oneness with Brahman.
25. They win oneness with Brahman—the seers whose sins are wiped out, whose doubts are resolved, who have mastered themselves, and who are engrossed in the welfare of all beings.
26. Rid of lust and wrath, masters of themselves, the ascetics who have realized Atman find oneness with Brahman everywhere around them.

---

*Almost certainly Gandhi quotes here from Proverbs 23:7 of the King James Version of the Bible, to which he frequently refers personally. However, the same observation can be made about the opening verse of the *Dhammapada*. Are there Buddhist, Hindu, Jewish, and Christian linkages, or perhaps simply eternal truth?

27–28. The ascetic is ever free—who, having shut out the outward sense-contacts, sits with his gaze fixed between the brows, outward and inward breathing in the nostrils made equal; his senses, mind, and reason held in check; rid of longing, fear and wrath; and intent on Freedom.

These shlokas refer to some of the yogic practices laid down in the Yoga-sutras. A word of caution is necessary regarding these practices. They serve for the yogin the same purpose as athletics and gymnastics do for the bhogin (who purses worldly pleasures). His physical exercises help the latter to keep his sense of enjoyment in full vigour. The yogic practices help in the yogin to keep his body in condition and his sense in subjection. Men versed in these practices are rare in these days, and few of them turn them to good account. He who has achieved the preliminary stage on the path to self-discipline, he who has a passion for Freedom, and who having rid himself of the pairs of opposites has conquered fear, would do well to go in for these practices which will surely help him. It is with such a disciplined man alone who can, through these practices, render his body a holy temple of God. Purity both of the mind and body is a sine qua non, without which these processes are likely, in the first instance to lead a man astray and then drive him deeper into the slough of delusion. That this has been the result in some cases many know from actual experience. That is why that prince of yogins, Patanjali gave the first place to yamas (cardinal vows) and niyamas (casual vows), and held as eligible for yogic practise only those who have gone through the preliminary discipline. The five cardinal vows are: non-violence, truth, non-stealing, celibacy, non-possession. The five casual vows are: bodily purity, contentment, the study of the scriptures, austerity, and meditation of God.

29. Knowing Me as the Acceptor of sacrifice and austerity, the great Lord of all worlds, the friend of all creation, the yogi attains to peace.

This shloka may appear to be in conflict with shlokas 14 and 15 of this discourse and similar ones in other discourses. It is not really so. Almighty God is doer and non-doer, Enjoyer and non-Enjoyer both. He is indescribably beyond the power of human speech. Man somehow strives to have a glimpse of Him and in so doing invests Him with diverse and even contra-dictory attributes.

Thus ends the fifth discourse, entitled "Sannyasa yoga" in the converse of Lord Krishna and Arjuna, on the science of Yoga, as part of the knowledge of Brahman, in the Upanishad called the Bhagavad-gita.

Discourse VI

This discourse deals with some of the means for the accomplishment of Yoga or discipline of the mind and its activities.

The Lord said:

1. He, who performs all obligatory action, without depending on the fruit thereof, is a sannyasin and a yogin—not the man who neglects neither the sacrificial fire nor he who neglects action.

Fire here may be taken to mean all possible instruments of action. Fire was needed when sacrifices used to be performed with its help. Assuming that spinning were a means of universal service in this age, a man by neglecting the spinning wheel would not become a sannyasi.

2. What is called sannyasa, know thou to be yoga, O Pandava; for none can become a yogin who has not renounced selfish purpose.
3. For the man who seeks to scale the heights of yoga, action is said to be the means; for the same man, when he has scaled those heights, repose is said to be the means.

He who has purged himself of all impurities and who has achieved even-mindedness will easily achieve Self-realization. But this does not mean that he who has scaled the heights of yoga will disdain to work for the guidance of the world. On the contrary, that work will be to him not only the breath of his nostrils, but also as natural to him as breathing. He will do so by the sheer force of will. See V.4.

4. When a man is not attached either to the objects of sense or to actions and sheds all selfish purpose, then he is said to have scaled the heights of yoga.
5. By one's Self should one raise oneself, and not allow oneself to fall; for atman (Self) alone is the friend of self, and Self alone is self's foe.
6. His Self alone is friend, who has conquered himself by his Self; but to him who has not conquered himself and is thus inimical to himself, even his Self behaves as foe.
7. Of him who has conquered himself and who rests in perfect calm the self is completely composed, in cold and heat, in pleasure and pain, in honour and dishonour.
8. The yogin who is filled with the contentment of wisdom and discriminative knowledge, who is firm as a rock, who has mastered his senses, and to whom a clod of earth, a stone and gold are the same, is possessed of yoga.
9. He excels who regards alike the boon companion, the friend, the enemy, the stranger, the mediator, the alien and the ally, as also the saint and the sinner.
10. Let the yogi constantly apply his thought to Atman remaining alone in a scheduled place, his mind and body in control, rid of desires and possessions.
11. Fixing for himself, in a pure spot, a firm seat, neither too high nor yet too low, covered with kusha grass, thereon a deerskin, and thereon a cloth;
12. Sitting on that seat, with mind concentrated, the functions of thought and sense of control, he should set himself to the practice of yoga for the sake of self-purification.

13. Keeping himself steady, holding the trunk, the neck and the head in a straight line and motionless, fixing his eye on the tip of his nose, and looking not around.
14. Tranquil in spirit, free from fear, steadfast in the vow of brahmacharya, holding his mind in control, the yogi should sit, with all his thoughts on Me, absorbed in Me.

Brahmacharya (usually translated "celibacy") means not only sexual continence but observance of all the cardinal vows for the attainment of Brahman.

15. The yogi, who ever thus, with mind controlled, unites himself to Atman, wins the peace which culminates in Nirvana, the peace that is in Me.
16. Yoga is not for him who eats too much, nor for him who fasts too much, neither for him who sleeps too much, nor yet for him who is too wakeful.
17. To him who is disciplined in food and recreation, in effort in all activities, and in sleep and waking, the discipline of yoga becomes a relief from all ills.
18. When one's thought, completely controlled, rests steadily on only Atman, when one is free from longing for all objects of desire, then one is called a yogin.
19. As a taper in a windless spot flickers not, even so is a yogin, with his thought controlled, seeking to unite himself with Atman.
20. Where thought curbed by the practice of yoga completely ceases, where a man sits content within himself, Atman having seen Atman;
21. Where he experiences that endless bliss beyond the senses which can be grasped by reason alone; wherein established, he swerves not from the Truth;
22. Where he holds no other gain greater than that which he has gained and where, securely seated, he is not shaken by any calamity however great;
23. That state should be known as yoga, union with the Supreme, the disunion from all union with pain. This yoga must one practice with firm resolve and unwearying zeal.
24. Shaking oneself completely free from longings born of selfish purpose; reining in the whole host of senses, from all sides, with the mind itself;
25. With reason held securely by the will, he should gradually attain calm and, with the mind established in Atman, think of nothing.
26. Wherever the fickle and unsteady mind wanders, thence should it be reined in and brought under the sole sway of Atman.
27. The yogin, cleansed of all stain, unites himself ever thus to Atman, easily enjoys the endless bliss of contact with Brahman.
28. Steady in the self, being free from material contamination, the yogin achieves the high state of perfect happiness in being connected with the Supreme.
29. The man equipped with yoga looks on all with impartial eye, seeing Atman in all beings and all beings in Atman.
30. He who sees Me everywhere and everything in Me, never vanishes from me nor I from him.

31. The yogin who, anchored in unity, worships Me abiding in all beings, lives and moves in me, no matter how he lives and moves.

So long as "self" subsists, the supreme Self is absent; when "self" is extinguished, the Supreme Self is seen everywhere. Also see note on XIII.23.

32. He who, by likening himself with others, senses pleasure and pain equally for all as for himself, is deemed to be the highest yogi, O Arjuna.

Arjuna said:

33. I do not see, O Madhusudana, how this yoga, based on the equal-mindedness that Thou hast expounded to me, can steadily endure, because of fickleness of the mind.
34. For fickle is the mind, O Krishna, unruly, overpowering and stubborn; to curb it is, I think, as hard as to curb the wind.

The Lord said:

35. Undoubtedly, O Mahabahu, the mind is fickle and hard to curb; yet, O Kauteya, it can be held in check by constant practice and dispassion.
36. Without self-restraint, yoga, I hold, is difficult to attain; but the self-governed soul can attain it by proper means, if he strives for it.

Arjuna said:

37. If one, possessed of faith, but slack of effort, because of his mind straying from yoga, reach not perfection in yoga, what end does he come to, O Krishna?
38. Without a foothold, and floundering in the path to Brahman, fallen from both, is he indeed not lost, O Mahabahu, like a dissipated cloud?
39. This my doubt, O Krishna, do thou dispel utterly; for there is to be found none other than thou to banish this doubt.

The Lord said:

40. Neither in this world, nor the next, can there be ruin for him. O Partha; no well-doer, oh loved one, meets with a sad end.
41. Fallen from yoga, a man attains the worlds of righteous souls, and having dwelt there for numberless years is then born in a house of pure and gentle blood.
42. Or he may even be born into a family of yogins, though such birth as this is all too rare in this world.
43. There, O Kurunandana, he discovers the intellectual stage he had reached in previous birth, and thence he stretches forward again towards perfection.

44. By virtue of that previous practice he is borne on, whether he will it or not, even he with a desire to know yoga passes beyond the Vedic ritual.
45. But the yogi who perseveres in his striving, cleansed of sin, perfected through many births, reaches the highest state.
46. The yogin is deemed higher than the man of austerities; he is deemed also higher than the man of knowledge; higher is he than the man engrossed in ritual; therefore be thou a yogin, O Arjuna!
47. And among all yogins, he who worships Me with faith, his inmost self all rapt in Me, is deemed by me to be the best yogin.

Thus ends the sixth discourse entitled "Dhyana yoga" in the converse of Lord Krishn and Arjun, on the science of Yoga, as part of the knowledge of Brahman in the Upanishad called the Bhagavad-gita.

∂iscourse vii

With this discourse begins an exposition of the nature of reality and the secret of devotion.

The Lord said:

1. Hear, O Partha, how, with thy mind riveted on me, by practicing yoga and making me the sole refuge, thou shalt, without doubt, know me fully.
2. I will declare to thee, in its entirety, this knowledge, combined with discriminative knowledge, which when thou hast known there remains here nothing more to be known.
3. Among thousands of men hardly one strives after perfection; among those who strive hardly one knows Me in truth.
4. Earth, Water, Fire, Air, Ether, Mind, Reason and Ego—thus eightfold are my prakriti divided.

The eightfold prakriti is substantially the same as the field described in XIII.5 and the perishable Being in XV.16.

5. This is My lower aspect; but know thou My other aspect, the higher—which if Jiva*by which, O Mahabahu, this world is sustained.
6. Know that these two compose the source from which all beings spring; I am the origin and end of the entire universe.
7. There is nothing higher than I, O Dhananjaya; all this is strung on Me as a row of hems upon a thread.
8. In water I am the savour, O Kaunteya; in the sun and moon I am the light; the syllable AUM in all the Bedas; the sound in ether, and manliness in men.

---

*That is, the vital essence.

9. I am the sweet fragrance in earth; the brilliance in fire; the life in all beings and the austerity in ascetics.

10. Know Me, O Partha, to be the primeval seed of all beings; I am the reason of rational beings and the splendour of the splendid.

11. Of the strong, I am the strength, divorced from lust and passion; in beings I am desire undivorced from righteousness.

Know that all the manifestations of the three gunas—sattva,* rajas,† and tamas‡— proceed from none but Me; yet I am not in them; they are Me.

God is not dependent on them, they are dependent on Him. Without Him those various manifestations would be impossible.

12. Befogged by these manifestations of the three gunas, the entire world fails to recognize Me, the imperishable, as transcending them.

13. For this My divine delusive mystery made up of the three gunas is hard to pierce; but those who make Me their sole refuge pierce the veil.

14. The deluded evil-doers, lowest of men, do not see refuge in Me for, by reason of this delusive mystery, they are bereft of knowledge and given to devilish ways.

15. Four types of well-doers are devoted to Me, O Arjuna; they are, O Bharatarshabha, the afflicted, the spiritual seeker, the material seeker, and the enlightened.

16. Of these the enlightened, ever attached to Me in single-minded devotion, is the best; for to the enlightened I am exceedingly dear and he is dear to Me.

17. All these are estimable indeed, but the enlightened I hold to be My very self; for he, the true yogi, is stayed on Me alone, the supreme goal.

18. At the end of many births the enlightened man finds refuge in Me; rare indeed is this great soul to whom "Vasudeva is all."

19. Men, bereft of knowledge by reason of various longings, seek refuge in other gods, pinning their faith on diverse rites, guided by their own nature.

20. Whatever form one desires to worship in faith and devotion, in that very form I make that faith of his secure.

21. Possessed of that faith he seeks to propitiate that one, and obtains there through his longings, dispensed in truth by none but Me.

22. But limited is the fruit that falls to those short-sighted ones; those who worship the gods go to the gods, those who worship Me come unto Me.

23. Not knowing My transcendent, imperishable, supreme character, the undiscerning think Me who am unmanifest to have become manifest.

24. Veiled by the delusive mystery created by My unique power, I am not manifest to all; this bewildered world does not recognize me, birthless and changeless.

25. Having the power to create this world of sense and yet unaffected by it, He is described as having unique power.

---

*That is, serene.

†That is, excitable.

‡That is, indifferent.

26. I know, O Arjuna, all creatures past, present and to be; but no one knows Me.
27. All creatures in this universe are bewildered, O Parantapa, by virtue of the delusion of the pairs of opposite sprung from likes and dislikes, O Bharata.
28. But those virtuous men whose sin has come to an end, freed from delusion and of the pairs of opposites, worship Me in steadfast faith.
29. Those who endeavour for freedom from age and death by taking refuge in Me, know in full that Brahman, Adhyatma and all Karma.
30. Those who know Me, including Adhibhuta, Adhidaiva, Adhiyajna, possessed of even-mindedness, they will know Me even at the time of passing away.

The sense is that every nook and cranny of the universe is filled with Brahman, that He is the sole Agent of all action, and that the man who imbued to Him, becomes one with Him at the time of passing hence. All his desires are extinguished in his vision of Him and he wins his freedom.

Thus ends the seventh discourse, entitled "Jananvijnana Yoga" in the converse of Lord Krishna and Arjuna, on the science of Yoga, as part of the knowledge of Brahman in the Upanishad called the Bhagavad-gita.

Discourse viii

The nature of the Supreme is further expounded in this discourse.

Arjuna said:

1. What is that Brahman? What is self-centered? What is Karma, O Purushottama? What is centered on things? And what centered on Divinity?
2. And who here in this body becomes free through sacrifice? And how at the time of death art Thou to be known by the self-controlled?

The Lord said:

3. The Supreme, the Imperishable is Brahman; its manifestation is Adhyatma; the creative process whereby all beings are created is called Karma.
4. That which is personal and physical is perishable; its cosmic and universal forms are transitory; and, O best among the incarnate souls, I am your Divinity in bodily appearance, reached through sacrifice.

That is, from Imperishable Unmanifest down to the perishable atom everything in the universe is the Supreme and an expression of the Supreme. Why then should mortal man arrogate to himself authorship of anything rather than do His bidding and dedicate all action to Him?

5. And he who, at the last hour remembering Me only, departs leaving the body enters into Me; of that there is no doubt.
6. Or whatever form a man continually contemplates, that same he remembers in the hour of death, and to that very form he goes, O Kaunteya.

7. Therefore at all times remember Me and fight on; thy mind and reason thus on Me fixed thou shalt surely come to Me.

8. With thought steadied by constant practice, and wandering nowhere, he who meditates on the supreme Celestial Being, O Partha, goes to Him.

9. Whoso, at the time of death, with unwavering mind, with devotion, and fixing the breath rightly between the brows by

10. the power of yoga, meditates on the Sage, the Ancient, the Ruler, subtler than the subtlest, the Supporter of all, the Inconceivable, glorious as the sun beyond the darkness—he goes to that Supreme Celestial Being.

11. That which the knowers of the Vedas call the Imperishable (or that word which the knowers of the Vedas respect), wherein the ascetics freed from passion enter and desiring which they brahmacharya, That Goal (or word) I will declare to thee in brief.

12. Closing all the gates, locking up the mind in the hridaya, fixing his breath within the head, rapt in yogic meditation;

13. Whoso departs leaving the body uttering AUM—Brahman in one syllable—repeatedly thinking on Me, he reaches the highest state.

14. That yogi easily wins to me, O Partha, who, ever attached to me, constantly remembers Me with undivided mind.

15. Great souls, having come to Me, reach the highest perfection; they come not again to birth, unlasting and (withal) an abode of misery.

16. From the world of Brahma down, all the worlds are subject to return, O Arjuna; but on coming to Me there is no rebirth.

17. Those men indeed know what is Day and what is Night, who knows that Brahma's day lasts a thousand yugas and that his night too is a thousand yugas* long.

That is to say; our day and night of a dozen hours each are less than the infinitesimal fraction of a moment in that vast cycle of time. Pleasure pursued during these incalculably small moments is as illusory as a mirage. Rather than waste these brief moments, we should devote them to serving God through service of mankind. On the other hand, our time is such a small drop in the ocean of eternity that if we fail of our object here, viz, Self-realization, we need not despair. She should bide our time.

18. At the coming of day all the manifest spring forth from the Unmanifest, and at the coming of Night they are dissolved into that same Unmanifest.

Knowing this too, man should understand that he has very little power over things, the round of birth and death is ceaseless.

19. The same multitude of creatures come to birth, O Partha, again and again; they are dissolved at the coming of Night, whether they will or not; and at the break of Day they are re-born.

*That is, eras.

20. But higher than the Unmanifest is another Unmanifest Being, everlasting; which perished not when all creatures perish.
21. The Unmanifest, named the Imperishable, is declared to be the highest goal. For those who reach it there is no return. That is my highest abode.
22. This Supreme Being, O Partha, may be won by undivided devotion; in it all beings dwell, by It all is pervaded.
23. Now I will tell thee, Bharatarshabha, the condition which determines the exemption from return, as also the return, of yogins after they pass away hence.
24. Fire, Light, Day, the Bright fortnight, and the six months of the Northern Solstice—through these departing men knowing Brahman go to Brahman.
25. Smoke, Night, the Dark Fortnight, the six months of the Southern Solstice—there through the yogin attains to the lunar light and thence returns.

I do not understand the meaning of these two shlokas. They do not seem to me to be consistent with their teaching of the Gita. *The Gita teaches that he whose heart is meek with devotion, which is devoted to unattached action and has seen the Truth, must win salvation, no matter when he dies. These shlokas seem to run counter to this. They may perhaps be stretched to mean broadly that a man of sacrifice, a man of light, a man who has known Brahman finds release from birth if he retains that enlightenment at the time of death, and that on the contrary the man who has none of these attributes goes to the world of the moon—not at all lasting—and returns to birth. The moon, after all, shines with borrowed light.*

26. These two paths—bright and dark—are deemed to be the eternal paths of the world; by the one a man goes to return not, by the other he returns again.

The bright one may be taken to mean the path of knowledge and the dark one that of ignorance.

27. The Yogin knowing these two paths falls not in to delusion, O Partha; therefore, at all times, O Arjuna, remain steadfast in yoga.

"Will not fall into delusion" means that he who knows the two paths and has known the secret of even-mindedness will not take the path of ignorance.

28. Whatever fruit of good deeds is laid down as accruing from (a study of) the Vedas, from sacrifices, austerities, and acts of charity—all that the yogin transcends, on knowing this and reaches the supreme and Primal Abode.

He who has achieved even-mindedness by dint of devotion, knowledge and service not only obtains the fruit of all his good actions, but also wins salvation.

Thus ends the eighth discourse entitled "Brahma Yoga" in the converse of Lord Krishna and Arjuna, on the science of Yoga, as part of the knowledge of Brahman in the Upanishad called the Bhagavad-gita.

ÐISCOURSE IX

This discourse reveals the glory of devotion.

The Lord said:

1. I will now declare to thee, who art uncensorious, this mysterious knowledge, together with discriminative knowledge, knowing which thou shalt be released from ill.
2. This is the king of sciences, the king of mysteries, pure and sovereign, capable of direct comprehension, the essence of dharma, easy to practice, changeless.
3. Men who have no faith in this doctrine, O Parantapa, far from coming to Me, return repeatedly to the path of this world of death.
4. By Me, unmanifest in form, this whole world is pervaded; all beings are in Me, I am not in them.
5. And yet those beings are not in Me. That indeed is My unique power as Lord! Sustainer of all beings, I am not in them; My Self brings them into existence.

The sovereign power of God lies in this mystery, this miracle, that all beings are in Him and yet not in Him, He in them and yet not in them. This is the description of God in the language of mortal man. Indeed He soothes man by revealing to him all His aspects by using all kinds of paradoxes. All beings are in him inasmuch as all creation is His; but as He transcends it all, as He really is not the author of it all, it may be said with equal truth that the beings are not in Him. He really is in all His true devotees; He is not, according to them, in those who deny Him. What is this if not a mystery, a miracle of God?

6. As the mighty wind, moving everywhere, is ever contained in ether, even so know that all beings, are contained in Me.
7. All beings, O Kaunteya, merge into my prakriti, at the end of a kalpa,* and I send them forth again when a kalpa begins.
8. Resorting to my prakriti, I send forth again and again this multitude of beings, powerless under the sway of prakriti.
9. But all this activity, O Dhananjaya, does not bind Me, seated as one indifferent, unattached to it.
10. With me as Presiding Witness, prakriti gives birth to all that moves and does not move; and because of this, O Kaunteya, the wheel of the world keeps going.
11. Not knowing My transcendent nature as the sovereign Lord of all beings, fools condemn Me as incarnated man. For they deny the existence of God and do not recognize the Master in the human body.
12. Vain are the hopes, actions and knowledge of those witless ones who have resorted to the delusive nature of monsters and devils.

---

*An "eon" in Sanskrit.

13. But those great souls who resort to the divine nature, O Partha, know Me as the Imperishable source of all beings and worship Me with an undivided mind.
14. Always declaring My glory, striving in steadfast faith, they do Me devout homage; ever attached to Me, they worship Me.
15. Yet others, with knowledge-sacrifice, worship Me, who am to be seen everywhere, as one, as different or as many.
16. I am the sacrificial vow; I am the sacrifice; I the ancestral oblation; I the herb; I the sacred text; I the clarified butter; I the fire; I the burnt offering.
17. Of this universe I am the Father, Mother, Creator, Grandsire; I am what is to known, the sacred syllable AUM; the Rig, the Saman and the Yajus;
18. I am the Goal, the Sustainer, the Lord, the Witness, the Abode, the Refuge, the Friend; the Origin, the End the Preservation, the Treasure house, the Imperishable Seed.
19. I give heat, I hold back and pour forth rain; I am deathlessness and also death. O Arjuna, Being and not-Being as well.
20. Followers of the three Vedas, who drink the soma juice and are purged of sin, worship Me with sacrifice and pay for going to heaven; they reach the holy world of the gods and enjoy in heaven the divine joys of the gods.

The reference is to the sacrificial ceremonies and rites in vogue in the days of the Gita. *We cannot definitely say what they were like nor what the soma juice exactly was.**

21. They enjoy the vast world of heaven, and their merit spent, they enter the world of the mortals; thus those who, following the Vedic law, long for the fruit of their action earn but the round of birth and death.
22. As for those who worship Me, thinking on Me alone and nothing else, ever attached to Me, I bear the burden of getting them what they need.

There are thus three unmistakable marks of a true yogi or bhakta — even-mindedness, skill in action, undivided devotion. These three must be completely harmonized in a yogi. Without devotion there is no even-mindedness, without even-mindedness no devotion. And without skill in action devotion and even-mindedness might well be a pretense.

23. Even those who, devoted to other gods, worship them in full faith, even they, O Kaunteya, worship none but Me, though not according to the rule.

"Not according to the rule" means not knowing Me as the Impersonal and the Absolute.

24. For I am the Acceptor of all sacrifices and the Master of ceremonies but not recognizing Me as I am, they go astray.

---

*Except that it was undoubtedly the same as the hoama juice used in Zoroastrian rites.

25. Those who worship the gods go to the gods; those who worship the manes* go to the manes; those who worship the spirits go to the spirits; but those who worship Me come to Me.
26. Any offering of leaf, flower, fruit or water, made to me in devotion, by an earnest soul, I lovingly accept.

That is to say, it is the Lord in every being whom we serve with devotion who accepts the service.

27. Whatever thou doest, whatever thou eatest, whatever thou offerest as sacrifice or gift, whatever austerity thou dost perform, O Kaunteya, dedicate all to Me.
28. So doing thou shalt be released from the bondage of action, yielding good and evil fruit; having accomplished both renunciation and performance, thou shalt be released (from birth and death) and come unto Me.
29. I am the same to all beings; with Me there is none disfavoured, none favoured; but those who worship Me with devotion are in Me and I in them.
30. A sinner, howsoever great, if he turns to Me with undivided devotion, must indeed be counted a saint; for he has settled resolve.

The undivided devotion subdues both his passions and his evil deeds.

31. For soon he becomes righteous and wins everlasting peace: know for a certainty, O Kaunteya that my bhakta never perishes.
32. For finding refuge in Me, even those who though are born of the womb of sin, women, vaishyas, and shudra too, reach the supreme goal.
33. How much more then, the pure brahmanas and seer-kings who are my devotees? Do thou worship Me, therefore, since thou hast come to this fleeting and joyless world?
34. On Me fix thy mind, to Me bring thy devotion, to Me offer thy sacrifice, to Me make thy obeisance; thus having attached thyself to Me and made Me thy end and aim, to Me indeed shalt thou come.

Thus ends the ninth discourse entitled "Rajavidya-rajaguhya Yoga" in the converse of Lord Krishna and Arjuna, on the science of Yoga, as part of the knowledge of Brahman in the Upanishad called the Bhagavad-gita.

ÐISCOURSE X

For the benefit of His devotees, the Lord gives in this discourse a glimpse of His divine manifestations.

---

*That is, ancestors.

The Lord said:

1. Yet once more, O Mahabahu, hear My supreme word, which I will utter to thee, gratified one, for thy benefit.
2. Neither the gods nor the great seers know My origin; for I am, every way, the origin of them both.
3. He who knows Me, the great Lord of the worlds, as birthless and without beginning, he among mortals, undeluded, is released from sins.
4. Discernment, knowledge, freedom from delusion, long suffering, truth, self-restraint, inward calm, pleasure, pain, birth, death, fear, and fearlessness;
5. Non-violence, even-mindedness, contentment, austerity, beneficence, good and ill fame—all these various attributes of creatures proceed verily from Me.
6. The seven great seers, the ancient four, and the Manus* too were born of Me and of My mind, and of them were born all creatures in the world.
7. He who knows in truth My immanence and My yoga becomes gifted with unshakable yoga; of this there is no doubt.
8. I am the source of all, all proceeds from me; knowing this, the wise worship Me with hearts full of devotion.
9. With me in their thoughts, their whole soul devoted to Me, teaching one another, with me ever on their lips, they live in contentment and joy.
10. To these, ever in tune with Me, worshipping me with affectionate devotion, I give the power of selfless action, whereby they come to Me.
11. Out of every compassion for them, I who dwell in their hearts, destroy the darkness, born or ignorance, with the refulgent lamp of knowledge.

Arjuna said:

12. Lord! Thou art the supreme Brahman, the supreme Abode, the supreme Purifier! Everlasting celestial Being, the Primal god, Unborn, all-pervading.
13. Thus have all the seers—the divine seer Narada, Asita, Devala, Vyasa—declared thee; and thou thyself dost tell me so.
14. All that Thou tellest me is true, I know, O Keeshave, verily, Lord, neither the gods nor the demons know Thy manifestation.
15. Thyself alone Thou knowest by Thyself, O Purushottama, O source and Lord of all beings, God of gods, O Ruler of the universe.
16. Indeed Thou oughtest to tell me all Thy manifestations, without a remainder, whereby Thou dost pervade the worlds.
17. O Yogin! Constantly meditating on Thee, how am I to know Thee? In what various aspects am I to think of Thee, O Lord?
18. Recount to me yet again, in full detail, thy unique power and Thy immanence, O Janardana! For my ears cannot be sated with listening to Thy life-giving words.

---

*That is, progenitors of humanity.

The Lord said:

19. Yea, I will unfold to thee, O Kurushreshtha, My divine manifestations—the chiefest only; for there is no limit to their extent.
20. I am the Atman, O Gudakeha, seated in the heart of every being; I am the beginning, the middle and the end of all beings.
21. Of the Aditas I am Vishnu; of luminaries, the radiant sun; of maruts,* I am Marichi; constellations, the moon.
22. Of the Vedas I am the Sama Veda; of the gods Indra; of the senses I am the mind; of beings I am the consciousness.
23. Of Ruddras I am shankara; of Yakshas and Rakshasas Kubera; of Vasus I am the Fire; of mountains in Meru.
24. Of priests, O Partha, know Me to be the chief of Brihaspati; of army captains I am Kartikeya; and of waters the ocean.
25. Of the great seers I am Bhrigu; of words I am the one syllable "AUM"; of sacrifices I am the Japa sacrifice; of things immovable the Himalaya.
26. Of all trees I am Ashvattha; of the divine seers, Narada; of the heavenly choir I am Chitraratha; of the perfected I am Kapila the ascetic.
27. Of horses, Know Me to be the Uchchaihshravas born with Amrita; of mighty elephants, I am Airavata; of men, the monarch.
28. Of weapons, I am Vajra; of cows, Kamadhenu; I am Kandarpa, the god of generation; of serpents I am Vasuki.
29. Of cobras I am Anata; of water-dwellers I am Varuna; of the manes I am Aryaman; and of the chastisers, Yama.
30. Of demons I am Prahlada; of reckoners, the time; of beasts I the lion; and of birds, Garuda.
31. Of cleansing agents I am the Wind; of wielders of weapons, Rama; of fishes I am the crocodile; of rivers the Ganges.
32. Of creations I am the beginning, end and middle, O Arjuna; of sciences, the science of spiritual knowledge; of debaters, the right argument.
33. Of letters, the letter A; of compounds I am the dvandva; I am the imperishable Time; I am the creator to be seen everywhere.
34. All-seizing Death am I, as the source of things to be; in feminine virtues I am Karta (glory), Shri (beauty), Vak (speech), Smriti (memory), Medha (intelligence), Dhriti (constancy), and Kshama (forgiveness).
35. Of Saman hymns I am Bright Saman;† of metres, Gayatri;‡ of months I am Margashirsha;§ of seasons, the spring.
36. Of deceivers I am the dice-play; of the splendid the splendour; I am victory, I am resolution, I am the goodness of the good.

---

*That is, storm deities.
†A popular hymn to Indra.
‡The aforementioned *Gayatri Mantra*.
§A month of devotion and dedication.

The "dice-play of deceivers" need not alarm one. For the good and evil nature of things is not the matter in question; it is the directing and immanent power of God that is being described. Let the deceivers also know that they are under God's rule and judgment and put away their pride and deceit.

37. Of Vrishnis I am Vasudeva; of Pandavas Dhananjaya; of ascetics I am Vyasa; and of seers, Ushanas.
38. I am the rod of those that punish; the strategy of those seeking victory; of secret things I am silence, and the knowledge of those that know.
39. Whatever is the seed of every being, O Arjuna that is I; there is nothing, whether moving or fixed, that can be without Me.
40. There is no end to my divine manifestations; what extent of them I have told thee now is only by way of illustration.
41. Whatever is glorious, beautiful and mighty know thou that all such has issued from a fragment of My splendour.
42. But why needs thou to learn this at great length, O Arjuna? With but a part of Myself I stand upholding this universe.

Thus ends the tenth discourse, entitled "Vibhuti Yoga" in the converse of Lord Krishna and Arjuna, on the science of Yoga, as part of the knowledge of Brahman, in the Upanishad called Bhagavad-gita.

discourse xi

In this discourse the Lord reveals to Arjuna's vision what Arjuna has heard with his ears — the Universal Form of the Lord. This discourse is a favourite with the Bhaktas. Here there is no argument, there is pure poetry. Its solemn music reverberates in one's ears and it is not possible to tire of reading it again and again.

Arjuna said:

1. Out of Thy grace towards me, thou hast told me the supreme mystery revealing the knowledge of the Supreme; it has banished my delusion.
2. Of the origin and destruction of beings I have heard from Thee in full detail, as also Thy imperishable majesty, O Kamala-patrakska!
3. Thou art indeed as Thou hast described Thyself, Parameshvara! I do crave to behold, now, that form of Thine as Ishvara.*
4. If, Lord, thou thinkest it possible for me to bear the sight, reveal to me, O Yogeshvara, Thy imperishable form.

---

*Meaning "lord," also a popular name, often spelled "Ishwar" in English.

The Lord said;

5. Behold, O Partha, my forms divine in their hundreds and thousands, infinitely diverse, infinitely various in color and aspect.
6. Behold the Adityas, the Vasus, the Rudras, the two Ashwins, the Maruts; behold, O Bharata, numerous marvels never revealed before.
7. Behold today, O Gudaskesha, in my body, the whole universe, moving and unmoving, all in one, and whatever else thou cravest to see.
8. But thou canst not see Me with these thine own eyes. I give thee the eye divine; behold My sovereign power!

Sanjaya said;

9. With these words, O King, the great Lord of Yoga, Hari, then revealed to Partha His supreme form as Ishvara.
10. With many mouths and many eyes, many wondrous aspects, many divine ornaments, and many brandished weapons divine.
11. Wearing divine garlands and vestments, anointed with divine perfumes, it was the form of God, all marvellous, infinite, seen everywhere.
12. Was the splendour of a thousand suns to shoot forth all at once in the sky that might perchance resemble the splendour of that Mighty One?
13. Then did Pandava see the whole universe in its manifold divisions gathered as one in the body of that God of gods.
14. The Dhananjaya, wonderstruck and thrilled in every fibre of his being, bowed low his head before the Lord, addressing Him thus with folded hands.

Arjuna said:

15. With Thy form, O Lord, I see all the gods and the diverse multitudes of beings, the Lord Brahma, on his lotus-throne and all the seers and serpents divine.
16. With many arms and bellies, mouths and eyes, I see Thy infinite form everywhere. Neither Thy end, nor middle, nor beginning, do I see, O Lord of the Universe, Universal-formed!
17. With crown and mace and disc, a mass of effulgence, gleaming everywhere I see Thee, so dazzling to the sight, bright with the splendour of the fiery sun blazing from all sides—incomprehensible.
18. Thou art the Supreme Imperishable worthy to be known; Thou art the final resting place of this universe; Thou art the changeless guardian of the eternal Dharma; Thou art, I believe, the Everlasting Being.
19. Thou hast no beginning, middle nor end; infinite is Thy might; arms innumerable; for eyes, the sun and the moon; Thy mouth a blazing fire, overpowering the universe with Thy radiance.

20. By Thee alone are filled the space between heaven and earth and all the quarters; at the sight of this Thy wondrous terrible form, the three worlds are sore oppressed, O Mahatma!*

21. Here, too, the multitudes of gods are seen to enter Thee; some awe-struck praise Thee with folded arms; the hosts of great seers and siddhas, "All Hail" on their lips, hymn Thee with songs of praise.

22. The Rudras, Adityas, Vasus, Sadhyas, all the gods, the twin Ashwins, Maruts, Manes, the hosts of Gandharvas, Yakshas, Asuras and Siddhas—all gaze on Thee in wonderment.

23. At the sight of thy mighty form. O Mahabahu, many-mouthed, with eyes, arms, thighs and feet innumerable, with many vast bellies, terrible with many jaws, the world's feel fearfully oppressed, and so do I.

24. For as I behold thee touching the sky, glowing, numerous-hued with gaping mouths and wide resplendent eyes, I feel oppressed in my innermost being; no peace nor quiet I find, O Vishnu!

25. As I see Thy mouths with fearful jaws, resembling the Fire of Doom, I lose all sense of direction, and find no relief. Be gracious, O Devesha, O Jagannivasa!

26. All the sons of Dhritarashtra, with them the crowd of kings, Bhishma, Drona, and that Karna too, as also our chief warriors—

27. Are hastening into the fearful jaws of Thy terrible mouths, some indeed, caught between Thy teeth, and are seen, their heads being crushed to atoms.

28. As rivers, in their numerous torrents, runs head-long to the sea, even so the heroes of the world of men rush into Thy flaming mouths.

29. As moths, fast-flying, plunge into blazing fire, straight to their doom, even so these rush headlong into Thy mouths, to their destruction.

30. Devouring all these from all sides, Thou lappest them with Thy flaming tongues; Thy fierce rays blaze forth, filling the whole universe with their lustre.

31. Tell me, Lord, who Thou art so dread of form! Hail to thee, O Devavara! Be gracious! I desire to know Thee, Primal Lord; for I comprehend not what Thou dost.

The Lord said:

32. Doom am I, full-ripe, dealing death to the worlds, engaged in devouring mankind. Even without slaying them not one of the warriors, ranged for battle against thee, shall survive.

33. Therefore, do thou arise, and win renown! Defeat thy foes and enjoy a thriving kingdom. By me have these already been destroyed; be thou no more than an instrument, O Savyasachin!

34. Drona, Bhishma, Jayadratha and Karna, as also the other warrior chiefs—already slain by Me—slay thou! Fight! Victory is thine over the foes in the field.

---

*Great Soul, the title most often bestowed on Mohandas Ghandi himself.

Sanjaya said:

35. Hearing this world of Keshave, crown-wearer Arjuna folded his hands, and trembling made obeisance. Bowing and all hesitant, in faltering accents, he proceeded to address Krishna once more.

Arjuna said:

36. Right proper it is, O Hrishikesha that Thy praise should stir the world to gladness and tender emotion; the Rakshasas* in fear fly to every quarter and all the hosts of Siddhas† do reverent homage.

37. And why should they not bow to Thee, O Mahatma? Thou art the First Creator, greater even than Brahma. O Anata, O Devesha, O Jagannivasa, Thou art the Imperishable, Being, not-being, and that which transcends even these.

38. Thou art the Primal God, the Ancient Being; Thou art the Final Resting Place of this Universe; Thou art the Knower, the "to-be-known," the Supreme Abode; by thee, O Myraiad-formed, is the universe pervaded.

39. Thou art Vayu, Yama, Agni, Varuna, Shashanka, Prajapati, and Prapitamaha! All Hail to Thee, a thousand times all hail! Again and yet again all hail to Thee!

40. All hail to Thee from before and behind! All hail to thee from every side, O All; Thy prowess is infinite, Thy might is measureless! Thou holdest all; therefore Thou art all.

41. If ever in carelessness, thinking of thee as comrade, I addressed Thee saying, "O Krishna!," "O Yadava!" not knowing Thy greatness, in negligence or in affection.

42. If ever I have been rude to Thee in jest, whilst at play, at rest-time, or at meals, whilst alone or in company, O Achyuta, forgive Thou my fault—I beg of Thee, O Incomprehensible!

43. Thou art Father of this world, of the moving and the un-moving; thou art it's adored, it's worthiest, Master; there is none equal to thee; how then any greater than Thee? Thy power is matchless in the three worlds.

44. Therefore, I prostate myself before thee, and beseech Thy grace, O Lord adorable! As father with son, as comrade with comrade, so shouldst Thou bear, beloved Lord, with me, Thy loved one.

45. I am filled with joy to see what never was seen before, and yet my heart is oppressed with fear. Show me that original form of Thine, O Lord! Be gracious, Devesha, O Jagannivasa!

46. I crave to see thee even as Thou wast, with crown, with mace, and disc in hand; wear Thou, once more, that four-armed form, O thousand-armed Vishvamurti!

---

*Meaning, demons.
†Perfect beings (Radhakrishna calls them "angels").

The Lord said:

47. It is to favour thee, O Arjuna, that I have revealed to thee, by My own unique power, this My form supreme, Resplendent, Universal, Infinite, Primal—which none save thee has ever seen.
48. Not by the study of the Vedas, not by sacrifice, not by the study of other scriptures, not by gifts, nor yet by performance of rites or of fierce austerities can I, in such a form, be seen by any one save thee in the world of men, O Kurupravira!
49. Be thou neither oppressed nor bewildered to look on this awful form of Mine. Banish thy fear, ease thy mind, and lo! behold Me once again as I was.

Sanyaya said:

50. So said Vasudeva to Arjuna, and revealed to him once more His original form. Wearing again His form benign, the Mahatma consoled him terrified.

Arjuna said:

51. Beholding again thy benign human form I am come to myself and once more in my normal state.

The Lord said:

52. Very hard to behold is that form of Mine which thou hast seen; even the gods always yearn to see it.
53. Not by the Vedas, not by penance, nor by gifts, nor yet by sacrifice, can any behold Me in the form that thou hast seen.
54. But by single-minded devotion, O Arjuna, I may in this form be known and seen, and truly entered into, O Parantapa!
55. He alone comes to me, O Pandava, who does My work, who has made Me his goal, who My devotee, who has renounced attachment, who has ill-will toward none.

Thus ends the eleventh discourse entitled "Vishvarupadarshana Yoga" in the converse of Lord Krishna and Arjuna, on the science of Yoga as part of the knowledge of Brahman in the Upanishad called the Bhagavad-gita.

Discourse xii

Thus we see that vision of God is possible only through single-minded devotion. Contents of devotion must follow as a matter of course. This twelfth discourse should be learnt by heart even if all discourses are not. It is one of the shortest. The marks of a devotee should be carefully noted.

Arjuna said:

1. Of the devotees who thus worship Thee, incessantly attached, and those who worship the Imperishable Unmanifest, which are the better yogins?
2. Those I regard as the best yogins who, riveting their minds on Me, ever attached, worship Me, with the highest faith.
3. But those who worship the Imperishable, the indefinable, the Unmanifest, the Omnipresent, the Unthinkable, the Rock-seated, the Immovable, the Unchanging.
4. Keeping the whole host of senses in complete control, looking on all with an impartial eye, engrossed in the welfare for all beings—these come indeed to Me.
5. Greater is the travail of those whose mind is fixed on the Unmanifest; for it is hard for embodied mortals to gain the Unmanifest-Goal.

Mortal man can only imagine the Unmanifest, The Impersonal, and as his language fails him he often negatively describes It as "Neti," "Neti" (not that, Not That). And so even iconoclasts are at bottom no better than idol-worshippers. To worship a book, to go to church, or to pray with one's face in a particular direction—all these are forms of worshipping the Formless in an image or idol. And yet, both the idol-breaker and the idol-worshipper cannot lose sight of the fact that there is something which is beyond all form, Unthinkable, Formless, Impersonal, Change-less. The highest goal of the devotee is to become one with the object of his devotion. The bhakta extinguishes himself and merges into, the object of his devotion. The bhakta extinguishes himself and merges into, becomes Bhagvan. This state can best be reached by devoting oneself to some form, and so it is said that the short cut to the Unmanifest is really the longest and most difficult.

6. But those who casting all their actions on Me, making Me their all in all, worship Me with the meditation of undivided devotion.
7. Of such, whose thought are centered on Me, O Partha, I become ere long the Deliverer from the ocean of this world of death.
8. On Me set thy mind, on Me rest thy conviction; thus without doubt shalt thou remain only in Me hereafter.
9. If thou canst not set thy mind steadily on Me, then by the method of constant practice seek to win Me, O Dhananjaya.
10. If thou art also unequal to this method of constant practice, concentrate on service for Me; even thus serving Me thou shalt attain perfection.
11. If thou art unable even to do this, then dedicating all to Me, with mind controlled, abandon the fruit of action.
12. Better is knowledge than practice, better than knowledge is concentration, better than concentration is renunciation of the fruit of all action, from which directly issues peace.

"Practice" (abhyasa) is the practice of the yoga of meditation and the control of psychis processes; "knowledge" (jnana) is intellectual effort; "concentration" (dhyana) is devoted

worship. If as a result of all this there is no renunciation of the fruit of action, "practice" is no "practice," "knowledge" is no "knowledge," and "concentration" is no "concentration."

13. Who has ill-will towards none, who is friendly and compassionate, who has shed all thought of "mine" or "I," who regards pain and pleasure alike, who is long-suffering:
14. Who is ever content, gifted with yoga, self-restrained, of firm conviction, who has dedicated his mind and reason to Me—that devotee (bhakta) of Mine is dear to me.
15. Who gives no trouble to the world, to whom the world causes no trouble, who is free from exultation, resentment, fear and vexation—that man is dear to Me.
16. Who expects naught, who is pure, resourceful, unconcerned, untroubled, who indulges in no undertakings—that devotee of Mine is dear to Me.
17. Who rejoices not, neither frets nor grieves, who covets not, who abandons both good and ill—that devotee of Mine is dear to me.
18. Who is same to foe and friend, who regards alike respect and disrespect, cold and heat, pleasure and pain, who is free from attachment;
19. Who weighs in equal scale blame and praise, who is silent, content with whatever his lot, who owns no home, who is of steady mind—that devotee of Mine is dear to Me.
20. They who follow this essence of dharma, as I have told it, with faith, keeping Me as their goal—those devotees are exceeding dear to Me.

Thus ends the twelfth discourse entitled "Bhakti Yoga" in the converse of Lord Krishna and Arjuna, on the science of Yoga, as part of the knowledge of Brahman in the Upanishad called the Bhagavad-gita.

Discourse xiii

This discourse treats of the distinction between the body (not-Self) and the Atman (the Self).

The Lord said:

1. This body, O Kauteya, is called the Field; he who knows it is called the knower of the Field by those who know.
2. And understand Me to be, O Bharata, the knower of the field in all the Fields; and the knowledge of the Field and the knower of the Field, I hold, is true knowledge.
3. What the Field is, what its nature, what its modifications, and whence is what, as also who He is, and what His power—hear this briefly from Me.
4. This subject has been sung by seers distinctively and in various ways, in different hymns as also in aphoristic texts about Brahman well-reasoned and unequivocal.

5. The great elements, Individuation,* Reason, the Unmanifest, the ten senses, and the one (mind), and the five spheres of the senses;
6. Desire, dislike, pleasure, pain, association, consciousness, cohesion—this, in sum, is what is called the Field with its modifications.

The great elements are Earth, Water, Fire, Air, and Ether. "Individuation" is the thought of I, or that the body is "I"; "the Unmanifest" is prakriti or maya; the ten senses are the five sense of perception—smell, taste, sight, touch, and hearing, and the five organs of action, viz.: the hands, the feet, the tongue, and the two organs of excretion. The five spheres of objects of the senses are smell, savour, form, touch, and sound. "Association" is the property of the different organs to co-operate. Dhriti is not patience or constancy but cohesion, i.e., the property of all the atoms in the body to hold together; from "individuation" springs this cohesion. Individuation is inherent in the unmanifest prakriti. The undeluded man is he who can cast off the individuation or ego, and having done so the shock of an inevitable thing like death and pairs of opposites caused by sense-contacts fail to affect him. The Field is subject to all its modifications alike.

7. Freedom from pride and pretentiousness, nonviolence, forgiveness, uprightness, service of the Master, purity, steadfastness, self-restraint;
8. Aversion from sense-objects, absence of conceit, realization of the painfulness and evil of birth, death, age and disease;
9. Absence of attachment, refusal to be wrapped up in one's children, wife, home and family, even-mindedness whether good or ill befall;
10. Unwavering and all-exclusive devotion to me, resort to secluded spots, distaste for the haunt of men;
11. Settled conviction of the nature of the Atman, perception of the goal of the knowledge of Truth—All this is declared to be Knowledge and the reverse of it is ignorance.
12. I will now expound to thee that which is to be known and knowing which one enjoys immortality; it is the supreme Brahman which has no beginning, which is called neither Being nor non-Being.

The Supreme can be described neither as Being nor as non-Being. It is beyond definition or description, above all attributes.

13. Everywhere having hands and feet, everywhere having eyes, heads, mouths, everywhere having ears, It abides embracing everything in the universe.
14. Seeming to possess the functions of the senses, It is devoid of all the senses; It touches naught, upholds all; having no gunas, It experiences the gunas.
15. Without all beings, yet within; immovable yet moving, so subtle that It cannot be perceived; so far and yet so near it is.

---

*Often translated as "ego," in translating this term as "individuation" Gandhi here shows his affinity with Jungian psychology, a connection frequently remarked upon.

He who knows It is within It, close to It; mobility and immobility, peace and restlessness, we owe to It, for It has motion and yet is motionless.

16. Undivided, It seems to subsist divided in all being; this Brahman—That which is to known as the sustainer of all, yet It is their Devourer and Creator.
17. Light of all lights, It is said to be beyond darkness; It is knowledge, the object of knowledge, to be gained only by knowledge; It is seated in the hearts of all.
18. Thus have I expounded in brief the Field, Knowledge and That which is to be known; My devotee, when he knows this, is worth to become one with Me.
19. Know that Prakriti and Purusha are both without beginning; know that all modifications and gunas are born of Prakriti.
20. Prakriti is described as the cause in the creation of effects from causes; Purusha is described as the cause of the experiencing of pleasure and pain.
21. For the Purusha, residing in Prakriti, experiences the gunas born in Prakriti; attachment to these gunas is the cause of his birth in good or evil wombs.

Prakriti in common parlance is Maya.* Prusha is the Jiva.† Jiva acting in accordance with his nature experiences the fruit of actins arising out of the three gunas.

22. What is called this body the Witness, the Assentor, the Sustainer, the Experiencer, the Great Lord and also the Supreme Atman, is Supreme Being.
23. He, who thus knows Pruusha and Prakriti with its gunas, is not born again, no matter how he lives and moves.

Read in the light of discourses II, IX, and XII this shloka may not be taken to support any kind of libertinism. It shows the virtue of self-surrender and selfless devotion. All actions bind the self. But if all are dedicated to the Lord they do not bind, rather they release him. He who has thus extinguished the "self or the thought of I and who acts as ever in the great witness," will never sin nor err. The self-sense is at the root of all error or sin. Where the "I" has been extinguished, there is no sin. This shloka shows how to steer clear of all sin.

24. Some through meditation hold the Atman by themselves in their own self; others by Sankhya Yoga, and others by Karma Yoga.
25. Yet others, not knowing Him thus, worship Him having heard from others; they too pass beyond death, because of devoted adherence to what they have heard.
26. Wherever something is born, animate or inanimate, know the Bharatarshabha that it issues from the union of the Field and the Knower of the Field.
27. Who see abiding in all beings the same Parameshvara, imperishable in the perishable, he sees indeed.
28. When he sees the same Ishvara abiding everywhere alike, he does not hurt himself by himself and hence he attains the highest goal.

---

*Illusion, or even delusion.
†Similar to *atma*, the cosmic self, Gandhi here uses the term preferred among Jains.

He who sees the same God everywhere merges in Him and sees naught else; he thus does not yield to passion, does not become his own foe and thus attains Freedom.

29. Who sees that it is Prakriti that performs all actions and thus (knows) that Atman performs them not, he see indeed.

Just as, in the case of a man who is asleep, his "Self" is not the agent of sleep, but Prakriti, even so the enlightened man will detach his "Self" from all activities, to the pure everything is pure. Prakriti is not unchaste; it is when arrogant man takes her as wife that of these twain passion is born.

30. When he sees the diversity of beings as founded in unity and the whole expanse issuing therefrom, then he attains to Brahman.

To realize that everything rests in Brahman is to attain to the state of Brahma. Then Jiva becomes Shiva.*

31. This imperishable supreme Atman, O Kaunteya, though residing in the body, acts not and is not stained, for he has no beginning and no gunas.
32. As the all-pervading ether, by reason of its subtlety, is not soiled even so Atman pervading every part of the body is not soiled.
33. As the one sun illumines the whole universe, even so the Master of the Field illumines the whole field, O Bharata!
34. Those who, with eyes of knowledge, thus perceive the distinction between the Field and the Knower of the Field, and (the secret) of the release of beings from Prakriti, they attain to the supreme.

Thus ends the thirteenth discourse, entitled "Kshetra-kshetrajnavibha Yoga" in the converse of Lord Krishna and Arjuna, on the science of Yoga, as part of the knowledge of Brahman in the Upanishad called the Bhagavad-gita.

διscourse xιυ

The description of Prakriti naturally leads on to that of its constituents, the Gunas which form the subject of this discourse. And that, in turn, leads to a description of the marks of him who has passed beyond the three gunas. These are practically the same as those of the man of secure understand (II.54–72) as also those of the ideal Bhakta (XII.12–20).

The Lord said:

1. Yet again I will expound the highest and the best of all knowledge, knowing which all the sages passed hence to the highest perfection.

---

*The transformative spirit of God.

2. By having recourse to this knowledge they became one with Me. They need not come to birth even at a creation, nor do they suffer at a dissolution.

3. The great prakriti is for me the womb in which I deposit the germ; from it all beings come to birth, O Bharata.

4. Whatever forms take birth in the various species, the great Prakriti is their Mother and I the seed-giving Father.

5. Sattva, rajas and tamas are the gunas sprung from prakriti; it is they, O Mahabahu that keep the imperishable Dweller bound to the body.

6. Of these sattva, being stainless is light-giving and healing; it binds with the bond of happiness and the bond of knowledge, O sinless one.

7. Rajas, know thou, is of the nature of passion, the source of thirst and attachment; it keeps man bound with the bond of action.

8. Tamas know thou, born of ignorance, are mortal man's delusion; it keeps him bound with heedlessness, sloth and slumber, O Bharata.

9. Sattva attaches man to happiness, rajas to action, and tamas, shrouding knowledge, attaches him to heedlessness.

10. Sattva prevails, O Bharata, having overcome rajas and tamas; rajas, when it has overpowered sattva and tamas; likewise tamas reigns when sattva and rajas are crushed.

11. When the light of knowledge shines forth from all the gates of this body, then it may be known that the sattva thrives.

12. Greed, activity, assumption of undertakings, restlessness, craving—these are in evidence when rajas flourishes, O Bharatarshabha.

13. Ignorance, dullness, heedlessness, and delusion—these are in evidence when tamas reigns, O Kurunandana.

14. If the embodied one meets his end whilst sattva prevails, then he attains to the spotless worlds of the knowers of the Highest.

15. If he dies during the reign within him of rajas, he is born among men attached to action; and if he dies in tamas, he is born in a species not endowed with reason.

16. The fruit of sattvika action is said to be stainless merit. That of rajas is pain and that of tamas ignorance.

17. Wisdom arises from Sattva and greed, from Rajas, likewise comes error; stupor and ignorance arise from Tamas.

18. Those abiding in sattva rise upwards, those in rajas stay midway, those in tamas sink downwards.

19. When the seer perceives no agent other than the gunas, and knows Him who is above the gunas, he attains to My being.

As soon as a man realizes that he is not the doer, but the gunas are the agent, the "self" vanishes, and he goes through all his actions spontaneously, just to sustain the body. And as the body is meant to subserve the highest end, all his actions will even reveal detachment and dispassion. Such a seer can easily have a glimpse of the One who is above the gunas and offer his devotion to Him.

20. When the embodied one transcends these three gunas which are born of his contact with the body, he is released from the pain of birth, death and age and attains deathlessness.

Arjuna said:

21. What, O Lord, are the marks of him who has transcended the three gunas? How does he conduct himself? How does he transcend the three gunas?

The Lord said:

22. He, O Pandava, who does not disdain light, activity, and delusion when they come into being, nor desires them when they vanish:
23. He, who seated as one indifferent, is not shaken by the gunas, and stays still and moves not, knowing it is gunas playing their parts;
24. He who holds pleasure and pain alike, who is sedate, who regards as same earth, stone, and gold, who is wise and weighs in equal scale things pleasant and unpleasant, who is even-minded in praise and blame;
25. Who hold alike respect and disrespect, who is the same to friend and foe, who indulges in no undertakings—that man is called gunatita.

Shls. 22–25 must be read and considered together. Light activity and delusion, as we have seen in the foregoing shlokas, are the products of indications of sattva, rajas and tamas respectively. The inner meaning of these verses is that he who has transcended the gunas will be unaffected by them. A stone does not desire light, nor does it disdain activity or inertness; it is still, without having the will to be so. If someone puts it into motion, it does not fret; if again, it is allowed to lie still, it does not feel that inertness or delusion has seized it. The difference between a stone and a gunatita is that the latter has full consciousness and with full knowledge he shakes himself free from the bonds that bind an ordinary mortal. He has, as a result of his knowledge, achieved the purpose of a stone. Like the stone he is witness, but not the doer of the activities of the gunas or prakriti. Of such jnani one may say that he is sitting still, unshaken in the knowledge that it is the gunas playing their parts. We who are every moment of our lives acting as though we are the doers can only imagine the state, we can hardly experience it. But we can hitch our waggon to that star and work our way closer and closer towards it by gradually withdrawing the self from our actions. A gunatita has experience of his own condition but he cannot describe it, for he who can describe it ceases to be one. The moment he proceeds to do so, "self" peeps in. The peace and light and bustle and inertness of our common experience are illusory. The Gita itself has made it clear in so many words that the sattvika state is the one nearest that of a gunatita. Therefore everyone should strive to develop more and more sattva in himself, believing that someday he will reach the goal of the state of gunatita.

26. He who serves me in an unwavering and exclusive bhaktiyoga transcends gunas and is worthy to become one with Brahman.

27. For I am the very image of Brahman, changeless and deathless, as also of everlasting dharma and perfect bliss.

Thus ends the fourteenth discourse, entitled "Gunatrayavibhaga Yoga" in the converse of Lord Krishna and Arjuna, on the science of Yoga, as part of the knowledge of Brahman, in the Upanishad called Bhagavad-gita.

διscourse xv

This discourse deals with the supreme form of the Lord, transcending Kshara (perishable) and Akshara (imperishable).

The Lord said:

1. With the root above and the branches below, the asvattha tree, they say, is impossible; it has Vedic hymns for its leaves; he who knows it know the Vedas.

Shvah means tomorrow, and ashvattha (na shvopi sthata) means that which will not last even until tomorrow, i.e., the world of sense which is every moment in a state of flux. But even though it is perpetually changing, as its root is Brahman or the supreme, it is imperishable. It has for its protection and supports the leaves of the Vedic hymns, i.e., dharma. He who knows the world of sense as such and who knows dharma is the real jnani; that man has really known the Vedas.

2. Above all and below its branches spread, blossoming because of the gunas, having for their shoots the sense-objects; deep down in the world of men are ramified its roots, in the shape of the consequences of action.

This is the description of the tree of the world of sense as the unenlightened see it. They fail to discover its Root above the Brahman and so they are always attached to the object of sense. They water the tree with the three gunas and remain bound to Karman in the world of men.

3. Its form as such is not here perceived, neither its end, nor beginning, nor basis. Let man first hew down this deep-rooted Ashvattha with the sure weapon of detachment;
4. Let him pray to win to that heaven from which there is no return and seek to find refuge in the primal Being from whom has emanated this ancient world of action.

"Detachment" in shl. 3 here mean dispassion, aversion to the objects of the senses. Unless man is determined to cut himself off from the temptations of the world of sense he will go deeper into the mire every day. These verses show that one dare not play with the objects of the senses with impunity.

5. To that imperishable haven those enlightened souls go—who are without pride and delusion, who have triumphed over the taints of attachment, which are ever in tune with the Supreme, whose passions have died, who are exempt from the pairs of opposites, such as pleasure and pain.
6. Neither the sun, nor the moon, nor fire illumines it; men who arrive there return not—that is my supreme abode.
7. As part indeed of Myself which has been the eternal Jiva in this world of life, attracts the mind and the five senses from their place in praktiti.
8. When the master of the body acquires a body and discards it, he carries these with him wherever he goes, even as the wind carries scents from flower beds.
9. Having settled himself in the senses—ear, eye, touch, taste, and smell—as well as the mind, through them he frequents their objects.

These objects are the natural objects of the senses, the frequenting or enjoyment of these would be tainted if there were the sense of "I" about it; otherwise it is pure, even as a child's enjoyment of these objects is innocent.

10. The deluded perceive Him not as He leaves or settles in a body or enjoys sense objects in association with the gunas; it is those endowed with the eye of knowledge who alone see Him.
11. Yogins who strive see Him seated in themselves; the witless ones who have not cleansed themselves see Him not, even though they strive.

This does not conflict with the covenant that God has made even with the sinner in Discourse. Akritatman (who has not cleansed himself) means one who has no devotion in him, who has not made up his mind to purify himself. The most confirmed sinner, if he has humility enough to seek refuge in surrender to God, purifies himself and succeeds in finding Him. Those who do not care to observe the cardinal and the casual vows and expect to find God through bare intellectual exercises are witless, Godless; they will not find Him.

12. The light in the sun which illumines the whole universe and which is in the moon and in fire—that light, know thou, is Mine;
13. It is I, who penetrating the earth up hold all beings with My strength, and becoming the moon—the essence of all sap—nourish all the herbs;
14. It is I who becoming the Vaishvanara Fire and entering the bodies of all that breathe, assimilate the four kinds of food with the help of the outward and the inward breaths.
15. And I am seated in the hearts of all, from Me proceed memory, knowledge and the dispelling of doubts; it is I who am to be known in all the Vedas, I, the author of Vendata and the knower of the Vedas.
16. There are two Beings in the world; kshara (perishable) and akshara (imperishable). Kshara embraces all creatures and their permanent basis is akshara.

17. The Supreme Being is surely another—called Paramatman who is the Imperishable Ishvara pervades and supports the three worlds.
18. Because I transcend the kshara and am also higher than the akshara, I am known in the world and the Vedas as Purushottama (the Highest Being).
19. He who, undeluded knows me as Purushottama, knows all, he worships Me with all his heart, O Bharata.
20. Thus I have revealed to thee, sinless one, this most mysterious shastra; he who understands this, O Bharata, is a man of understanding, he has fulfilled his life's mission.

Thus ends the fifteenth discourse, entitled "Purushottama Yoga" in the converse of Lord Krishna and Arjuna, on the science of Yoga, as part of the knowledge of Brahman in the Upanishad called the Bhagavad-gita.

Discourse XVI

This discourse treats of the divine and the devilish heritage.

The Lord said:

1. Fearlessness, purity of heart, steadfastness in jnana and yoga-knowledge and action, beneficence, self-restraint, sacrifice, spiritual study, austerity, and uprightness;
2. Non-violence, truth, slowness to wrath, the spirit of dedication, serenity, aversion to slander, tenderness to all that lives, freedom from greed, gentleness, modesty, freedom from levity;
3. Spiritedness, forgiveness, fortitude, purity, freedom from ill-will and arrogance—these are to be found in one born with the divine heritage, O Bharata.
4. Pretentiousness, arrogance, self-conceit, wrath, coarseness, ignorance—these are to be found in one born with the devilish heritage.
5. The divine heritage makes for freedom, the devilish for bondage, Grieve not O Partha; thou art born with divine heritage.
6. There are two orders of created beings in this world—the divine and the devilish; the divine order has been described in detail, hear from Me now of the devilish, O Partha.
7. Men of the devil do not know what they may do and what they may not do; neither is there any purity, nor right conduct, nor truth to be found in them.
8. "Without truth, without basis, without God is the universe," they say; "born of the union of the sexes, prompted by naught but lust."
9. Holding this view, these depraved souls, of feeble understanding and of fierce deed, come forth as enemies of the world to destroy it.
10. Given to insatiable lust, possessed by pretentiousness, arrogance and conceit, they seize wicked purposes in their delusion, and go about pledged to uncleaned deeds.

11. Given to boundless cares that end only with their death, making indulgence or lust their sole goal, convinced that this is all;

12. Caught in myriad snares of hope, slaves to lust and wrath, they speak unlawfully to amass wealth for the satisfaction of their appetites.

13. "This have I gained today; this aspiration shall I now attain; this wealth is mine; this likewise shall be mine hereafter;

14. "This enemy I have already slain , others also I shall slay; Lord of all am I; enjoyment is mine, perfection is mine, strength is mine, happiness is mine;

15. "Wealthy am I, and high-born. What other is like unto me? I shall perform a sacrifice! I shall give alms! I shall be merry!" Thus think they, by ignorance deluded;

16. And tossed about by diverse fancies, caught in the net of delusion, stuck deep in the indulgence of appetites, into foul hell they fall.

17. Wise in their own conceit, stubborn, full of the intoxication of self and pride, they offer nominal sacrifices for show, contrary to the rule.

18. Given to pride, force, arrogance, lust and wrath they are deriders indeed, scorning Me in their own and others' bodies.

19. These cruel scorners, lowest of mankind and vile, I hurl down again and again, into devilish wombs.

20. Doomed to devilish wombs, these deluded ones, far from ever coming to Me, sink lower in birth after birth.

21. Three-fold is the gate of hell, leading man to perdition—Lust, Wrath, and Greed; these three, therefore, should be shunned.

22. The man who escapes these three gates of Darkness, O Kaunteya, works out his welfare and thence reaches the highest state.

23. He who forsakes the rule of Shastra and does but the bidding of his selfish desires, gains neither perfection, nor happiness, nor the highest state.

Shastra does not mean the rites and formulae laid down in the so-called dharmashastra, but the path of self-restraint laid down by the seers and the saints.

24. Therefore let shastra be thy authority for determining what ought to be done and what ought not to be done. Ascertain thou the rule of the shastra and do thy task here accordingly.

Shastra here too has the same meaning as in the preceding shloka, Let no one be a law unto himself, but take as his authority the law laid down by men who have known and loved religion.

Thus ends the sixteenth discourse, entitled "Daivasurasampadvibhaga Yoga" as part of the knowledge of Brahman in the Upanishad called the Bhagavad-gita.

ðíscouRse xvíí

On being asked to consider Shastra (conduct of the worthy) as the authority, Arjuna is faced with a difficulty. What is the position of those who may not be able to accept the authority of

Shastra but who may act in faith? An answer to the question is attempted in this discourse. Krishna rests content with pointing out the rocks and shoals on the path of the one who forsakes the beacon light of Shastra (conduct of the worthy). In doing so he deals with the faith and sacrifice, austerity and charity, performed with faith, and their divisions according to the spirit in which they are performed. He also sings the greatness of the mystic syllables AUM TAT SAT—a formula of dedication of all work to God.

Arjuna said:

1. What then, O Krishna, is the position of those who forsake the rule of Shastra and yet worship with faith? Do they act from sattva or rajas or tamas?

The Lord said:

2. Threefold is the faith of men, an expression of their nature in each case; it a sattvika, rajas or tamasa. Hear thou of it.
3. The faith of every man is in accord with his innate character; man is made up of faith; whatever his object of faith, even so is he.
4. Sattvika persons worship the gods; rajas ones, the Yakskas and Rakshasas; and others—men of tamas—worship manes and spirits.
5. Those men who, wedded to pretentiousness and arrogance, possessed by the violence of lust and passion, practice fierce austerity not ordained by shastra;
6. They, whilst they torture the several elements that make up their bodies, torture Me too dwelling in them; know them to be of unholy resolves.
7. Of three kinds again is the food that is dear to each; so also are sacrifice, austerity, and charity. Hear how they differ.
8. Victuals that add to one's years, vitality, strength, health, happiness and appetite; savoury, rich, substantial and inviting, they are dear to the sattvika.
9. Victuals that are bitter, sour, salty, over-hot, spicy, dry, burning, and causing pain, bitterness and disease, are dear to rajasa.
10. Food which has become cold, insipid, putrid, stale, discarded and unfit for sacrifice is dear to the tamasa.
11. That sacrifice is sattvika which is willingly offered as a duty without desire for fruit and according to the rajasa.
12. But when the sacrifice is offered with an eye to the fruit and for vain glory, know, O Bharatashreshtha, that is rajasa.
13. Sacrifice which is contrary to the rule, which produces no food, which lacks in the sacred text, which involves no giving up, which is devoid of faith is said to be tamasa.
14. Homage to the gods, to brahmanas, to gurus and to wise men; cleanliness, uprightness, brahmacharya and non-violence—these constitute austerity (tapas) of the body.

15. Words that cause no hurt, that are true, loving and helpful, and spiritual study constitute austerity of speech.
16. Serenity, benignity, silence, self-restraint, and purity of the spirit—these constitute austerity of the mind.
17. This threefold austerity practiced in perfect faith by men not desirous of fruit, and disciplined, is said to be sattvika.
18. Austerity which is practiced with an eye to gain praise, honour and homage and for ostentation is said to be rajasa; it is fleeting and unstable.
19. Austerity which is practiced from any foolish obsession. Either to torture oneself or to procure another's ruin is called tamasa.
20. Charity, given as a matter of duty, without expectation of any return, at the right place and time, and to the right person is said to be sattvika.
21. Charity, which is given either in hope of receiving in return, or with a view of winning merit, or grudgingly, is declared to be rajasa.
22. Charity given at the wrong place and time, and to be the underserving recipient disrespectfully and with contempt is declared to be tamasa.
23. AUM TAT SAT has been declared to be the threefold name of Brahman and by that name were created of old the Brahmanas, the Vedas and sacrifices.
24. Therefore with AUM ever on their lips, are all the rites of sacrifice, charity and austerity performed, always to the rules, by Brahmavadins.
25. With the utterance of TAT and without desire for fruit are the several rites of sacrifice, austerity and charity performed by those seeking Freedom.
26. SAT is employed in the sense of "real" and "good"; O Partha, SAT is also applied to beautiful deeds.
27. Constancy in sacrifice, austerity and charity, is called SAT; and all work done for those purposes is also SAT.

The substance of the last four shlokas is that every action should be done in a spirit of complete dedication to God. For AUM alone is the only Reality. That only which is dedicated to It counts.

28. Whatever is done, O Partha, by way of sacrifice, charity or austerity or any other work is called Asat if done without faith. It counts for naught hereafter as here.

Thus ends the seventeenth discourse, entitled "Sharaddhatrayavibhga Yoga" in the converse of Lord Krishna and Arjuna, on the science of Yoga, as part of the knowledge of Brahman in the Upanishad called the Bhagavad-gita.

Discourse xviii

This concluding discourse summed up the teaching of the Gita. It may be said to be summed up in the following; "Abandon all duties and come to Me, the only Refuge" (66). That is true renunciation. But abandonment of all duties does not mean abandonment of action; it means abandonment of the desire for fruit. Even the highest act of service must be dedicated to Him, without the desire. That is Tyaga (abandonment), that is Sannyasa (renunciation).

Arjuna said:

1. Mahabahu! I would fain learn severally the secret of sannyasa and of tyaga, O Hrishikesha, O Keshinishudana.

The Lord said:

2. Renunciation of actions springing from selfish desire is known as sannyasa by the seers; abandonment of the fruit of all action is called tyaga by the wise.
3. Some thoughtful persons say: "All action should be abandoned as an evil"; others say: "Action for sacrifice, charity and austerity should not be relinquished."
4. Hear my decision in this matter of tyaga,* O Bharatasattama; for tyaga too, O mightiest of men, has been described to be of three kinds.
5. Action for sacrifice, charity and austerity may not be abandoned; it must needs be performed. Sacrifice, Charity and austerity are purifiers of the wise.
6. But even these actions should be performed abandoning all attachment and fruit; such, O Partha, is my best and considered opinion.
7. It is not right to renounce one's allotted task; its abandonment, from delusion, is said to be tamasa.
8. He who abandons action, deeming it painful and for fear of straining his limbs, he will never gain the fruit of abandonment, for his abandonment is rajasa.
9. But when an allotted task is performed from a sense of duty and with abandonment of attachment and fruit, O Arjuna, that abandonment is deemed to be sattvika.
10. Neither does he disdain unpleasant action, nor does he cling to pleasant action—this wise man full of sattva, who practices abandonment, and who has shaken off all doubts.
11. For the embodied one cannot completely abandon action; but he who abandons the fruit of action is named a tyagi.
12. To those who do not practice abandonment accrues, when they pass away, the fruit of action which is three kinds: disagreeable, agreeable, and mixed; but never to the sannyasins.
13. Learn, from me, O Mahabahu, the five factors mentioned in the Sankhyan doctrine for the accomplishment of all action:
14. The field, the doer, the various means, the several different operations, the fifth and the last, the Unseen.
15. Whatever action, right or wrong, a man undertakes to do with the body, speech or mind; these are the five factors thereof.
16. This being so, he who, by reason of unenlightened intellect, sees the unconditioned Atman as the agent—such a man is dense and unseeing.

---

*Abandonment (not quite as severe as renunciation).

17. He who is free from all sense of "I," whose motive is untainted, slays not nor is bound, even though he slay all these worlds.

This shloka though seemingly somewhat baffling is not really so. The Gita *on many occasions present the ideal to attain which the aspirant has to strive but which may not be possible completely to realize in the world. It is like definitions in geometry. A perfect straight line does not exist, but it is necessary to imagine it in order to prove the various propositions. Even so, it is necessary to hold up ideals of this nature as standards for imitation in matters of conduct. This then would seem to be the meaning of this shloka: He who has made ashes of "self," whose motive is untainted, may slay the whole world, if he will. But in reality he who has annihilated "self" has annihilated his flesh too, and he whose motive is untainted sees the past, present and future. Such a being can be one and only one—God. He acts and yet is no doer, slays and yet is no slayer. For mortal man and royal road—the conduct of the worthy—is ever before him, viz. ahimsa—holding all life sacred.*

18. Knowledge, the object of knowledge, and the knower compose the three fold urge to action; the means, the action and the doer compose the threefold sum of action.
19. Knowledge, action, and the doer are three kinds according to their different gunas; hear thou these, just as they have been described in the science of the gunas.
20. Know that knowledge whereby one sees in all beings immutable entity—a unity in diversity—to be sattvika.
21. That knowledge which perceives separately in all beings several entities of diverse kinds, know thou to be rajasa.
22. And knowledge which, without reason, clings to one single thing, as though it were everything, which misses the true essence and is superficial is tamasa.
23. That action is called sattvika which, being one's allotted task, is performed without attachment, without like or dislike, and without a desire for fruit.
24. That action which is prompted by the desire for fruit, or by the thought of "I," and which involves much dissipation of energy is called rajasa.
25. That action which is blindly undertaken without any regard to capacity and consequences, involving loss and hurt, is called tamasa.
26. That doer is called sattvika who has shed all attachment, all thought of "I," who is filled with firmness and zeal, and who seeks neither success nor failure.
27. The doer is said to be rajasa who is passionate, desirous of the fruit of action, greedy, violent, unclean, and moved by joy and sorrow.
28. That doer is called tamasa who is undisciplined, vulgar, stubborn, knavish, spiteful, indolent, woebegone, and dilatory.
29. Hear now, O Dhananjaya, detailed fully and severally, the threefold division of understanding and will, according to their gunas.
30. That understanding, O Partha is attvika which knows action from inaction, what to be done from what ought not to be done, fear from fearlessness and bondage from release.

31. That understanding, O Partha, is rajasa, which decides erroneously between right and wrong, between what ought to be done and what ought not to be done.
32. That understanding, O Partha, is tamasa, which shrouded in darkness, thinks wrong to be right and mistakes everything for its reverse.
33. That will, O Partha, is sattvika which maintains an unbroken harmony between the activities of the mind, the vital energies and the senses.
34. That will, O Partha, is rajasa which clings, with attachment, to righteousness, desire and wealth, desirous of fruit in each case.
35. That will, O Partha, is tamasa, whereby insensate man does not abandon sleep, fear, grief, despair and self-conceit.
36. Hear now from Me, O Bharatarshabha, the three kinds of pleasure. Pleasure which is enjoyed only by repeated practice, and which puts an end to pain,
37. Which, in its inception, is as poison, but in the end as nectar, born of the serene realization of the true nature of Atman—that pleasure is said to be sattvika.
38. That pleasure is called rajasa which, arising from the contact of the senses with their objects is at first as nectar but in the end like poison.
39. The pleasure is called tamasa which arising from sleep and sloth and heedlessness, stupefies the soul both at first and in the end.
40. There is no being, either on earth or in heaven among the gods that can be free from these three gunas born of prakriti.
41. The duties of Brahmanas, Kshatriyas, Vaishyas, and Shudras, are distributed according to their innate qualifications. O Parantapa.
42. Serenity, self-restraint, austerity, purity, forgiveness, uprightness, knowledge and discriminative knowledge, faith in God are the Brahmana's natural duties.
43. Valour, spiritedness, constancy, resourcefulness, not fleeing from battle, generosity, and the capacity to rule are the natural duties of a Kshatriya.
44. Tilling the soil, protection of the cow and commerce are the natural functions of a Vaishya, while service is the natural duty of a Shudra.
45. Each man, by complete absorption in the performance of his duty, wins perfection. Hear now how he wins such perfection by devotion to that duty.
46. By offering the worship of his duty to Him who is moving the spirit of all being, and by whom all this is pervaded, man wins perfection.
47. Better one's own duty, though uninviting, than another's which may be more easily performed; doing duty which accords with one's nature, one incurs no sin.

The central teaching of the Gita *is detachment—abandonment of the fruit of action. And there would be no room for this abandonment if one were to prefer another's duty to one's own. Therefore one's own duty is said to be better than another's. It is the spirit in which duty is done that matters, and its unattached performance is its own reward.*

48. One should not abandon, O Kaunteya, that duty to which one is born, imperfect though it is; for all action, in its inception, is enveloped in imperfection, as fire in smoke.

49. He who has weaned himself of all kinds, who is master of himself, who is dead to desire, attains through renunciation the perfection of freedom from action.

50. Learn now from Me, in brief, O Kaunteya, how he, who has gained this perfection, attains to Brahaman, the supreme consummation of knowledge.

51. Equipped with purified understand, restraining the self with form will, abandoning sound and other objects of the senses, putting aside likes and dislikes,

52. Living in solitude, spare in diet, restrained in speech, body and mind, ever absorbed in dhyanayoga, anchored in dispassion,

53. Without pride, violence, arrogance, lust, wrath, possession, having shed all sense of "mine" and at peace with himself, he is fit to become one with Brahman.

54. One with Brahman and at peace with himself, he grieves not, nor desires; holdings all being alike, he achieves supreme devotion to Me.

55. By devotion, he realizes in truth how great I am, who I am; and having known Me in reality he enters into Me.

56. Even whilst always performing actions. He who makes Me his refuge wins, by My grace, the eternal and imperishable haven.

57. Casting, with thy mind, all action on Me, makes Me thy goal, and resorting to the yoga of even-mindedness fix thy thought ever on Me.

58. Fixing this thy thought on Me, thou shalt surmount all obstacles by My grace; but if possessed by the sense of "I," thou listen not, thou shalt perish.

59. If obsessed by the sense of "I," thou thinkest, "I will not fight," vain is thy obsession; thy nature will compel thee.

60. What thou wilt not do, O Kaunteya, because of thy delusion, thou shalt do, even against thy will, bound as thou art by the duty of which thou art born.

61. God, O Arjuna, dwells in the heart of every being and by His delusive mystery whirls them all, as though set on a machine.

62. In Him alone seek thy refuge with all they hear, O Bharata. By His grace shalt thou win to the eternal haven of supreme peace?

63. Thus have I expounded to thee the most mysterious of all knowledge; ponder over it fully, then act as thou wilt.

64. Hear again My supreme word, the most mysterious of all; dearly beloved thou art of Me, hence I desire to declare thy welfare.

65. On me fix thy mind, to Me bring thy devotion, to Me offer thy sacrifice, to me make thy obeisance; to Me indeed shalt thou come—solemn is My promise to thee, thou art dear to Me.

66. Abandon all duties and come to Me, the only refuge. I will release thee from all sons; grieve not!

67. Utter this never to him, who knows no austerity, has no devotion, nor any desire to listen, nor yet to him who scoffs at Me.

68. He who will propound this supreme mystery to My devotees, shall, by that act of highest devotion to Me, surely come to Me.

69. Nor among men is there any who renders dearer service to Me than he; or shall there be on earth anymore beloved by Me than he.

It is only he who has himself gained the knowledge and lived it in his life that can declare it to others. These two shlokas cannot possible have any reference to him, who no matter how he conducts himself can give flawless reading and interpretation of the Gita.

70. And the man of faith who, scorning not, will but listen to it—even he shall be released and will go to the happy worlds of men of virtuous deeds.
71. Hast thou heard this, O Partha, with a concentrated mind? Has thy delusion, born of ignorance, been destroyed, O Dhananjaya?

Arjuna said:

72. Thanks to Thy grace, O Achyuta, my delusion is destroyed, my understanding has returned. I stand secure, my doubts all dispelled; I will do thy bidding.

Sanjoya said:

73. Thus did I hear this marvellous and thrilling discourse between Vasudeva and the great-souled Partha.
74. It was by Vyasa's favor that I listened to this supreme and mysterious Yoga as expounded by the lips of the Master of Yoga, Krishna Himself.
75. O King, as often as I recall that marvellous and purifying discourse between Keshave and Arjuna, I am filled with recurring rapture.
76. And of often as I recall that marvellous form of Hari, my wonder knows no bounds and I rejoice again and again.
77. Wheresoever Krishna, the Master of Yoga, is, and wheresoever is Partha the Bowman, there rest assured are Fortune, Victory, Prosperity, and Eternal Right.

Thus ends the eighteenth discourse, entitled "Sannyasa Yoga" in the converse of Lord Krishna and Arjuna, on the science of Yoga, as part of the knowledge of Brahman in the Upanishad called the Bhagavad-gita.

book six

THE Z FACTOR

introduction

The Texts

David Bruce

S OME VERSION OF "AS FAR AS THE EAST IS FROM THE WEST" IS A POPULAR EXPRESSION IN ALMOST every culture, because no matter where you live on planet Earth, the sun comes up in the east and sets in the west. The midpoint between sunrise and sunset, however, is where the sun is the highest. In *Three Testaments*, and now more explicitly in *Four Testaments*, Brian Arthur Brown identifies a "high noon" midpoint between the larger religious traditions that dominate the East (eastern Eurasia, south Asia, Southeast Asia, and China), on the one hand, and the larger religious traditions that dominate the West (western Eurasia, Africa, and North and South America), on the other. The irony is that what should be as obvious as the sun at midday is in fact still obscure and partly hidden by the cloud cover of academic assumptions. The influence of Zoroastrianism on Judaism via the Babylonian captivity has been pondered for more than a century; yet it is still only a peripheral concern in the study of Christian origins. Brown successfully moves the question of Zoroastrian influence into the mainstream of New Testament scholarship and is among the first to engage Muslim scholars on this issue in a manner that is sensitive to Islamic faith and teaching.

In the *Analects* we read, "Tsze-lu asked, saying, 'What qualities must a man possess to entitle him to be called a scholar?' the Master said, 'He must be thus, earnest, urgent, and bland: among his friends, earnest and urgent; among his brethren, bland.'"[1] By this prescription, Brown is writing for friends rather than fellow scholars, because he is anything but bland. In his typically breathless pace, Brown generates legitimate excitement about what the explorations of Vedic-based Zoroastrianism can mean for mutual understanding among the major religious traditions. If he sometimes seems to overstate his case, it is not so much that he is offering a solution in search of a problem as that he is sketching an outline that will require a host of scholars with various forms of expertise to fill in over the next few decades—such is the fate of a pioneer. Before I summarize what Brown has accomplished leading into Book VI, let me first lay out what he has not—and is not claiming to have—accomplished so far.

Brown is not claiming to have found the original "fountainhead" of the seven major religious traditions. He is well aware that Vedantic and Hebrew traditions predate Zoroaster; his challenge here is to the entrenched view that Eastern and Western religious traditions developed in relative isolation from one another. It is, in fact, odd that this view has been so rarely challenged, given that it is the assertion of a negative—which, in history as in metaphysics, is nearly impossible to prove. In some circles the isolation hypothesis has been invoked to explain some of the stark contrasts between Eastern and Western religious traditions, especially as they regard the personality and historical involvement of God, the nature of the soul, and the goal of human striving. In other circles, ironically, the isolation hypothesis has been invoked to explain some of the striking similarities between Eastern and Western traditions, toward the goal of supporting a sociologically functionalist view of religion as addressing common concerns, separating it from the content of metaphysical claims. For all sorts of reasons, it is time to put this assumption to rest.

Brown is not claiming to have found the mechanism by which one or more religious traditions give birth to another. He is instead sensitive to the multiplicity of means by which cultures seed one another, including conquest, abduction, nonmilitary missionary efforts, incidental commercial travel, intellectual curiosity, and individual spiritual hunger. The means by which ancient Judaism came into direct contact with Zoroastrianism would have been profoundly different from the way in which Jesus might have experienced something of Buddhism, or Southeast Asia might have first encountered Islam. Brown also understands that historical causation is rarely as straightforward as A causing B. Religion is carried in the arms of art, music, dance, literature, and language, and it involves politics, economics, the presence or absence of heroes, and other accidents of history. If Brown's work is heuristic in tone, it is not determinist in nature.

Brown is not claiming to have found a pure, primordial religious tradition tragically displaced by localized corruptions. Knowing that no single writer or community can speak authoritatively for hundreds of millions of adherents of a religious tradition, Brown has previously made every effort to let the three major Western traditions, and now the four major Eastern traditions, speak for themselves. The choice to publish major religious texts—and not merely excerpt them—from each major Eastern tradition removes a degree of editorial control while upping the ante on academic integrity. There is here no attempt to conceal the differences in conceptualities or in religious practices by homogenizing or syncretizing them in some reductionist humanistic amalgam.

So what does Brown actually accomplish in this compendium?

First, Brown shows us how certain archetypes transcend cultural specificity. Light and darkness, the heavens and earth, purity and defilement, reality and illusion—all these are perennial themes finding expression in the major religious traditions of the world. Brown's chief concern, of course, is to highlight how these perennial themes are also foundational expressions in Zoroastrianism, indicating how Zoroastrianism remains the most likely vehicle of linguistic transmission of these thematic elements from east to west or west to east. As Brown develops his historical thesis, he points to Vedic and Semitic sources more ancient than Zoroastrianism or any of the current major religious traditions, but he is aware that unless these sources were conveyed in images that resonated in something we might fearfully call "the human condition," they would not have been adopted. He neither ignores the archetypal nor reduces religious claims to psychological phenomena. As an adherent of a particular religious tradition myself, I am aware of the temptation to emphasize the distinctive elements of my tradition as justification for participation in that tradition. Brown's thorough documentation of parallel language and imagery undercuts such partisanship and calls the honest seeker to humble appreciation of the insights of others.

Second, Brown highlights the universal tension between transcendence and immanence. As long as humans have pondered the meaning of their existence, its context has been critical. What is my place in my family? In my tribe or clan? In my homeland? In my ethnic or linguistic ancestry? In the human race? In the cosmos? When one reaches the most transcendent levels of existence, how do we speak intelligibly about that Reality? Is that which is greatest and highest in fact knowable, and if so, how? How do we compare the particular claim of "The Lord is God, the mighty God, the great king over all the gods"[2] with the metaphysical assertion that "higher than the Unmanifest is another Unmanifest Being, everlasting; which perished not when all creatures perish"?[3] It is not always obvious that we are talking about the same Reality, or seeing it the same way, or even comparing claims that are categorically equivalent.

Raising the question of the nature of this Reality in turn raises the question of our relationship to that Reality. All of the scriptures in this volume appear to me to render some expression of the thought expressed by the Apostle Paul when he said that "all have sinned, and fallen short of the glory of God."[4] In the *Tao Te Ching*, the *Analects*, the *Dhammapada*, and the *Bhagavad Gita*, humankind is characterized as being on a journey, as becoming as much as being, as seeking enlightenment or attunement, atonement or at-one-ment with Reality. The path toward this fulfillment (salvation) is regarded as essentially linked, fused, or even identified with the Reality we seek. Existentialist theologian Paul Tillich coined the term "Ultimate Concern" to indicate the unity of the quest with the goal itself.

Perhaps because *humility* is so universally regarded as a necessary element in the spiritual quest, all religious traditions in both the East and the West emphasize the need for the quester to be assisted in that quest. In the West, that assistance is typically spoken of as the intentional activity of God through human instruments; in the East, that assistance is more typically characterized as the activity of divine or human intermediaries (incarnations of Brahman in Hinduism, bodhisattvas in Buddhism; sages in Taoism, teachers in Confucianism). In both East and West, the complete dependence of the intermediary on God/Reality is key, in some respects modeling or paralleling the spiritual quest. In all cases, the Heavenly Reality *attracts* and *redeems* the quester.

The means by which the Heavenly Reality redeems us is one of the clearest ways to distinguish among religious traditions. In the Western traditions, the Heavenly Reality is typically regarded as being "self-identified" as "personal." God's redeeming action is personal, and human personhood is considered ultimately enduring. The means of redemption is personal: the heroic prophet-deliverer reconnects people (individually and collectively) to a personal God. In the Eastern traditions, the Heavenly Reality is typically regarded as being impersonal. Heaven's redeeming action calls the quester to transcend the needs of personhood. The means of redemption is transpersonal: the faithful teacher exemplifies transcendence of egoism for the greater good/Good.

While the modalities are distinct (though painted here with far too broad a brush), they are hardly opposed. In both East and West, there is ample discussion that God/Reality is best thought of as transcending personhood, and yet expressed in personal terms so as to be accessible to persons. For me, this is seen most clearly in the celebration of the Eucharist, a ceremonial sharing of bread and wine in which Christians believe Jesus to be *personally present*. The net effect of this is that in both East and West the Heavenly Reality is considered the redemptive force, whether "active" in the sense of intervening in human affairs or in the sense of exuding a spiritually magnetic pull.

Third, Brown highlights the relationship of history and religious truth. This treads on thorny ground. In an illustration that hits close to home for me, it has been grimly remarked that there was never any difficulties in war-torn, terrorist-troubled Northern Ireland that couldn't be cured by amnesia. Analogous to that is the intuition that if all religious traditions could be reduced to a set of perennial principles, the gulf between Eastern and Western religious traditions could be more or less bridged. That isn't about to happen. While all seven major religious traditions share an allegiance to sacred texts, recognize a multiplicity of spiritual species (spirits, angels, etc.), prescribe methods for spiritual advancement, and outline ethical responsibilities, the Western traditions regard history as the distinct medium of human fulfillment.

While Eastern traditions appreciate and recognize the influence and impact of historical persons—Lao Tzu, Gautama, Confucius—their larger interpretive framework views these persons as especially enlightened expositors of that which was perennially true. Western traditions, in contrast, see historical persons as effecting permanent change in the spiritual "economy." Abraham was the historical progenitor of a people who would bear a unique covenantal relationship with God; Moses would deliver a new and permanent law to govern that people; David would begin a royal dynasty to which God would commit unique and irrevocable blessing; Jesus would die to bear the sins of the entire human race and rise from the dead in anticipation of the end of time; Muhammad would be the first to recite the Holy Quran, revealing God's final word to humanity. In lesser and more debatable fashion, rabbis would consolidate the canon of Hebrew Scriptures, councils would codify the Christian faith, and caliphs would claim divine authority to govern.

The three Western traditions we are to examine in relation to their Vedic Eastern connections might dispute the veracity of one another's historical claims, but the notion that historical claims could bear religious significance has been widely acknowledged for millennia among them. Beginning with the development of modern scientific methods, however, such claims began to be regarded as problematic. In Europe, historical method itself began to be exercised as a discipline independent of theological considerations, and historians questioned whether it was possible for historical claims to uphold religious dogma. Soon, all historical claims that involved supernatural intervention were deemed inherently problematic, and academic historians would systematically exclude accounts of the miraculous. In the twentieth century, Christian theology in particular would begin in many circles to redefine Christian faith in terms earlier proposed by *les philosophes* and other philosophers of the Enlightenment, viewing the Christian religion—and all other religions along with it—as universal truths mythologized for popular consumption. Many Jews and Muslims have cautiously joined this movement to, in effect, "Easternize" Western religious traditions.

The difficulty with this approach is that the very *identities* of Western religious traditions are rooted in historical claims. Judaism loses its power if there is no historical reality to the emergence of the Jewish people and the codification of the Torah. Christianity loses its specificity if there is no historical reality to the life, death, and resurrection of Jesus of Nazareth and the creation of the Church. Islam loses all its missionary impetus if there is no historical reality to the claim that God revealed the Quran to Muhammad. I may be very much misinformed, but I don't believe that the value of the *Bhagavad Gita* is seen as depending on the historicity of the conversation between Arjuna and Krishna in the same way that the authority of Jesus's teaching is dependent on his identity as the Son of God being confirmed by his resurrection from the dead. Western religions each require their historical claims to act as touchstones for their present-day communities; in Europe and North America, those Christian communities that have disconnected themselves from traditional historical claims have experienced rapid decline, probably because they quickly become indistinguishable from their surrounding culture.

Finally, Brown turns strangers into family. When my wife and I were courting, we would share thoughts and perspectives and stories with each other in order to get to know one another. While there were many similarities in our past (we grew up, after all, in the same country, speaking the same language), it was important for us to listen carefully not only to *what* the other was saying but also for those subtle tones that conveyed *how* the other was impacted by what they were relating. By inviting us to read one another's scriptures and exploring historical linkages between them, Brown invites the reader to recognize that the major religious traditions of the world share significant commonalities. I confess that it had been thirty years since I read the *Gita* or the *Analects* in their entirety, and while I am at fifty-one years of age a more profoundly committed Christian than I was at twenty-one, I am nevertheless—or is it *because* of my increased commitment?—more appreciative of the family resemblance of the scriptural traditions of Judaism, Christianity, Islam, Taoism, Confucianism, Buddhism, and Hinduism.

I cannot glibly reconcile all the distinctive claims of the world's great religious traditions: Am I to live again in the flesh *and* seek to escape from the flesh in Nirvana? Do I acknowledge Jesus as the only begotten Son of God *and* allow for Krishna as an incarnation of the divine? Can I agree that propriety is the highest ideal *and* attempt to live the life of the sage? Yet I can easily name important resonances between the *Dhammapada* of the Buddha and the Sermon on the Mount of the Christ, as Professor Sharma does with themes in the *Analects* and the *Bhagavad Gita*. Faced with the tremendous wisdom embodied in these Eastern texts, I can choose to be respectful rather than dismissive of what I do not (yet?) understand.

It is true that there can never be a complete translation of one language into another, even when those languages are contemporary. How much more must this be so in the case of scriptures written centuries—and, in some sense, worlds—apart? History and culture are important, and religious experience incorporates the richness of life rather than abstracting from it. Just as I can never completely share the identity of another person, I can never quite understand what it means to be a Christian and an adherent of another religion. And yet I am married, I do have friends, and I can open my heart to a stranger—especially when it is pointed out that the stranger and I are actually distant cousins. In the world of religion, there is ultimately no "us" and "them" but a larger "us" than we ever imagined. We are indeed entering a New Axial Age.

Book VI offers specific and convincing proposals that show links between the Eastern Vedic traditions via Zoroaster and the Western monotheistic religions that may be more historically grounded than mere coincident similarities addressing common human experiences. While this work will have Eastern religionists talking more among themselves and also open up conversations between them and the West, the larger impact may be actually within the Western religions.

While they may find some commonality with Zoroastrians and other Eastern religions with "avatars" or incarnations of messiah figures, Jews insist that redemption is not a function of the messiah but of God alone. Christians may agree that the Saoshyant messiah is indeed the redeemer or "savior" of the whole world rather than just any one people, but they believe that it was Jesus who paid the "ransom" in this regard. Muslims expect the return of Isa al-Masih, Jesus the Christ, but many of them see a greater role for the Mahdi who will precede him as the Elijah or John the Baptist figure. All three will be resonating with the Saoshyant motif being related to their own perspectives as elaborated in Book VI.

Indeed, there is little, if anything, that will not please orthodox Jews, Christians, and Muslims in their particular chapters of Book VI, allowing for their idiosyncratic theological positions as it does. How can it be possible that this traditional material also reads so well for more liberal and progressive practitioners of Judaism, Christianity, and Islam? This accomplishment is a seminal achievement that will have the adherents of the three Western monotheistic religions talking within their traditions, with each other, and now with their Zoroastrian and other co-religionists of the East.

Finally, it goes almost without saying that one enduring legacy of this work is the establishment of the "Z" factor in identifying putative Zoroastrian passages or influences in the scholarly analysis of the Hebrew, Christian, and Muslim scriptures. This development establishes once and for all that each of the three have Vedic/Eastern connections, which, while not necessarily foundational, are of enduring significance.

preface

New Frontiers in Scriptural Studies

WHILE EACH OF THE SCRIPTURES IN THIS COMPENDIUM ARE EDIFYING AND OF INTEREST on their own merits, the question remains about what profundities may exist in the relationship between the religions of the East and the West as possibly evidenced in their sacred texts. We can now show some of those links in direct connections, but with three of the four Eastern religions and all three Western religions, the connection provided by the extant scriptures of Zoroastrianism is especially pertinent. This loose correlation will be enhanced should a happy accident or archaeological discovery actually succeed in acquiring the new Holy Grail of missing sections of the Zoroastrian Avesta sometime in the near future. In this regard the relationship between monotheism and monism as it existed in the sixth century BCE may be of special interest in the twenty-first century given the increasing interconnectedness of societies and ideas.

The "evidence" for a close and direct relationship between Zoroastrian and Jewish priests and scholars in Babylon can be divided into three categories: circumstantial, collateral, and absolute proof. The absolute proof of Vedic and Zoroastrian influence in Hebrew Scriptures seems to consist in small but concrete things like the sudden emergence of *Redeemer* as an actual name for God and the hitherto strangely unnoticed appearance of the name *Krishna* in the book of Esther. Additionally, the circumstantial and collateral evidences are so abundant that a pattern emerges that is almost impossible to ignore. With Christianity this pattern gets unexpectedly stronger, and it is perhaps even more so in Islam, where previous revelations are confirmed, corrected, or amplified. In both these latter cases, this is an interesting new development with even less basis in scholarship of the nineteenth and twentieth centuries than in the case of Judaism, where at least substantial hints existed prior to this study.

In *Three Testaments: Torah, Gospel, and Quran* we considered the merits of Christian Bibles that highlight the words of Jesus in red ink and Jewish Bibles that highlight the creation story and scriptures of environmental interest in green. This was in contemplation of a Bible with Zoroastrian-related verses highlighted in bold type, and we might have extended this model to the Quran, marking bold the Z passages freshly revealed to Muhammad, according to Muslim understanding. We demurred from doing this in the scriptural portions of that compendium because this science was still embryonic in both the Hebrew Scriptures and the New Testament, and the Islamic contribution needed more work than our team was prepared to undertake, despite the involvement of a Quranic translator and an Arabic linguist.

Despite the advances being made in this investigation, as will be illustrated now in Book VI, neither Jewish nor Christian scholarship has advanced sufficiently to print such a Bible in confidence that all evidence has been accounted for, and the investigation within the Muslim community has not been advanced to any appreciable extent in the few years between these compendia. Were such a purely scriptural publication of the three Western texts to be printed, we might refer to the Zoroastrian passages in bold as "the Z factor," a nomenclature we at least hope to see adopted now in all such studies in much the same way that J, E, P, D, and other initials are regarded in studies of the Hebrew Torah. In New Testament studies we use Q for traces of a document hidden between the lines of the three synoptic (look-alike) gospels and S for the "signs gospel" behind John's Gospel. The designation M is becoming established in Quranic studies to identify the Meccan surahs, as over and against the longer Medina surahs, known as Md. While no scriptural compendium with such verses in bold is possible at this juncture, it is entirely appropriate to adopt the Z nomenclature for academic study purposes in all three Western scriptures.

There is a thin line between identification of Z passages attributable to Zoroastrian material and simple similarities between all or most religions, but we should now be able to make the correct distinction. For example, while the Quran condemns lying as a general principle, there are no particular verses that appear to represent the previous revelation to Zoroaster about the destructive power of the Lie, strident enough to be translated with a capital L. However, the Jewish sect that compiled the Dead Sea Scrolls deprecate their enemies with titles like "The Man of the Lie" and "The Spouter of Lies," which, while not scriptural, could give such passages Z standing in academic circles. Indeed, Jesus denounced Satan as a "Liar" and "The Father of Lies,"[1] the kind of Z factor references that would certainly qualify for bold print. With further evidence to follow, as a starting place for scriptures to be identified as Z, the following three chapters conclude with three lists of putative Z verses in the Hebrew, Christian, and Islamic Scriptures. They should be regarded as tentative but recognizable as being Z, with circumstantial evidence, collateral substantiation, and solid proof in various measures.

11

israel in exile

God as Israel's Only Redeemer

Almost six million Jews live in America, perhaps about fourteen million in the world—not so many that their religion deserves as much attention as it gets. But if you read the papers, you know that "Jews is news"—and, among religions, so is Judaism. With just over 0.1 percent of the world's population, Jews have won 22 percent of all Nobel Prizes, rising to 50 percent in some recent years. Another six million Jews live in Israel and two million more are spread around the world, principally in France, Great Britain, Canada, Argentina, South Africa, Russia, and Brazil, with tiny groups scattered almost everywhere. All of them think being Jewish defines a critical part of their being; many of them believe that Judaism tells them the meaning of life. Moreover because the Hebrew Bible, the Torah—which, according to the great sages, defines Judaism—is affirmed by Christianity and Islam as God's revelation, Judaism is news to most of the world.[1]

EXAMINATION OF WHAT MAY HAVE HAPPENED BETWEEN ZOROASTRIANS AND JEWS IN BABYLON has been going on for some time, though most expert scholars of Zoroastrianism and many Zoroastrian scholars (the two separate streams of inquiry) have by and large moved on to other considerations in Iranian and related studies in recent years. Notable exceptions are the work of Yaakov Elman and Geoffrey Herman, though their inquiries are limited to the relationships between Jews and Zoroastrians in the Seleucid, Parthian, and Sassanian periods. In a fresh approach, we entertain something new in this investigation by working backward from Judaism in Babylon to a Zoroastrianism that then appears to have erupted like a volcano immediately previous.

Until now, most biblical inquiries in this area of study have moved from what we know, think, or guess about Zoroaster, forward to what influence or impact some kind of Zoroastrianism may have had on Judaism and other ancient cultures. In earlier years when scholars tried (almost in vain) to locate and define Zoroaster, they could see little specific direct connection between him and Judaism or anything else. As information has continued to emerge, we can now start with Judaism in Babylon, and document how Judaism developed dramatically and rapidly in tension with something that appears to be new on the Mesopotamian scene at about the time of the Babylonian Exile. That "something" looks like Zoroastrianism, sounds like Zoroastrianism, and acts like Zoroastrianism, so it must be Zoroastrianism, or something we must invent that is too much like Zoroastrianism to call it anything else.

The easiest example is the ongoing debate as to whether Zoroaster believed in "One God" or was a "Two God" dualist or even a "Best God" henotheist. Setting aside the monistic alternative that was still embryonic in the West, it is impossible to resolve that question within Zoroastrian evidence available to us at this time. But since the Jews observing Zoroastrians on location in Babylon and writing up reports within a generation (as verified by Dead Sea Scrolls) declared Zoroastrians to be monotheists like themselves, or close to the henotheism *cum* monotheism they often practiced, we can say there is powerful Jewish evidence that early Zoroastrians practiced a religion akin to monotheism. We know that Zoroastrianism developed a monistic cult later on, and eventually became largely dualistic, though typical Zoroastrians "on the street" today maintain the monotheism was there in the earliest texts, remained a subtext throughout history, and is practiced still.

Moreover, Jews like Deutero-Isaiah (as we sometimes refer to Second Isaiah) could not possibly have considered Cyrus as a Messiah candidate if they thought of him as worshipping a "pantheon" of gods, as is sometimes suggested. So, regarding Zoroastrian monotheism, QED! The argument that the Jews thought they were worshipping the same God as the Zoroastrians has other support, too intricate for this brief space, but the same approach can now be applied to other complex questions about the Zoroastrianism encountered by the Jews and adopted by them, such as the Last Judgment, angelology, demonology, salvation, and paradise.

Judaism arrived in Babylon with the bare bones of its scriptural Torah and returned to Jerusalem fifty years later with the Torah nearing completion as we have it, its monotheism reinforced, and its messianism more clearly delineated, plus an increasing scriptural corpus in which we find salvation by a God in the role of a Redeemer, angelology, demonology, fire-sacrifice liturgies, perpetual fire on its altar, resurrection, a Last Judgment, paradise, and the book of Job. These all appear for the first time in Israel at this precise and brief juncture, and are later epitomized by reports of God's revelation to Daniel as he comes out of the Ulai River in a scene highly reminiscent of Zoroaster's experience described in the Avesta.[2] These and other related elements of the Hebrew Scriptures have never been addressed systematically, though they have been recognized in an indistinct fashion, whereas the stunning Zoroastrian presence in the New Testament and the Quran is only now beginning to be appreciated at all.

Twentieth-century studies of the Torah among Jews, Christians, and some Muslims were dominated by the "Documentary Hypothesis" of the Pentateuch, the Jewish Torah. This divinely inspired communal document includes contributors traditionally identified by many but not all scholars, clergy, and congregation members in four clusters of sources—J, E, D, and P—with various subsets, such as H (holiness), R (a "redactor," probably Ezra) and others more recently identified. The latest of those to be identified is Z, referring to traces of Zoroastrianism. J refers to sections in which God is referred to as Jehovah,[3] E where the divinity is called Eloh[4] in Hebrew (Allah in Arabic), and D recalls the speeches of Moses. The priestly tradition, known as P, key to some of the arguments in this book, originated in Jerusalem among elite temple priestly scholars descended from Aaron.

After regaining status among the exiles in Babylon, the priests continued work and flourished under Persian monarchs who were well-disposed toward them, possibly in creative tension with Zoroastrian priests who shared their monotheism at that time. In the return to Jerusalem, according to this thesis, they finished their work under Ezra, who published J, E, and D integrated with P in the name of Moses. P may then have included the Z subset of Eastern lore and sacred Vedic material, only now identified as such. This Z factor connects the Hebrew Scriptures indirectly but significantly with Hinduism and Buddhism. For those unfamiliar with this "critical" or analytical appreciation of the scriptures, a downloadable chart of the sources of the Pentateuch is available free of charge on my website.[5]

The Z elements would include the Vedic origins of imagery in the first chapter of Genesis, and the rituals of purification introduced in the return to Israel by Nehemiah, the Jewish "cup bearer" for the Zoroastrian monarch who had successfully lobbied King Artazerxes for permission to supervise the reconstruction of the city of Jerusalem. These Z examples are added to the more obvious list above but need more explanation than some, so let us compile the list of such topics with brief notes of elucidation as required, knowing that this is grist for PhD theses to come, where each of the following may deserve a chapter.

While other non-Hebraic influences can also be detected, the following eighteen concepts were but dimly foreshadowed in Hebrew Scriptures prior to the interaction between Jews and Zoroastrians during the Exile. When we examine the same list in reference to the New Testament, it is obvious that we are sorting and sifting, filtering, and combing through the same material to determine the outlines of the point we are making. This will be followed by a respectful approach to the Islamic Quran, believed to be a fresh revelation, confirming, correcting, and amplifying these and other "previous revelations."

angelology

This concept was foreshadowed in Hebrew Scriptures by indiscernible spirits in various guises, though these are hardly distinguishable from God, as when Hagar is comforted by a presence in the desert, when Jacob wrestles with an "angel" who turns out to be the Lord, and, most notably, when Moses deals with the Angel of the Lord at the burning bush, only to realize it was indeed the Lord God. Even these early J (Jehovah) accounts may have originally been simple references to appearances of God, modified by Ezra in these and other final texts following the return to Jerusalem.

By then Jewish theology was insisting on the complete transcendence of God and the concept of angels was readily at hand from the encounter with Zoroastrianism. Clearly defined descriptions of angels begin with Ezekiel during the Exile.[6] Spirits or "angels," by redaction or in translation, then evolved rapidly from mere messengers or divine agents charged with functions of the moment to spirits controlling natural phenomena. There were such angels in later Jewish apocryphal books as well, of whom four of seven "archangels" were named in the Bible itself as Gabriel, Michael, Raphiel, and Uriel, all very much in the precise Zoroastrian model. The Zoroastrian mold is unchanged in the Quran and in the New Testament, where all seven appear in the book of Revelation, as will be seen. In the Hebrew Scriptures and apocryphal books, after the Exile and return, these powerful figures, all new to Israel, controlled the affairs of nations (Daniel 10:10–21), the stars, the planets, and the winds (Enoch 19:1; 40:4–5; 60:12), healing (Tobias 3:17), death (2 Baruch 21:23), and the four seasons (Enoch 82: 13), all a far cry from the indistinct spirits previous to the engagement with Zoroastrianism in Babylon. The Jewish and Christian idea of a personal "guardian angel" would have been also inspired by the Zoroastrian figure of the fravashi, the divine guardian-spirit of each individual human being.

creation

Likewise, the creation stories in the Bible put the Jehovah spiritual inspiration into the local Mesopotamian "Garden of Eden" lore found in chapter two, and precedes it in Genesis 1:1–2:3 with the older Vedic seven-day creation story refined by P, the priestly work in Babylon. This incredibly inspired priestly team drew from both local sources and revelations directly offered to the Hebrew community by the Divine during a churning cascade of inspiration in the Babylonian setting, perhaps the most fulsome spiritual encounter between two groups in the history of the world. The evidence that the Vedic sources of Zoroastrianism were the first to contemplate the reality or the symbolism of the seven-day creation is so well established that a review here would be superfluous, except to acknowledge that there were seven planets visible to the primitive Aryan eye. That old Vedic illustration became the foundational context for angelology, creation, demonology, and other realities adopted by other Mesopotamian entities even before the Hebrews adopted and refined them. The Vedic creation story, honed in the Babylonian version and adopted in creative tension with Zoroastrian interlocutors, merely needed the Jewish sensitivity to the divine inspiration available to them to become the spiritual masterpiece in Genesis with which the whole world is familiar.

demonology

This concept was also foreshadowed in Hebrew Scriptures by indiscernible "spirits" in early Hebrew stories and documents in the Torah, but tracking the switch to a more clear-cut demonology is more complex than the above presentation about angelology. This is because in Israel and in all of its neighbors, the world appeared "swarming" with devils since bad news garnered most of the press, then as now. However, the pattern seen in angelology can be traced in demonology, if not tracked with the same precision. Post-Babylon, the demons and devils in Israel were discernibly better defined, as in Leviticus 17:7 and 2 Chronicles 11:15, where the murky allusions to demons in the past are supplanted by sacrificial goat demons, one of the clearest emulations of Zoroastrian ritual practice, written up in Hebrew Scriptures from both Babylonian and post-Babylonian eras, according to the experts who are confident in this critical science.

The shift from vague forces of evil to a more Zoroastrian type of demons with defined spheres of influence may have evolved further without much recognition to date in the intertestamental period, but is not fully developed until clearly Zoroastrian portions of the New Testament, to be examined in the next chapter. The case of Satan is the exception, where the model seen in angelology is present again as a completely functioning demon, so much so that we give it treatment on its own below, showing this and other clear traits before and after Babylon.

final judgment

The stark enduring power of Zoroastrian doctrine, and images of it, is nowhere more dramatically illustrated than in the Muslim employment of the *Chinvat Bridge* imagery of final judgment, which will be dealt with in chapter 14. It is mentioned here to make the point that neither Christians nor Muslims necessarily got their Zoroastrian material from Jewish sources, and that the Jews did not just happen to make this stuff up while they were under Zoroastrian influence and domination. The Jews certainly had little or no notion of a final judgment prior to the Exile, and yet they had a fully developed "eschatology" upon their return to Jerusalem just fifty years or so later. It was no doubt "revealed" to them by God, but there can be little doubt about the identity of the mouthpieces employed by the Divinity. Both exilic and post-exilic prophets (Ezekiel 13:5, Joel 2:31) put an eschatological twist of future finality on the phrase "The Day of the Lord," used earlier (Amos 5:18, Isaiah 2:12) when it had referred merely to God's judgment of Israel's enemies and of Israel's vindication on this earth.

This borrowing of a Zoroastrian meaning may be a good illustration of how the transition from early Vedic beliefs migrated through Zoroastrianism to Jews and Christians, to be "confirmed" (or "corrected") by Muslims. It may illustrate how such images and their meanings also migrated east, either directly from Vedic sources or as reinforced by Zoroastrian Magi and other influences. In the East it is not "the Lord" who will judge, as in Western iterations of this teaching, but *Yama* (Sanskrit: यम), a *dharma-pala*, a wrathful divinity, who judges the dead and presides over *naraka*. This underworld place of torment of the wicked is usually translated as hell in English by Sarvepalli Radhakrishnan, Mohandas Gandhi, and others. Yama, appearing in this role in Hinduism, Jainism, and Theravada Buddhism, was certainly present in Babylon once the Zoroastrians arrived. His re-presentation in the change of Jewish perceptions and expressions parallels the change in the understanding of hell itself, to be documented below, in both East and West.

Zoroastrian influence on Judaism is also evident in the evolution of Jewish ideas about good, evil, and the End of Time. Zoroastrianism, from the beginning, has taught that time and God's creation have a beginning, a middle, and an end-time in which all souls will be judged. The Zarathushtrian teachings were later elaborated and illustrated with Jewish mythological motifs, many of them borrowed from the pre-Zoroastrian, Indo-Iranian gods and goddesses, as well as myths of cosmic conflict from ancient Mesopotamia. Later Zoroastrianism also teaches a specific sacred timeline, a historical structure for the created world. The Zoroastrians are often credited with introducing eschatology, or an understanding of the End of Time and its events, into all the religions of the world, both West and East.

fire sacrifice

Mention has been made of the remarkable inclusion of fire-sacrifice rituals in the post-exilic edition of the Torah's book of Leviticus. Campfires and hints of desert rituals in the rest of the Torah hardly hold a candle to this radical departure from the simplicity in worship practices of the Hebrews in the desert as described in various early documents in the Torah and beyond, as carried forward from Babylon into the Second Temple. During the compilation of sacred resources in Babylon, and under the influence of Zoroastrian priestly confreres, the scribes working on the teaching scrolls of the Torah must have suddenly "remembered" a sense of holiness associated with fire in those desert moments of sacred memory. Though obviously ceremonial and part of tradition, but uncertain about the precise elements in such liturgies, these scribes may have turned to their Zoroastrian colleagues for descriptive material or, thus prompted, may have been inspired to recall stories of sacred moments in Israel's desert experience. Copied, remembered, or a combination of both, the first ten chapters of the book of Leviticus were regarded as sufficiently important to present them as part of a unique scroll format, half the length of other scrolls in the Torah. While fire sacrifice does not appear in even a single reference in pre-Babylonian sections of the Torah, the priestly Levitical document lays out detailed instructions for those assistants charged with organizing worship, including fire sacrifices, which were designed to be taken forward to the Second Temple upon the return that was then on the horizon. Indeed, Leviticus 1:1–10:20 devotes ten entire chapters of the Bible to matters and specific details regarding fire sacrifice, the first, sudden and only treatment of this subject in the Torah in a section written in parts of the priestly document composed in Babylon under Zoroastrian influence.

funerary practices

Ezekiel, another of the exiles, while yet in Babylon, had a vision of a valley full of dry bones. They were possibly the bones of exiles who had perished there. He heard a noise in his head and saw vision of a shaking of the bones; they came together, bone to bone, and flesh came upon them, and skin covered them, and breath came into them, and they lived and stood upon their feet. And the Lord said to Ezekiel, "Prophesy and say: 'the Lord will open your graves and bring you into the land of Israel, and will put his spirit into you, and will place you in your own land.'"[7] It is difficult to credit this passage as indicating that during the years in Babylon, Jewish practice emulated the Zoroastrian custom of exposing corpses of the dead to become dry bones as nature takes its course, but even without specifics, we can surely assert with confidence that there is a certain Zoroastrian connection to Ezekiel's "valley of dry bones." Nobody else we know of had this practice.

hell

The general concept of hell in the earliest Hebrew Scriptures is that of *sheol*, simply the place of the dead, good, bad, and indifferent. In Ezekiel, during the Exile, there is a shift toward its presentation as a prison or a place of consignment for those who are outside the community of God's people, like the Egyptian Pharaoh (Ezekiel 31:1–32), the Assyrians and Elamites (Ezekiel 32:22–24), Meshech, and Tubal, the chiefs and princes (Ezekiel 32:26). This may accord with Zoroastrian practice, but there is little evidence for that other than the timing of a shift in Jewish thought (working backward, remember?). The *coup de grace* in this regard is in the less often recognized but equally prevalent post-Babylon use of the Hebrew word *gehenna* to introduce the fiery hell that carried over into Christian Scriptures and was confirmed by the revelation to Muhammad in the Quran.

The word *gehenna* is derived from the image of *Hinnom*, remembered as a ravine south of Jerusalem, which during the days of the monarchy was the scene of an idolatrous cult involving the passage of children through fire (2 Kings 23:10; 2 Chronicles 28:3; and Jeremiah 7:31 and 32:35). In the post-exilic era, the image of *gehenna* was used in a metaphoric sense to denote a place of fiery torment reserved for the wicked either immediately after death or after the final judgment. References to *sheol* had been occasionally tinged with punishments among other images, but the distinct concept of a blazing hell (a lake or abyss of fire) only emerges post-Babylon (Daniel 7:10; Enoch 18:11–16, 27:1–3, and 90:26; Judith 16:17; and the apocryphal Assumption of Moses 10:10). The site was Judean, but there can be no doubt that the imagery was straight from the Avestan doctrine of the ultimate judgment of the wicked in a stream of molten metal in underworld of *nakara*, described in Yasna 31:3 and 51:9, learned in Babylon during the Zoroastrian era and connected with a sordid image from Israel's own past.

This image, found in post-exilic documents, apocryphal and intertestamental writings, and both the New Testament and the Quran (as will be seen), is still preached by fundamentalist Christians, ultra-orthodox Jews, and Wahhabi Muslims to this day, but there can be no doubt where the Jews got it before they passed it on. Even Jeremiah, the first to employ this Zoroastrian imagery, used it in dire prophecy (Jeremiah 19:2–10), and one can hear its judgmental echoes from Texas to Sierra Leone today. If ever there were an image bequeathed to the modern world from specifically Zoroastrian sources, and also connected with Eastern religions and their texts, it would be this image of hell and the associated final judgment on the Day of the Lord, picked up by the Jews in Babylon, adapted to their own experience, and used and abused by them and others ever since.

í am

The name I AM, as the appellation of God, is without question from the Hebrew source, where Moses is confronted by God at the burning bush and self-identified in that manner. The Zoroastrian prayer book referred to as the Little Avesta, described earlier, takes up the Mosiac theme of God's self-revelation as the I AM and elaborates upon it in a passage believed to be as old as the Gathas of Zoroaster himself, who describes God in the following phrases:

> I AM the Keeper,
> I AM the Creator,
> I AM the Maintainer,
> I AM the Discerner,
> I AM the Beneficent.

This is as fulsome as it gets in reference to the belief that Zoroaster not only lived sometime after Moses but also got his introduction to belief in One God from the Israelites living in exile in his homeland, prior to the revelation he experienced for himself at the river. In this case we are referencing the connection as from the Hebrew source to the Zoroastrian, instead of the other way around. Hinduism in the *Bhagavad Gita* would have received this appellation of the Divine from its reformed Vedic sources, who got it from the Israelites. Not even Jesus who uses the I AM motif in the New Testament (see below) can match the persistent recurrence of the I AM motif as spoken by Krishna in the *Gita*: I AM Action, I AM the Doer, I AM Born from Age to Age, I AM the Origin and the End of the Universe, I AM the Savior, I AM the Light, I AM the Sweet Fragrance of the Earth, I AM the Reason of Rational beings, I AM the Splendor of whatever is Splendid, I AM Strength, I AM Desire, I AM Exceedingly Dear, I AM the Sacrificial Vow, I AM the Sacrifice, I AM the Father and the Mother of the Universe, I AM the Sacred Sound of AUM, I AM Deathlessness and also Death, I AM the Source of All, I AM Vishnu, I AM Indra, I AM the Wind, I AM Everlasting Time, I AM Victory, I AM Silence, I AM Rapture, I AM the Goal, the Sustainer, the Lord, the Witness, the Abode, the Refuge, the Friend, the Origin, the End, the Preservation, the Treasure house, the Imperishable Seed[8] (for the first forty instances), I AM in forty additional examples, and, finally, I AM Who I AM[9]—the essential doctrine at the heart of Judaism as picked up and used by Zoroastrians, Hindus, and Christians in particular.

messiah

Prophecies in the earlier chapters of Isaiah and elsewhere make it clear that Jews had an expectation of an anointed "messiah" before arriving in Babylon (Deuteronomy 18:15; 2 Samuel 7:14; Isaiah 7:14; Isaiah 8:23–9:2; Isaiah 9:5; Isaiah 11:12; Psalm 2; Psalm 16; Psalm 22; Psalm 34; Psalm 69; Psalm 110; and elsewhere). There is also the possibility that the prophet of the same name, often called Second Isaiah, who prophesied during the Exile and extended the scroll, might have redacted the earlier Isaiah prophecies back into those earlier chapters. This is unlikely, because the earlier vision of the messiah was of a figure who would come in real time to bless and bolster the community once and for all, but in a normal historical sense. If the Zoroastrians did indeed receive the revelation of One God from the Jews in the first place, it could well be that the beginnings of their own messianic vision also came from the Jews a generation or two before Babylon. Regardless of that possibility, interesting and attractive as it may be, the fully developed Zoroastrian messianic vision was of a figure known as the *Saoshyant*, a word meaning Redeemer, though sometimes translated as Savior. This figure was one who transcended time in appearing at the beginning of time, was expected soon in the fullness of time, and to appear in association with final judgment at the end of time. The Jewish messianic vision as prophesied during and after the Exile (Isaiah 53:5; Jeremiah 31:15; Daniel 9:24–27; Micah 5:2 or 5:1 in Jewish Bibles; Haggai 2:6–9; Zechariah 9:9; Zechariah 12:10) resembled the Zoroastrian vision more than the earlier Jewish vision, though it reserved the role of Redeemer to a function of God alone. That is to say, the Jewish messiah was not a "personal savior," but would lead the Jews to victory and national redemption.

paradise

Any and all of the above examples can be developed to show the Vedic origins, the Zoroastrian connection, the adoption by Jews in Babylon, and links back to Hinduism, Buddhism, and even Taoism and Jainism, as well as forward to Christianity and eventual "confirmation" by Islam. Sometimes these exercises may trigger PhD theses by those developing their specialties; in other cases the connections are almost self-explanatory. The latter is the case with paradise, though a little more information could be of interest. The Vedic Rig Veda scriptures hold that the physical body is destroyed but recreated and reunited with the soul in Paradise (the Third Heaven) in a state of bliss. In the Zoroastrian Avesta this paradise is defined as the "Best Existence" and the "House of Song," a place of the righteous dead. The Hebrew word *pardes* is borrowed directly from the Persian, and it does not appear as a future "heaven" anywhere before the post-exilic period. It occurs in the Song of Songs 4:13, Ecclesiastes 2:5, and Nehemiah 2:8, in each case meaning "garden," the original Persian meaning of the word *pairi-daeza* being "enclosed garden." Xenophon uses it in this exact manner to describe the royal parks of Cyrus the Great in his *Anabasis* historical account. This is quite outside the religious usage in the Avesta, but it shows how later Jewish writers were able to connect it with the Garden of Eden, even though that connection was never made in the earlier pre-exilic portions of these documents.

In Second Temple–era Judaism "paradise" came to be associated with both the Garden of Eden and prophesies of restoration of Eden, transferred to heaven. The Septuagint version uses the word around thirty times, both of Eden (Genesis 2:7, etc.) and of Eden restored (Ezekiel 28:13, 36:35, etc.). In the Apocalypse of Moses, Adam and Eve are expelled from paradise (instead of Eden) after having been tricked by the serpent. Later, after the death of Adam, the Archangel Michael carries the body of Adam to be buried in Paradise, which is in the Third Heaven again there. In Rabbinical Judaism the word *pardes* recurs in parable-like stories. The Zohar of Kabbalah thought gives the word a mystical interpretation, associating it with the four kinds of Biblical exegesis: *peshat* (literal meaning), *remez* (allusion), *derash* (anagogical), and *sod* (mystic). The initial letters of those four words then form פַּרְדֵּס—*PaRDeS*, which was in turn felt to represent the fourfold interpretation of the Torah, in which, for Kabbalists, *sod* (the mystical interpretation) ranks highest. Its appearance in English literature and elsewhere will be touched on below, but there is no question about where the concept of paradise comes from or when it became extraterrestrial.

perpetual fire

The references to perpetual fire are fewer, and could be considered scant except for the placement and timing, which fits the painting we are restoring. In Leviticus, chapter 6, we find perpetual fire on the altar of Israel, again suddenly and without precedent in the Torah, integrating the perpetual fire from Zoroastrian altars with H, the Hebrew Holiness Code. Somewhat later, in 2 Chronicles 7:1, Ezra remembers the use of fire at least once on the altar, a P document recalling that "When Solomon had ended his prayer, fire came down from heaven and consumed the burnt offering and the sacrifices; and the glory of the LORD filled the temple," a most convenient redaction into a later document but not mentioned in the earlier account of the same occasion in 1 Kings 8:54, an account of the exact same event with the fireworks not noticed at that time, or at least not recorded.

The recorded instructions in Leviticus 6:12–13 is succinct in its context of introducing fire sacrifice, as mentioned earlier. "The fire on the altar shall be kept burning on it. It shall not go out, but the priest shall burn wood on it every morning; and he shall lay out the burnt offering on it, and offer up in smoke the fat portions of the peace offerings on it. Fire shall be kept burning continually on the altar; it is not to go out." (Of course, Job reset the sacrificial fire every day too, but all agree that Job was not originally a Hebrew document.)

In ancient Persia the Zoroastrian altars were tended by dedicated priests and represented the concept of "divine sparks," or *amesha spenta*. Period sources indicate that three "great fires" existed in sacred sites during the Achaemenid era of Persian history.

In identical fashion, this eternal flame was a component of the Jewish religious rituals performed in the Second Temple in Jerusalem, where a commandment required a fire to burn continuously upon the Outer Altar. Modern Judaism continues a similar tradition by having a sanctuary lamp, the *ner tamid*, always lit above the ark in the synagogue. In the Torah, there is just one clear priestly redaction setting the practice in the desert in verses just before the precious Zoroastrian gems in the book of Leviticus. In Exodus 27:20–21 a priestly appendix, P, is added to a mixture of J, E, and P material, older material supplemented by later priestly inserts, according to all who subscribe to the documentary hypothesis in any form. The P appendix, almost certainly added in Babylon or later, reads:

> And thou shalt command the children of Israel, that they bring thee pure oil olive beaten for the light, to cause the lamp to burn always. In the tabernacle of the congregation without the veil, which is before the testimony, Aaron and his sons shall order it from evening to morning before the LORD: it shall be a statute for ever unto their generations on the behalf of the children of Israel.

An interesting biblical account of Zoroastrian–Jewish contact, as well as an early attestation of Middle Eastern petroleum, appears in the second book of the Maccabees (which is not found in Jewish Bibles, and only in Catholic and Orthodox Christian versions). This document dates from about 124 BCE, which places it among the latest books of the Old Testament, but so late that the Jewish canon does not recognize it. In the first chapter of this book, there is a story of how the Jewish altar fire was restored to the Temple after the Captivity. Jewish Temple practice required a continuously burning flame at the altar (Exodus 27:20) though this flame did not have the special "iconic" quality of the Zoroastrian sacred fire. Nevertheless, during the restoration of the Jewish Temple, this story arose and is repeated in the book of the Maccabees, four hundred years later: "When the matter (restoring the fire) became known and the king of the Persians heard that in the place where the exiled priests had hidden the fire a liquid had appeared, with which Nehemiah and his people had purified the materials of the sacrifice, the king, after verifying the facts, had the place enclosed and pronounced sacred."[10] This shows that as late as the time of the composition of 2 Maccabees, the Jewish writers were aware of the Zoroastrian reverence for fire—and also that, if the story is true, the Zoroastrians saw and respected similarities in practice between their own religion and that of the Jews. The fiery liquid cited here is petroleum, called "naphtha," an expression that arises from a combination of Persian and Hebrew words.

purification Rites

Both the Greek Septuagint version and the Latin Vulgate Bible named the book of Nehemiah "Second Ezra," and while the two books of Ezra and Nehemiah are now separate in most Christian Bibles, they appear to have once been joined together in a single scroll, and they appear as one book in most Hebrew texts today. Many scholars accept that in a portion of the book ascribed to Nehemiah he tells how he, as the "cup bearer" at the court of king Artaxerxes in the Persian capital, Susa, is informed that Jerusalem is without walls and resolves to restore them. He has the king's ear and is granted the wherewithal to complete his vision, which he does over two terms as governor.

Mary Boyce has pointed out that the cup bearer's main responsibility was purification, and the job had ritual as well as hygienic aspects. Without much doubt, Nehemiah was an authority on Zoroastrian rites of purification, both ceremonial and practical, a major concern among Zoroastrians today who believe in the efficacy of harmony between these two realms. Before consecration to God there must be purification from defilement. The only places outside the book of Nehemiah where a certain type of ritual purification takes place are 2 Chronicles 29:15 and Ezra 6:20, and they are both written by Ezra as the scribe and religious official at Nehemiah's right hand. When we read more of this in the book of Nehemiah, it appears that, as governor, Nehemiah himself may have dictated such references to Ezra.

In Nehemiah 12:30 the ceremonial dedication of the walls of the rebuilt city is described and the account is emphatic that both priests and Levites purified themselves by offerings and ablutions, and the gates and the wall were purified by being sprinkled. Speaking of the several thousand who participated in the ceremonies, we read in Nehemiah 12:45, "They performed the service of their God and the service of purification, as did the singers and the gatekeepers," both as a sign of the dedication and to remove defilement from the path of the sacred procession.

While not a ritual drawn from Jerusalem's own previous history, the action was important enough to be confirmed as recorded by Ezra in Nehemiah 13:22, a day later after the momentous reading of the finally completed scrolls of the Torah (as we have it) and in preparation for the Sabbath Day as evening fell and on the morrow: "Then I commanded the Levites to purify themselves and go and guard the gates in order to keep the Sabbath day holy." This fastidiousness could have reflected ceremonial life in Susa, much as it does among Parsee Zoroastrians in Mumbai today. These references are included here to simply make the point that Israel now had a Zoroastrian socioreligious patina.

Redeemer

It would be of more than passing interest to know if any clear linguistic markers exist in the extant Avesta texts to link it with the Hebrew and Christian Scriptures. One such example in the Hebrew Scriptures was discovered in researching *Three Testaments* with the help of online collaborators, many of whom were members of the Jewish online research facility H-JUDAIC, which kindly provided access to an even wider group of Jewish scholars who joined in the pursuit of an answer to this puzzle. Many of these scholars in Europe, South Africa, Australia, and Israel joined with the Jewish members of our team in North America to search for at least one linguistic marker absolutely connecting the Torah to the Avesta.

We found what we were looking for after intense research by several scholars examining the biblical use of the Hebrew word *gaol*, which is usually translated "nearest *kinsman*," "blood *avenger*," or even "*vindicator*." In no translation of the Torah itself, from the old King James Version to the respected Jewish Tanakh and everything in between, is *gaol* ever translated as *Redeemer* in those first five scrolls or books. That word is reserved almost exclusively for translations of Second Isaiah. *Gaol* as *Redeemer*, as a noun referring to God, is not found even once in the Torah! Nor is it found in First Isaiah or any other prophet, with one exception—coincidently, Jeremiah. It is found three times in wisdom writings, possibly connected to Zoroastrian precedents themselves. But such a specific use of *gaol* in the sense of *Redeemer* appears thirteen times in Second Isaiah alone. We are quite certain that we know the reason, given the time and place of his writing, so a cluster of that magnitude becomes a "linguistic marker" if the context holds up in some unique pattern.

Not only was Second Isaiah active as a prophet during the interface between Zoroastrian and Hebrew priests, but he also showed his special interest in the Zoroastrian concept of the *Saoshyant*, as evidenced by his description of the Zoroastrian monarch, Cyrus, as possibly "God's Anointed" or Messiah. *Saoshyant* is a figure of Zoroastrian eschatology who brings about the final renovation of the world for good. In popular literature, the word *Saoshyant* is often translated by the Hebrew word *Messiah*, somewhat erroneously. The most correct translation of the Persian / Avestan word *Saoshyant* in English is *Redeemer*.[11] The Hebrew and Christian translators in every age all caught that meaning from the context in Second Isaiah, so *Gaol / Redeemer* as a noun, and as a name for God, is the "linguistic marker" that establishes a literal connection between the Hebrew Torah and the Zoroastrian Avesta in a manner similar to the twenty or more such examples connecting the Quran to previous Zoroastrian revelations, though none of those examples are as uniquely definitive.

An examination of every occurrence of "Redeemer" in the Tanakh shows clearly how this title for the Zoroastrian "messiah" is adopted by Second Isaiah. It is even adapted by him in terms of a more sophisticated Jewish theology, showing God himself to be the one who alone "redeems" Israel. The theological sophistication of this concept in this context cannot be overstated. Second Isaiah must be party to the growing understanding among Jews in Babylon that the Saoshyant / Messiah will appear at the end-time of history, but, as if to argue the point of redemption here-and-now with Zoroastrian priestly colleagues, he insists on the point that *God alone is Israel's Redeemer*. This is a point that Jews have had to pursue in later conversations with Christians and others, but one initially established at the moment Israel first adopted the Redeemer imagery from Zoroastrianism. Were we to highlight "Z" words in bold in the biblical text, as suggested in "The Z Factor" of the preface to Book IV, we might have begun with the first chapter of Genesis, and possibly all of Leviticus, but in Isaiah the word "Redeemer" would be highlighted in bold again and again, as occasionally elsewhere, prior to additional references in the final prophets. The following verses from the Hebrew Tanakh version of the Bible spike the post–Torah Hebrew Scriptures with a clear Eastern religious Zoroastrian concept.

Second Isaiah 41:14 states, "I will help you, declares the Lord. I, your Redeemer, the Holy One of Israel." (God has a new name in all these texts, though deliberately connected to God's old name, especially in the phrase "the Holy One of Israel," an earlier appellation by none other than First Isaiah.)

Second Isaiah 43:14 says, "Thus said the Lord, Your Redeemer, the Holy One of Israel: 'For your sake I send to Babylon.'" (Babylon is frequently the scene of action of the Redeemer God.)

Second Isaiah 44: 6 states, "Thus said the Lord, the King of Israel, Their Redeemer, the Lord of Hosts: I am the first and the last, And there is no God but me." (In this context, there is also an affirmation of monotheism, as might be expected.)

Second Isaiah 44:24 says, "Thus said the Lord, your Redeemer, Who formed you in the womb: It is I, the Lord, who made everything." (Equally prominent in answer to the Zoroastrian question about the source of creation.)

Second Isaiah 47:4 says, "Our Redeemer—the Lord of Hosts is his name, is the Holy one of Israel." (It would be impossible to be more direct in this regard than this affirmation. When Second Isaiah attributes worship of Israel's God to Cyrus, the joint identity of the Hebrew and Zoroastrian God is made possible in a phrase like the above.)

Second Isaiah 48:17 says, "Thus said the Lord, your Redeemer, The Holy One of Israel: I am the Lord your God." (Driving the point home, this identification of the title Redeemer with Israel's God is a deliberate campaign by Second Isaiah. He has an agenda not found elsewhere in the Hebrew Scriptures.)

Second Isaiah 49:7 states, "Thus said the Lord, The Redeemer of Israel: The Holy One of Israel chose you." (The people are assured that the broader context takes nothing away from Israel's sense of uniqueness.)

Second Isaiah 49:26 says, "I, the Lord, am your savior, The Mighty One of Jacob, your Redeemer." (A more messianic thrust, combining Jewish history with Zoroastrian vision.)

Second Isaiah 54:5 says, "The Holy one of Israel will redeem you (most other translations: 'will be your Redeemer'), He is called God of all the Earth." (Taking the universality of the Saoshyant and attributing the role of redemption to God himself.)

Second Isaiah 54:8 states, "I will take you back in love, said the Lord, your Redeemer." (A connection of love with redemption, rare for Hebrew Scriptures to this point, but germane to the identification of Zoroastrian influence.)

Second Isaiah 59:20 states, "He shall come as a Redeemer to Zion." (The universal agenda notwithstanding, the particular agenda of Israel is specifically supported.)

Second Isaiah 60:16 says, "You shall know that I the Lord am your Savior, I, the Mighty One of Jacob, am your Redeemer." (The concepts of savior and redeemer are again closely associated, except that where Zoroastrians place the messianic vision into the future work of a divinely appointed individual, and Christians pick up messianic themes as referring to Christ, the theological understanding of Second Isaiah comes through again, identifying *God himself* as the saving redeemer, a theological sophistication perhaps more typical of Jewish tradition generally.)

Second Isaiah 63:16 says, "You, O Lord, are our Father. From of old, Your name is Our Redeemer." (Except that "from of old" in Israel, God's name was never any such thing! To the Jews, this is a new name for God, and the direct source is now obvious.)

I have attributed this use of the Zoroastrian name "Redeemer" for the messiah to Second Isaiah, though part of that might reflect the work of a Third Isaiah or group of Isaiah's later disciples who may have stood in that tradition in post-exilic times, seen in the last three examples above. The few other rare uses of this name for God may also actually connect with the Zoroastrian identity. The Tanakh gives us Redeemer as a name for God once in Jeremiah and twice in the Psalms.

Jeremiah 50:34 says, "Their Redeemer is mighty, His name is the Lord of Hosts. He will champion their cause—So as to give rest to the earth, and unrest to the inhabitants of Babylon." (Among the oracles in the book of Jeremiah, chapters 30 and 31 have such a marked similarity to the style of Isaiah 40–55 and such a clear dissimilarity from the rest of Jeremiah that they may even be an insertion from something written by Second Isaiah, according to certain text experts.[12] More likely, given what we know now about Zoroaster's dates and Jeremiah's ministry among exiles in Babylon, Egypt, and possibly earlier among the Scythians, this is a final clue that there was interplay between Zoroaster's ministry and that of Jeremiah.)

Psalm 19:15 says:

> May the words of my mouth
> And the prayer of my heart
> Be acceptable to You,
> O Lord, my rock and my Redeemer.

Psalm 78:35 says, "They remembered that God was their rock, / God most high, their Redeemer." (In both cases these psalms may indicate random usage, innocent of awareness of Zoroastrianism, though we should not be too sure. That is where the critical interface took place, but these psalms are of undetermined date and wisdom literature in particular may reflect a longer connection with Zoroastrianism, and even the Saoshyant doctrine, translated as Redeemer, possibly a usage of an acceptable idiom from outside Israel.)

A traditional concordance also lists another Wisdom example in Proverbs 23:11 as an instance of *gaol* being translated as *Redeemer* in the King James Version, which is followed by the Revised Standard Version, and the New Revised Standard Version, but not the Tanakh or other translations. The point is that *gaol* as a noun, capitalized, and used as a title for God in the Divine role as *Saoshant / Redeemer* is extremely rare, and never found in the Torah in any version. It is confined almost exclusively to Second Isaiah, and there it is repeated again and again in the writing of the very prophet who answers Zoroaster's questions, suggests Cyrus as a candidate for messiahship, and then develops the sophisticated theological concept of God himself acting as the *Redeemer*. The clustering of this particular usage of *gaol*, the manner in which it is used, and its parallels in the dominant religious culture surrounding the Jews at the time of writing make it a genuine linguistic marker, establishing a textual linkage between the Hebrew Scriptures and a uniquely Zoroastrian expression at a most significant level.

Finally, beyond the specialized usage of *gaol* / *Redeemer* in Second Isaiah, there is one other dramatic usage of this word in the wisdom writings of Hebrew Scripture. It qualifies as a connecting "linguistic marker" if we can be persuaded that the book of Job may itself be Zoroastrian in origin (see below). This particular usage is the clincher in any case, as either an instance of "Redeemer" as a loan word in a loaned book or as an example of a concept shared with the community of wisdom references, which are related to the Zoroastrian Lord of Wisdom.

Resurrection

The first reference to resurrection in the Hebrew Scriptures is in Isaiah 26:19, which is part of the early Isaiah material, dated as a block well before the Babylonian Exile. This particular verse is part of what is sometimes called the *Isaianic Apocalypse* in chapters 24–27, which is sometimes regarded as the best example of something written by Second Isaiah in Babylon and redacted back into the First Isaiah material.[13] That resurrection verse reads, "Your dead shall live, their corpses shall rise. O dwellers in the dust, awake and sing for joy! For your dew is a radiant dew, and the earth will give birth to those long dead."[14]

Despite being traditionally attributed to the first prophet Isaiah, who lived in the eighth century BCE, the *Isaianic Apocalypse* is sometimes considered post-exilic because of its numerous polemics against Babylon, which was not a threat or a subject of concern to Israel during the earlier prophet's lifetime. The apocalyptic tone also fits with Second Isaiah in Zoroastrian style and not earlier, and other telltale signs concluding with the restoration of the righteous to Jerusalem, expected then by Jews in Babylon, not in rural Judea. According to that theory, the references to refugees from previous exiles are inserted to authenticate the prophecy. "On that day a great trumpet will be blown, and those who were lost in the land of Assyria and those who were driven out to the land of Egypt will come and worship the Lord on the holy mountain in Jerusalem."[15]

The resurrection verse is of interest because it addresses the question of whether Jews got the vision of even more profound resurrection imagery in Babylon, or in this case was it possibly the other way around. We should be aware that Isaiah 26:19 possibly predates our earliest textual evidence of Zoroastrian references to resurrection. Just as it is maintained that Zoroaster received his understanding of One God and the messiah from Israelites soon after the early prophet Isaiah, might he not have received the revelation about resurrection from the same source? Again, this presupposes a late date for Zoroastrianism, just before the Exile, but it also points to the intensity and almost intimacy of conversations, trust, and sharing of beliefs between Jewish and Zoroastrian priests in Babylon, with the possibility that the teaching went both ways.

In the *Gathas*, Zoroaster discusses the judgment of all humans when the soul leaves the body and goes straight to hell or paradise as the case may be.[16] This was not yet regarded as an end-of-time event for all people; indeed, only community and religious leaders were deemed worthy of eternal life.[17] The more sophisticated Zoroastrian vision of resurrection as an eschatological event turns up in Yasht sections of the Avesta written during the Achaemenid Dynasty of descendants of Cyrus, but so late as to appear to us as possibly more derivative from the Jews than something they received in Babylon. This resurrection, at the appearance of the messianic Saoshyant, is introduced thus: "Ahura Mazda created many and good creatures in order that they shall make the world perfect and in order that the dead shall rise up, that the Living One, the Indestructible, shall come, the world be made perfect at his wish, the Victorious Saoshyant and his companions, so that he may make the world perfect, unchanging, undying, uncorrupted, undecaying, ever-living, ever-growing."[18] So we can say with some certainty that Zoroastrians believed in resurrection during the Achaemenid period while Jews were still in Babylon, and that their understanding resembled that expressed in the *Isaianic Apocalypse* of Hebrew Scripture, but in this instance it is difficult to suggest that the early Isaiah material was derived from anything the Zoroastrians shared with Jews in Babylon. The opposite may be the case, though the exchange of ideas must have been fascinating as the two communities received their "revelations" in this matter while stimulating each other.

The concept of resurrection is developed now to the level where the person's body will be re-established post-mortem, reunited with the soul, and made immortal.[19] This should not be confused with the simple resuscitation of the corpse in which mortal existence is merely resumed, as we find in the Elijah–Elisha narrative (1 Kings 17:17–24; 2 Kings 4:31–37, 13:20–21). The dramatic vision of Ezekiel's valley of dry bones is considered in reference to burial practices, but proclaimed right in mid-exile experience, it is a striking witness to the eschatological theology of the full doctrine. We cannot say which party was teaching the other, or whether Jews and Zoroastrians were working together, but something dramatic concerning resurrection was going on in Babylon between Jews (including the Pharisees as the party of the resurrection) and Zoroastrian scholars, priests, scribes, and believers. Two later examples of resurrection in the Hebrew Scriptures fit the picture as found in the book of Daniel, which has been dated to the Maccabean period but set in the Exile where this matter fomented with such grand consequence.

> At that time Michael, the great prince, the protector of your people, shall arise. There shall be a time of anguish, such as has never occurred since nations first came into existence. But at that time your people shall be delivered, everyone who is found written in the book. Many of those who sleep in the dust of the earth shall awake, some to everlasting life, and

some to shame and everlasting contempt. Those who are wise shall shine like the brightness of the sky, and those who lead many to righteousness, like the stars forever and ever.[20]

And further, "But you, go your way, and rest; you shall rise for your reward at the end of the days."[21]

salvation

According to the revelation received by Zoroaster, a good and an evil force struggle for mastery in the universe. Humanity has to decide on which side to align itself in this battle. The righteous would pass to their reward in heaven and the wicked would be cast into hell, both initially regarded as temporary states. That is where things stood during the interface between Zoroastrians and Jews in Babylon. Jews don't often use the term *salvation*; rather, they sometimes speak of *redemption*, especially in the post-exilic period. Judaism of the Second Temple period (and prior in Babylon) considered the concept of salvation more communal and national than exclusively personal, as Zoroastrianism and modern Christianity view it. The salvation of the individual Jew was connected to the salvation of the entire people.[22] Ideas regarding the Messiah's role in salvation did not present a consensus, though an exception to this would be the Qumran community, whose literature has a highly developed sense of messianic intervention. Even in the Qumran literature however, one can see evolving thought about the Messiah where a two-Messiah theory evolved to a belief in a single Messiah as represented by Melchizedek, who resolved the issue of the Messiah being both king and priest as the agent of personal and corporate salvation.

satan

The Hebrew word "Satan" translates into English as "Adversary," the very devilish persona that appears near the heart of Zoroastrian doctrine, where it caused much the same confusion as it does among Jews, Christians, and Muslims whenever they permit it to assume too great or too little importance. The Jews had their own prototype in the appearance of the serpent in the third chapter of Genesis, and a nameless spiritual adversary who appears in the book of Numbers, but the fully developed persona of Satan materializes first in the book of Job, still regarded by many as the very oldest text in the Bible. After the Exile and return the appearances of Satan conform to that Job image, as in Zechariah 3:1–2, immediately after the return.

the book of job

According to Mary Boyce, the great English authority on Zoroastrianism, when God meets with the heavenly beings in Job 1:6 it is a scene resembling the Council of Heaven between Ahura Mazda and the Immortals described in the Avesta.[23] The biblical picture of God in the book of Job presiding over a council of lesser beings in His heavenly entourage, none of whom were fully "divine," does match with that of the yazatas in Zoroastrianism.[24] The reference to the "sons of God"[25] in Job is an easy connection to "the Immortals." The appearance of Satan gives the book a Zoroastrian stamp, as mentioned above.

From internal evidence we know that the book of Job is not Jewish; the text itself says that Job was from Uz, that he was the greatest man of all the people in the East, and it provides other clues that it is Vedic in origin. There are parts of the text that appear adopted as "whole cloth" from an Eastern document, parts that are evidently new in the Hebrew version, and long sections, we assume to have been cherished by Zoroastrians in Babylon, that have editorial touches which gently and authentically add spiritual flourishes from the Jewish editors.

In spite of its prominence in the Bible, few (if any) scholars, Jewish or Christian, conservative or progressive, believe that this is a Jewish document. It has been amended and brought into the Jewish canon, where it stands out as the major link with Eastern religions. It is philosophical and theological, not entirely compatible with any Eastern source we know of, and likely not specifically Zoroastrian in origin, either, though it has unmistakable Vedic affinities. By its tone and content, Manichaeism could be considered a likely source, were it not for the fact that apparently the Jews got the book of Job, much as we have it, some two hundred years before Manichaeism appeared on the world scene. The version the Jews acquired in Babylon has sufficient providence at this point to be sure that it happened during the Exile, though it would appear that Zoroastrians had previously edited the text of this master work to make it fit their agendas as well. The Jews acquired the book early enough in the period of Zoroastrian rule that the Sassanian dualism of later Zoroastrianism has not elevated Satan in the story to the level of quasi-equality as a rival to God. Satan is still God's somewhat insubordinate servant, and he even does God's work by testing a righteous man. This points to a Zoroastrianism of One God immediately before or during the Exile, one of the dating mechanisms of pristine Zoroastrianism by our technique of reading backward from its encounter with Judaism.

The general Zoroastrian ethos is brought to a head in two particular verses related to the present discussion: "I know that my Redeemer liveth, and that he shall stand at the latter day upon the earth."[26] It is impossible to ignore the strength of the Zoroastrian connection in Job, traditionally regarded as Eastern and ancient anyway, but, with a resurrection motif, this passage continues: "Though after my skin, worms destroy this body, yet in my flesh I shall see God."[27]

There is additional supporting evidence or at least hints corroborating the idea that Job could be found in the lost Zoroastrian Avesta texts, our "Dead Zee Scrolls," which were still circulating when Israel was in Babylon. Despite its universally agreed non-Hebraic context, the story uses the name Yahweh for God, a parallel to the suggestion in Isaiah[28] of an association between the Eastern God of Cyrus and "YHWH," the latter making Zoroastrianism the only other non-Hebraic employment of the holy name in the Hebrew Scriptures. These are all indications that Job was originally Zoroastrian or cherished by them, and possibly reworked for Hebrew readers in the same way the creation story is reworked in chapter 1 of Genesis.

We may presume that the prologue and the epilogue of Job are lifted directly from the Avesta version, and that the dialogue is produced in freestyle translation, enhancing the Zoroastrian material with Hebrew spiritual sensitivity and theological sophistication. It would be easy to find objections, but Job came from somewhere, and its use of Redeemer as a title for God, or for the Messiah/Saoshayant, in the context of resurrection on the last day is too much for even Muslims to ignore from a greater distance in time, far less Christians or especially Jews.

In addition to the above connections, in his book *Religions of the Silk Road*, Richard Foltz draws our attention to additional Zoroastrian links to the Hebrew text in the book of Esther, noted by a range of his respected colleagues, whom he quotes as attesting to the ongoing conversations in Babylon during the Sassanian era. The book of Esther "provides explicit examples of (Zoroastrian) traditions such as court protocol, which also continued through the Islamic period. The drinking custom mentioned in Esther 1:8, and echoed in the tenth-century Arab writer al-Jahiz, is one example. Others are the function of the chamberlain in Esther 6:4–5, and the role of Eunuchs in 1:10."[29]

James Russell says, "The plotter, Teresh, and the disloyal minister's wife, Zeresh, appear to be reflections of the demons Taurvi and Zairik in the Avesta. Together they can be seen to represent the (Zoroastrian) paradigm of 'the lie' (*druj*) opposed to the kings law (*dätä*), and by extension lewdness vs. chastity, and violence vs. the pacifism of the righteous."[30] And Almut Hintze writes, "The Jewish festival of Purim, which comes out of the Esther story, was likely derived from the ancient (Zoroastrian) springtime festival of *Fravardigan*, which like Purim, began on the fourteenth day of the month of Azar and also included an exchange of gifts."[31]

After a century of neglect, the connection between Zoroastrianism and Judaism is beginning to get more detailed attention as a link between Eastern and Western religions that will serve as the model for deeper investigation of Christian and Islamic links and initial analysis of the connections between Zoroastrianism and the monistic religions farther east.

Some of the items on the above list do actually appear in the Torah, elements of which preceded the Exile, but none of the above entries appear in any strand or cluster of Torah material (except in the priestly source, which may have begun in Jerusalem before the Exile, was largely formulated during the Exile in Babylon, and was edited into the finished product of the Torah as we have it today, completed by Ezra and his team of scribes shortly after the return, and read for the Jewish public as representing the Law of Moses). These comments include assumptions more fully described in *Three Testaments: Torah, Gospel, and Quran*, but, taken as a whole, a pattern emerges that explains the radically expanded Jewish religion, comparing before and after the Exile. The consistency of development in that very short period of time, all related to the long-term theological evolution of Israel, allows for the claim that it is all compatible with the teachings of Moses.

The connections between Zoroastrianism and Judaism are the most striking because they may have had some previous history of significance in an encounter between Israelite exiles and Zoroaster, and because the Jews lived in the vortex of Zoroastrian influence during the Exile. Looking backward from Judaism in this way illustrates the immediacy between Zoroaster's own life and the beginning of the Axial Age, and it also shows us more about Zoroastrianism and its relationship to the Vedas and to the Eastern religions throughout the length of the Silk Route. Foltz gives us another interesting and very specific example of the interconnectedness in Kushan, part of the Sogdian region (Uzbekistan), where we will suggest in Book VII that the quest for the full text of the ancient Avesta might be pursued by archaeologists. Foltz quotes Jan Nattier as follows:

> The most popular representation of the Buddha in Kushan art is Maitreya, the "Future Buddha," some of whose soteriological and eschatological qualities seem to echo those of the Zoroastrian Saoshyant and the Jewish and Christian Messiah. In a particularly striking parallel, in Buddhist mythology, Maitreya will be welcomed by a disciple named Kasypa. The name of a similar figure in Zoroastrianism, awaiting the Saoshyant, is Karashaspa.[32]

The time is drawing near when "Scriptural Reasoning" classes will be able to move on to theological reasoning in discussion of, for example, Kasypa, Karashaspa, Elijah, John the Baptist, and even the al-*Mahdi* of Islam in relation to *Isa al-Masih* and possibly others.

z-related passages in hebrew scriptures

Genesis 1:1–2:3
Exodus 27:20–21
Leviticus 1:1–10:20
Leviticus 17:7
2 Chronicles 7:1
2 Chronicles 11:15
2 Chronicles 29:15
Ezra 6:20
Nehemiah 2:8
Nehemiah 12:30
Nehemiah 12:45
Nehemiah 13:22
Esther 1:8
Esther 1:10
Esther 2:21
Esther 6:2
Esther 6:4–5
Job 1:6
Job 2:1

Job 19:25–26
Psalm 19:15
Psalm 78:35
Ecclesiastes 2:5
Song of Songs 4:13
Isaiah 26:19
Isaiah 41:14
Isaiah 43:14
Isaiah 44:6
Isaiah 44:24
Isaiah 41:14
Isaiah 47:14
Isaiah 48:17
Isaiah 49:7
Isaiah 49:26
Isaiah 53:5
Isaiah 54:5
Isaiah 54:8
Isaiah 59:20

Isaiah 60:16
Isaiah 63:16
Jeremiah 50:34
Jeremiah 19:2–10
Jeremiah 31:15
Ezekiel 1:4–28
Ezekiel 10:3–22
Ezekiel 13:5
Daniel 7:10

Daniel 9:24–27
Daniel 10:10–21
Daniel 12:1–3
Daniel 12:99
Micah 5:2 (5:1 in many Jewish Bibles)
Haggai 2:6–9
Zechariah 3:1–2
Zechariah 9:9
Zechariah 12:10

z passages ín jewísh apocryphal and íntertestamental wrítíngs

Enoch 18:11–16
Enoch 19:1
Enoch 27:1–3
Enoch 40:4–5
Enoch 60:12
Enoch 82:13

Enoch 90:26
Tobias 3:17
2 Baruch 21:23
Judith 16:17
Assumption of Moses 10:10
2 Maccabees 1:33–34

12
jesus as a zoroastrian saoshyant, the redeemer of the world

According to one of the accounts of the life of Jesus in the New Testament, he himself once posed to his immediate followers the question of who people thought he was and how they interpreted what he was doing and saying. "Who do people say that I am?" he asked them at a place called Caesarea Philippi (Mark 8:27). The followers offered several answers. Some people, they reported, thought he was Elijah, the Jewish prophet who was expected to return to earth just before the end of the world. Others thought he was some other prophet. Then Peter, one of the disciples, when asked to give his own answer to the question, told Jesus he was the "Messiah," the ambiguously defined figure most of his fellow Jews were hoping would soon appear and help them to overcome the national captivity and religious persecution they were suffering under the Roman Empire.[1]

DIRECT TRANSMISSION OF VEDIC TRADITIONS, NOT THROUGH JUDAISM BUT STRAIGHT FROM Zoroastrianism, the largest state religion on Israel's borders, would have come into Christianity through cultural osmosis, but also through awareness of Zoroastrianism and appreciation of it by Jesus himself. It is widely assumed that Jesus never went anywhere outside Israel (except possibly to Egypt as a baby). In *Three Testaments* we charted all the places he went outside Israel according to the New Testament on a map, using a mix of modern, ancient, and current country names. Egypt, Israel, and "Palestine" are easily recognized, but not even clergy or scholars would easily rhyme off his trips to Lebanon, Syria, and Jordan; yet the Bible records such trips by Jesus into territory where Zoroastrianism was still functioning as a state religion in various guises or in subsumed identities.[2]

For our purposes here, we will simply draw attention to one such trip, where Jesus visits the cities of Tyre and Sidon in present-day Lebanon. In the Gospel of Mark, the trip was taken to get away from the demanding multitudes; Jesus went there because he knew people in a house he had been to before who would shield him from the crowds.[3] Even there, though, visiting with non-Jews (almost certainly Zoroastrians of some description, possibly Sabaean), people recognized him as the Jewish Messiah from across the border, one they, too, could relate to as possibly the Saoshyant they had been looking for. Just as the boy Jesus learned in the temple what the Messiah was to be, he may have learned on previous trips to Lebanon what the Saoshyant represented. He was thus prepared for the questions by a Syro-Phoenician woman who confronted him about healing and ministering to non-Jews.

For those who find this a radical departure from Judaism as the "single parent" of the church they grew up in, we ask them to suspend judgment until we wade through the now expanding list of Zoroastrian connections we may see in the New Testament. Some of them are reflected in incidents involving Jesus, others are received by Christians through the filter of Judaism, and still others may now be seen as received directly from the Zoroastrian parent into early church traditions. Non-Christians, Western and Eastern, may simply find this exercise to be an interesting adjunct to the growing awareness of the relationship between Christianity and Zoroastrianism, and a similar exploration of Islamic connections yet to come, all revealing a profound relationship between West and East, generally through the Zoroastrian stimulation experienced by monotheists and monists alike.

angelology

Various apocalyptic writings survive from the "intertestamental" period, such as the book of Enoch, a compilation of spectacular visions about angels, among other things. While such writings are regarded as scriptural by Roman Catholic and Orthodox Christians, many Protestants may not realize that when they reverted to the smaller Jewish canon, they were losing connection with a body of texts also regarded as scriptural in the early church and quoted in the New Testament by Saint Paul and other writers. It is in such places that we find many of the references to angels that have found their way into Christian tradition, obviously from Jewish transmission, and not directly from Zoroastrianism in this case.

creation

We are taking the issues explored in Hebrew Scriptures alphabetically briefly through the New Testament for comparison sake, but certain observations can only be fully understood by reference farther down the list. The New Testament doctrine of creation would be one of these, for it bears no relationship to the Hebrew rendition, and is totally Zoroastrian. The New Testament teaches that the universe was created by Jesus as the cosmic and eternal Christ. "All things were made through him, and without him was not anything made that was made."[4] "By him all things were created, in heaven and on earth, visible and invisible, whether thrones or dominions or rulers or authorities—all things were created through him and for him."[5] This bears no relationship to the Genesis version but matches up precisely with Zoroastrian doctrine that the Saoshyant was present in creation. This may be a stunning realization for some Christians, but not for Hindus, for example, who see Krishna in a similar light when he says, "I AM the source of all spiritual and material worlds. Everything emanates from Me. The wise who perfectly know this engage in My devotional service and worship Me with all their hearts."[6]

It is the Zoroastrian connection that links East and West so profoundly in this and in so many other ways, just as apparent in this instance as the presence of the very word KRiSHNA in the Hebrew text of Esther.

demonology

Tracing specific sources of demonology is more difficult than angelology simply because not all neighboring Mesopotamian and other religions had angels, but they all had demons, at least to the extent of reporting, like modern media that reports bad news and evil events far more frequently than more positive stories. The Zoroastrian demon influence in first-century Christianity becomes evident in the writings of Gnostic and Jewish sects like the Essenes of the same era. Due to archeological finds such as the "Dead Sea Scrolls" and the "Nag Hammadi Library," the modern world can know what these ancient devotees believed—and some of these beliefs show direct Zoroastrian influence. This is especially true in the Jewish text known as the "Essene Manual of Discipline," which, like the apocalyptic texts, describes a war between the Spirit of Light and the Spirit of Darkness, as well as the Spirit of Truth and the Spirit of Error, and an ultimate End-Time when the battle will be won.

Though the Gathas are half a millennium older, this Essene text sometimes sounds almost exactly like them: "For God has established the two spirits in equal measure until the last period, and has put eternal enmity between their divisions. An abomination to truth are deeds of error, and an abomination to error are all ways of truth."[7] Other demons also appear, but Zoroastrian demonic spirits of darkness and error in opposition to light and truth are featured in the New Testament where, as in the Dead Sea Scrolls, the faithful are described as the "children of light"[8] and part of the army of God, supported by him and by his angels against the princes of darkness who still surround them.[9] In this way, despite the welter of demons in the New Testament, it is possible to distinguish the Zoroastrian influence, though not to say whether it is direct, derivative, or both.

final judgment

The apocalyptic idea of the End of Time, as well as a Final Judgment by God when that end arrives, owes a great deal to Zoroastrian thinking. Rabbinic Judaism tended to drop the earlier Jewish interest in the Final Judgment, which peaked between the

Exile and the birth of Christianity. Christians picked up the theme in such dramatic fashion that we might suspect indirect influence of Zoroastrianism through Judaism and its sects and possibly direct influence from Zoroastrianism itself (though we know not how). In the book of Revelation, the final battle between God and Satan, after the latter had been bound for a millennium (a Zoroastrian concept), ends with the chief of demons "cast into the lake of fire and brimstone . . . and . . . tormented day and night for ever and ever."[10] This language could not be more Zoroastrian. On the positive side, for those judged fit for eternal life, the final judgment in Zoroastrianism triggers the reunion between soul and future body that occurs at the end of "time" when the resurrection of all God's people is completed in the communal *Frashegird*, the Kingdom of God.

fire sacrifices

Unlike the clear connection between Leviticus and the Zoroastrian fire rites observed by Jews in Babylon, there is nothing in Christian Scripture or church practice that connects Christianity to its Vedic or Zoroastrian antecedents in reference to fire sacrifices, though many churches adopted and still keep the eternal flame burning above their altars (see below).

funerary practices

Despite the tenuous connection in the prophecy of Ezekiel, as quoted above, the post-exilic Jews did not discernibly adopt much (if anything) from Zoroastrian funerary practice. Christians, to the contrary, have dabbled with the Vedic (though not Zoroastrian) practice of cremation through the centuries. We might suppose that the connection is coincidental were it not for the fact that Christians have always referred to their final rites as "funerals" from a chain of words back to the Sanskrit word for fumes. The non-Jewish tradition of Jesus's three days in the grave[11] is identifiable as the three-day pause practiced in Zoroastrian funerary rites even still today: "For the first three nights after the breath has left the body the soul hovers about the lifeless frame and experiences joy or sorrow according to the deeds done in this life. On the dawn of the fourth day the soul takes flight from earth."[12] The entire Easter motif is more Zoroastrian than Jewish, despite contextual elements reflected in Hebrew prophecy. If there is a link to Vedic practice in Christian funerary practice, including the case of Jesus, it came directly from their Zoroastrian neighbors, and not through the Jews.

hell

The molten hell of Zoroastrianism was transposed to Judaism during the Exile and identified with the Jewish memory of Gehennah, the smoldering dump outside Jerusalem where legend even then had it that children were sometimes sacrificed to the god Moloch during the excesses and debauchery of the later kingdom. That image of fire was the principal one elaborated upon and adopted by Christians. Gehennah was even translated as "hell fire" in the King James Version of the Bible,[13] and the description of hell as a place of "everlasting fire"[14] where there is "weeping and gnashing of teeth"[15] inspired the poetic visions of Milton's *Paradise Lost* and the Inferno section of Dante's *Divine Comedy*, both overtly Christian but covertly Zoroastrian in many respects.

i am

Jesus would have noted the distinct collection of Little Avesta "I AM" sayings in his travels among the Zoroastrians, and he was inspired to do the same thing and to make it a feature of his ministry. The Mosaic burning bush expression of I AM, as employed by Zoroaster, is applied by Jesus to his role as Saoshyant Messiah and would be written in bold as related to the Z motif.

There are actually seven I AM sayings by Jesus (which just happens to be the sacred number for Jews, derived from the Zoroastrians, who adopted it from the Vedic source). The seven I AM sayings are scattered, as something to which he kept referring, but they are all reported in the Gospel according to Saint John, by an author who obviously picked up on a favorite theme of Jesus:

1. "I AM the bread of life."[16]
2. "I AM the light of the world."[17]
3. "I AM the door of the sheep."[18]
4. "I AM the good shepherd."[19]
5. "I AM the resurrection, and the life."[20]
6. "I AM the way, the truth, and the life."[21]
7. "I AM the true vine."[22]

Zoroaster's deliberate focus on the I AM phrase as the name for God is easily identified, but anyone who questions the deliberate nature of Jesus's use of the phrase need look no further than his dispute with the Pharisees about his claim to predate Abraham as a divine figure. He says to them, "Before Abraham was, I AM."[23] Jews will not take these words as warrant for belief in his messianic identity, and Muslims may stick to their reservations about one God with three personas, but the twisted syntax of this quotation makes it clear that Jesus is making a point. He does not say, "Before Abraham was, I was," which would be the normal grammatical construction of the phrase. He goes out of his way to make it clear that he is speaking with the voice that came to Moses from the burning bush; he says, "Before Abraham was, I AM."

It is worth noting in passing that this offers progressive Christians a way out of the painful conundrum in which, shortly thereafter, he appears to some to suggest that only Christians can ever get to heaven. He says, "I AM the way, the truth, and the life. No one comes to the Father except through me."[24] If it is his habit to speak with the voice that addressed Moses from the burning bush, then here he is not speaking with merely the voice of Jesus of Nazareth, the man of Galilee. It is clear that in these words to the disciples, he is teaching them that anyone who knows the great I AM, as revealed to Moses, the "I am what I am," the "sacred ground of being," will be saved from perdition or "go to heaven."

messiah

It is in the context of the coming Saoshyant that the story in the second chapter of Matthew's Gospel of the Magi should be read. These astrologers, who are certainly to be regarded as Zoroastrians, were following the savior-signs of their own religion when they sought out the infant Jesus in a perhaps apocryphal New Testament story. Whether or not the Zoroastrians received their expectation of a virgin-born redeeming savior from the Israeli exiles, or vice versa in Babylon, the Christian understanding, and that of Jesus, is patently different from the hope of at least some Jews that a Messiah would come to reestablish the throne of King David, protect and support the Jewish people, and restore the glory of Israel. Jesus presents himself as more interested in saving the world than restoring the throne of Israel. Zoroaster taught that after him would come "the man who is better than a good man,"[25] the Saoshyant: "The meaning of Saoshyant is 'one who will bring benefit' (redeem or pay a ransom); and it is he who will lead humanity in the last battle against evil."[26] While both Zoroastrianism and Judaism subscribed to the image of a virgin birth to convey that this figure comes at God's initiation, by definition Jesus might be seen more as a Zoroastrian Saoshyant than as a Jewish Messiah, and he came to this defining of his role not in the temple as a twelve-year-old but in the direct experience of Zoroastrianism that passed on the same imagery to the followers of Krishna in India. We have yet to consider where and when Jesus might have had such direct contact. The parallels between Buddha's teaching and that of Jesus are well recognized; those between Jesus and Krishna need more investigation.

paradise

Zoroastrian souls in Paradise were not thought to achieve complete bliss until the whole believing community reached the state of *Frashegird*, a kind of Kingdom of God. In Vedic teaching, soon after each blessed soul reached Paradise it was reunited with its new body, to live again a happy life of full sensation, just a short step before reincarnation on earth. Zoroaster's own teaching short-circuited that pattern in his teaching that the soul in Paradise must wait for its "future" body in Frashegird when "the earth will give up the bones of the dead."[27] The Jewish view is less clear on this point in the scriptures, but the Christian understanding coordinates well with the Zoroastrian and builds on it. Saint Paul, known as Saul in his days as a Pharisee activist, writes to the Christians in the early (still Jewish) church at Philippi about the enemies of God, "I tell you, even with tears, their end is destruction: their god is their belly and their glory is in their shame; their minds are set on earthly things."[28] He continues, "But our citizenship is in heaven, and it is from there that we are expecting a Savior, the Lord Jesus Christ."[29] He concludes, "He will transform the body of our humiliation that it may be like his glorious body, by the power that also enables him to make all things subject to himself."[30] But none of that is completely fulfilled until the climax of both terrible and glorious events described in the book of Revelation conclude with "a great multitude that no one could count, from every nation, from all tribes and peoples and languages standing before the throne,"[31] where they are redeemed. It is easy to conclude that the Christian position comes from a direct connection, the occasion for which is not yet clear, but Revelation could stand as both a preface to the apocalyptic Quran and an appendix to the Avesta.

perpetual fire

As recorded, "And thou shalt command the children of Israel, that they bring thee pure oil olive beaten for the light, to cause the lamp to burn always."[32] We will not find an echo or a reporting of those words in the New Testament, nor will we find "the fire shall ever be burning upon the altar; it shall never go out"[33] among the several hundred quotations from the Hebrew Scriptures in the Christian Scriptures. Yet a majority of Christians follow this practice inherited by Jews from Zoroastrians in their churches. Orthodox and Catholic churches strictly observe the practice with an "altar light" suspended from the ceiling above the altar, and in Anglican cathedrals and in certain Lutheran congregations a "sanctuary lamp" hangs or stands. There may be other candles during the services of worship, especially two standing on the altar to represent the divinity and the humanity of Christ. The candle, light, or lamp that remains perpetually burning may serve as an example of Zoroastrianism coming into the church through its Jewish parent who adopted it in Babylon and continue the practice as described in the previous chapter.

purification rites

Most New Testament uses of words for purity relate to cleanness of some type, with an echo of the Hebrew Scriptures as in "Let us approach (the house of God) with a pure heart full of faith, and with our hearts sprinkled clean and our bodies washed with pure water"[34] (a reference to baptism). Most such references may be seen as symbolic, and if the Jews did add certain Zoroastrian purification rites to their religion under the influence of Nehemiah, the power of such rites was condensed by Christians into the "ritual" sacrifice of Jesus as the Lamb of God, a more distinctly Hebraic learning. There are other references to a pure heart, and the person who is in right relationship with God is to live a life of purity, which is listed among the Christian "virtues," but this does not rise to the level of ritual. While Jesus appears generally observant of Jewish cultural and religious purity rituals, he cautions against making such dietary rules more important than ethical observance, as when he teaches the multitude, "there is nothing outside a person that by going in the mouth can defile, but the things that go out of the mouth are what defile a person."[35] For Christians, the purification through sacrifice effected through the death of Christ is preeminent and does not need repeating.[36] While certain Christians make its reenactment in the "sacrifice of the mass" into a ritual as complex Zoroastrian rites today, there is no ritual connection with either Jewish or Zoroastrian practices in the matter of purification rites.

Redeemer

God as a redeemer, a function embodied in the role of the Saoshyant, was central to the Zoroastrianism encountered by the Jews in Babylon. While perhaps influenced by the Saoshyant image during the Exile, Second Isaiah makes it clear that God alone is the Redeemer of Israel, which means that redemption is not accomplished through another agency like the evolving understanding of the messiah's role, thus falling short of the later Christian belief that the Messiah (Saoshyant/Redeemer) is God in person (not the Jewish understanding, nor the later Muslim version). The Christian reversion to the Zoroastrian understanding of the Saoshyant/Redeemer/Messiah is almost certainly an indication of direct contact, probably by Jesus himself. It is not necessary to adopt the "Jesus in India" legends as history, despite their strength in a prevalence that often surprises Western Christians, who generally believe that if it did not get recorded in Western scriptures, it did not happen. That is the position of most Christians in spite of the New Testament teaching that he did so many other unrecorded things that the whole world could not hold the books required to describe them.[37] More attention needs to be given to the New Testament passages that indicate his travels in Zoroastrian regions, possibly beginning during his "lost years," the time between his bar mitzvah in Jerusalem at the age of twelve and his reappearance in ministry at the age of thirty.[38]

Resurrection

Our investigation of the links between Zoroastrian and Jewish teachings about resurrection were especially thorough, partly in preparation for consideration of Christianity where this doctrine or putative observation of the resurrection of Jesus, first by the disciples, followed by multitudes, became the essential touchstone of the new religion. Yet when we get to it in Christianity, it is as impossible to simply recapitulate succinctly as it would be to adequately summarize the Jewish quintessential concept of the People of God or the Islamic *sine qua non* doctrine of the Quran. For the purposes of this study, it might be simply maintained that the New Testament verses about resurrection most resembling Zoroastrian doctrine are those that speak of the general resurrection, rather than the specific resurrection of the Messiah/Saoshyant, all of which come so late in the final Common Era sections of the Avestan canon that they might be suspected of borrowing from Christians instead of the other way round.

However, whether derived from conversations with Zoroastrians during the Exile or not, the Hebrew Scriptures are replete with verses that Christians have found easily applicable to the resurrection of the Messiah. This should not be regarded as the petulant imaginings of a new sect attempting to justify its existence through selective quoting from the scriptures of the parent religion, but rather as the use of what was then their own scripture to make sense of their recent experience, as they perceived it, an experience that they found difficult to fathom without scriptural warrant. The question of how much Zoroastrian and how much Jewish influence is found in the Christian doctrine of Resurrection is perhaps overshadowed by reference to a Far Eastern story they both treasured, and which is specific in this regard, as noted below in the note on the book of Job.

RiveR Rites

We have speculated about the growing realization that Jesus must have traveled during his "missing years," and almost certainly was exposed to Zoroastrian lore and practices during that time and subsequently. The fact that post-exilic Jews made so little of the Zoroastrian river rites might make us think that when Jesus deliberately chose public baptism in the Jordan River to launch his ministry, he may have only recently returned from travels in Zoroastrian territory. This river rite was insisted upon by Jesus despite protests by John the Baptist, and it was replete with the divine voice, and even followed by an encounter with "the tempter," exactly as recorded concerning Zoroaster, whose mantle he took at that moment as extended to the Saoshyant Messiah. The lack of significant Jewish precedence makes this one of the evidences amounting to proof of a direct connection between Jesus and Zoroastrian teachings.

salvation

In Zoroastrianism, as it evolved through the Sassanian era and into the Common Era, it was believed that at the climax of the struggle between good and evil, Ahura Mazda, known then as Ormazd, would triumph over Ahriman, or Satan, and the Saoshyant, as God's agent, would resurrect the dead for judgment. The righteous would pass to their reward in heaven and the wicked would be cast into hell, but both were temporary states. A meteor would finally strike the earth, causing a flood of molten metal. All would have to pass through this torrent as an ordeal of purgation. The reaction of each to this test would be determined by the extent of their faithfulness and service in the cause of good. After this ordeal, everyone would become immortal, and all those who Ahriman had harmed or corrupted would be renewed. Salvation thus took the form of deliverance from postmortem suffering, and ultimate restoration was assured to all after suffering the degree of purgation that the nature of their earthly lives entailed. From this it may be surmised that the Christian vision of personal salvation owed little to the Jewish model of redemption in the corporate context, and much to the Zoroastrian tradition. This particular Zoroastrian model was not even known by Zoroastrians in Babylon during the Exile. From the known dates of later Avesta material, it is clear that it was circulating in the contemporary and less lofty Zoroastrianism of the time of Christ, and through the early church era as later Christian Scriptures were developing. This again implies a direct connection, perhaps by Jesus, but more likely by John and others in the early church. The ransom theology of Paul, also clearly related to another Zoroastrian model, would support the theory of direct awareness in the church, such theology not being seen in the Jewish heritage of Christianity.

satan

In Christianity the classical doctrine of the Devil is almost exactly identical to the Zoroastrian concept. The Devil, or Satan, is a being who is evil, through pride, just as Zarathushtra's evil spirit is evil, and both seek to corrupt humanity. Both regard evil as more than somebody's bad idea, believing rather that the spirit of evil itself is ignored at humanity's peril. This devil, as Christians have traditionally believed, not only roams about attempting to corrupt people but also has corrupted the physical world, just as Ahriman does in the later Zoroastrian teachings. Christianity also adopted Jewish—and Zoroastrian—apocalyptic myths about cosmic battles and the upcoming end of the world into its own doctrine. The Christian book of Revelation, the last book in the New Testament canon, is a later example of a form that goes back all the way through its Jewish sources to the distant, ancient worlds of Iran and Mesopotamia.

the book of job

In the oldest book of the Bible, written even before the Pentateuch was completed as the Torah we know, Job prophesied from the ash heap where he suffered. He declared, "I know that my redeemer liveth, and that he shall stand at the latter day upon the earth. And though after my skin, worms will destroy my body, yet in my flesh shall I see God."[39] The last friend to visit Job in his misery is Elihu, whose name actually means "God in Person," a persona who is seen by Christians as a Christ figure or a prophecy of Christ. This is yet another hint of the Vedic Zoroastrian origins of the book of Job, since Zoroaster was the first to prophesy a Redeeming Messiah who will appear in person at the climax of time. Elihu assures Job that God has promised to deliver him and, most remarkably from a Christian perspective, this deliverance is because God has provided a "ransom,"[40] a familiar Zoroastrian motif. Twice in the Christian gospels it is emphasized that Jesus came "as a ransom for many."[41] This theology is then echoed by Saint Paul, who writes, "There is one God and one mediator between God and men, the man, Jesus Christ; who gave himself as a ransom for all."[42]

We do not know, and we may never know, if anything placing Jesus in India is true, or if he only went to Persia, or perhaps just to Syria—the latter trips for which the biblical record is univocal, suggesting that the visits recorded there were subsequent to previous travels. For that matter, if Jesus and his parents made it all the way to Egypt soon after his birth (a trip some regard as apocryphal), the likelihood that a shorter trip was made by Jesus to at least Zoroastrian Syria is actually immense, even without the biblical record. The young man from Nazareth would have often crossed the Galilee, from which point he could have reached Syria any day before noon. He may well have gone farther, but our minimal projection takes this speculation out of the sphere of the bizarre and into the realm of the perfectly reasonable. If a young Muhammad was exposed to Eastern Zoroastrianism, for better and for worse, in caravan trips to Syria from even farther away, and if Jesus's family found refuge in Egypt to be within reach, we should almost certainly conclude that Jesus traveled at least short distances as a single, young man, unless he was totally devoid of interest in even the nearer reaches of the wider world. If such travels did take place, we should expect that they would be reflected in the stories of his life, his teaching, and his ministry—and we now see that they are.

The river baptism that launched his vocation and the I AM motif used throughout his ministry are all related to the connection in which we now see clear Zoroastrian imprints on both Christmas and Easter, as more fully documented in *Three Testaments: Torah, Gospel, and Quran*. Recapitulation and elaboration of those points may be in order if we are to realize that the Zoroastrian motif is as profoundly significant in the Christian Scriptures as we now recognize it to be in the Hebrew Scriptures.

In the New Testament we have identified Zoroastrian elements with the appearance of the Magi in the birth narrative. The Roman holiday on December 25 was previously dedicated to Mithra, the Vedic deva of light who had been reformed by Zoroaster into an "Immortal," or angel, and celebrated as "the Unconquered Sun" on the then winter solstice, when the light began its annual comeback. Was it mere coincidence that Christians took that as the appropriate date to celebrate the birth of Christ? It was Jesus himself who later said, "I AM the *light* of the world,"[43] perhaps speaking as much as Saoshyant as Messiah. The Zoroastrian motif continues in his teenage years when Jesus was growing up with increasing "Wisdom" and in favor with the people of humanity.[44] The Zoroastrian motif occurs next in the baptism of Jesus with a river scene revelation reminiscent of Zoroaster's commissioning, and in the immediate appearance of "the tempter." We have clear indications of his exposure to Zoroastrianism in Sidon and Tyre, where a Syro-Phoenician woman challenges him to admit that the Messiah is the savior of all people rather than one who would merely restore the throne of his own people. Throughout his ministry he makes use of the I AM phrase in a manner reminiscent of Zoroaster's use of God's phrase to Moses at the burning bush in the Little Avesta. Jesus also exhibits an emphasis on the Last Judgment not seen since Zoroaster. We might even ask whether Jesus reinterpreted the Hindu "born again" theme to make it available and pertinent to this life. There is no Hebraic precedent for this concept, but a superabundant Vedic/Zoroastrian/Hindu tradition of rebirth exists, of which we now believe Jesus may have had knowledge.

At the end or climax of his life Jesus concluded his ministry profoundly in the Zoroastrian mode during the events leading up to and during the crucifixion and resurrection. At his preliminary trial, the high priest, Caiaphas, asked him, "Are you the Messiah, the Son of the Blessed One?" The earliest gospel has Jesus answer specifically, "I AM."[45] He then goes directly to Zoroastrian imagery, speaking again to Caiaphas, "You will see the Son of Man . . . coming with the clouds of heaven"[46] (a resurrection saying of the prophet Daniel in Babylon, whether apocryphal or historical). The gospel story ends with a penultimate closing scene with the repentant thief—"today you will be with me in *paradise*" (not "heaven")—in which Jesus appears to be operating in full Zoroastrian mode, leading to a three-day funereal event like the Zoroastrian models, and with no Jewish parallel. Finally, since Babylon there had been certain views and hints of resurrection theology among the Jews, and Christians managed to portray the resurrection of Jesus as fulfillment of Jewish expectation. Suffice it to say simply that those expectations were not nearly as intense or as specific as the Zoroastrian doctrine of the Saoshyant at the time of Christ. The Eastern influence of Zoroastrianism in Western monotheistic traditions can at last be recognized for what it is in Judaism and Christianity.

When the church regained its bearings in Jewish heritage late in the twentieth century, it was necessary to recognize that putative foundational connections to Greek philosophy and Egyptian religion, while reflecting a Mediterranean interchange in the first mission era, had been exaggerated. In this study, there is no intention to undo the recovery of the essential Jewish connection, but there is every intention to make the point that through Zoroastrianism (which had disappeared from Western radar screens) Asia figures at least as prominently in the Christian message as Europe or North Africa ever did, and it almost rivals Judaism in our claim that it is almost foundational for the church. The church's understanding of creation of the universe by the Messiah, the perpetual light, hell, purgatory, and paradise all imply a direct connection with Zoroastrianism beyond the personal experiences of Jesus, as does the church understanding of salvation, the "ransom" theology of Saint Paul, the apocalyptic material in Revelation, and liturgical remnants in church liturgy. At a minimum, we may assert that the usual Christian view of Jesus as both "Lord and Savior" points to the dual heritage of Davidic messianism (Lord of the realm in Israel) and Zoroastrian Saoshyant (the savior of the world).

z-related passages in the new testament

Matthew 5:22	Matthew 19:1
Matthew 8:12	Matthew 20:28
Matthew 12:40	Matthew 27:63
Matthew 15:21–28	Mark 7:24–37
Matthew 16:13	Mark 8:27
Matthew 18:8	Mark 8:31

Mark 9:31
Mark 10:1
Mark 10:34
Mark 10:45
Mark 14:62
Luke 9:22
Luke 9:28
Luke 16:8
Luke 18:33
Luke 24:7
Luke 24:46
John 1:3
John1:5
John 1:28–29
John 3:16–17
John 4:6
John 6:35, 41, 48–51
John 8:12
John 9:5
John 10:7–9
John 10:11–14

John 10:40
John 11:25
John 12:35
John 12:36
John 12:46
John 15:1–5
John 21:25
Acts 10:40
Acts 26:18
2 Corinthians 6:14
Ephesians 5:8
Ephesians 6:12
Philippians 3:19
Philippians 3:20
Philippians 3:21
Colossians 1:16
1 Timothy 2:6
1 Thessalonians 5:4
1 Thessalonians 5:5
Revelation 7:9
Revelation 20:10

13
chinvat bridge: the final judgment

Zoroastrian Scriptures and "Previous Revelations" Corrected and Confirmed in the Quran

The study of Islam as a religion (and of the Quran) as providing the "presiding idea" and dominating principle of a major world civilization is of great significance not only because it makes better known the worldview of more than a billion people (second only to Christianity with over two billion people) ranging from blue-eyed Slavs and Berbers to blacks, from Arabs to Malays, from Turks and Persians to Chinese. It is also significant because Islam and its civilization have played a far greater role than usually admitted in the genesis and development of European (and including American) civilization. Today Islam constitutes the second largest religious community in Europe and has a population of the same size as Judaism in America (or surpassing in 2015). But most of all, the study of Islam is significant because it concerns a message from God revealed within that very Abrahamic world from which Judaism and Christianity have issued forth. The Islamic revelation is the third and final revelation of the Abrahamic monotheistic cycle and constitutes a major branch of the tree of monotheism. It is, therefore, a religion without whose study the knowledge of the whole religious family to which Jews and Christians belong would be incomplete.[1]

IN SPITE OF GENEROUSLY INCLUSIVE AND RELATIONAL SENTIMENTS IN THE QURAN, WITH MUCH beauty and both personal and communal fulfillment in countless situations, Islam appears to reel through the twenty-first century, with conflicts between Muslims and others exceeded only by conflicts between Muslims and Muslims. This may not be very different from the horrors of the "world wars" in the twentieth century, mainly between Christians, with their anti-Semitism resulting in the Holocaust of Jews. While readily conceding the importance of Islam and the validity of its core message, the question to arise in the current context is "Who speaks for Islam?"

The answer to that question is the Holy Quran! Muslims may not much agree with each other, but they all agree that the Quran is the basis of their faith, more even than the Prophet Muhammad, and certainly more than the various traditions of interpretive jurisprudence, as important as they are. We begin this analysis of echoes of the East in the Quran with an acknowledgment that in bringing critical analysis to our study of the Islamic Scriptures, nothing in this compendium is premised on views that are in particular conflict with Muslim traditions of understanding the Quran. Indeed, properly understood, the Quran may be said to confirm all truths of the previous revelations.

The Muslim view is that the Quran was revealed directly to Muhammad in a series of recitations that were written down by family members he called the People of the House. Many of these revelations are similar to stories in the Hebrew and Christian Scriptures, some of which Jewish and Christian scholars would agree have become "jumbled" in the collecting and transmission of communal documents inspired by God. Muslims are traditionally of the view that all the material in the Quran was revealed freshly to Muhammad, "correcting" more than Jews and Christians would think necessary, but basically "confirming" and "amplifying" the previous revelations. This understanding possibly includes material from the Zoroastrian Scriptures as known to the Sabaeans who were "People of the Book" but with no book of their own except the Avesta, then in wide circulation throughout the Persian Empire locations where Sabaeans lived.

Muhammad did not copy or edit these revelations from any earthly "source," but no Muslims contend that he was the only resident of Arabia unfamiliar with the stories of Abraham and all the other prophets before receiving the fresh revelations. Rather, it could be after discussion with local Jews and Christians (or Salman, his Zoroastrian "Companion") that God would reveal the story or information afresh, in either its uncorrupted original content or a new format required for presentation to Arabic audiences and to humanity. Muhammad's first wife was Christian, as were other women he married later in life, in a "polygamy" identical to the culture of the earlier Torah. Two other wives were Jewish, and his circle included many Jews and Christians, including a monk who first recognized him as a prophet and a cousin of his first wife who first recognized the Quran as being from God. Of all the persons named in the Quran, all but one or two are found in Hebrew or Christian Scriptures or both, most of them being prophets. The amplifications of their stories without biographical detail presume that the Muslim reader already knows David and Goliath, Mary and Jesus, and all the others, just as the Christian reader is presumed to know Jonah, Job, and the cast of characters from the Hebrew Scriptures, making the Quran the third and final testament of the Abrahamic trilogy.

There are Muslim fundamentalists in our time who take the Quran literally rather than as a literary expression of profound spiritual truths in verses that, in the Quran, are called "ayahs" or symbols, meant to be recited or breathed as the breath of God. There are Jewish and Christian fundamentalists who have limited understanding of the profound depths of their own scriptures, but the vast majority are informed by the poetic and literary character of the Bible. In the Muslim community there is a sensitivity to radical extremism that we join in respecting, but only to the extent that fundamentalist Jews and Christians also require patient understanding and restricted influence. Over the centuries there have been wise and appropriate traditions of Quranic interpretations, and even today many classic translations have more words in footnote explanation than words in the text itself.

Our approach is to simply recognize the Muslim belief that previous revelations were given afresh to Muhammad, corrected, confirmed, and amplified. Our investigation will simply point to situations in which many versions of the stories in the Quran appeared previously, to be corrected or confirmed in the Quran according to Muslim understanding. Certain Muslim and non-Muslim scholars have been known to take a more radical approach in suggesting the Quran is a bad copy of other material, or that it was written by someone else, but nobody associated with this project would advance such views, and they are completely unnecessary in appreciation of the relationship between the Quran and the previous revelations. That said, there is a plethora of connections of interest to our study, which we present one item at a time in the expectation that discovery of the long-lost text of the Avesta will eventually be of particular benefit in Quranic studies. Even without that, there are many connections between Islam and the Zoroastrianism we now see as the parent of both monism and monotheism, the Oneness of God East and West.

A nonscriptural overlap between Islam and Zoroastrianism continues in the Iranian national epic, the *Shahnamah*, from the ninth- or tenth-century CE Samanid Dynasty. The Muslim author, Ferdowsi, saturated the poem with Zoroastrian ideas, like attributing the origins of the Iranian people to a battle against the Zoroastrian figure, Angra Mainyu the destructive spirit. This is a work that established the Iranian language in written form as a bulwark against the Arabic language. The Iranian/Persian ethnic identity has always maintained Zoroastrian imagery as a fallback or default characteristic, and Iran today maintains a Zoroastrian presence in parliament, under the constitution, unbroken since 1906 and even through the 1979 Islamic Revolution. Indeed, Ayatollah Sadughi proclaimed, "We Muslims are like the branches of a tree, if our roots are cut off, we shall shrivel up and die."[2]

Counterintuitive to Western media reports and some evidence to the contrary in recent times, Islam has traditionally been more tolerant of minorities than has Christian Europe. The Druze, Yazidis, Mandeans, Gnostics, Yarsans, Shaktas, Christians, Jews, Zoroastrians, and dozens of other sects are under pressure these days. But they stand in contrast to the situation in Europe where Druids, Albegensians, Cathars, Wicca, devotees of the Norse pantheon, and dozens of other religious minorities have been eliminated, along with the secrets of Stonehenge, except for the Jews who nearly met the same fate as recently as the twentieth century. The Islamic parallel to the Jewish persecution in Europe is the jeopardy in which the Baha'i find themselves in Iran, but Zoroastrians at least remain a protected minority.

At the height of Islamic culture during Europe's dark ages, the Iranian University of Gundesshapur had a curriculum that included Greek and Chinese texts, and, more germane in reference to Zoroastrianism, it even included courses in Sanskrit.[3] This is in stark contrast to the current situation in Muslim cultures illustrated by a decision at the Prince Mohammed Bin Fahd University in Saudi Arabia, rejecting the gift of a library copy of *Three Testaments: Torah, Gospel, and Quran* by one of its professors in 2014. The lead librarian wrote to him, saying, "While the Library does have a few resources on Judaism and Christianity, we do not have any materials that are a comparative study of Judaism, Christianity, and Islam. I feel the intent of this book could be misconstrued by certain library users."[4]

While no cultural connections between Islam and Zoroastrianism are as convincing as the religious hints in the Quran itself connecting the two, we have the good fortune to have had this subject investigated by an impeccable Islamic scholar and jurist, who bases much of his information about Zoroaster on research done by an earlier historian of equally good repute, writing during the early years of Islamic expansion. Our scholar, Abu Ja'far Muhammad ibn Jarir al-Tabari (839–923 CE), was a prominent and influential Persian jurist, historian, and exegete of the Quran from Tabaristan, known as Mazandaran in modern Iran. His primary source was Hisham Ibn Al-Kalbi (737–819 CE), an Arab historian, born in Kufa, who spent much of his life in Baghdad. He specialized in records located in Palmyra, Syria, which was the final stronghold of Zoroastrian intellectual life in the transition to Islam, a city where the ancient ruins were destroyed as recently as 2015. Al-Kalbi's book, *Djamharat al Nasab* ("The Abundance of Kinship"), was translated into German by Werner Caskel (*Das genealogische Werk des Hisam Ibn Muhammad al Kalbi*) in 1966. It is the information from Al-Kalbi as distilled by al-Tabari that interests us, given its ancient provenance.

First, these worthies convey a report that Zaradusht bin Isfiman (an Arabic adaptation of the name "Zarathustra," and his surname, "Spitama") was an inhabitant of Israel and was a servant of either the prophet Jeremiah or his disciple Baruch.[5] The direct connection with Israel is by modern accounts erroneous, but this may reflect the speculation by ourselves and others that Zoroaster was connected with Israelite exiles. A connection with the prophet Jeremiah in research of such ancient provenance is especially germane to our thesis developed earlier by other means.

Second, according to this information, Zaradusht defrauded his master, who cursed him, causing him to become leprous (see the story of Elisha's servant Gehazi in the same region of Syria at 2 Kings 5:27 of the Hebrew Scripture to consider how such tales are based on oral realities). The renegade Zaradusht then eventually made his way to Balkh (in current-day Afghanistan), his ancient center according to our modern research also. Here, according to Al-Kalbi, via al-Tabari, he converted Bishtasb (known to us as Vishtāspa), who in turn compelled his subjects to adopt this religion of the Magians.[6] Also interesting, recalling another tradition in a related document published between 681 and 683 CE, al-Tabari claims that Zaradusht was accompanied by a Jewish prophet at the court of Bishtasb/Vishtāspa. Zaradusht translated the prophet's Hebrew teachings for the king and convinced him to convert to the faith they shared with the Jews, which we are to understand also represents the faith confirmed in the revelations given to Muhammad in the Quran—in one view held in early Islam.

Finally, just as those Zoroastrians were not known by that name (which, as mentioned earlier, does not even appear in the Avesta, for the same reason that "Jews" are never mentioned by that name in the Torah, nor are "Christians" called such in the gospels), Tabari notes on his own authority that these new believers had previously been "Sabaeans in the Magian religion."[7] This is very significant since, with the assistance of modern Islamic scholars,[8] the Sabaeans mentioned as People of the Book in the Quran are acknowledged as Zoroastrians in *Three Testaments: Torah, Gospel, and Quran*. Tabari is the first to make this assertion, which solves innumerable problems in reference to the Islamic identification of both the Sabaeans and the Zoroastrians (Magians) as People of the Book in relation to their presence in the Quran.[9]

angelology

In the Arabic of both Christians and Muslims, angels are called *mala'ika*, from the word meaning "to assist or help." In Islam, it is believed that before the creation of humans from clay or earth, angels had been created out of light, not a far stretch from the Immortals of Zoroastrianism, associated with the star-like planets. They are without gender and have no need of food, drink, or even sleep. Angels do not have free will so they are instinctively obedient, worshipping God and carrying out His commands. The Quran says, "They do not disobey God's commands as received; they do exactly what they are commanded."[10] "Everything in the heavens and every creature on the earth is to prostrate before God, as do the angels. They are not puffed up with pride. They fear their Lord above them and do everything they are ordered to do."[11] Angels are involved in carrying out duties in both the unseen and the physical worlds.

Seven angels are mentioned by name in the Quran, with a description of their responsibilities, again not too far distant from Zoroastrian concepts as seen in the appearance of the seven Immortals, and archangels, as they are called in the Hebrew and Christian texts:

Jibreel (Gabriel): communicating God's words to His prophets[12]
Israfeel (Raphael): blowing the trumpet to mark the Day of Judgment
Mikail (Michael): in charge of rainfall and provisions required for life
Munkar or Nakeer: questions souls in the grave about their faith and deeds
Malak Am-Maut: Angel of Death who takes possession of souls after death
Malik: the guardian of hell
Ridwan: the guardian of heaven

creation

Modern Islamic commentators are fond of describing the creation of the heavens and the earth, in terminology akin to the "Big Bang Theory," which resonates with creation verses in Quranic teaching. The Quran says that "the heavens and the earth were joined together as one atom, before We split them asunder."[13] Following this cataclysm, God "turned to the sky, which was all as smoke. He said to it and to the earth: 'Come together, willingly or unwillingly.' They said: 'We come together in willing obedience.'"[14] Thus everything from atoms to planets took shape, cooled down and came together in patterns following the natural laws that God established in the universe.

The Quran then states that God gave the sun, the moon, and the planets their own individual courses or orbits: "It is He Who created the night and the day, and the sun and the moon; all the celestial bodies swing along, each in its rounded course."[15] Like the Vedic prototype as reformed and developed by Zoroaster, Jews, Christians, and Muslims all believe in a linear concept of time, beginning with a creation, progressing through the ages of history, and an end of time in this world culminating in the establishment of paradise or heaven. While there is no question that Zoroaster was using a linear time model, the previous Vedic concept was one of cyclical time through eternity, and it is this previous Vedic model that was adopted through the East, including the four religions under consideration in this compendium. Through recent Communist influence in China and British influence in India, everyday life appears to be conducted on the Western model in the East in the twenty-first century, religion notwithstanding.

The Quran in particular has a whole chapter dedicated to descriptions of the end times, the judgment of the dead, and the eternal reward and punishment of saints and sinners—an eschatology similar to the storyline of the Christian book of Revelation and to some elements in the Jewish books of Isaiah and Daniel, all demonstratively cast in the Zoroastrian mode. If Zoroastrianism was a stimulus to religious thinking, or promoted openness to revelations, it is clear that as with the monistic/monotheistic divide, advancement could occur in different directions without denying the timing, the Silk Route connections, or other aspects that affected these developments, loosely or tightly coordinated as they might be.

The descriptions of creation in the Quran are limited in details, presuming every Muslim's knowledge of the biblical account of events of the seven days and the creation of humans from a piece of clay, referred to as "primordial soup" by some scientists, mixed with "single drop of sperm" in the Quran. Rather, to engage the reader in contemplating the lessons to be learned from it, the act of creation is frequently spoken of in a way designed to highlight the Creator, Who is behind it all.

> Verily in the heavens and the earth there are signs for those who believe. And in the creation of yourselves, and the fact that animals are scattered through the earth, are signs for those of assured faith. And in the alternation of night and day, and that fact that God sends down sustenance from the sky, and revives therewith the earth after its death, and in the change of the winds, are signs for those who are wise.[16]

Just as it is impossible to read the New Testament without knowledge of the things referred to in the Hebrew Scriptures, the succeeding creation accounts make it clear again that we are dealing here with a divine trilogy of Torah, Gospel, and Quran, but with a possible backdrop in eastern Vedic imagery as reformed by Zoroaster.

demonology

In contrast to the angels in Islamic theology, demons known as *jinn* are said to possess free will. Except for their chief, Iblis or Satan (both terms used in the Quran), the jinn (a plural word with a singular form *jinnī*) are not always necessarily evil, and from them we get the English word "genie," first employed in the translations of *The Book of One Thousand and One Nights*. Made from smokeless fire by God, as humans were made of clay and angels of light, jinn are frequently mentioned in the Quran. The *Sūrat al-Jinn*[17] is named after the jinn, and the Quran also mentions that Muhammad was sent as a prophet to both "humanity and the jinn," and that prophets and other messengers were sent to both communities. The social structures of the jinn communities resemble those of human beings; they have kings, courts of law, weddings, and mourning rituals. They are normally invisible to humans, but humans can be seen clearly by jinn, who can possess them. Jinn have the power to travel large distances at the speed of light and are said to live in their own remote communities in mountains, seas, trees, and the air. Just like humans, jinn will be judged on the Day of Judgment and will be sent to Paradise or Hell according to their deeds. We might note in passing that while "progressives" in many of these religious traditions have difficulty "believing in" a literal existence of angels and demons, and relegate jinn to the status of leprechauns in Ireland, it is often these very progressive thinkers who insist that intelligent life may exist beyond earth or move among us in "alien" forms.

fire sacrifices

If little or nothing could be found in the Christian Scriptures related to fire sacrifices, the Quran goes a step further in offering strident condemnation of practices involving fire, a change understood as "correction" of corrupt scriptural records concerning previous revelation, especially Zoroastrianism in this regard.

final judgment

The connecting element referenced in the title of this chapter is especially germane as a place to begin this phase of our comparative investigation. The Chinvat Bridge is the Zoroastrian "bridge of judgment," sometimes called the *Chinvat Peretu* or "bridge of the requite." It is described under the first name in the extant Avesta[18] as the "sifting bridge" that separates what we might call heaven and earth. To gain Paradise (the third heaven), the soul of the dead person (which remains on earth near the body for three days) must cross the bridge, which appears narrow to sinners and wide to the just. It is guarded by two four-eyed dogs, exactly identical to the four-eyed dogs of *Yama*, the Hindu ruler of the netherworld who guards the gates of hell, an indication of just how wide this Eastern tradition is by the time it reaches Islam. In Zoroastrian Scripture three servants of God act as sentinels on the bridge: Obedience (*Sraosha*), Covenant (*Mithra*), and Justice (*Rashnu*), who question, council, and judge. The Chinvat Bridge is sometimes identified with the rainbow, or with the Milky Way, and the souls that successfully cross it become One with Ahura Mazda. For Muslims, this bridge is called the *As-Sirat*, which every soul must cross on Judgment Day to enter Paradise. It is as thin as the blade of a sword for everyone, and the fires of hell burn below to scorch sinners to make them fall, while the just are enabled to speed across, arriving at the Lake of Abundance. In the following, narrated by Muhammad's Companion, Abu Sa'id Al-Khudri, not in the Quran but in the Haddith, the Zoroastrian inspiration is the obvious foundation of this element of Middle Eastern sacred lore:

> We, the companions of the Prophet said, "O Allah's Apostle! What is the bridge?" He said, "It is a slippery bridge on which there are clamps and hooks like a thorny seed that is wide at one side and narrow at the other and has thorns with bent ends. Such a thorny seed is found in Najd and is called As-Sa'dan. Some of the believers will cross the bridge as quickly as the wink of an eye, some others as quick as lightning, a strong wind, fast horses or she-camels. So some will be safe without any harm; some will be safe after receiving some scratches, and some will fall down into Hell. The last person will cross by being dragged over the bridge."[19]

funerary practices

In Islamic practice a funeral (*janazah*) can be subject to regional, ethnic, and sectarian customs, but within the *sharia* framework of Islamic law based on the Quran. This requires washing, both minor ablutions (*wudu*) and full body (*ghusl*), before shrouding and burial of the body, followed by prayer (*salah*), all normally within twenty-four hours of death. Cremation of the body is forbidden. We include such information only for comparative purposes and to illustrate the lack of any Zoroastrian or other Eastern influence at this point.

hell

Hell, or *jahannam* (from the Hebrew *gehenna*), is mentioned frequently in the Quran. It has seven doors[20] leading to a fiery crater that has levels similar to Dante's *Inferno*. The lowest of these rings of fire contains the *Zaqqum* tree[21] of poisoned fruit, and a stream of boiling pitch, reminiscent of our Zoroastrian precedent that so influenced Jewish and Christian imagery. The level of descent to hell depends on the degree of offenses. Suffering is both physical and spiritual. Being a Muslim does not enable a sinner to avoid hell, but it is not clear whether bad Muslims remain in hell forever. Non-Muslims (*kafir*), however, especially those who persecute Muslims, will be punished eternally in the opinion of most Muslim commentators. Others note that in mercy, grace, and compassion, God can rescue people from hell as God chooses, and hell may be actually emptied after the Final Judgment and the working out of its consequences. The heterodox Ahmadi position is that "Life after death is actually the starting-point of further progress for man. Those in paradise are advancing to higher and higher stages in knowledge and perfection of faith. Hell is meant to purify those in it of the effects of their bad deeds, and so make them fit for further advancement. Its punishment is, therefore, not everlasting."[22]

i am

In Islam there are traditionally ninety-nine names for God, most listed in the Quran, to which is added the highest Name (*al-ism al-ʾaʿẓam*), the Supreme Name of God: *Allāh*. While it is obvious that this is the Arabic pronunciation of the generic pre-Islamic Semitic name of God, given in Hebrew as *Eloh*, Muslims far from Arabia have sometimes imagined that it appears only in the Quran as a sacred name that should not be used by non-Muslims, Arab speaking or otherwise. Suffice it to observe in this connection that while I AM (*ehyeh asher ehyeh*, or I Am what I Am in the King James Version) is found in the scriptures of Jews, Zoroastrians, and Christians, no equivalent is found in the Quran, and it is never used by Muslims in spite of respect for the other scriptures.

messiah

In the Quran the Messiah is *ʿĪsā al-Masih* in Arabic (though spelled *Yasūʿ al-Masih* by Arab Christians), more fully *Īsā al-Masih Ibn Maryam*, Jesus the Christ, son of Mary. Far more than "merely" a prophet as charged by Christian Islamophobes, he is the Messenger of God who was sent to guide the Children of Israel (*banī isrāʾīl*) and to provide a new scripture, *al-Injīl* (the Gospel). He was born of the Virgin Mary (who appears far more often in the Quran than in the Bible) and was devoted to her, engaged his disciples, and performed miracles of healing (which no other prophet ever did, in Islamic understanding). Jesus appeared to be crucified but did not die; he ascended to paradise and will return in a "second coming" to prepare believers and to usher in the Day of Judgment. He is not part of a Holy Trinity and does not personally "redeem" the people, but his role is more specifically religious than the Jewish image of the Messiah. Again, this is more like the Zoroastrian Saoshyant, though to this point we have no linguistic markers or other evidence linking the messianic motif in the Quran to the Avesta. In Islam, Jesus is regarded as a precursor to Muhammad, and is believed by Muslims to have prophesied the latter's coming in the promise of a Comforter, Paraclete, or "Advocate" (an "Ahmad" in Arabic, which is part of Muhammad's name) as attested in the Quran itself.[23]

paradise

Paradise (*firdaws*) is also called "The Garden" (*Janna*), as in the Quranic quotation, "O soul who is at rest, return to thy Lord, well-pleased with Him, well-pleasing Him. So enter among My servants, and enter My garden."[24] The first of these Arabic words is one of the clearest linguistic markers of Persian providence, and the second is an image tightly connected to Zoroastrianism, both given freshly to Muhammad by God in confirmation of the earlier revelations to People of the Book. Paradise is a higher plane of physical and spiritual pleasure, where the believers live in lofty mansions[25] and partake of fine food and good drink,[26] and faithful men are attended by virgin companions called *houris*,[27] another of the clearest of Persian linguistic markers and the most-quoted benefit of paradise in the Quran.[28] There are seven levels of such heavens, again related more to previous revelations in Zoroastrianism than to Jewish or Christian precedents.[29]

perpetual fire

The above comments about fire sacrifices in general would also apply here.

purification rites

Purification rites in Islam are mainly centered on the preparation for ritual prayer, taking the form of ablution, in a lesser form (*wudu*), and greater form (*ghusl*), depending on the situation. The greater form is obligatory by a woman after she ceases menstruation, on a corpse that didn't die during battle, and by men after sexual activity. *Ghusl* is optionally used on other occasions—for example, just prior to Friday prayers—whereas *wudu* would be appropriate before prayers on other days. Ideally ritual purification remains valid for a full day but becomes invalid on the occurrence of certain acts: flatulence, sleep, contact with the opposite gender (depending on the school of jurisprudence), and the emission of blood, semen, or vomit. Some schools of jurisprudence require that ritual purity is necessary before touching or holding the Quran. The parallels with previous revelations in Zoroastrianism (both ancient and modern) are obvious, somewhat less so with Judaism, and least with Christianity.

redeemer

In the Last Days, according to the Islamic tradition, a Redeemer will appear in the person of the Mahdi (*Guided One*) who will rule for seven, nine, or nineteen years (according to various traditions) before the Day of Judgment, when the Mahdi will banish evil from the world. There are no references to the Mahdi in the Quran, but Muhammad spoke about him in some of the less authoritative Hadith, so, as important as the concept may be, it is not part of the Revelation. The Mahdi will be challenged by the Anti-Christ but will be assisted to victory by Jesus in his second coming. Especially in Shia traditions of Persian Iran, this figure appears to relate to the Saoshyant imagery of the previous revelations to Zoroaster, perhaps sharing those attributes with the Masih, as described above. Shia Muslims believe the Mahdi has been born already but disappeared and will remain hidden from humanity until reappearing from *Occultation* to bring justice to the world, an event that is the subject of frequent adventist frenzy in some places these days.

Resurrection

According to Islamic tradition, the souls of the deceased repose in their graves awaiting resurrection on the Day of Judgment, though they do anticipate their individual eternities by faith, wherein those destined for paradise are already at peace and those destined for hell will suffer distress in anticipation. On the Last Day the resurrection is a physical phenomenon in which God will re-create the decayed body: "Could they not see that God who created the heavens and the earth is able to create the like of them?"[30] Only then will resurrected humans and jinn be judged by God according to their deeds. Each person's eternal destiny is calculated on a balance of good and bad deeds in life. As indicated above, the Day of Judgment is described as passing over hell on a narrow bridge in order to enter paradise. Those who fall, weighted by their bad deeds, may remain in hell forever, where they are "resurrected" to torment, not unlike Jewish and Christian literal understandings, all of which have their origins in Zoroastrian belief.

River Rites

There is no Islamic derivative of the Vedic–Zoroastrian river rites or water rites so obviously emulated in the Jewish and Christian stories of Daniel and Jesus, but an indirect connection to the ZamZam tradition may relate to similar human needs or instincts in Divine providence. The Well of Zamzam is located within the now expanded al-Haram mosque in Mecca, Saudi Arabia, the well itself being twenty meters (sixty-six feet) east of the Kaaba shrine. Muslims believe that Abraham (Ibrāhīm) had refurbished the House of God on the foundation of the original shrine, constructed by Adam (Adem), and today called the Kaaba, a building toward which Muslims around the world face in prayer, five times each day. According to Islamic belief in a story found not in the Quran but in the Bible, the Zamzam is a miraculously generated fountain or spring that was identified when Abraham's infant son Ishmael ('Ismā'īl) was thirsty and crying for water. Islamic tradition holds that the Zamzam Well was revealed to Hagar (*Hājar*), the second wife of Abraham and mother of Ishmael, as recorded in the Bible at Genesis 17:20. Abraham had left this wife and their son at a spot in the desert and departed. The desperate Hagar ran seven times back and forth in the scorching heat between the two hillocks of Safa and Marwah, looking for water. Getting thirstier by the minute, the infant Ishmael kicked the ground with his feet, whereupon water rose to the surface. In another version of the story God sent his angel, Gabriel (*Jibra'il*), who clipped the earth with his wing and the water bubbled forth. The name of the well comes from the phrase *Zomë Zomë*, meaning "stop," a command repeated by Hagar during her attempt to contain the spring of water. During their participation in the *hajj* pilgrimage, millions of pilgrims visit the well every year in order to drink its holy water.

salvation

In contrast to Jewish guilt motifs and the Christian doctrine of Original Sin (the belief that all humans are self-centered at birth, needing both grace and nurture to become God-centered), Islam teaches us that human beings are born without sin and are naturally inclined to worship God without any intermediary action by parents, priests, or a savior. At times of challenge in life, each person is to maintain this state of grace by good deeds, following God's commandments and striving to live a righteous life. If one falls into sin, sincere repentance is in order, but the Final Judgment is also based on the surplus of good works over evil deeds, rather than the free grace of God offered to a repentant sinner. In these regards, again Islam appears closer to the previous revelations on the Zoroastrian model, an observation that is consistent with many of our examples but in need of connecting links if regarded as anything more than common human response to the revelations. Such indications may be among those we anticipate finding in the lost sections of the Avesta, the "Dead Zee Scrolls," in Iran or to the north and east, if such texts are ever located.

satan

In Islam, Satan, or "Shaytan," is also (and even more frequently) known as Iblis, the jinn who refused to bow before Adam. We read the words of God: "It is We Who created you and gave you shape; then We bade the angels prostrate to Adam, and they prostrate; not so Iblis; He refused to be of those who prostrate." God asked, "What prevented thee from prostrating when I commanded thee?" Iblis replied, "I am better than he: Thou didst create me from fire, and him from clay."[31] For his disobedience, God cursed Iblis to *Jahannam* (hell) for eternity but gave him a reprieve until the Day of Judgment after Iblis appealed his sentence. Iblis then determined to use this time to lead men and women to become sinners to prove humanity's inferiority and justify his act of defiance. The primary characteristic of Iblis is hubris, but he has no influence other than the power to present evil suggestions to humans and other jinn. For refusing to abide by the will of God, Iblis was cast out of paradise, and thereafter he was called "Shaytan" (Satan).

the book of job

A segue to the book of Job in the Quran is the teaching that upon his reprieve from God, Iblis (Satan) vowed that he would use his time on earth to lead all men and women to become sinners to prove humanity's inferiority and justify his act of defiance. The Quran describes Job as a righteous servant of God, who was afflicted by suffering for a lengthy period of time. It clearly states that Job never lost faith in God and forever called to God in prayer, asking Him to remove his affliction: "And Job, when he cried unto his Lord, (saying): Lo! Adversity afflicteth me, and Thou art Most Merciful of all who show mercy."[32] The narrative continues to show how after many years of suffering, God ordered Job, "Strike with thy foot!"[33] At once, Job struck the ground with his foot, and God caused a cool spring of water to gush forth from the earth, from which Job could refresh himself. The Quran says that it was upon that sign of obedience that God relieved Job's pain and suffering, returned Job's family to him, blessed him with many generations of children, and granted him great wealth. The extent of Islam's confident reliance on the Hebrew Scriptures (collectively referred to as *Taurat*: Torah) is indicated by this masterful and succinct footnote to the Job narrative in the classic translation of the Holy Quran by Abdullah Yusuf Ali:

> Job (*Ayub*) was a prosperous man, with faith in Allah, living somewhere in the northeast corner of Arabia. He suffers from a number of calamities: his cattle are destroyed, his servants slain by the sword, and his family crushed under his roof. But he holds fast to his faith in Allah. As a further calamity he is covered with loathsome sores from head to foot. He loses his peace of mind, and he curses the day he was born. His false friends come and attribute his afflictions to sin. These "Job's comforters" are no comforters at all, and he further loses his balance of mind, but Allah recalls to him all His mercies, and he resumes his humility and gives up self-justification. He is restored to prosperity, with twice as much as he had before; his brethren and friends come back to him; he has a new family of seven sons and three fair daughters. He lived to a good old age, and saw four generations of descendants. All this is recorded in the Book of Job in the Old Testament. Of all the Hebrew writings, the Hebrew of this Book comes nearest to Arabic.[34]

The thread of Zoroastrian connection to the book of Job, which we know to be of Eastern provenance, appears to be lost in the Islamic tradition, especially since later Muslim scholars place Job in Arabia, as a descendant of Noah and an ancestor of the founders of Rome. These ill-informed Muslim speculations are unfortunate, or symbolic at best, and nobody claims them to be revelations. The evidence above is sufficient to link the book of Job of Western monotheism to its Vedic progenitors through Christian and especially Jewish connections, supported by Zoroastrian details indicated in the Bible, including those pointed out by Mary Boyce as previously referenced.

We see the reflection of Hebrew and Christian Scriptures in the Quran, but the issue of the place of Zoroastrian Scriptures in the Quran now falls into the category of what, in conversation, is sometimes called "the elephant in the room"—that is, something clearly obvious but rarely discussed or acknowledged. Since the Roman Empire and the reign of Alexander the Great are mentioned in the Quran, and since regional religions like Judaism and Christianity are discussed, how could it be possible that the Quran makes no mention of Persia and Zoroastrianism, Arabia's most powerful neighbor and its most significant religious influence at the birth of Islam, respectively? It may be that these influences are actually addressed in the Quran, but in such a manner that they are so pervasive as to be almost invisible, forming the context of much of the Islamic Scripture. Just as water is invisible to fish and air is invisible to humans, it may be only in an interfaith study like this one that the "water" (Persia) and the "air" (Zoroastrianism) of the Quran can be seen and identified as Sabaean.

The facts about Salman El-Farsi, Muhammad's Persian companion, are well known, though also usually mentioned only in passing. We recognize Z Persian "loan words," like *paradise* (heaven) and *houri* (beautiful maiden), that somehow form part of the revelations from God in the Quran, much like the *Chinvat* or *As-Sirat Bridge* that appears in the Hadith. The number of such markers in the Quran itself will grow exponentially as we proceed. Among putative linguistic markers that have been suggested as appearing in the Quran are the following, especially validated when they appear in clusters as they do in both the Avesta and the Quran: *adversary, angels, archers, bountiful* (or *beneficent*), *cattle, choice, compassion* (or *compassionate*), *cow, creation, demons, dominion, fire, firmament, freedom, gardens, horses, immortal, judgment, law, lies, mercy* (or *merciful*), *order, pasture, path* (or *way*), *resurrection, righteousness, rivers, salvation, seven, sin* (*deviate* or *go astray*), *soul, sun, shining* (or *radiant*), *thunder, truth, water, wind, wisdom, world,* and *usury*. Certain nouns in the Avesta are also connected with particular adjectives, and the coupling is repeated again and again in the Quran: *water flowing,* or *water flowing under, straight paths, swift horses, six days,* as well as *sun, moon,* and *stars* as usually connected.

Many of these words are in common use in every kind of document or literature, but they do appear to have special meaning in the Avesta, and when found in clusters in the Quran they may be suspect as related to the previous revelations to Zoroaster, now corrected or confirmed. We further suggest the possibilities that Avesta chapters known as *Fargans* (teachings on purity) may be a link to the *Furqan* (Criterion) of the Quran, that scores of Avesta verses are critiqued in the Quran, and that material from dozens of the more recent and corrupt Avesta chapters is specifically condemned in the Quran, often at length. The references to Zoroastrian Scripture are presented in the Quran in a manner similar to the appearance of material previously revealed to Jews and Christians, which is more easily identified simply because we have their scriptures to compare, whereas 80 percent of the Avesta has been destroyed.

Jews and Christians are not necessarily expected to agree with this perception, but fruitful discussion and mutual growth in understanding requires that in learning about the Quran, they might appreciate the Muslim perspective on the Quran as being as legitimate as the Jewish communal perspective of the Torah and the Christian focus on the person of Jesus in the Gospel. Additional truth may lie elsewhere, but let us at least begin by always recognizing what Jews, Christians, and Muslims believe about their own scriptures, an approach more fully elucidated in *Three Testaments: Torah, Gospel, and Quran*, but also essential to this investigation of Eastern links where we apply the same criterion to them as well.

Muslims may need convincing that the Avesta is as prominent between the lines in the Quran as the Bible is, but they would have no objection to this proposition in principle. Muhammad did not believe the revelations he received were of a different essence than the truth from God as it had been revealed to Jews and Christians earlier, or to Zoroastrians, "Sabaeans," and possibly others.

In some cases, especially in reference to Zoroastrianism dualism as practiced at the time of Muhammad, the critiquing would have been negative and the amplification was corrective. At the same time, as we might discover, whenever the material to be re-presented was of pristine Zoroastrian teaching, it would be embraced as generously in the Quran as are the treasured aspects of Jewish and Christian Scriptural teachings. The Avesta-related passages are not always recognized, simply because the originals no longer exist, but finding echoes of them in the Quran may be quite possible as a feature of programs in religious studies today.

Most of the suspected reflections of Avestan revelations appear in the Medina portions of the Quran. This would indicate that at some point late in his prophetic life, most likely under the influence of Salman, formerly a Zoroastrian, Muhammad was exposed to those portions of Avesta Scripture passed down from Zoroaster himself, as well as the later portions that would have troubled him and were followed by condemnations from on high. The splendor and power of many Zoroastrian recitations from the pervasive surrounding culture would have impressed Muhammad that God had indeed spoken, much as his intuition that earlier revelations were meant to build directly on the Jewish foundation and the Christian community. None of this should be taken as implying that Muhammad used Zoroastrian Avestas as direct sources, any more than he used the Hebrew or Christian material as it was given to him by Jews and Christians, but there can be little doubt that Zoroastrian/Sabaean material from the Avesta appears in the Quran, and that it represents something of the revelations in the vast and sprawling Vedic, Chinese, Indian, Jain, and other Eastern scriptures. In every case it seemed clear to Muhammad that the material was re-presented by God in a fresh revelation, and everyone who has heard the Quran recited has to be impressed by its powerful witness to this assertion.

The breakthrough in understanding the role of the Zoroastrian Avesta occurs when we recognize that along with the Roman Empire and the empire of Alexander the Great, both mentioned in the Quran, the Persian Empire loomed large in Muhammad's own personal experience. Along with what sometimes appeared to be a corrupt Judaism and a corrupt Christianity (which they may have been in Muhammad's experience), God also spoke to him of a corrupt Zoroastrianism, but, as with Judaism and Christianity, there was also much to be confirmed and amplified in the prophecies of Zoroaster.

If we are now able to identify the Avesta-related material and such critiques in the Quran, we might see not only a reflection of the Zoroastrianism that needed to be purified but also, in addition to this connection with the whole of the East, some aspects of pristine Zoroastrianism as it affected Judaism and Christianity in earlier periods, though previously unrecognized. Examples would include the most ancient Vedic roots of the creation story in the Hebrew Scripture and the messianic theology related to the Saoshyant as now understood in the Christian Gospel. Such Avestas, the method of their rediscovery, and their impact on critical analysis of Hebrew and Christian Scriptures are more fully introduced in our earlier presentation of *Three Testaments*. But there is detailed work ahead that may occupy scholars for years to come.

The list of Z-related passages in the Holy Quran at the end of this chapter is to be regarded as preliminary, tentative, experimental, and in need of modification or development. This specific type of critical analysis is relatively new in the current Muslim environment, but if even the concept is accepted as valid, it breaks new ground in illustrating the principle that clusters of material in the Quran can be identified as relating to God's previous revelations to Zoroaster, as maintained by the Sabaeans and others in the Arabia of Muhammad's lifetime.

Many other faint echoes of Z material are also intertwined with unique Quranic revelations, with verses reflecting Hebrew and Christian threads already loosely woven into the fabric, sometimes all four being identifiable in one surah. Such material was revealed afresh to Muhammad, though, just as some verses of Hebrew and Christian Scriptures appear almost verbatim from the Bible record, the opening and closing of the Quran, chapter 1 and chapters 113 and 114, may have an almost literal affinity with the Avesta—a matter for Muslim scholars to eventually adjudicate. In a more general sense, anything in the Quran that is related to the Day of Judgment, for example, should be correlated (directly or indirectly) to earlier Zoroastrian revelations, just as references to the law given to Moses are correlated to the Hebrew revelations and allusions to Jesus as the Messiah are correlated to the Christian connection. Zoroastrian echoes, faint or strong, may be heard in about a third of the chapters or "surahs" of the Quran, traditionally identified in English by Roman numerals (by A. Yusuf Ali, for example, in the most widely circulated translation of the Quran in English), an irony matched by the use of Arabic numerology everywhere else in the scriptures of this study.

The importance of this issue is simply that, unlike the Hebrew or Christian view of their sacred texts, Islam claims that its scripture correctly re-presents the true and valid revelations of God to all the peoples of the world. In reference to Eastern religions, it is possible to regard this as happening through the Quran's dealing with Zoroastrian Scriptures in a manner consistent with its presentation of material found in the Hebrew and Christian Scriptures, since the Avesta may be seen as prototype, antitype, or inspiration for all the primary scriptures of the East.

z-related passages in the holy quran

Surah I:2–7
Surah II:177, 214–15
Surah III:15–18, 190–200
Surah IV:57, 122–24, 174–75
Surah V:122–23
Surah VI:1–70
Surah X:1–23, 41–60
Surah XI:1–6
Surah XIV:48–52
Surah XVI:1–56, 61–83, 90–100
Surah XVII:11–14
Surah XVIII:32–49
Surah XIX:61–87
Surah XXIII:1–11
Surah XXIV:35–46
Surah XXV:1–31, 45–77
Surah XXVII:59–75, 83–90
Surah XXIX:2–13
Surah XXX:11–60
Surah XXXI:2–11

Surah XXXIII:21–27
Surah XXXVI:2–12, 68–83
Surah XXXIX:1–3, 5–21, 32–75
Surah XLVII:1–28
Surah LXI:1, 10–13
Surah LXIV:1–6
Surah LXV:8–12
Surah LXVI:6–8
Surah LXVII:1–30
Surah LXXX:1–42
Surah LXXXI:1–29
Surah LXXXIV:1–25
Surah XCIII:1–11
Surah XCIV:1–8
Surah XCV:1–8
Surah XCVIII:7–8
Surah XCIX:1–6
Surah CXII:1–4
Surah CXIII:1–5
Surah CXIV:1–6

book seven

THE "DEAD ZEE SCROLLS"

introduction

Searching for the "Dead Zee Scrolls"

Richard Freund

W HEN THIS PROJECT BEGAN IN 2012, BRIAN ARTHUR BROWN ASKED IF I WOULD BE prepared to write a foreword to the *Four Testaments* book in reference to the search for what he calls the "Dead Zee Scrolls" and their value in understanding Eastern scriptures, as well as their relationship to the scriptures of the West. As it turned out, the task to do the foreword to the entire work was given to Francis Clooney, described elsewhere as the *éminence grise of comparative theology*, and I am to introduce the section on archaeology, my own academic specialty. This I am pleased to do, since the zeal that Dr. Brown has displayed for telling the story of the Zoroastrians, and his view that the original texts of their scriptures are still out there waiting to be discovered, is both refreshing and extremely intriguing. Such a discovery might well impact the study of Eastern scriptural texts in a manner not unlike the impact the Dead Sea Scrolls have had upon the Western texts.

Just over 150 years ago, German biblical scholars often questioned whether the Hebrew Bible was very ancient. With extant manuscripts of the Hebrew Bible in their day of just over one thousand years old, many speculated that the Hebrew Bible was the invention of late Hellenistic and rabbinic Judaism and had been retrojected into an ancient period to give it greater authority. The discovery some seventy years ago of the Dead Sea Scrolls changed everything. That accidental discovery and the deciphering of the more than nine hundred manuscripts over the next sixty years proved that the Hebrew Bible was indeed ancient, but the study of the scrolls also showed us just how much we did not know about religion from the canonized texts passed down in the major world religions.

Brown's quest in this book for defining the parameters of the original Zoroastrian Avesta and its influence in the development of other religions in the Middle East and

Asia reminds me of the New Testament scholars' reasonable search for an original ancient manuscript presumed to lie behind the Gospels. One of the original texts behind
the Gospels is called "Q" by New Testament scholars, short for the German word for
Quelle, or the "source." There are complete seminars in major conferences every year
attempting to understand what "Q" was, despite the fact that no document like "Q"
has ever been found. We are now at that stage with the "Dead Zee Scrolls."

I am associated with archaeological excavations of Bethsaida, a first-century CE city
by the northeast shore of the Sea of Galilee, where students and scholars gather every
year hoping to discover just a small fragment of a text from Q. Bethsaida was one of
the original places for the meeting of Jesus and the Apostles in the first century CE.
Unfortunately, the climate in this area is cold, damp, and extreme. Although we do not
hold out too much hope that Bethsaida will have preserved even a very small fragment
of the so-called "Q" document, we do recognize that the material culture of the site
gives us a piece of the story. Brown's search for the "Q" of Zoroastrianism (or "Z," as
he would have it) is admirable. The interplay between the oral and written traditions
of the world's religions may preserve much more of value than we ever imagined.

why written documents are rare

My students are always surprised to hear that ancient written materials are rarer than
gold or silver in excavations. The idea of writing on stone or wet pottery, preparing an
animal skin for writing, or creating a usable papyrus page is an involved, multistep
process. The creation of the inks needed to write on the latter materials and the skills
necessary to write at all are rarely seen to be as involved as they really are.

First, we must understand that most of the religions of the world, even those that
have produced canonized texts, were passing on their traditions in an oral fashion
both before the writing took place and after. Often, if we have learned anything from
the past one hundred years of work on ancient biblical texts, this meant that writing
was reserved for times of crisis, celebration, or culminating moments in the religious
group's history. In most other cases, the oral tradition seemed to work just fine. More
important, oral and written traditions seem to have coexisted throughout time. Today,
if you enter an Islamic madrasa, a Jewish yeshiva, or a Hindu temple, you will still
find children and adults learning by rote the text of the Quran, the Talmud, and the
Vedas as if the printed text did not exist. It is seen as an effective hedge to the written
text. People in antiquity simultaneously valued and used "oral" and "written" traditions to transmit their most important accounts from generation to generation because
writing was so difficult and precarious.

The "original" Avesta may itself have passed through this process. Oral traditions
were also seen by ancients as infinitely more reliable than scribal traditions, which
were limited by the actual size of the parchment (later paper) that they had secured
for writing. In addition, the ancients seem to have written down far less of their most
important texts than we might think (the writing was reserved for more mundane items

such as receipts, decrees, and contracts, which were a more practical use of writing). Finally, because the conditions for preserving ancient writing (notice that caves that are in dry and remote desert areas figure in many of these scenarios of preservation) are far more precarious than most of us ever imagined, it is surprising that we have as many ancient manuscripts as we do have. However, we can be now quite certain that more are on the way.

what the discoveries of new nanuscripts of ancient texts tell us about religion

What do the discoveries of texts in the wall of a synagogue in Cairo in the 1890s; the discoveries in Buddhist caves in western China in the early 1900s; the discovery of Gnostic Gospels in the deserts of Nag Hamadi, Egypt, in 1945; and the Judean desert's Dead Sea Scrolls in 1946/1947 all have in common? They all remind us that unexpected treasures were discovered not by ecclesiastical leaders or scholars but by local people and purely by accident. These accidental discoveries remind us that we should always be vigilant and not have too much hubris about what we think we know about the beliefs of any ancient religion.

where to look: hidden in the wall of a synagogue in cairo

Although known about by Europeans in the eighteenth century, the Cairo Ben Ezra Synagogue Geniza (literally, "hidden" in Hebrew) was a wall of the synagogue that was devoted to "hiding" manuscripts that were not necessarily religious texts but were deemed to be of some significance, perhaps just because they were written at all. The tendency to bury ancient texts that could no longer serve a ritual purpose, or when they were no longer able to be repaired, was a cross-religious problem. Religious institutions are wonderful places to bury manuscripts that are no longer usable but contain sacred teachings. We know that even in antiquity people spent enormous amounts of time and energy hunting down heretics from the canonized textual traditions, and it is not surprising to find that these heretics were actually preserving part of a religious tradition that was in transition. Also, Buddhists, Muslims, and Jews seem to have had a problem decommissioning their ancient texts, so they just hid or buried them, waiting for them to naturally decompose.

In 1896, the twin sisters Agnes S. Lewis and Margaret D. Gibson returned to England from Egypt with fragments from the Cairo Geniza that they considered to be of interest and showed them to Professor Solomon Schechter at Cambridge University. Schechter, already aware of the Geniza (but not of its significance), immediately recognized the importance of the material. A strange story that emerges from the Geniza which affects our search for the "Dead Zee Scrolls" has to do with one medieval manuscript in particular that Schechter identified as being from an ancient sect of Jews that goes back much earlier. Fifty years later, in the Dead Sea Scrolls, the same manuscript was found—except it was a version that was almost a thousand years older than the one that Schechter found in the Geniza. The discovery of any original manuscript has a ripple effect upon the totality of manuscripts because so few have survived. We now know that the Cairo Geniza is a collection of some 300,000 Jewish manuscript fragments that revolutionized our understanding of Jewish life and culture in antiquity, not just in the Middle Ages. We exhibit a single example of such a Zoroastrian Avesta Scripture found early in the twentieth century in our appendix, fully expecting that more may soon be found.

HIDING IN CAVES IN CHINA

I am so pleased to see that Brown has preserved the name of my favorite archaeologist of all time in his writing. Marc Aurel Stein was the quintessential explorer of the nineteenth and early twentieth centuries, and I have been following his work for years (I even have been invited to follow in his footsteps to excavate in Kashmir—but doing so is far more difficult now than it was in Stein's time). Stein had the idea that the ancient Silk Road, with its many caves, enclaves, watchtowers, and caravan stops, was the place to look for the history of the movement of ideas from the Middle East, India, and China. Stretching from the eastern shore of China to the city of Istanbul in modern-day Turkey, ancient merchants moved along stretches of a road that originally may have included what was called even earlier the "Incense Route" and later the Silk Route. It even led to trade throughout the Mediterranean. While Chinese merchants themselves probably never made it as far as Istanbul, they had middlemen who felt comfortable traveling from east to west and back. These traders traded not just goods but also stories, and probably their religious texts as well.

In the early 1900s, Stein stunned the world with thousands of manuscript discoveries in Chinese caves along the Silk Road in western China. The Mogao Caves or Dunhuang Cave documents were first discovered in a sealed cave by a Taoist monk named Wang Yuanlu on June 25, 1900. From 1907 onward he began to sell them to Western explorers, notably Stein, most of whose discoveries are at the British Library in London, and Paul Pelliot, whose discoveries are at the Louvre Library in Paris. While most of the known collections are in London and Paris, so much more is in Chinese archives and still in unexplored caves in China that have never been completely deciphered. There are thousands of unexplored ancient Silk Road caves that may yet provide new understandings of the people that moved along the ancient route from ancient Babylonia to Afghanistan and to China in the times that are of interest to us in this quest.

To illustrate the importance of these caves, let me point to two documents that I have been investigating. One is in the British Library, Or.8212/166 (D.XIII), and exhibited in our appendix. Written on paper, this document is one of the earliest Jewish texts on paper anywhere. It is a simple thirty-seven-line text about the trading of sheep and the sale of clothing written in a Persian dialect using Hebrew letters. This was a common Jewish ethnic method for maintaining Jewish identity—the creation of a Jewish language that would be readable by Jews from that region but when read aloud would sound like the Persian of that region. In the same way, Eastern and Central European Jews used a German dialect written in Hebrew letters called "Yiddish," Iberian Jews used a Spanish dialect written in Hebrew letters called "Ladino," and Jews who lived in Arabic-speaking countries wrote in an Arabic dialect written in Hebrew letters. What Or.8212/166 (D.XIII) shows is that Jews maintained records in a quasi-religious language of Jewish Persian that incorporated words from the Bible, the Talmudim, and their local Persian neighbors. But when we combine this document found by Stein with a document found by Pelliot in a later expedition in the cave,[1] we find that the Jews who deposited these texts in this cave were more than just itinerant merchants—they were Jews who maintained their religious ideas through prayers and in their business. These Paris and British Library documents are really a two-in-a-million find, since so many of the documents found in the caves were just stacked up together. The Pelliot document was a never-before-seen prayer that, while resembling the canonized prayers of the rabbis, was nevertheless different from the prayer book.

DISCOVERIES IN CAVES IN THE MIDDLE EAST

The discoveries made more recently in the Middle East deserve, I think, a mention in this regard, since Brown has referred to them in passing. In December 1945, a discovery by two brothers, Muhammad and Khalifah Ali, in a sealed jar of the Nag Hammadi site (twelve books plus eight leaves from the thirteenth book—a total of fifty-two different tractates from Gnostic Christians living in the area in the second and third century CE), changed forever the way we view the diversity of ancient Christianity and what the New Testament (Gospels) really contain. The Gnostic Christians preserved stories of Jesus's life that are not included in the canonized Gospels. Mostly what these texts revealed was how much we did not know about what Jesus's life meant to many Christians, regardless of their acceptability in the debates about canonization and authenticity.

The greatest discovery of ancient texts in the modern period has to be the discovery of the Dead Sea Scrolls in salt-soaked caves in the Judean desert some twenty-five miles from Jerusalem. Brown's search for the "Dead Zee Scrolls" by that name pays homage to this discovery, which revolutionized our understanding of ancient Judaism and Christianity. In the winter of 1946, a discovery by two Bedouins in the Judean desert in caves along the Dead Sea changed the way that Jews, Christians, and Muslims view their own religious texts today. The scrolls were not all biblical texts. Scholars realized for the first time that the ideas of the apocalypse (the end of the world), the conflict between the children of "light and darkness," and the quasi-messianic figure who would lead them, were all well known to this group of people who wrote the scrolls before Christianity and before rabbinic Judaism. The people who wrote and placed these texts in the caves to preserve them for some future generation of followers were doing something that perhaps most ancients did in times of crisis. The Dead Sea Scrolls, which were generally limited to only eleven caves (of the hundreds of caves along the Dead Sea) found in close proximity to the ancient village of Qumran, showed us just how a single discovery has a ripple effect upon religious ideas.

Now, seventy years after their discovery, all nine hundred–plus manuscripts have been assembled from hundreds of thousands of small fragments. The texts tell us about the canon of the Hebrew Bible, views of ancient sectarians, and the interpretation of ancient biblical ideas in a period that precedes the rise of rabbinic Judaism and early Christianity. They also remind us that the thousands of caves along the Dead Sea rift valley may yet reveal even more preserved textual materials as our techniques to retrieve these texts become more sophisticated. It is this type of discovery that Brown is hoping for with the search for the "Dead Zee Scrolls." The area that Brown has identified, caves and other locations along the Silk Road, are clearly among the best places to look for the Avesta and perhaps other Zoroastrian-related texts. Perhaps, with time, the political complications that now impede this work will make it possible.

ARE THERE MORE UNEXCAVATED CAVES OUT THERE TO BE FOUND?

The short answer is "yes!" There are many areas around the world where there are caves and buried structures that may preserve ancient texts. The Silk Road is a good place to start. The problem is access and systematic excavation. Excavations are multiyear, expensive, and often inefficient ways to gain knowledge. They are generally destructive and the question is: Where do we start? We have been identifying areas for investigation for twenty years using two or three different types of geophysical non-invasive techniques that map the subsurface of areas before we ever excavate. Then, when we excavate, we can do "pinpoint" excavations. We have recently adapted two techniques that were originally used in gas and oil exploration to help identify and design retrieval of gas and oil below the surface. We now use them to figure out what lies below the surface in archaeological sites and assess how best to extract what is found there.

Electrical resistivity tomography (ERT) is a technique that uses electricity to reflect what is located up to fifty feet below the surface of the ground, and ground-penetrating radar (GPR) uses FM radio waves to reflect up to fifteen feet below the surface. Operating them in tandem, we have identified caves and subsurface areas of buildings, tombs, and even destroyed areas that contain a variety of materials below the surface that the computer software can interpret. Stone, bone, metal, glass, fired pottery, and such all reflect the signal differently. The mapping allows us to place what is below the surface on a GPS-coordinated map and do excavations with much greater precision than ever imagined. The maps we have (with GPS locations) mean that in the future, when access for excavation is possible, we can go with local collaborators and retrieve what is in the location. But these techniques still require access to the location. In remote areas this remains a major hurdle. We have sometimes used satellite imaging of a location that may locate some features on the surface that mask sites below the surface, but access to those sites continues to be problematic.

Recently, use of airplanes, helicopters, or drones mounted with LiDAR (light detection and ranging) equipment has given us hope that many areas on the ground could be pinpointed even in remote areas with tree cover. LiDAR has many applications in the field of archaeology including aiding in the planning of field campaigns, mapping features beneath forest canopy, and providing an overview of broad, continuous features that may be indistinguishable on the ground, but ultimately we must have access to an identified site.

In a sense this is both complementary and very similar to the goals of our projects which we do on the ground, but instead of doing it on the ground, it is done through a type of aerial photography and laser detection and technology. LiDAR can also provide archaeologists with the ability to create high-resolution digital elevation models (DEMs) of archaeological sites that can reveal micro-topography that are otherwise hidden by vegetation. The elevation mapping is in itself invaluable in the search for buildings, caves, and hidden features. Unfortunately, LiDAR without a follow-up project like ERT or GPR provides maps that cannot be easily truth-tested. However, LiDAR-derived products can be easily integrated into a Geographic Information System (GIS) for analysis and interpretation. This is only a short list of the work that can be undertaken to find ancient repositories in caves. The list of opportunities is impressive but it always comes down to finding the right partners in country to collaborate in these enterprises.

what will be found?

Every year I read about new areas that have uncovered important finds. I am glad to see that Brown reads the same reports that I do. In the beginning of 2012, it was announced in the media that a cache of Jewish documents had been found in caves in Afghanistan. I was surprised, as were many other scholars, to discover that caves in Afghanistan contained so much Jewish material. I visited the collection that was eventually acquired by the Hebrew University of Jerusalem and is now in the national collection. It shows me again that treasures lie buried in far-flung places, and each discovery forces us to remember just how much we do not know about ancient religious texts. While these materials did not contain the types of foundational texts found in the Dead Sea Scrolls, they did contain written documents that we had never seen before.

In 2014, I did a Fox News interview on a small pottery shard that had eight letters on it that had been found in the excavations of Jerusalem. I spoke about how rare it was to find written materials from the tenth century BCE, and how rare it was to find written materials that survive from antiquity at all. I spoke about the nature of ancient Hebrew writing of this period, and finally the reporter asked me what the shard said. I said what I knew at the time: "We know exactly what it says but we just do not yet know what it means."

Ancient writing samples matter for another reason. Over the course of time an ancient tradition usually "morphs" from its original setting and meaning and becomes what the preserver of the ancient tradition understands the tradition to say to his or her own generation. I am reminded of the "Virgin Mary" traditions, which moved from a relatively benign citation in the book of Isaiah to its translation in Greek, to the hundreds of pages in the Church Fathers literature interpreting the mystery of the Virgin Mary. If we have learned anything from Brown's testaments project, it is how the recasting of traditions happens, and why, by studying the actual texts of ancient traditions, and studying how they were recast or interpreted in different areas of the world, we have a better chance of understanding what the actual meaning of the text was. To illustrate from a sister tradition, the Quranic words urging "modesty" in dress for Muslim women have been recast time and again; discoveries about details of dress in the prophet's own time would be instructive and perhaps helpful in the current societal context.

the final testament

We have made remarkable finds in caves, deserts, buildings, and often museum collections. The essence of what we do not know is as important as what we pretend to know from the world's religions based solely upon the canonized texts that we have in our possession.

While we love to think about the great modern archaeological discoveries of antiquity as being the product of scientific expeditions conducted by elite groups of specialists, the fact is that most of the discoveries that are made, even today, are by people living in the region who stumble upon a location that has been abandoned. Caves, ancient dwellings, cemeteries, and even religious institutions often house the remains of ancient texts that no longer are readable but were still held to be sacred. Ancients decided that these religious texts deserved a proper burial, but thankfully not all of these locations were known to religious officials who often decided that one text or another no longer served the interests of the religion and needed to be suppressed, not copied, or seriously censored. When we think about the religious texts that dominate the world's religions, we often think of them as a corpus of documents that have been passed down from generation to generation. In fact, the history of the ancient texts of most of the religions of the world is filled with canonical and noncanonical texts. Texts were recognized as ancient but not accepted into the final version of the religion's most sacred writings.

It is estimated that we have preserved only a fraction of the religious ideas and texts of the world's religions. Most never succeeded in attaining the final theological stamp of approval, or often the religious tradition of one text or another was targeted for extinction by the accepted theological authorities. The testaments that we preserve and value are not only the edited and canonized texts that appear in these pages. There is another testament just waiting to be discovered in the caves, deserts, religious buildings, and institutions around the world. The work of *Four Testaments* is only the beginning of the story, and the "Dead Zee Scrolls," if and when we find them, are merely part of a larger picture, East and West. The Final Testament is the testament that was written in the hearts and minds of the followers, and the material culture that they left behind may be the only way to recover those ideas that did not make it into the texts in our possession.

pReface

A Model for the Twenty-First Century

Zoroastrianism crossed paths with Judaism and is a generation or more older than Taoism, Confucianism, Buddhism, and the Hinduism of the *Bhagavad Gita*. It is also a progenitor of the spiritual aspirations of Christians and Muslims who came later. Zoroastrianism is miniscule in numbers of adherents today and only a remnant of its scriptures has been available for hundreds, even thousands of years, considering two eras of decimation and destruction. But Zoroastrianism may have been a conduit for reformed Vedic concepts which influenced all major Eastern religions in some ways and impacted on Western religion in other ways. Might a new appreciation of the role of Zoroastrianism be another beginning of a New Axial Age on the basis of religious understanding?

—Brian Arthur Brown

THE *TAO TE CHING* IS A TRIP TO THE PLANETARIUM FOR A VIEW OF THE UNIVERSE AND A perspective on life. The *Analects* is a survival manual for existence in life, depending on human experience to provide examples of what works and what is worthy of emulation. The *Dhammapada* is a GPS, a Global Positioning System, which correctly centers us in the situation in which we find ourselves. The *Bhagavad Gita* is a universal guidebook, providing step-by-step directions to the destination.

The 20 percent of the Zoroastrian Avesta we have in hand as this compendium goes to press is but the tip of the iceberg. Canadians tell the world that when an iceberg rolls over, the tsunami effect can capsize ships out in the ocean or devastate coastal communities if the rollover takes place close to shore. Such a rollover of the text of the Avesta is what we expect to happen very soon. We hope this compendium and its predecessor can help prepare the affected religious communities to endure the rollover and thrive in the future, though some of them may feel themselves to be at sea while others believe they have remained grounded on the shore.

Professor Richard Freund has given us the scientific tools we need to chart the discovery of one or the other of the full texts of the Avesta, copies of the first original, destroyed by Alexander the Great, or copies of the reconstituted second version, destroyed by Muslim decree. Both Greeks and Muslims believed that they obliterated all copies, as impossible as that now seems.

In the quest for this "Holy Grail" of the world religions, Book VII looks at previous such discoveries, the Seal of Cyrus in particular, many of which seemed equally as improbable until they were found. We review the developments of the last hundred years in Zoroastrian studies, leading to the current launchpad excitement as the search gets ready to really lift off. This chapter explores the history and the geography of the anticipated location of the find. We conclude with a perspective on what this will mean to the world, and to world religions in particular, and an exhibition of similar documentary discoveries, none of which were even known before the twentieth century—a comment sure to be repeated someday about the discoveries in the twenty-first century, almost certainly including the "Dead Zee Scrolls."

The Seal of Cyrus was found in the same general region where it was produced among the same religionists in the precise era we are considering. Certain other observations might be made by way of addressing lingering doubts that a complete Avesta will be found. For example, while there was only one actual "Seal" of Cyrus, there may have been as many as twenty thousand copies of the Avesta made in ancient times, and in as many as twelve languages, so there were plenty of such scrolls or texts, even allowing for exaggeration. Moreover, the Avesta was the principal scripture of the Sogdian people for over a thousand years, and they "kept the faith" in their pivotal management of trade through the whole central portion of the Silk Route. Nor were they the only people to be using this text with various levels of devotion and at different times within periods before and after Alexander, and also before and after the Muslim advance into Central Asia. We simply observe the greater likelihood of the discovery of these "Dead Zee Scrolls" happening in Uzbekistan rather than Iran, Turkey, China, Turkmenistan, Kazakhstan, Kyrgyzstan, Tajikistan, Afghanistan, Pakistan, or India, all of which also have Zoroastrian sites under exploration. Like the discovery of Troy, the finding of the Seal of Cyrus was a deliberate Indiana Jones type of operation; the finding of the Dead Sea Scrolls and the Nag Hammadi Library were accidents. The finding of the Avesta may combine the Indiana Jones search techniques, accidental possibilities, and the high-tech sophistication described by Freund in a triangulation that will almost certainly bring results, and possibly soon.

An exhibition of related documents unearthed in the same area, though found several strata levels closer to the surface, will be presented in the appendix. A valuable bibliography will complete the back matter of this volume, though we expect the discussion to continue from scholarly reviews of this book to supermarket tabloid sensational reporting of the discovery of the "Dead Zee Scrolls" when it happens, and from university and seminary classes to congregational and family discussions as a new appreciation of the world religions unfolds.

The Vedic tradition is germane to our Eastern "testaments," linked to the West by a Zoroastrianism that itself influenced both Eastern and Western religious developments from one end of the Silk Route to the other in the sixth century BCE. The explosion of related archaeological discoveries in the next years of the twenty-first century should be of tremendous interest to our readers. The archaeological tourist industry in Central Asia is shifting from uncertain and seemingly risky programs originating in Istanbul to four- and five-star tours from Beijing for Europeans and Americans, as well as increasing junkets for visitors from various parts of the East. Archaeological digs and expeditions by well-qualified experts from abroad are increasingly complemented by local government and local university explorations, especially in China and in other parts of the eastern end of the old Silk Route, where most of the action is taking place. Readers should begin to watch for both discovery announcements and for increasing opportunities to visit the area, from either Istanbul or Beijing. Each discovery is treated like "the find of the century," and the opening paragraphs of the following sample of very recent newspaper clippings illustrate how each new site is considered proof of the "true" original context of the Zoroastrian religion:

"archaeologist says central asia was cradle of ancient persian religion"

IOL News Service, July 31, 2005—The Mysterious Magian civilization which flowered in the desert of Turkmenistan 3,000 years ago was the cradle of the ancient Persian religion of Zoroastrianism, Greco-Russian archaeologist Victor Sarigiannidis claimed here on Friday. He said the theory would provoke controversy amongst his fellow archaeologists, but said his excavations around the site of Gonur Tepe have uncovered evidence of sacrifices consistent with the Zoroastrian cult in a huge palace, seven temples and a vast mausoleum. They feature superb mosaics depicting griffins, wolves and lions, as well as a marble statue of a ram and finely highlighted vases in gold and silver, according to Sarigiannidis, a member of the Russian Science Academy.[1]

"zoroastrian temple discovered in duhok"

Kurdistan, Iraq, 22 August, 2006—Duhok's Director of Antiquities, Hasan Ahmed Qassim, has announced the discovery of a Zoroastrian temple near the Jar Ston Cave, a famous ancient site. The temple is believed to be the most complete to have been unearthed in this region, being made up of five sanctuaries, three of which were carved into rock, with the remaining two having been constructed from stone blocks. The discovery is being hailed as the most significant archaeological development in the region in recent times.[2]

"uzbek archaeologists discover ancient temple of zoroaster"

Samarkand, November 25, 2013—The oldest temple of Zoroastrians in Central Asia has been discovered by Uzbek archaeologists in Khorezm. This finding convincingly evidences that the state of ancient Khorezm is the cradle of Zoroastrianism. The temple is situated on the left bank of the Amu Darya. The valley of this great Asian river became the birthplace of the oldest organized religion in the world, and the territory of the creation of one of the first written monuments in the history of mankind, the Avesta. It was the encyclopedia of spiritual and cultural values of the people of Central Asia.[3]

"major zoroastrian tombs in china's xinjiang uygar autonomous region"

China Daily, 09/05/2014—Archaeologists in Northwest China's Xinjiang Uygar Autonomous Region have discovered major Zoroastrian tombs, dated to over 2,500 years ago. These massive tombs, now being excavated, are the world's earliest traces of the religion of Zoroastrianism so far. This is leading to startling speculation about the religion's origins. "All the evidence leads to one conclusion: Zoroastrianism originated in the east on China's Pamir Plateau. We have found the earliest and largest scale Zoroastrian ruins, with all the typical symbols of this religion. Of course, there is the possibility that there are other undiscovered ruins elsewhere in the world, but at this moment, it's a logical conclusion that the origin of the religion is here, not in Persia," said Wu Xinjiang, Director, Archaeological Inst., Chinese Academy of Social Sciences.[4]

These brief samples are but an indication of the intense scrutiny of the region, mostly north and east of Iran, where earlier attention to Zoroastrian origins and artifacts was focused. While most of the physical materials that have come to light to date do highlight the Eastern ethos of this religion, there have been scant examples of the written materials which will be of interest to the whole world when found. Our appendix exhibiting written materials from in and around Dunhuang, China, proves beyond a shadow of doubt that tremendous quantities of texts were produced, and though only one "Dead Zee Scroll" was found there, the remainder is somewhere, waiting to be discovered.

14

among the ruins

Tablets and Cylinders

THE BRITISH MUSEUM IS IN POSSESSION OF THE CLAY CYLINDER THAT WAS ORDERED TO BE made and exhibited by Cyrus as king of Persia, in order to make known his policy of religious toleration, and that is said to represent the first "bill of rights" in human history. A replica is on display at the United Nations headquarters in New York to reflect the universality of its message. This "Cyrus Cylinder" was discovered in Babylon in 1879, just after archaeologists also made the discovery of the legendary city of Troy. In a manner similar to the way that the discovery of Troy disproved the view that Homer's *Iliad* was fiction, the finding of the Cyrus Cylinder gave substance to echoes in classical literature that ascribed the highest ideals to this leader of the world's first superpower, ideals that were widely regarded as mere idealizations until the cylinder was found. It is difficult to imagine that such other important information from such times has been lost for two-and-a-half millennia, but we are now realizing that Zoroaster and his message may have been as close as Cyrus all along, though still hidden from our sight.

Hormuzd Rassam, an Assyrian Christian from Mosul, was perhaps the most prolific archaeologist in the Middle East in the nineteenth century. His discoveries included the tablets containing the Gilgamesh epic from Babylon, the world's oldest-known example of written literature, as well as the Cyrus Cylinder, a famous declaration issued in 539 BCE to commemorate that Persian monarch's conquest of the Babylonian Empire and to announce his progressive and spiritually based policies. Rassam's experiences in obtaining these artifacts among others may help us understand why the recovery of the Avesta Scriptures is taking so long. In February 1879, when Rassam visited the ruins of ancient Babylon on behalf of the British Museum, he found the site devastated, razed to the ground, looted many times over the centuries, and even its few remaining bricks being sold off as a cheap building material.

Rassam states, "Indeed, the annihilation of that city was so effectual that one wonders whether the accounts given of its greatness and magnificence by different Gentile historians were true. . . . I found it would be only a waste of money and labour to excavate at Imjaileeba (the site of the principal old palace), where former diggers had left nothing unturned to find what they wanted."[1]

Rassam writes about the clumsy efforts of untrained local assistants: "The damage done by such mode of searching is incalculable, inasmuch as the Arab style of digging is too clumsy. . . . In nine cases out of ten, they break or lose a large part of their collections, and worse than all, they try to make a good bargain by breaking the inscribed objects, and dividing them amongst their customers." He adds, "I myself bought, when I was in Baghdad, a most valuable Babylonian terra-cotta cylinder for the British Museum, which had met with the same fate. The discoverer had tried to saw it in two, and in doing so the upper part broke into fragments, some of which were lost altogether. The saw that was used for that purpose must have been very rough, as it gnawed off nearly half an inch of the inscription."[2]

Rassam had to make deals with the locals. First, he employed for cash those whose profession it had been to steal the bricks; next, he allowed them to keep and sell the bricks, provided they would not steal any artifacts they uncovered. Despite sites that had been already ruined and decayed, it was through such bargaining that humanity did retrieve at least the Gilgamesh Tablet and the Cyrus Cylinder with the priceless information they contain. Techniques improved dramatically through the twentieth century, and in the twenty-first century such sites are treated with almost operating room spotlessness. What may make our goal achievable is the fact that the Avestas we seek were probably deliberately hidden and may have thus escaped the ravages of time and the vagaries of human activity. Caches of artifacts from Babylonia and the Persian Empire of the period are not the only potential sources of what we seek. They may be the best known and most thoroughly researched so far, but we are just beginning, and the search areas north and east from there are less thoroughly decimated by looters.

Do we have evidentiary examples of Professor Richard Freund's technology in reference to any site we know well enough to examine in ongoing explorations of tombs or caves? In August 2015, British Egyptologist Nicolas Reeves was examining the tomb of Tutankhamen, or King Tut, as the world knows him best, prior to restricting tourist visitors who are now shunted to a nearby replica of the world's most famous tomb, discovered intact and full of treasure by Howard Carter. Reeves noticed for the first time that careful observation revealed hairlines beneath the artwork on the stone walls, possibly outlining doorways to additional rooms. As he pondered the possibility that some other royal figure could also be buried there, Queen Nefertiti came to mind, since her final resting place is unknown, and especially since she may have worn a beard and ruled as the Pharaoh Smenkhare, after the death of her husband, Pharaoh Akhenaten. Her name means "the beautiful one has come," and we made reference to this princess who had possibly come from Mitanni in what is now a Kurdish portion of old Syria, a great niece of Abraham's clan who brought a proto-monotheism to Egypt, where it was adopted by her husband, the Pharaoh Akhnaten, when she became queen. Nefertiti is also of interest in our story as the mother of Ankhesenpaaten, who married her stepson, "King Tut," when he was eleven years of age. The necessity of immediately producing a male heir to protect the line causes some scholars of the Hebrew Scriptures to believe that Ankhesenpaaten would have had good reason to pluck a male infant from the Nile where he had been hidden by Hebrew slaves. With her prepubescent husband unable to produce an heir, she would have claimed him as her own baby (at least in public), named him after Tutmose, and raised him in the palace as a royal prince.

As Reeves looked at the wall art depicting pharaonic images, it then struck him that one pharaoh depicted several times had especially beautiful facial features and a very long neck beneath the beard. He immediately realized who might be buried behind the wall—clues in plain sight for nearly one hundred years to some fifteen million visitors per year. Others had previously noticed that King Tut's tomb was small for a king and that the design was more like tombs elsewhere built for Egyptian queens. Reeves speculated that when Tut died unexpectedly at age nineteen, no tomb had been prepared over the years of his brief reign, but his stepmother Nefertiti had died just ten years earlier and her burial chamber could have been sealed off to provide a small but fabulous tomb for Tutankhamen.

He took his theory to Egyptian antiquities minister Mamdouh el-Damaty, who inspected the site with him and approved Reeves's request to use infrared thermography to see if the north wall was different from the rest of the stone in which the tomb had been excavated. He authorized high-resolution x-ray imaging of the wall in the manner described to us by Freund. The tests indicated that the north wall was at a very different temperature than the bedrock of the other walls, indicating a free-standing partition, as described in an Associated Press release on September 30, 2015.[3] It was enough for the Ministry of Antiquities to send to Japan for the world's best x-ray imaging equipment (of the kind described to us by Professor Freund) and to authorize further investigations under supervision by Reeves. The world is holding its breath in anticipation of what could be the most important archaeological find since 1922.

Our own search for sites that could produce similar dramatic discoveries of the "Dead Zee Scrolls" carried on in the months while the investigation in Egypt proceeded, even as compilation of the text of this book continued. Mention has been made of Dunhuang, and at last we are ready to summarize what happened there and elsewhere in the twentieth century, germane to our quest, and to begin the twenty-first-century pursuit for the "Dead Zee Scrolls" in eastern China, Uzbekistan, and contiguous areas.

15

from aurel stein to mary boyce and beyond

Controversies in the Twentieth Century and Resolution in the Twenty-First

SIR MARC AUREL STEIN (1862–1943) WAS A HUNGARIAN ARCHAEOLOGIST WHO SPENT MOST OF HIS life in the service of the British Empire in India and north of India in Central Asia. He recovered and published the text of what is almost the only native history of India from before the Muslim invasions and conducted some of the first archaeological surveys of Iran and Iraq, and in his old age he pioneered the use of aerial photography in archaeology, a precursor to our own *modus operandi* from air and space.

Stein's most important Central Asian expeditions began in 1900 and ended in 1916 when, with an energy and style compared to the modern fictional Indiana Jones,[1] he began a project related to the earliest and largest paper archive in the ancient world. One hundred years later the largest such international collaborative effort in history is known as the International Dunhuang Project, centered at the British Museum in London, but with materials, staff, and extensive facilities in Tokyo, Beijing, New Delhi, Paris, St. Petersburg, and Berlin.

In May 1900 Stein entered the Taklamakan Desert in the southwest of what is now the Xinjiang Uyghur Autonomous Region of northwest China, in a rough inhospitable climate where vestiges of buildings bespoke the more prosperous days of eras gone by. Traveling east, he uncovered Buddhist paintings and sculptures and Sanskrit texts in various ruins. At Niya he found over a hundred wooden tablets written in an early Indian script in 105 CE, the earliest physical documents of Indian provenance yet to be discovered. Stein also discovered a trove of ancient coins dating from early Silk Route trade during the Han Dynasty, as well as household artifacts like a carved stool, a Persian rug, an antique mousetrap, a walking stick, part of a guitar, and a bow in good working order. Stein's discoveries made him famous and convinced the Indian government to fund his second expedition, though in the meantime archaeologists from seven countries began the task of recovery of artifacts that found their way to museums in Russia, Europe, America, and various parts of Eastern Asia.

Stein began his second expedition in 1907, and in that year he stumbled upon a paper archive in a sealed-up military watchtower over a series of caves overlooking the city of Dunhuang, yielding over forty thousand documents, many of which are still being deciphered. Abbot Wang was the leader of a monastic group in charge of the caves known as the Mogao Grottoes, or the Caves of the Thousand Buddhas. The theory is that he had opened the old military archive in the year 1900 and attempted to interest the Chinese government in preservation of the material, or to sell enough to undertake the project himself. Stein purchased thousands of manuscripts written in Chinese, Sanskrit, Sogdian, Tibetan, Turkic, and Uighur. Among these manuscripts were rich Buddhist paintings and the world's oldest printed document, the *Diamond Sutra*, from 863 CE. Once the importance of Stein's collection became sensationalized through the world press, the Chinese government tried to prevent further expeditions.

Other collectors and robbers made things difficult, but, after some negotiation, Stein returned to Dunhuang in 1915, his third exploration of the area; he obtained some more documents from the cave temples and unearthed a number of spectacular silks from previously pillaged tombs. His appreciation of the leftovers from the grave robbers marked the conclusion of Stein's career in those parts. He did go on to donate and catalog hundreds of his artifacts, manuscripts, and silks at the British Museum, almost the only such material to have survived the political upheavals and confusion in China that followed soon after. Stein's discoveries were limited to materials from a couple of centuries on either side of the fifth century CE, about a thousand years after the flourishing of Zoroastrianism in that same area. But the Stein collection contains at least one copy of a prayer from the ancient Avesta. It is a prayer also found in extant portions of the Avesta but far older than any such manuscript in the possession of the modern Zoroastrian community, hinting at more to be found at deeper substrata or other locations. The International Dunhuang project is the model of international collaboration we hope to see fulfilling the quest for a complete Avesta, but before that happens we may need another Aurel Stein to head the search.

In the last century attempts were made to establish an understanding of Zoroastrianism, a religion long obliterated by the vicissitudes of history and the rivalries that both refined and decimated its heritage. Those initial twentieth-century attempts failed largely because of scholarly disputes on how to date and read the surviving material and the external references. However, by the end of that century a consensus on many such issues emerged around the findings of Mary Boyce at the University of London's School of Oriental and African Studies, published in 1977 after a year of life "on the ground" in the Zoroastrian villages of Iran. Professor Boyce remained ambivalent about Zoroaster's precise dates, but she at least succeeded in establishing to the satisfaction of all that his "mythical" European dates of 6500 or 6000 BCE are to be replaced by dates somewhere between 1200 and 1000 BCE at a minimum. These later dates work plausibly with the theses of this compendium and *Three Testaments:*

Torah, Gospel, and Quran, though not as well as the traditional Persian dates placing his birth late in the seventh century BCE and his death mid-sixth century BCE, about a generation before Cyrus came to power in Babylon.

A separate effort to date Zoroaster by the Persian records received its impetus from earlier European scholarship in 1947 when Ernst Emil Herzfeld, a German (Jewish) archaeologist and Iranologist at Princeton University (taking refuge from the Nazis), published new evidence just a year before he died.[2] As the culmination of a lifelong investigation, Herzfeld produced evidence supporting the Persian view that the King Vishtāspa (German, Wistaspa / Greek, Hystaspes), who is named by Darius I as his father, was the very same king named by Zoroaster in the Gatha sections of the Avesta as his royal patron. This would coincide precisely with the time period in the traditional Persian record. Herzfeld's views found immediate support and further convincing arguments by the German scholar W. B. Henning,[3] published in 1951. Henning upheld the authenticity of the Persian view of Zoroastrian tradition as presented by Hassan Taqizadeh, an Iranian politician who was an authority on Middle Eastern calendars. The growing consensus picked up enough momentum that it produced a popular view among literary sophisticates, expressed in *Creation,* a novel by Gore Vidal. That story was narrated by the fictional grandson of Zoroaster in 445 BCE, describing encounters with aged figures of the Axial Age during his travels.[4]

In the strictly academic sphere, opponents of the traditional Persian dates continued to support the dominant European position, situating Zoroaster at around 1000 BCE. This still works in our view about an understanding of the Oneness of God coming from Israel to Zoroaster, since we find Moses next door at a still earlier time, but does not fit as well regarding pristine Persian Zoroastrian influence on the Jews in Babylonian Exile. In opposition to the traditional Persian position supported by Herzfeld and Henning, the supporters of the dominant European view were led by Gherardo Gnoli, professor of Iranian philology at University of Naples "L'Orientale" from 1965 to 1993, an authority in the non-English-speaking world perhaps on a par with Mary Boyce.

Opposing scholars who were lining up to side with the old Persian position now included William W. Malandra and R. C. Zaehner, outspoken American and British scholars, respectively, but in 1977 they were all overshadowed by Mary Boyce, who published the fruits of her year spent in the Zoroastrian village of Sharifibad in Iran. Henning himself was the respected mentor of Mary Boyce, but she never quite agreed with his dating. The publishing of her diary of life among the Zoroastrian villagers appeared to answer all questions, including a perhaps gratuitous treatment of the dating issue.

It appeared that Herzfeld, Henning, Taqizadeh, Vidal, Malandra, Zaehner, and others had failed to carry the day in one of the more engaging scholarly debates of the twentieth century. Then, shortly before his 1996 election as president of the Italian Institute for Africa and the East, upon reconsideration of the Darius–Vishtāspa matter, Gherardo Gnoli dramatically changed sides, accepting that Zoroaster may indeed have been an early contemporary of Cyrus, living in the sixth century BCE rather than around 1000 BCE. Malandra immediately wrote a new review of *Textual*

Sources for the Study of Zoroastrianism, by Mary Boyce, in the *Journal of the American Oriental Society*[5] in which he challenged her position on the 1000 BCE era dates. Her supporter Shapur Shabazi replied with grace in the *Bulletin of the School of Oriental and African Studies* as follows:

> On the basis of a King List and several allusions in medieval sources, many scholars have insisted that an authentic Zoroastrian "tradition" placed Zoroaster in the sixth century B.C. This theory was demolished in 1977, but recently Professor Gherardo Gnoli has restated it in great detail and with seemingly sound arguments.[6]

According to Mary Boyce, Shabazi himself was not personally convinced, but the conversion of Gnoli to the Persian traditional view was the beginning of movement toward that position, and at least openness by Mary herself and other leading Iranists, which has continued and is in line with our thinking. In spite of this consensus, however, there are still respected scholars of Zoroastrianism who cling to the dates between 1000 and 1300 BCE, mainly for philological reasons, since it is clear that the Gathas composed by Zoroaster himself employ a language from that earlier era. The answer to that is found in twentieth-century Christian hymns and prayers written in Shakespearean English, the "noble" form of the language employed more than three hundred years earlier in the beloved King James Version of the Bible. In similar fashion, as he reinterpreted proto-Vedic scriptural traditions for his time, Zoroaster would have been inspired to authenticate his words by the use of the still revered Vedic language and cadence from that earlier era. Mormon, Baha'i, and other modern "scriptures" are introduced in old English for the same reason.

The views of Mary Boyce on this and related matters were conveyed by her to this author in a series of lengthy telephone conversations between England and Canada in the winters of 2004–2005 and 2005–2006, during consultations in regard to writing the book *Noah's Other Son*. She had a concern that her efforts had failed to establish an adequate connection between Judaism and Zoroastrianism in Babylon, a neglected area of study, in her view, and one she was anxious to have addressed. It was not possible to include her wise counsel in that regard in *Noah's Other Son*, but the second winter of conversations was especially poignant, as she conversed lying down from what would become her deathbed a few months later. A commitment was made to address this issue in a subsequent publication—namely, *Three Testaments: Torah, Gospel, and Quran*—and she also took a certain delight in sharing her perspective on the "battles" over the evolving consensus regarding Zoroaster's dates.

She never did commit to a change of her own published position, though she often acknowledged that her mentor, Walter Henning, favored the sixth-century dates, and she was forthcoming in suggesting how the Persian position could be supported and maintained. It was she who suggested, perhaps as an original thought, that the philological issue of antiquated language could be resolved by reference to the practice of Christians and others of authenticating their new works by the use of Shakespearean English as the most noble form of English, and that the King James translators were perhaps the first to employ this technique (or "trick," as she called it), since that form of English was also archaic, even by the time the "Authorized Version" of the Bible was published, adding its own imprimatur to the tradition that lasted four hundred years. This would be almost exactly the length of the validating throwback employed by Zoroaster.

So where do we go to find the original (or post-Alexander reconstituted) text of the Zoroastrian Avesta? There are a number of possibilities, but one stands out. A legend that survives in the language of the Pali canon of Buddhist writings relates how Silk Route merchants began spreading the Buddha's teachings, even within his lifetime, and that they were especially well received in the Zoroastrian stronghold of Bactria a generation after Zoroaster, since the teachings were compatible, some of them being almost the same. According to the legend, two brothers named Tapassu and Bhallika had visited the Buddha and became his disciples. They returned to Bactria and built temples dedicated to the Buddha in the original Zoroastrian stronghold.[7]

This would appear to have sent devotees who chose to cling to orthodox Zoroastrian traditions to Sogdiana, an ancient Persian province in the region just to the north, for refuge. The population of Sogdiana was thoroughgoing in its loyal Zoroastrian devotion, even while welcoming Buddhists and other religions there, in accordance with Zoroastrian liberality, but with different results. Sogdiana was becoming established as an ethnic entity in Zoroaster's own time and appears to have become the default position refuge for Zoroastrians from anywhere in the Persian Empire, right up until practically the last gasp of that religion as a major influence in the world, a final transition in the face of the advance of Islam a thousand years later.

Sogdiana flourished as the main thoroughfare of the Silk Route for most of a thousand years, independent—sometimes under Greek rule, sometimes Chinese, eventually under Islamic domination—but always flourishing and always maintaining its evolving Zoroastrian traditions. This happy state of affairs lasted until a time of great Sogdian influence in China itself, when the Sogdians backed the wrong horse in a Chinese rebellion and had to hide their identities and assimilate. Of the many publications about the Silk Route, the story of Sogdiana is perhaps told best by Professor Jenny Rose of Claremont University, herself of Zoroastrian ancestry, in her book *Zoroastrianism* and in an article titled "The Sogdians: Prime Movers between Boundaries."[8]

Rose sets the scene in the ancient world for our search for the Avesta in Sogdiana around its ancient capital of Samarkand, still the capital of what is now modern Uzbekistan. Rose herself does not accept our exact dates, nor does she adopt our technique of reading backward from Babylon to the evidence about Zoroastrian origins immediately prior to the Jewish exile. In her writings she offers little direct reflection on the two occasions when the Avesta was banned and "destroyed" throughout the Persian Empire, first by Greeks and later by Muslims, but our readers can pick these things out for themselves by now. The upshot of the matter is that the vibrant trade community that became the default center for Zoroastrian refugees in times of conflict was itself overcome in circumstances that prompted Zoroastrian devotees to become masters of disguise and subterfuge with respect to their culture, language, and religion.

The missing portions of the Avesta, referred to by us as the "Dead Zee Scrolls," may someday be found elsewhere, anywhere from Babylon to Chengdu. Our money is on the likelihood that, like Roman artifacts of the same era found recently beneath the streets of London, England, the "Dead Zee Scrolls" will be found beneath the streets of Samarkand in Uzbekistan or in one of the ancient treasure troves in its environs.

Meanwhile, back in Egypt, the further investigation of what lay behind the wall in King Tutankhamen's tomb was producing results. A special three-day examination was authorized with Egyptian, British, and Japanese experts on site from November 25 to November 27, 2015. At a news conference on Saturday, November 28, Japanese expert Hirokatsu Watanabe confirmed with "at least 90 percent certainty" that a large room of undetermined size certainly exists and has objects within it that will remain unidentifiable pending further study of the images in a lab in Japan. Nicolas Reeves was ecstatic in his comments: "Clearly it does look from the radar evidence as if the tomb continues as I have predicted. If I am right, it is a corridor continuation of the tomb which will end in another burial chamber. It does look as if the tomb of Tutankhamen is a corridor tomb and it continues beyond the decorated burial chamber. I think it is Nefertiti and all the evidence points in that direction."[9]

Antiquities Minister Mamdouh el-Damaty gave his opinion that if it is a tomb, it might be that of Kiya, another wife of Pharaoh Akhenaton—indeed, Tutankhamen's own mother. Then, speaking in English, he announced, "We can now say that we have to find behind the burial chamber of King Tutankhamen another chamber and another tomb." No destructive digging is to take place in the immediate future, and, pending reports from the lab, the next authorized step is likely to be miniscule drilling to insert lighting and a camera. Still nothing definitive, but the world's interest is only increasing. Those of us associated with our own quest for the "Dead Zee Scrolls," perhaps in a cave in China or beneath the streets of Samarkand, are encouraged to believe that Professor Richard Freund's equipment really works and that it is only a matter of time before the discovery of our own "Holy Grail" would undergo similar tests.

epilogue

The Resurrection of Zoroaster: A Prophet from the East for the Twenty-First Century

THE ZOROASTRIAN CONNECTION PROVIDES THE LINK BETWEEN EASTERN AND WESTERN religions, as well as between monism and monotheism. Zoroaster himself is the prophet we may need for the twenty-first century insofar as his prophetic insight provides the model we may need for life in multifaith societies. We see this model in the reign of Cyrus in Persia, applied in high relief in the case of his relations with the Jews. We see it also in the practice of Zoroastrians in Sogdiana and in the inclusive attitude of Sogdians throughout the length of the Silk Route over the thousand years of their stewardship of that trade corridor. In Bactria the devotees living in Zoroaster's original Balkh stronghold were so taken with the Indian Buddhism, which emerged next door as a new religion that developed in the wake of Zoroaster's influence, that they adopted it as a natural evolution, the way Manichaeism, Nestorian Christianity, and ultimately Islam developed or came to be accepted in various other places in the religious evolution of the Persian Empire, where this happened (for the most part) without violent reaction. The dominance of Islam, the Crusades, inquisitions, and holocausts were all of another era.

This may be the model needed for the similar evolution of interfaith coexistence in a New Axial Age of multicultural milieu in urban societies in many parts of the world today, and even out in the new rural realities of North America and elsewhere. It does not hurt this trend that we can now identify Zoroastrian linkages connecting Hinduism, Buddhism, Taoism, and other traditions with Judaism, Christianity, and Islam. The latter in particular has an understanding in the Quranic teaching that God has provided prophetic witnesses to the revelation of His word in every society, even if to be interpreted afresh in their own tradition or corrected from corruptions. Something like that might be adopted and applied among all believers as a basis for dialogue, an evolution of understanding, and a foundation for the mutual respect that appears so lacking in the resurgence of religion in many developing parts of the world and its denigration in developed societies.

This suggests that the purpose of our study is not the acquisition of esoteric information but the practical addressing of perhaps the most pressing issue of our time. "Faith relations" of the twenty-first century are replacing "race relations" of the twentieth century even before the latter is adequately resolved. However, in the awful autumn anguish of racial tensions in 2014, the example of white and black congregations in Titusville, Florida, opting to worship together in the face of racial turmoil was an indication that faith relations may even be the key to race relations. This approach is urgently required in Egypt, the Ukraine, Burma, Germany, Iraq, France, and many other places. It can be facilitated by application of the genesis of interfaith activities at a new level suggested by this study. Religion is among the most acute problem areas of our world, but it also has the capacity to be the leading edge of the solution, with all believers and practitioners remaining loyal to their traditions and, at the same time, respectfully comfortable in their understanding of others in mutual sharing of insights, studies, and faith-motivated activities. Zoroastrianism could be the model, not uniting East and West but engendering mutual respect.

The discoveries at Dunhuang may be a precursor of the most exciting breakthrough yet to come in the unearthing of the "Dead Zee Scrolls." While we can acknowledge that, like "Q," the full text of "Z" might never be found, we have come far enough in this study to possibly implement some of the further insights that would come if we did. However, that question being addressed, there is no reason why we should not at least pursue "the quest for the historical Zoroaster" and undertake a more serious archaeological search for the Zoroastrian Avesta Scriptures with some hope of success.

Though the results were not what everybody expected, the spectacular success of new high-tech instruments in the recent high-profile Egyptian investigation indicates that we are almost certainly on the cusp of dramatic new discoveries in many parts of the world where ancient cultures flourished. Zoroastrian religion, and the related Persian cultural influence in the ancient world, was dominant or influential across the Silk Route for approximately one thousand years. This is less than the rise and fall of Egyptian civilization over a period of three millennia, but Persian rule and Zoroastrian influence extended over a larger area than the Egyptians could claim, and they have had a more pervasive sway over the planet, from India and China to the Middle East and Europe, as well as transmitted influence from Europe to Africa and the Americas. Astounding gaps in our understanding, particularly regarding Zoroastrian religion as the conduit of Vedic influence to the seven world religions and many local traditional religions, are surely about to be addressed in the vortex created by accidental folk discoveries and high-tech resources, which can provide answers to questions as yet unasked.

As the twenty-first century unfolds before us, the International Dunhuang Project provides a model for Zoroastrian studies among the leading universities, museums, libraries, and related institutions that have such departments in many parts of the world. We need something like that to coordinate the exciting discoveries made year by year in Samarkand, Bukhara, Tashkent, more remote corners of Uzbekistan, western China, and elsewhere. China itself is assuming a new and more vigorous role in a region where it appears eager to exert economic and political influence. In this regard, China seems ready to cooperate with others in archaeological projects and even religious research in the pattern established by its participation in the International Dunhuang Project. A partial list of individuals, institutions, sample publications, and centers where such efforts were recently or are currently undertaken with informal connections to each other might be of interest at this point (see table 1).

Table 1

Leading Scholars	Usual Location	Current Institution	Publications, DVDs, etc.
Xinru Liu	Beijing	New Jersey College	The Silk Road
Martin Schwartz	Berkeley	University of California, Berkeley	various articles
Philip Kreyenbroek	Kassel	Gottingen University	Living Zoroastrianism
Geoffrey Herman	Jerusalem	Hebrew University	Jews, Christians, Zoroastrians
Albert de Jong	Leiden	Leiden University	Traditions of the Magi
Susan Whitfield	London	British Library	Life Along the Silk Road
Almut Hintze	London	University of London	Change & Continuity in Zoroastrian Tradition
François De Blois	London	University College	Persian Literature: Royal Asiatic Society
Jennifer Rose	Los Angeles	Claremont University	Zoroastrianism
Richard Foltz	Montreal	Concordia University	Religions of the Silk Road
Valery Hansen	New Haven, Connecticut	Yale University	The Silk Road, A New History
Yaakov Elman	New York	Yeshiva University	Iran, the Magi, and the Jews
Boris Marshak*	Samarkand	Moscow University	Legends of Sogdiana
M. L. West	Oxford	Oxford University	Hymns of Zoroaster
Frantz Grenet	Paris	Collège de France	Bulletin of Asia Institute
Étienne de la Vaissière	Paris	Ecole des Hautes Etudes	Sogdian Traders
Gherardo Gnoli*	Naples	University of Rome	Encyclopaedia Iranica
Ito Gikyo	Kyoto	Kyoto University	Ito Artifact Collection
Enrico Raffaelli	Toronto	University of Toronto	Sih-rozag in Zoroastrianism
J. P. Mallory	Belfast	Queens University	In Search of IndoEuropeans
David W. Anthony	Oxford	Hartwick College	The Horse, the Wheel and Language

*Recently deceased

Students and readers of this compendium are invited and encouraged to look for opportunities to be associated with any developing network attempting to establish formal or informal links between the above agencies and persons. To remain connected in the short term, those who have such interest may receive a monthly blog report on developments by contacting the author and contributing editor of this volume directly.

Meanwhile, the appendix to this work may whet appetites for the deluge of written materials that may be confidently expected to descend upon us in the course of the twenty-first century, maybe even within the next decade. The documents in our appended exhibition were all discovered within the twentieth century. None of these manuscripts were in possession of scholars prior to that time, nor were they even known to exist, much like those yet to come in our time. For that matter, when these documents were found it often took some time for academics and researchers to recognize them for what they are. We are just getting started in the search for the "Dead Zee Scrolls," and what better place to begin than with some old inscribed bones from China that indicate the extent of Chinese cultural intercourse with the Persian Empire at the approximate time of Zoroaster? These bones show the influence of Cyrus, who as a child very possibly knew that special prophet and grew up to participate in the propagation of related ideologies to the West through the interface between Zoroastrian priests and Jewish scholars in Babylon, and to the East into India and even areas of China, where Magi had already paved the way and continued to operate.

The Edict of Cyrus was thought to be as legendary as the Trojan War until the discovery of the Cyrus Cylinder in the pre-dawn of the twentieth century. The fact that copies were in widespread circulation in the ancient world is only now being realized, a reality that suggests that somewhere, and soon, we will also find ourselves in possession of material from the "Dead Zee Scrolls," whether on potshard, bone, parchment, leather, or metal (as illustrated in the appendix that follows). We preface this fascinating exhibition with material from the website of K. E. Eduljee, our guide from within the Zoroastrian community. The point of this final material on the Cyrus Edict is to illustrate the likelihood of discovering other important material from the same era—namely, the "Dead Zee Scrolls."

APPENDIX

Images of the Original Eastern Testaments

and Tantalizing Hints of Things to Come

preface: the edict of cyrus and the chinese cuneiform bones

K. E. EDULJEE OF ZOROASTRIAN HERITAGE, HERITAGE INSTITUTE[1]

In 1928, Xue Shenwei, a Chinese traditional doctor was shown two inscribed fossilized horse bones that bore a script that was unknown to him [and presumably to the then owner(s) of the artifacts as well].

The bones had been found somewhere in China. Seven years later, Xue decided to purchase the bones. He bought the first in 1935 and the second in 1940. Xue presumed the writing on them was in an unknown ancient script once used in ancient China.

In 1966, during the Chinese Cultural Revolution, Xue buried the bones for safe-keeping. Years later, when he thought the threat of the bones being confiscated or destroyed had passed, he dug up the bones and, in 1983, took them to the Palace Museum in Beijing's Forbidden City for examination and assessment. The inscription collection of the Palace Museum is the largest of its kind in China and Xue likely hoped that the museum's curators and experts might be able to shed some light on the script. It was then that Xue learned that the script on the bones was not a lost Chinese script, but cuneiform. In 1985, shortly before his demise, Xue donated the bones to the Museum naming the seller(s) from whom he had earlier purchased the bones.

Palace Museum specialist Wu Yuhong determined that the cuneiform text on one of the bones under consideration bore similarities to the text on the Babylonian Cyrus Cylinder. As he could not identify the text on the other bone, the Palace Museum sent images of the script on the two bones to the British Museum for further study.

At this juncture in the narrative, we need to turn our attention to the ongoing analysis of the (incomplete) text contained on the Cyrus Cylinder found in Babylon. In 2009, Wilfred Lambert, a retired professor from Birmingham University, and Irving Finkel, Curator of Cuneiform Collections at the British Museum, had determined that the text on some additional tablet fragments in the British Museum's possession were part of Cyrus's proclamation. These fragments had been uncovered by Hormuzd Rassam in Dailem (a site near but separate from Babylon). Shortly after this discovery by Lambert, his colleague Irving Finkel, assistant keeper, Department of the Middle East, similarly identified another tablet fragment. Perhaps, now aware of the possibility that the text on the Cyrus Cylinder was not unique to the Babylon temple where the cylinder had been found—that it might have been only one instance of Cyrus's proclamation being distributed throughout Cyrus's empire—Finkel reexamined the images of the Chinese bones. He now determined that the text on the second bone that had not been previously connected to Cyrus, was also part of Cyrus's proclamation.

It is of some interest to note that inscribed animal bones have been discovered in China dating back to the fourteenth to twelfth centuries BCE. Such inscriptions are the oldest surviving examples of the Chinese script used to write complete and meaningful sentences. The inscribed bones are referred to as oracle bones. The bones in our example shown in figure 4 of this appendix are from a scapula (shoulder blade) of an ox. About ten thousand oracle bones are known to exist. Nearly all known Chinese oracle bones are from Xiaotun (also Yinxu or Yin Xu) located three kilometers northwest of Anyang, the ancient capital of the late Shang Dynasty. Anyang itself is located in the northern province of Henan not far from the eastern terminus of the Silk Roads, namely, the cities of Zhengzhou and Luoyang.

This region would have been very familiar to Iranian traders, especially Sogdians who had colonies along Chinese sections of the Silk Roads. The largest number of oracle bones date to the reign of Wu Ding, who died around 1189 BCE. The oracular use of the bones involved the interpretation of patterns of cracks that appeared on the bones after subjecting them to heat via a heated metal rod. The text on the bones records the interpretation of the oracle and the date of its production. We make this note since the use of inscriptions on bones is very specific to one area of China known to ancient Iranian (Persian) traders, and where they have been found in great abundance.

Finkel communicated his finding to the Palace Museum and at the same time requested better images of the text. The request prompted Chinese Assyriologist Dr. Yushu Gong to make a set of rubbings of the bone inscriptions using black wax (on white paper). The resulting contrast provided a more distinct representation of the script on the bones than had the previous photographs.

At about the same time that the communication between Finkel and Gong had been taking place, the British Museum and the Iran Heritage Foundation cosponsored a two-day workshop on new discoveries concerning the Cyrus Cylinder to be held on June 23 and 24, 2010. Yushu Gong carried the cuneiform bone rubbings with him to the workshop in London, where he presented them to the participants. The findings of the workshop were announced to a public information session on the evening of June 24—by presenters Neil MacGregor, Irving Finkel, Matthew Stolper, and John Curtis.

Irving Finkel, curator of Cuneiform Collections at the British Museum, contemplates a black wax rubbing of the Chinese cuneiform–inscribed horse-bone text. (Courtesy of the British Museum)

Finkel had determined that both the script and the text on the Chinese bones were similar to, but not identical to, those on the Cyrus Cylinder. The peculiarity of the text on the Chinese bones—with every twentieth word transcribed literally—was that they were linguistically correct. In addition, the individual wedge-like strokes of the cuneiform characters had a slightly different v-shaped top compared to the Babylonian standard. The shape of the top of the characters was similar to the form used by scribes in Persia. Finkel therefore stated, "The text used by the copier on the bones was not the Cyrus Cylinder, but another version, probably originally written in Persia, rather than Babylon." Questions about the certainty of this adjudication were raised later, including qualms expressed by Finkel himself.

But if the writing on the bones was a forgery written by someone with no knowledge of the cuneiform script, one could reasonably expect a number of errors and even a made-up script. Regardless of the authenticity of the Chinese bones as a legitimately distributed copy of Cyrus's edict, whoever made the bone inscriptions would have had to have access to a Persian version of Cyrus's edict. This in itself is a further indication that Cyrus's edict was not limited to Babylon and for this reason alone, the text merits serious consideration as a copy of the edict that had been circulated throughout Cyrus's realm. That version could have been written not as a clay inscription, but on any substrate. It could have been carved on stone or written with ink on leather as well as parchment.

There wasn't sufficient time at the workshop for an in-depth analysis of the Chinese cuneiform bones. That would require further debate. Nevertheless, what was beginning to take hold was the concept that the Cyrus's Cylinder was not just another foundation deposit—it was part of a larger distribution of Cyrus's edict. The corollary to this concept was that Cyrus had intended the edict to be a universal policy of governance throughout his empire.

Christian Jesuits arrived in India in 1541 CE to a literate community of religious scholars. Along with their small Bibles, we can only speculate about what other books are on display here at the court of King Akbar in this artwork from around 1558. (*Jesuits at the Court of an Indian Prince* (gouache on paper), Indian School (sixteenth century) / Private Collection / Otus / Index / Bridgeman Images)

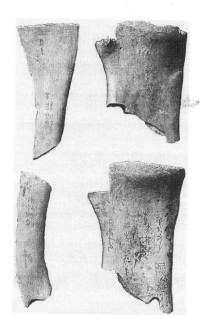

Fourteenth- to twelfth-century oracle (ox) bones from Xiaotun, China. Excavated in 1945. (Courtesy of the Schøyen Collection, Oslo and London)

Ashem Vohu: "Holiness is the best of all good: it is also happiness." This is the copy of a fragment of a copy of the ancient Avesta referred to by Professor Richard Freund in his introduction to Book VII. It is a prayer that the Zoroastrian community happens to have already, though this is a copy at least a thousand years older than those cherished in recent centuries. It was found by Aurel Stein in Dunhuang, at the Chinese end of the Silk Road, in a trove of material, dating from the fifth to the ninth centuries CE. Admittedly, what we are looking for ultimately dates back even a thousand years before that, to the pristine or classical Zoroastrian era in the same general area or even somewhat to the west of Dunhuang in the locale of old Sogdiana, modern Uzbekistan, where the search continues on a daily basis at the present time "beneath the streets of Samarkand." (Courtesy of the International Dunhuang Project, British Library, Or.8212/84)

The second-century BCE Ma-wang-tui Lao Tsu Ms2. manuscript of the *Tao Te Ching* is germane to this study, both as a specific instance in which unexpected finds move the dating of earliest available scripts of a tradition back by many centuries and as the basis for the translation used in this compendium. (Courtesy of Harvard University)

the analects

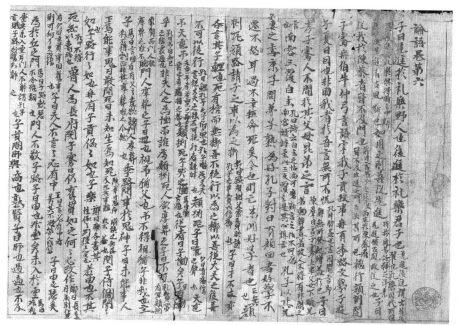

On his website, Robert Eno, late of Indiana University, describes such a page as "a leaf from a medieval hand copy of the *Analects*, dated 890 CE, recovered from an archaeological dig at Dunhuang, in the Western desert regions of China. That manuscript has been determined to be a school boy's hand copy, complete with errors, and it reproduces not only the text (which appears in large characters), but also an early commentary (the small, double-column characters). Recovery of that particular copy of the text was unusually valuable, because the second century CE commentary it includes (in smaller characters) is a famous one by a great early scholar that has otherwise been largely lost." (Courtesy of the International Dunhuang Project, British Library, Or.8210/S.4106)

the diamond sutra

The world's earliest dated printed book was found in a cave 1907 by the archaeologist Marc Aurel Stein in northwest China. It had been hidden near Dunhuang on the Silk Road, with thousands of other manuscripts and printed items. It is the earliest example of block printing to bear a date: "the 13th of the fourth moon of the ninth year of Xiantong" (i.e., May 11, 868 CE). Though written in Chinese, the text is one of the most important sacred works of the Buddhist faith, founded in India. It was first translated from Sanskrit into Chinese at about 400 CE. (Courtesy of the International Dunhuang Project, British Library, Or.8210/P.2)

the heart sutra

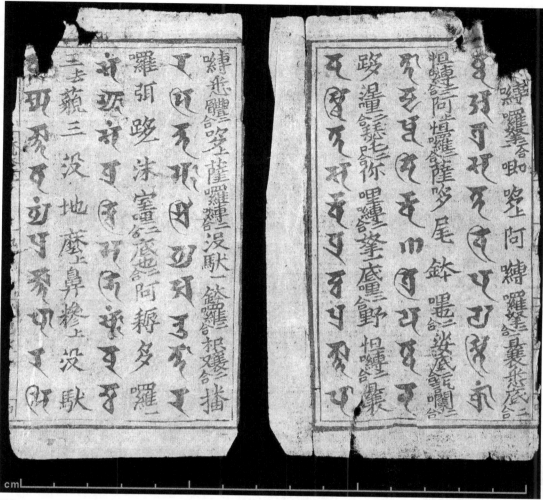

This text was produced in the Western Xia state of China (1038–1227) during the twelfth or thirteenth centuries CE and hidden in a stupa outside the city walls of the abandoned Western Xia fortress city of Khara-Khoto in Gansu. It was obtained by Marc Aurel Stein during his later expedition of 1913–1916. In the British Museum it is exhibited alongside the *Diamond Sutra* in the "early printing" display because of its production by early block printing techniques. It is written in Sanskrit with a phonetic transcription in Chinese in an era in which, until recently, it was believed that China had no connections with India, Iran, or the West. (Courtesy of the International Dunhuang Project, British Library, Or.12380/3500)

the dhammapada

"If you want honor, wealth, or, after death, a blissful life among the gods, then take good care that you observe the precepts of a moral life" (*Dharmapada*, 4b.; Conze 1959: 84). (Courtesy of the International Dunhuang Project, British Library, Or.8210/S.782)

baghavad gita

There were no copies of the *Bhagavad Gita* found at Dunhuang, nor have any been found to date at any other of the celebrated sites of ancient provenance. There are Hindu devotees and some scholars who wish to place its origins back with the Vedic Scriptures (to which the *Gita* actually refers), but a date around 400 BCE is generally accepted. Victor Mair has produced evidence that it had links to, or a common source with, the *Tao Te Ching* in China during the Axial Age, when ideas and theologies were being shared along the Silk Road. (Courtesy of the India Office Library, British Library, Add.26457-folio # 17r)

Who knew there could be so many Jewish texts sealed up with the others among ancient Silk Road documents discovered at Dunhuang? Richard Freund says, "This document is one of the earliest Jewish texts written on paper anywhere." Ancient Jewish parchment documents at such locations in Western China were actually voluminous, physical evidence of business, cultural, and religious interchanges in the ancient world, which, when speculated upon at the beginning of this compendium, may have seemed almost far-fetched by some of our readers. We know now that the "Lost Tribes of Israel" traveled to China and India as well as to Africa and Europe. (Courtesy of the International Dunhuang Project, British Library, Or.8212/166 [D.XIII])

postscript to the appendix

Were our readers among those who wondered whether Nefertiti's tomb had been behind the burial chamber of King Tutankhamen for more than three millennia, hidden behind a wall of artwork seen by millions of tourists every year since 1922? It took infrared scanning and other high-tech devices described by Professor Freund in this book to investigate what lay behind door-shaped cracks in the wall that were spotted in the summer of 2015 by Nicholas Reeves, a British archaeologist now associated with the University of Arizona and funded by National Geographic. We followed that investigation as it unfolded during the compiling of this compendium merely to illustrate the possibilities of finding the "Dead Zee Scrolls" through the use of similar technologies in this century. We are entering an era that is certain to produce more artifacts and scrolls than even imagined in the twentieth century, including earlier manuscripts of *Tao Te Ching*, *Analects*, *Dhammapada*, *Bhagavad Gita*, and Avesta, the "four fingers and a thumb" described in our prologue and discussed within various sections of this compendium and exhibited in this appendix.

As author of this work, when I recall the times that I visited Tutankhamen's tomb, oblivious to the hidden chambers right at hand, I think of those who may find it difficult to imagine the Avesta Scriptures being so close at some other site. The sketch on the next page is a composite of my own recollection of Tut's tomb, speculative diagrams of preliminary inquiries, and the results of putative scans performed on April 2, 2016. We present this exploration to both Zoroastrian scholars and scholars of Zoroastrianism as encouragement in their quests to know more about the source of the religious stimulation along the Silk Road not long after Nefertiti's lifetime. In just such a place we may find the "Dead Zee Scrolls," representing the tradition that may have led or contributed much to the *Tao Te Ching*, the *Analects*, the *Dhammapada*, the *Bhagavad Gita*, and the spiritual communities that grew out of those testaments. We know now that they all also share connections with the Torah, the New Testament, and the Quran, in humanity's quest to know and serve one God in various manifestations, expressed in monotheistic terms and in ultimate unity with all.

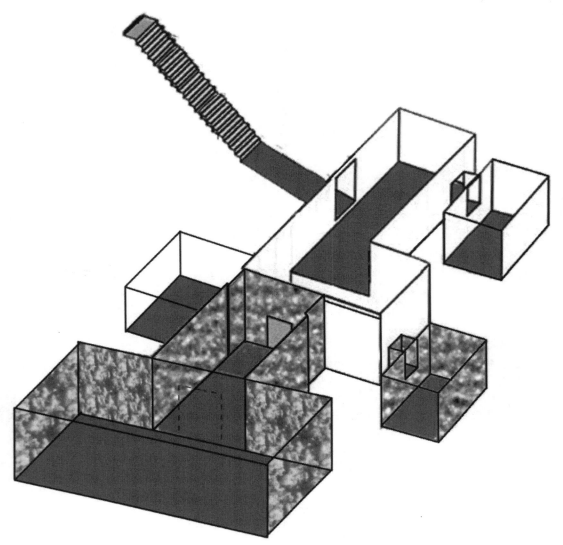

Who Knows What Lies Hidden in a Tomb?

notes

prologue

1. Rasiah Sugirtharajah, *The Bible and Asia* (Cambridge, MA: Harvard University Press, 2013), 44.

2. Norman Cohn, *Cosmos, Chaos & the World to Come: The Ancient Roots of Apocalyptic Faith* (New Haven, CT: Yale University Press, 2001).

3. J. C. Hindley, "A Prophet Outside Israel? Thoughts on the Study of Zoroastrianism," *Indian Journal of Theology* II, no. 3 (1962), 107.

4. Brian Arthur Brown, *Three Testaments: Torah, Gospel, and Quran* (Lanham, MD: Rowman & Littlefield, 2012).

book one: from the foundations of the earth to our common spiritual ancestors

INTRODUCTION

1. Esther 1:14.

2. Isaiah 7:14.

3. Numbers 24:17.

4. Cyril Glassé, *The Second Coming of the Judeo-Zoroastrian Jesus of the Dead Sea Scrolls* (New York: Revelation, 2014), 164–65.

5. Cyril Glassé, *The New Encyclopedia of Islam,* fourth edition (Lanham, MD: Rowman & Littlefield, 2013), 570.

6. Ibid., 571.

EXORDIUM

1. Ζωροάστρρης.

2. New Persian, *Zardushi.*

3. K. F. Geldner, *Encyclopaedia Britannica,* eleventh edition, vol. 28 (New York: Encyclopaedia Britannica, 1911), 1040.

4. Ibid.

5. Ibid.

6. Ibid.

7. Ibid.

8. Ibid.

9. Ibid.

10. Yasna, 9, 1.

11. Yasna, 57, 8.

12. *Arda Vīrāf*, I, 2.

13. Geldner, *Encyclopaedia Britannica*, 1040.

14. Iranian *Mithra*.

15. *Asha* = Vedic *rla*.

16. Yasna, 44, 9.

17. Yasna, 30, 3.

18. Reference has been made to Zoroaster's natural monotheism, but it is not difficult to understand how the religion sometimes veered off course to dualism, supposing the evil spirit to be a god. That spirit is the spirit of falsehood and is itself false, whereas Ahura Mazda represents the complete oneness of God in all that is true.

19. cf. *Bundahish*, I, 4.

20. Yasna, 31, 11.

21. *Garō demāna*.

PREFACE

1. Rustam Azimov, "Zoroastrian Fire temple at Khorazm," *Uzbekistan Today*, November 20, 2013.

CHAPTER ONE

1. According to the Quran and Muslim tradition as described in Brian Arthur Brown, *Noah's Other Son: Bridging the Gap between the Bible and the Qur'an* (New York: Continuum, 2007).

2. William Schmidt, *The Origin of the Idea of God* (New York: Rowman & Littlefield, 1984).

3. As quoted by Karen Armstrong, *The Great Transformation* (New York: Random House, 2007), 8.

4. Daniel 8:16.

5. Luke 1:19.

6. Luke 1:26.

7. Quran 96:1–3.

8. Genesis 12:1.

9. Genesis 28:12.

10. Genesis 32:24–28.

11. Exodus 3:2.

12. Exodus 19.

13. Acts 9.

14. *Achsenseit* or "axis time" in Karl Jaspers, *Vom Ursprung und Ziel der Geschichte* (The Origin and Goal of History) (New York: Yale University Press, 1953).

15. Jaspers's use of the German word *Achse* is translated equally as *axis* or *pivot*.

16. Daniel 5.

17. William Barclay, *The Revelation of John*, Vol. 1 (Philadelphia: Westminster Press, 1976), 122.

CHAPTER TWO

1. Zadspram 20–21.

2. Yasna, 31.8, 33.6–7, 43.5.

3. Yasna, 33.6, 13.94.

4. 2 Kings 17:6 and 1 Chronicles 5:26.

5. Arnold J. Toynbee, *A Study of History*, abridged by D. C. Somervell (New York: Oxford University Press, 1987), 387.

6. Jeremiah, chapter 3.

7. Jeremiah, chapter 47.

8. Cf. Bundahishn 34:1–9; Arda Wiraz 1:1–5; Denkard 7.7:6; Zadspram 33:11–12, quoted in Maneckii N. Dhalla, *History of Zoroastrianism* (Bombay: AMS Press, 1938), xxxi.

9. Al-Biruni, *The Chronology of Ancient Nations* (orig. 1000 CE), vol. 3, translated by C. Edward Sachau (Whitefish, MT: Kessinger, 2004), 17.

10. Émile Benveniste, "The Persian Religion According to the Chief Greek Text," *Journal des savants* 4, no. 1 (1931), 15.

11. Genesis 5:27.

12. Genesis 9:29.

13. This helpful illustration was introduced by Jenny Brown to my students in a seminary class who were having difficulty recognizing the potential for confusion in the ancient world's change from lunar to solar dating.

14. Susan Whitfield, *Life Along the Silk Road* (Los Angeles: University of California Press, 1999).

15. Sol A. Nigosian, *The Zoroastrian Faith* (Montreal and Kingston: McGill-Queens University Press, 1993).

16. Karen Armstrong, *The Great Transformation* (New York: Random House, 2007).

17. "Evil-merodach" in the books of Nehemiah and Ezra.

18. Esther 1:14.

19. Yasna, 13, 51.12, and 53.1.

20. Yasna, 13, 51.12, and 53.1.

21. Luke 3:23.

CHAPTER FOUR

1. Karl Jaspers, *Vom Ursprung und Ziel der Geschichte* (The Origin and Goal of History) (New York: Yale University Press, 1953). The debate on the "Axial Age" continued in the 1970s under the title "The Age of Transcendence." In a series of conferences since then, Shmuel N. Eisenstadt published his edited collection, *The Origin and Diversity of Axial Civilizations* (Albany, NY: SUNY Press, 1987).

2. Jan Assman, "World Religions and the Theory of the Axial Age," in *Dynamics in the History of Religions Between Asia and Europe*, edited by Volkhard Krech and Marion Steinicke (Leiden and Boston: Brill, 2012), 255.

3. Karl Jaspers, *The Way to Wisdom: An Introduction to Philosophy* (New Haven, CT: Yale University Press, 2003), 98.

4. Frederick Haberman, *Tracing Our Ancestors* (Villa Rica, GA: Kingdom Press, 1934), 129.

5. An ancient nation in modern Uzbekistan that disappeared during the Middle Ages.

6. K. F. Geldner, *Encyclopaedia Britannica*, eleventh edition, vol. 28 (New York: Encyclopaedia Britannica, 1911), 968.

CHAPTER FIVE

1. As detailed in the Avesta's *Dinkhard* iv, 21; v, 34; vii, 5, 11.

2. Pliny the Elder, *Natural History*, Volume XXX, 2.

3. Yasna, 8:1–27.

4. Yasna, 33:1–7 and 33:10–14.

5. Yasna, 43:5–8.

6. Yasna, 46:1–3.

7. Yasna, 44:1–5 and 44:8–12.

8. Yasna, 48:1–12.

CHAPTER SIX

1. Maneckii N. Dhalla, *History of Zoroastrianism* (Bombay: AMS Press, 1938), 331–32.

2. Yasna, 72:10.

3. Yasht, 13:56.

4. The author's own rendering of Yasna 27:13, in which "guru" is often rendered "teacher" by Western translators.

5. *The Way of Truth*.

6. Rig Veda, 10:129.

7. Victor Mair, "Religious Formation and Intercultural Contact in Early China," in *Dynamics in the History of Religions Between Asia and Europe*, edited by Volkhard Krech and Marion Steinicke (Leiden and Boston: Brill, 2012), 97.

8. G. W. F. Hegel, *Lectures on the History of Philosophy* (1805–1806), translated by E. S. Haldane (1892–1896), available at https://www.marxists.org/reference/archive/hegel/works/.../hpconten.htm, accessed February 12, 2016.

9. Theodore Goldstucker, *Literary Remains of the Late Professor Theodore Goldstucker* (London: W. H. Allen, 1879), 32.

10. *The Westminster Review*, Volumes 78–79 (1862), 478.

11. F. Max Muller, *Three Lectures on the Vedanta Philosophy* (Whitefish, MT: Kessinger, 2003), 123.

12. H. P. Blavatsky, *H. P. Blavatsky's Collected Writings*, volume 13 (Wheaton, IL: Quest Books, 1982), 308–10.

13. Matthew Stewart, *The Courtier and the Heretic* (New York: W. W. Norton, 2006), 106.

14. Girija Viraraghavan, "The History of Roses in India," IndianRoseFederation.org, Pune, India, accessed August 20, 2013.

15. The *Spinoza-huis*, or Spinoza Museum in Rijnsburg.

16. Samuel Cramer, "Mennoniten," in *Realencyclopedie für Protestantische Theologie and Kirche*, 24 vols, 3rd ed., edited by J. J. Herzog and Albert Hauck (Leipzig: J. H. Hinrichs, 1896–1913), 611.

17. Frank Thilly, *A History of Philosophy* (New York: Holt & Co., 1914), § 47.

18. "I believe in Spinoza's God who reveals himself in the orderly harmony of what exists, not in a God who concerns himself with fates and actions of human beings." These words were spoken by Albert Einstein, upon being asked whether he believed in God by Rabbi Herbert Goldstein of the Institutional Synagogue, New York, 24 April 1921, published in the *New York Times*, 25 April 1929; from Ronald W. Clark, *Einstein: The Life and Times* (New York: World Publishing Co., 1971), 413; also cited as a telegram to a Jewish newspaper, Einstein Archive 33-272, from Alice Calaprice, ed., *The Expanded Quotable Einstein* (Princeton, NJ: Princeton University Press, 1929).

19. *Stanford Encyclopedia of Philosophy*, vol. 5, 33 (see http://plato.stanford.edu/entries/pantheism/#Per).

20. *Stanford Encyclopedia of Philosophy*, vol. 1, 32c1.

21. *Stanford Encyclopedia of Philosophy*, appendix I.

22. *Stanford Encyclopedia of Philosophy*, vol. 1, 17s1.

23. *Stanford Encyclopedia of Philosophy*, vol. 5, 19.

24. Harold Bloom, "Deciphering Spinoza, the Great Original—Book review of 'Betraying Spinoza. The Renegade Jew Who Gave Us Modernity.' By Rebecca Goldstein," *New York Times*, 16 June 2006.

25. Ephesians 1:22.

26. 1 Corinthians 12:14–18.

27. John 17:20–22.

28. Ephesians 4:15.

29. Genesis 1:28.

30. Exodus 3:14.

book two: the taoist testament

INTRODUCTION

1. With excerpts from Victor H. Mair, "Religious Formation and Intercultural Contact in Early China," in *Dynamics in the History of Religions between Asia and Europe*, edited by Volkhard Krech and Marion Steinicke (Leiden and Boston: Brill, 2012), 92–95.

2. This statement succinctly encapsulates the reason for considering Taoism to be monistic, since the Way, sometimes translated as the Flow, is shown to be a living, all-inclusive reality of life-energy embracing everything in the universe.

3. Also known as the *I Ching*, the *Book of Changes* is an ancient divination text and the very oldest of the Chinese classics.

4. Several above paragraphs are from the introduction to Professor Mair's translation of *Tao Te Ching*, re-presented here with his warm support for this project, and the permission of his publisher, Bantam Books at Random House.

5. More extensive documentation for the facts concerning Magi in China presented in these paragraphs may be found with illustrations in Victor H. Mair, "Old Sinitic *ˀmʸag*, Old

Persian *maguš*, and English Magician," *Early China*, vol. 15 (1990): 27–47, and extensive bibliographic references for Mary Boyce regarding Zoroastrianism in this volume.

6. See Robert Eno, "Shang State Religion and the Pantheon of the Oracle Texts," in *Early Chinese Religion. Part One: Shang through Han (1250 BC–220 AD)*, edited by John Lagerwey and Marc Kalinowski (Leiden: Brill, 2008), 41–102.

7. Mair, "Religious Formation and Intercultural Contact in Early China," 92.

8. Victor H. Mair, *Tao Te Ching, The Classic Book of Integrity and the Way* (New York: Bantam, 1990), 147.

9. Victor H. Mair, *Wandering on the Way* (Honolulu: University of Hawaii Press, 1994), xviii.

PREFACE

1. Liu Xiaogan, *Our Religions: Taoism* (New York: Harper One, 1993), 231.

book three: the confucian testament

INTRODUCTION

1. *Tao Te Ching* 19 (#56 in earlier traditional versions).
2. The *Analects* of Confucius, *Analects* 4:24.
3. *Analects* 15:23.
4. *Analects* 19:7.
5. *Analects* 17:9.
6. *Analects* 14:26.
7. *Analects* 12:5.
8. *Avot* 3:21.
9. *Analects* 12:15.

PREFACE

1. *Analects* 14:34.
2. Tu Wei-ming, *Our Religions: Confucianism* (New York: Harper One, 1993), 141.
3. James Legge, "James Legge—A Short Biography" in *The Illustrated Tao Te Ching*, edited by Andrew Forbes and David Henley (Chiang Mai: Cognoscenti Books, 2012), ASIN: B008NNLKXC.
4. Tim Franks, *Reporting from China*, BBC radio documentary broadcast internationally in English, 12 July 2014.
5. Yu Dan, *Confucius from the Heart: Ancient Wisdom for Today's World* (New York: Atria Books, 2006).

book four: the buddhist testament

INTRODUCTION

1. Detailed in the preface that follows.
2. A Scythian tribe, fitting well with our thesis of a Zoroastrian connection.

3. Luke 2:25–28, a remarkable "coincidence" noted by the Dalai Lama and Marcus Borg in their collections regarding parallels between Buddhism and Christianity.

4. Another of the now famous life story parallels between Buddha and Jesus, suggesting a common source in Zoroastrianism, where the story is told earlier.

5. Ezekiel 36:31.

6. Galatians 5:22–23.

7. Galatians 5:19–21.

8. Latent in Vedic teaching, possibly hinted at in Zoroastrianism, and now to become explicit in both Buddhism and a revived Hinduism.

9. The Zoroastrian formula.

PREFACE

1. Masao Abe, *Our Religions: Buddhism* (New York: Harper One, 1993), 71.

2. Jack Kornfield, *Bringing Home the Dharma* (Boston: Shambhala, 2011).

3. See bibliographical entries for Thich Nhat Hanh and Elaine Pagels, Elmar R. Gruber and Holger Kersten, Markus Borg, and the Dalai Lama, all of whom have written complete books on the subject.

4. Information taken from *New York Times*, April 5–6, 2014, the international weekend edition.

5. Quoted by William R. LaFleur in Masao Abe, *Zen and Western Thought* (Honolulu: University of Hawaii Press, 1989), 209.

6. A rendering by the author, to emulate the essence of the sutra in the delightful ethos currently in vogue.

7. Genesis 2:24 and Mark 10:8.

8. A rendering by the author that gets to the heart of the matter.

9. *Ātman* is a Sanskrit word that means "inner self" or "soul" and is one of the terms that may remain untranslated in both the *Dhammapada* and the *Bhagavad Gita*.

book five: the hindu testament

INTRODUCTION

1. M. K. Gandhi, "Crime of Reading Bible," *Young India* VIII, no. 35 (September 2, 1926), 308.

2. *Bhagavad Gita*, 2.54, emphasis added.

3. *Analects*, 8.4.

4. *Analects*, 13.3.

5. *Analects*, 13.3.

6. *Analects*, 14.27.

7. *Analects*, 15.23.

8. *Analects*, 16.8.

9. *Analects*, 16.10a.

10. *Analects*, 16.10b.

11. *Analects*, 17.24.

12. *Analects*, 19.25.

13. See 12:21 and 16:7.

14. XII:13–20; XIV:21–27; and XVIII:49–56.

15. *Sthitaprajña*, XII.19.

16. *Sthitaprajña*, XVIII.52.

17. Quran, 41:34–35.

PREFACE

1. Arvind Sharma, *Our Religions: Hindusim* (New York: Harper One, 1993), 3.

2. Ellen Barry, "Gandhi's Face Imprinted on a New Brand of Leadership," *New York Times*, International Weekly, September 30, 2014, p. 4.

3. 1 Corinthians 6:19.

4. Meaning: nonviolence.

5. Meaning: renunciation.

6. Khushwant Singh, quoted in Renuka Narayanan, *The Book of Prayer* (Mumbai: Viking India, 2001).

7. Rudyard Kipling, *Rewards and Fairies* (London: Macmillan, 1919), 175.

8. Kipling, *Rewards and Fairies*, 175.

9. Victor H. Mair, *Tao Te Ching: The Classic Book of Integrity and the Way* (New York: Bantam, 1990), 41.

10. Barbara Stoler Miller, *Bhagavad-Gita: Krishna's Counsel in Time of War* (New York: Bantam, 1986), 18.

11. *Bhagavad Gita*, book 3, stanza 38.

12. *Tao Te Ching*, chapter 54, lines 6 and 7.

13. *Bhagavad Gita*, book 8, stanza 12.

14. *Tao Te Ching*, chapter 19, lines 4 and 5.

15. Mair, *Tao Te Ching*, 141 and 142.

16. Ibid., 146.

17. Proverbs 23:7, King James Authorized Version.

18. *Bhagavad Gita* 10:35: "Of Saman hymns I am Bright Saman; of metres, I am Gayatri."

19. Beginning with a traditional doxology, often untranslated even when recited in English, addressing the mantra that follows to God, making this both a prayer and a meditation.

20. Rig Veda 3.62:10 in the International Alphabet of Sanskrit Transliteration.

book six: the z factor

INTRODUCTION

1. *Analects* 13:28.

2. Psalm 95.

3. *Bhagavad Gita*, VIII.20.

4. Romans 3:23.

PREFACE

1. John 8:44.

CHAPTER ELEVEN

1. Jacob Neusner, *Our Religions: Judaism* (New York: Harper One, 1993), 293. (Updated statistics supplemented by Neusner's brother-in-law, Professor Elihu Richter, at the Oxford Round Table, August 2014.)

2. Daniel 8:2–16.

3. Or, more correctly, Yahweh spelled with a "J" in German.

4. Most often in the plural as Elohim.

5. The chart is accessible at www.BrianArthurBrown.com.

6. Ezekiel 1:4–28 and 10:3–22.

7. Ezekiel 37:12.

8. *Bhagavad Gita* IX.18.

9. *Bhagavad Gita* XVIII.55.

10. 2 Maccabees 1:33–34.

11. "benefactor, strengthener, saviour, redeemer" [lit. "who sets about benefitting, etc."] (Hum 11); beneficent (lit.); a prophet, religious leader; future savior or messiah (k517). (Courtesy of Jospeh H. Peterson's dictionary of common Avesta words, located at http://www .avesta.org/avdict/avdict.htm#dcts.)

12. For example, John Barton in an entry on "Source Criticism," *The Anchor Bible Dictionary*, vol. 6.

13. Marvin A. Sweeney, *Isaiah 1–39*, Volume XVI of *The Forms of the Old Testament Literature*, edited by Rolf P. Knierim and Gene M. Tucker (Grand Rapids, MI: Wm. B. Eerdmans, 1996), 316.

14. Isaiah 26:19.

15. Isaiah 27:13.

16. Yasna, 31:20, 46:10.

17. Mary Boyce, *Zoroastrians: Their Religious Beliefs and Practices* (London: Routledge, 1979), 14.

18. Yasht 19, verses 10, 11, and 89.

19. James H. Charlesworth, *Resurrection: The Origin and Future of a Biblical Doctrine* (New York: T&T Clark, 2006), 2.

20. Daniel 12:1–3.

21. Daniel 12:9.

22. Isaiah 33:22; 51:4–5; 52:7–10.

23. Personal conversation with the author in January 2015.

24. Mary Boyce, in personal conversations with the author, January 2006, in support of her observations in her 1982 *History of Zoroastrianism*, then in revision despite her ill health.

25. Job 1:6 and 2:1.

26. Job 19:25 (King James Version), familiar phraseology from Handel's *Messiah*.

27. Job 19:26.

28. Isaiah 45:1.

29. Shaul Shaked, "Iranian Functions in Esther," in *Irano-Judaica*, edited by Shaul Shaked and Amnon Metzer (Jerusalem: Ben-Zvi, 1982), 292–303, as quoted by Richard Foltz in drawing such resources together.

30. James Russell, "Zoroastrian Elements in the Book of Esther," in *Irano-Judaica II*, edited by Shaul Shaked and Amnon Metzer (Jerusalem: Ben-Zvi, 1990), 33–40, as quoted by Richard Foltz.

31. Almut Hintze, "The Greek and Hebrew Versions of the Book of Esther and Its Iranian Background," in *Irano-Judica III* (Jerusalem: Ben-Zvi, 1994), 34–39, as quoted by Richard Foltz.

32. Jan Nattier, "The Meaning of the Maitreya Myth: A Typological Analysis," in *Maitreya: The Future Buddha*, edited by Alan Sponberg and Helen Hardacre (Princeton, NJ: Princeton University Press, 1988), 47, note 60, citing Przyluski—all part of the welter of resources on related matters assembled by the redoubtable Richard Foltz in his brilliant analysis of *Religions of the Silk Road*.

CHAPTER TWELVE

1. Harvey Cox, *Our Religions: Christianity* (New York: Harper One, 1993), 363.

2. Matthew 15:21–28, 16:13, and 19:1; Luke 9:28; Mark 7:24–37, 8:27, and 10:1; John 1:28–29 and 10:40. The map of Jesus's travels is available for download at www.BrianArthurBrown.com.

3. Mark 7:24–31 (found also at Matthew 15:21–28).

4. John 1:3.

5. Colossians 1:16.

6. *Bhagavad Gita* 10.8.

7. *Essene Manual of Discipline*, in *The Dead Sea Scrolls*, edited by Millar Burrows (New York: Random House, 1988).

8. Luke 16:8; John 12:36; 1 Thessalonians 5:5; and Ephesians 5:8.

9. John 1:5, 8:12, 12:35, and 12:46; Acts 26:18; 2 Corinthians 6:14; Ephesians 6:12; 1 Thessalonians 5:4.

10. Revelation 20:10.

11. Matthew 12:40; Mark 8:31, 9:31, and 10:34; Luke 9:22, 18:33, 24:7, and 24:46; Acts 10:40.

12. This typical passage is found in Yt. 22.1–36 and compares with Yasht, Yt. 24.53–64.

13. Matthew 5:22.

14. Matthew 18:8.

15. Matthew 8:12.

16. John 6:35, 41, 48–51.

17. John 8:12 and 9:5.

18. John 10:7–9.

19. John 10:11–14.

20. John 11:25.

21. John 14:6.

22. John 15:1–5.

23. John 8:58.

24. John 14:6.

25. Yasna, 43:3.

26. Mary Boyce, *Zoroastrians: Their Religious Beliefs and Practices* (New York: Routledge, 1979), 42.

27. Yasna, 30:7.

28. Philippians 3:19.

29. Philippians 3:20.

30. Philippians 3:21.

31. Revelation 7:9.

32. Exodus 27:20–21 (King James Version).

33. Leviticus 6:13 (King James Version).

34. Hebrews 10:22.

35. Mark 7:15.

36. Hebrews 9:13–14.

37. John 21:25.

38. As indicated in Mark 7:24, where it is obvious that he is returning to an area where he knew people, though no previous visit to Tyre is mentioned in scripture.

39. Job 19:25–26.

40. Job 33:24.

41. Matthew 20:28 and Mark 10:45.

42. Timothy 2:5–6.

43. John 8:12 and 9:5.

44. Luke 2:52.

45. Mark 14:62.

46. Daniel 7:13.

CHAPTER THIRTEEN

1. Seyyed Hossein Nasr, *Our Religions: Islam* (New York: Harper One, 1993), 427.

2. Quoted by Monica M. Ringer in "Iranian Nationalism and Zoroastrian Identity," in *Iran Facing Others: Identity Boundaries in Historical Perspective*, edited by Abbas Amanat and Farzin Vejdani (Basingstoke, UK: Palgrave Macmillan, 2012), 216.

3. Gerard Russell, *Heirs to Forgotten Kingdoms* (New York: Basic Books, 2014), 95.

4. Correspondence forwarded by the professor to the author.

5. Karl-Heinrich Büchner, *Beobachtungen Über Vers Und Gedankengang Bei Lukrez* (Berlin: Weidmannsche Buchhandlung, 1936), 105.

6. Büchner, *Beobachtungen Über Vers Und Gedankengang Bei Lukrez*, 105.

7. Büchner, *Beobachtungen Über Vers Und Gedankengang Bei Lukrez*, 105.

8. Brian Arthur Brown, *Three Testaments: Torah, Gospel, and Quran* (Lanham, MD: Rowman & Littlefield, 2012), 413.

9. A matter discussed cautiously by A. Yusuf Ali in footnote 76 of his classic translation of *The Holy Quran: Translation and Commentary* (Beirut: Dar Al Arabia, 1934), 33.

10. Quran 66:6.

11. Quran 16:49–50.

12. And in Iran the Archangel Jibreel of Islam is still called by his ancient Zoroastrian name of *Sraosh* in popular culture!

13. Quran 21:30.

14. Quran 41:11.

15. Quran 21:33.

16. Quran 45:3–5.

17. Quran 72.

18. Yasna 71 and in the Vendidad at Fargard 19.

19. Sahih Bukhari, *Hadeeth*, Volume 9, Book 93, Number 53, translated by Muhammad Muhsin Khan (Chicago: Kazi, 1996).

20. Quran 39:71; 15:43.

21. Quran 17:60; 37:62–68; 44:43; and 56:52.

22. Muslim.org, an Ahmadiyya website.

23. Quran 61:6.

24. Quran 89:27–30.

25. Quran 39:20; 29:58–59.

26. Quran 52:22; 52:19; 38:51.

27. Quran 56:17–19; 52:24–25; 76:19; 56:35–38; 37:48–49; 38:52–54; 44:51–56; 52:20–21.

28. In spite of nasty inferences in the European press, the English word "whore" (German *Hure*, Danish *hore*, Swedish *hora*, Dutch *hoer*, Proto-Germanic *hōrōn*, masculine form Gothic *hors*, Proto-Germanic *hōraz*) is properly to be regarded as stemming from the Proto-Indo-European verb root *keh₂-, or "to love" (with an original meaning of "lover"), and is therefore not etymologically related to the Arabic (Semitic, and thus non-Indo-European) word *houri*, despite other legitimate questions about this genuinely Quranic reference by the time they reach Hadith.

29. Quran 17:46; 23:88; 41:11; 65:12.

30. Quran 17:100.

31. Quran 7:11–12.

32. Quran 21:83.

33. Quran 38:41.

34. Ali, *The Holy Quran*, note 2739.

book seven: the "dead zee scrolls"

INTRODUCTION

1. Bibliothèque nationale de France, manuscript Hebreu #1412.

PREFACE

1. "Archaeologist Says Central Asia Was Cradle of Ancient Persian Religion," *IOL* scitech, July 31, 2005.

2. "Zoroastrian Temple Discovered in Duhok," *Kurdish Globe*, August 22, 2006.

3. "Uzbek Archaeologists Discover Ancient Temple of Zoroaster," *Uzbekistan News*, November 25, 2013.

4. "Major Zoroastrian Tombs in China's Xinjiang Uygar Autonomous Region," *China Daily USA*, September 5, 2014.

CHAPTER FOURTEEN

1. Hormuzd Rassam, *Asshur and the Land of Nimrod* (New York: Eaton & Mains/Curts & Jennings, 1897), 266–67.

2. Ibid., 260.

3. Miriam Mazen, Associated Press, in *National Post* (Toronto), September 30, 2015.

CHAPTER FIFTEEN

1. For example, see Justin M. Jacobs, "Confronting Indiana Jones: Chinese Nationalism, Historical Imperialism, and the Criminalization of Aurel Stein and the Raiders of Dunhuang, 1899–1944," in *China on the Margins*, edited by Sherman Cochran and Paul G. Pickowicz (Ithaca, NY: Cornell University Press, 2010), 65–90.

2. E. E. Herzfeld, *Zoroaster and His World* (Princeton, NJ: Princeton University Press, 1947).

3. W. B. Henning, *Zoroaster, Politician or Witch-Doctor* (Oxford: Oxford University Press, 1951).

4. Gore Vidal, *Creation* (New York: Random House, 1981).

5. William W. Malandra, "On the Date of Zoroaster," *Journal of the American Oriental Society* 114 (1994): 498–99.

6. Shapur Shabazi, "The 'Traditional Date of Zoroaster' Explained," *Bulletin of the School of Oriental and African Studies* 40 (1997): 25–26.

7. Hsuan-tsang (or Xuanzang), *Records of the Western Countries* (*Ta T'ang Si Yu Ki*), in *Buddhist Records of the Western World*, vol. I, trans. Samuel Beal (New Delhi: Oriental Reprints, 1969), 47–48.

8. Jenny Rose, "The Sogdians: Prime Movers between Boundaries," *Comparative Studies of South Asia, Africa and the Middle East*, 30, no. 3 (2010): 410–19.

9. Kareem Fahim, Associated Press, "Hope for Nefertiti's Tomb," *New York Times*, November 28, 2015.

appendix

1. See www.zoroastrianheritage.com.

bibliography

Abazov, Rafis. *The Palgrave Concise Historical Atlas of Central Asia*. New York: Palgrave Macmillan, 2008.

Abe, Masao. *Zen and Western Thought*. Honolulu: University of Hawaii Press, 1989.

———. *Our Religions: Buddhism*. New York: Harper One, 1993.

Al-Biruni. *The Chronology of Ancient Nations* (orig. 1000 CE). Volume 3. Translated by C. Edward Sachau. Whitefish, MT: Kessinger, 2004.

Ali, A. Yusuf. *The Holy Quran: Translation and Commentary*. Beirut: Dar Al Arabia, 1934.

Amanat, Abbas, and Farzin Vejdani, eds. *Iran Facing Others: Identity Boundaries in Historical Perspective*. Basingstoke, UK: Palgrave Macmillan, 2012.

Anthony, David W. *The Horse, the Wheel and Language: How Bronze-age Riders from the Eurasian Steppes Shaped the Modern World*. Oxford: Princeton University Press, 2007.

"Archaeologist Says Central Asia Was Cradle of Ancient Persian Religion." *IOL* scitech. July 31, 2005.

Armstrong, Karen. *The Great Transformation*. New York: Random House, 2007.

Barclay, William. *The Revelation of John*. Volume 1. Philadelphia: Westminster Press, 1976.

Beckwith, Christopher I. *Empires of the Silk Road*. Princeton, NJ: Princeton University Press, 2009.

Benveniste, Émile. "The Persian Religion According to the Chief Greek Text." *Journal des savants* 4 (1931).

Blavatsky, H. P. *H. P. Blavatsky's Collected Writings*. Volume 13. Wheaton, IL: Quest Books, 1982.

Bleeck, Arthur H. *Avesta*. Hertford: Muncherjee Horsmusjee Cama, 1864.

Bloom, Harold. "Deciphering Spinoza, the Great Original—Book review of 'Betraying Spinoza. The Renegade Jew Who Gave Us Modernity.' By Rebecca Goldstein." *New York Times*, 16 June 2006.

Borg, Marcus. *Jesus and Buddha, the Parallel Sayings*. Berkeley, CA: Ulysses Press, 2004.

Boyce, Mary. *Zoroastrians: Their Religious Beliefs and Practices*. London: Routledge, 1979.

———. *Zoroastrianism*. Chicago: University of Chicago Press, 1984.

———. *Zoroastrians*. London: Routledge, 2001.

Bromberg, Carol Altman et al., eds. *Bulletin of Asia Institute*. Volume 19. Bloomfield Hills, MI: Asia Institute, 2005.

———. *Bulletin of Asia Institute*. Volume 20. Bloomfield Hills, MI: Asia Institute, 2006.

———. *Bulletin of Asia Institute*. Volume 22. Bloomfield Hills, MI: Asia Institute, 2008.

Brons, A. *Ursprung, Entwickelung und Schicksale der altevangelischen Taufgesinnten oder Mennoniten*. Amsterdam: Johannes Muller, 1912.

Brown, Brian Arthur. *Noah's Other Son: Bridging the Gap between the Bible and the Qur'an*. New York: Continuum, 2007.

———. *Three Testaments: Torah, Gospel, and Quran*. Lanham, MD: Rowman & Littlefield, 2012.

Bruce, David. *The Resurrection of History*. Eugene, OR: Wipf and Stock, 2014.

Büchner, Karl-Heinrich. *Beobachtungen Über Vers Und Gedankengang Bei Lukrez*. Berlin: Weidmannsche Buchhandlung, 1936.

Bukhari, Sahih. *Hadeeth*. Volume 9. Translated by Muhammad Muhsin Khan. Chicago: Kazi, 1996.

Burrows, Millar, ed. *The Dead Sea Scrolls*. New York: Random House, 1988.

Butler-Bowdon, Tom. *Tao Te Ching: The Ancient Classic*. West Sussex: Capstone, 2012.

Calaprice, Alice, ed. *The Expanded Quotable Einstein*. Princeton, NJ: Princeton University Press, 1929.

Charlesworth, James H. *Resurrection: The Origin and Future of a Biblical Doctrine*. New York: T&T Clark, 2006.

Clark, Ronald W. *Einstein: The Life and Times*. New York: World Publishing Co., 1971.

Cohn, Norman. *Cosmos, Chaos & The World to Come: The Ancient Roots of Apocalyptic Faith*. New Haven, CT: Yale University Press, 2001.

Cox, Harvey. *Our Religions: Christianity*. New York: Harper One, 1993.

Cramer, Samuel. "Mennoniten." In *Realencyclopedie für Protestantische Theologie and Kirche*. 24 vols., edited by J. J. Herzog and Albert Hauck, 3rd ed. Leipzig: J. H. Hinrichs, 1896–1913.

Dalai, Lama. *The Good Heart: A Buddhist Perspective on the Teachings of Jesus*. Somerville, MA: Wisdom Publications, 1998.

Dan, Yu. *Confucius from the Heart: Ancient Wisdom for Today's World*. New York: Atria Books, 2006.

Darmesteter, James. *The Zend-Avesta*. 3 vols. Oxford: Oxford University Press, 1880.

Dhalla, Maneckii N. *History of Zoroastrianism*. Bombay: AMS Press, 1938.

Doniger, Wendy. *The Hindus: An Alternate History*. London: Penguin, 2010.

Eisenstadt, Shmuel N., ed. *The Origin and Diversity of Axial Civilizations*. Albany, NY: SUNY Press, 1987.

Eknath Easwaran. *The Dhammapada*. Tomales, CA: Nilgiri Press, 2007.

Eno, Robert. "Shang State Religion and the Pantheon of the Oracle Texts." In *Early Chinese Religion. Part One: Shang through Han (1250 BC–220 AD)*, edited by John Lagerwey and Marc Kalinowski, 41–102. Leiden: Brill, 2008.

Étienne de la Vaissière. *Sogdian Traders: A History*, translated by James Ward. Leiden: Brill, 2005.

Finkel, Irving, ed. *The Cyrus Cylinder*. London: I.B. Taurus, 2013.

Foltz, Richard. *Religions of the Silk Road*. New York: Palgrave Macmillan, 2010.

Freund, Richard. *Digging through the Bible*. Lanham, MD: Rowman & Littlefield, 2009.

———. *Digging through History*. Lanham, MD: Rowman & Littlefield, 2012.

Fronsdal, Gil. *The Dhammapada*. Boston: Shambhala, 2006.

Geldner, K. F. *Encyclopaedia Britannica*. Volume 28. Eleventh edition. New York: Encyclopaedia Britannica, 1911.

Gershevitch, Ilya. *The Avestan Hymn to Mithra*. London: Cambridge University Press, 1967.

Ghandi, Mahatma. *The Bhagavad Gita*. New Delhi: Young India, 1931.

"Gandhi's Face Imprinted on a New Brand of Leadership." *New York Times*. International Weekly. September 30, 2014. p. 4.

Glassé, Cyril. *The New Encyclopedia of Islam*. Fourth edition. Lanham, MD: Rowman & Littlefield, 2013.

———. *The Second Coming of the Judeo-Zoroastrian Jesus of the Dead Sea Scrolls*. New York: Revelation, 2014.

Goldstucker, Theodore. *Literary Remains of the Late Professor Theodore Goldstucker*. London: W. H. Allen, 1879.

Gruber, Elmar R., and Holger Kersten. *The Original Jesus: Buddhist Sources of Christianity*. Shaftsbury, Dorset: Element Books, 1995.

Haberman, Frederick. *Tracing Our Ancestors*. Villa Rica, GA: Kingdom Press, 1934.

Hansen, Valerie. *The Silk Road: A New History*. New York: Oxford University Press, 2012.

Henning, W. B. *Zoroaster, Politician or Witch-Doctor*. Oxford: Oxford University Press, 1951.

Herzfeld, E. E. *Zoroaster and His World*. Princeton, NJ: Princeton University Press, 1947.

Hindley, J. C. "A Prophet Outside Israel? Thoughts on the Study of Zoroastrianism." *Indian Journal of Theology* II, no. 3 (1962).

Holy Bible. *New Revised Standard Version*. Iowa Falls: World Bible Publishers, 1989.

Hsuan-tsang (or Xuanzang). *Records of the Western Countries (Ta T'ang Si Yu Ki)*. In *Buddhist Records of the Western World*. Volume I. Translated by Samuel Beal. New Delhi: Oriental Reprints, 1969.

Jacobs, Justin M. "Confronting Indiana Jones: Chinese Nationalism, Historical Imperialism, and the Criminalization of Aurel Stein and the Raiders of Dunhuang, 1899–1944." In *China on the Margins*, edited by Sherman Cochran and Paul G. Pickowicz, 65–90. Ithaca, NY: Cornell University Press, 2010.

Jaspers, Karl. *Vom Ursprung und Ziel der Geschichte* (The Origin and Goal of History). New York: Yale University Press, 1953.

———. *The Way to Wisdom: An Introduction to Philosophy*. New Haven, CT: Yale University Press, 2003.

Kipling, Rudyard. *Rewards and Fairies*. London: Macmillan, 1919.

Kjellberg, Paul, and Philip J. Ivanhoe, eds. *Essays on Skepticism, Relativism and Ethics in the Zhuangzi*. Albany: State University of New York Press, 1996.

Kornfield, Jack. *Bringing Home the Dharma*. Boston: Shambhala, 2011.

Krech, Volkhard, and Marion Steinicke. *Dynamics in the History of Religions Between Asia and Europe*. Leiden and Boston: Brill, 2012.

Legge, James. "James Legge—A Short Biography." In *The Illustrated Tao Te Ching*, edited by Andrew Forbes and David Henley. Chiang Mai: Cognoscenti Books, 2012. ASIN: B008NNLKXC.

Liu Xiaogan. *Our Religions: Taoism*. New York: Harper One, 1993.

Liu, Xinru. *The Silk Road in World History*. New York: Oxford University Press, 2010.

Mair, Victor H. "Old Sinitic ˙myag, Old Persian *maguš*, and English Magician." *Early China* 15 (1990): 27–47.

———. *Tao te Ching, The Classic Book of Integrity and the Way*. New York: Bantam, 1990.

———. *Wandering on the Way*. Honolulu: University of Hawaii Press, 1994.

———. "Religious Formation and Intercultural Contact in Early China." In *Dynamics in the History of Religions between Asia and Europe*, edited by Volkhard Krech and Marion Steinicke. Leiden and Boston: Brill, 2012.

Mair, Victor H., and Mallory, J. P. *The Tarim Mummies*. London: Thames and Hudson, 2000.

"Major Zoroastrian Tombs in China's Xinjiang Uygar Autonomous Region." *China Daily USA*. September 5, 2014.

Malandra, William W. "On the Date of Zoroaster." *Journal of the American Oriental Society* 114 (1994): 498–99.

Mallory, J. P. *In Search of the Indo-Europeans*. New York: Thames and Hudson, 1989.

Michie, David. *The Dalai Lama's Cat*. Sydney: Hay House, 2012.

———. *The Dalai Lama's Cat and the Art of Purring*. Sydney: Hay House, 2013.

———. *The Dalai Lama's Cat and the Power of Meow*. Sydney: Hay House, 2015.

Miller, Barbara Stoler. *Bhagavad-Gita: Krishna's Counsel in Time of War*. New York: Bantam, 1986.

Muller, F. Max. *Three Lectures on the Vedanta Philosophy*. Whitefish, MT: Kessinger, 2003.

Nanavutty, Piloo. *The Gathas of Zarathustra*. Ahamedabad: Mapin, 1999.

Narayanan, Renuka. *The Book of Prayer*. Mumbai: Viking India, 2001.

Nasr, Seyyed Hossein. *Our Religions: Islam*. New York: Harper One, 1993.

Nattier. Jan. "The Meaning of the Maitreya Myth: A Typological Analysis." In *Maitreya: The Future Buddha*, edited by Alan Sponberg and Helen Hardacre. Princeton, NJ: Princeton University Press, 1988.

Neusner, Jacob. *Our Religions: Judaism*. New York: Harper One, 1993.

Nigosian, Sol A. *The Zoroastrian Faith*. Montreal and Kingston: McGill-Queens University Press, 1993.

Prabhupada, A. C. *Bhagavad-Gita as It Is*. Los Angeles: International Society for Krishna Consciousness, 1979.

Radhakrishnan, S. *The Dhammapada*. New Delhi: Oxford University Press, 1950.

Rassam, Hormuzd. *Asshur and the Land of Nimrod*. New York: Eaton & Mains/Curts & Jennings, 1897.

Rose, Jenny. "The Sogdians: Prime Movers between Boundaries." *Comparative Studies of South Asia, Africa and the Middle East* 30, no. 3 (2010): 410–19.

———. *Zoroastrianism*. London: I.B. Tauris, 2011.

Russell, Gerard. *Heirs to Forgotten Kingdoms*. New York: Basic Books, 2014.

Saraswati, Dayananda. *Srimad Bhagavad Gita*. Mylapore: Arsha Vidya Research and Publication Trust, 2012.

William Schmidt. *The Origin of the Idea of God*. New York: Rowman & Littlefield, 1984.

Shabazi, Shapur. "The 'Traditional Date of Zoroaster' Explained." *Bulletin of the School of Oriental and African Studies* 40 (1997): 25–35.

Shaked, Shaul, and Amnon Metzer, eds. *Irano-Judaica*. Jerusalem: Ben-Zvi, 1982.

———. *Irano-Judaica II*. Jerusalem: Ben-Zvi, 1990.

———. *Irano-Judaica III*. Jerusalem: Ben-Zvi, 1994.

Sharma, Arvind. *Our Religions: Hinduism*. New York: Harper One, 1993.

Slingerland, Edward. *Confucius Analects*. Indianapolis: Hackett, 2003.

Stausberg, Michael, and Yuhan Sohrab-Dinshaw Vevaina, eds. *The Wiley-Blackwell Companion to Zoroastrianism*. Chichester, West Sussex: John Wiley & Sons, 2015.

Stewart, Matthew. *The Courtier and the Heretic*. New York: W. W. Norton, 2006.

Sugirtharajah, Rasiah. *The Bible and Asia*. Cambridge, MA: Harvard University Press, 2013.

Sugirtharajah, Sharada. *Imagining Hindus*. London: Routledge, 2003.

Sweeney, Marvin A. *Isaiah 1–39*. Volume XVI of *The Forms of the Old Testament Literature*, edited by Rolf P. Knierim and Gene M. Tucker. Grand Rapids, MI: Wm. B. Eerdmans, 1996.

Ten Elshof, Gregg A. *Confucius for Christians*. Grand Rapids, MI: Wm. B. Eerdmans, 2015.

Thich, Nhat Hanh, and Elaine Pagels. *Living Buddha; Living Christ*. New York: Riverhead, 1995.

Thilly, Frank. *A History of Philosophy*. New York: Holt & Co., 1914.

Toynbee, Arnold J. *A Study of History*. Abridged by D. C. Somervell. New York: Oxford University Press, 1987.

Tu Wei-ming. *Our Religions: Confucianism*. New York: Harper One, 1993.

"Uzbek Archaeologists Discover Ancient Temple of Zoroaster." *Uzbekistan News*, November 25, 2013.

Vidal, Gore. *Creation*. New York: Random House, 1981.

Viraraghavan, Girija. "The History of Roses in India." IndianRoseFederation.org. Pune, India. August 20, 2013.

West, E. W. *Pahlavi Texts of Zoraratrianism*. Oxford: Oxford University Press, 1860.

Whitfield, Susan. *Life Along the Silk Road*. Los Angeles: University of California Press, 1999.

"Zoroastrian Temple Discovered in Duhok." *Kurdish Globe*, August 22, 2006.

index

about the author

After a lengthy career as a minister of the United Church of Canada, east, west, north, and central, **Brian Arthur Brown** is currently scholar-in-residence at the historic and progressive First Baptist Church of Niagara Falls, New York, and minister emeritus for St. John's–Stevensville United Church in Fort Erie, Ontario. He is the author of nineteen previous books on the quest for peace and harmony between aboriginal natives and other Canadians; French and English in Canada; Canadians and Americans in war and peace; and, since 2001, Jews, Christians, and Muslims worldwide, culminating in *Three Testaments: Torah, Gospel, and Quran,* in use around the world and the predecessor to *Four Testaments: Tao Te Ching, Analects, Dhammapada, Bhagavad Gita.*

Brown holds a bachelor's degree in classics from Dalhousie University in Halifax, a master's degree in theology from McGill University in Montreal, and a doctorate in organizational behavior from the University of California, and he has done post-doctoral studies in executive leadership at Harvard University. He is currently a member of the Oxford Round Table at Oxford University and in 2015 was elected as a fellow of the Royal Society for the Arts.

Married for well over fifty years, Brian and Jenny Brown live within earshot of the thunderous Niagara Falls and maintain connections with "co-religionists" worldwide.

about the contributors

David Bruce is a Roman Catholic writer and theologian, following a lengthy career in the ministry of the United Church of Canada. He is the sole author of the four-volume series *Jesus 24/7* and was a major contributor to *Three Testaments: Torah, Gospel, and Quran*. Dr. Bruce is currently noted as the author of *The Resurrection of History*, a popularization of his 2014 PhD thesis from St. Michael's University College at the University of Toronto.

Francis X. Clooney, a Jesuit, is professor of comparative theology at the Harvard Divinity School, director of the Center for the Study of World Religions at Harvard University, and professorial research fellow at the Australian Catholic University. With a doctorate in South Asian languages and civilizations (University of Chicago, 1984), he taught at Boston College for twenty-one years before coming to Harvard. His primary area of scholarship is theological writings in the Sanskrit and Tamil traditions of Hindu India. Clooney is regarded by many as the *éminence grise* in the developing fields of comparative theology, "religious studies," and interfaith conversations.

K. E. Eduljee ("Ed") is the founder of the Heritage Institute in British Columbia, Canada, and the author of several monographs, as well as the *Zoroastrian Heritage* website and blog. He is currently writing the *Immortal Cypress*, an epic in verse. An articulate Parsee and meticulous scholar of both history and religion, in his proficient use of social media he communicates with both the general public and the Zoroastrian community.

Richard Freund is the director of the Maurice Greenberg Center for Judaic Studies, University of Hartford. He has directed six archaeological projects in Israel and three in Europe, as well as archaeological oversight in Burgos and Cadiz, Spain, and a research project at the extermination camp at Sobibor, Poland. Freund is the author of six books on archaeology and over one hundred scholarly articles, and he has appeared in fifteen television documentaries, including as a featured guest in a 2004 Nova special and *Finding Atlantis* on the National Geographic Channel in

2011. His books from Rowman & Littlefield, *Digging Through the Bible* and *Digging Through History*, are widely available.

Mohandas Gandhi—No introduction is necessary and none would be adequate, except to emphasize that the founder of modern India and leader of nonviolent political change in the twentieth century, while more an activist than a scholar in areas like law and politics, became a scholar of Buddhism, Christianity, and Hinduism in reference to scriptural texts and political and social application.

Karl Friedrich Geldner (1852–1929) was professor of Sanskrit and comparative philology in the University of Marburg and the pioneering author of *Vedische Studien*, his still definitive work on Vedic studies. Geldner is regarded as having "proven" that the Avesta format is historically related to the Vedic meters of the *gayatri* family in the Rig Veda, and that the meters of the Gathas were recited, unlike the meters of the Younger Avesta, which are mostly sung. This situates the early Zoroastrian Scriptures as freestanding Vedic contributions to religious developments across the East, particularly Hinduism and Buddhism, independent of the Vedic connections to the Western corpus (as discussed in Book VI of this compendium).

Cyril Glassé is the author and editor of *The New Islamic Encyclopedia* from Rowman & Littlefield, generously endorsed by Huston Smith, as well as other works and articles, including the recent *The Second Coming of the Judeo-Zoroastrian Jesus of the Dead Sea Scrolls*. An Islamic immigrant to the United States, originally from Russia via various Middle Eastern countries, Glassé lives in New York City, where he works as a cultural guide to the city and as an educational consultant.

Victor H. Mair is an American sinologist and professor of Chinese at the University of Pennsylvania. In addition to countless articles and twenty books of his own, Mair has edited the standard *Columbia History of Chinese Literature* and *Columbia Anthology of Traditional Chinese Literature*. Mair is a longtime advocate for writing Mandarin Chinese in an alphabetic script (viz., pinyin), which he considers advantageous for Chinese education, computerization, and lexicography. He is widely regarded as the leader in the growing appreciation of exterior influences in the development of civilization in ancient China.

Jacqueline Mates-Muchin is senior rabbi at Temple Sinai in Oakland, California. Following ten years of rabbinical service, she recently spent a six-month sabbatical in Israel. Her earlier scholarly focus produced *The Analects of Confucius and Its Parallel in Early Rabbinic Thought* as a reflection of her Chinese and Jewish traditions as the first Chinese American rabbi.

Sarvepalli Radhakrishnan, an Indian philosopher and statesman, was the first vice president of India and the second president of India (1962–1967). One of India's influential twentieth-century scholars of comparative religion and philosophy, he was Spalding Professor of Eastern Religion and Ethics at Oxford University (1936–1952). His philosophy, grounded in Advaita Vedanta, reinterpreting this tradition for a contemporary understanding, earned him an enduring reputation as a bridge builder between India and the West.

Arvind Sharma has been a member of the faculty of religious studies at McGill University since 1987, where he lectures on Hinduism and comparative religion at the world launch site of comparative religion under Willfred Cantwell Smith (before the latter's relocation to Harvard, where he founded the Center for the Study of World Religions). Sharma himself has held fellowships at the Center for the Study of World Religions as well as at the Center for the Study of Values in Public Life, the Center for Business and Government, John F. Kennedy School of Government at Harvard University, and the Brookings Institute. He also received a Maxwell Fellowship and was elected fellow of the Royal Asiatic Society, London.